CHICKEN SOUP
FOR THE HORSE
LOVER'S SOUL

Chicken Soup for the Horse Lover's Soul
Inspirational Stories About Horses and the People Who Love Them
Jack Canfield, Mark Victor Hansen, Marty Becker, Gary Seidler, Peter Vegso,
Theresa Peluso
Published by Backlist, LLC,
a unit of Chicken Soup for the Soul Publishing, LLC. www.chickensoup.com
Copyright ©2012 by Chicken Soup for the Soul Publishing, LLC. All Rights
Reserved.

Front cover design by Andrea Perrine Brower
Originally published in 2003 by Health Communications, Inc.

Back cover and spine redesign by Pneuma Books, LLC

Distributed to the booktrade by Simon & Schuster. SAN: 200-2442

Publisher's Cataloging-in-Publication Data
(Prepared by The Donohue Group)

Chicken soup for the horse lover's soul : inspirational stories about horses
and the people who love them / [compiled by] Jack Canfield ... [et al.].

   p. : ill. ; cm.

   Originally published: Deerfield Beach, FL : Health Communications, c2003.
   ISBN: 978-1-62361-011-1

   1. Horses--Anecdotes. 2. Horse owners--Anecdotes. 3. Human-animal
relationships--Anecdotes. 4. Anecdotes. I. Canfield, Jack, 1944-

SF301 .C47 2012
636.1   2012944080

PRINTED IN THE UNITED STATES OF AMERICA
on acid free paper
21 20 19 18 17 16 15   03 04 05 06 07 08 09 10

CHICKEN SOUP FOR THE HORSE LOVER'S SOUL

Inspirational Stories About Horses and the People Who Love Them

Jack Canfield
Mark Victor Hansen
Marty Becker, DVM
Gary Seidler
Peter Vegso
Theresa Peluso

Backlist, LLC, a unit of
Chicken Soup for the Soul Publishing, LLC
Cos Cob, CT
www.chickensoup.com

Contents

v

5. ON COMPANIONSHIP AND COMMITMENT

6. AND . . . THEY'RE OFF!

Introduction

As our ancestors sat cross-legged around fires in caves for warmth and protection, the rhythmic pounding of wild horses' hooves broke the silence. The thundering sound echoed across time and space.

Primitive cave art in Lascaux, France and classic stories of horses carrying Roman legions, Spanish invaders, and Native Americans to war contrast with modern images of horses racing across our television sets carrying the Lone Ranger, Roy Rogers and Ben Cartwright. Mounted horse racing was popular in the Greek Olympics almost 700 years before Christ. Today, tapes of 4-H shows are re-played in living rooms and photo finishes are simulcast at racetracks around the country.

Mourned by warriors, immortalized by Hollywood and cherished by little girls, the special relationship between mankind and horses not only exists historically, it still flourishes today. The magic of the relationship between horse and human lies not in its strength and longevity; it lies in the mystery of how two different species can be drawn so closely to one another.

Watch as a little girl, only a hock high, holds an apple in her hand as this massive animal takes it gingerly into its mouth. So delicate she is, in contrast to the horse's massive size and strength. The eternal instinct to flee is subdued as a rider climbs onto a horse's back; a position this prey animal should find threatening, yet there is no fear, only a mutual shared trust.

In a marvelously symbiotic relationship, horses give humans speed, stamina and strength, while we provide them with a steady food supply and protection from predators.

We have shared a destiny for thousands of years as the horse's role in our lives has changed from utilitarian to one of emotion and pleasure. Within the past hundred years, horses were as much a part of our daily lives as our cars and tractors are today. Long before airplanes and cell phones, the horse had become integral to our very existence and ability to communicate, as it not only moved faster and farther than almost any animal, it could and would carry a human upon its back. For early man, the experience of riding was as close to flying as he could possibly get.

Horses manifest an extraordinary sense of fun, frivolity and joy. Good old-fashioned "horse play" is an essential part of a horse's daily life; something we humans would do well to mimic. Many of us come home from work feeling like a human piñata—beaten but not quite broken—slip on our boots and head for the barn where we bury our heads in our horses and take in their aroma. Sharing time with a horse elevates senses, expands awareness and amplifies this thing called life.

Horse lovers scrimp on groceries so our horses can eat the best. We won't go to the doctor if we're flat on our back in bed, yet we call the vet if our horse has the equivalent of a cold. This dedication and commitment is rewarded by a soft nicker, a gentle ruff of breath, the quiet reassurance of a neck to cradle, a flawless dressage move, a fluid jump, a record-breaking time around the barrels or a blue ribbon from the county fair. That's all a horse lover needs.

For all their strength, horses can touch with amazing gentleness. For all their speed, they can gloriously harness their "stay apparatus" and stand three legged for hours in the sun. For their size as the largest domesticated animal, they allow waiflike riders to control them with simple pressure of a leg. It is in these amazing contradictions that we find ourselves lost in the mystery of the bond between our two species.

Saying good-bye to one of these magnificent animals causes us to reflect on this partnership. While we find it brimming with warm memories, we grieve for their loss as we would for any other family member. These themes of extreme sadness and joy were shared in many of the stories we considered for this book.

The stories in *Chicken Soup for the Horse Lover's Soul* were selected to give you a richer, deeper understanding of the bond between humans and horses. You will find stories so moving that they will test the limits of your tear ducts while others will have you laughing out loud or running to give your horse a hug and a treat. Other stories shine an illuminating light on the horse's unique versatility, intelligence and intuitiveness; or their strength, stamina and athletic prowess. You will welcome new foals and say good-bye to others. But, when all is said and done, that mysterious spell cast upon little boys and girls by ponies and stories like *Black Beauty* still cannot be explained. The mystery isn't meant to be solved, but enjoyed.

Ranchhands to city slickers, rodeo queens to seniors who never lost their love for horses, will see themselves saddling up in the stories of *Chicken Soup for the Horse Lover's Soul*. As you read, no doubt you'll be reacquainted with old friends, recall sad and happy experiences, or decide to delight someone with a gift that they will beam upon receiving.

Happy tales and happy trails.

1

A SPECIAL BOND

Somewhere in time's Own Space
   There must be some sweet pastured place
   Where creeks sing on and tall trees grow
   Some Paradise where horses go,
   For by the love that guides my pen
   I know great horses live again.

Stanley Harrison

The Racking Horse

A horse is worth more than riches.

Spanish Proverb

The first time Bart told me about his horse Dude, I knew their bond had been something special. But I never suspected that Dude would deliver a wonderful gift to me.

Growing up on a 100-year-old family farm in Tennessee, Bart loved all animals. But Dude, the chestnut-colored Quarter Horse that Bart received when he turned nine, became his favorite. Years later when Bart's father sold Dude, Bart grieved in secret.

Even before I met and married Bart, I knew all about grieving in secret, too. Because of my dad's job, our family relocated every year. Deep inside, I wished we could stay in one place where I could develop lasting friendships. But I never said anything to my parents. I didn't want to hurt them. Yet sometimes I wondered if even God could keep track of us the way we moved from place to place.

One summer evening in 1987, as Bart and I glided on our front-porch swing, my husband suddenly blurted out, "Did I ever tell you that Dude won the World Racking Horse Championship?"

"Rocking horse championship?" I asked.

"Racking," Bart corrected, smiling gently. "It's a kind of dancing that horses do. Takes lots of training. You use four reins to guide the horse. It's pretty hard." Bart gazed at the pasture. "Dude was the greatest racking horse ever."

"Then why'd you let your dad sell him?" I probed.

"I didn't know he was even thinking about it," Bart explained. "When I was seventeen, I started a short construction job down in Florida. I guess Dad figured I wouldn't be riding anymore, so he sold Dude without even asking me. Running a horse farm means you buy and sell horses all the time, and that's what Dad did.

"I've always wondered if that horse missed me as much as I've missed him. I've never had the heart to try to find him. I couldn't stand knowing if something bad . . ." Bart's voice trailed off.

After that, few nights passed without Bart mentioning Dude. My heart ached for him. I didn't know what to do. Then one afternoon while I walked through the pasture, a strange thought came to me. In my heart, a quiet voice said, "Lori, find Dude for Bart."

How absurd! I thought. I knew nothing about horses, certainly not how to find and buy one. That was Bart's department.

The harder I tried to dismiss the thought, the stronger it grew. I did not dare mention it to anyone except God. Each day I asked him to guide me.

On a Saturday morning three weeks after the first "find Dude" notion, a new meter reader, Mr. Parker, stopped by while I was working in the garden. We struck up a friendly conversation. When he mentioned he'd once bought a horse from Bart's dad, I interrupted.

"You remember the horse's name?" I asked.

"Sure do," Mr. Parker said. "Dude. Paid $2,500 for him."

I wiped the dirt from my hands and jumped up, barely catching my breath.

"Do you know what happened to him?" I asked.

"Yep. I sold him for a good profit."

"Where's Dude now?" I asked. "I need to find him."

"That'd be impossible," Mr. Parker explained. "I sold that horse years ago. He might even be dead by now."

"But could you . . . would you . . . be willing to try to help me find him?" After I explained the situation, Mr. Parker stared at me for several seconds. Finally, he agreed to join the search for Dude, promising not to say anything to Bart.

Each Friday for almost a year, I phoned Mr. Parker to see if his sleuthing had turned up anything. Each week his answer was the same: "Sorry, nothing yet."

One Friday I called Mr. Parker with another idea. "Could you at least find one of Dude's babies for me?"

"Don't think so," he chuckled. "Dude was a gelding."

"That's fine," I said. "I'll take a gelding baby."

"You really *do* need help." Mr. Parker explained that geldings are unable to reproduce. Then he seemed to double his efforts to help. Several weeks later, he phoned me on a Monday.

"I found him," he shouted. "I found Dude!"

"Where?" I said, wanting to jump through the phone.

"On a farm in Georgia," Mr. Parker said. "A family bought Dude for their teenage son. But they can't do anything with the horse. In fact, they think Dude's crazy. Maybe dangerous. Bet you could get him back real easy."

Mr. Parker was right. I called the family in Rising Fawn, Georgia, and made arrangements to buy Dude for $300. I struggled to keep my secret until the weekend. On Friday, I met Bart at the front door after work.

"Will you go for a ride with me?" I asked in my most persuasive voice. "I have a surprise for you."

"Honey," Bart protested, "I'm tired."

"Please, Bart. I've packed a picnic supper. It'll be worth the ride, I promise."

Bart got into the Jeep. As I drove, my heart beat so fast that I thought it would burst as I chatted about family matters.

"Where are we going?" Bart asked after thirty minutes.

"Just a bit farther," I said.

Bart sighed. "Honey, I love you. But I can't believe I let you drag me off."

I didn't defend myself. I'd waited too long to ruin things now. However, by the time I steered off the main highway onto a gravel road, Bart was so annoyed that he wasn't speaking to me. When I turned from the gravel road to a dirt trail, Bart glared.

"We're here," I said, stopping in front of the third fence post.

"Here where? Lori, have you lost your mind?" Bart barked.

"Stop yelling," I said. "Whistle."

"What?" Bart shouted.

"Whistle," I repeated. "Like you used to . . . for Dude. Just whistle. You'll understand in a minute."

"Well . . . I. . . . This is crazy," Bart sputtered as he got out of the Jeep.

To humor me, Bart whistled. Nothing happened.

"Oh, God," I whispered. "Don't let this be a mistake."

"Do it again," I prodded.

Bart whistled once more, and we heard a sound in the distance. What was it? I could barely breathe.

Bart whistled again. Suddenly over the horizon, a horse came at a gallop. Before I could speak, Bart leaped over the fence.

"Dude!" he yelled, running toward his beloved friend. I watched the blurs of horse and husband meet as if they were performing in one of those slow-motion reunion scenes on television. Bart hopped up on his pal, stroking his mane and patting his neck.

Immediately, a sandy-haired, tobacco-chewing teenage boy and his huffing parents crested the hill.

"Mister, what are you doing?" the boy yelled. "That horse is crazy. Can't nobody do nothing with him."

"No," Bart boomed. "He's not crazy. He's Dude."

To everyone's amazement, at Bart's soft command to the unbridled horse, Dude threw his head high and began racking. As the horse pranced through the pasture, no one spoke. When Dude finished dancing for joy, Bart slid off him.

"I want Dude home," he said.

"I know," I replied with tears in my eyes. "All the arrangements have been made. We can come back and get him."

"Nope," Bart insisted. "He's coming home tonight."

I phoned my in-laws and soon they arrived with a horse trailer. We paid for Dude and headed home.

Bart spent the night in the barn. I knew he and Dude had a lot of catching up to do. As I looked out of the bedroom window, the moon cast a warm glow over the farm. I smiled, knowing that my husband and I now had a wonderful story to tell our future children and grandchildren.

"Thank you, Lord," I whispered. Then the truth hit me. I'd searched longer for Dude than I'd ever lived in one place. God had used the process of finding my husband's beloved horse to renew my trust in the friend who sticks closer than a brother.

"Thank you, Lord," I whispered again as I fell asleep. "Thank you for never losing track of Dude—or me."

Lori Bledsoe as told to Rhonda Reese

A Rocky Rescue

The Lord was ever present in Mama's daily life. So it was natural for her to invoke his assistance for any task that proved difficult—from the piddling ones that hardly seemed to require divine intervention to those that were knottier and more difficult to resolve. I can remember being no more than seven or eight years old and watching her as she pitted all the strength of her five-foot-tall body into popping the lid from a jar of canned green beans. It wouldn't budge.

Mom stopped and sighed. Then holding the stubborn jar in her left hand, she raised her eyes heavenward and said, "Lord, I'd like to feed these beans to my family for dinner, but I need your help in getting this lid off. Thank you, Lord."

Her tone was reverential and totally respectful, but the little prayer was delivered in an attitude of one friend talking to another. Matter of fact. Affectionate. But, most importantly, confident of receiving an answer.

Mom lowered her eyes and put her right hand on the lid. She gave a twist and off it came, so easily that it appeared oiled.

I can remember being impressed, even as a youngster, by Mom's faith. I believed in her and I believed in God, but for whatever reasons, I just couldn't muster up that closeness to him that she enjoyed. There were times when I wondered how in the world she could talk so much to someone she'd never seen. I asked her about it once, and she told me she had seen him. Of course, she went on to explain that she saw him in the flowers and trees and stars and in a host of his other creations. That was fine, but it wasn't what I had in mind.

Mom didn't read the Bible a lot, but curiously she managed to find various passages relating to horses. You see, I was a horse nut and I had my very own big, black, wonderful Tennessee Walker. His name was Bob's Merry Legs and he was far more than just a horse. He was a friend. He listened to all of the secret things that welled up inside my heart. The broad white blaze on his face caught my tears. His ears moved back and forth as he strained to catch every syllable that I uttered to him. Mom knew that if there was any way to reach me with God, it was through horses.

So she read to me passages from Job, with the Lord speaking of the horse's might and majesty. She told me how Jesus would come back one day and he'd be riding a big white horse as all of his saints rode horses behind him. I could envision the scene. It made my heart beat faster and my pulse race with excitement. I imagined an even grander cavalcade, with angels on horses, their robes flowing downward over the animals strong withers and backward across their muscled rumps. Then when I went outside with Bob, I pictured him in heaven and thought Jesus might be proud to ride him.

Every morning that there was school, I got out of bed, dressed, ate breakfast and went outside to visit with Bob before catching the yellow bus that I rode for a total of three hours each day. One morning I went through my routine and then headed for the barn, snatching some sugar cubes as I passed the kitchen counter. I went out the back door, whistling and calling for my friend. His routine was as predictable as mine. He would hear my whistle and call, look out the barn door and then come romping into the paddock to whinny and hang his head over the fence. This particular morning, however, something was wrong. There was no Bob. I panicked.

"Bob?" I called again. I opened the paddock gate and went into the barn. He wasn't there. I went back to the paddock and from the angle of the barn doorway, I spotted the problem. There was a section of fence down and Bob obviously had wandered off. I was frightened.

I ran back to the house and told Mom that I wouldn't be going to school—a rather presumptuous announcement for a ten-year-old fifth-grader.

"What are you talking about?" she asked.

"Bob's missing."

She didn't repeat what I'd said. Mom was like that. In a crisis, she always had an immediate grasp of the situation.

"I'll go get Daddy," she responded. "You wait here."

I could hardly stand still. My best friend was out there somewhere. I knew it would take Mom only a few minutes to drive to the field where Daddy was working in the cotton. That's where I was raised: on a 100-acre cotton farm that was crisscrossed with dozens of dirt roads. Bob and I knew all of them.

It seemed like forever, but no more than ten minutes could have passed when Daddy pulled into the backyard in his truck with Mom behind in her car.

Mom got out. Daddy didn't. He yelled for me to get in the truck. I did and he started driving.

We covered those dirt roads, but there was no Bob. Daddy was trying not to show it, but I knew he was getting worried. Suddenly, he said, "I'm going across the main dirt road to Mr. Rogers' place." There was something about the way he said it that made my skin prickle. I can still remember the feeling.

We crossed the main road and headed toward a huge gravel pit. Daddy stopped a safe distance from the rim and we got out. We looked down and there, appearing very small, was Bob. I immediately started to cry as if my heart had broken.

Knowing that tears wouldn't help Bob, I wiped my eyes, hiccupped three or four times, edged closer to the rim of the gravel pit and looked down. I could see that Bob's right rear foot was cocked off the ground so that it was bearing no weight—a sure sign that it was injured. There was no use asking or even wondering how or why he'd gotten into the pit. The only concern was getting him out.

We lived in a tiny, rural community. There were no such things as rescue helicopters or even much in the way of emergency assistance. Daddy began walking around the rim and I followed. He came to a spot where the wall of the pit gradually sloped and a sort of trail led to the bottom. Bob, who wasn't wearing shoes, had left hoofprints in the dirt that was still soft from a rain three days before.

Daddy and I looked at one another.

"I have to go down and get him," I said.

"No way," Daddy responded. "You'll get hurt, your mother will kill me and I have no idea what else will happen. But I do know that you're not going down there."

I wiped away the last of the tears and looked Daddy straight in the eye. "Then how will we get him?"

"I'll go," Daddy answered.

"He won't follow you, and you know it," I said. "I'll be fine. I can scoot down and, then coming back up, I'll have Bob to hold on to. He won't let me fall." Suddenly, I knew I was speaking the truth. Bob was my best friend and that meant I was the one to rescue him. And I was his best friend, which meant he'd do all he could to keep me from harm.

Nevertheless, Daddy was torn.

"There's no choice, Daddy."

He knew I was right.

"We don't have a lead rope," he said.

"We don't need one. Bob's wearing a halter. Besides, I know he'll follow me without a rope or a halter."

Daddy knelt down and double-tied my tennis shoes, shortening the laces and tightening the knot. He got up and stood back. I knew that was his way of giving me his permission. I sat down at the top of the trail and started scooting, kicking rocks as I went.

I don't know how long it took me to reach Bob. I remember it seemed to take hours to scoot all the way to the bottom of the gravel pit and I shredded my jeans in the process.

When I was three-quarters of the way down, Bob hobbled in my direction and started whinnying. I thought of Mama. I knew what she would do.

"Lord," I breathed, "I know I have no business doing this, but my friend needs help. I know you like horses or you wouldn't have them in your Bible. I don't know if I can do this, Lord, so I'd sure appreciate it if you'd give me a hand. Thank you." I didn't realize it then, but I must surely have sounded just like Mama.

I reached the bottom and turned around to wave at Daddy. I immediately wished I hadn't because it made me think of the climb we'd need to make to get out of the pit. I reached up and patted Bob on the neck.

"You silly, silly horse," I crooned. "Why'd you ever get out and why in the world did you come here?" He looked at me as if to apologize for causing so much trouble.

"Okay," I said, "I know your foot hurts, but you don't have a choice—just like I didn't have one. I'll help you, but you'll have to help me, too." I took hold of his halter with one hand and put my other hand on the side of his neck to help steady me. We were ready when I suddenly halted.

"Lord," I said matter-of-factly, "we're going to need all the help you can give us. I'm just a kid and I'm scared. I know Bob's scared, too. Just please don't let us fall, Lord. Just let me and my friend get to the top. Thank you, Lord."

I was about to start forward when I stopped again. "Lord," I said, "if you were thinking about sending any angels down here today, it would sure be good if you could send some to go all around us. Maybe they could let us just sort of lean on them. Thanks again."

This time we started up, each step placed slowly and

carefully, Bob maneuvering his bulk along the narrow trail as small rocks scattered from under his feet. I plastered myself as close to him as possible. Every time I extended one foot forward, I said, "Please, Lord, don't let us fall." I don't know how many times I repeated those words as I slipped and fell to my knees perhaps dozens of times. Bob stopped with each slip. I stopped anytime he seemed to favor his hurt foot.

Eventually, we made it to the top, two best friends holding on to one another. I learned that day what it meant to take risks for a friend and, just as importantly, I learned what kind of relationship I could have with someone I'd never seen. Mama was right . . . as usual. And today, when I can't wrestle the lid from a jar, I simply stop and say, "Lord, I need some help to do this." It never fails, the lid slips off so easily it appears to be oiled.

Diane M. Ciarloni

Cowboy Heart

*It is not enough for a man to know how to ride;
he must know how to fall.*

Mexican Proverb

"Silt, Colorado!" hollered the Greyhound bus driver as he pulled off to the side of the road.

I grabbed my small bag and climbed off the bus. At the edge of the road was a large man who was standing beside an old army jeep.

"Are you Roger Kiser?" he asked me.

"Yes, sir," I replied.

"My name is Owen Boulton. I own the Rainbow K Ranch," he said as he stuck out his hand to shake mine.

I had been sent to Colorado by the juvenile judge in Florida so that I could work on a ranch. It was a program that had been set up to help troubled teenagers.

Within a week of my arrival at the Rainbow K, I had been turned into a full-fledged cowboy. I had been assigned a large horse, named Brownie, and had been given a full outfit of Western wear, as well as a list of never-ending duties, which started at around 4 A.M. each day.

Things went rather well for the first couple of months. We

worked from 4 A.M. until 6 P.M., seven days a week. We bailed hay, branded cattle, collected chicken eggs, mended fences and shoveled manure.

The best part was my horse, Brownie. I guess she had been given that name because she was brown in color. In addition to my other daily chores, I fed her, bathed her and brushed her.

Every morning when I came out to collect the eggs from the chicken coop, Brownie was waiting for me by the gate. I would walk over and pat her on her side. She would toss her head backward and make a strange sound as if she were blowing through her lips. Slobber would fly everywhere.

"I bet you sure could whistle loud if you had some hands," I would tell her. She would stomp her feet and turn around in a circle.

There were not very many things on the face of this earth that I loved when I was a young boy. But that horse was one thing that I would have died for.

After we ranchhands had eaten breakfast one morning, I was told to go with several of the older men to repair fences up on the northern range. We loaded the jeep with fencing materials and tools and off we went. It was almost 7 P.M. when we got back to the ranch.

As we drove up to the barn, I saw about twenty ranchhands all sitting around in a circle. I got out of the jeep and walked toward the crowd.

"What's going on?" I asked.

"It's your horse, Brownie. She's dead," said one of the men.

Slowly I walked up to where Brownie was lying in the corral. I bent down and patted her on her side. It took everything I had to keep from crying in front of all those men.

All at once, the corral gate opened and Mr. Boulton came riding in on an old tractor. He began scooping out a large hole right next to Brownie.

"What's he gonna do?" I yelled out.

"We always bury the horses right where they drop," said

one of the ranchhands.

I stood to the side while he dug the hole for Brownie, wiping the tears from my eyes as they rolled down my cheeks. I will never forget that feeling of sadness for as long as I live.

When the large hole had been dug, the men all stood back so that Brownie could be moved into it. Mr. Boulton lowered the tractor's big scoop and moved toward Brownie.

"PLEASE, MR. OWEN, SIR! Please don't move Brownie with that tractor bucket. You'll cut her and mess her up!" I yelled as I ran out in front of the tractor, waiving my hands and arms.

"Look here, boy," said Mr. Boulton. "We have no choice but to do this when a horse dies. She is just too heavy to move by hand."

"I'll get her in the hole. I swear I will, Mr. Owen, sir," I screamed as loud as I could. I ran over to Brownie and I pushed on her head as hard as I could, but she barely moved. I pushed and pushed, but her body was just too heavy. Nothing I tried to do would move her any closer to the hole. Finally, I stopped pushing. I crumbled there in the dirt, with my head resting against Brownie's side.

"Please don't use that bucket scoop on Brownie," I pleaded over and over.

One at a time, the ranchhands began to get down off their horses. Each positioned himself around the large brown horse and together they began to push and pull with all their might. Inch by inch, Brownie moved toward the large hole in the ground. All at once, she began to slide downhill. I raised her head as best I could, so that her face would not be scarred. The next thing I knew, I was being pulled down into the hole.

Suddenly, everything went totally silent. I just sat there at the bottom of the hole with Brownie's head resting on my lap. Dust and dirt settling all around me.

Slowly, I got to my feet and I placed her head flat on the ground. Then I positioned each of her legs so they were straight. I removed my Western shirt and I placed it over her

face so that dirt would not get into her eyes. I stood there
crying as my best friend was being covered with earth.

Most of that night I stayed in the barn, cleaning Brownie's
stall. I cried until I could cry no more. I guess I was just too
embarrassed to go back to the bunkhouse with the rest of
the ranchhands.

Early the next morning, I walked back to the bunkhouse
to shower and change clothes before going out to collect the
chicken eggs. As I entered the small wooden house, I noticed
that the ranchhands were up and getting dressed. There on
my bunk was eight dollars and some change. On a match-
book cover was written, "Buy yourself a new Western shirt."

When I looked up, all the men were smiling at me. One of
them said, "You may be a city boy, R.D. [that's what they
always called me], but you definitely have the heart that it
takes to be a real honest-to-goodness cowboy."

I wiped my swollen red eyes and I smiled real
proud-like.

Roger Dean Kiser

A Good Horse Is Hard to Find

A Good Horse Is Hard to Find. *Reprinted by permission of Boots Reynolds. ©1997 Boots Reynolds.*

Shadow

It started to snow outside, and hoping for a bit of diversion from the typical Minnesota winter weather, we decided to go to a horse sale in town, We watched with interest as the fancy horses with shiny coats came parading in. Some had glitter on their hips or festive red and green ribbons in their manes because it was just before Christmas. There were horses of all colors, shapes and sizes, and everyone was in a bidding frenzy,

Lots of people were going to get expensive horses for Christmas it seemed. Some of the animals had experience working cows and some had experience in the show ring. Others could earn their keep by pulling a sleigh. Eager to own the finest prospects, a number of people in the crowd were bidding hundreds and even thousands of dollars.

"Here's a four-year-old sorrel mare, 15.3-hands high, with forty-two halter points," the auctioneer bellowed. "Her bloodlines include Sonny Dee Bar, Tender Six and Zanzabar Joe. Do I hear five thousand, five thousand one, five two?"

I was fascinated by the spectacle. Every magnificent horse that came through had a story and bloodline that the auctioneer read. The crowd would "ooh" and "aah" in response and then the bidding war would begin. A couple over here, then a man over there and a lady in front of me all bid on the same horse, until he was "going, going, gone!" Then the next horse entered and the process started all over again, taking at most, ten to fifteen minutes per horse. Fifty to sixty horses were sold that day.

Eventually, they got to the last one, a skinny little black pony. The crowd roared with laughter. The pony was led in by a fifteen-year-old boy, who sat on her and then jumped up and down on her back, proclaiming, "She's broke to ride." She had big brown eyes under a long forelock that was full of dried manure and weed seeds.

"She's going to take some time to clean up," the auctioneer stated. "And she needs a few groceries to fatten her up."

Then, looking around, he asked, "Anybody know the story on this one?"

One of the helpers whispered something into his ear and he announced, "The owner forgot about this one out in the pasture and now he wants to get rid of her. She is not registered. There's no pedigree that we know of. Okay, who will give me three hundred for the old mare?"

The crowd was still laughing.

"How about two? Okay, one! Will anybody give me fifty bucks for her?"

The crowd continued to snicker at the lonely, forgotten little pony.

"Okay, get her out of here!" he told the boy who led her in.

So she turned her head as if to say good-bye then hung her head and walked out. The boy put her back in her stall and proceeded to help the new owners with their horses. One by one, the horses clip-clopped, by her stall to meet their new families. The lonely little black mare just hung her head.

Every time a person walked by, her ears would perk up and she would raise her head in anticipation that maybe, just maybe, someone wanted her. But then there would be only more snickers and the sound of fading footsteps. Finally, she would drop her head. The pony turned around so she didn't have to watch the other horses parade by.

It broke our hearts to watch this. We just looked at each other and nodded. Randy went one way and I went the other. We found the auctioneer and said, "Will you take ten dollars?"

He looked at us, puzzled, "For what?" he asked.

"The little black mare," we said excitedly.

"SOLD!" he said with a shake of his head and a smirk.

Without access to a proper horse trailer, we loaded her into the bed of my Toyota pickup, and to a chorus of titters and guffaws, headed for home.

For the last two years of her life, Shadow had the neighborhood kids begging to ride her, brush her or just be by her side, dreaming of the adventures tomorrow would bring for the both of them. We laugh when we remember the faces of those folks at the auction and the sight of the dirty old pony in the bed of our pickup. But the joy and the laughter we had sharing life with Shadow far exceeded the laughter at the sale barn that night.

T.C. Wadsworth

Old Twist

The majestic eye peered through the opening in the stall door. It was a gaze that reflected years of success and experience as a champion reining horse. It also conveyed gentleness and wisdom. It belonged to an old Quarter Horse named Twist. Now past thirty years old, he had spent the last few years relegated to the rank of dependable trail companion for his owner. But inside the rough, aged exterior, the heart of a true winner still beat with the same spirit to be part of a rider's life. This spirit had not faded even as younger horses arrived at the barn and took up more and more of Twist's owner's time. Little did I know the effect that the old champion's spirit would have on my daughter.

A few years before, my daughter Stacy had had a bad experience with a runaway horse. She was just eight at the time, and a terrifying fall accompanied the disaster. Although she broke no bones, her confidence, love for horses and the desire to learn to ride were shattered. No matter how her mother and I tried, we had no success in healing the damage caused on that fateful day. But as I stood there and saw Stacy look into the eye of the old fellow in the stall, I knew this was going to be the beginning of a special relationship.

Fortunately, Stacy's accident had not diminished her love for animals in general, and this small opening was all that Twist needed to establish a special bond. Stacy was now thirteen years old, which is a critical age for all young ladies to handle. It is a time when special bonds are not easy to form, but so crucial to possess. Would Twist be able to wipe away Stacy's reluctance to get back into a saddle after five years? It was as if Twist recognized the challenge and the importance of victory. It wasn't a blue ribbon, trophy or award that was at stake, but the heart of a child, and what a special medal of victory he then would possess.

In the days and weeks that followed, my daughter began to express daily interest in coming to the barn with me and my wife. We were careful not to interfere. We did not dare disrupt the magic of the old man at work. Though she said she was there to see the barn cats, Stacy would seek out Twist. She took the initiative to spend time with him, feeding, brushing, combing and stroking him from head to hoof, all the while talking to him about her life.

Though age had taken away some of the tone of the old Quarter Horse's muscles, it had not lessened his ability to strike the stance of a champion as he stood quietly while she groomed him.

Then one day as my wife was readying one of our horses for a ride, Twist's owner noticed the old guy's eager expression and desire to be included, too. So the owner asked Stacy if she wanted to get Twist ready and take him out for a ride. In response, Stacy looked once again into the old man's eye. I can't say that he winked at her, but it was that moment their two spirits met and completed the bond that had been forming over a couple of months. Continuing to look deep into his eyes, Stacy didn't speak, she only nodded yes.

Moments later, I stood there as they rode off together, Stacy winning renewed confidence and desire, and Twist winning his medal of a child's heart. I had not seen his head held higher or his walk more regal than in that first minute.

As this first ride turned into many more, Twist took very good care of his young friend and slowly replaced her fear with confidence. I nearly cried the day I looked across the field and caught sight of Stacy and Twist cantering back to the barn. Her long hair was pulled back and flowing in the breeze in a way that seemed to mimick the appearance of the old man's tail. He had won. He had beaten fear, removing years of bad memories and replacing them with moments of happiness that are etched forever not only in my daughter's heart but mine as well. I know I always will be grateful for what Twist did for my family. I will forever remember the time I looked deep into the eyes of this champion and saw the love of a child looking back at me.

Tom Maupin

A Silent Bond

Never thank yourself; always thank the horses for the happiness and joy we experience through them.

Hans H.E. Isenbart

Apparently, my trainer found the fuzzy chestnut named Tic Tac giving pony rides someplace in Texas. I always had a problem believing that this fiery steed could have come from such humble beginnings. Of course, he was no fiery steed, but I was ten years old at the time, filled with high hopes for my riding career, and no successful rider was without a feisty mount, right? Tic Tac would be mine.

The first time I rode the 15.3-hand Morgan–Quarter Horse cross, he reared up so high that I heard the Lone Ranger's theme song play in my head. Maybe we should have named him Silver. Of course, that would not have fit him at all. My mother, watching my lesson from the edge of the ring, was mortified as she saw us suspended in midair. I, on the other hand, was thrilled with Tic Tac's obvious energy and spirit.

My trainer at the time had a remarkable ability to instill within me an immense amount of confidence. Every time I watched her ride, I sat in awe, hoping to be just like her. She made me believe that I could ride anything, anywhere, any-time. Over the years, this overconfidence often has resulted in catastrophic spills, broken bones and countless bruises, but it also has given me the courage to get back on.

I rode many horses in the barn in exchange for helping to muck stalls, clean tack and bring in the horses from the pasture. I grew to love the work and relished the smell of manure and sawdust as every horse-crazy girl does. Although I appreciated the chance to ride other horses, Tic Tac was always my favorite. I was terribly upset when other people rode him during their lessons and I secretly hoped that he would pull another vertical rear and scare them into riding another horse the next time. But he never did. Everyone fell in love with him, just as I had.

We never knew Tic Tac's birthday, so I let him share mine. Each November 9 I brought out a bag of birthday treats and set them by his stall. Then after a bareback gallop in the pasture, I sat with him for hours as he ate his grass, apples and carrots and I sipped Dr Pepper. I never talked to him, the way that many people chat with their horses. I hardly ever said a word, because I never felt I had to.

Tic Tac taught me many lessons that have served me well over my twenty-plus years in the saddle. One slippery day after a Texas rainstorm, I pointed him toward a tiny pile of branches on the ground. As his front feet began to leave the earth, he slammed on the brakes, startling me. Tic Tac never stopped at a fence. A little disappointed in him, I dug my heels into his side and coaxed him over the jump. He hesitated and then carefully popped over it. But the footing on the landing side was too soggy to support his legs, and they slipped out from under him. Both of us went tumbling into the mud. As I sat in the muck, looking up at Tic Tac, who had safely made it back to his feet, I noticed a stream of blood oozing down his soft muzzle. I immediately felt a flood of guilt for having urged him to jump when he knew better. Taking him back to the barn to tend to his still-bleeding scrape, I silently vowed never to question his instincts again. Lesson learned: When you've built trust with a horse, respect it.

On March 9, 1988, I began my daily walk to the barn. I was early and the horses were still turned out. Because the geldings were always in the rear pasture, I headed in that direction and looked for Tic Tac's halter on the fence, but it wasn't there. Scanning the grounds, I couldn't find him anywhere. I felt deflated because I thought that someone must be riding him. Returning to the barn, I found a friend who looked at me with sad eyes, and explained that Tic Tac had been taken to the veterinary clinic.

It must be colic, I thought. He had had several bouts of colic in those two years, but never before was it serious enough for him to have to travel to the clinic in Katy, Texas.

The next few hours were a blur. I remember my mom returning to the barn about an hour after she dropped me off. Someone must have called her to comfort me. I was numb as I sat in the driveway, waiting to see the trailer pull up, but eerily knowing that when it did, it would be empty.

While I waited for the rusty two-horse to rattle in, at least twenty different barn mates came to sit with me at various times. I have no recollection of what they said to me or even who they were. The words and the faces blended together and all I could do was stare down the road and recall every second of the past two years that I'd spent with Tic Tac.

After hours of waiting, the phone rang, and eventually someone handed it to me. I told my hand not to reach for the phone and I urged my legs to run, but they ignored me. Slowly, I placed the phone to my ear and began to walk toward Tic Tac's stall. On the other end, a tearful trainer and best friend told me what I already knew. Tic Tac was gone.

By the time she was able to force out the words, I was in his stall and could see an imprint in the shavings where he had been lying, probably trying to roll to ease his belly pains. My legs gave way and I collapsed, trying to relieve the pain that suddenly covered my entire body like a second skin.

At that time, I thought I'd never leave his stall because it was the only connection I had to him. I walked over to the feed bin and traced every line, hoping to feel the soft muzzle that was once scraped by my ignorance. I ran my hand through his water trough, begging to hear the muffled sound of his gentle gulps.

Eventually, my mom eased me from the ground and took me home. The house was silent and oddly still. My entire world seemed changed. My siblings and friends didn't know how to act around me. On one hand, they knew I was terribly sad and they felt bad for me, but on the other, they probably thought I was nuts because he was just a horse.

Since then, I've been on countless other horses and have had greater success in the show ring than I ever could have had with Tic Tac. Nevertheless, that special bond never has been and never will be duplicated. I'm reminded of this each time I find myself talking to a horse.

Every March 9 between 1988 and 1995, I couldn't bring myself to dry my tears and face the world. I wouldn't go to school. I wouldn't go to work. I wouldn't even go to the barn. My parents understood and never forced the issue. They let me sit in my room, holding a picture of Tic Tac. Sometimes, I reminisced about all of our wonderful times together. Other times, I relived that painful day of loss.

A couple of years ago, I decided not to be a slave to March 9. Instead of grieving, I spent that day in silent celebration of a remarkable relationship with a fuzzy chestnut with a crooked blaze. I don't regret those years I spent mourning that day. After all, never before had I experienced such an incredible sense of loss and abandonment, all of it made worse by the fact that I never said good-bye. But then again, I never said a word to Tic Tac because I never had to.

Tiernan McKay

Daddy Always Said "Yes" to Horses

He has galloped through young girls' dreams, added richness to grown women's lives, and served men in war and strife.

Toni Robinson

The only "no" I ever heard from my dad Jim turned out to be "no problem." From the time I was a little girl to the time that my dad died, he called me Baby Teresa. Most everyone said he spoiled me and I could only nod my head or smile in agreement.

Every girl's dream is to have a horse. My daddy agreed.

When I was just three years old, I got my first horse. It was a beautiful Palomino rocking horse made of plastic. Cradled in a metal frame and suspended by giant springs, he was my pride and joy, and I could maneuver that horse like a jockey going down the homestretch. I loved my plastic Palomino, but soon he wasn't good enough.

I didn't want to be limited by earthly bounds. I wanted a swinging horse that was suspended in the air. My daddy agreed.

He took the rocking horse from the frame and suspended it

with ropes from a ceiling beam in our basement. Not knowing that the attachment was only temporary, I ran and leaped onto the horse's back just like they did in those old Western movies. But unlike the cowboys in the movies, I didn't ride off into the sunset. I was carried off to the emergency room in my father's arms. When I had landed on the Palomino's plastic saddle, the ropes had pulled loose from the ceiling and I crashed face first onto the concrete floor. When I woke up in the emergency room, I had a concussion, two black eyes and a bruised ego.

When I returned home, the horse was gone, clandestinely put out to pasture, I learned years later, at a friend's house.

When I was ten years old, my next horse was the real deal: a certified hay-munching, apple-eating, horse-apple-producing Arabian cross. Just four years old, Sandarrow was a mighty mite. He'd been advertised in the local paper as gentle and calm. He was the first horse we ever looked at. I wanted him the moment I laid eyes on him. My daddy agreed.

Sandarrow was light yellow, almost white, with a short strong neck. Stocky, strong and surging with unrestrained power, he certainly was not gentle and calm. He was more of a rodeo horse than a kid's horse. Nothing scared Sandarrow or restrained him for long. Halters? He'd break them. Barbed-wire fences? He'd walk right through them. When I took him to the local county fair for 4-H, he climbed the six-foot wooden stall door as if he were a monkey with hooves, and then he strode out into the alleyway, wearing a silly horse grin. He hightailed it out of the fairgrounds, through town and into the countryside, racing around meadows, taunting my daddy to catch him.

This was the early 1960s, before safety helmets, protective clothing, rider safety training and the other precautions we take for granted today. Sandarrow preferred to ride bareback: that is, with no rider at all. To achieve his goal, he would often rub me off on fences, run under low-hanging branches, buck like a bronco or speed off like a Formula One racer.

One day when I was eleven, I decided to have a quick ride before a dance recital, so I jumped on Sandarrow without bothering to put on my shoes or his saddle. He ran down the hill by our house, weaving like an equine bobsled, through the trees and toward the garden where my daddy was working. I don't think I touched Sandarrow's back the whole way down the hill.

When we got to the garden fence, Sandarrow started bucking. I could see my dad's eyes bulging with fear as I bounced up and down on his back as if I were jumping on a trampoline. Finally, Sandarrow spun and off I flew, landing flat on my back.

With the wind knocked out of me and dazed from a concussion, I couldn't move from where I'd landed. Sandarrow stomped on my right foot, breaking nearly every bone. Then, my daddy said, he kicked with both feet, narrowly missing my head.

Terrified, my daddy scooped me up in his arms and ran with me back to our house, which was a short distance down the hill. My daddy was a small man and I was almost as large as he was. But I remember how strong he felt, how fast he moved and how he kept looking down into my tear-filled eyes, reassuring me, "You'll be okay, Baby Teresa. Daddy has you." He wanted to get rid of Sandarrow after the accident, but I begged to keep him. Daddy agreed.

The rest of the summer, I still rode Sandarrow. This time however, I wore a cowboy boot on one foot and a cast on the other.

Before I knew it, Daddy's girl had grown up and I was longing to acquire a new horse to keep at the Pi Phi sorority house at the University of Idaho. Actually, what I was interested in now was horsepower. I wanted a car of my own and had my eye on a vintage Chevy Corvette that a boyfriend in the military service was offering to me because he was going on assignment overseas. I could see my friends and myself cruising the mountain roads of the Palouse in that car, Daddy disagreed.

Oh, he did get me a Chevy, though, a compact Chevy Vega, which, because it used oil like crazy, couldn't pass a gas station. Still, my father, a logger by trade, babied the car almost as much as he babied me and kept it running for nearly ten years.

My daddy was always very active and enjoyed robust health until he was eighty-one. That year, Mother Nature, snuck up on him and started pulling him down. First, he lost the vision in his right eye, then he had a heart attack from which he recovered. But then he was hamstrung by terminal lung cancer. From the time a diagnosis was made, he lived only a month. But during that time, we pulled out old photo albums and looked at pictures of the rocking horse and my black eyes, Sandarrow and Baby Teresa's baby blue car.

After my father passed away, I went into his room alone to soak up the essence of this diminutive man who was a giant to me. I smelled his Levi's and fingered the suspenders that were still attached. I held his watch and the glasses that were on the dresser. Inside the dresser, I found a cloth bag containing all of my baby teeth. Apparently, the tooth fairy and my daddy were good friends.

Finally, I sat on the edge of the bed he'd slept in for more than sixty of his eighty years and I looked at his nightstand. There was a Beetle Bailey alarm clock, a 1920s-era art deco lamp and a worn, faded, diorama about the size of a deck of cards.

I moved in close. This was a Minnie Mouse diorama that my daddy had bought me at Disneyland when I was only six years old. It featured Minnie riding a horse into the sunset. Unbeknownst to me, Daddy had customized it, putting a lock of my hair on Minnie's head and a picture of me in the painted sky behind her. My mother Valdie later told me that for more than forty years, this horse sat by my father's head and every night he would pat the top of the diorama and say, "Good night, Baby Teresa."

Tears burst forth as I called out to God to take good care of this man who never said no to a girl who wanted a horse. He agreed.

Teresa Becker

Syd and Roanie

The wind of heaven is that which blows between a horse's ears.

Arabian Proverb

Syd Parkin is fifty-nine years old and still regrets standing only five feet, three inches tall. Not because he is too short, but rather because he is too tall to be a jockey. On the one-year anniversary of surviving a life-threatening aneurysm, Syd rode to the top of a mountain ridge, where he and his horse Roanie had a very special bonding experience. He credits Roanie for teaching him to appreciate all the little miracles and blessings each day has to offer. Syd put it this way: "Even on your worst day, if you look hard enough, you can find one good thing. For instance, I almost died, but I got two great things: Roanie and a second chance at life."

They were partners for five years and spent time together every day. Then one afternoon, while on a simple trail ride, some unknowing teenagers on rental horses came charging up behind them. They startled Roanie while crossing a cement road and in a split second Syd's and Roanie's lives were forever changed. Roanie slipped, fell down hard, doing the splits, and shattered his pelvis.

Syd and several veterinarians did everything in their power to rehabilitate his faithful partner. Despite all of their efforts over an agonizing ten months, Syd had to face the heartbreaking reality that Roanie would never recover. He was advised to put him down. Syd confided to me: "I just can't do it yet. I don't know if it's really the right thing to do." I told him to trust his own judgment. "You'll know when it's time." Syd responded, "I just wish Roanie could give me a sign so I'd know."

I asked for and was granted a moment alone with Roanie. His strong animal instinct to survive was palpably low. I spoke softly, "How ya doin', Roanie boy? Not too good, huh? I know you've been fighting real hard. You look tired boy. Your dad loves you so much. I think maybe you're hanging on because you're feeling how hard it is for him to let you go. Roanie, he just needs a sign from you that it's okay. I promise I'll help look after your dad. So if you can, please let him know it's okay to let you go."

I fought back tears that fell anyway. As I looked deeply into his big, soft, soulful eyes, I got a strong sense that Roanie had understood every word I'd said.

I returned to Syd and asked if there was anything else that I could do. He replied, "No. I'm calling the vet tomorrow to make the appointment." He broke down saying, "I just can't be there when he goes down. I won't be able to take seeing him hit the ground." I promised Syd that I would be there and that I would be looking into Roanie's eyes so that he would go while looking into a familiar, loving face. Syd nodded okay, but this provided little comfort. "If I were a *real* man, a *real* cowboy, I could do it." I told him not to be so hard on himself. "Not being able to watch doesn't mean you're less of a man. On the contrary, it means you're a kind, loving, sensitive man who loves his horse too much to witness something too painful to see."

He thanked me for my offer and said he'd take me up on it. All night I wondered if I'd be able to keep my promise. It's difficult to explain what I felt, except to say that as impossible as being there was going to be, it would be even more impossible not to be there.

I called Syd the next day, and he told me that the veterinarian was coming to put Roanie down. "But it's okay. When I went to see him this morning, Roanie gave me a sign. Now I know it's the right thing to do." The appointment was set for eleven o'clock the next morning. I arrived at ten-thirty to discover that Syd had spent the entire night in Roanie's stall. He had written him a three-page letter and read it to him. Neither of them got much sleep. Syd was doing his best and to his credit, he mustered up enough strength to help me put out orange parking cones to reserve the spot closest to Roanie's stall for the veterinarian and for the truck that eventually would be hauling Roanie away.

The hauling truck arrived first. It was clean and white with a shiny sterile-looking metal bed. My eyes quickly looked away for all too soon, I would witness the precious cargo its coldness would hold. The stable was hushed with unusual stillness and a reverent quiet. I believe the other horses knew what was going on. The veterinarian arrived on time. Syd apologized: "I've never done this before, so you're going to have to talk me through this. Do I just bring him out here by the truck?" The veterinarian nodded yes. I put my hand on Syd's shoulder, trying to transfer all the love and support I could as we walked slowly but deliberately to Roanie's stall. "Breathe," I said as a reminder to Syd and myself. Roanie was munching on a feast of his favorite treats that Syd had prepared for him. Syd slowly undid Roanie's halter from the pipe corral. As Roanie sweetly lifted his head to cooperate, as he had done a thousand times before, I was never more impressed with a man's courage—nor strength of heart—as I watched Syd tenderly slip that halter on Roanie's face for what was so painfully the last time. Every action, every word he spoke echoed under the enormous weight of *"this is the last time."*

Syd stood beside his friend and stroked him with a loving touch. "You're a good boy. I love you, Roanie boy." He then lifted Roanie's mane, put his face against the horse's neck and inhaled several times, rubbing his nose back and forth, savoring and taking in every molecule of what he called the greatest smell on earth. "Just one more," he said with tears streaming down his face. As long as I live, I will never forget the way he smelled that horse's neck. Then Syd looked into Roanie's eyes and said, "Good-bye boy. I love you, Roanie. Thanks for being my friend."

As Syd led the horse out of his stall, again I placed my hand on his shoulder and said, "You will smell him again, you know. He will come to visit you in his spirit form and you will feel him around you." Syd nodded. In previous weeks we had discussed the idea that our spirit or life energy never dies, that it leaves our earthly body, but lives on. I told him how my mother's spirit comes to me in the form of hummingbirds, how I have sensed my Aunt Nancy's presence in butterflies, and that Roanie would find a similar way to visit him.

However, in this harsh moment of earthly mortality, Syd had to do the impossible. He led his beloved partner to the hauling truck. It was the longest, most difficult fifty feet they ever walked. The veterinarian gave Roanie a strong sedative. Roanie started to get wobbly. Syd said his final good-byes. Afraid that Roanie might stumble and fall, I pleaded, "Syd, go. Please. Go now." I don't know how, but he managed to find the strength to leave and he headed for the bridge where I was to meet him when it was all over. But now it was time for me to fulfill my promise.

The sedative was doing its job. The veterinarian administered the fatal injection. I stood my post and held Roanie's gaze. As he slowly descended and gently lay on the ground, his breath blowing hard through his soft pink nostrils, I went down with him, never taking my eyes off of his.

"It's okay boy. You did good. You are so loved. So loved." I stroked his face. He lay very still and although he did not appear to be breathing, I asked, "He's not gone yet, is he?" The veterinarian felt for his pulse. "No, not yet," he responded. Still stroking his face, with my heart breaking, I mustered up as much humor as I could. "Now listen, Roanie, when you get to heaven, I want you to trot right up to Trigger and bite him on the butt. You tell him he wasn't the only star. You were just as loved." What more could I say to my noble friend?

"Roanie, your dad is standing on the bridge," I continued. "He loves you so much. If you can, please boy, let him feel you. Let him feel your spirit as you pass. Good-bye, boy. I love you, Roanie." I kissed his face and looked to the veterinarian. "He's gone now, isn't he?" After checking for a pulse, he solemnly nodded yes. I kissed Roanie one last time, stood up, collected myself, then cut a small lock of hair from his mane, which Syd had requested, and a lock from his tail. I removed Roanie's halter and lead rope for what was truly the last time. One last soft pat on his face. "Okay," I said. "Thank you."

I stood as if on guard as they hoisted Roanie into the truck. As soon as they were out of sight, I headed for the bridge that Syd, Roanie, my horse Annie and I had ridden across so many times before. As I approached him, I prayed for any words that might offer him some measure of comfort. We just grabbed each other and hugged. I started to cry. Syd said, "It's okay." I looked at him. "Really, I'm okay. The whole time I was waiting, the wind was blowing strong on my back. Then suddenly, I felt this warm gush of wind blow into my face. It was Roanie. I felt him go through me. He was telling me he was all right."

Syd and I walked the rest of the way across the bridge, telling Roanie stories, thus beginning our path of grieving and healing. I am happy to say that since then, Syd has gotten another horse Bodie. My horse Annie and I were honored to go along on their maiden ride together. We rode to the same mountain ridge where Syd had had his life-changing bonding moment with Roanie. As we stopped to admire the beautiful valley below, bathed in the pinkish gold light of the setting sun, a hummingbird suddenly appeared, stopped directly in front of us and hovered there for about ten seconds. We shared a knowing smile. "Syd, I believe we just had a visit!" Syd responded simply: "Yup, just another one of those small miracles you can see every day if you look for them."

Judy Pioli Askins

A Horse with Heart

With a coat the color of smooth beach sand, and a silky mane and tail of the richest ebony, T.J. stood more than 16 hands tall. His heart was unbelievably full of love and loyalty. His kind eyes and soft breath were always a comfort. He understood me. He never uttered a word of disappointment on the many occasions that I'd seek the solace of his sleek neck and strong shoulders. He never failed to carry my burdens away.

Even as a three-year-old, he was a joy to ride. Whether we were galloping bareback across Mr. White's wheat fields in the middle of the night or schooling extensively in the ring, he always seemed to enjoy himself. His ears flicked forward with his nicker of anticipation of our ride as I entered the barn that damp day in April.

"Ready to go out and play, boy?" I questioned him even though I knew he was more than ready to go. The gleam in the depths of his eyes affirmed my assumption.

"I have been waiting for you all day," he seemed to say.

I brought out my brushes and began to curry his coat and massage his favorite spots. At a spot just in front of his withers, I circled with extra pressure while he craned his neck forward in sheer delight "Oh, yeah . . . right there . . . feels so good!" he seemed to communicate to me and I smiled at his pleasure. After knocking the dirt off of him with a brush, I wrapped his legs in navy blue polo wraps to support them and pushed my comfy saddle up onto his broad back. I shimmied into my chaps and stuffed my hair into my helmet. I was just as excited as he was for this ride because today was the first day with no rain in more than a week. I helped him slip his noble head into the bridle and I fastened the buckles. Then we walked out of the barn toward the driest spot on the farm.

As he walked to warm up, I watched the sun tease us by peeking out from behind the clouds and then scooting out of sight again as if afraid of its reflection in the puddles. I urged T.J. into a trot with a tiny bit of pressure from my lower legs. I was so proud of how responsive he was that day, moving out for me and then collecting as I asked him. We worked in some circles and figure eights. We practiced his transitions, which were as smooth as butter. T.J. had come a long way from being a "spaghetti noodle" two-year-old to the balanced horse that he was that day. The footing felt good enough for a canter, and neither of us could resist it. His canter was wonderfully fluid as he stretched across the ground. Again, we worked a few circles and figure eights at the canter, this time with simple lead changes in the middle. As a change from the routine workout, I decided to try a couple flying lead changes with him. We'd worked on them before and T.J. knew how to do them. We proceeded across the pasture on his left lead, keeping a balanced straight line all the way to the corner. When we were almost to the corner, I simply shifted my weight to ask for the opposite lead. I felt T.J. shift his body with me as he executed the maneuver, but something was not right. Where was his left hind leg? I could not feel it beneath us where it was supposed to be.

When T.J. had used his left hind leg to thrust over to the right lead, he had pushed off on a slick spot of mud. His hind end slipped out from underneath him and we unceremoniously headed for the ground. With my legs still astride him, we landed in motion. Lying on his side, T.J. was sliding swiftly toward a six-inch-square post in the three-rail board fence. Because I was still on his back, pinched between his side and the ground, I watched in agony as I waited to be smashed between his back and the fence post. In what seemed like slow motion, I glanced at my horse. I thought about how horrible it would be if I could never gallop bareback across the wheat fields with him again. I thought about how much I loved him.

In the space of a heartbeat, T.J. bunched every muscle in his body and flipped over me so that now he was the one sliding into the fence, legs first. His massive body slammed into the fence with enough force to level the six- by-six post. Immediately after he hit the fence, I slid into him. All that I could hear was both of us breathing, trying to suck air into our lungs while we sorted out what just had happened. Slowly, I pulled myself to my feet on rubbery legs. I reached down and stroked his coat as I stepped around him to survey the damage.

"Easy, boy. You're okay." I tried to soothe him even though he was much calmer than I was. T.J. just lay still while I untangled the splintered boards from between his legs. I dragged the broken post out of his way and urged him to try to stand up. He pulled his front legs over, stretched them out in front of his chest and pushed his neck out for balance as he struggled to rise from the ground. After a quick glance to see that all four legs were still intact, I swung my arms around his neck in a fierce hug. A few minutes passed and, through my tears, I stroked his face and kissed him.

We stood there for a while, just taking everything in. Then gingerly, we walked back to the barn so that I could take a closer look at him. T.J. walked away from that fence with a couple scrapes on his legs and belly, but without major injuries that required veterinary attention.

I was only bruised and a little sore, which was pain that I was grateful to bear, considering how devastating that day could have been. I still do not know exactly how T.J. was able to roll over me in the air without touching me. I do not need to know. I do know that he willingly chose to sacrifice himself for me that day. He loved me that much. His heart was full of love and loyalty. He showed me his love every day. He showed me the depth of his devotion that damp April day, and I will never forget it.

Jerri Simmons-Fletcher

Sleeping Baby

"Kori! Kori! Has anyone seen Kori?" my sister Suzi asked, running into the kitchen. Kori was my fourteen-month-old niece. She recently had learned to walk, go up and down stairs and push open doors.

"Oh, have you checked upstairs?" I asked, not bothering to look up from my favorite cartoon.

"Of course I have! I've checked everywhere!"

My mother and little sister Trudy entered the kitchen.

"She's not in the bedrooms," my mother said, concerned.

"Maybe she's fallen asleep somewhere," I said.

My mother began barking orders. "Jennilyn, you check the closets. I'll check the yard and the swings. Suzi, you check with the neighbors. Trudy, go to the barn and see if she's with Grandpa."

Everyone began a frantic search. Frequent shouts of "She's not in here!" resounded throughout the house.

Soon Suzi returned from the neighbors. "They haven't seen her!" she gasped, catching her breath.

Grandpa strode swiftly through the back door. "She's not in the barn. I've checked the stables and around the pond."

"The pond!" A look of horror filled my sister's face.

"She's not in the pond. The water's crystal clear today. I promise she's not there." Gently, he hugged Suzi. "We'll find her."

"I'll go check the attic again," Suzi sniffled, holding back tears.

"And we'll all go check around the fields," commanded my father.

I looked at my watch. Nearly an hour had gone by. The sun was high in the sky and the warm summer breeze shifted the tall grass in the field. *That looks like a good place for a baby to get lost,* I thought as I parted the knee-high grass under my feet. I could see Trudy searching on the far side of the field. Behind her, our three horses were grazing.

Suddenly, Trudy was running toward me and shouting, "I found her! I found her!"

I ran into the house. "Trudy found her! Trudy found her!"

"Where? Is she okay?" my sister cried, bounding down the stairs from the attic.

"She's in the field!" I hollered.

Just as we were racing out the door, Trudy raced in.

"The horses are protecting her. She's okay. Get Dad," cried Trudy. "The horses won't let me in."

Excitedly, we all raced to the field. The horses were still on the far side, standing guard. As we drew closer, we could see the horses, head to tail, forming a tight circle. Lady Star whinnied as we approached.

In the center of the circle, Kori was sleeping peacefully on a bed of grass.

Jennilyn McKinnon

A Gift of Gold

A pony is a childhood dream. A horse is an adult treasure.

Rebecca Carroll

Some moments feel like magic. It is as if I can hear and feel the presence of my daughter Emily while taking my summer-evening riding lessons. While I am preparing to ride in my first horse show, I am experiencing something I will hold dear to my heart for a long time. These magical moments give me hope, joy and a calm inner peace because next week it will have been three years since I lost my daughter in a tragic car accident.

Emily was nine years old when she fell in love with an old bay mare. I watched the tender relationship between a young girl and her first horse blossom. Emily's love for her horse consumed her life and after she'd taken a few riding lessons, I knew she was hooked. I was immediately designated Horse Show Mom.

I spent many chilly winter evenings and lots of sweltering summer days watching Emily ride in lessons and school for shows. My little girl progressed from looking slightly scared and frustrated to looking confident and self-assured. In the process, I learned enough equine terminology so I could talk the talk. But the hardest thing to learn was how to act cool and calm when my little darlin' fell off her horse!

Our days were busy, preparing for shows. There was always work to be done: cleaning tack, washing and grooming the horse and finding the right chaps to match Emily's show clothes. There were weekly trips to the dry cleaners, as well as submitting entry forms and writing checks—lots of them. My role as Horse Show Mom was hard work, but very rewarding. Little did I know that the memories of those moments would need to last me for a lifetime.

After much anticipation and many sleepless nights, the long-awaited events arrived. Show days were fun, exciting and exhausting for all of us. In the show ring, there is a partnership of two, but behind the scenes, three often work together—the horse, the rider and the Horse Show Mom—to present the perfect package. Painting hooves, polishing boots and French-braiding Emily's hair were only a few of my duties. I will always remember telling my little equestrian to "Sit up and smile!"

Ah, the years flew by, and Emily grew tall. To keep up with the stiff competition she needed to upgrade to a larger and fancier horse. After we spent many months searching for the perfect match, Parker came into our lives. He was kind and forgiving, and sturdy and strong, and soon he became our treasured friend. The three of us became an integral part of the "family" at our barn. We had many good times together, laughing, crying and experiencing many fabulous and frantic moments.

When Emily turned seventeen, she announced that she was not going to show her horse anymore. She wanted to spend more time with her high school basketball team than with her dappled-gray gelding.

I was heartbroken at the news. "What about Parker? What about your friends at the barn? What about your trainer?" I couldn't believe it was over and I guess what I was really saying was "What about me?"

I had to settle for visiting the barn with carrots for some of my old equine friends and watching other kids practice for horse shows. But I still yearned for those early-morning moments, hearing the horses nicker in anticipation of what was to come and watching them march up the ramp of the horse trailer.

Well, many years have passed and my memories are sweet. Somehow, I feel close to Emily while spending time with horses. At times, the memories are bittersweet and tears spill from my eyes. Other times, I can smile and laugh. And at age fifty, I find that those memories now are getting me ready to ride in my first horse show. Now it is my turn to execute the proper leg, hand and body position to sit the jog and to pick up the correct lead for the lope.

My Paint gelding Murphy is a beautiful and talented animal. He moves with great ease in a solid way. He is definitely a "been there, done that" kind of guy. And somehow I think he knows he is a cherished friend who is helping me heal a broken heart.

As the sun sets, a cool breeze touches my face. I cluck for the jog and Murphy's transitions appear effortless. I sit tall in the saddle, my eyes up, my heels down and my hands light. I am doing something that I had watched my daughter do endless times. But this time, I am on board the horse, gently gliding around the arena as though I have done it a million times.

We trot figure eights over some poles in the center of the ring with a loose rein and graceful, rhythmic motion. For a novice, it is not an easy task, riding patterns over obstacles and keeping the pace forward and even. It takes a considerable amount of concentration and skill. Yet, with a steady cadence, we perform the task easily. Murphy and I approach the center pole in a straight line (almost every time) and are able to change directions subtly without a second thought as we cross the obstacle.

Well, this time I am "a top," and the sweetness of Emily's silent messages ring through my being. As if she is perched on my shoulder, not two of us, but three softly glide around the ring, and I hear her comments surround me like silken scarves wrapped around my soul.

It is possible that these moments mean more to me than any judge's scorecard might show. I am sure my handsome steed knows that he is part of this celebrated blessing. Preparing for competition gives me goals and something to look forward to. But the sound of Emily's quiet voice in my mind as the sun sets and the breeze touches my face is more precious than a world of blue ribbons or any prize I might earn in the show ring. It is a gift of gold that will forever glisten in my heart.

"Relax Mom. Just feel the motion and listen with your body. Keep the pace even, for he knows his job. Be soft with your hands and he will take good care of you.

"And, oh yeah, Mom. Sit up and smile!"

Robin Roberts

Chance of a Lifetime

Think, when we talk of horses, that you see them
Printing their proud hooves in the receiving earth;
For 'tis your thoughts that now must deck our kings.

William Shakespeare

It was a blistering hot day in June, when a man came to my small horse farm in Missouri, asking for some goat's milk. He needed it for his teenage nephew's new Quarter Horse filly because she was deathly ill. The man said two veterinarians had examined the foal and concluded that it would cost thousands of dollars to save her. His nephew didn't have that kind of money and planned to shoot the foal instead. The uncle told the teenager, "Give me twenty-four hours to try to save her." I gave him all the goat's milk I had and offered to help in any way I could. The man said, "You know, this filly just might end up here with you!" I thought he was joking. He wasn't.

The next day, a truck pulled into my driveway with the three-week–old foal lying on the flatbed, being held by the man's daughter. The man gently lifted the bright red filly off the truck and laid her on the grass. A makeshift pen was set up around her. It was under a shady tree, just outside my back door, so I could easily check on her every hour, day and night.

I have multiple sclerosis, which has gotten steadily worse, and I wasn't looking for a new project when this foal arrived on my doorstep. In fact, just before she got here, my husband Dave and I had decided to sell half of our horses, along with all of our goats and most of our farm birds. I wanted to lessen my work load. Still, I gladly accepted when the man asked me to help save this filly. He emphasized there was no money to pay for any more vet bills. He added, "Nobody expects her to make it through the next day or two." I took that as my cue to prove everyone wrong.

After the man left, I checked over every inch of the poor creature's tiny, frail body. She was in horrible shape, with fever sores in her mouth and pressure sores all over one side of her body. Her joints were grotesquely swollen and disfigured by a bacterial infection called neonatal septicemia. She looked like a skeleton, barely covered with skin and clumps of hair. She had a high fever, due to the life-threatening bacteria circulating in her bloodstream. She couldn't stand up or even lift her head. Her helpless brown eyes were sunken from dehydration, yet there was a twinkle in those eyes that captured my heart. I loved her from the moment I first saw her.

I didn't own her, but I'd become responsible for her. In those first few hours, I put together a basic medical kit and treated her wounds. She was desperate for nourishment. I searched the Internet and found that goat's milk is the next best thing to mare's milk for feeding a foal. So, I milked my goats, put the milk in a bottle with a foal nipple on it and just squirted what I could into the filly's mouth. She got some of it, but not enough. Finally, out of desperation, at four in the morning, I brought my goat Megan over to the filly. I held Megan's teat to the foal's mouth and she took to it immediately! She wasn't strong enough to hold her head up, but with my help, she was able to nurse directly from Megan. She drank until she couldn't hold anymore. My first hurdle was overcome.

By the next day, my efforts to feed the filly every half-hour were paying off. She seemed better. By the third day, she was able to sit up by herself. I kept reminding myself that she wasn't mine, but it did no good. I felt like she belonged to me much more than she belonged to the teenage boy who didn't care whether she lived or died. Her will to live was strong and she deserved to be given a name. I decided to call her Megan's Chance in honor of Megan, the old white nanny goat who had supplied milk, companionship and the chance for this little angel to live. Chance became her nickname.

Megan would groom Chance just as if she were her own baby. It was amazing and touching to watch an old goat mothering a young filly. Megan would lie down on the grass next to Chance and the two of them would pass the time in quiet contentment. The other animals on the farm also sought to comfort her. The geese and one of my chickens adopted her and stayed next to her most of the time. Our dog, a Yorkie–Pom mix named Pookey, would go up to Chance as she was lying on the ground and whisper into her ear. That seemed to bring a smile to Chance's face.

As the days wore on, the bond strengthened between Chance and me. She'd whinny when she heard me coming to see her. Just the sound of my footsteps lit a spark in her. Secretly, it warmed my heart to know that she didn't whinny to anyone else. I was her special mama, and she was my special child. It took awhile for me to realize that Chance would enrich not only my life, but also the lives of many people around the world.

I frequent several equine message boards on the Internet where horse lovers and owners get together to visit and trade thoughts on dealing with horse problems. When I first asked for advice about Chance, I had no idea that word of her troubles would spread the way it did. E-mails came flooding in to me from people who offered suggestions and words of support and who asked to see photos of her. I started a daily on-line diary on my Web site, where people could read the latest news about Chance and her struggle to live. I posted new pictures of her almost every day.

All over the world, people were falling in love with this determined little soul. The on-line horse-loving community watched with great interest as Chance and I experienced our ups and downs from day to day. Thousands shared my joy when Chance began gaining weight and sat up by herself for the first time. People were thrilled as her mouth ulcers and pressure sores healed. And when her fever shot back up and her joints began to swell again, I didn't cry alone.

There were days when the two of us were extremely tired, yet we kept up the fight. As we would rest together in the grass, I would tell Chance, "You have to keep trying. So many people are hoping and praying and sending their love." Chance would put her head in my lap as I'd hold her, stroke her and kiss her muzzle. Her lovely eyes were still saying, "I'm not giving up yet, Mama. I'm just resting."

As news of Chance's brave struggle spread over the Internet, people wrote to me saying they were doing acts of kindness in her honor. Some helped animals and others helped people needing assistance. More and more lives were indirectly touched by Chance and her courage. I felt so proud that I was able to share this wonderful little spark and watch it grow exponentially. We were all part of a miracle that was spreading.

Chance's health experienced lots of ups and downs as summer dragged on. Overall, she failed to improve as much as I'd hoped. I knew she needed to see a veterinarian, so I contacted the man who'd brought her to me and asked that his nephew give her to me officially. He did. At last, Chance was legally mine.

We went to the veterinarian and were told that most foals with this illness die. Only when it's caught at the very beginning is there any hope of recovery. The bacteria were out of control, destroying Chance's joints as well as one of her eyes. The veterinarian said that her vital organs eventually would be attacked. It was only a matter of time before

Chance would have to be put to sleep.

My goal now became simple. I wanted to help Chance experience the joys of being a horse as much as possible before her time was up. Against all odds, she was soon trying to stand up. The first time she stood, with her body contorted and her legs twisted, I laughed and cried with joy. Then she took her first steps: another milestone! She started to walk more. Several times a day, I would help her to stand and then balance her, as she would stroll all over the yard.

Chance seemed determined to see what the world had to offer her. She was carefully supervised as she met other horses on my farm. She nickered almost uncontrollably the first time she saw them. She quivered with excitement. We were watching yet another miracle in this filly's life. And through all of this, my health was holding up, which was also miraculous.

Suddenly, at two and a half months old, Chance seemed to grow tired of the fight. She had tasted green grass, enjoyed painless days and made many friends in the other animals and people who often came to visit her. Chance knew what unconditional love felt like and her very existence had spread love and hope throughout the world. Now God seemed to be letting her know it was almost time to come back home to him.

Chance no longer had a desire to get up and was content to pass the hours and days with her head in my lap. She must have felt my sadness because she would lift her head, time and time again, and nuzzle my face, asking for kisses and hugs. Somehow though, her eyes let me know that it was okay to let her go.

One Wednesday morning, I made a difficult phone call asking the veterinarian to end Chance's life the following Saturday. Then I went out and talked with Chance about it, telling her how selfish I was feeling and that I just wasn't ready to let God have her back yet. But as I was sitting there, a bird landed on the fence post just three feet from us. I turned to get a better look, expecting it to fly away, but it continued to sit there, looking at us. Then I heard the sound of flapping wings getting louder and louder. I looked up to see a flock of geese circling overhead. There was no honking, just the noise of dozens of wings. I sobbed and said out loud, "Okay God, you can have your angel back. Just please make sure she, too, gets strong beautiful wings."

Saturday morning at the veterinarian's office, Chance laid her head in my lap, as she'd done so many times before. She closed her eyes, stretched hard and sighed with contentment. The sedation went into her body, she fell asleep in my arms, and the air was sucked from my lungs as Chance took her last breath. At that moment, I knew she'd awakened in heaven.

Three days after we had laid Chance to rest under the trees at our pond, I went to visit her grave. On the dirt right above her body was a beautiful perfect feather. God kept his promise. Chance had gotten her wings.

Denise Bell-Evans

Throwing My Loop

There are times when you can trust a horse, times when you can't, and times when you have to.

Anonymous

Old ranchers often say that a man is allotted one special horse in his lifetime. I have had mine. She was a chocolate bay mare with an irregularly shaped star on her forehead. Her name was Susie and she was my friend and partner a long time ago. She taught me a most valuable lesson—one that changed my life.

I loved Susie the first time I saw her. She was standing in a pasture with a large number of mean old Brahma bulls. She had an ugly scar running from her right knee to just above the hoof. The man who owned her said he didn't know what caused the injury, but he doubted she would ever be able to run much. I thought he was wrong. I was sixteen years old and she was just two. I knew it was only a matter of time until we were pretty famous as roping partners.

The old fellow let me pay for her a little at a time. After umpiring an infinite number of Little League games, lifeguarding at the local pool and mowing yards, I finally was able to make Susie mine. Actually, to say that she was mine is not quite right. I never really owned Susie. We just joined up. Like so many important things in our lives, maybe it was always meant to be.

My dad and uncles taught us a few things. More importantly, they got us help from some old calf ropers who knew what they were doing in terms of training a roping horse. Susie and I practiced long hours and after a couple of years, we were fairly competitive at small rodeos.

She was always calm in the box and had really good speed. She would spring out of there like a fighter jet, running real low and hard, and put me right where I needed to be every single time. It was effortless to rope on her. Once I threw my loop, this filly would stop in her tracks as if she'd hit a brick wall. She worked the rope really well and if everything went right, we were tough.

For instance, if Susie and I drew a lightweight calf that ran real slow with his head sticking up like a chicken, man, I was good! I could just throw my loop on him, flank him and, as long as he didn't fuss or kick, I could wrap him up, and we would take home the money. Yep, it was easy if everything went perfectly.

Problem was, everything didn't always go perfectly.

I handled this imperfection of life primarily by doing two things: I whined a lot and blamed everybody on earth but myself and old Susie. I couldn't blame Susie because she was as good a roping horse as a man could want. She always did her part.

Mostly, in my view, my parents and teachers caused the problems. When I was little, my mom and dad were really nice folks. Momma made up my bed, took out the trash and cared for everything and everybody. Teachers were nice, too, when I was in the first, second and third grade. We just had to do a little coloring in books, eat lunch and dessert, then take a nap. I had a good life as a little kid.

Then I turned into a teenager, and everybody seemed to change on me overnight. Suddenly, my mom was waking me up every morning, saying things like, "You need to get up and make up your bed, water the horses, take out the trash, mow the yard and help out around here." Frankly, I was shocked. I tried to explain to her that I simply did not do these sorts of things. Then my dad would come home and take her side every time.

Even worse, though, were my teachers. One day we're taking naps and eating chocolate cake, and the next thing you know, we're diagraming sentences and doing word problems in arithmetic.

Yep, things were rough.

That was when my downhill slide began. My parents and teachers were on me all the time, wanting me to work and learn something new every single day, but I didn't. None of it was my fault, of course. In my view, how on earth was I supposed to learn anything if I got all the bad teachers? Then these teachers would put Cs, Ds and Fs on my report card, and my parents would start yelling all over again.

Unfortunately, things got worse. My Cs, Ds and Fs from middle school and high school turned into thirteen Fs in college. I never passed a course, but it wasn't my fault. Once again, I'd gotten all the bad teachers. A counselor even diagnosed my problem. He gave me a test that found I had a below-average IQ. Whew, was I relieved! Now I had the perfect excuse not to ever try.

Things went downhill even more, and with my parents, teachers and coaches on me all the time, I came up with a plan that only a twenty-year-old could think of. Because I was pretty good with a rope and I had the world's best roping horse, I knew that old Susie and I could make it out there on the road. All we needed was a little luck.

My dad tried to explain to me that if I wasn't winning at every small rodeo now, it wasn't likely that I was going to win at the big ones. He tried to get me to see how my lack of ability was going to become even more apparent when Susie and I were up against heavier cattle. And he pointed out other problems of life on the road. But what did he know?

After all, he was old. He was forty, for goodness sake.

So I loaded up Susie in a little one-horse trailer and we hit the open highway. We were two young kids off to rope a dream. I was going down the road singing, "Old Susie was long and lean, a roping machine and her eyes were green," and all I could see in my rearview mirror was a dusty little Texas town that I no longer needed.

It all started off great. We won a little here and there. But there is nothing like life and the open road to teach a fella what's important. I learned many things on that road.

I learned that my daddy kept a good roof over our heads. Growing up under a roof that didn't leak never seemed very special until it wasn't there. I learned that no one in America was interested in whether I ate. Certainly no one would cook my food for free, but I remembered that my momma had always done exactly that. I also learned that the cattle were heavier than I had ever seen and the cowboys were better than I ever imagined and then that little town in Texas didn't seem so dusty after all.

On a cool night in Colorado, Susie and I were up in a roping event. We hadn't eaten on Thursday or Friday. We had drawn a small calf and desperately needed to win some money so we could eat. I knew we would be okay because old Susie would put me right there, and because I was good with a rope, we would be fine.

I backed her into the box, and she was as calm as she always was. I called for the calf, and just like a fighter jet, she took off. Even though she had to be hungry, she was giving me all she had. She put me right there like she always did. I leaned just a bit and knew that supper was only ten or eleven seconds away as I let my loop fly.

And I missed him. Just completely missed him.

That was bad, but things would get worse. I had to stand by a waste barrel that night and wait for a family to throw away half-eaten food so I could feed my friend. As I watched my partner reduced to eating garbage because of me, I tried so hard to think of someone to blame, but there was no one there but me. I had done this to my friend.

The longer I stood there, the more painful the experience became. I suddenly understood that my parents and teachers had not been trying to do anything but help me. They had done all that they could do to prevent my ending up at a place like this, but I wouldn't listen. Now I realized that if I couldn't take care of my horse, it was very unlikely I could provide for a spouse or a child. My horse had always done her part. I had never done mine.

The great English theologian C.S. Lewis once said, "Every conversion begins with a blessed defeat." That night was my defeat. I made a resolution to be different.

There are others who have had a similar experience. Long ago, a physician named Luke wrote about someone who must have been a lot like me. His dad tried to help him, too, but like me, this young man wouldn't listen. He spent all his money and ended up just like me, broke, hungry and full of regret.

Now, I'm certainly no preacher, but that doesn't mean cowboys can't learn from the Bible. This fellow that Luke wrote about was wasting his life until he realized that he needed his family, friends, and teachers—all the people who are sent to help us. The Bible says this young man "came to himself" and the prodigal son then knew that it was time to go home and live a different life.

And I came home, too. I have sinned many times since, but not academically. Even with my below-average IQ, I never made another B, C, D or F in school. I don't tell you this story to boast, but rather to give you what Emily Dickinson called "that feathered thing": hope.

It's just a matter of using the gifts that you have been given, applying yourself and living by that old cowboy line "When you get bucked off, get up and get back on!" In short, do your part. I learned that lesson from a very special horse. Her name was Susie and she was long and lean and a roping machine.

We have a horse farm now and some evenings at dusk, I walk in the pasture. I look at the pretty green hills behind my barn, and sometimes the breeze rustles gently and the hay meadow sways softly as if it's one living thing. And just for a minute, I can still smell Susie. I can feel her under me, running hard with her head low, giving me everything she had.

I also remember a man is allotted one special horse in his life. Fortunately, I've had mine.

Michael Johnson

Nerf Spurs. © *Cartoon copyright by Mark Parisi, printed with permission.*

2

HORSES AS TEACHERS

The educated horse is a thinking horse, and it seems that he understands that every now and then something happens that he must chalk up as a mistake and be done with it.

Dennis Murphy in Practical Horseman

The Language of Horses

Above all, a horse should never be chastised out of foul mood or anger, but always with complete dispassion.

François Robichon de la Guérinière

As a very young boy, I was sure that horses had a language and if I could speak that language, I could train them in a new and entirely different way. So it was at the age of eight that I set a life goal for myself to be able to communicate fluently with horses.

We lived on a horse facility in Salinas, California, at the time, and I spent every waking hour trying to communicate with the untamed, domesticated horses.

The summer I was thirteen, I went to Nevada for three weeks for a job. I had been hired to help capture wild mustangs. This was the first opportunity I'd had to work with totally wild horses. Determined to make the best use of my time, I rose early each day and rode a long way into the desert, where I used binoculars to study the habits of the mustang herds that lived there.

I was utterly spellbound by these horses. I would sit for hours and hours, watching those beautiful animals as they ran, grazed and played in the wide spaces of the desert.

What astonished me most was how the wild horses communicated with each other. They rarely used sounds; instead, they used a complex language of motion. The position of their bodies, and the speed and direction of their travel were the key elements of their language. And by varying the degree of rigidity or relaxation in the eyes, ears, neck, head and the position of the spine, a horse could signal anything he needed to communicate.

As I watched I thought: *Could this convince a wild horse to let me get close enough to touch him without him running away?*

So that I could easily spot him, I picked a horse with unique markings, and tried to herd him away from the others. For many days, I tried every way I could think of to get near him. But he always sensed me and he was off before I was even close. One day, I got lucky and came up behind him in a small canyon. At last, I had his full attention. Then, using only my body to convey the signals I'd seen the horses use with each other, I persuaded the wary stallion to stand still. He studied me silently as I moved closer and closer. He was watchful but he wasn't afraid. Barely breathing, I took the step that brought me within an arm's reach of him. I avoided his eyes as I stretched my hand toward him and laid it softly on his neck. It lasted only a few seconds, but it was enough. I watched him gallop away, my chest exploding with joy. I had communicated with a horse!

My desire to learn to communicate with horses became a deep inner passion that I fiercely hid from the rest of the world. Unwilling to share with anyone what was most important to me, I was usually alone, except for the horses. The only thing that mattered to me was my life's dream.

Every summer, I returned to Nevada for three weeks to work, continuing my research in the desert. Four years later, when I was seventeen, I progressed so far that I not only touched a wild mustang, I saddled, bridled and rode one without once using any pain or intimidation to do so. Proudly, I rode the wild horse back to the ranch. The ranchhands who saw me ride in called me a liar when I told them what I'd done. They insisted the horse I rode must once have been a domesticated horse who had run away and ended up with the mustangs. Deeply hurt, I realized the futility of my dreams. With no one to believe in me, it was *my* spirit that was broken.

I eventually got over the humiliation of being ridiculed and decided to continue my training methods, but I vowed I would never again tell anyone what I did.

And so I became a horse trainer. I used my experiences with every horse I worked with to learn more and more about the language of horses. It was a slow but satisfying education.

Once, when I was about twenty-five, a family hired me to tackle a problem mare. She was a beautiful horse, intelligent and extremely talented. But during her training, a previous owner had inadvertently mishandled her and she had developed a serious problem. She wouldn't stop. She would blast away like a rocket and refuse to be halted, crashing through fences and slipping and sliding as she made dangerously sharp turns. She was diabolically treacherous. A short time earlier, the mare had almost killed her owner's daughter. The family was going on vacation and they asked me to sell the horse for them for whatever I could get for her. They had heard I was good with difficult horses and they knew that in order to sell her, someone would have to be able to bring her to a stop from a run. No one else was willing to try.

This mare was the most dangerous horse I had ever seen, but I used everything I had absorbed over the years to help her. Moving slowly and keeping my communication with her to just the basics, I earned her trust. Building on that trust, I continued to communicate with her, and soon her resistance melted. Our progress was swift and remarkable from that point on. It had seemed impossible, but within a few days, she was transformed.

While the owners were still away, I showed the mare in a

competition and she took first place. I brought her prize, a very expensive saddle, to the home of her owners. I wrote them a note, explaining that she had improved enough to win this saddle and under the circumstances, I felt that they should reconsider selling her. I pinned the note to the saddle and left it in the dining room for them to find upon their return.

They were ecstatic about the change in their horse and were thrilled to be able to keep her. This mare went on to become a world-class champion. Her owners found a new willingness in her and a sweet temperament that made her presence in their family even more precious than her value as a show horse.

Many times over the next thirty years, using the simple tools of gentleness, respect and communication, I managed to turn troubled horses around and experienced the satisfaction of seeing them return to loving families.

Today, the lonely work I began in the high deserts of Nevada so many years ago is full of recognition and satisfaction. I have achieved goals beyond the simple desires of a young boy of eight, but I still find myself watching quietly, this time inspired by others as they follow my path, as they work and learn, as they become fluent in the language of horses.

Monty Roberts with Carol Kline

Riding the Edge

Competitive riding should be classical riding at its best.

Charles de Kunffy

During the summer of 1961, most of us at Rock Creek Stables traveled from Louisville to county horse shows throughout Kentucky. I was only twelve, but my parents and our trainer Jim had high ambitions.

The year before, they had purchased Bubbling Fancy after she won the Five-Gaited Pony Championship in Lexington. Dad planned a display wall for the trophies he knew we were going to win. Jim laid plans to ready us for the World's Grand Championship.

Instead, they watched for two years while I struggled to handle this high-stepping, spirited chestnut Saddlebred. Jim just scratched his chin and drawled, "Yup, she's a lotta horse." I was a skinny, four-foot, ten-inch tall girl with nerves of steel when it came to horses and no stomach whatsoever for riding in front of crowds.

I had my own ambitions. In addition to wanting to overcome fears about showing, I yearned even more to find the connection with Fancy that I had with Sugar, my trail horse.

When Sugar and I galloped across the open meadows, we were one body, one heart, racing melded and timeless against the wind. Fancy and I might hit moments where Jim shouted "Right thar!" but we were still disconnected, striving out-of-sync toward a good performance.

Jim pushed hard against my fears, entering us in a show every week. When we arrived in Harrodsburg, Kentucky, in late July, there weren't many shows left before the World's Championship in August.

At the Harrodsburg show, the barns teemed with activity: trainers unloading horses, grooms dragging bales of hay, harnesses being slapped on skittish roadsters, high-strung Saddlebreds whinnying their excitement. Smells of fresh popcorn and hot dogs wafted above the scent of tanbark, leather and horses.

Mom and I stepped into the makeshift tack room, where she helped me dress. My jacket, jodhpurs, boots and derby hat all matched. Their deep chocolate brown color showed off my long hair and Fancy's coat. The contrast was like wheat against dark earth.

Meanwhile, a groom brushed Fancy until she glistened. On went her show bridle and cutback saddle. Another groom knelt to fasten white leather cuffs around her front hooves to protect them from being kicked by her rear feet during a high-speed rack, the most thrilling of her five gaits.

Then they led Fancy, snorting and prancing, out of her dark stall. Jim bent over, knit his hands together for me to step into and boosted me onto her back.

We warmed up in the practice ring, working three of our five gaits—walk, trot and slow gait—leaving out the canter and rack, saving Fancy for the show ring. Fancy quivered with excitement and chomped on her bits. When Jim cracked his bull whip into the air, we bounded forward, her legs now tightly coiled springs.

"Right thar!"

But tension flooded my body as I glimpsed High Parader nearby. A small bay pony, he was winning a lot of shows that summer. High Parader was more cute than beautiful, but he rarely made a mistake. This was the first time our paths had crossed.

A loudspeaker blared, "Five-gaited ponies you're up!" Following Jim's strategy, I held Fancy back. Everyone else trotted in a bunched cluster up the dirt path into the show ring. The ring attendant moved to close the gates. Then we burst up the ramp and into the ring at full trot, Fancy's tail streaming high and long behind us. It worked: The crowd gasped; the judge turned to see what had captured their delight. Posting low in the saddle, hands steady on the reins, I smiled, but my anxiety spiked with the attention.

Intent on trotting fast, I pushed Fancy right to the edge, that point where she wanted to break gaits into a gallop. I picked my spot among the twelve horses in the ring—a clear position by the outer rail, where the judge could see Fancy's gorgeous form against the white wood fence.

Four times High Parader and his rider tried to pass us in front of the judge so that he would see only them. Each time, I had to act quickly to rein in Fancy but not so harshly that she would break her stride. Then I turned her short to cross the ring to a new spot. It was tricky because I wanted her pushing that edge, stepping high and fast into that tight margin where any sudden change increased the risk of breaking into another gait and losing points.

The class progressed, first in one direction, then we turned to repeat our gaits in the opposite direction.

As soon as we reversed direction, it happened. Fancy broke into a gallop. I hadn't felt it coming. I reined her in quickly until she trotted again. We were on the back side. Did the judge see us? I struggled to refocus.

Eventually, we reached the climax of the class, the call for the last, but most exciting, gait.

"Rack on!" the announcer shouted. The grandstands roared.

High Parader pounded close behind us. I gave Fancy the slightest signal through the rein. She accelerated into a rack.

Suddenly it clicked. We hit that sweet spot I longed for and we were one single creature united in motion. This time I let her energy loose, let her explode down the straightaway in a fast, high-strutting rack that launched the crowd to its feet. This time I could sense even the slightest change in her step, and before she could break stride into a gallop, I'd flick one hand, subtly signaling her on the side where she was about to step. Because I did it at precisely the right moment, this steadied her in her brilliant, flowing rack. Riding at the edge was scary. I had the feeling that I was just this side of totally out of control. A misstep here not only could break our stride, it could hurl me into a rolling crash amid dirt and flying hooves. But Jim had taught me that the edge, if we could hold it, was where we looked dazzling, so the edge was where I rode her. It was hair-raising and at the same time sheer joy, an infinite moment where nothing existed except this one pristine blur of motion that Fancy and I had become.

Suddenly, the class was over and the riders sent to one end of the ring to await the awards. We paced in the shadows, Fancy huffing hard under me. We had broken out of a trot for less than ten strides, but it had been a break just the same. Had we lost? Had High Parader fumbled, too? But he never did. His strength was a dull but dependable performance because he was never pressed to the dangerous yet exhilarating edge.

The loudspeaker called fifth place, fourth, third, second. . . . *Oh please, make it High Parader!*

"Second place, Number 186, Bubbling Fancy, Jane Douglass up."

Back at the barn, Mom and dad ran up as I dismounted.

"Second place is a great accomplishment, honey," said my dad, hugging me. "You should be proud!"

I shook my head.

Then I remembered the small carrot I had saved for Fancy. I touched her damp neck and held out the carrot. She surprised me with a nicker.

I smacked my forehead with recognition.

"Fancy! We did it!"

I didn't know about our prospects for the World's Championship in three weeks, but I did know this: I had forgotten to fear the cheering crowd because Fancy and I had found our connection.

Jane Douglass Rhodes

Big Brother Is Watching

A cowboy is a man with guts and a horse.

Will James

In the year after my father died, there was nothing I wanted more than a trophy. I was twelve and the hope of placing a trophy on my dresser woke me up in the middle of the night. All of my friends had trophies, from soccer and football, from raffle-ticket sales and BMX races and chess tournaments. One friend even had a trophy in the shape of deer antlers because he'd shot a thirteen-point buck. Any of those would have elated me. I believed they would have given me back something my father's absence had taken away. The problem was that I had no skills or talents that would yield a trophy.

My older brother Alan had shelves of trophies, too. He had some from Little League, but most came from horse shows. Before my father died, he had bought each of us a horse. Mine was a pinto pony that I named Colonel because of a white star on his shoulder. Alan's was a Quarter Horse, fourteen hands high, named Otis. Alan ran the barrels and did poleracing, and when he kicked Otis's sides and hollered for him to come on, they were nothing but run. Colonel always wanted to follow, and I could feel him gathering power and speed in his gallop, but I was afraid of falling, so I'd pull on the reins and we'd lag behind, able only to watch Alan ride.

After my father died, my mother rarely went to the stable where we boarded the horses. In fact, she really didn't go anywhere. She cut back on her hours at work and stopped going to play bridge. Mostly, she stayed in her room—in just a year it had become *her* room, not *their* room—watching infomercials, eating chocolate and chain-smoking. Alan ran a lot of errands for her and cooked our meals and paid our bills with money he made waiting tables.

This was also the year I started smoking. And I was spending time with the crowd at school that set fire to bathroom trash cans. I liked the feeling I got from being around everything I'd been told to stay away from. I might have been scared to let Colonel burst into a run beneath me, but I wasn't afraid to cut class and play video games at the mall. I liked that after I back-talked a history teacher, girls suddenly knew who I was. I liked the new heavy metal music I listened to and the way I'd learned to spit phlegm onto the ceiling. I appreciated the depths to which my grades dropped. I enjoyed hanging out with kids who, like me, had no trophies and who couldn't care less.

My brother didn't like this behavior, and when the worst of my report cards arrived in the mail, he rode with me into the pasture and interrogated me. To all of his questions—"What do you think you're doing? Who do you think you're fooling? Why are you throwing everything Mom and Dad worked for down the toilet?"—I answered: "I don't know." And the truth was, I didn't know. I was adrift, floating away from everything I'd known.

Alan started picking me up from school, denying me the opportunity to carouse with the smokers and bullies, and we drove to the stable to ride until night fell. Through all of this, I still loved riding and still found comfort in being around Colonel, but I hated being made to ride. After a week of forcing me to spend my afternoons exclusively with him, I took a self-righteous stand and told Alan that I refused to be chaperoned like this. I listed all the ways I thought he was treating me unfairly, and he let me work myself into a fury. When I'd exhausted all of my angles, Alan said, "I entered you in the horse show. It's in two weeks."

I was stunned, appalled and incredulous. I was thrilled, but I didn't let on. I huffed, "Why?"

He was cleaning Otis's hooves. Without looking at me, he said, "You want a trophy, right?"

The next week is a blur in my memory. Although I hated to admit he had such sway with my emotions, Alan's implied challenge completely refocused my attentions and my loyalties. Suddenly, I thought of nothing except strategies for running barrel events faster and methods to cut time off my pole races. I distanced myself from the smokers and bullies. When Alan picked me up after school, I asked him to drive faster to the stable. By week's end, Colonel and I had lit upon a new rhythm and we rode hard and fast, the way I'd always watch Alan ride. The night before the junior rodeo, I could already feel the trophy in my hands, the promising weight of its dignity. I could see my reflection in that golden angel's breasts.

Alan had entered me in four events, and in the first three, I floundered. My nerves sizzled in my knees and I made mistake after mistake, missing barrels I should have circled, steering Colonel to the left when we clearly should have gone right. I was on the verge of tears and in the full throes of anger. I was furious with Alan for subjecting me to my own shortcomings and with my mother for venturing back into the world to watch me fail. I was furious with my father for dying and furious with myself for being my pitiful self.

The last event was running poles and to everyone's surprise, I didn't do half bad. My time was nowhere near the fastest, but it seemed solid enough to secure me seventh place, the last place that would receive a trophy. Colonel and I watched the other riders. Before the last competitor, I was still in seventh. My mother smoked cigarette after cigarette, while Alan casually set out to find a port-o-potty. I asked how he could leave at a time like this—I couldn't stop smiling—but he just shrugged and said, "When you have to go, you have to go."

The last rider started off badly, missing a pole that would have to be circled before the run was over. The trophy was as good as mine. Then the rider hit his stride, and the second half of his run was flawless and breathtakingly swift. My heart stalled.

He'd finished two-tenths of a second faster than I had. He'd knocked me out of seventh place; he'd taken away my trophy.

But this is, as I've said, a story about my brother.

When he found me after the last rider he claimed not to have heard the judges announce the time that had beaten me out. He claimed that I'd heard incorrectly, that I was mis-remembering my own time. I thought he was making light of my situation, and I stormed off. How could I have not heard the right time, how could I have thought I'd ridden slower than I had?

When the announcement came during the awards cere-mony, I was sitting under a mesquite tree, imagining ways to ingratiate myself back into the crowd of smokers and bul-lies, the kids who'd never wanted a trophy. I was only half-listening to the announcer, so when he called my name—and Colonel's—his voice didn't really register. It was a voice from a dream, the voice of a ghost. He said I was in seventh place, that I should come claim my trophy. He called my name again, like a question this time. "Donald Keyes, you out there?" None of this seemed real. For a split second, I thought the voice was my father's.

I can still remember running toward the corral as if my life depended on it. I can hear and feel my boots hitting the hard dirt of the arena, can hear the crowd laughing gently as they applaud. I can see Alan and my mother clapping, my mother wiping her eyes, my brother giving me a smug thumbs-up. I can remember wondering how I could have made the mistakes Alan had cited, hearing the wrong time, underestimating my own score. I can remember letting those mistakes go, releasing them with some of the pain that came from losing my father, some of the anger I had toward him for leaving us and some of the anger I had at myself for being so angry with him. It's strange how our minds work, how hope can become a stand-in for a father, the same way an older brother can. It's strange how our deepest wounds heal right before our eyes, yet we never notice this until the scars are gone.

I've always known that I didn't win that trophy, just as I've known that the reason the judge handed it to me had everything to do with Alan. I don't know where he went during that last rider's turn, but I suspect he ducked away to the judges' booth and somehow convinced them that awarding his little brother a trophy was maybe one of the most important things they would do in their lifetimes. Maybe he just presented my case—a young father who died suddenly, a mother who would never recover, the wrong crowd, the hours and hours of practice—or maybe he handed the judges twenty dollars, maybe a hundred. I imagine he did whatever he had to do, no matter what the cost. I imagine when he reads this—we haven't broached the subject for twenty years—he'll deny the allegations with typical stubbornness and dismiss them with kindly fraternal disinterest. He'll say I've always had a talent for making up stories, which is why I became a writer and university professor.

And I'll say, No. I became a writer and professor and a man, because he had faith in me. I'll say he knew what I needed when I didn't, that he reached out and cared for me when I was more trouble than I imagined. I'll say he taught me how to ride and how to live. And I'll say, Thank you. Again and again, my brother, thank you.

Don Keyes

God Bless Little Horse Lovin' Souls

Whenever you observe a horse closely, you feel as if a human being sitting inside were making fun of you.

Elias Canetti

Our nine-year-old daughter Lindsay was extremely excited about entering her young gelding in his first schooling show. After riding and taking lessons for several years, Lindsay had some show experience under her belt, but this was the first time she was going to enter with a horse of her very own. And because Snickers was only a three-year-old, it promised to be a big day for both of them.

We'd tried to instill in Lindsay the concept that winning ribbons isn't what showing should be all about. It was a tough message to get across because, heck, she's just a kid, and what child wouldn't want to come away from a show with proof of how well she had done? To help her understand this, we'd asked Lindsay to set a goal for herself, consisting of two specific accomplishments that she'd like to achieve with Snickers in the ring that day. That way, if she reached her goal, she'd be a winner regardless of how she placed in the class. After much thought, she came up with two ideas that were pretty straightforward: keep Snickers moving and don't let him cut the corners. Perfect!

About to enter the ring for her class, Lindsay was very excited. Snickers looked magnificent, groomed to within an inch of his life and braided to the hilt. Lindsay was equally well turned out, from her glossy black boots to the top of her velvet helmet. One look at her and it was obvious that she was bursting with pride.

I took a moment to remind her to focus on her goal and to just try her best. Because this was Snickers's first show, I told Lindsay not to expect too much from him, and how important it was that the experience be a positive one. She gave me a big smile and a thumbs-up and proceeded into the ring.

As it turned out, they did extremely well in the class. Snickers behaved like an old veteran, totally unfazed by it all. Lindsay kept him going forward nicely and she didn't let him cut the corners of the ring. Although they didn't place, she had accomplished her goal, and I was thrilled for them.

As I ran over to offer my heartfelt congratulations, I saw that Lindsay was bent over in the saddle with her arms wrapped around Snickers's neck, hugging and patting him. When she raised her head to look at me, I couldn't help but notice that her eyes were filled with tears.

"Sweetie, what's wrong?" I asked. "You guys were absolutely amazing!"

"Oh, Mom," she replied in a shaky voice. "Snickers did such a good job and I'm so proud of him."

Then, just before the tears really started to fall, she managed to add: "I understand all about the ribbons and stuff, but I'm afraid that Snickers is just too young not to be upset about it!"

Patricia Carter

Encounter with a Dangerous Spy

A horse gallops with his lungs, perseveres with his heart, and wins with his character.

Frederico Tesio

I confess. I do not like riding horses.

I would sooner run with the bulls of Pamplona than ride a horse. I would sooner bungee jump. I would sooner go over Niagara Falls in a barrel.

I am, to use the politically correct term, "equine challenged."

So you can imagine my reaction when Barbara Orr, an otherwise nice woman from Ojai, California, asked me if I wanted to try to ride an ill-tempered wild mustang named Tornado.

Actually, Barbara asked if I wanted to ride a mild-mannered, well-trained Thoroughbred named Spy. But, really, what's the difference? Neither has a seat belt.

"NO WAY!" I said, explaining that I had never ridden a horse in my life and now was no time to break my streak— or my leg.

Correction. Let me be more specific. I have never before ridden a live horse, which is not to say that I had never been on a bucking bronco. Twice, in fact, I had.

The first time was at age three when I rode one of those spring-suspended hobby horses. It was a dangerous toy: no seat belt. I got thrown over the front. Faulty stirrup, I think. And I lost my two top front teeth, I kid you not.

As they say, if you get thrown from a horse, you've got to get right back on. I did. Well, at age four. This time I got aboard a mean merry-go-round wild bronco named Cyclone as I recall. Or it should have been.

As the story was told to me after I regained consciousness —and after a trip to the emergency room—the carousel went around once, twice, three times, when my dad finally noticed that I was no longer on Cyclone. That's right, I got bucked off, thus becoming the only person in history to ever require a dozen stitches on the forehead due to a runaway merry-go-round horse.

I have worse luck with ponies than someone who loses the rent money at the track. Personally, I have forever since thought that horse sense means being smart enough not to get on a horse.

Trying to weasel out of falling off Spy, I confessed my equestrian mishaps to Barbara. After she stopped laughing and wiped the tears from her eyes, she said she would give me a free lesson.

Not usually one to look a gift horse in the mouth, I looked at the bit in Spy's mouth and said, "ARE YOU CRAZY? CAN YOU IMAGINE WHAT A REAL HORSE WOULD DO TO ME?"

"Chicken," said Orr.

"Darn right," I said.

"Fraidy cat," Ms. Orr-nery said.

Horse feathers. Dirty pool. I may be a chicken, but I am no fraidy cat. I gathered my courage up.

I got up on Spy.

Then I made my second mistake. I looked down. Vertigo. I suddenly realized where the phrase "On your high horse" originated. Horses are tall.

Spy, to be precise, stands 16.1, that's 16 hands (with a hand equaling four inches) plus one more inch. Or, if my math is correct, about eleven feet at the shoulders.

Barbara also told me that Spy, a beautiful gray Thoroughbred, weighs about 1,250 pounds, although I have to question that. I mean, really now, how did Barbara get Spy to stand still on the bathroom scale?

Anyway.

As if I weren't already shaking enough in my boots (okay, shaking in my Nikes) Barbara says: "On a 1,200-pound animal with a mind of its own, there is a potential for danger."

No duh! On a twenty-pound carousel horse with no mind of its own there is a potential for danger.

Barbara instructed me on how to make Spy turn. In addition to gently pulling the reins—left to go left and right to go right, simple even for a sportswriter—you simultaneously also squeeze with your right leg to go left and your left leg to go right.

I kept getting confused and would squeeze with my right leg while pulling the right rein. Poor Spy didn't know what to do, because, in effect, I was telling him to turn right and left at the same time.

"Don't kick him, squeeze him like a tube of toothpaste," Barbara further instructed me. Bad analogy. She obviously has not seen the mess I leave around the sink with the cap off.

Somehow, I figured out left means right and right means left and I got Spy to go where I wanted him to go. Or, if he didn't, I would just pretend I wanted to go where he took me.

Making a "cluck, cluck" sound gets a horse to walk. To go faster, you make a kissing sound and give a squeeze with your heels in his ribs.

I did the latter and had an instant flashback to when I was three because I almost got thrown from the saddle. Spy took off as if he'd seen a rattlesnake. Barbara called it "loping," but the truth of the matter is that Spy was galloping at Kentucky Derby speed—at least eighty miles an hour, I swear.

At this point, I think Barbara was impressed with my

natural ability because she said, and I quote, "I've never seen anyone ride a horse like you do."

The biggest problem I had was that I'd laugh out loud with delight at the fun I was having, and Spy would take my laugh as a "Whoa!" and stop.

In all, I rode for an hour and fifteen minutes. I would have gotten off sooner but I was having too much fun. Also, I forgot how to make Spy stop. Fortunately, Spy finally heard Barbara laughing at me and took it as a "Whoa!"

Despite the snickering, I had about as much fun as you can have with your clothes on. Toward the end, I was making Spy do figure eights and figure sevens and even some figure threes. I made him go fast, slow and even backward. I don't want to brag, but after seeing me, the birds started whistling the theme song to *Bonanza*.

Barbara was a miracle worker, but I learned a few things the hard way. One, a city slicker should never ride a horse for an hour and fifteen minutes the first time out because you won't be able to walk for three days afterward.

Two, I learned that you should always take your wallet out before riding a horse. All that bouncing around bent my credit cards so much that they don't work, even the ones that aren't maxed out over my limit.

Yes, I was a little sore. But, hey, no stitches were required. And I returned home with all my teeth, which, of course, explains why my smarty-pants wife did not believe me when I limped through the front door and proudly told her I had ridden a real horse.

Her exact words: "I don't believe you."

After she stopped cackling, she added: "So then, Hoss, how come you aren't missing any teeth? Where are your new stitches?"

By the way, Barbara Orr informed me, and with a little too much delight I might add, that Spy competes under the show name Just for Laughs. I think that is called painful irony.

Woody Woodburn

Between a Rock and a Hard Place

Between a Rock and a Hard Place. *Reprinted by permission of Boots Reynolds.* ©*1987 Boots Reynolds.*

Standing Ground

It was one of those frosty days when you can see your breath white and sparkling in front of you even though it's midday. The frost was feathered on the fence line and it sparkled on the horses' whiskers. I must have been eight or nine years old and feeling very big because I was to help Dad with the horses that day. Dad was telling me to stand in the downed fence line and turn the horses back if they came my way. We needed the bunch of them to go up the fence line and not through to the other pasture. There was only so much daylight to work with and Dad was always saying not to burn daylight.

I remember seeing them coming, the whole bunch of them running toward me, their heads and tails high as if they were having the best time making fresh tracks in the snow. I knew Dad was counting on me to hold them, but they were coming fast and they didn't look like they were going to turn just because I was standing there. I remember them passing in a rush as I felt myself shrinking up and feeling small and helpless. I hadn't moved, but I felt invisible.

Then came Dad, with a look of frustration on his face that I had seen before. Then I was filled with an awful feeling of shame and guilt. I was the cause of wasted hours and effort. We would have to go find the horses, get them back in and try again to send them up the line toward the barn. I was keenly aware of the ache of cold in my fingers and the fact that because of my failure we would be in the frosty air much longer. I wanted to blow away in the wind and become even smaller than I had felt as the band of horses and ponies rushed past me with such fun in their eyes.

I knew that Dad was annoyed and I felt the tears well up in my eyes as he came to the fence line. I stared at the ground. I had let him down and I didn't dare cry on top of it. He looked at me and said with clenched teeth and a level voice, "You have to hold your ground. If you think they are going to rush you, stand your ground and let them know you're there." I knew he would have yelled had it been my older brothers who had let the horses through and the knowledge only shamed me more. I didn't know how I was going to make myself bigger, but I knew we couldn't afford the time it would cost if there were a repeat of my performance.

By the time we had the horses back onto the right side of the fence line, they were really having fun, blowing and snorting as they crossed over the fence line and past my post once again. Now came the test. Dad looked at me with those clear blue eyes as if to say, "Hold 'em!" I had to keep them inside that fence. As they came toward me again, blowing and bucking, I could feel the sweat deep down inside my clothes and the scratchy frost on my collar. Fear started to creep up and stiffen my shoulders. I looked at them all in one glance. Midnight was leading the way, his shiny black coat glistening in contrast to the snow. Silver Bell, my little sorrel pony, was not far behind with her head thrown up and her eyes dancing. Dad was in the distance slowing to watch and wait. I locked my eyes on him and felt his words sink into my body: hold your ground. Hold my ground! I pulled my shoulders back and thought *I am big enough to hold my ground.* I felt frozen in place and I threw my arms wide and yelled "Ha! Ha!"

Midnight whirled, and I felt his breath as his feet threw

snow and mud against me, but I held my place and didn't give in to that sinking feeling that had made me feel so small the last time they came through. As he whirled, I saw the rest begin to turn up the fence line and I began to jump up and down and yell. I felt a tingle all the way down to my stiffened toes. I had held my ground! They had seen me and known that I was big enough to stand firm!

Dad waved me in behind them as they turned up the fence line and we followed them in. Dad didn't say anything about that morning to anyone, not even me. But the look on his face made me know that he was proud of me, and that was enough. That, and knowing that the horses had seen something different about me that second time around.

Starr Lee Cotton Heady

That Ol' Black Magic

The sight of that pony did something to me I've never quiet been able to explain. He was more than tremendous strength and speed and beauty of motion. He set me dreaming.

Walt Morey

I had one horse, a beautiful Tennessee Walker named Bob. He was all I needed and, if the truth be known, I didn't really need him all that much. Then, a few days following my fourteenth birthday, a neighbor friend told me about a black mare.

"She's really pretty," he said, "but she's wild. She's been running on about forty acres with a dozen or so mules. The guy who owns the land told me she's been there at least three or four years, which is why she's so wild. He also told me her owner hasn't paid board for her in eighteen months or more."

I was listening. I knew there was a point to this story and I also knew he hadn't made it yet. I was familiar with all of Robert's idiosyncrasies. He was seventeen with a flair for the dramatic.

"Anyway, Mr. Burns, he's the one who owns the place,

told me we can have her if we can catch her. Actually, I was thinking of you and not me since we already have more horses than we can feed or need."

"What do you mean *have her?*" I queried.

He shook his head. "I mean just what I said. We can have her. Free. For nothing. All we need to do is catch her."

"And just how wild is she?" I asked.

He grinned and then he laughed. "Pretty darned wild. Wanna' go look at her?"

The trip was short, and we caught Mr. Burns walking back to the barn with a couple of empty buckets. A black mare was standing in the middle of the mules gathered around some hay and a little grain in a corner of the field nearest the house.

I sat in Robert's truck with the window down, looking. The mare would be beautiful with some loving attention and care. As things were, her long mane and tail were matted with burrs. Her forelock was no better, standing straight out from her forehead in a compact burr column, making her look like a ragamuffin unicorn. Her feet were grown out to the point of being inhumane and, even from a distance, I could see that one eye was infected.

"It was probably a thistle," I said.

"What?" answered Robert.

"Her eye," I said. "The right one is infected. She probably poked a thistle in it.

"Just how would you propose to catch her?" I continued. "We sure couldn't walk up to her and slip on a halter and lead rope, especially if she stays bunched inside those mules. Do you know how hard those things kick? And they'll run right over you if they can't get in a good kick."

Robert chuckled. "Yeah, I know that, but here's what I was thinking. Mr. Burns already is feeding them in a corner. We ride over here on our horses and tie them to the fence, within easy smelling distance of the mules and the mare. We come over here the night before and string a second set of wire. We make it long enough to reach from one side of the corner to the other."

I rolled my eyes skyward. I already knew where he was headed, but I let him go on and assume the dramatic role of mastermind. It cost me nothing and it made him feel good. He went through his entire plan, ending with trapping the mules and the mare in the corner of the pasture and then releasing the mules, one or two at a time, while keeping the mare snared.

"And you really and truly think this will work?" I queried in dismay.

"Look," he said in an irritated tone, "this is a free horse. Free! She's not a spring chicken, but she's still plenty young enough to have a baby or two, and how many times have you said that's what you've always wanted?"

Yes, I thought, I definitely wanted this mare and, yes, I definitely would like to breed her. I smiled and shook my head in the affirmative. We got out of the truck and greeted Mr. Burns, filling him in on our plan. He was skeptical and made us promise to tell our parents and, further, make them promise not to sue him should anything happen to us. We agreed.

Suddenly, owning the mare became a reality. I pictured her in our barn. I mentally named her Black Magic because, obviously, she was black and, not so obviously, because it would be sheer magic when (not if) we caught her. I was even thinking about a chocolate-colored stallion named Soldier. Mr. Diggs, another neighbor, owned him. He'd be a perfect match for Black Magic. The mare was as good as mine and we hadn't made the first move toward trapping her.

The plan was in place and we began executing it the following evening. We twisted smooth wire around the gnarled, crusty tree branches that served as posts, checked in with Mr. Burns and then went home. The next day, we rode our horses back and arrived just as Mr. Burns was dumping the feed. We began working and we worked and we worked until darkness fell and Mr. Burns switched on all five of his big, outside floodlights.

We kept working until all of the mules were out and only the mare was in. She was upset, nervous, constantly moving, switching her ears back and forth and flaring her nostrils. She also was exhausted. Now what?

"If we leave," said Robert, "the mules will come back and aggravate her. I'm afraid she'll hurt herself trying to get out."

"Fine," I rebutted. "So what do we do with her?"

It was Mr. Burns who solved the knotty problem. "That corral over there is old, but it's sound and sturdy," he said. "It would put quite a bit of distance between the mare and the mules, and I don't think she could break out of it or hurt herself."

"But how do we get her over there?" I asked.

"Doing the same thing you've already done," he responded. "I have some hog wire in the barn. String it from either side of the corner to the corral gate. That'll make a sort of alley. Then herd her over there."

Thirty minutes later, the "walls" were up. The mare, who was covered in lather and wild-eyed, whirled around and looked at the gaping opening. She was confused. We kept our voices calm and started shooing her toward the alleyway leading to the corral. It was a frightening, rather torturous process, but it finally worked. Black Magic was actually in the corral.

The following day began weeks and weeks of hard work. We did everything possible to gentle the mare. Soothing voices. Special treats. Hours of sitting calmly and silently outside her corral gate. More hours standing motionless inside the gate.

Nothing worked. She refused the treats. She bolted as soon as we took one small step in her direction. She'd been in the corral for three weeks and, still, all we could see of her eyes were the whites. Worse, she was losing weight at a nearly alarming rate. She munched uninterestedly at the hay, and not even that if she saw anyone around.

"How could she get this wild?" I asked Mr. Burns.

"Don't know," he answered. "I guess God created some

animals to be wild and others he created to be part of a person's life. The wild ones have a different spirit. I've seen folks try to force the first ones into the second group, and I can tell you, the result is pitiful. You could call it broken. I hate to tell you this, but I think this mare belongs to the first group."

Somewhere, deep inside my soul, I think I heard the truth in Mr. Burns' voice, but I wasn't ready to give up. She had a name. She was no longer just the black mare. She was Black Magic. And she had a breeding to Soldier coming up and I could already imagine see her long-legged baby running like the wind across the pasture. I just needed to work harder.

And I did work harder, and Black Magic refused to respond. There were moments, very fleeting moments, when I caught a different look in her eyes. It was the faintest of all possible hints that she would like to be a part of my life but, unlike me, she'd accepted that it wasn't meant to be.

Now that I'm much, much older, I look back and smile. I think of Black Magic and me like an ill-fated, star-crossed pair of lovers. The attraction was there, but it would be fatal. It was just a matter of who recognized it first. In this case, it was Black Magic.

I knew what had to be done. Black Magic's coat had turned dull. Her eyes were becoming sad and lackluster. She was a different horse than the one we'd worked so hard to capture two months earlier. It was time to turn her loose and, somewhere inside my fourteen-year-old soul, I knew it was more than turning loose just one black horse. I knew it was also turning loose my dreams and hopes. Although I didn't realize it then, it was also finding out that sometimes the best way to show love is to turn something or someone loose. I also learned that sometimes it's better not to capture something in the first place.

The hog-wire alleyway was still in place. I opened the corral gate and waited until Black Magic turned her head toward the opening. She eyed it. She stood still and then looked at me. She watched me and waited. All I did was nod my head. I still don't know how, but she knew what I was telling her. She didn't run. She just trotted down the alley-way and into the pasture where the mules had waited for her for the entire two months. She stopped once and looked back at me.

A kid can't possibly know what he is learning as life's equations fall into some sort of sequential order. And certainly no one ever knows what form the teachers will assume, since God sends all kinds. In this case, it was a black mare with burrs in her mane and tail, and outgrown feet. I learned about freedom and sacrifice. I learned about caring enough to let go, a lesson I've carried with me each time I've been faced with putting a beloved animal to sleep. I learned that sometimes people and animals enter our lives for only a short time, passing through the portals of our hearts just long enough to leave us with the results of an important lesson or the seeds of a life-changing idea.

Black Magic was a teacher. I never went to see her again. For whatever reason, it seemed that merely visiting her would break apart something very special. It was as if a piece of that hog wire was keeping us attached and, even though I'd learned about freedom, I didn't want to cut us apart forever.

I never did get a mare and I never did get a foal. But that was just as well because there was no room for them in the corner of my heart that was still occupied by the black mare and her imaginary chocolate-colored foal. Now, all these many, many years later, I can still feel the spell woven by that ol' Black Magic.

Diane M. Ciarloni

One Good Horse

A *man on a horse is spiritually as well as*
physically bigger than a man on foot.

John Steinbeck

I was born the only son of a respected Montana cowboy. He was a man cut from the old cloth, quick with his fists when called upon, the last of the wild-horse runners. He was a good hand in the hills, a poker player and horse trader, more comfortable among men than women and children.

From my mother I inherited a slight, wiry frame and an artistic nature. From my father, I inherited expectations.

Because of my father's horse-trading, horses of all shapes, colors and dispositions passed through our corrals. If they were not too bad—no obvious pawing, kicking, biting or pitching of themselves over backward—I was expected to ride them.

The good horses sold quickly at a profit. The bad ones stayed longer.

My father was also a horse breeder. Later, his herd would show the good blood of foundation Texas-bred performance horses and AAA running stock. But it began with mustangs: jug-headed, blue roan mares and white-eyed stallions.

My father was also an opportunist. Whatever fad entered the horse world, he followed: Shetlands, Appaloosas, whatever the public wanted.

"I wish you would get some good horses on this place," I often heard my mother scold him.

But the barbs did not pierce his thick Irish hide. A "good" horse was any horse that made money.

At the age of ten, I was given my first horse to break. It was a blue roan we called Ribbon Tail, the product of a half-Shetland mare and a leopard Appaloosa stallion. He was to be my bar mitzvah, the horse that would make me a cowboy.

He was my nightmare.

Ribbon Tail had wood for brains and iron for will. He would respond not to love or discipline, training or torture. He was a barn-sour, stiff-necked, thick-hided curse to a little boy who dreamed the contradictory dreams of poetry, painting and pleasing his father.

Try as I might, I could not break the blue roan. I slept dreading the morning. I awoke with a sickness in my stomach and heart. I was raised being told, "A good cowboy made himself a hand on any horse he rode." It was the cowboy, I had been trained to believe, not the horse. So Ribbon Tail was not the failure. I was.

My sentence with the blue roan lasted two years. It was hard time. He humiliated me at brandings, roundups, anyplace where men and horses gathered.

And worse, I humiliated my father.

Finally, my father tried putting other boys on Ribbon Tail, fellows my age and older, boys more aggressive and fearless than I. But they failed, too. On any given day, no one was capable of making Ribbon Tail leave a corral.

When my mother finally talked my father into selling Ribbon Tail, I was relieved, but not ecstatic. By then, I was numb. My early love of horses was all but gone, and I considered myself a failure, a pariah of the plains.

It was a surprise then, when my father came home from

an auction a year later with a new horse for me. It was a yearling Paint stallion. Dad had been attracted by his splashy sorrel and white coloring.

"What is his breeding?" my mother asked.

"Dunno," Dad said. "No papers. He's probably a crop-out from a Quarter Horse herd."

I named the horse Gusto, and he changed my life.

I started Gusto when he was a two-year-old. He had a soft, kind eye and he liked people. The first time on him, I eased off a corral rail onto his bare back and rode him around the pen without a bridle. He reined naturally and was so smooth that I bragged to cowboy friends, "You can roll a cigarette on him at a gallop."

Gusto took to cows like he was part heeler, nipping calf tails on the long trail to our summer pasture. But mostly, he was a healer. With his gentle responsive ways, he closed the wounds in my soul that Ribbon Tail had left open and bleeding.

My father said nothing. Compliments were not his way. But anyone could see his chest swell with pride at the mention of Gusto.

Gusto was never to be a big horse. He stood under 15 hands and his back was a little too round. But he had a good hip, deep girth and more heart than one horse should carry. He would begin a hard day at a brisk walk, cover country and work cattle for hours in the heat and bring you home in the evening with the same rhythmic pace.

Gusto made anyone a hand. When we sorted pairs, he and I did most of the cutting. When it came to branding, he and I pulled the calves to the fire. When a big outside circle had to be ridden, either I rode Gusto or my father did.

He made us all forget the mean little roan we had called Ribbon Tail.

Gusto and I seemed inseparable, but graduation from high school and the blossoming of my creative side would finally put the miles and years between us.

I was riding a big circle the day the newspaper called. I

was eighteen and my writing career had started. I got off Gusto that day and I would never get on him the same again. I was leaving the ranch, moving from the tack room to the newsroom, my trail taking me to two different newspapers in Montana, free-lancing in California and New Mexico, and a stint with the information office of the Air Force.

With me gone, my younger sister Debbie claimed Gusto and began training him on barrels and poles. He thrived on competition, winning buckles, ribbons and trophies, and setting one indoor arena record.

When Debbie married, Gusto became my father's horse. With no children in the house, his companion on those long circles in the badlands was my mother, and sometimes she rode the Paint.

I was twenty-six years old when my father passed away and I returned to the ranch. Gusto was thirteen, his best years behind him, but I had come home to relearn cowboying. He served as coach for me and my wife, a city girl who learned to ride on his back. When my two children became old enough to set a saddle, Gusto took care of them.

The last time I seriously rode Gusto, he was nineteen. I could feel the arthritis stiffening his shoulders and the spring leaving his legs.

At the age of twenty-two, Gusto was retired. He still wintered at home, but his summers were spent across the road in the "rough section," in the company of mares and foals or yearlings.

"What are you going to do when Gusto dies?" a friend once asked me. "You are going to have to sell the ranch," he answered himself, stating in one sentence what a symbol Gusto had become.

He was always there, grazing the creek bottoms or standing on a high gumbo hill swatting flies. Strangers sometimes stopped and inquired about him. Some wanted to buy him. One fellow just stopped to say that Gusto was the prettiest horse he had ever seen.

But age was creeping up.

Always an easy keeper, Gusto began losing flesh. Always the king of the remuda, he was now on the bottom of the pecking order. New young horses treated him rudely, disrespectfully. He lay down often, rose slowly and painfully unhinged himself to walk.

One cold winter day after the morning feed, he lay down on the sun-warmed corral floor and went to sleep. He awoke hours later, after the other horses had long since left the corral. He seemed disoriented, almost panicky, as he struggled to his feet. He left the corral desperately, nickering as he walked, calling out like an old man who had fallen asleep on a park bench and awakened to find his family gone.

I kept putting off putting him down.

What will you do when Gusto dies? kept spinning in my head. And all the time, his arthritis worsened.

Finally, one November I knew I could not make Gusto endure another Montana winter. He was now twenty-six years old, which is old for a horse. I saddled my best horse, a registered Paint gelding, and rode out into the rough section. I found Gusto keeping company with a pregnant mare.

I dismounted, stroked Gusto's head, put my arms around his neck, and told him good-bye.

The next day, I left for a week-long elk-hunting trip. The grave had already been dug on a high cedar-topped ridge that overlooks the Sunday Creek valley. My son, now fourteen, rode out and brought Gusto in. My veterinarian put Gusto down.

When I knew it was done, I came home.

I have been ranching for twenty-three years now. I have endured some terrible droughts and harsh winters. Part of my heart has become tough and pragmatic. I know what has to be done and how to do it.

But another part of my heart is soft, vulnerable. It is the part that Gusto healed.

John L. Moore

Take a Deep Seat

Always smile when you are riding because it changes your intent.

James Shaw

When I decided to take riding lessons I had just turned fifty. I wasn't an athletic man. The chances of getting a broken neck on my first horse seemed pretty good. I wasn't in shape, and as it turns out, you don't just sit there. Nope. Not in English saddle, you don't.

"Get your heels down!" my instructor yelled. She was seventy if she was a day and she still had a figure so trim she dared to wear Lycra leggings under a gray sweatshirt and got away with it. I knew why later, when she went into the hayloft and started throwing huge bales around all by herself.

Her hair was coal black and her skin so smooth that teenage boys probably whistled at her in the mall. But when you got up close, you barely noticed a hardness to her that must have been a face lift and surely her hair was dyed, and you bet she had on plenty of makeup. Still, I didn't look as good as she did, and I doubted I'd live as long.

One day, they put me on a big gelding named Burt.

"You're looking sharp," Bev yelled at me. "You couldn't ride a boxcar with the doors shut, but you look good just sitting there."

"Why, Bev, that's the first compliment you ever gave me."

"Don't get used to it."

I could see her as a ballet teacher. I could see her with a long cane that she pounded on a dance floor as she moved her little swans around like puppets.

"Fascist!"

She laughed. Neither of us took the other too seriously. She knew I'd never be one of her fifteen-year-old equitation students, and I was just glad she was old enough to understand my jokes.

"Take a deep seat," she said.

I didn't know what that meant, and she was so busy yelling about my right foot turning out, that I forget to ask. Naturally, I did the wrong thing. I sat back on my tailbone as the horse trotted and I couldn't find the rhythm. I was supposed to rise up with the horse's outside leg and lower down with the inside. I was supposed to look good. Instead, I bounced around like one of those little monkeys they tie to a dog at the state fair.

"Stop that bouncing. Don't you sit around the corner. Darn you, post!"

I'd lost a stirrup by then. I was looking off to the side and trying to find it when I lost one rein. The obedient horse, good old Burt, went right where I'd pointed him—into a mammoth pile of sawdust.

Burt stood there up to his knees in the wood shavings they used to line the floors of the stalls and then he turned his head looking at me as if he was saying, "You dork!"

Bev just stared.

It was the kind of stare that required a witty response, so I said, "Oh yeah!" and I backed the horse out. I backed him an extra six steps just to show that I could.

"If there was a backward show, you'd win a blue ribbon." Bev ran a hand over her face. She did it again and then turned around. Her shoulders were shaking.

"Well, don't cry about it."

She turned around and tears were rolling down her face. She was about to bust a gut, laughing at me. "Oh good lord!" she said. "Have you ever seen anyone ride before?"

"Roy Rogers . . . Hopalong Cassidy."

"Not cowboys. English riders!"

I got down and she started complaining about that. "That's not how you dismount. I've told you before. Gimme those reins." Her fingers had started angling away from the palms. I could see arthritis in her future. And I knew about the show-ring accident that ended her career. I'd heard how she was dragged and that her back would never be the same.

"I'm going to do this once," she said. "You understand? I'm doing it because I like you, but you're an idiot." She took a halfhearted swipe at my head and said, "Boost me up."

She didn't weigh any more than my twelve-year-old daughter. I almost tossed her over the horse.

Bev squinted at me and shook her head again. "Now you watch."

What came next was a lesson in oneness. Bev moved with the horse so that the animal was free to trot as if he had no rider, no rider at all. Bev wasn't posting—going up and down with the horse—she was floating above him. She was allowing the horse total freedom and yet she was somehow totally in control.

I stood in the center of the arena and she rode around me. At first, she tried talking, explaining the intricacies of her movements. But quickly a look of bliss came upon her face and she forgot all about teaching.

As she floated above old Burt, I saw the years fade away until I was sure I saw a young woman still beautiful and still in the prime of her life.

Then her grin changed and I knew she was hurting.

She pulled the horse up in front of me. "Help me down," she said. "I'm old."

"Bev, you'll never be old as long as you live," I said. "I'm helping a goddess dismount."

"Yeah right. Don't think sucking up will get you anywhere. You're going back on that horse and ride another hour."

"Yes ma'am."

"And when you're done, write me a check." She walked away with just the slightest of limps and I knew she'd probably have a backache tonight.

"Thank you!"

She turned and flashed me a grin. "I haven't been on a horse in a long time," she said. "It was worth the pain pills I'll have to take tonight."

"It was worth it to me to see a truly glorious rider."

I think she blushed just a little. Then she stomped away, turning my lesson over to an eighteen-year-old girl whose smile would never be quite as big or as wonderful as Bev's was that day.

Gary Cadwallader

3

THESE AMAZING ANIMALS

The old mare watched the tractor work,
a thing of rubber and steel,
ready to follow the slightest wish
of the man who held the wheel.
She said to herself as it passed by,
you gave me an awful jolt,
but there's still one thing you can't do,
you cannot raise a colt.

George Rupp

Sgt. Reckless, a Mighty Marine

I figured they'd at least offer me a blindfold or maybe a cigarette. My commanding officer marched back and forth in front of me and I could hear the crowd outside growing restless.

"You know why you're in here, don't you? I'm saving your life. You've ruined hers. You've destroyed her reputation along with that of the baby."

"It's a foal, sir. It's a foal, not a baby horse," I replied meekly.

"I don't care what the technical term is. The fact remains you have ruined its life, its mother's reputation and, in all probability, made a laughingstock of the Marine Corps!" he growled. "Now, sit yourself down and think about the consequences of your actions while I go out there and see what I can do to straighten out this mess!"

So this was how it was going to end. I had survived the war only to face a firing squad stateside for telling the truth. I was only doing my job.

"Join the Marines and see the world!" the poster promised. Unfortunately, I missed the fine print that said I'd have to walk. It was 1953. The draft was still on for the Korean Conflict, so for me it was either get drafted or join the service of my choice. The Marines said they needed a few good men, but they would take me anyway. They were behind in their quota they said.

Boot camp—tent camp—Korea. That didn't take long. They were further behind than I thought. After losing half of our regimental staff to dysentery, they transferred me from cooking for the enlisted men to cooking for the officers up on the hill. They said they could keep a better eye on me and if just one officer got sick, they would transfer me to reconnaissance.

It was in recon that I first heard about the little horse Reckless. It seems a Lt. Pederson of the Recoilless Rifles Platoon, Anti-Tank Company, fifth Marine Regiment had bought her off the racetrack in Seoul, Korea, for $250. Reckless was bought for the sole purpose of serving as an artillery packhorse, and what a packhorse she became.

Those 75 mm rounds she carried weighed over twenty pounds apiece and, fully loaded, she could replace six men packing ammo up those steep hills to gun placements. This little sorrel, blaze-faced mare was quite a war-horse, quickly gaining the respect of the men of the entire fifth Marine Regiment. She stood only about 14 hands high, but she had the heart and soul of a true marine. Her stamina and determination were incredible.

During one battle, she carried more than 800 rounds to gun positions in front of enemy lines. The North Koreans must have been shocked to see her working her way through the war-ravaged brush, looking like some prehistoric, hump-backed monster covered with large scales. Her strange appearance resulted from the men placing flak jackets over her fully loaded packs to protect her from being hit by shrapnel from the shells exploding around her.

As it was, she was wounded twice. In one courageous battle called Outpost Vegas, this little mare made more than fifty trips to gun positions, carried more than 9,000 pounds of recoilless ammo and covered more than thirty miles. She was wounded on one of those trips, but she bravely finished her quest and thus was given the name Reckless by her squad. Her real name was Ah Chim Hai, which roughly translated meant "morning flame."

It's interesting to note that once the squad leader showed Reckless the locations of the gun placements, she would make the trips to the front lines and back by herself with no additional human guidance. For her heroic feats, Reckless received the Korean Service Medal with three battle stars, the United Nations Service Medal, the National Defense Service Medal and two Purple Hearts. She was a true marine heroine.

Whenever the fifth Marines pulled back from the front lines for some well-deserved R and R, Reckless was right there with them. She especially enjoyed snacking on the chocolate wafers and large crackers from the men's C rations. Being a true marine, she often washed these down with a mixed drink of Coca-Cola and beer.

During one of these relaxing moments, her squad remembered that Reckless had been a racehorse before becoming a war hero, and the men issued a challenge to Native Dancer, winner of the Preakiness and the Belmont, to a matched race. This would be her crowning glory!

Thank goodness the Vanderbilts didn't respond to the challenge because the results might have been very embarrassing. Reckless just didn't quite match up to the caliber of Native Dancer. But this was just a small setback for the marines, who saw this as more of a challenge than a defeat. They had even bigger and better plans for their little heroine.

When word was released to the press that Reckless would be coming to the United States to be stationed with the First Marine Division at Camp Pendleton, California, the governor issued a proclamation welcoming her to the state. She was invited to attend all kinds of functions befitting a dignitary of her status. Ed Sullivan even wanted her shipped back to New York City to be a special guest on his television show honoring the Marine Corps' birthday. Unfortunately, the ship transporting her to the United States got held up by a storm at sea and she missed the show.

Reckless was given a hero's welcome at Camp Pendleton

and promoted to the rank of sergeant. Her life became one parade after another. On these occasions, the fifth Marines would send someone to the base stables, where she had her own paddock and stall. They'd groom her and put on her blanket with all her medals and sergeant stripes and take her down to the parade grounds. She'd stand proudly beside the reviewing stand while the troops paraded by in full-dress uniform fit for the occasion. Then the warm California sun would take its toll. Her head would lower, her ears, eyelids and bottom lip would start to droop, she'd cock one hind foot and then start to snore. She was the only enlisted marine who could actually sleep through a parade and get away with it.

Now, unbeknownst to Reckless, some high-ranking public relations officers decided it would be a great idea to arrange a "marriage" between her and some famous Thoroughbred racehorse sire. The plan called for their offspring to be entered in and, no doubt, win the Kentucky Derby, thereby propelling Reckless and the Marine Corps even further into the limelight.

After the consummation of this marriage, Reckless was taken back to the base stable and turned out for daily frolics with the stable horses. At night, she was led back to her private stall and paddock, where she was queen of the stable and she knew it.

Before going any further, I must explain that in the armed forces, officers know everything. The enlisted men do not. That's just the military way, which means that most officers find it unnecessary to inform the enlisted ranks of their plans. This is exactly what happened with Reckless and her Derby-winning colt. We knew nothing about the officers' plans and most of the enlisted men would be discharged or transferred before the foal's birth.

It was at this time that Reckless and I crossed paths. After my "Korean vacation," I'd been transferred to special services and assigned to the base stable. One of my jobs was to help promote the annual Navy Relief Rodeo by being a trick roper and rodeo clown. Our base commander at the time was a strong supporter of the rodeo and through his efforts, we received some bucking horses and bulls for the sailors and marines to practice on.

One of the young bucking horses had gotten kicked in the chest and needed stitches. After a visit to the veterinarian, he was turned out with the stable horses so it would be easier to catch him when it came time to take out the stitches. The next morning when Reckless was turned out, the crew gathered to see her put this new guy in his place. To their surprise, they discovered, first, that he was a stallion, and second, that Reckless was in love. By the time they got her back to her paddock and the young stallion into a corral, Cupid had shot all his arrows.

"You can probably brush off most of those scuff marks and comb out her ruffed-up mane," I explained. "But I don't know how you're going to get that smirk off her face." We all agreed not to tell anybody about this and swore an oath of secrecy.

Apparently, the arranged marriage had failed, and no one had informed the powers that be to check her in twenty-eight days to see if the ink had dried on the license. All was forgotten until one day I looked up and saw a staff car and veterinarian's truck parked outside Reckless's paddock. After the vet had checked her over, the staff car pulled up to the office where I was and the officers unloaded with big smiles on their faces. One proudly announced that Reckless was going to have a baby.

It was at this point that I became very confused. Why were they so excited about her being in foal with a common bucking horse? I didn't know about the earlier marriage with the champion stallion, and they didn't know about her affair with the rodeo bronc. I was fully expecting to be blamed for her condition while quietly wondering who'd let the cat out of the bag. Instead, I was being ordered to make a big sign to put along the main base highway that ran by her paddock. They explained that they wanted everybody to be aware of the expected arrival and its gender once it got here.

The sign was to say, "It's a . . . ." and then the appropriate sign of "Boy" or "Girl" was to be put up when the foal was born. Also, whoever was on duty at the time of the blessed event was to call the special services officer immediately and he would notify the press.

Well, it seems the foal came about a month later than expected, and you can guess who was on duty the night it happened. Actually, it was about daylight when I looked out and saw her cleaning him off. So as instructed, I hung the "Boy" sign, made the phone call and started my morning chores. Suddenly, the driveway filled with staff cars and news media.

They were driving Reckless nuts. She was frantically trying to maneuver between the colt and the flashing cameras. I told the newspeople to step outside the paddock and I'd lead her past them so they could get the shots they wanted. The officers beamed with pride as the cameras clicked. When they were finished, I turned Reckless loose, and she scurried to the backside of her paddock with her wobbly legged offspring in tow.

While heading back to the barns, I heard one of the officers mention the Kentucky Derby. As I stopped to listen more closely, one of the reporters turned to me and asked in a very loud voice, "What is the name again of that famous sire that's the daddy of this colt?"

I proudly answered, "Well, sir, he ain't very famous, but he's one of our best bareback broncs. You know, a buckin' horse."

You could have cut the silence with a knife. My CO grabbed my arm and invited me immediately into the office for a "debriefing" while the other officers and the news media were left in a very disgruntled and confused state. During my meeting with the CO the entire story of the corps' plans for Reckless was brought to my attention. I learned all about the tremendous amount of time and energy devoted to developing a PR strategy to keep her name in the spotlight and to make her even more famous.

In just a few seconds, I had managed to dishonor the reputation of a war heroine and destroy a huge public relations campaign for the marines.

My enlistment was up shortly after Reckless had her colt. After recent research, I discovered that she fell in love two more times. None of those offspring were derby winners either. Reckless spent the rest of her life at Camp Pendleton in the lap of luxury. She passed away in the spring of 1968. It was a well-earned retirement for such a brave and courageous little mare. A monument was erected in her honor at the base stable where she still rules to this day.

Boots Reynolds

Sgt. Reckless

The Guiding Sight

"She's a card and she cracks me up every day. I ask her to give me some sweets, and she does, coming close to me and planting a kiss on the nose!"

(Dan Shaw of Ellsworth, Maine must be talking about his girl-friend, right? Well, maybe not.)

"When we go to the mall, my wife goes one way *(Wife! Uh-oh. Now we have trouble . . .)* and I go the other. I'll ask Cuddles to find the escalator. 'Now find the elevator, then find the elevator button.' She puts her nose near the button, so I know what to press."

(Aha! Cuddles must be a dog! That's it!)

"If she needs to go outside, she'll tap on the floor with her tiny hoof. If I don't answer right away, she'll tap and neigh. Then, if I still don't answer, she'll tap, neigh and cross her back legs."

(Neigh? Back legs? It can't be. But it is . . . a horse!)

Cuddles is the first official guide horse, assisting Shaw, who is blind, carefully down the aisles of his grocery store, across busy streets and even to his seat on an airplane. Cuddles is a miniature mare who stands approximately twenty-four inches tall at the base of the mane and could possibly live to the ripe old equine age of forty.

Miniatures were first imported to the United States in the

early 1900s as workhorses to take advantage of their small size and great strength in pulling ore carts in coal mines. Cuddles doesn't pull Shaw, but gently leads him where he can't see to go safely himself, even navigating New York City's top tourist sights. Cuddles is the first guide horse to go to the top of the Empire State Building, to the Statue of Liberty and down into the cavernous and noisy subway. She also toured the famous toy store, FAO Schwarz, no doubt to look over the stuffed horses on display.

Shaw, age forty-six, began losing his sight to retinitis pigmentosa—"It's in the genes," he says—when he was seventeen and couldn't imagine himself with a white cane or a guide dog. He'd experienced overwhelming grief from the previous loss of a pet dog. Then he heard about The Guide Horse Foundation in North Carolina. There, miniatures undergo eight months of training to deal with those normal things that occur in human life that might otherwise spook a horse. Police horses are trained the same way.

Cuddles responds to Shaw's more than twenty-five vocal commands, and she can see very well in almost complete darkness, something with which Dan is all too familiar. Yes, she frequently goes in his house to watch television with him and perform other more necessary duties. Litterbox trained, no, but the little horse does tap on Shaw's door with her tiny sneaker-clad hoof when Nature calls.

Shaw says Cuddles has allowed him "to feel free for the first time in twenty years." Now, he leads a full life, he says, which includes connecting with people and animals in ways he never would have imagined.

He recalls one notable moment, of many, from his New York City adventure. In front of the famed and elegant Plaza Hotel on the edge of Central Park, Shaw decided to take Cuddles for a ride in a carriage pulled by large draft horses.

"I let Cuddles pick out her own horse, so she walked up and down the sidewalk and sniffed each one, finally settling on her choice. I think the two kind of spoke to one another, the huge horse and the little one."

Their joint sojourns to Shaw's favorite nearby fishing hole are highlights of his leisure time: "It's about a mile and a half away, and I went with a person the first three times. You go down a paved road, down a dirt road, across a bridge and down a path. Now, I just say, 'Let's go fishing, Cuddles,' and off we go. She knows the way. When I get there, she eats grass while I fish. No, I haven't taught her to tap once for bass, twice for trout yet," laughs Shaw.

The two share remarkable communication, he believes. "She's so smart. If I'm in her corral and I'm walking toward something I shouldn't be, she'll block me. If I call, she'll come right to the gate."

Her keen intuition averted probable injury to Shaw in the summer of 2002, when they visited a local horse show. Shaw made an oral presentation about his buddy and they received a standing ovation. "We don't do tricks," he affirms. "Guide dogs don't do tricks."

He remembers that it was terribly windy as the two stood by a show corral and a huge canopy, the latter anchored by heavy metal pipes and other weights.

"Suddenly, out of nowhere, Cuddles yanked me to the side, about ten paces," recounts Shaw. The canopy came crashing down where the two had just stood, pipes and all. "If she pulls me, I always go with her," he says. "It's said that horses can sense danger before it happens. I believe it."

Shaw thinks his miniature maintains a unique perspective of him, the human. "She's accepted me as part of her herd. It's like when a horse goes blind in its herd. Another horse will take care of it. She's taking care of me."

Shaw wants to take care of Cuddles and he does. After attending a special school, he was able to continue his beloved craft of woodworking. He still makes birdhouses, arbors, furniture and buildings. He built a barn for Cuddles and her miniature barn mate, twenty-eight-inch tall Nevada. "I feel that because of what Cuddles does for me, the least I can do is let her be a horse," says Shaw. The structure features a television, a heated water bucket and other amenities befitting his best friend. He stresses that it's critically important to him that Cuddles have her "down time."

Shaw has accrued so many fun experiences that he's telling them in two books: *Dan Meets Cuddles*, and the second, *Adventures of Dan and Cuddles*, which was penned especially for second and third graders "who've seen us in *Weekly Reader* and *National Geographic for Kids*," explains Shaw.

Shaw calls Cuddles "one awesome little deal. Whenever you think you know her, she always comes up and does something else. She's the little soldier when she gets dressed in the morning with her harness and boots. But when they come off, she's just the playful little horse."

Shaw feels a connection with another human–animal partnership saga: Morris Frank had the first Seeing Eye dog in America, a female named Buddy, and Frank subsequently helped establish the first school for such dogs in America. He wrote a book, *First Lady of the Seeing Eye*, made into a Disney TV movie in 1984. The film was entitled *Love Leads the Way*.

Its title is appropriate for Cuddles, says Shaw. The tiny horse is leading him lovingly and carefully through his life while paving the way for other visually impaired individuals to gain amazing insight, if not real sight, when they, too, acquire their own guide horses.

Stephanie Stephens

The Stallion and the Redwing

It was about the most beautiful sight on our southwestern Ohio farm: the stallion and the redwinged blackbird.

Day after day during early summer, the redwing perched in the highest branch of the three small trees—a hawthorn, a wild cherry and a crab apple—that grew in a clump along the back lane that led from the barn to the far pasture. Beneath these trees, none more than twenty feet tall, our dappled-gray Welsh stallion stood in the shade, idly switching his tail at the flies.

Often, for an hour or more at a time, the redwing sat there, alert, apparently on guard, as its mate went to and fro to her nest secured in several tall weeds in the uncut hayfield. It chattered constantly with a tick, tick, tick.

They certainly were aware of each other's presence, the horse and the bird. And all was at peace between them. Whether there was any communication is something I did not wonder about at the time. I know it was a stunningly beautiful picture, complete only when both of them were in it.

Late in the summer, the redwing and his family departed for the winter. According to a log I had kept, they would return the first week in March.

It was in October that the stallion, more than twenty years old, died. We buried him with grief and dignity, as befits a herd sire, in a deep grave along the fence that led south from the corncrib. The grave was exactly twelve steel fence posts from the gate. I counted them carefully and then recorded the location in my log so that we could find the grave in later years.

When the redwinged blackbirds had not returned to the farm by the first week of March, I became uneasy. As I went to the barn early on the seventh to do the chores, I wondered what might have happened. Then I heard it, far away, but unmistakably the tick, tick, tick of a redwing. Whether this was chirp, monologue or song, it was a welcome sound, like hearing from a dear old friend.

I went to the doors on the east side of the barn and pushed them open. I knew just where to look. The redwing would be sitting in the very top of one of the three small trees, facing the field where its mate later would build a nest.

I strained my eyes. I searched every branch and limb, which did not yet bear leaves. The redwing should be there. It wasn't. Yet, I could hear it. Tick, tick, tick.

After standing there puzzled for a full minute, I became convinced that the bird's voice must have been coming from some other direction. I went outside the barn and looked up at the towering silver maple next to the overhang. The bird sometimes spent time up there. But it was not there now. It was nowhere in sight.

I went beyond the corncrib. Then, more by chance than anything, I saw it. Down along another fence that stretched southward from the corncrib, the bird was perched atop a steel post. I could see it clearly. It was spreading its wings in the fashion of the species, calling out tick, tick, tick. Tick, tick, tick your-ee-ee-ee.

Yet it was all a little strange. I had never seen the bird in that spot before. And it was odd that it remained there, clinging in the stiff breeze to the very top of the fence post.

I waved my arm, but it did not frighten the redwing away. It continued its song.

As my eye measured the distance, something clicked in

my mind and I began counting the fence posts between the bird and me. One, two . . . seven, eight . . . ten, eleven, twelve. The redwing was sitting on the twelfth post—the one closest to the stallion's grave.

It took me a while to organize my thoughts. I counted again. Yes, the bird was on the twelfth post, as close to the stallion's grave as it could get.

I went to the house and checked back through my log. The redwings had left the farm a full two months before the stallion had died. How, then, could the bird know that the stallion was buried at a spot far from its usual perch? Had it come here to sing over the grave?

I might have dismissed it as mere coincidence. I might even have forgotten it, except for one fact: On the morning of March 5, the following spring, I heard the familiar sound of a redwinged blackbird. Tick, tick, tick. Without even thinking, I ran to the corner of the corncrib and gazed down along the fence row. There was the bird, not on the ninth post or the fifteenth post, but on top of the twelfth post.

It was singing over the stallion's grave just as it had the previous spring. It remained there for twenty or thirty minutes and then flew to the clump of three trees along the back lane. Never once, after that first day of its return, did I see it go back to the grave.

The redwing returned on March 3 the year after that and on March 8 the fourth year. It always alighted on the twelfth post the first day of its return before going anywhere else, and there it seemed to talk briefly to the stallion buried beneath the dense pasture grass.

This spring the redwing did not return. It is past April 1, and I know I shall not see it again. Like the stallion, it has undoubtedly lived out its life.

Although it is not here, I still see it in my mind's eye, in the clump of three small trees and atop the twelfth steel post. And I continue to ponder the relationship between the bird and the stallion. Does there develop an affinity, a kinship between nature's creatures that we, mere humans, cannot comprehend or explain? Does some understanding, some loyalty, exist that rivals or even transcends anything that exists among men?

Only the stallion and the redwing knew.

Gerald W. Young

A Change of Command

"Do you need some help?"

"No, I can do it myself," came Bill's grumbled reply.

I circled my restless young Paint and watched Sundance stand patiently as Bill fumbled with the saddle hitch.

The sorrel Quarter Horse was from excellent breeding stock, lean with good muscle tone. Only the graying hairs on his face hinted of his age, which was twenty-four. For fifteen of those years he'd belonged to me. The rider, like the horse, hid his years well. Silver hair peaked out around a black Stetson hat. The tanned face remained unlined despite years in the sun. And like the horse, the man was fit and trim. When working with the horses, his steel-blue eyes sparkled with a clarity otherwise missing those days and a smile touched his lips.

Slight arthritis had somewhat slowed the horse. Alzheimer's disease had slowed the man. With no family of his own, Bill had become a part of mine, and I worried about letting him continue to ride as I worried about when to take away the keys to his car.

Sundance and I remembered horse shows where he and Bill had competed in barrel-racing and pole-bending events. We remembered long leisurely trail rides and running flat-out across the prairie, pretending we were in the wilds of Montana instead of rural Illinois.

Sundance worked well for me, but had a special bond with Bill, a visible excitement when they rode together. Whenever Bill eased into the saddle and lightly touched the big gelding with the tips of his spurs, the horse pranced, eager to run, ready to perform. Only the gentle touch of a spur and Bill's hands on the reins told him it was time for action.

I hid the spurs a while back, and Bill didn't seem to notice. Horse and rider no longer ran the way they used to. Rides were kept to a walk and trot around the arena and out into the pasture. I kept an eye on them and worried.

I hesitated when Bill asked to ride one crisp October morning. The vacant look in his eyes had become more pronounced, and although I wanted him to be active for as long as he could be, I didn't want him hurt. I also couldn't say no.

Bill finally got the cinch tightened and climbed into the saddle. He settled himself with a big sigh. Sundance eased forward at a slow pace, and contentment softened the rider's face. Bill asked for a trot, and I watched the horse's reluctance.

"This horse is acting pretty . . . ," Bill searched for the words he wanted. "He seems pretty sluggish today."

I nodded. "Well, he's getting older and his joints are a little stiff in the morning. Be patient with him."

Bill grunted an undecipherable response when his commands remained unanswered. After several requests, the horse gently broke into a smooth jog trot.

Sundance concentrated on the ground ahead, carefully measuring his stride. I glimpsed Bill's hand ease toward the saddle horn once for balance.

Bill cued the horse to canter—whether by conscious intent or from years of riding, I wasn't quite sure. Sundance continued in his easy trot. When asked again for a canter, the gelding looked toward me, and I hoped I had conveyed my concern to the horse.

I pulled my Paint to a stop and watched, my heart skipping a beat now and then.

Bill touched the horse with his right heel and gave a voice command at the same time. "Canter, canter." Sundance hesitated, shook his head slightly and slowed to a walk.

With a sigh, Bill reached down and patted Sundance on his neck. "Okay, boy. We'll take it easy on you today."

I tried to swallow around the lump in my throat and smile in spite of the tears in my eyes. My heart settled its rhythm, and I felt at peace at what I'd witnessed between horse and rider. I no longer feared letting Bill ride. Where once Bill had been in command, the control had shifted to the horse. Sundance knew the man was different from the rider who had once urged flying lead changes through the poles, from the man who had ridden like the wind across the prairie. The horse I loved was protecting the friend we both loved.

Sandra Tatara

From One Mom to Another

For a hundred and fifty years, in the pasture of dead horses, roots of pine trees pushed through the pale curves of your ribs, yellow blossoms flourished above you in autumn, and in winter frost heaved your bones in the ground—old toilers, soil makers; O Roger, Mackerel, Riley, Ned, Nellie, Chester, Lady Ghost.

Donald Hall, "Names of Horses"

I will never be persuaded that animals don't understand tragedy and don't communicate with each other because I witnessed an extraordinary episode between Christie and Dixie, two Belgian mares who never appeared to even like each other, until Dixie turned to Christie in her last hours.

Dixie was scarred, scared, undernourished and wild-eyed when I first saw her. Her nose had been broken numerous times from what the owner said was "smacks on her head with a two-by-four for being bad." I didn't need another Belgian, but I dug deep in my pockets, borrowed and scraped, and came up with the money to buy her. I rationalized that maybe, eventually, after bringing her back to health, I could use her as a brood mare. Under all the mud and dirt, I saw some promising conformation.

Christie's history couldn't have been more different than Dixie's. Christie came from a loving home, had the best of care and much preferred being with people than with other horses. She was my first draft horse and she came to the farm a year or so before Dixie. I knew she was special and I knew she would help me safely learn all the ins and outs of owning and driving a draft horse. She never disappointed me.

Dixie, although lacking Christie's people skills and trust, turned into an excellent, caring mother and gave me nice, strong colts each year that she was bred. During a routine visit, I asked our veterinarian to look at Dixie. Something just didn't look right. She was eating, drinking and taking care of Pinkie, the colt she had a month earlier, but she just looked what horsepeople describe as "off."

After taking her temperature we found she was running a fever. Perhaps she had some kind of uterine infection from the birth, although she had no outward signs of illness. We did some uterine cultures and the veterinarian told me to give her some medication to get her temperature down.

But a few hours later, Dixie started getting sicker. Although her temperature was down, she wouldn't eat, she seemed uncomfortable and she wasn't passing stool. She was obviously more distressed and starting to show signs of colic. I put in another call to our veterinarian but our usual doctor, whom I knew and trusted, was not on call. A new, young associate with little equine experience arrived in her place. I wasn't in a position to wait, and figured that she was better than no veterinarian at all.

Several times throughout the evening, the veterinarian returned to administer pain medication, but Dixie's pain increased. She became more and more uncomfortable and finally was unable to nurse Pinkie. Pinkie was confused and hungry, and he didn't understand why his mother, usually so attentive, wasn't paying attention to him. On the veterinarian's final visit of the evening, she gave me a syringe full of pain medication and instructions to administer the shot in three hours. She explained that it was a safe dose of a long acting drug that would make Dixie more comfortable.

I slept in the paddock that night with Dixie, watching her, walking her, trying to help her with Pinkie and hoping to see some improvement. At the appointed hour, I gave her the last shot. Within a few minutes, she seemed more at ease, even making her way over to the fence line that adjoined the paddocks where the other horses were lined up and watching her quietly, as if standing vigil, their hay in untouched piles.

Dixie wasn't a social horse. I seldom saw her show interest in the other horses. She never had anything to do with Christie. Typically, if one of the herd came near her fence she would charge and pin her ears, strongly telling the intruder to stay away.

That night, everything changed.

Astonished, I watched Dixie touch noses with all the horses in line. Next, she stood across the fence from Christie. I thought this was strange, but she seemed so calm now. I began to get hopeful even as Pinkie seemed more confused and upset.

Dixie and Christie continued their silent conversation for several more moments until Dixie turned, looked at the others again, walked to the center of the paddock and lay down.

I kept my distance. I didn't want to disturb her when she needed to rest, so I sat down at the edge of the paddock and just watched her.

I watched as Pinkie, now quiet and subdued, slowly made his way over and stood beside his mother. With a gentleness that belied his anxiety and hunger, Pinkie smelled Dixie's hooves, her legs and her tail, and ever so lovingly nuzzled her mane and pressed his nose to hers. With a final sniff, he turned and walked to the fence line joining the other horses. I knew then that Dixie was gone.

I slowly walked to the center of the paddock and wished my Dixie farewell. Eventually, I glanced over to see Christie still standing in the spot where she and Dixie shared their last moment. To this day, I swear Christie had tears running down her face.

I was numb and in shock. Dixie was gone. I had a month-old colt who needed to eat and no way to feed him. I sought advice from others who had raised orphan foals.

Pinkie would have nothing to do with a bottle. He rejected it, and I worked all day trying to get fluids into him. He had been creep-feeding since birth, eating small amounts of supplemental food, but wouldn't take anything by mouth. He turned up his nose at his favorite grain. He wanted his mother.

As I was working with Pinkie, I noticed how agitated Christie was, running the fence line, calling out. It was a behavior totally out of the norm for her. She had weaned her own colt six weeks before. She hadn't much liked being a mother and wanted nothing to do with him after three months. She had been a good mother but when the time came to wean him, she gladly booted him out of her paddock without a second glance, and her milk supply had dried up in a few days.

Feeling exasperated, I walked outside to try one last time with the bottle. As I passed Christie's paddock I stopped to see if I could figure out why she seemed so agitated. I stood there, not believing what I saw. Her udder, which had been empty and had returned to normal size, was full! I expressed some fluid into my hand—it was milk! She paced the fence line almost frantic, calling to Pinkie and not taking her eyes off him.

Now, I understood the significance of what had happened at the fence line before Dixie died.

I decided to take a chance. I put Pinkie in Christie's paddock. He was exhausted, hungry and depressed. I stood close by in case Christie rejected him. Instead she trotted up to Pinkie, nuzzled him and pushed him around until he was close to her udder. He started to nurse. He drank his fill then quickly lay down and slept with Christie standing vigil over him until he woke up and ate again.

Christie adopted Pinkie as her own. He started creep-feeding again the next day, and with the help of Christie's milk grew into a strong, vigorous colt. A much better mother to Pinkie than she had been to her own colt Pete, Christie continued to produce an abundance of milk for another three months and watched over her adopted son until he went to his new home.

I know I was sent to bring Dixie home and give her a few happy years. I still get tears in my eyes when I remember her at the fence line that night, calmly and quietly touching the noses of the horses she'd previously wanted nothing to do with.

On that sad night I saw a miracle. On that sad night I found hope. On that sad night I witnessed the power of love.

Thank you, Dixie.

Chris Russell-Grabb

A Leap of Faith

Everything depends upon myself and my horse.

Mamie Francis

Babe leaped out at me from a newspaper story about the National Cowgirl Museum and Hall of Fame.

She merited mention as the mount of Mamie Francis, a famous equestrienne of nearly a century ago. The story explained why the museum was moved from the Texas Panhandle town of Hereford to Fort Worth and why an elite coterie of cowgirls, women writers and artists, and leaders are revered and remembered for their contributions to the Western way of life.

Mamie (billed as "Miss Mamie," born as Elba Mae Ghent) and Babe (a white Arabian mare whose real name was Lurlene) made their living diving from a fifty-foot tower into an impossibly shallow, ten-foot-deep tank of water. They performed their high-diving act 628 times from 1908 to 1914, for the amusement of audiences and a paycheck.

The New York American (July 12, 1908) called Mamie's act "the most dangerous of all the circus thrillers." *The Gazette Times* (Pittsburgh, July 25, 1909) gushed: "Her self-poise is the best indication of nerves of steel."

A photo published in Philadelphia's *The Daily Evening Telegraph* (July 8, 1909) proves the peril. Babe and Mamie have just made their leap. Babe's ears are forward and alert, her tail flies perpendicular to the ground. Mamie's long, dark hair streams straight back—testimony to their breakneck speed—as she sits balanced and confident on Babe's back. It was unlikely work for Mamie, a small-town Wisconsin girl who couldn't swim.

Danger was their daily fare. The daredevil girl, always dressed all in white, and her white diving mare stunned the thousands who watched their act. They headlined in Cincinnati, Pittsburgh, Philadelphia, and in the most-celebrated playground of all—New York's Coney Island.

While their leaps provided royal entertainment for revelers, it was dangerous business for Babe and Mamie. Each leap, always a leap of faith, made them money and fame, and ready candidates for the obituary page.

Horses are grounded creatures, born to crop grass at ground level, and to run and roam together in social groups . . . herds . . . for companionship and protection. There's safety in numbers, with lots of eyes on look-out for predators lurking behind a bush or in the trees. Bad things come from above and being away from the herd.

But here Babe was, poised on the precipice of a tower, against instincts developed by her forebears from surviving millions of years in the wild. She waited until all was still and quiet, for just the right moment, when she felt as one with Mamie. Then she leaped. Mamie never forced her.

Faith in each other kept them climbing the ramp . . . and jumping. On one dive, the tank collapsed when they hit the water, and they were buried under mud, dirt, canvas and water. Mamie's chest caved in and she was in danger of drowning. Luckily, a Good Samaritan was watching from the wings. He jumped in and pulled Mamie out from under Babe and the debris, and out of the tank. Babe managed to scramble out on her own. As more help arrived, her rescuer—a man with athletic, quick reactions and a good heart—disappeared into the din and clatter of the carnival. Mamie didn't know him and never got to thank him.

On July 11, 1908, in full view of a happy Coney Island crowd of 30,000, Babe inched to the tower's edge, her skin quivering with anticipation. The moment to leap was upon them. Suddenly, the whistles of a steam calliope pierced the quiet and shattered Babe's concentration. She lost her balance and teetered, and before Mamie could steady her, they tumbled into the water below. The crowd feared the worst. Could they have survived? Attendants pulled Mamie from the tank. But no Babe. She was thrashing about, drowning on the bottom of the tank. Precious seconds passed as workers rushed to get a rope around her. Two minutes passed as Babe kicked and struggled, making rescue impossible. Five minutes passed. Finally a lone diver, a hero among horses, dived into the tank. He swam down to Babe, who was probably unconscious by now, and passed the rope under her body. The men wrenched Babe out as death knocked on her door.

Two hours later, Babe walked out of Coney Island's Dreamland under her own horsepower. Horses remind us, in their simple ways and simple faiths, that there is hope in life. And as long as there is life, there is hope.

Mamie was a sprite of a girl, and on horseback as in life, she was tough as West Texas boot leather. Her grandson Tom Shelton says, "She was afraid of no one and of nothing."

She respected the dangers of the high dive, but embraced the excitement: "Oh, the glory of it all. I just close my eyes, take a deep breath, and await the splash."

Mamie's boss, C.F. "California Frank" Hafley, appreciated her talents and liked her so much he married her in 1909. Mamie is so beloved among cowgirls that she was posthumously inducted into the National Cowgirl Hall of Fame in 1981.

She told *The Gazette Times* (Pittsburgh, June 26, 1910) that she dived for money:

"After a while, I will be able to retire and live on my ranch without bothering over money matters. Until then, I must take the chance of accident involved in the high dive on horseback. But . . . I have minimized the chance . . . not by any trickery or chicanery, but by skill. Everything depends upon myself and my horse."

Mamie might have leaped for money. But Babe leaped for Miss Mamie.

Gayle Stewart

Riding in the Alaskan Bush

Living in Alaska, we often encountered wildlife, especially moose. In the winter, when the snow was deep in the mountains, they would come down into the valley and be thick through the trees. I have awakened and opened the drapes of my room downstairs to be face-to-face with a moose eating grass outside my window. I have waited at the bus stop countless times with a moose contentedly eating a tree a short distance from me. It became second nature to sing or talk for the entire quarter of a mile walk to the bus stop in the dark so that they knew that I was a person.

During cross-country ski trips, we encountered dozens of them. They bedded down on our property with their calves and, on a few unlucky occasions, ate our bushes down to the nub despite our repeated attempts to scare them away by banging pots and pans from the safety of our second-story deck.

Dustee, my lovable horse, was known to be frightened of moose when they would venture too near and he would snort and run at dangerous speeds through his pasture. When I walked out to the balcony and called his name, he would rush over to the fence as close as he could get and fix his eyes upon me. He would stand frozen, not looking away, as if it would all be okay as long as I was there. I would stay out there with him until the moose had gone.

Despite acknowledging their well-deserved reputation, we didn't consider the moose a danger. In all the years, no one in our family was ever hurt or threatened by them. That changed one day as I was returning from a trail ride, traveling down a power line toward home. I always carried a folding hoof pick in my pocket in case the occasional stone or other debris become lodged in Dustee's foot. As we were riding along, I realized that something was bothering him and I stopped to check it out. I stepped off and went to his left foreleg, kneeling down and placing his leg on my knee so I could pry the stone loose.

Suddenly, I froze, the hair on my neck stood on end and I had the distinct feeling of being watched. Instinct told me I was in imminent danger. I remained there, kneeling down and completely unable to move. I have never been one to freeze in dangerous situations. As a matter of fact, I am usually the first to act and address critical issues in emergency situations. But not this time. I was only able to turn my head, and there, over my left shoulder, was one of the most dangerous creatures known to man: an angry moose.

The sight of a moose about to attack is difficult to describe. She stood only about fifteen feet away, teeth bared, ears flat back on her head. Standing six feet tall at the shoulder, she towered over me as I kneeled there, the hair on her back standing up. I had no time to react before she charged. I watched her come, unable to look away from the awesome sight. Then I felt my horse's leg rise off of my knee and out of my hand, and the next moment his front legs landed squarely in front of me. I was directly underneath his belly, looking out between his outstretched legs, watching as his neck stretched down and his head snaked down low toward the ground.

He assumed the posture of the angry moose, but stood stock-still. His teeth were bared and his ears were flat back as he crouched over me, staring at the moose. I only vaguely realized in that split second what was happening. The moose had stopped, ears flat and teeth still bared, her nose only a few feet from my horse's, her angry eyes locked on his. There was utter silence, as only there can be in the wilderness. No wind, no leaves rustling. It seemed that we all were holding our breath.

Then, from over my right shoulder I heard a rustling. It was the pitter-patter of little feet, small hooves moving in the woods. I watched from the corner of my eye as a very young, very cute calf moose walked nonchalantly out of the woods, passed by us and calmly walked by the angry moose that still threatened like a terrible thunder cloud. The calf disappeared into the brush. Agonizing seconds passed as I waited there under my determined protector until the cow moose relaxed her posture and turned to disappear quietly into the woods.

My sweet horse turned his head, looked at me with his beautiful eye and nuzzled me gently as if to say, "It's all right now. You can come out." Words can't express the kindness that glowed in those dark chocolate eyes and the love that was shown.

He stood, quietly waiting, as I crawled out from beneath his belly. He placed his legs back where they belonged, I mounted and away we went toward home. After what we had been through together, our peaceful departure was a relief and a letdown at the same time. For bravery above and beyond the call of duty, Dustee deserved a medal at the very least. But the best I could do, and I think he understands, is award him the trophy of my heart. He never will be forgotten.

Laurie Wright

Instincts of a War Mare

I was born loving horses. As my mother tells it, my first three words were "da-da," "ma-ma" and "horsey." I come from many generations of city folks, my great-grandfather being the only one to have owned a riding horse. So, it's my conviction that God gave me this passion for horses. And it's Marguerite Henry (author of *King of the Wind*) and Walter Farley (author of *The Black Stallion*) who focused that passion onto Arabian horses.

I was blessed with understanding parents, who saw to it that I began riding lessons at the age of six and who bought me a horse seven years later. Because we lived in a neighborhood with less than an acre of wooded land and no barn, the mare lived in the backyard with the screened porch as her stall. She joined in with the family each evening, watching television through the glass doors that separated the den from the porch.

Two years later, we moved out into the country to a small seven-acre farm that had fenced pastures and a three-stall barn. Right next door was this beautiful, green-eyed albino stallion who was owned by an equally beautiful brown-haired, blue-eyed boy. Ah, love was in the air. The stallion was gelded, but the boy and I were married five years later.

Seven years after that, we had our own farm and

eventually, we began boarding horses to help offset the cost of our collection of Arabians. We now have a small herd of straight Egyptian brood mares and a very talented young show horse, Raasuwl SCA. My husband Donald and I do all the work on the farm, which means many long, but rewarding, hours each day.

One cold, windy evening last February, I was finishing up the chores at the barn. Don had already gone to the house to bring in the dogs and cats for the night, and I just had to shift the mares from their pasture to the paddock by the barn. The mares know the routine: I open the gate and they charge through and gallop to the paddock where their buckets of sweet feed are waiting.

They always run through in the same order: first, Hazara, the undisputed alpha mare; then Mataalah, Inaaya, Yum-Yum and, always last, Khatira Moniet. Katie, as we call her, is the lowest-ranking mare within the herd. She is just as pretty as she can be, the image of her great-grandmother the famous Egyptian mare Moniet El Nefous, but this doesn't carry a bit of importance with the other mares. Katie is always made to be last: last through the gate, last to get to her bucket, last to get to choose a flake of hay, last to get to drink from the water tubs and last to get her belly scratched when Don and I are out visiting with the mares.

And if once in a while she dashes ahead and gets somewhere first, she is reprimanded with snapping teeth and flying heels. We like to give her some extra attention when we can, particularly extra scratching and extra carrots, while we make the other mares stay back.

So, on this evening as I went to swing the gate open, the mares were bunched up, waiting for their run to the barn. All except for Katie, that is. She was standing back about fifty feet out of harm's way. As I gave the gate a push, a gust of wind caught it and pushed it right back at me. Hazara had already started her charge and as she dodged to avoid the gate, her shoulder rammed into my chest and sent me flying ten feet through the air. I landed on my back and my head slammed against the frozen ground, knocking me out cold. The first thing I was aware of as I began to come to was the sound of hooves all around me and the pressure of what I thought was a fence post against my side. As my vision cleared I looked up and there was Katie standing above me.

The other mares were milling all around me, but Katie was standing very calmly over me, protecting me. What I thought was a fence post against my side was actually her front leg. It took me about ten minutes to even try to get to my feet, and she stood guard over me the entire time, keeping the other mares away. As I tried to stand, she lowered her head and let me grab her mane and pull myself up. When she was satisfied that I was safely on my feet, she touched her nose to my face and then calmly walked away through the other mares and once again took her place about fifty feet away.

Since childhood, I have read the stories about the loyal Arabian war mares who would stand guard over their riders who had fallen during battle, risking their own safety for that of their masters. I had wanted those stories to be true, but I always wondered if they weren't just exaggerated, romantic tales. Now I know that they are true. I have my own "war mare" who certainly risked her safety to come to my aid. I have loved Katie since we bought her ten years ago, but because of what transpired on that wintry day, she now holds a very special place in my heart. And there is always that one extra carrot in my pocket that is just for her.

Christina Donahue

The Man Whisperer

For three generations, Sandy MacPherson's family had owned a farm in the county of Angus in northeast Scotland. Mainly, the farm had been prosperous, raising black Aberdeen Angus cattle for beef, some sheep and raspberries. Sandy's wife Jean ran a riding school and the horses were her "family."

Unfortunately, as the changing times made farming harder, the MacPherson's farm struggled to survive. Sandy was old-fashioned. He believed that running the farm was "a man's job" and that his wife and children could not really understand the position in which they found themselves.

Sandy found great consolation in spending time with the horses, particularly with a horse named Wallace that Sandy had delivered himself many years before. Standing in the stable in the early evening, Sandy would stroke Wallace, get a whinny in response, and then the man would explain all his worries to the horse. Sandy could unload on the silent but responsive Wallace all the worries he could not bear to share with his family.

Unfortunately, Sandy's other solace was vodka. When he went to visit Wallace and drink from a vodka bottle hidden in the hay, he would explain it as "going to tidy up in the stable and settle everyone down for the night."

Sandy's wife Jean was one of those quiet women, who said

little but saw and anticipated everything. Her cousin was the local lawyer, her nephew was the local accountant, and she probably knew more of their precarious financial position than her husband.

Jean knew that when Sandy went off to the stable heavy with the burden of farm worries, and came back an hour or so later with his burden considerably eased, he had been at his secret vodka bottle. She would ignore the odd slurred word that Sandy never even knew he let fall. She would give him coffee to get rid of the smell that Sandy fully believed vodka never left on his breath.

Standing one day looking into the warm and wise eyes of Wallace, Jean asked him, "What are we going to do about Sandy, Wallace?" As she stroked the horse and he butted her with his head in response, she suddenly began to form an idea.

The clever Jean slipped into the stables every evening while Sandy was out on the farm and took out his secret vodka bottle. She would pour the vodka into a jug, fill the vodka bottle with water and then brush the neck with the real vodka. This way, when Sandy opened the bottle, it still smelled of vodka.

For more than two months, this process went on, and each evening, Sandy would return, his burden duly lightened by his vodka. When one day his accountant finally told him that the farm was no longer making enough money to survive, he stroked Wallace with tears on his cheeks and asked, "What am I to do. How can I tell them?" Wallace moved his head against the troubled man's face almost as if he were wiping the tears away, and Sandy hugged him.

Jean took Wallace out for a ride the next morning, looking over the land they all loved so much. She was about to turn and head for home when, to her surprise, Wallace resisted and went a few steps to his right. Jean frowned, but said, "What is it Wallace. Where do you want to go?"

He trotted in the direction of the old raspberry fields. Once, they had been very lucrative with a profitable raspberry crop. Over the years, the local canneries that had bought the fruit had closed down, and now they were empty. Wallace trotted on, down toward two old farm cottages. In the heyday of the farming life in Angus, they had been homes for some of the farm workers, but now they were in ruins.

Jean dismounted from Wallace and studied where he had brought her. Suddenly she cried out, "Wallace, you're a genius," and she threw her arms around him and hugged him. Like all geniuses, Wallace accepted the praise that was his due and nodded his head a little in acknowledgment.

Jean had a word with her cousin, and two days later he asked Sandy to stop by. "There may be a way to raise quite a bit of capital. Sell the old raspberry fields for a housing development," he said. "You could have quite a few houses there. The demand for country homes in the county of Angus is at a peak. You could make a fortune!"

Sandy took a little convincing, but over the months, he began to see that this was, indeed, going to bring in a lot of money.

Finally, he stood one night in the stable telling Wallace, "Things are great boy. It's like a miracle, as if God knew how worried I was and just solved all of my problems."

The next morning, Jean found the vodka bottle was untouched and it continued that way. When there was some thunder, Sandy heard one or two of the horses crying a little, and he put on his jacket. "I'll just go and see that they are okay. Wallace, in particular, doesn't like thunder."

Sandy came back just as soon as the storm passed over. "He is fine now. I really seem to have a way with horses, particularly Wallace. I calmed him right down. I think my always talking to him has been good for him. Maybe there is a bit of the horse whisperer in me."

Jean smiled and the next morning went to the stable. As she stood there stroking Wallace, he turned his head to look at her and she smiled. "I know, you clever boy. You have helped him and all of us enormously, but particularly Sandy. I think there is more than a bit of a 'man whisperer' in you, hmmm?" Wallace nodded his head and lowered it for his rewarding hug.

Joyce Stark

The Pilon

Far back, far back in our dark soul the horse prances. . . . The horse, the horse! The symbol of surging potency and power of movement, of action in man!

Apocalypse

In the Tex-Mex slang of south Texas, the word *pilon* (pronounced peh-lone) means "a little something extra." But because Spanish is a musical language that wraps a rainbow of emotions around a single word, it also has a much broader meaning. A *pilon* is an unexpected gift and an unanticipated blessing, although it probably won't be recognized as such when it is received because a *pilon* will usually come disguised as a problem, a trouble, an annoyance, an inconvenience. Yet, true to the magical nature of a *pilon*, it will turn out to be the silver lining in the dark cloud.

My *pilon* came to me when we decided to buy a mule. We had recently moved to the country and had bought our son a gelding. Because my husband and I had been raised as country folks, we knew it was only a matter of time before we would be faced with the problem of finding a companion for the gelding. Many horses are not happy living alone. We didn't want to invest in another horse right away, so we decided to get a mule, which could do double duty as both a companion for the gelding and as a guard animal for the sheep. After much searching, we finally found what the advertisement said was an "excellent pack animal." As we hooked up the trailer and loaded the family in the truck, my husband and I decided that, unless the mule had only three legs, he was coming home with us, regardless.

We arrived with checkbook in hand and were shown a short, gray animal with long, floppy ears and a black stripe running down the middle of his back

Quickly deciding that this was the mule for us, we turned to the seller to finalize the agreement. As we said, "We'll take the mule," the seller, misreading our eagerness for gullibility, added this stipulation to the sale: "I'll sell you the mule if you take the little horse, too."

What little horse? I wondered as I looked around the pen. All I could see was the mule, but the man was walking toward another pen before I could even voice my question. We followed, full of curiosity at this unexpected snag.

As we rounded the barn, we saw the little horse. It was a foal, about four or five months old, although it was hard to tell. At the sound of human voices, the foal had begun racing around the pen at breakneck speed, trying to escape. She was in pitiful condition. Her belly was swollen with worms, her mane and tail were matted and tangled, she was covered with mud, and I could see several large gashes on her legs, where she had tangled with some wire. Her coat was dull and lifeless. She raced around the pen, nostrils flaring, with a wild look in her eye. My husband had already begun to back up, telling the man, "No, we're not in the market for a horse." My eyes, however, were drawn to that poor foal. She was scared to death, but something, perhaps it was in her gaze or in the arch of her neck, told me that in spite of her pitiful condition, she had pride.

I interrupted my husband and drew him off to the side. "There's something about this foal," I whispered.

"She's a mess," he replied. "The vet bills alone are going to be more than she's worth."

Using my best female logic, I answered, "Well, we need a mule, so let's go ahead and take the package deal." I guess I had that look in my eye, because my husband just sighed and turned around to write the man the check.

It took us four hours to catch the foal. We chased her around the pen, tried to box her in and watched dumbfounded as she sailed over the fence. We clambered over the fence after her. Just as we were about to give up, miraculously, we caught her. We loaded her into the trailer, jamming her up against the mule and tying her securely so she wouldn't try to jump through the roof. I prayed all the way home. When we pulled into the ranch, the gelding had smelled the new arrivals and was trumpeting his welcome. As we turned them all in together, I thought I caught a look of gratitude in the foal's eyes.

The veterinarian was not very optimistic when he saw the foal the next day. He checked her, dewormed her and immunized her, but left the ranch saying that he couldn't guarantee that she wouldn't have a lot of future problems. I named her Senisa, which is the name of a plant that grows all over south Texas. For most of the year, it is a gray-leaved mousy little bush, but when it rains, it suddenly bursts into beautiful purple blooms. I was hoping that with some love and attention, the foal would be like that tough little desert bush.

Senisa exceeded everyone's expectations. Within two months, she had a beautiful, glossy black coat that was as soft as a kid glove. Her wounds had healed and she was healthy. As she grew older, she became very territorial about "her" ranch. She ruled the roost in the barn, with the gelding and the mule content to bask in her glow.

One day, Senisa repaid my rescue of her by rescuing me. I had heard some barking down by the barn and had raced out of the house to see what was going on. Some stray dogs had gotten into the area and were snarling and growling at two lambs in a small pen. Without thinking, I ran into the pen to protect the lambs. As I held the lambs and turned to face the dogs, I realized that I hadn't brought the gun with me and grew scared as I watched the dogs tear at the fence. They were operating as a hunting pack and I knew that if they got into the pen, they would attack me to get at the lambs. I was desperate and alone and wondering what in the world I could do, when I caught a black flash out of the corner of my eye.

I turned my head to see Senisa racing across the pen and charging directly at the dogs! Her hooves were flying and her head was down and weaving as if she wanted to slash and bite them. The dogs didn't realize Senisa was charging them until she was almost upon them. They turned away from the fence with a yelp and ran out of the pen, down the hill and through the pasture, with Senisa chasing them all the way. They slithered out of a hole under the fence and were gone, never to return.

That day, I truly understood what they mean in Tex-Mex when they comfort someone going through difficult circumstances by saying, *"Es un pilon."* Bad times are only "a little something extra" in your life. Persevere and work through the trouble because tucked into every bad circumstance is a *pilon,* a magical pocket of beauty or love that is waiting for you, if only you have the eyes to see it.

Nancy Minor

Shawnee

Shawnee was a high-stepping, head-up, tail-arched three-year-old the first time we saw her. She pranced down the street in the Fourth of July parade, her owner and his small grand-daughter on her back. A glowing sorrel with large white splotches here and there, Shawnee had a big white blaze down her face. Her eyes were large, liquid and intelligent; her body tall and beautiful. My eyes followed her and her riders down the street. We were looking for a younger horse because our Strawberry was getting old, and my husband Jim had told me about Shawnee. "She's half Quarter Horse and half Arab," he said. "Hank told me he just broke her to ride this year, but she's coming right along on the cow bit. He wants a lot for her, but I'm thinking hard about it."

I shifted our six-month-old son Dan from one hip to the other and stepped forward to see Shawnee better. "Okay," I told Jim. "But I want to ride her before you buy her." I wasn't much of a horseperson, preferring my own two feet to those of a horse even when it came to chasing cows. "Yeah," Jim replied. "I told Hank we'd meet him at the Blue after the parade and take a good look at the horse." The Blue was where Jim's brother-in-law worked and there was a nice big parking lot behind it.

Jim got on Shawnee and rode her around for about a half

hour. When he returned, he told me, "I'll hold Dan, you go ahead and give her a try." I did, thinking it was a good thing I'd worn clean jeans to the parade that day instead of a skirt and blouse. Shawnee was huge, but I managed to get into the saddle without help, and she started walking along the alley. I turned her into the next street, away from Main and all the cars and people. Shawnee seemed calm, neither shying away from people crossing the street in front of us nor swerving when cars came up behind her and passed slowly. People were accustomed to horseback riders in our small town, especially during the Fourth of July festivities, with the big parade and rodeo going on.

I neck-reined Shawnee down yet another street and headed back in the general direction of the Blue. Suddenly, a young boy ran into the street and tossed a lighted firecracker right under Shawnee! I touched her flanks with my heels and she leaped instantly into a run. The firecracker went off with a terrific bang behind us, but Shawnee slowed to a walk when I pulled on the reins. She never let on she even heard the firecracker. I knew right then and there that we had a new horse.

Hank took our check that day, but said it would be the next day before he could bring her out to the ranch. "Okay with us," Jim told him. "We'll be there."

The next day, Hank came riding in on Shawnee, followed by his wife in their pickup. "I decided just to ride her out," he said with a grin. "She's a real good horse, and it'll be a while before I get another one like her." We had to laugh, knowing Hank said that about every single horse he raised, broke and then sold. I well knew what would come next, so I went inside to start the coffee perking, leaving our son playing in the yard.

"Well, get down and come on in for some coffee," Jim told him. "The wife just baked some cookies a bit ago, and I think they're still warm." They tied Shawnee to the gatepost and trooped inside.

"Where's Dan?" I asked. "Oh, he's playing with that Tonka

truck in the side yard," Jim told me. Dan loved that big old Tonka truck, and because he couldn't do much more than crab-crawl, we didn't worry too much about it. I served the coffee and set out a plate of cookies to go with it, then walked to the door, intending to go out to get Dan. I stopped short, with one hand on the door, and let out a faint scream.

"What's wrong?" Jim came swiftly to the door. I pointed, wordlessly, out the door. Hank and his wife hurried to the kitchen window. Shawnee was standing, front feet spread out, her head down, looking between her legs. And there, standing underneath her belly, hanging on tight to a front leg with one hand, reaching up trying to scratch her tummy, was our six-month-old son!

I couldn't have said a word had I tried. Jim however, was a typical ranchman. He was always calm, cool and collected. And he acted! He went out the door, easy as you please, talking all the time in that slow, gentle manner he used with animals and children. "Easy does it, old girl. Don't you move now. You just stand real still until I can grab that boy under you. Easy now, girl." Jim moved forward, still talking soothingly to Shawnee, until he could reach down and lift our son out from under her. Shawnee had raised her head and given him one rather exasperated look, before lowering her head to that small mite of humanity still trying his cooing best to pet her stomach.

After he had Dan safely in his arms, Jim slumped a little— the only sign he ever showed that he had been worried and afraid. Then he held Dan so he could touch Shawnee's nose. Shawnee reached out and velvety horse nose met tiny boy hand. It was an instantaneous mutual admiration society. The mutual love and respect didn't end until we buried our beloved Shawnee nineteen long years later.

Jan Roat

The Wedding

I have run a small carriage business for about eleven years. We offer a horse-drawn carriage for romantic rides, weddings, engagement proposals—those occasions when something unique makes the moment even more memorable.

Dealing with brides-to-be can be great fun or absolutely awful. I've had some meet me on their wedding day in tears. Others have been just as calm as could be. I've had some say to please take them for a ride somewhere—anywhere—because they weren't up to getting married.

One spring day, I got a call from yet another bride-to-be. She was thrilled that she had found someone who offered a carriage for weddings. This young woman knew exactly what she wanted us to do at her wedding. We were to pick her and her dad up at her house, drive them to the church and then drop them off. That seemed simple enough, I thought. Before accepting the job, I drove to her house to see what was involved.

I always do this because I've gotten into some tight situations by not checking before saying I'd do the affair. I don't want anything happening to the people riding in my carriage or to my horses. It looked like an easy drive along a quiet country road to the desired church and I agreed to do the job. The bride was very pleased and paid for the whole thing on the spot.

On the day of the wedding, we arrived, clean horse, sparkling carriage, in our tuxedos, all set to have a good time. The bride's father came out, looking glum. He told us that something terrible had happened the night before and suggested that we see it before we drove into something that we might not be able to handle. We had no idea what he meant, but my partner took off in a car with the bride's father to take a look. They returned.

"Eh, no big deal," I was told. "There was a little house fire close to the street we would be driving on. Don't worry about it."

Off we went at a crisp walk. My mare Lynn was enjoying herself as usual. She always liked to take drives in new places. Round the hill, all the way to the bottom and out of the woods to the little town we drove. The town was one street in width, with cars parked on both sides, leaving us little room to navigate. I had figured we'd be okay when I first looked at the route, but today there had been a house fire.

The house was right next to the street, not five feet away from where we would pass. It was totally gutted, with timbers still smoldering, some still burning a little. There were fire trucks in the street with engines running, lights on and buckets reaching across the burned cars to spray water on the small fires.

Television newspeople were clustered around their vans carrying cameras. Microphones and cords ran everywhere. It seemed as if every town resident was milling around, watching. Above, TV news helicopters were flying low, people hanging off the sides with cameras. Police were trying to direct traffic through this little street without mishap, and the street now looked to be only six feet wide: just big enough for a Percheron horse pulling a wedding carriage.

Our destination was the church across the street, about fifteen feet beyond the burned house. The whole area was a solid chain of vehicles with no where to drop off a bride-to-be. *Would Lynn ever make it through this chaos?* Talk about sensory overload for a horse! I began to have doubts about proceeding, not wanting to ask my horse to deal with it all. A "little house fire . . . no big deal," my foot.

Lynn got much taller than her actual 17.2 hands when she saw what was in front of her. I imagine her eyes must have been wide open, taking everything in. I could hear what she was thinking loud and clear:

"WHAT in the world is all THIS? Smells funny. Big trucks! Who is that odd looking man in the street and why is he flapping carrot colored things? I don't think I want to be here anymore!"

Lynn hesitated, but kept walking forward, snorting the odd smells, seemingly fascinated by the man waving that orange flag for traffic control. I asked her to walk on and walk on she did, right past the noisy fire trucks, right past the newspeople, over the cords, looking with amazement at the burned house and up at the firemen in those buckets high in the air. She went forward all the while.

When she got to the traffic controller, she stopped. He stopped flapping his flag, thinking she might be scared. *Scared?* After having run the gauntlet of these terrifying sights and smells? Naaah, she just wanted to see if his flag tasted good. When he realized what she wanted, he laughed out loud and let her sniff his orange flag. Obviously, Lynn didn't think too much of it and proceeded down that crowded street to the church.

Throughout the journey, the bride and her father were totally quiet. We arrived on time, stopped in the middle of the street and the bride's dad helped her down from the carriage.

I expected her to rush up the steps to the church. Instead, she walked around to the front of my carriage to see Lynn.

Face-to-face, they stood. The bride told Lynn what a brave horse she was and thanked her for getting her to the most important affair of her life without a problem. Then she reached her arms around Lynn's big gray face and gave her a kiss on her forehead. Lynn lowered her head for this, knowing somehow it was a good thing to do.

We unhitched in the street a little further away from the

hubbub, cooled Lynn off and left, grateful that nothing else bad happened.

Later that month, I got a notice from the post office of a package delivery. The mailman couldn't fit it into the mailbox at the farm. When I picked up the package, it was addressed to Lynn at the farm's address, and sure enough, it was big.

Inside the box was five pounds of fresh carrots and a note. The kind young woman who got married that day a month before hadn't forgotten Lynn's bravery. She had set up deliveries of fresh carrots to the farm every month for a year, a box each month for every minute that Lynn had carried her through that scary town.

I'm proud to say that Lynn shares her treats with the rest of the horses, but I'm prouder still of Lynn's bravery that day. She dug deep and did things most horses would have panicked over and refused. Not that mare. She came through with flying colors and delivered in style, creating special memories for a beautiful bride on her wedding day.

Kris DeMond

Andy's Wish

The first time I saw him was through a small window in a horse trailer. I saw only his eye, but it looked right through me and pierced my soul. Andy, a Thoroughbred stallion, either was going to find a home with me or be ground up into a small can of dog food.

After a four-hour drive in silence, we were home and I had no idea what to do with Andy. I didn't know what to expect. I only hoped that I could handle what was to come. I opened the rusty trailer door and could see long legs encrusted in manure. He was covered by a horse blanket that at one time must have been green, but now it was heavily soiled with urine stains and tied together with hay-baling twine.

This stallion was as proud as any I had ever seen and he had a severe hatred for man. His piercing eyes glared, he was prepared at any moment for the fight of his life. I noticed the blanket was deeply embedded into his skin. I had no idea how long he had been jailed in its clutches. I was able to walk him carefully to a stall while he reared to his staggering height and shouted that he had arrived, never acknowledging my existence.

After the shock of seeing such a poorly managed animal, I was at my wits end with what I should do first, knowing that this stallion needed more than my experience justified. I placed him in a comfortable stall with an attached paddock. Although the stall I made for him was bedded deeply in pine shavings for comfort, Andy had the idea that being able to see the outdoors was his greatest comfort. He stood for hours in the corner of his paddock riveted by the sight of the green mountains that surrounded him. He gulped gallons of fresh air, enjoying a silent thrill that he wasn't willing to share. I knew that the breeding ranch he had come from had kept him in a small, enclosed stall, he was knee-deep in his own manure and he had only a small window at the very top of his stall for fresh air. He was beaten daily with a two-by-four and made to withstand the torture of a chain against his gums. He left his jailed existence only if the ranch manager needed his sperm. Other than that, his life didn't matter. He existed solely for himself.

I had to tranquilize Andy to remove his blanket of torture. The knotted ties had to be cut apart and the embedded fabric slowly peeled from his hide. The wounds were horrendous and I contemplated how I would be able to care for them, considering his obvious hatred for people. But the wounds appeared to be the least of my worries. This poor stallion was so undernourished that I could see every bone in his body, and his coat was in shambles, puckered by sores and lacking any glow. He was green and crusted with old feces. I had to cut off the majority of Andy's tail because it was so tangled. Because of this, he couldn't even perform the simple maneuver of swatting a pesky fly. The simplicity of a horse's life had been taken from him, and it was up to me to see that he found it again.

In the weeks that followed, I spent hours in Andy's stall, talking softly to him, groveling for his attention. At first, he ignored every attempt I made. Then slowly, his ears began to perk up at the sound of my voice. I managed to doctor his wounds by enticing him near the paddock fence with grain. Then I would reach inside the fence line and swipe salve into the open sores. I was able to hose off his coat, and he began to take on the shine of a copper penny with each layer of crust that was removed. His eyes changed their focus and his beautiful sculptured head inspired me as he looked toward the hills each evening at sunset.

After a few months, Andy began to fill out and I could see the elegant form he must have had as a young colt. He was a sight to behold even during this metamorphosis. He began to allow me to brush him and his eyes began to soften more with each passing day. I smiled when I saw him swat at a fly and it brought tears to my eyes to see him roll in the splendor of his clean pine shavings. Regardless of what he had been through, he was now home.

To my amazement, my $1 rescue horse turned out to be a true bargain. I discovered that Andy was an ex-racehorse who had won several stakes races. His sire was a full brother to the great Northern Dancer and his dam a granddaughter of the famous Man o' War. Andy was bred and trained at the Florida farm that had produced Affirmed. His future as a money-earning racehorse was right on track until he suffered a broken knee joint and was put out to stud.

How he ended up in my hands was a pure miracle. I had always imagined owning a racehorse from the time I was a child reading *The Black Stallion*, riding horses in my dreams. It seemed that fate had brought us together in some twisted irony of survival.

As I worked with Andy, it became apparent that he held as much admiration for me as I held for him. He began to nicker when I walked down the barn aisle and he would stand in his paddock to watch me walk away when the day was over. He began a habit of biting the fence when I came near so that he could contain his excitement while I scratched his head and stroked his delicate ears. He didn't know how to handle affection and it was very possible that he had never experienced it before. I was happy to give him what he deserved.

Today, Andy is the ripe old age of twenty-five and he is still full of life. We have come a long way. His eyes now focus on me with sweetness each and every day. His nickers are now soft neighs and his affection for me rivals mine for him. He doesn't hold any grudges. Through me, he has forgiven his abusers. He sired a few colts that look just like him. Andy allows me to heal his wounds, trim his feet and scratch his ears without question. His remarkable spirit shines through and I am able to imagine just how extraordinary he must have been in his younger days of glory. Through him I hear the sound of the trumpets announcing a race, I hear the blast that opens the gate and I feel his powerful strides reaching for every wire. When I close my eyes, he allows me to dream, and when he closes his, I allow him absolute reassurance.

Vikki Marshall

Great Finesse

It was only my second day on the job at a Woodford County horse farm, when my boss stopped by the barn to see how I was doing. "When you finish here," he requested as he peered through the open door of the stall I was bedding, "just pop down to the second paddock on the right and bring in Great Finesse. She is blind, so be careful with her. She doesn't need much to eat, she doesn't move around enough to keep the weight off. Just give her a handful of feed to make her feel like she is getting something. Give her a good old brushing and pick her feet. Then you can put her back out. She needs something to look forward to each day."

When I finished bedding the stall, I did as he'd asked. I had seen blind horses on other people's farms, but I had never cared for one myself. Most of the blind horses I had seen were jumpy and erratic, a bit frightening to get close to. Great Finesse was quite large, and the thought of bringing her through the tight confines of the gate and the barn doorways was a bit daunting. I walked out to where she was standing in the center of the field. As I approached, I noticed that she had a peculiar way of cocking her head sideways, almost as though she were trying to determine my location by tilting her head so that the sounds of my feet in the grass and my voice reached her ears at different times. The expression on her face was a bit curious, but trusting.

I clipped a shank onto her halter and said hello. Then I turned and walked toward the gate. Great Finesse showed no hesitation at following me. In fact, she stepped up beside me and placed her head along my shoulder and arm. I quickly realized that she was using me for a guide, following subtle cues through my arm and shoulder the way a blind person might follow subtle cues through the harness of a guide dog. Not only that, but if I touched her, she stopped. If I pushed against her, she moved away. Most horses push against you if you push, and pull away if you pull. Great Finesse had learned to trust her handlers enough to follow cues even from a stranger.

Suddenly, the gate didn't seem so daunting. I placed her safely along the fence, away from the gate, while I unhooked the chain and flung the gate open. I used my body to hold it open and used my hands to guide her safely through. She didn't even touch the gate, let alone bang her hips. All the way to the barn, Great Finesse rested her head against my arm, walking in exactly the same position as a blind person following a sighted guide. At the barn, I gave her that handful of feed as a reward. Then I groomed her from head to toe, picked her feet and painted them with hoof dressing, and turned her back out.

The next day, when I brought her in for the same routine, I quickly realized that she jumped every time I did something in a different order from what I had done the day before. She seemed to have memorized the way I did things so that my movements wouldn't startle her. As long as I worked the same way I had the day before, she was quiet. When I changed my routine, she was startled. From that day on, I always did things in exactly the same way with this remarkable mare.

When I mentioned her behavior to my boss, he smiled and replied, "We worked very hard to get her that way."

"How did you train her?" I queried.

"Well, we knew it was coming, you see, so we had a bit of time to prepare."

"She wasn't always blind?"

"No, she had a progressive eye disease. She lost the sight in one eye and most of the sight in the other. Because she could see only shadows, she became quite nervous and upset. She was too valuable a mare to lose. She is quite well bred and has produced several stakes winners. Her limited vision caused her enough distress that our veterinarian finally decided it would be kinder to surgically blind her so she wouldn't see ghosts and monsters in the shadows.

"Because I had a bit of time to prepare before the surgery," my boss continued, "I spent a great deal of time figuring out how to make the transition easier for her. She is on a late foaling schedule. She doesn't usually foal until late April, so I began by choosing a paddock that is situated between the foaling barn and the brood mare barn, where we put the late foals. The paddock I chose for her has access to both barns with gates at the nearest point, so she doesn't have to be moved. She stays there year-round. She has good shade for summer and a windbreak for winter.

"I wanted to make sure she wouldn't hit the fences or the waterer," my boss explained. "So I had the maintenance crew lay tanbark six feet wide around every obstacle. Then I began training the mare by walking her around the field, letting her feel the tanbark under her feet and then letting her touch the fence. Soon she knew to stop when her feet hit tanbark."

"That was pretty smart," I said, genuinely impressed. "I have seen some blind horses who would barely shuffle or who would move only in tight circles in the middle of the field. She seems pretty confident out there."

"That was the idea. I didn't want her to be frightened. The last thing we worked out was companionship. The rest of the mares travel around the farm through the year as their needs change. They foal up in the foaling unit, which is rather like a maternity ward. We even have our own neonatal unit next to the office. Once they have foaled, they come to the brood-mare barns. We fill up Broodmare One, up on the hill first. When it is full, the rest come down here. When we wean, the babies stay here in familiar surround-ings and the mares go to a big field across the road, where they are too far away to hear the babies fuss. The babies stay here until the yearlings leave for the track, then they go to the yearling barns. Once the babies are gone, the mares come back here until it is time to go to the foaling barn again."

"So I guess you couldn't give her a mare for a companion because they need to be able to travel," I surmised.

"That, and we were afraid a sighted mare might hurt her."

"So what did you do?" I asked.

"We got her a llama."

"Oh yeah, I saw him up in the far corner of the field. A big brown critter! He always looks scared."

"That's Tipper. He is Great Finesse's companion. They don't hang out together much, but at least she isn't alone."

"What do you do when she foals?"

"The first year we put a bell on the foal. She did great. The mare was an even better mother than before she lost her sight. This year, the plan is to use a nurse mare for the baby to give Great Finesse a break. It is a bit harder for her because she can't see."

"You all really did a good job with her. She is very calm and trusting and confident."

"Well, we tried, you know, but what you are describing, she learned herself."

Just then, I heard galloping hoofbeats. I looked up just in time to see Great Finesse galloping across her field! She moved with all the grace of a sighted horse in her familiar territory. When her feet hit the tanbark, she changed course as effortlessly as any horse. *How aptly named she was,* I thought. Through the efforts of her caretakers and her own great finesse she had learned to cope with the obstacles of her condition and to function happily in her sightless world.

Thirza Peevey

A Job for Missy

*You never know how a horse will pull until you
hook him to a heavy load.*

Paul "Bear" Bryant

God, find that little horse a home. All she needs is a job, I prayed,
blinking back tears. I watched Missy leave the auction ring
on her way to the killer pens. I hefted my saddle onto my
shoulder and followed her out.

Missy was deep shiny black with a tiny white spot on her
right rear heel. Her big head and light haunches spoke of her
mustang ancestry almost as clearly as the Bureau of Land
Management (BLM) brand under her mane. I had known her
almost a year and she had won my heart with her incredible
work ethic and endurance. Originally, her owners had
brought her to me desperate to fix her bad habits.

She liked to bite and she was vicious with her heels. She
was very hard to catch even in a pen. Sometimes she bucked
and only a very severe bit kept her from running away. But,
according to her owners, she hadn't always been like that.
When they had tried her out, Missy was easy to handle and
seemed to enjoy being groomed and ridden.

I called the BLM's Wild Horse Adoption Program and

found out the rest of the horse's history. She had been adopted as a three-year-old by a family that didn't know much about horses. She was too much for them to handle and they sold her to a horse trader who sent her to a feedlot to be trained to work cows. She excelled there under expert handling and hard work, and the trader thought she would make a good pleasure-riding horse.

So what had happened to this mare? Even poor handling as a youngster shouldn't have caused such terrible habits to resurface years later.

I worked at a livestock auction where horses were used to move the cows from sellers' pens to sale ring and then to the buyers' pens. It's a good place to find out what a horse is made of. There are loudspeakers, people running, cows bumping and banging, tight quarters and other horses, and they all teach a young horse a lot in a hurry. I took her to work and rode her. Her earlier training came back in a rush. She was quick to stop a cow from turning back and willingly plowed through the yearlings packed in the alley. Within minutes she remembered the cues to sidepass so I could open gates with ease from her back. I was impressed. Most horses find sale-barn work daunting.

I called the owner with a glowing report.

"Ride her a little longer. She gets bad if you ride her very long," the owner said.

The next sale, I rode her for eleven hours with only a few minutes to drink and one thirty-minute break to eat. Missy never slowed. She loved chasing cows. Finally, ashamed of myself for riding her so hard when she obviously wasn't going to cause problems, I switched horses. For the rest of the auction, Missy tried to chase cows from across the fence, ignoring her feed and water.

Early the next morning when I started catching horses to return to the auction, Missy hurried to the gate.

"You worked hard enough yesterday, you don't need to go today."

Missy whinnied, pawing at the gate. When I walked by

with two other horses, Missy charged down the fence line, screaming her displeasure. Afraid she was going to hurt herself, I grabbed a halter. Ordinarily, it took mental games and time to catch Missy, but this morning, she stood at the gate and shoved her nose in the halter. She danced expectantly at the trailer and leapt in as soon as the door swung wide enough.

Surprised, I shut the door and headed for town. The horse could stand tied at the auction and rest.

Missy refused to stand quietly tied to the post. She bit at the cows through the fence and paced the length of her tether until she wore a hole around the post. She chewed her lead rope. When she started kicking at the other horses, I gave in. Missy stood very still while I saddled and bridled her, but she almost trod on my heels as I lead her into the alley.

Long hours pulled the fat off the mare and built muscle in her haunches. The work also wore her feet down. Missy stood quietly as her shoes were nailed on. She never even offered to kick.

As long as Missy was working, she was happy. If she had a week off, her attitude took a sharp turn for the worse. Her mustang ancestry gave her incredible stamina, but her own spirit drove her to perform. If I was riding Missy, I needed only two horses when everybody else needed three or four. Her work ethic earned her admirers among the cowboys at the auction.

Six months later, I sent her home. She immediately reverted to her old tricks. She hated occasional short pleasure rides. Her owners couldn't catch her. She began kicking again. She bucked. She ran away. She was worse than ever.

They sent her back. She met me at the gate and stuck her nose in the halter, ready to go to work. I tried using her for day work on ranches, thinking maybe it was open space that was causing her problems. Missy worked day after day without argument. I found other people to ride her at the auction, thinking maybe she had bonded with me. Missy didn't care who was riding as long as she was working. I called the owners and explained that Missy needed a job where she could work hard every day. She would never be a pleasure horse. The owners weren't interested in competitive trail riding or endurance races.

"Sell her," they said.

I couldn't afford another horse, and mustangs rarely sell well, especially in ranch country. Sick at heart, I rode her through the auction ring. She gave a flawless performance, but only the killer buyer bid. The gavel fell at $350. Just because she wasn't a registered horse, my hardworking little partner was going for dog food. Almost physically ill, I stripped off the tack and watched her leave the ring.

I tried to forget Missy, but every time I battled some chicken-hearted, lazy blue-blooded colt, I remembered her.

Almost a year later, I was gathering cattle on a big rough-country ranch when another cowboy began talking about a neighbor kid and his horse.

"You never saw such a horse," the cowboy said. "Toughest thing on four feet. Chris may be only eleven, but he is hell on horses. I didn't think they'd ever find something tough enough for Chris, but they picked this mustang out of the killer pen for almost nothing. That kid must ride ten hours a day. If he ain't in school, he's riding. Why, the other day, I saw him fifteen miles from home, halfway to town. He said he was headed into town to spend the night with a friend. That little black mare was loping along, ears forward, happy as she could be, not blowing a bit." The cowboy shook his head in admiration.

My heart jumped painfully. "Any white on her?" I asked.

"She's got a spot on her off hind foot. Other than that, she's glossy black. What a horse!"

Lynn Allen

4

HORSES AS HEALERS

Horses change lives. They give our young people confidence and self-esteem. They provide peace and tranquility to troubled souls, they give us hope!

Toni Robinson

I Got It, Dad!

There are only two kinds of people in the world: horse lovers and the other kind.

I was the horse lover in my family. My sister was a dancer, my mom liked to bowl and my dad liked to golf. My son, Caton Ryder (Caton after the wise man Cato, and Ryder meaning horseman) is a horse lover, too.

Caton was born in Clements, California, in 1983. Shortly after his birth, something didn't seem quite right. Concerned, we took Caton to the pediatrician, who said, "Oh yeah, that's just strabismus," meaning his eyes are crossed a little bit. "His head has extreme molding," the doctor continued, "which happens sometimes when the baby comes through the birth canal."

Still concerned, Caton's mother and I continued taking our son to various doctors. Finally, it was the eye doctor who said, "This is not an eye problem. There is definitely something more serious going on here."

We immediately took three-month-old Caton to Oakland Children's Hospital. By the time we got there, Caton had slipped into a coma. It turns out that he had a condition called hydrocephalus—excessive fluid in the cranium. The duct that normally goes into the circulatory system is closed off, so the fluid enters the brain cavity and has no way to be released. The typical consequence is wasting of the brain and loss of mental powers. The solution for this problem, we were told, was to immediately implant a shunt that goes from the cranium down into the peritoneum in the abdominal area.

After a hurried series of tests and scans, the doctors told us that if Caton lived through the night, he would probably never walk or talk and he would certainly be greatly challenged.

Caton lived through that night and as he grew up he had a number of surgeries, including the shunt surgery and an operation to help his eyes. Life became more precious every day, and things were going pretty well.

Caton's always been a big boy, today, at twenty years old, he's six feet, four inches tall and he weighs about 230 pounds. I think the combination of being big and having certain physical and mental challenges has presented an interesting situation in his development. It seemed to me that rather than crawling then walking, and doing things in a certain order that seemed more normal, Caton tended to get good at fine-motor details before he managed gross-motor skills. He became more dexterous than mobile.

When Caton began walking, he would fall a lot and it would take him a long time to get anywhere. At times, he would start heading north and wind up going west. But even when Caton was very young, I'd snuggle him in front of my saddle and off we'd ride. Riding gave him a sense of rhythm and motion, and by being "tall in the saddle," he could focus on something in the distance. Eventually, Caton became fairly confident, and it was time for him to ride by himself.

At the time, I had a great horse named Sparky. He and I had scored well in reining cow horse classes and the Snaffle Bit Futurity. I used a lot of voice commands in those days to teach horses to walk, trot, canter, stop, back up and turn, so I knew Sparky would focus on me, even with Caton on board.

I remember the first time I put Caton on Sparky. I strapped my son into the saddle with a seat belt arrangement and led the two into the round corral. I couldn't believe how balanced Caton was. It was as though his sense of pride and accomplishment simply overwhelmed any physical difficulties. His balance was extraordinary, as it is today.

I managed to walk more than a few miles as I led the two of them around for weeks. Then I saddled up and rode next to them in the round corral, doing figure eights, turns and stops. After riding alongside for months, I finally sent Caton and Sparky (who pretty much kept one ear on me and my voice) around the corral on their own.

Caton could steer the horse pretty well, but he couldn't get Sparky to go forward without my help. Then, one day Caton had an epiphany. Talk about being a proud daddy! I remember the moment well.

Caton came up with the idea that if he could get his thoughts from his head through his body, down his legs and to his feet, the horse could feel it and would actually move. Caton started putting together thoughts that caused action. Watching this process was amazing. The horse would pick up a foot and put it down and the two of them would gain some yardage. Caton and Sparky now could actually propel themselves across the round corral without Dad's assistance.

Pretty quickly you could predict the process: Caton would smile, think, send his thoughts down to his feet, and Sparky would lope off across the arena, stop at the fence and turn around. A connection between human and horse had reached an understanding, a relationship.

This is when Caton really started to "wake up." It used to take him ten minutes to get across the arena on foot, and now he could do it in one minute because he had a partner named Sparky. Something special had happened, and I knew the horse was responsible.

We rode together more and more, Caton still sporting his seat belt for security. He wanted to accomplish other things with horses, and as fate would have it, the phone rang one day. We were invited to the French Ranch in Salinas, managed by our friends Hira and Corinne Reed. It was time to gather the cows and calves for branding, and the Reeds needed a few extra hands.

Caton, now six, couldn't wait to go. He was so excited about his first real roundup! So we loaded the horses and down the highway we went, two cowboys and their trusty steeds.

We stayed in the bunkhouse that night, just like all self-respecting cowboys did in the movies. We got up at o'dark early (about 4 A.M.), when the sky was still pitch black, of course, and the smell of coffee was drifting in the air. Caton quickly put on his clothes, including his chaps and cowboy hat. That buckaroo was ready to ride. We wandered over to the house and chowed down on a cowboy breakfast (the stick-to-your-ribs kind) of beans, bacon and eggs, and the best biscuits and freshly churned butter any ranchhand ever tasted.

Our two horses came up to the corral gate, ready to start the day. I saddled Sparky, secured Caton in the saddle and ponied them up the draw between two rolling hills. Within an hour it was getting light, and Caton declared, "I got it, Dad." I turned them loose, after saying a quick prayer. We could now see the cows and calves, the cows bellowing at the calves to join up as we started gathering the lot. Pretty quickly, the herd was headed in the right direction, and we started driving them the four-mile journey. "Caton and I and a few other cowboys had a good bunch in front of us, maybe 300 to 400 cows and their 300 to 400 calves.

Caton was riding over here and then over there, helping where he could. It was a beautiful spring morning in the California hills, and I was sure a proud dad that day, watching Caton ride. There was a little group of calves, about thirty of them up on a knoll, bawling for their moms. I said, "Caton, go up there and get those calves." He did a perfect job. Instead of going straight toward them, he went up and around on the hill so he didn't spook the calves.

Caton rode up on this group of calves, slapped his leg a couple of times and shouted, "Heeeyaaa! Get along little doggies, it's your misfortune and none of my own. . . ." A finer, more appropriate cowboy tune there wasn't, and how he remembered the lyrics was beyond me! That brief moment is etched in my memory as though it happened ten minutes ago.

That seemed to be the beginning of the beginning. Since then, Caton has become a good rider and he's often in the limelight during my demonstrations. He's learned how to swim, ride a bicycle, snow ski, dribble a basketball— lots of things. He drives everything on the ranch—including his father—crazy and he is even learning how to drive a vehicle.

I've carried this story in my heart for twenty years. Horses are the partners who opened the door for my son, transforming him, offering him opportunities. For that I am grateful.

May the horse be with you!

Pat Parelli

Chrysalis

A horse is the projection of people's dreams about themselves; strong, powerful, beautiful and it has the capability of giving us escape from our mundane existence.

Pam Brown

Ellen was a fat girl.

She didn't start out that way. But by the time she was halfway through elementary school, her lack of coordination and competitive spirit had made her the laughingstock of her more athletic peers.

No matter the game, Ellen was always chosen last. Chosen last in kickball, because she couldn't catch or run. Chosen last in badminton, because she had never once managed to hit the birdie over the net. Chosen last in red rover, a game even a klutz ought to be able to play.

Junior high was worse.

There was a real physical education class instead of mere playground games, and every day Ellen suffered the indignities of not being able to shoot a basketball through a hoop or skip rope without tripping or even perform a respectable side-straddle hop.

And so she turned to food for comfort.

By the time she started high school at age fourteen, five-foot-five Ellen was tipping the scales at almost 200 pounds. Her family's efforts to help her lose weight did no good. She turned up her nose at the special salads her mother fixed for her. She refused her father's invitations to take brisk walks with him. She ignored her sister's warning that a girl her size would never have a boyfriend.

Ellen would toss her head and roll her eyes at her family. Then she'd grab a bag of potato chips or a box of cookies and flounce on the recliner in the den, where she'd spend hours lost in the pages of a book.

More than anything, she loved to read about horses. And that's what finally gave Ellen's father a brilliant idea.

"There's a woman at work who's looking for a stable-hand," he told Ellen one evening. "Somebody to feed her horses and clean the stalls and things like that. I told her you might be interested in the job."

"She wouldn't want me," Ellen replied.

"Why not?"

"Because I've never been near a horse."

"I told her that. But I also told her you've been reading about them all your life. She's willing to teach you every-thing from the ground up. And she's also offered to pay minimum wage and to let you ride whenever you want."

Ride? Ellen's heart beat faster. Somebody was actually offering to let her ride a real horse?

Don't be silly, the voice inside her whispered. *Had Dad not told this woman that his daughter was a clumsy tub of lard who could barely keep her balance on a bicycle?*

No way would she be strong or coordinated enough to ride a horse. And pity the poor animal that had to carry her weight on his back.

"I told her we'd drop by her place Saturday morning to see about it," her father said.

So that was that.

Pat Cunningham lived on a small farm not far from town.

Dressed in jeans and cowboy boots, she was waiting for Ellen and her father as they pulled into the gravel driveway.

"So you're the girl who loves horses," she said to Ellen, smiling and holding out her hand. "C'mon, let me show you around."

She led Ellen to the barn and gestured toward a wheelbarrow and manure fork. "Every day, these stalls have to be mucked out and then spread with fresh sawdust. The water and feed buckets get scrubbed and filled, the tack room swept and tidied, the gates and fences checked. Think you're up to it?"

"Um . . . I guess so," Ellen stammered.

"Good," Pat replied. "The school bus comes right by here every afternoon. When you're done with the chores, I'll run you home in my truck."

"Where are the horses?" Ellen asked shyly.

"Oh, yes, the horses," Pat said. She gave a long, low whistle and within seconds, two beautiful horses trotted up to the barnyard gate.

Pat pointed to the bay gelding. "That's Thunder. Don't let the name scare you. He's as gentle as a lamb. And the sweet mare beside him is Buttermilk. Which one do you want to ride first?"

Before Ellen could protest, Pat had the horses hitched to fence posts.

She showed Ellen how to lift their feet and use a hoof pick to dislodge sticks and rocks from around their shoes.

She showed her how to use the currycomb and finishing brush and how to remove cockleburs from their manes.

Finally, she showed her how to put on blanket and saddle, bridle and bit.

"I'd like you to ride at least one of them every day you're here," Pat said. "Both, if you have time. They really need the exercise."

Ellen felt tears welling up in her eyes. How could she tell this kind woman that she was nothing but a fat girl who had no earthly idea how to ride a horse?

"But, I've never . . . never actually been on a horse. All I've ever done is read about them."

"Then it's high time you learned," Pat said. "Stand there beside Buttermilk and put your left foot in the stirrup. Then bounce a couple of times on your right foot and spring into the saddle."

But try as she might, Ellen couldn't stretch her leg high enough to get her foot anywhere near the stirrup.

"Hold on a second," Pat told her. "Let's try the milk crate." She fetched it from the barn and helped Ellen climb onto Buttermilk's broad back.

"There are a couple of things to remember. Heels down. Hands on the reins like so. Relax. This is supposed to be fun! Now follow me."

Pat swung into Thunder's saddle and headed toward the pasture. Buttermilk followed, with Ellen gripping the reins so tightly that her knuckles turned white.

But it didn't take long before she began to relax. Pat was right. This was fun. In fact, Ellen couldn't remember when she'd ever had such a good time.

Pat showed her how to go from a walk to a trot, and promised that she'd be cantering in just a short time. "You're a natural," she told Ellen. "I'm sure lucky to have run across you."

So Ellen became a stablehand. Every day after school, she cleaned stalls and scrubbed buckets and swept the floor of the tack room.

After that, she rode. Some days she rode Thunder. Other days she rode Buttermilk. On good days, she rode them both.

And as the days turned to weeks and the weeks to months, Ellen the fat girl slowly evolved into Ellen the equestrian. Her flab became muscle and her clumsiness, grace. She glowed with a self-confidence that was obvious to everyone around her.

It was near the end of the school year when a heavyset girl sat down beside Ellen on the bus one afternoon.

"My name's Stacy. I hear you work with horses," the girl said hesitantly. "Do you need an assistant? I've never ridden before, but I read about horses all the time."

"Why don't you get off here with me and we'll go talk to my boss," Ellen said, smiling to herself. She was pretty sure she could guess what Pat's answer would be.

"We're lucky to have run across you, Stacy. Who do you want to ride first—Thunder or Buttermilk?"

Jennie Ivey

That Kid Is on Zoloft

We've heard the familiar saying that "the best thing for the inside of a man is the outside of a horse." Well, it is true that horses have an uncanny ability to unlock something deep within the recesses of the human mind.

It was spring on the Cocolalla Creek Ranch, nestled in the mountains of northern Idaho, and the warming sun was pushing up a carpet of lush, green grass in the meadows. When my husband Tom and I checked on the horses that morning, we found that one was injured after having gotten into a squabble with another horse the night before.

The injured horse was a Norwegian Fjord named Olaf, a small, stocky draft horse that looks like a fawn-colored teddy bear with a personality to match. No wonder he lost the fight.

Dawna, our barn manager, brought him into the barn, cross-tied him in the alleyway and started to treat his wounds. Although the wounds were not serious, Olaf was bleeding and trembling from the pain. At this time, the North Idaho Children's Mental Health Psychological Therapy Group was also using the indoor arena on the ranch. The group brings in children who have been abused and helps them overcome their fears and problems by working with horses. This hippotherapy program is called the Healing

Partners Equestrian Therapy Program.

A twelve-year-old boy was part of that program. Fair-headed and freckled, with a slight build, Shane had just been released from the hospital and was very fragile, having had a cast removed from his arm the very day of his visit to the ranch. Shane watched for some time from a distance, then hesitantly walked up to Dawna and asked what she was doing. Dawna told him about the horse fight and showed him Olaf's wounds. Shane winced at the sight of the gaping wounds and asked if Olaf was in pain. Dawna replied tenderly, "Yes, it hurts, and he is in pain, but look how trusting he is to let me help him and how strong Olaf is not to cry out or run away."

Reaching up and stroking Olaf's muzzle, the boy whispered to the trembling horse, "I did the same thing, too, when I was hurt."

Dawna then asked if Shane would like to help groom Olaf. Eagerly, he took the brush that was in her hand and allowed her to guide the first few strokes to make sure it wasn't too hard or too soft, but just right. She noticed his knees and hands were shaking.

"What's wrong, honey?" Dawna asked.

"I'm scared all the time because my stepfather used to hurt me," replied Shane in a whisper. "He beat me up just like that bigger horse did Olaf."

At that point, Olaf dropped his big shaggy head and the boy and horse snuggled into a single, quiet mass. Tears gushed like a mountain spring and Shane told Dawna of the pain he had suffered and the wounds inflicted upon him.

Dawna told Shane that whenever he felt scared, shaky, sad or alone, all he had to do was brush Olaf or think of Olaf when he wasn't around. Shane agreed and proudly pronounced to Dawna, "I take a drug called Zoloft that helps calm me down and not be so afraid. From now on, I think Olaf should be called Zoloft because that's what he does for me."

Indeed, this shaggy, four-legged Zoloft became the miracle drug that broke through the darkness that surrounded this withdrawn child and let him come back into the light.

About this time, I walked into the barn and went up to the group to see what was going on and to say hello. I got down on a knee and talked eye-to-eye for a little while with Shane. When I turned to leave, Teresa, a therapist with the group, came up to me and quietly told me about Shane and how his stepfather had sexually abused and badly beaten him. She said that for more than nine months Shane, had not spoken a word about what had happened to him to anyone outside of her and his immediate family.

"With Olaf, I mean Zoloft, it was perhaps the first time Shane realized that others suffer as well," explained Teresa with thankfulness in her eyes. Shane went on to take a short ride on Zoloft that day and every other day he came to the ranch. Although every ride was another step toward recovery, Teresa summed up Shane's magical first ride on Zoloft by saying, "That was the first time in ten months that I saw Shane calm. That horse opened the door to saving this child."

As a postscript to this story, Teresa reports that Shane got tremendous therapeutic value from standing tall in court and telling the truth in front of the perpetrator, his stepfather. The prosecutor said that Shane's incredibly powerful testimony in court made it possible for his stepfather to be charged with two extra counts. He was taken directly to jail. If recommendations are taken and predictions come true, this evil man will be convicted and sentenced to twenty-five years in prison for his crimes. A heavy sentence would truly be icing on the cake for Shane.

Teresa went on to say, "From my experience as Shane's counselor, I know that Zoloft (that is, the four-legged one) helped this injured young man to feel a sense of power, control, calmness and confidence that he did not have before."

Now when you see Shane proudly riding around the arena, you can really say, "That boy is on Zoloft and it's really helping him!"

Marguerite Suttmeier

Hey, Lady!

"Hey, lady, can I walk Tostada?" came the small voice from somewhere in the dark behind me.

I jumped six inches and rapped my knuckles on the gate I was opening.

Spinning around, I searched the blackness. A short, hunched form was barely visible in the reflected light from the distant street lamp.

"Little John," I said. "What are you doing out this late? Won't your mom be worried?"

The small boy, who lived in the housing project about a half mile from the boarding stable I managed, looked up at me and said, "Nah, she's in jail. Can I walk Tostada?"

I had seen Little John hanging around the stable on the weekends. He was a round little boy, who walked with his shoulders slumped and his head hanging down. He always looked at the ground and wouldn't look you in the face when you spoke to him. He never replied to any questions.

However, he did talk to the show horses in their stalls. They seemed to enjoy the little person and would put their heads over the stall doors to snuffle him on the neck. He mostly just stood there and let the horses nuzzle him. Rarely, he would reach out and tentatively touch their soft noses.

Little John's speech was slow when he would stay to talk.

Most of the time he would scurry away when people approached him. Fetal alcohol syndrome was the term I heard from the professionals who boarded horses at the barn.

"Lady," said the insistent boy, his voice breaking, "can I walk Tostada?"

"Sure, Little John," I replied, and I turned back to the gate to halter my gray Anglo-Arabian mare Misata.

Little John had come by to visit her a few times while I was at the barn and had once gathered the courage to ask her name. He couldn't pronounce Misata, but in an attempt to get her name, he hit upon a word he knew. To Little John, she was Tostada.

That night, my normally energetic, spooky horse walked with her head down next to the small person who had his hands wrapped tight around the lead rope. I held the other end, tensely hoping Misata would behave.

Finely tuned and in show shape, Misata was a handful for experienced riders. Her favorite class was the Arabian costume class, where she would race wildly around the arena, bells and tassels streaming out behind her, trying to outrun every other horse in the class.

That night, she stepped calmly thought the gate. I handed the middle of the lead rope to the boy.

Walking with his head down, in his normal fashion, Little John could not see where he was going in the dark. He stumbled. Misata, who usually had to be jerked to a halt, stopped and stood still.

"Look up, Little John," I said softly as I breathed relief that Misata hadn't spooked at the sudden movement.

Little John helped me finish my chores, and then I took him down to the local police station, where a young officer gently talked to the young boy and set him up with a place to stay.

The next Saturday, as I was mucking stalls, a small voice whispered, "Hey, lady, can I help?" Little John stood in the doorway, looking at the ground.

"Tell you what," I said. "You scrub up all those water buckets and I'll let you sit on Tostada." For the first time, Little John looked me in the eye, "Really?"

He diligently set to work with the scrub brush. About halfway through the sloppy job, one of the buckets splashed up water into the boy's face. Words erupted from the small person that scalded my ears.

"Little John, we do not talk that way in my barn."

"Teacher lets me," he said without looking at me.

"In my barn, you do not talk that way, ever," I said. "If you want to talk like that, you need to leave." Through tumbles and falls and bumps and bruises, Little John never let fly a foul word again.

When he finished the water buckets, I took Misata out of her stall. She walked out instead of bolting through the door and stood calmly as Little John ran a brush over her down-stretched neck and front legs.

The mare, who never stood for me to mount, was still as I tried to boost the round, rolled up little boy onto her back. He was like a deadweight.

"Little John," I asked, "do you want to ride?"

He nodded, still looking down.

"You can't stay on a horse unless you look up and ride straight," I told him. "If you look at the ground, you will end up on the ground."

The boy stared up at the normally fidgety horse who was standing calmly just for him, and then he looked up at me. "Okay," he said.

I boosted him onto Misata's back. He instinctively curled into a fetal position and started to slide off her side. The mare shifted her weight to stay under the boy.

"Sit up," I reminded him.

He looked up, wrapped his hands in the mare's thick gray mane and smiled the first smile that I had ever seen on his eight-year-old face.

That was our first ride of many that summer. Little John rolled over Misata's shoulder more than once as he learned the importance of sitting up straight. The mare stopped each time, waiting for her young charge to climb back to his feet and then back on her back, where she seemed certain that he belonged.

"Stay, Tostada," he would croon, as he pulled her next to a fence so he could climb up and on. For him, she did.

He worked his way up from scrubbing buckets to picking stalls. He was determined to earn his way and be responsible for every minute he spent with his Tostada.

He worked in the barn and rode almost every day. He began to walk straight and look people in the eye.

And finally, that August, Little John's Tostada carried a proud young boy in the town's parade. The tall white mare walking carefully through the balloons and bands was not Misata, my fiery show horse, but the calm steady support of a young man who had little else in the world.

Jeanette Larson

Thursdays Are Special

Horses and children, I often think, have a lot of the good sense there is in the world.

Josephine Demott Robinson

Sometimes he would come on Thursday and not even be able to get out of the car because of the seizures. Still he came, week after week.

His caretakers said he knew when it was Thursday, even though he knew little else and could not communicate how he knew. He could see, but not speak, could not even sit up unassisted. Yet, he knew when it was his day to go ride. He was only ten, and he didn't live to his teens.

Nevertheless, his story, which includes horses and horsepeople who made him smile and gave him something to look forward to one day a week, must be told.

Many years have passed and many children have benefited from various therapeutic riding programs. But none touched me as much as this one boy. He required a steady horse, one with patience with his rider's inability to balance and an understanding of the boy's need to occasionally lay his face on the mane and just breathe in horse smells. We had several wonderful horses that filled the bill.

One volunteer would walk beside this youngster on the right and help hold him in the saddle, one would control the horse and another would walk on his left to steady him and be his instructor for the day. Any breakthroughs, no matter how small, were recognized and rewarded. A smile, an attempt to move a hand or leg in the right direction, even attention focused on the instructor or the horse were considered achievements.

One week, he was in very good spirits. This followed several weeks when he was either too ill to come or he had suffered seizures in the car and was forced to miss his lesson with the horses. But that day, he smiled. He seemed alert and willing.

We were stopped and waiting for another rider to be helped when my young student reached out and touched my hair. My hand was on his leg, so I knew he was steady, even though my eyes weren't on him. I looked around and knew he was trying to tell me something. The horse stood motionless, as if he knew his movement could distract or confuse his rider.

"What?" I asked. It was unusual for him to reach out and touch, to even control his hands enough to do so. He reached out again and stroked my hair, as he sometimes did to the horse's mane on good days.

I realized that my waist-length hair was back in a ponytail, and that he wanted it to hang down. Perhaps he wanted to see it, like the horse's tail in front of us, free and swinging. Or perhaps I had worn it down in other classes with him and it wasn't the same today. For whatever reason, I knew he wanted me to free that ponytail, so I did. He looked at me, managed to touch his hands together a couple of times in what he used as clapping, and he smiled at me.

Approval.

Our lesson continued and he seemed to have a better time that day than I could remember him having in any other class. He reached toward me and I put my head so he could touch my hair several times while we were walking along.

I didn't know as his attendant carried him back to the car that it would be the last time I saw him. He missed several weeks, then I went back to college. I found out months later that he died not too long after that.

But instead of mourning, I thought of him in heaven, running out to his favorite horse, not having to wait until Thursday or for his attendants to help him. He and his horse would gallop across clouds, with him laughing and the horse's tail streaming freely behind as the wind sang through their hair.

There is a heaven for horses and for little boys who know what day they ride, even when they don't know much else. I'm grateful for having seen that desire, and for understanding that God gave us horses and little boys and that they all aren't the same, nor should they be.

Kimberly Graetz Herbert

A Beach Day

And God took a handful of southerly wind,
blew his breath over it and created the horse.
Bedouin Legend

"We need to go to the beach." Martha was right. We needed it more than anything right now. We were three friends. Three middle-aged friends. In the suburbs. With horses. We'd been riding together for years and didn't ever intend to stop.

Martha was the most accomplished rider. She was tall, lean and supple. Her face was tanned and her eyes sparked with excitement. She had the resources to buy the best horses and the athleticism and drive to excel at dressage. Her horse was Mars, a licorice-black Friesian with a long forelock that draped his face and graceful feathery hair on his fetlocks. With Martha astride, his muscled body glistened and bunched under her command.

Kerry was fearless, opinionated and had a will of iron. Compact and strong, she could lift fifty-pound feed bags onto her shoulder with a smile. Her whole life had been steeped in horses and she had a solution to any horse-related problem that arose. She rode Shasta, a big dappled

Hanoverian mare with an attitude to match Kerry's. Shasta was smart, too smart in my opinion, and had a good sense of what she could get away with.

I was the busy one, working too hard, raising two kids and getting involved in a multitude of community activities. I had spent my adult life trying to squeeze riding into spare moments. I didn't own a horse, but was always negotiating and conniving to get a ride. I was not the best rider of the group, but the most relaxed. Once I found the time to get on a horse, I was totally in the moment and felt Zen-like in my peace. I had been riding Cort, a hardworking bay who pretended, not too convincingly, to hate all humans. He was a sucker for a good neck scratching and gingersnaps. Like me, he also was middle-aged, but sometimes suffered under the delusion that he was a hot-blooded yearling and acted that way.

In this early spring season, life had just thrown all three of us some pretty serious curve balls. Martha's situation was the saddest. Her husband had just passed away from cancer, and she was now facing the reality of a life alone. Kerry, who never feared any horse, had recently hopped on a neighbor's pony in an ice-slicked paddock. The pony reared, twirled and lost his footing, and Kerry was thrown onto her back. Two broken vertebrae and two millimeters from paralysis, she was told never to ride again. She didn't listen. I had just been laid off from a twelve-year office job due to a faltering economy, and couldn't sleep at night, worrying about money and even more, the loss of my professional identity.

A beach day was prescribed. We lived thirty minutes from the ocean, where there was a wide beach with an inviting stretch of sandbars at low tide. So, on that chilly March morning, we loaded the three horses into a spacious trailer and headed out. In the parking lot at the beach, the sand drifted across the asphalt and the salty smell of the ocean made the horses' nostrils flare. They were excited, shifting their weight and stamping their feet while we tacked up. Their mood was infectious and we found ourselves as eager as the horses.

We started out trotting three abreast across the sand as if we were the Three Musketeers, black, gray and bay in beautiful alignment. The gulls screeched over our heads and dogs let off their leashes bayed and loped behind us. We laughed aloud in pleasure and imagined us as a scene in a perfect movie where nothing ever goes wrong.

But it wasn't to be a movie-perfect day. Kerry moved Shasta into the shallow water to avoid a rocky patch and the big mare decided the water was just too cold and veered back out. A war of wills ensued. Martha and I watched in amusement as horse and rider set a zigzag path: in the water, out of the water, in the water, out. Forced once more into the water, Shasta was fed up. She glanced back at Kerry and slowly collapsed onto her side in peaceful, nonviolent protest. Kerry leaped off at the last moment and stood there, drenched to the thighs in the frigid water, holding the reins of a supremely stubborn horse. Shasta had made her point and soon stood up, shook and cheerfully nuzzled Kerry for a treat.

Happy that no one was hurt, we set out again, this time walking straight out into the bay on a narrow spit of rocky sand that was littered with broken shells and terminated almost at the horizon in an abandoned lighthouse. We walked and talked almost to the end, then turned and headed back toward the beach. Now it was Cort, my aged mount, who decided he was once again a yearling and it was time to run. His head lowered and oblivious to the snaffle bit that I was futilely pulling on, he took off at a full gallop. He could not be stopped. I flew past the other two and caught a glimpse of their laughing faces. My Zen-like peace was left a quarter-mile back and I clung to his back in total panic. Back on the main beach, Cort slowed on his own and waited calmly for the others to catch up. I could swear I saw that horse wink at the other two.

It was almost time to go home. Pools of water barely two inches deep were forming all over the sandbars. Martha rode Mars into one large puddle, then stopped. As Kerry and I watched, Martha straightened her back and moved the reins slightly in her hands. Mars tightened his muscles and started a piaffe, perhaps the most beautiful dressage movement, where the horse trots in place almost in slow motion, his feet rising and falling in the same spot. Mars was awesome. He was a black shadow on the sand, moving in a dream-like sequence. And because of where Martha had placed him, with every step, a sheet of fine water sprayed upward from his hooves. I looked at Martha's face and her eyes were gazing far away and I could see that her soul was flying free.

The air had changed from chilly to cold. The sun was low and the dogs and their owners had all gone home. We quickly and quietly loaded the horses and eased our tired legs into the truck. Not much was said, but we knew our problems had been forgotten, for a day at least. Tomorrow we would have to deal with loneliness, health and money. But not today.

"Hey, Kerry?" It was Martha.

"Yeah?"

"What do people without horses do?"

Tracy Van Buskirk

Damsel in Distressed Work Boots

God forbid I should go to any heaven where there are no horses.

R.B. Cunningham Graham

In my mid-forties, I left a safe, perfectly paved, colorless highway and made a hairpin turn that sent me reeling down a rutted route of self-discovery. My rest stop, my refueling place, was a five-acre ranch on a quiet country road. It became my new home. It offered serenity, healing and the company of nature.

The house came together quickly. I unpacked boxes with a sense of permanence. Everything claimed a place of belonging. I worked hard all day and started sleeping deeply at night. The day my son declared that our new house felt like home, I breathed a sigh of relief. It was the first sign that we were going to be okay. The nesting came naturally, and once the house felt safe and secure, I focused on the rest of the property. It was time to bring my horses home.

The day the hay was delivered, my horses moved in. I climbed the stack of alfalfa to knock off the top bales, and looked down a sheer fourteen-foot wall. I realized I was stuck. I called out for my eleven-year-old son, and he braced the ladder as I fearfully eased down. We didn't have wire cutters, so I popped open the bale by twisting a broom handle until the wire weakened. Without feeders or water troughs, I had to toss the hay on the ground and fill large plastic buckets with water. The next morning, as the sun came up, I fed my horses for the first time.

I picked up the manure fork and wrapped my manicured hands around the cool steel handle. My movements were awkward. Time and again, the fork tines stabbed the ground and the flying manure missed the large mouth of the trash can. My arms ached and I had angry red blisters on my hands. I paused to straighten my back and catch my breath. My horses were eating their breakfast contentedly, and I listened to their slow methodical chewing and the soft rumble of their noses as they blew out bits of alfalfa. The manure, some still steaming, simply smelled healthy. My poor horses were corralled in single-rail fencing with wire curling up the rotted posts. They looked as though they'd moved to the wrong side of the tracks. Where was their silver spoonful of white fencing and pasture grass?

In my previous life of Riley, we had a lovely gentleman's ranch with plenty of hired help. I was indoctrinated by the mantra of my marital years: If you had horses, you had help. One of our longtime employees was supposed to move with us. But I couldn't replace his salary, so I was on my own. Kitchen utensils, needlepoint scissors and light bulbs fit my hand perfectly. Tools, shovels and wheelbarrows did not. I felt physically defeated by the sheer work of taking care of my horses. Trembling with dismay at the injustice, I expected to be rescued. Where's Waldo, my knight in shining work boots, when it's time to feed? Blanket the horses? Pick up manure? And what about the disrepair? Who was going to fix everything? More importantly, how was I going to pay for it?

My seven-year-old trail horse, sweet reliable Buddy, became the financial sacrificial lamb. I was consoled when he went to a loving home. I knew he would be well cared for and, in turn, Buddy became the benefactor of safe new fencing, shelters from the sun and pelting rain, and spacious sand pens with permanent feeders and automatic waterers.

My biological clock adjusted to livestock hours. My designer jeans were replaced with Wranglers and work boots. Our dogs, wiggling their morning greeting, led the way to the hay barn. The wheelbarrow became my most cherished tool. I used it to schlep hay, transport manure, off-load supplements and cart tools and trash and firewood. That scratched blue bathtub body, supported in a steel frame with sturdy fat wheels, became my constant companion. I needed it more than the luxury car in my garage. It was as necessary to my job as a wrench is to a mechanic, medicine to a doctor or a case library to an attorney. I couldn't work without it.

An "Aha!" moment came as I was heaving manure cans into the dumpster. I didn't hurt anymore. I was efficient in my chores. I could throw manure as an intact pile or one nugget at a time across a twelve-foot stall. I could toss hay without getting it in my hair and bra. I could feed and clean in less than an hour, brushing off my hands with accomplishment. I paused and realized that if I was willing to do this kind of work, it must be in alignment with my soul. I reflected on my previous life, a socialite with a full calendar, and discovered that nowhere in society were my needs better met than in the company of my horses. Because of them, I'd learned how to work and I was proud of it.

The first winter, I struggled with the weather. It brought drenching rain, sticky clay soil that made me six inches taller with each trip to the barn, and a dumpster overflowing with manure. Twice daily, I bundled up and begrudgingly left the warm house to take care of my horses.

With the next winter approaching, and my memory of the grueling one past, I dreaded the thought of inclement weather. But I treated it like childbirth and I was better prepared the second time around. I had fresh hay stacked to the rafters—it was tiered and I owned hay hooks for moving it around. I had fleece shirts, down vests and heavy hooded raincoats, rubber boots, warm gloves and earmuffs, too. My body was strong and my hands were capable. More importantly, I had come to love the daily contact with my horses. I loved the gentle whinny of their greeting and their soft blinking eyes as they watched me round the corner with my trusty wheelbarrow. I tried to explain it to my mom, "When my horses are blanketed and eating their dinner in clean bedded stalls, when the sounds are contented and the light soft, it reminds me of nursing mothers comforting their hungry babies. It's nurturing and, for me, it offers a deep sense of communion with mothers everywhere."

One early evening, as I stomped the sand off my boots on my way back to the house, my life suddenly felt familiar. It felt good and honest and real. I shrugged out of my coat and boots and paused in our warm kitchen in my stocking feet. My son was quietly concentrating on his homework, our roasting dinner promised comfort and I was overcome with contentment. I felt that I understood Kahlil Gibran's description of comfort, "That stealthy thing that enters the house as a guest, and then becomes a host, and then a master." I knew for sure that I was home.

Paula Hunsicker

Riding the Road to Recovery

As Jane entered her forty-ninth year, her life could not have been more perfect. She had a career in the air force, achieving the rank of senior master sergeant, and she was happily married to a great guy. She was an accomplished musician and equestrian, valued by friends for her warmth, generosity and humor, and admired by peers for her discipline, determination and focus.

Just three years earlier, Jane had won the coveted spot of lead violinist for the U.S. Air Force Strolling Strings. She was the first woman to hold this distinguished position in the group's nearly fifty-year history. As part of this talented ensemble, she performed at the White House and at diplomatic functions throughout the United States and around the world.

In her free time, Jane could be at the barn with her beloved fifteen-year-old horse Clear Screen, also known as Leroy. An elegant pair, this 17.2-hand, dark bay Thoroughbred and his five-foot, nine-inch rider built a successful show record in both the ladies sidesaddle and hunter divisions. Everything was going smoothly until April 2000, when fate had another plan for this beautiful, determined woman. Suddenly, a favorite pastime became the catalyst for dealing with a life-threatening illness.

There was a family history of breast cancer and Jane knew she was considered high risk. She followed the recommended prevention and early-detection plan that included regular breast examinations and mammograms. Until the day she discovered the lump, her exam results always were negative.

A battery of tests led to referrals to several specialists. The agonizing process of identifying the lump and undergoing the appropriate treatment began. Just as in riding, determination and patience paid off. Days waiting for test results seemed like an eternity. The bad news, "You have cancer," was followed by the good news, "Thankfully, you caught it early."

Despite the fact that Jane's breast cancer was diagnosed as Stage I, she opted for a very aggressive treatment plan of surgery, radiation and chemotherapy. With her family history, she didn't want to take any chances.

In early May, she underwent a lumpectomy and lymph-node biopsy. Her first question to the doctor after the procedure was, "Will I be able to compete in a horse show in eighteen days?" Four days after the operation, Jane was riding again, but her ordeal was far from over. Additional testing revealed that the bad cells were a little more widespread than initially thought. As a result, her diagnosis was changed to Stage II breast cancer.

In addition to being an accomplished rider, Jane was an avid runner in top physical condition, but there was no way she could have prepared for the emotional blow. In one of the few times she expressed her doubts, she told me, "The reclassification of my illness from Stage I to Stage II was my darkest moment. I felt totally defeated, like this was the end of the world. How could my body have betrayed me? If my tumor was small and discovered early, how could the cancer have spread so quickly?"

The end of May marked the start of the chemotherapy phase: eight treatments, three weeks apart, concluding with six weeks of radiation, five days a week. All this time, Jane was calculating the show schedule because during the previous year she and Leroy had competed and won ribbons at prestigious horse shows including the Pennsylvania National, the Washington D.C. International and the National at Madison Square Garden in New York City.

By the second treatment, Jane's hair had fallen out. This didn't bother her as much as expected, and wearing a wig offered some unexpected advantages. A lifelong brunette, Jane quipped, "I've always wanted to be a blonde!"

Her winning attitude rarely faltered, and where riding had always been her temporary escape from the pressures of everyday life, it now served the added purpose of enabling Jane to keep control over at least part of her normal routine.

With her doctor's approval, she continued to ride as much as possible. Knowing that Leroy was at the barn waiting kept Jane up and moving. Ever since she had purchased Leroy as a four-year-old, a strong bond had existed between the two. I remember her telling me, "I felt that Leroy rallied to be the strong one. Instead of me taking care of him, the roles reversed, and now he was taking care of me. On days I was sick, depressed or wobbly, he was extra careful."

The road to recovery for Jane was taken one day at a time. Riding and competing with Leroy continued to be the focal point and primary goal. Jane set her sights on returning to the show ring just four and a half months after her breast cancer was diagnosed.

When the big day came, Jane transported Leroy to the Middleburg Classic Horse Show in The Plains, Virginia. The moment she had so eagerly awaited turned out to be uncomfortably long, dusty and hot. Although she was not awarded the blue ribbon that day, Jane was clearly the winner to her friends and fellow competitors present to cheer her on.

Jane's struggle with cancer continued and she faced many obstacles. "When you have cancer, your biggest fear is that the disease changes everything and your world spins out of control. Riding is the best therapy because it puts life into perspective. I know I am still me," she confided.

Two years after she felt that lump, Jane returned to the Middleburg Classic. Her health now restored, she felt strong enough to compete in all three classes of the side-saddle division.

The victory was especially sweet when the tricolor reserve champion ribbon was awarded to Jane and her partner through it all—her horse Leroy.

Lisa B. Friel

The President's Escort

*The one thing I do not want to be called is "First
Lady." It sounds like a saddle horse.*

Jacqueline Kennedy Onassis

The four-beat cadence of the riderless horse echoed the
beat of a country's broken heart.

On those two November days, Black Jack carried in his
empty saddle the grief of a nation. He was vigorous and brilliant, strong, proud and stepping off in his own direction, not
unlike the young, fallen American president he was there to
honor.

Black Jack was on duty as the riderless horse in the full honor
funeral of President John F. Kennedy in Washington, D.C., on
November 24 and 25, 1963. The day of the assassination, Friday,
November 22, had dawned bright and warm in Dallas, Texas,
but a day full of promise suddenly turned dark.

Now President Kennedy was gone and the country was in
mourning. The funereal pomp and ceremony befitting a president was playing out, with Washington as stage and the world
as audience. Black Jack's role was center stage.

He paraded in a place of privilege in the cortege, only a
few feet behind the 1918 artillery caisson that bore the

President's coffin draped in an American flag, and in front of the procession of international dignitaries and family, and the president's widow Jacqueline.

Mrs. Kennedy understood history was at hand. At her request, the funeral reprised many of the rites of President Abraham Lincoln, America's first assassinated president, who died April 15, 1865. Presidents Kennedy and Lincoln both lay in state in the black-shrouded East Room of the White House and in the Great Rotunda of the U.S. Capitol. Church bells rang and a procession trailed through the streets of Washington. Riderless horses—Black Jack for President Kennedy, Old Bob for President Lincoln—provided proper escort.

Black Jack escorted the president's coffin to the Capitol, the White House, St. Matthew's Cathedral, and finally across Memorial Bridge to Arlington National Cemetery.

His empty saddle symbolized an ancient military tradition of mourning the leader who will ride no more. In the saddle's stirrups was a pair of spit-shined black boots, reversed and facing backward, allowing the leader to look over his troops one last time. A silver saber hung on Black Jack's right side. These were trappings of a military officer.

As president, Kennedy was commander-in-chief. Black Jack was military, a soldier on a mission from the Caisson Platoon. The Caisson Platoon is part of the U.S. Army's Third U.S. Infantry, known as The Old Guard, based at Fort Myer, Virginia. The Old Guard is the army's official ceremonial unit and escort to the president. The unit also escorts fallen soldiers and American heroes to their final resting places. The lion's share of its duty is in Arlington National Cemetery, adjacent to Fort Myer.

Black Jack's handler during the Kennedy services was nineteen-year-old Pfc. Arthur Carlson, a six-foot, two-inch tall army soldier from Alabama, who did his best to handle his handful of horse.

"He was spooked," Carlson said more than thirty-five years later.

Black Jack skittered at forty-five-degree angles, and jigged and pranced down Constitution Avenue, Pennsylvania Avenue, Connecticut Avenue, all along the route. At the White House, where they waited for the coffin to be placed on the caisson, he kept circling Carlson. He was impatient with the skirl of the Black Watch bagpipes and the relentless, muffled drumrolls. This was duty different from his typical, quiet missions in Arlington. Thousands of people crowded curbsides to watch. It was all new and noisy. And historical. A loose horse would have sullied perhaps the twentieth century's most solemn ceremony.

Black Jack's anxiety level rose just as the services got underway. Early on Sunday, November 24, the platoon contingent gathered in the courtyard of the Treasury Department building for the first procession, to move the president's body from the White House to the Capitol. A chance encounter with a steel grate frayed the gelding's nerves.

"When we went to leave that courtyard, we were to pass through a street-level tunnel that penetrated the building. There was a grate—a large steel grate that had been left propped up against the wall—and I was following the caisson leading Black Jack," Carlson remembers. "A wheel on the caisson, snagged on that grate and the caisson started dragging it on the stones and making an awful noise, which was magnified being in that tunnel.

"And it just scared that silly horse out of his wits. He decided to stay scared for two days. He danced for two days. He danced and tossed his head."

Carlson said he was hardest to control "when I was supposed to be standing still, like outside the White House, outside the Capitol and outside the cathedral, where he stomped my foot."

Somehow, Carlson hung on to Black Jack and maintained the dignity required of the occasion, a feat he credits in no small measure to the determination inherent in his Swedish ancestry. "Much determination. Not good for much else, but my God, we're determined," he said.

"At the time, I was in full military mode, that is, completely focused on the mission. That was it. I didn't allow anything else in. I was just trying to do my small part the best I could."

Carlson's and Black Jack's "small part" remains an enduring image of the Kennedy funeral.

Black Jack was handsome, not a big horse at 15 hands and not a purebred of any breed. He was a Morgan–Quarter Horse crossbred gelding, who kept his date with destiny when he was transferred from the Fort Reno, Oklahoma, Remount Station to Fort Myer on November 22, 1952, eleven years to the day prior to the assassination.

His tiny feet—"He could have stood on a biscuit," Carlson says—precluded his being ridden or used to pull the heavy caissons. His good looks qualified him for duty as the caparisoned or decorated horse in military funerals. As is required for all GIs, Black Jack was assigned a serial number, his was 2V56, which was branded on the left side of his neck. He was the last horse the army branded with "US," which marked his left shoulder.

Why was Carlson, a private with no previous horse experience, conscripted into the prestigious service as "cap walker?" Easy.

"I was tall, slim and had good posture. Still do."

Black Jack's military resume also featured a shared January 19 birthday with Confederate General Robert E. Lee (Lee was born in 1807, Black Jack in 1947) and a name honoring General of the Armies John J. "Black Jack" Pershing, the American military commander in World War I. Coincidentally, the nickname of Mrs. Kennedy's father Jack Bouvier also was Black Jack.

He served with The Old Guard for twenty-four years and paraded in thousands of funerals for the famous and the not-so-famous rank and file, including Presidents Herbert Hoover and Lyndon B. Johnson, and General of the Army Douglas MacArthur.

The horse from Oklahoma lived a long and full life as the

platoon's patriarch and most famous resident. On birthdays, he enjoyed media coverage and butter-pecan cakes baked by a colonel's wife, who was a devoted fan. He received hundreds of letters and birthday cards, including one hand-drawn birthday card in 1975 from a little girl in West Virginia named Mary Lou Retton, who made her own history in 1984 when she won an Olympic gold medal in gymnastics.

Black Jack died at an elderly twenty-nine in 1976, the year of America's bicentennial. He is buried near the flagpole on Fort Myer's Summerall Field parade grounds. A bronze plaque marks his grave, and the Black Jack Museum in the Caisson Platoon stable honors his memory.

The memories of that November, though it was so long ago, remain seared in America's soul. The red, white and blue of the American flag, whipping in the wind at half-staff. Six matched gray horses pulling the high-wheeled caisson and coffin. A black-veiled widow lighting an eternal flame at the grave. And the proud spirit of a riderless horse. They provided the theater, a place for the country to cry.

Gayle Stewart

Fly, Misty, Fly!

Why am I so dumb, Misty?

It was a sparkling cold winter's day when I came out to ride. In the high mountains of southern Idaho, riding is usually a summer pastime. Winter riding took a certain amount of nerve and preparation, and at the time, I had neither. I just had to get out: out of my house, out of my life for a while. So, I came out to the farm where I boarded Misty, my old Morgan mare. I was halfway through my junior year in high school and it wasn't going well, not well at all.

"I can't see why it makes a word wrong if you spell it a little differently. Why can't they see what I meant, not how I spelled it? F-r-i-e-n-d or f-r-e-i-n-d? They look like the same word to me, so it doesn't matter how many times they grade me wrong. I can't tell which is right. I'm so stupid."

I caught Misty with a halter, brushed her thick winter coat and warmed the bit between my hands so that the cold metal didn't "bite" her tongue. No matter how upset I might be with my life, none of the lessons I had learned about how to care for horses ever left me. They'd been taught to me by Mr. Codding, who owned the farm where I boarded Misty. Mr. Codding would board horses for kids who lived in town, but we never forgot that he had the last word on how they were to be treated.

But it does matter if I confuse greater than or less than, or if I put the decimal point at 00.1 or 0.01. If I say it out loud, I can hear the difference, but they look the same. I understand the math, but I can't write down what I understand. And every time my math teacher makes me take a turn at the board to solve problems, everyone can see how dumb I am. If I have to go up to that board again to work out a problem, I think I will die. Mom'll just kill me if I flunk a math class. Well, no, she won't kill me. She'll just be so disappointed. Why can't I be smart like she is?

Mr. Codding had shown me how to warm a bit before asking a horse to take it in his or her mouth. You took off your gloves and warmed it with your own hands. Better your hands got a bit cold than a cold bit hurt your horse's tender mouth.

I'm not sure he would have approved of my taking Misty out on that cold winter day. Even without wearing slippery shoes, a horse could lose his footing on a snowy road. But I had to get out, get away—far away—from my problems. I hadn't told anyone where I was going. I needed some healing and fortunately, had the presence of mind to seek out a horse.

Of course, Dad says that the only reason to send me to college would be to get my "M.R.S." degree. I wish he hadn't made all those people at his dinner party laugh at me when I said that that wasn't it, that I wanted to go to college to learn. Maybe he's right. I'm too dumb to go to college. I can't even spell, for crying out loud, and I'm flunking math. It's a good thing I didn't tell him I want to go to college to be a scientist. He'd think that was a real hoot.

I leaned against Misty's muscular neck, buried my face in her mane and inhaled her sweet horse scent. Together we stood and breathed. Her strength and calm presence steadied me.

I decided to ride around the section. A section is one square mile, which is how our county roads were laid out. Where I grew up riding, we kids mostly rode in the fields or in the barrow pit next to the roads. (No one knows why those in southern Idaho call the ditch next to the road the barrow pit, but that is the term everyone used.) The barrow pit is not the best place to ride because it can have trash in it, but it was all we had. A dirt road was the best thing, of course. And that is why I headed around the section. The back mile, the one that ran parallel to the Codding's farm, was all dirt for its entire one-mile distance. And there were only two farms on it. So there was a lot of space for us to stretch out and run or enjoy all the kinds of horseplay that teenaged girls could think of. That made it a favorite place to ride.

Only today, I didn't have any girl friends with me and I wasn't in the mood for play.

If I can't do math, I can't be a scientist. That's what Mom says. She says that a scientist needs to be able to measure and test things.

I climbed up the fence and got on Misty's bare back. It's nicer to ride a horse bareback in the winter because your legs are right next to the animal's warm body. My body moved automatically in rhythm with Misty's. My hands connected with her mouth and we were one. All my life, I had been a complete klutz. I couldn't catch a baseball to save my life or kick the big rubber balls we used to play kickball. I couldn't walk on the top of fences the way that my friends did. I was always the last to get picked for any team and my physical education class was torture. But the first time I got on a horse, I found some mysterious coordination that had missed me in every other physical endeavor I had ever attempted. On a horse, I was graceful and strong.

Sandy is going to medical school. She gets straight As. John is going into engineering. He breezed through Algebra II as if it was easier than walking. Whenever they talk about the future, I just tell them I plan to be a goat herder. They think it's funny. I've never told a soul what I really want to do. They would laugh and laugh if I did. But I'll tell you, Misty. I want to be a scientist and watch animals like Jane

Goodall and I want to be a veterinarian. Isn't that silly? It is harder to get into vet school than to get into med school and you need good grades. I'll never get good grades. If I flunk algebra, I won't make it to college at all because my grades will be too low, so I've got to drop it before I flunk it. But if I can't do the math, I can't do the chemistry I would need to be a scientist. You see, Misty, there is no hope. This is a stupid dream.

I want this to all go away, Misty. I want wings so that I can fly. Tommy flies all the time, you know. He's doing drugs again. He says it is wonderful to be high. He says I'd feel happy all the time if I got high with him. But if I did, I couldn't come and be with you. Tommy does dumb things all the time when he is high. I couldn't risk doing something dumb and maybe hurting you. That's a risk I won't take.

We had gotten to the back road. It was a mile long with snow packed over the dirt. Almost no one drove on it and no one knew I was there. If I fell off on that cold winter's day, it would be a long time before anyone would think to look for me there. But the thought that I might fall off Misty never crossed my mind. For me, the rest of my life was risky. This was real and necessary.

I dropped the reins and carefully knotted them so that Misty wouldn't trip over them. I wouldn't need them. The road was straight and ran for a mile before it met the north–south road. Misty would tire and slow before we reached it. If I needed to, I could ask her to slow with my voice and I trusted her to listen. In the past, when I had lost my balance and started to fall, she always slowed and moved to stay under me. Misty wouldn't let me fall now. The rest of my life was falling to pieces all around me: my parents' divorce, my school failure, my friends, my beliefs, my broken dreams. But Misty wouldn't let me fall.

I wrapped both hands in her mane. I leaned forward and gently asked her to run. She surged ahead, powerful and strong. My long hair flew back in the wind, like her mane. The road blurred beneath us. Cold wind blew tears from my

eyes onto my icy face. I closed my eyes and felt her powerful muscles surging as she carried me with her. She was
blowing now, emitting a rhythmic puffing sound from her
nostrils. It sounded like the beating of feathered wings.
Faster and faster, farther and farther, Misty was carrying me
away from my hopelessness.

Fly, Misty, fly.

I came back from that ride renewed and determined to continue. A year and a half later, I entered college. My parents
sold Misty to some family friends who wanted to use her for
breeding and for their daughter to ride in 4-H. So Misty had
more souls—equine and human—to nurture. My path was
rockier. I entered college as a music major, but switched to
zoology, only to find that my mother was right and I didn't
have the math skills for chemistry. I switched again to psychology, still hoping to study animal behavior. Fortunately,
the college dorms were on the same side of campus as the
livestock barns, and whenever things got too overwhelming,
I would go and watch the horses. The barn guys got used to
me as a regular fixture, perched up on the fence watching the
horses eat their evening meal. I completed the psychology
degree and started another degree, this time in animal sci-
ences. By this time, I had been joined by Larkin, Misty's son.
He would take me flying when everything threatened to
overwhelm me.

It wasn't until I was in graduate school that my learning disability, called dyslexia, was discovered. The psychologist who
tested me, an old professor of mine, was astonished by the
results. "How did you do so well in my class with so severe a
learning disability?" he asked me.

I rarely had time to ride while I was going to veterinary
school. Yes, I finally made it to vet school, although it was a
struggle to get in because no one believed that a dyslexic
could pass the grueling curriculum. After hours of classes
and studying, I would come home and seek out Larkin in the
pasture. I would stand by his shoulder, lean against his muscular neck, bury my face in his mane, inhale his sweet horse

scent and breathe with him. His powerful essence gave me the strength to go on.

Riding horses is easy. Climbing back in the saddle of life when you repeatedly fall off, now, that is a lot harder. I kept going because of my mother's belief in me and because my love of animals and my desire to learn about them were stronger than my fear of failure—and because I had a horse carrying me.

Janice Willard, DVM, MS

Like Pegasus, Laughter Takes Flight

The first time I ever saw a group of live horses I was ten years old. A dozen horses appeared at one of the busiest intersections in the city where I lived with my mom, grandparents and a variety of aunts, uncles and cousins. I distinctly recall that each horse carried one of "Newark's Finest" fully outfitted in riot gear. The shields, weapons and boots blended with the horses to form menacing images.

Newark, the largest city in the state of New Jersey, was in the middle of civil unrest that summer and riots had erupted throughout the city. The governor had dispatched the National Guard and the mounted police to restore order. As a child, the sights and sounds terrified me and my first impression of horses would forever be tied to riots, violence and looting. It would take more than a decade for that association to change.

Eleven years later, I was a college student majoring in journalism and working part-time for a weekly newspaper. A prominent resident volunteered her time every week "walking horses" for a nonprofit organization. Somewhere, there was a connection to disabled children who were confined to wheelchairs. "Cover the story," I was told. "It should make good copy."

Somehow, I just could not reconcile the two images in my

mind: a group of fragile, disabled children with a herd of wild, thrashing horses. These contradictory images occupied my thoughts as I followed the directions to Crossroads Farms in western New Jersey. As I drove, I couldn't help but admire the breathtaking landscape with its rolling hills, open spaces and white rail fences. It was a far cry from the congestion, traffic and urban chaos with which I had associated horses.

When I arrived at Crossroads Farms for my interview, I noticed a specially equipped school bus, outfitted with a hydraulic wheelchair lift, parked near the entrance. Inside the vehicle were six children, each occupying his or her own motorized wheelchair. As their teachers and caregivers maneuvered the wheelchairs from the bus, it was evident that the children were struggling to contain their enthusiasm. Laughter, shouts of cheer and hand clapping were evident everywhere. Even to the most casual observer, the looks on these children's faces brought to mind Christmas morning, Disneyland and a visit to the Hershey's Chocolate Factory.

Volunteers, including the woman I was featuring in my story, were waiting to escort the children from the wheelchairs onto a special staging area. As the volunteers pushed each wheelchair up a ramp, the children were gently lifted from the confines of their mobile apparatuses. Below the ramp, six horses patiently waited for their precious cargo to be placed on each of their backs.

Taking in the situation, I was completely awed by the scene unfolding before me. One by one, each child was secured in a special saddle. Three volunteers were assigned to each child: one leading the horse, and two flanking the child. The horses seemed to sense the fragility of their cargo and took special care not to jostle or bump the child.

The children, in turn, were ecstatic. Their faces were not big enough to hold their smiles and their bodies were too small to contain their joy. The horses slowly began walking down the rustic paths and the children were absolutely delighted. As they were led away, they bantered back and forth, "I'm flying!" "I love my horse." " I feel like an angel. These horses are like wings."

From my vantage point, it wasn't difficult to understand their frame of reference. While they were atop the horses, they were freed from the metal, the bars and the arms of the wheelchairs that almost perpetually surrounded them. In addition, their perspective astride the horse was a high one. For once, they were at least the same height as the adults who cared for them. No one was looking down at them. For the next thirty minutes, they were as tall as, or taller than, their caregivers, and their laughter was sent heavenward.

I continued to watch them and pondered the comparison to angels' wings. Although these children were still confined to the limitations of a physical existence here on earth, their horses were, indeed, like angels' wings, providing them with the opportunity to experience a freedom they could never have imagined.

As their laughter continued to ring out, I was reminded of the Greek legend of Pegasus, the white winged stallion. The most beautiful creature in the ancient world, this elegant equine was so revered that Zeus, the king of the gods, created a constellation of the winged horse to light the night sky. I am delighted to report that the descendants of Pegasus are alive and well in northwest New Jersey. For as Pegasus transported the thunderbolts of Zeus across the sky, these "winged" horses carry a more precious cargo—the souls of children, who, for a brief moment, can soar through the air as their laughter is released to the heavens.

Barbara A. Davey

At the End of His Rope
. . . a Winner!

When Jerry Long, of Capitan, New Mexico, first meets the at-risk, emotionally and physically challenged children he counsels in the Horses N' Hearts program at Lincoln County Schools, he directs them to convey a positive first impression, no excuses. Excuses just don't belong in Long's world. And he ought to know.

His directives: "No fish handshakes. Firm grips. Stand up straight. Look me in the eye. Smile."

Then he tries, over three or four days, to match names he's previously memorized with the students who line up to make contact with him. They try to confuse him, to elicit incorrect responses from him in a game of wits for all players, made even more challenging because Jerry is blind. He's also diabetic and fifteen years ago he underwent a kidney transplant.

Long's own twelve-year-old American Quarter Horse, Heza Exclusive Man, nicknamed Duke, plays an integral role in the therapy, just as horses play a major role in this human volunteer's motivation. A champion team roper then and now, Long uses Duke as an instrument to teach lessons of coping with life and its challenges, something Long well understands. He wants the youngsters to learn to be responsible for their actions.

A father and grandfather, Long, holds a Master of Education degree. He was a public school teacher, counselor and administrator for thirty years when diabetes took his sight and caused kidney failure, ultimately resulting in his retirement and in his abandonment of riding and roping. Even though battling depression at the time, he found work and inspiration as transition coordinator with the Texas School for the Blind and Visually Impaired in Austin, helping blind students prepare to reenter that sometimes fearful place, the "real world." All the while, he dreamed of returning to his beloved sport of team roping. In that Western discipline, riders pair up to catch a cow by galloping toward it and then tossing ropes around the steer's humanely wrapped horns.

One day, when Long was with a friend who missed a steer at a local roping, he jokingly told his sighted buddy, "I'm an old, fat, bald-headed blind man, but I can do better than that. Quit making excuses. Just tie some bells on him, and I'll do at least that well!"

He hadn't, of course, planned on following through with his pronouncement.

When the two chums got together next, Long's comrade coerced and chided him into getting on a horse and picking up where Long had left off before losing his sight. With "my heart in my throat," Long recalls, he rose to the challenge. He roped seven times and caught two steers. He was, literally, "back in the [roping] saddle again," and it felt just like old times.

Now, he competes and wins against "regular" ropers, his only concession as a blind rider being a set of bells affixed to the cow's horns. Long is so adept, in fact, that he recently played the lead in an educational video about roping. He ran 108 steers and roped 99 percent of them. In roping, a seventy percent average is considered admirable by anyone.

Long, who's an in-demand public speaker, says he tries to inspire people, to motivate them. "We all face different challenges and our character is determined by the way we meet those and contend with them." He's also a Christian who just wants "to treat people the right way."

He doesn't write down his speeches—he couldn't see them, of course—and he endeavors to speak from the heart. His audiences find much value in his messages and they tell him so.

About his sporting successes, he's reflective. "It takes a pretty brave person to team rope with a blind guy," laughs Long. There are many who might say it's Jerry Long who's not short on determination, drive and courage.

For him, there are more kids to help, more adults to inspire and more cattle to rope. Oh, and if he adds another shiny winner's belt buckle to his collection, that would be just fine, too.

Stephanie Stephens

"I'm sorry, sir, but roping horses are a dime a dozen."

Roping. *Reprinted by permission of Steve Sommer and Francis Brummer.* ©2002 *Steve Sommer and Francis Brummer.*

Don't Fence Him In

A good rider on a good horse is as much above himself and others as the world can make him.
                                                    Lord Herbert

I'm standing in the entry hall of a 116-year-old Victorian-style home, the wooden floors creaking beneath my shoes. "What time does his bus come?" I ask, shifting my weight to hear the floors again.

"It stops at our door at 8 A.M.," his mother replies.

The eighteen-year-old high school senior staring out the window chimes in. "No, it doesn't. It comes at 7:50." Then I hear the roar of the school bus as it moans up the hill to the Max Meadows, Virginia, home of David Taylor.

I look at my watch. It's 7:50.

David flashes a smile in my direction as he walks off the porch, makes his way across the yard and climbs up the steps of his school bus. "He loves being right," his mother Judy tells me as she waves good-bye.

Doesn't every normal teenager? I think to myself. And perhaps that's the best way to describe David.

I became friends with David in 1998 when he ran over my foot with his wheelchair while we were at the American

Quarter Horse Youth World Championship Show.

He attends a public school, just outside Max Meadows, where he walks to class like the hundreds of other students scurrying about the hall. He plays sports, plays bass drum in the band, swims, skis, rides an American Quarter Horse and goes to dances. Heck, he even dates. If you didn't know any better, you'd swear that David is just another typical high school kid intent on proving that his parents are never right.

But the fact that David is able to do any of this is nothing short of a miracle. David was born two months prematurely in what his mother describes as a backwoods hospital some sixty miles from Roanoke, Virginia. On the way from that facility to a more modern one, David died and was resuscitated five times. Later, Judy was given the grim news about her newborn.

She was told that he would require surgery to implant a shunt into his head to release a dangerous buildup of fluid on his brain known as hydrocephalus. The doctor said that her son also had seizure disorders and would likely have impaired hearing and speech. Later, David was diagnosed with cerebral palsy, which affected his mobility.

"The doctors told me that *if* he lived, he would be a vegetable," Judy explains. "But I would look into his eyes and see this spark. There was just something about him. I thought with any infant who refused to die five times over, I wasn't willing to accept their opinion."

David is the youngest of four children and the only boy. To survive, he would have to be strong, independent and work harder at the everyday tasks that able-bodied people take for granted.

After learning to walk at four, David had hamstring and heel surgery to help his balance and to straighten his legs. Then his doctors recommended horseback riding lessons.

"This was fourteen years ago and horseback riding as therapy was practically nonexistent," Judy explains. "But we found him a Shetland pony and started him riding."

It wasn't long before David outgrew his pony and

ultimately acquired his first American Quarter Horse.

"Then he started walking better," Judy says. "He started talking better. He even started breathing better, which helped so many other things. I am convinced it was that horse and the way he moved that helped him so much."

Today, David has advanced from therapeutic riding to competing in various shows. He competes at local shows and has been to the All American Quarter Horse Congress every year since 1997. He has competed at the American Quarter Horse Youth Association World Championship Show each year since 1998.

"It doesn't bother me being handicapped in an able-bodied world," David says. "But I don't want people to make me a handicapped person in a handicapped world. That's why I want to ride in Quarter Horse shows. I love my Quarter Horse and hope someday that I can show my skills against other people of similar ability."

Every day except Tuesday, David can be found riding English and Western in the field next to his house or in his neighbor's arena. Tuesdays are reserved for water therapy, another activity that has contributed to his independence. His therapist is an affable, gregarious young guy named Jason, whom David affectionately calls Buddha Belly. As they spend an hour in the water stretching, playing catch, walking against a current and wrestling, Jason tells me that he's never seen anyone work harder than Slim Fast, his nickname for David.

The water also helps his balance once he's on horseback. When David rides, he is not strapped on. He uses no special equipment and for the most part, he does everything him-self, short of tossing the saddle up and pulling the cinch. And yes, everything includes falling off.

"Oh yeah, he's fallen," Judy admits with a giggle. "Right in front of the judge once." Like any teenager, David rolls his eyes away from his mother.

David's horse is a twenty-year-old sorrel mare named Judy Meyers. He acquired her in 1997 and is quick to point out that she's not named after his mother.

"I love this horse," David says proudly. "She knows me and we're getting better the more we work together. She helps me run barrels and poles, and do reining. We're practicing a lot for trail and learning English [style riding]."

For safety reasons, David can compete only in individual pattern classes.

David's voice shakes as he and Judy work into a trot and they circle my body as if it's a barrel to prove they're getting faster.

"She won't hurt you," he says. "It's just Judy." *No*, I think to myself, *it's not just Judy. This is an amazing horse keenly aware of who's on her back and where each pound of his nearly six-foot-tall body is.*

After David finishes using me for barrel practice, we head inside, where he sets the table, fixes a quick lunch and says grace before we eat.

During the meal, we talk about his future. David, an avid NASCAR fan who collects signed memorabilia from his countless trips to the races, is expected to have a normal life span with continued riding and therapy. He is not mentally handicapped and will graduate with a regular high school diploma. He is planning a move to North Carolina in the hope of getting a job in auto racing. Judy teases and says that as soon as her youngest moves away, she'll begin remodeling the house, starting with his bedroom. "I've waited a long time to do it," she says.

"Yeah, but I get to keep my horse," David pops back. Then he goes silent for a minute. "She gives me the chance to be part of the real world."

Tom Persechino

Regalito

Regalito is a Spanish name that means special little gift, and he was, in more ways than one.

Little girls who love horses dream of riding great white horses with long wavy manes and tails. Although mostly in the middle part of "middle age," I had never lost that little girl's dream. My husband Arthur gave me Regalito for our thirtieth wedding anniversary. That was the first special little gift. Regalito is a Spanish Andalusian stallion. He is beautiful, noble and above all, huggable.

Since the age of four, I have ridden horses. They are the love and passion of my life—after Arthur, of course!

After his five-day journey from California, Regalito arrived at our farm in Louisiana. He immediately made himself at home. How proud and noble he was. But, with great pain and sadness, I knew I would never sit on his back and share in the exultation of his dance; for, indeed, when Regalito moves, it is like a dance.

For five years, I had been unable to ride because I suffer tremendous pain and lack of mobility from a devastating disease called fibromyalgia. This disease robs you of the joy of movement; every step is a painful effort.

Because I could not ride horses, I started painting them in watercolors. All my feelings for these wonderful creatures

came out in vivid shades of green and blue, copper and silver, turquoise and gold. Many of the paintings have sold,
but one stays with me: the painting of Regalito that I did a
year before I even knew of his existence. I think I must have
conjured him up. He was, in fact, the magical horse who
changed my life.

After Regalito arrived at the farm, I had a new working
student come over to ride him. I taught Bobby dressage and
in turn he taught Regalito. The days, weeks, months and
then a year went by as I watched Bobby ride my beautiful
white stallion. Sometimes it felt as if my heart would burst
from wanting to ride him so much. I watched day by day
thinking, *If only that were me.*

Then one day as I sat in my usual place in the viewing
stand by the riding ring teaching Regalito and Bobby, the
thought came to me, *Why not me? Why not me?* Regalito is the
kindest horse, so gentle and willing. We had built such a bond
in the year he had been with us. I knew he would never hurt
me. Somehow he knew that I was fragile.

So today is the day, I said to myself. *If I don't ride him today, I
will explode with all this emotion!* Aloud, I said to Bobby, "Wait
a minute while I go change into my riding pants. I'm getting
on Regalito!"

Of course, Bobby's surprise was immense and he said,
"Are you sure?"

I replied, "I've never been so sure of anything in my life.
The time is now".

I mounted Regalito with stiffness and difficulty; the
mounting block made it easier. Bobby held the stallion's
head, but it wasn't necessary. Regalito stood as still as a
statue. He seemed to be saying, "What's taken you so long?"

I felt completely at home on his back, almost as if I'd
slipped a foot into an old shoe. Regalito and I were made for
each other. I sat in the saddle and all the pent-up emotion
came out. Tears of joy rolled down my cheeks. I had done
what I had thought was an impossible task a year ago. I was
sitting on the back of my beautiful white stallion.

It took me a few moments to compose myself. Regalito just stood quietly and waited, and then we walked away into a land where horse and human merge. I was weightless on my horse. I felt no pain and for these moments on his back, I was well again.

Regalito gave me back the second special gift, the gift to be myself. With generosity of spirit and great care, he carried me around the riding ring, doing intricate dressage movements with lightness and ease.

Daily I danced with my horse, daily my body moved and daily I became stronger, regaining a lot of my range of motion and certainly regaining the joy and passion of my life.

Thank you, Arthur, for my special little gift. Thank you, Regalito, for living up to your name and giving me the greatest gift of all: a reason to get up in the morning and feel again and again the joy that riding brings to my life and the healing it brings to my body and soul!

The Bond
For Regalito

I looked into his eyes and saw his soul.
He looked into my eyes and saw my soul.
He was my horse and I his person.
We knew each other's thoughts, each other's feelings.
We trusted one another.
We took joy in each other's company.
He was my horse—I his person!
We shared a bond, a bond of love.

Diana Christensen

Touched by an Equine

Emma arrived at the ranch on a typical Saturday morning about two and a half years ago. She was five years old and absolutely beautiful, with blue-green eyes, sun-kissed golden brown hair and a smile that would melt even the coldest of hearts. Emma came to us because she was clinically diagnosed with autism, a complex developmental disability that typically appears during the first three years of life. This precious child behaved like a windup toy.

"Emma, come here." "Get out of the tack room." "No, don't eat the ball." "Emma, sit down." "NO, Emma," her mother's words rang constantly. It would take two people to keep Emma still. On more than one occasion, she got into one of the stalls and tried to eat the horse's rubber mats. Emma, to say the least, was in her own world.

I'll never forget the day, the very moment that she first got on Horse Angel Dottie. When Dottie began to carry her new rider around the ring, the transformation was immediate. Gone was the uncontrollable child. In her place was a beaming, relaxed confident little girl. Wow!

Ever since I've known Emma, she's spoken only gibberish. "Saa Pa awom nes sapa nom," she would say, smiling and laughing to herself. I longed to know what she was trying to say and I could see in her eyes that she wanted me to understand. We communicated on a different level, thanks to Dottie.

Emma's been riding every week since her first visit. She's an excellent equestrian. She loves to ride and has no fear. I take some credit for her riding prowess and courage, but the real honors go to Dottie.

Emma had been riding for about eighteen months when she came for her usual Saturday lesson on an unusually hot, humid and dusty day. Nobody felt like working on this dog-day afternoon, especially yours truly and our Horse Angel Dottie. Nevertheless, as we stepped into the arena, I instructed Emma to give Dottie a little kick and say "walk," just as I had done a thousand times before. I tugged gently on Dottie's lead rope and started to move forward when, all of a sudden, I heard a little voice say "walk." I stopped dead in my tracks. So did Dottie, whose ears were already pricked to the rear. "Emma, oh my God, Emma, you said walk. You said WALK!" I shouted at the top of my lungs. "Your first word, Emma, your first word, and Dottie and I heard it." I don't know who was more touched by that one fantastic word, Dottie, Emma or I. Emma was smiling and clapping her hands. She knew. Tears were streaming down my face. And Dottie, well, she quietly walked on, just as she'd been told. I felt an overwhelming joy and gratitude for that incredible moment and this wonderful Horse Angel. I believe with all my heart that this is the reason Emma is speaking today.

Emma's vocabulary has increased to include the words whoa, yes, no, peanut butter, red, blue, yellow, green, the numbers one through ten, and Dottie's and my personal favorite, "I love you."

Melody Rogers-Kelley

Going Where No Horse Has Gone Before

The first time I was invited to bring miniature horses to a nursing home, I asked the activities coordinator if she wanted to schedule an alternate date in case bad weather on the appointed day should prevent the residents from coming outside to see the horses.

What a surprise when she said, "Oh, but I thought they could come inside. Can't they?" And so we did.

Once inside, I handed my pooper-scooper dustpan and broom to the nearest staff member and asked her to bring up the rear. She didn't even flinch.

Immediately, staff members and residents who probably never had expected to have the opportunity to see or touch a horse surrounded us. Once you love horses, you always will, but the responses we've had at the nursing homes are as varied and surprising as the people themselves.

During one visit, we brought two of our little horses into a room where people lined the walls in a semicircle of chairs, wheelchairs and hospital beds.

We told them a little bit about each horse, then walked them around the center of the circle. If someone reached out, we brought the horses over to be petted, but we stayed far enough away so that those who didn't want to touch wouldn't have to.

The lady sitting in the first wheelchair looked up at me, and I thought she was going to say something, but she didn't, so I went past her around the circle. When I came back to her, she looked again as if she were going to speak and I paused, but still she said nothing.

Unexpectedly, my mare Taj stepped forward and put her head on the folded hands in the woman's lap. Underneath, I saw one finger move against the soft muzzle resting there. Then I saw tears on the woman's cheeks. I hadn't known that she was paralyzed, unable to speak or to reach out. Taj, however, had sensed her wishes with unfailing accuracy.

The stories the residents tell us of their experiences—their long-past racing-stable days, the ice cuttings at the river before refrigerators were common, the time the barn burned, or the day their old mare ran away with the plow—give us vivid images of their "good old days" that we enjoy as much as they enjoy our horses.

It's easy to get caught up in the wonderful memories of these visits, but to get back to the real world I need only to remember one quiet man last summer.

He was sitting in an armchair in the circle of residents, his chin resting in his hand, calmly watching the flurry of activity while the horses made their last circuit of the room before leaving that day.

As I approached him, I was asking if anyone had any more questions before we left. He looked up at me when I stopped in front of him.

"Why, yes," he said thoughtfully, "Do you know when we eat?"

Apparently, everyone's world doesn't revolve around horses!

Carole Y. Stanforth

Billie Girl

When you are buying a horse, take care not to fall in love with him, for when this passion hath once seized you, you are no longer in a condition to judge his imperfections.

Sleur de Sollesell

One morning during the summer of 1994, I found myself standing inside the barn in front of one of the stalls. We had recently lost our daughter's beloved first pony, Rounder, to colic, and staring at that empty stall made me feel very heavyhearted. How would we ever replace Rounder?

Since moving to our small rural town of Agua Dulce, California, in 1977, my husband Don and I had filled our lives with horses while raising our four children and running our local water-well business. I knew I needed to find another perfect horse for our family. When my girlfriend called and asked me to go with her to look at a horse, I didn't hesitate to say yes and I hooked up my horse trailer. Little did I know that would be the day that Billie Girl would come into our lives.

As we drove into the feed-store parking lot, I was filled with excitement. There were so many horses to look at. My girlfriend was unsuccessful in her search, but I felt very drawn to a sweet-looking Paint mare. I was able to take her home for a couple of days to try her out. Then, I would get back to the horse trader with a decision.

That night, my husband walked into the barn and was surprised to see an occupant in the once-empty stall. He asked what her name was and I told him she didn't come with one. After a little discussion, we decided to name her Billie Girl after our friend Billy who had died just that day from a five-year battle with cancer.

For the next two days, Billie Girl passed every test I put her through with flying colors. All we had left to do was the vet check. When all was said and done, the veterinarian had shocking news for us. Billie Girl had cancer. My family was devastated and yet concerned about the quality of the mare's life in the future. After much thought and prayer, I called the horse trader with my sad news. His first response was uncompassionate as he told me to just bring her back and I could look at any of his other horses. Trying to hide my frustration, I responded, "I don't want to do that. Billie Girl has cancer and is unsellable, so please just give her to me." But his last response chilled me to the bone. "I can get a dollar a pound for her at the auction, so just bring back my horse!"

Late that night, I walked into the barn feeling extremely discouraged. I went into Billie Girl's stall and wrapped my arms around her neck. Pressing my cheek against her warm velvety coat, I could feel my discouragement start to fade and a peaceful, tranquil feeling came over me. As I listened to her munching hay in the quiet of the night, I asked, "Oh, Billie Girl, what do I do?" At that moment, she pulled back and put her muzzle to my face. As I held her head and breathed into her nostrils, she blew four consecutive warm breaths into my face. It was as if she was sending me a message of love and gratefulness. I knew, in that instant, that Billie Girl was here to stay.

The next morning, I excitedly told Don about my experience the night before with Billie Girl. We both knew we needed to arrive at a price the horse trader would accept.

After much emotional discussion, we agreed upon an amount and put it into a sealed envelope.

As I drove to the feed store and walked into the front office, I could see the puzzled look on the horse trader's face. I'm sure he was wondering, *Where's my horse?* I walked up to him and said, "I don't have your horse because she is at home. I really believe you should give her to me, but since that doesn't seem to be an option, what is the lowest amount you will take?" I will never forget how long it seemed to take for him to respond. He sat back in his tilted chair with hands clasped behind his head. After staring a few moments at me, he simply said, "Nine hundred dollars." I handed him that sealed envelope filled with nine $100 bills and quietly asked for a bill of sale. I still get chills today thinking of that amazing moment.

Billie Girl became a favorite of our family. She was a babysitter for all who rode her, including my nonhorseman husband, our nine-year-old year old son Matt and our five-year-old son Aaron. She was such a good babysitter that one month after she became ours, Aaron was galloping her with a group of riders down a sandy beach—one of his favorite memories.

We were blessed with four fun-filled years, a year for each breath she once blew to me the night she became our Billie Girl!

Laurie Henry

Passages of Time

One pretty Saturday morning in midspring, I stood watching in wonderment as Sheba, our old gray mare, cantered in happy circles around our nine-year-old daughter. Helen was standing in the middle of the pasture, halter and lead rope in hand, looking completely exasperated as Sheba ran circles around her. After all, Helen had awakened early this morning in eager anticipation of riding her brand-new horse for the first time.

But not if she couldn't catch her! I watched as Sheba lightly sailed over a low practice jump hurdle set up in the pasture. With head high, ears pricked forward and tail sailing on the wind as Arabians tails are wont to do, this old horse was the picture of beauty and lighthearted gaiety. I glanced across the paddock and saw that my husband, too, had stopped to watch this scene play out. We had just bought Sheba three days earlier and had found her to be gentle and very approachable in the pasture. But now she was happily evading my daughter's attempt to halter her. However, she was not running away to the far corners of the pasture, just circling within a few yards of Helen. Then, as we stood watching, Sheba simply stopped running and walked quietly over to the water tank for a drink.

A few moments later, while Helen was pleasantly grooming

Sheba, I asked my husband what he thought of the incident. "They looked to be 'happy circles' to me," he said. We both had a tingly sense of having received a message from this animal. She seemed to be expressing her gratitude for having been rescued from the crowded horse dealer's corral and coming to live with us. Indeed, before buying her, I had taken the old horse aside and quietly told her that if she would teach my young daughter to ride, she could have a home with us for as long as she lived. Now, Sheba seemed to be answering me with a resounding "yes!" Little did I know then just how much she would do for us.

It is a couple of years later and I am again standing in the same pasture, watching the same horse, the same gentle canter, but this time my handicapped daughter Mary Elizabeth is astride. Grandpa is with me, watching with tears in his eyes. Shaking his head in amazement, he is saying, "I never would have believed it." Helen went on to become quite an accomplished rider, pursuing such diverse equestrian activities as dressage lessons and exercising young Thoroughbreds on the track. But of my three children, it is Mary Elizabeth who loves horses as much as I do.

Although a couple of years older than Helen, she has always been developmentally behind her younger sister. Mary Elizabeth was born prematurely, deaf and with an impaired nervous system. She couldn't crawl or sit like other babies. She learned to walk with the support of a wheeled walker. She graduated to a pair of crutches in kindergarten. By first grade, she could walk unassisted but fell often. Her run looked more like a controlled fall. She found it difficult to stand without constantly moving to maintain her balance and she usually sat down or propped against something for support. In addition, she has severely reduced sensation in her arms and legs, which hampers her fine-motor control. Her deafness adds another handicap in itself.

But Mary Elizabeth loves animals, especially horses. As Helen began to learn how to ride, it soon became apparent that Mary Elizabeth intended to be included in this new activity. I was aware of riding programs for the handicapped and knew that Mary Elizabeth would benefit from riding. However, with her poor balance, I never thought that she would be able to ride without someone walking along-side the horse to steady her in the saddle. She never has been able to ride a bicycle and the two activities seemed similar in my mind.

One surprise followed another and through it all, I have been astonished repeatedly by Sheba's patience and under-standing. Without any spoken words, the horse always does exactly what our deaf daughter "tells" her, such as positioning herself perfectly next to strange objects for mounting, or standing still with a slipped saddle hanging from her belly. Time and again, this old mare has demon-strated her intelligence, instead of the more usual and expected equine behaviors, to accommodate Mary Elizabeth.

Grandpa was right to be moved to tears of awe that day as we stood in the pasture witnessing Mary Elizabeth's demonstration of riding bareback at a canter across the field with only a set of reins clipped to the halter—a feat even her teenage brother wouldn't attempt! Over the years, Sheba has very generously shared her capable legs and willing spirit so that our very special daughter can experience an unaccustomed freedom and equality in her otherwise handicapped life.

Mary Gail Cooper

Aul Magic

A horse can lend its rider the speed and strength he or she lacks, but the rider who is wise remembers it is no more than a loan.

Pam Brown

When Betsy removed his halter, our spirited chestnut stallion whinnied loudly, wheeled away and kicked up his heels, racing the wind around the arena as his golden coat gleamed in the sunshine, obviously delighting the kids in the audience. Afterward, however, the proud Arabian stallion stood quietly at the arena fence as the children gathered to pet him.

I had introduced Aul Magic+/ to the audience as The Red Stallion comparing him to Walter Farley's Black Stallion, an equine hero from literature and the movies. He certainly lived up to that introduction at the special presentation at the therapeutic riding school that day. Schools like the one we were visiting provide physical therapy to the disabled, but they also supply emotional therapy through the bond that develops between horses and people.

Magic, too, is exceptionally good at bonding with people of all ages. He thrives on attention and hugs, and we enjoy sharing him with those who otherwise wouldn't get a chance to interact with such an affectionate and responsive horse.

On this particular occasion, as Magic performed, walking without wearing a halter or any other equipment, his trainer Carolyn Resnick invited an autistic boy into the arena to walk with the stallion.

With the characteristic detachment of autism, the boy stared downward, never looking up, as he was guided by his teacher toward the horse. The boy's head remained down and his gaze stayed firmly fixed on the ground as he stood with the stallion in the arena.

When the proper cue was given, the entire group, including the stallion, stepped forward. The boy, head still down, was gently encouraged by his teacher to walk with the others.

After a few steps, again on cue, everyone stopped walking. Magic, too, immediately stopped and stood at Carolyn's side.

When the group walked forward again, Carolyn eased back, giving up her place at Magic's shoulder to the boy. At first, the stallion lagged behind the boy, remaining beside her as he had been taught. With Carolyn's encouragement, however, Magic soon realized that the boy was now leading the parade and the horse began walking beside him.

The group continued walking and stopping, walking and stopping across the arena, with Magic always at the boy's side. During the entire time, the boy's eyes never left the ground, as though he were not even part of this parade, much less its leader. Yet whenever the boy stopped, the stallion stopped and stood beside him. When the boy took a step, Magic stepped forward as well.

When the little group stopped for the last time, the autistic boy finally raised his eyes from the ground. For the first time, he looked up at the beautiful stallion that had been his walking companion. As I watched from outside the arena, there seemed to be a sudden hush of expectation. If there was any noise from the crowd or any other sound I no longer heard it.

In the sunshine, Magic's coat gleamed like golden silk. I watched, fascinated, as the boy reached upward to stroke the stallion's glistening neck. *Perhaps,* I thought, *if even this boy can manage to reach out to another creature, there is hope for the rest of us.*

The remarkable interaction between the boy and the stallion ended as swiftly as it had begun. The boy's arm returned to his side, his eyes resumed their fixed downward stare and he was led shuffling from the arena.

But I will never forget that glorious day when an autistic boy reached out to caress a gentle Arabian stallion. I'll remember, too, the shining tears in the eyes of those who understood the significance of that gesture.

Sharon Byford-Ruth

5

ON COMPANIONSHIP AND COMMITMENT

Is it the smell of their body as I hug their long neck,
or the scent only a horse has that I can't forget?
Is it the depth of their eyes as they contentedly rest?
No, it's just being around them that I like the best.

Teresa Becker

A Horse in the House

It was more than two decades ago, as Easter was approaching, that my family waited for Martha, our cream-colored Quarter Horse brood mare, to have her annual foal. All of us—my husband Arthur, our ten-year-old son Marc and twelve-year-old daughter Karla—considered the birth of a foal a big event on our farm in Mandeville, Louisiana.

That year, Martha was taking her time. She was already three weeks overdue. When my husband had to go away on business, I was left to oversee the birth alone. I spent many nights sleeping in the stable next to Martha's stall, wondering each evening if this was finally going to be the night.

On the night before Easter Sunday, Martha at last went into labor. When I heard her pacing restlessly, I got up from my folding cot and ran to her stall. Fifteen minutes later, she gave birth to a small golden-haired foal. Martha nickered once, licked her newborn foal and lay down to rest.

But ten minutes later, Martha was up and turning around again as though she wanted to give birth a second time. I couldn't believe it. Equine twins are rare, and from what I knew, when a mare carries two foals, she usually aborts them or they are born dead. But sure enough, Martha gave birth to another foal. This one was dark brown with three white socks and a big white mark on its forehead.

Though Martha's foals were small, I was relieved that they were both alive and seemed healthy. It wasn't long before they wobbled to their feet and began pushing each other to get to their mother's milk. After the foals had nursed, I thought my troubles were finally over and I went back to the house for my first good night's sleep in weeks.

The next morning, the children and I let Martha and her foals out to pasture. We named the reddish-gold filly Amber and her darker sister Ebony. It was a delight to watch them trying out their legs and exploring the world.

But it soon became evident that Martha was having a problem accepting Ebony. When Amber ran, Martha cantered protectively after her, but when Ebony tried to follow them, the mare pushed her away. Then, to our horror, she kicked at the foal, striking her baby on the head.

Though Ebony was thrown off balance, she didn't seem harmed or fazed by the blow. In fact, she continued to run after the two other horses. But later that morning, Ebony began to have what appeared to be a seizure. Repeatedly, her legs stiffened, her body arched and she fell to the ground.

Each episode left her more weak and helpless. It was heartbreaking to see her struggle to her feet only to fall down again.

In desperation, I called all over town to find a veterinarian. I knew if Ebony became too weak to nurse, she would die. But it was Easter Sunday and the local veterinarians were either away or busy with other emergency calls. Finally, at 6 P.M. I managed to reach one. When I explained what had happened, he came straight over.

The veterinarian suspected that the kick to Ebony's head had caused a blood clot that was putting pressure on the brain. He thought that this was the reason for her convulsions, and injected her with steroids to help dissolve the clot. For hours, we watched over Ebony in the freezing barn, hoping for some sign of improvement. But Ebony stayed weak and helpless. Finally, it became so cold, I decided there was only one thing to do: bring Ebony into the house.

I padded the floor of my bedroom with pillows and towels and the veterinarian helped me carry the foal inside. He gave me some formula and told me to feed Ebony from a baby bottle. Then, having done all that he could, he left me alone with her.

Ebony had to be fed every twenty minutes. Between feedings, I lay on my bed, trying to get some rest. The situation seemed hopeless and my mind and body were heavy with despair. I was exhausted both physically and emotionally from the effort of trying to keep Ebony alive.

I must have dozed off, because the next thing I knew I was suddenly awakened by a nuzzle and a soft nicker from a wet little nose.

It was Ebony. She had gotten up and come to my bed for her bottle. Though she still was weak, I was overjoyed to see her on her feet again. As I watched her suck greedily at her bottle, my fatigue vanished and I felt a wave of joy. Ebony was going to pull through and live after all!

Three days later, Ebony was running in the fields as strong and as healthy as any other foal. But when we tried to return her to Martha, the mare again kicked her away. It was clear that I now had another child—an equine daughter—to raise.

At that point, Ebony had to be fed every half hour. To make feeding her easier, we kept her in the house, leaving the patio door ajar so she could come and go as she pleased. Whenever she was hungry, she came into the kitchen, nickering for a bottle.

My son Marc became her playmate. Every day after school, he and Ebony ran in the fields together. When Ebony tired of playing, she came inside and lay down on the living-room carpet to nap or watch TV. It seemed completely natural to have this large and rather gawky creature sharing our home with us.

Then, as Ebony grew older and even larger, we began to put her in the barn at bedtime and gradually reduced her bottle feedings. But during the day, she still had the run of the house. Like most toddlers, Ebony was curious and wanted to get into everything. She walked from room to room, looking for things to play with. One day, she found Marc's school report on the kitchen table and promptly chewed it up. The teacher said Marc's excuse, "My horse ate my homework," was a new one for her. Another day, I caught her gleefully pulling tissues from the box on my bedside table. What a mess!

When Ebony was three months old, we decided that it was time to wean her from the bottle and encourage her to become a horse. We took her out to pasture and left her to play with her sister Amber and our other horses. At first, Ebony protested. But she soon adjusted to her new life and happily settled into the herd.

For many years after her stay in our house, I still considered Ebony my daughter, even though she became a fine, healthy horse, well able to take care of herself.

That's why I was pleased to discover that the feeling seemed mutual because if ever I left the door of our house open, guess who walked right in? It startled our guests, but for us, Ebony would always be welcome—our horse in the house.

Diana Christensen

Side by Side

It had been a great day at the barn. Everything was going smoothly, the sun was shining brightly, everything was perfect. Then the telephone rang and I was shaken back to the reality of my job as owner of a horse-rescue operation.

It was almost midnight when my new charges arrived after their nearly twelve-hour journey. I recall walking around the trailer to get a first look at the two aged mares recently confiscated from their home by authorities.

They eyed me cautiously. We opened the trailer and began to unload them, careful to keep them close to one another to help them feel secure in their new surroundings. The fear in their eyes screamed, "How much more can we take? How long will this nightmare go on?"

We slowly led them down the barn aisle, past the curious eyes of their new stablemates, and placed them in a stall together. Rushing to a corner, they stood shaking, their heads buried. Only occasionally did one of the mares, Dee, look around. Rosie, Dee's companion, seemed the most traumatized. She was unwilling to lift her head and her eyes were hollow and distant—a dull blank stare where blazing light should have been. Lethargic, she refused to look at us. Both of the mares ignored offerings of small amounts of water and hay. I settled in and continued to monitor them through the night, but nothing changed.

I knew Dee and Rosie's history and it was a sad one. When the authorities arrived to investigate a complaint about neglected horses, they found no hay, grain or bedding on the property. Dee and Rosie were literally eating the wood off the barn to try to stay alive. These two horses had been kept not only in the same barn, but in the same stall for nearly twenty-eight years. Tomorrow would be the beginning of my real challenge: to introduce these two terror-stricken horses to the life they had been denied.

For the first two weeks, I tried to gain their trust but my slow, deliberate movements stirred only more fear in their hearts, where fire and spirit should have been. Finally, a few mornings later, I entered the barn to find Rosie looking over her stall gate. When she saw me, her whinnies filled the barn. I approached her, talking softly and through tearful eyes, I saw the faintest hint of a spark in her gaze. She and Dee still backed away and refused my touch, but they were interested in their surroundings and showing signs of life.

I hung feed buckets in the stall, placing them so Dee and Rosie could touch one another as they ate, but they refused. They would eat only if allowed to share the same bucket. The same was true with water.

Five weeks passed before I had gained enough of their trust to attempt to take them outside. Holding a lead line in each hand, I had to be sure they could feel one another before they were calm enough to handle. Their eyes once again filled with fear, but they reluctantly followed me from the barn.

I was told that neither had touched grass since the age of six months. When their hooves touched it, they panicked. The whites around their eyes showing, nostrils flaring, they snorted and screamed as each of them tried to raise all four feet simultaneously. I quickly worked to get them back in the barn and into their stall. There, they once again retreated into the corner where they shivered and shook with fear. I had lost everything I had gained, but only for a short time.

A week later, I tried again. Although the experience was still traumatizing, they trusted me enough to walk with me for a short distance. Over the next fifteen minutes, I learned their fear of birds, butterflies, water puddles and vehicles. From that day forward, a daily trek would be part of our routine.

Soon, they trusted me enough that I could open their stall door and they would run from the barn, make two laps around it and then return to their stall together. What a beautiful sight to see them trying to accustom themselves to a new situation in a world that had been so cruel to them.

Two months would pass before I could separate them and give each her own stall. The stalls were side by side with an open grid between them so that they could see and touch each other. I placed their hay bags back to back so it appeared that they were eating together. Each had her own hay, and plenty of it, but still feared that the other would be hungry. Rosie would take a bite of hay and eat it. The next bite would be dropped to the floor, where she would use her nose to push it under the stall wall to Dee. Any hay that fell to the ground was given to Dee.

Four months after the girls (as they had become known to everyone at the farm) had arrived, I decided to try to turn them out in a small paddock. The experience did not go smoothly. They had seen only one other horse in their lives, so when their stablemates began getting close to the fence that bordered the fields, they once again panicked. The girls would race one full lap of the paddock at top speed and then stand shaking at the gate, waiting for me to save them from their newest danger. Each new experience was an insurmountable obstacle to them, but patience and repetition would work every time.

Thirteen months passed and it was time to try them with the other horses; time to see if they could lead a normal life. I turned them out in a small field with five other horses. The first few days, Rosie and Dee stayed together. Eventually, Rosie began to socialize and seemed to love her new life. She would run and kick up her heels and "talk" to anyone who would listen. Dee, on the other hand, was reserved and feared her fieldmates. But as always, Rosie and Dee were together at feeding time and Rosie always made certain that Dee had enough to eat. At the end of the thirteenth month, Dee also began to socialize with the others and to live her life as a normal horse.

The beginning of the fourteenth month would bring new changes for all involved with our horse rescue operation. For three years, we had rented facilities and now we had purchased our own farm. All of our horses, at that time numbering eighteen, loved the new land—seventy acres of rolling hills for running and grazing and enjoying life! Rosie and Dee would thrive on the lush pastures with their nightmare past behind them. Finally, the light returned to Rosie's eyes, and I could sense the fire and spirit in both their hearts.

The world couldn't have been better, at least until the Sunday morning I went to feed and Rosie didn't come to her bucket. This was unusual because she was always the first to her place. I fed the other horses and then set out to look for Rosie. The search was short. Next to the fence, only fifty yards behind our house, lay Rosie. I called to her and she raised her head and nickered. She tried to get to her feet, but failed.

As I approached her, I called her name again, and once again she tried to stand. Again and again she tried, but her efforts were futile. Exhausted, she collapsed. Looking her over, I couldn't find anything wrong or see why she wasn't able to get up, but on closer inspection, I found what appeared to be a bullet hole between her eyes. It had been covered by her forelock.

I phoned the veterinarian and after what seemed like hours, he arrived. A careful examination determined what I feared: Rosie would have to be destroyed. Both the sheriff and the veterinarian confirmed that she had been shot with a high-powered rifle with a scope. A trespasser with a rifle outlawed in our state had once again shattered Dee's world and had stolen away Rosie's newfound life.

A reward was set and the search was now on for the killer of the beautiful white horse who, after surviving decades of abuse and neglect, had just learned to live. The sheriff advised us that Rosie was to be left in the field for at least four days. In the event that the person was found, the bullet might have to be surgically removed from Rosie's brain as evidence so that it could be matched with a specific rifle.

My concern now turned to Dee. For twenty-eight years she had lived side by side with Rosie. How would she survive now? I covered Rosie with a heavy tarp and tied it for her privacy as well as protection. When I returned the next day to feed, Rosie was uncovered and Dee was standing guard over her body. When I put grain in their buckets, Dee would paw Rosie's body and whinny to her. As I led Dee to her feed, she kept calling Rosie to "come to eat." When Dee finished eating, her guard duties continued.

For five days, I would cover Rosie's body only to find her uncovered the next day with Dee by her side. The fifth day we would bury Rosie, but for nearly two weeks after that Dee would continue to guard the place where Rosie had lain and continue to call her for supper each night.

It has been five years since Rosie's death. Her killer was never found, although other horses within a ten-mile radius of our farm also were shot and had to be destroyed. Dee, at the age of thirty-eight, is now arthritic but otherwise in good health. She still lives her life in the rolling pastures of our farm.

Dee's trust in us has continued to grow. She comes to me when I call her and she can be handled as easily as a newborn kitten. The pain of her past seems to have faded away, but I sometimes see that faraway look in her eyes and I wonder what thoughts are passing through her mind. As she stares across the fields, is she searching for Rosie? Does she realize she'll never have far to go to find her? Rosie will always be with her, standing by her side by side.

Sissy Burggraf

My Friend Bob

I was short. He was tall.

I was white. He was black.

My vocabulary was above average for a third-grader. His . . . . Well . . . . I was the only one who understood him when he spoke.

I was a nine-year-old girl. He was a gorgeous six-year-old Tennessee Walking Horse whose registered name was Bob's Merry Legs. He had the most velvety black coat I'd ever seen. His four white stockings and broad white blaze made him look even blacker than he was. He was at least 16 hands tall which meant that he towered over me.

I wanted him as soon as I saw him enter the sale ring. Daddy had brought me to the auction, but I'm sure he had no idea what would happen.

I couldn't take my eyes off the glorious-looking creature. I was quite certain my life would be nothing but pure happiness if I could have him and, by contrast, I was equally certain it would be nothing but misery if I were denied him.

I knew begging and pleading would get me nowhere. In our family, one made a simple request and then waited for the parental decision.

"How will you take care of him?" asked Daddy. Look at him. He's huge. You won't even be able to get on his back.

"They want $125 for him," continued Daddy. "That's a lot of money, but that's not all. We'll need to feed him and pay for visits from the veterinarian every now and then. We're talking about a very expensive situation here."

I looked him square in the face, eyeball-to-eyeball. "I could give you my entire allowance until he's paid off," I said.

Looking back over all those years, I have no idea how Daddy kept a straight face.

"And how much allowance do you get?" he asked.

"A quarter every week." I responded.

"Hmmm," he said, "if my mental arithmetic is correct, you'll need almost fourteen years to pay him off. That's a long time."

I dropped my head and looked down at the dirt. My visions of having the beautiful black horse in the pasture at our small farm were fading quickly. Now, my focus was to keep my bottom lip from quivering.

"Are you sure about this? A horse is a lot of responsibility, you know. It's different from having a dog or a cat."

I shook my head in the affirmative.

"Okay," said Daddy. "Go over to the man in the red plaid shirt, the one leaning against the fence. Ask him if the horse is still for sale for $125 and ask him if he can deliver him to our farm."

A grin split my face so wide I could feel the shape of my cheeks changing. I ran to the man, began talking to him, pointing first at Bob and then at Daddy. He nodded his head "yes" to both of my questions. I started to run back to Daddy, but changed my mind. I knew he'd take care of the business part. What I needed to do was introduce myself to Bob.

The big black horse had been moved to a small corral. I climbed to the top rail of the fence, threw over one leg at a time and perched there.

"Hey, Bob," I said. "You're beautiful. You don't know me yet, but I already love you. We're going to have wonderful times together."

The horse tossed his head before walking to me. He stopped three feet short, then stretched out his neck and flared his nostrils in an attempt to pull my scent into his nose. Slowly, I held out my hand. Bob snuffled across my small palm, his warm breath the most wonderful sensation I'd ever felt. I knew at that moment we'd bonded. Nothing else was needed. Bob settled in at the farm immediately. No fuss. No special fanfare.

My parents set limits on the freedom we could enjoy. The railroad track one mile east and the bridge three-quarters of a mile to the west were the boundaries. There were numerous dirt roads crisscrossing our farm and I could ride anywhere I pleased on those.

Bob learned my schedule. He began prancing and whinnying sometime between 4:05 and 4:15 in the afternoon, but Daddy made him wait until 4:20 before he opened the paddock gate. Bob walked on his own, with no bridle or rider, down the long driveway to the edge of the cattle gap and waited, looking expectantly in the direction he knew the school bus would come. I would find him neighing furiously by the time the bus door opened and I stepped out.

My daddy wouldn't go anywhere without wearing one of those dapper fedora hats, and Bob loved them. He waited for Daddy to walk past him and, quick as lightning, he darted over, snagged the hat with his teeth and snatched if from Daddy's head. The horse seemed to laugh and was extremely pleased with himself, knowing he'd exposed the man's very large bald spot. Fortunately, Daddy learned quickly that chasing Bob down was not the thing to do. It wasn't a fair match and Bob always won. Instead, Daddy would just ignore the situation, and try as hard as he could not to acknowledge the sight of Bob running around with the hat dangling from his big yellow teeth. Eventually, after being ignored, Bob would walk over and drop the hat at Daddy's feet.

Three years after Bob came to live with us, Mama and

Daddy decided that I could ride beyond the railroad tracks and the bridge. That was really great, but there was one major problem: I couldn't convince Bob that we had permission to expand our universe. He absolutely refused to cross the tracks or the bridge. It was frustrating as well as humiliating. Finally, Daddy came and led him across both former boundaries while I sat in the saddle. Somehow, Bob equated that action with receiving the official okay from an authority figure.

I had my first date on Bob, graduated grade school and moved into high school. Unlike some girls, though, I didn't leave behind my passion for horses in general and for Bob in particular.

He was still my very best friend and he still met me each day at the end of the driveway. Very seldomly did we skip a day of riding, but if we did, I sat in the pasture with him. Our conversations were long and slow and deep. There was nothing about me he didn't know, and he kept my secrets ever so well.

I was completing my sophomore term and Bob was sixteen. His coat was still jet black and his step still had all the fire and prance of a much younger horse. I visited him each morning before catching the school bus, but on one particular morning, something was seriously wrong.

He was on the ground in his paddock, drenched in sweat. He'd swing his beautiful head toward his side and try to nip himself, telling me he was experiencing painful stomach cramps. He looked at me. I knew he was asking for help and I also knew he had a serious case of colic.

I ran to the house, slamming the door behind me, snatching the receiver from the wall phone and dialing the veterinarian. Mama came from the kitchen, drying her hands on a dish towel.

"What's wrong?" she asked.

"It's Bob. Colic. I called the vet." I answered, short of breath from the run as well as from fear and from struggling to hold back tears.

Mama walked to me and patted my shoulder. "It'll be okay," she said. "I'll go get Daddy so he can help." She got into her car and drove to the field where he was working on his tractor. They returned together.

"We need to get him up if we can," he said to me. We set off for the paddock at a run. Daddy put a lead rope on Bob's halter. "You coax him," he said. "He'll listen to you."

"Bob," I sobbed. "Please, Bob. Get up. Please. Please. I need you, Bob."

The big horse lumbered to his feet and when he was standing, I gasped. He looked as if he'd lost a hundred pounds overnight. Daddy handed me the lead rope. "Walk him," he said. I could tell from his look and the tone of his voice that he thought the situation was bleak. With tears running down my face, I started walking the black horse.

The veterinarian arrived, jumping quickly from his seat. He grabbed a stainless-steel bucket from the back of his truck and poured in mineral oil until it was half-full.

Then he stuck a pump with a long, clear plastic tube attached to it into the bucket. He walked over to Bob, pinched his nostrils together and began feeding the tube through his nose, down his throat and into his stomach. Then the veterinarian began pumping the oil into the tube, hoping to dislodge the impaction that was the source of Bob's pain and move it out. He pumped and pumped and pumped, but nothing happened. Bob's front legs started buckling at the knees.

"Don't let him go down," the veterinarian yelled. "We don't want him to roll. If he does, he could twist that intestine and then we don't have a prayer."

I held on to my horse, my heart breaking, knowing he was miserable. I knew how he longed to lie down, but I tugged and strained on the lead rope. "Please, Bob," I prayed. "Stand up, Bob." And, for the first time since the ordeal began, I allowed myself to say the word, the awful word. "Please, Bob. Please don't die," I breathed.

"I can't do anything more," the veterinarian said. "Just keep walking him as much as you can."

Both Bob and I were exhausted, but I walked him and stroked his face. Finally, he touched my cheek with his nose. I suppose I knew what would happen. I suppose I wasn't surprised when he yanked the rope from my hand and crumpled to the ground, looking like a million broken pieces of black glass.

He stretched out his neck, and I lay down on the grass next to him. "I love you, Bob. You've been the best friend I could ever have." He knew what I said. He always did.

Daddy worked all day to dig Bob's grave, way back in the middle of a small thicket of trees and vines. He knew a decent burial was all I'd accept for Bob. I missed school for an entire week, crying every day.

All these many years later, my heart still feels the tug of a lead rope whenever I think of Bob.

Daddy is dead and Mama is more than eighty years old.

The farm has long since been sold and rows of houses cover the pastures and fields.

There's a house built over the grave now.

Sometimes, when I'm home visiting Mama, I imagine the people living in that house. They are unaware of the history the earth holds, but I wonder if every so often they hear a whinny and just for a minute see the silliest thing: a big, black horse with a fedora dangling between his teeth, trying to entice someone into a game of tag.

Diane M. Ciarloni

The Magic Carpet Pony

Gypsy gold does not chink and glitter. It gleams in the sun and neighs in the dark.

Gypsy Saying

At nine, I had already shown my determination to ride through several years of being overmounted until, at last, Daddy got serious about finding me a proper pony. He went looking one day with $300 in his pocket, just in case he found the right animal. At one farm, he saw a 13-hand Welsh pony with a a flashy bay coat that shined like a new penny. Daddy just thought, "Wouldn't it be fabulous to own a pony like that?"

After two months of looking, Daddy realized that he couldn't settle for anything less. He paid $800 for Jupiter, an exorbitant sum in those days. But when I found that note in my Christmas stocking—"Dear Robin, I am waiting for you down at the barn. Please come soon. Jupiter"—I'm sure my ecstasy was worth $800.

As Jupiter and I rode out across the fields, it was as if I'd been given a magic carpet. Jupiter took me anywhere I wanted to go, from the winner's circle to the ends of my imagination.

Of course, he did it on his terms. Jupiter was too independent to be anybody's lackey. He dutifully carried me over hill and dale and post and rail, but only after I'd spent an hour trying to catch him. When I fell off on my first fox hunt, Jupiter galloped away, totally unremorseful. "If you're not good enough to stay with me, that's your problem," he seemed to say.

Jupiter wasn't above asserting his independence in the show ring, either. Every so often, he would refuse a fence just to remind me that I rode—and won—at his sufferance. Most of the time, though, he suffered me to win, providing me with a wall full of ribbons and a truckload of silver trays, plates and goblets.

He ran away from me in the pasture, he ran away with me in the hunting field and he lorded over the dogs and the other horses with his well-aimed kicks, so why did we love him so? It was his indomitable spirit. When it came to that go-for-the-gold, never-say-die, thrill-of-a-lifetime effort, the Black Stallion had nothing on Jupiter.

Jupiter had the right stuff and he knew it, too. I rode that little pony over a lot of fences that I'd hesitate to jump with a horse today. Daddy saw him jump out of a paddock over a four-foot fence in the snow one time, then make a circle and jump back in, just for fun. His exuberance was excessive at times, but you had to love him for it.

There was talk of selling Jupiter when I outgrew him. After all, ponies are expensive pets and they live forever. But it never quite happened.

My friendship with Jupiter actually deepened in high school. Some afternoons I took off cross-country on Jupiter and dealt with the disappointments of teenage life. So what if I didn't get chosen to be a cheerleader? So what if the wrong fellow asked me to the dance? I didn't have time to practice being peppy or agonize over adolescent crushes with a barn full of horses to ride.

Soon it was college and marriage and talk of the day when my little girl would have Jupiter to ride. But instead of a daughter, I had a divorce.

Divorce was still somewhat scandalous in those days and I wrestled with guilt and feelings of failure. One afternoon, I tacked up Jupiter for a long ride. He didn't look much like the magic-carpet steed of my childhood, with his shaggy brown winter coat. He was well into middle age and had mellowed a bit, but I thought he could still save the Alamo. Sure enough, the moment I got on him and felt that familiar step, I was flooded with a feeling of security.

As I began making a life of my own, I found that Jupiter was not just a solace in troubled times, but a role model.

Jupiter never asked how high the fences were or whom he had to beat. He just jumped. After he had demolished the competition in his own division, he cheerfully out-jumped horses that stood a foot taller. Once, I even had the nerve to enter him in a barrel race. When we rode into the ring—a chubby-cheeked girl with pigtails on a fat pony wearing an English saddle—the cowhide cowboys snickered. But Jupiter flew around the course, his little legs a blur as he circled the barrels without even slowing down. He won, beating the state champion barrel racer in the process. It was no more than I expected of him, but those cowboys were flabbergasted.

His attitude rubbed off on me and helped me get my first job. There wasn't even an opening at the local magazine when I called for an interview. Looking like an English pony up against Western horses, I went to see the editor. But, Jupiter-like, I knew I could do the job. The self-confidence must have worked, because the editor hired me.

Years later, my second marriage gave me a second chance at a lot of things, among them recreating my happy childhood. In high spirits, I went to reclaim my pony, who had been loaned to a succession of little girls.

When I found him, I was appalled at the toll the years had taken: He was thin, one ear was crumpled over and he had something wrong with one eye. Furthermore, although it was late summer, he had the long coat of the last winter.

I cried all the way home. When I unloaded him, I really

was afraid he'd keel over and die before I could get him into the barn. I began shoving grain at him and called the veterinarian. Two days of grain feeding later, Jupiter had perked up considerably.

After a week, I couldn't stand it any longer. I got on him. He walked around a bit and then we trotted. Then he broke into a little canter and, to my astonishment, tried to run away. Oh, you spunky pony!

My husband quickly became enamored of the pony, and together we nursed and fed and groomed him. For three years, I enjoyed seeing my old pony in the pasture, knowing he was loved and well cared for.

Jupiter was twenty-eight the day he lay down in a quiet corner of the pasture and died.

I spent the day much as anyone making funeral arrangements for a loved one. I called my husband in tears, and he began to look for a backhoe. Daddy called and we cried together. "Remember the time . . . ?" In between calls, I braided a lock of Jupiter's tail to keep.

Daddy came over for the wake and we told Jupiter stories. I kept waiting for the neighbors to come calling with pies and hams.

I got out some old pictures, but the best images were in our minds. Daddy shook his head and laughed occasionally at some memory. And we all got choked up. I'd never seen my daddy cry before. In fact, I wondered a bit at his sentimentality, driving thirty miles on a weeknight just to talk about an old pony.

"I'll always picture him jumping the paddock fence in the snow," Daddy said. "You know, that pony had more heart than any horse I've ever seen. He had to, because he didn't have enough leg to jump half the things I saw him go over."

"Is that why you never sold him?" I asked. Daddy shrugged sheepishly.

I reminded him of his motto about owning horses: "You should never have a horse that isn't for sale."

"Oh, I put a price on Jupiter," he said. "But fortunately, no one took me up on it." That was the first I'd heard of that. "What were you asking for him?" I inquired.

Daddy smiled, his eyes shining again. "I figured one day that watching you and that biggety little pony take on all comers was worth about a million dollars. Maybe nine hundred thousand. I didn't want to be unreasonable."

Robin Traywick Williams

Handled with Care

The name Buttercup evoked visions of a small, butter-yellow flower. The horse with the same name couldn't have been more different.

My daughter Lauren is six years old. Three months premature, she was diagnosed with spastic diplegia, a form of cerebral palsy. Lauren uses a walker for mobility. Her balance is too poor for Lofstrand crutches. Now, though, after a surgery meant to reduce her high muscle tone, Lauren's balance should get better. Horseback riding will be her first true test.

Therapeutic horseback riding is Lauren's release. It gives her something to do on a weekly basis that most children only dream of doing.

Her first horse, Robin, was a rather smallish pony. Brown with white spots, Robin plodded along faithfully week after week. The next year, Lauren rode Jeannie, the one-eyed wonder, gentle and small. She rode Jeannie up until the time of her surgery. For about ten weeks, she did not ride at all, then in the fall, she returned in time for the last lesson before the year-end show.

It was then that Lauren met Buttercup, who is well-groomed, caramel in color and BIG. So much for my image of delicate yellow flowers.

Lauren seemed calm about the whole idea of riding a big horse. I, on the other hand, was busy trying not to have a heart attack.

I have trusted these virtual strangers with the safety of my daughter, but now I questioned putting her on the back of this big horse. My sanity was intact. I was calm, cool and outwardly in control. With that reality check, I decided I had good reason to be worried.

"Where's Jeannie?" I asked, trying to keep the quiver of nervousness out of my voice.

"Jeannie has a sore foot."

Buttercup was led around the ring a couple of times to warm her up in preparation for Lauren's lesson. This gave me a chance to see the horse in action. She appeared calm enough. Her eyes were kind. No doubt about it, Buttercup was beautiful and big.

Lauren was thrilled. Her little body stiffened with excitement as it always does when she is happy about something.

Buttercup was brought around to stand in front of us. I swallowed my reservations and fear and lifted Lauren onto Buttercup's broad back. Marcella, the occupational therapist, rounded up Lauren's side walkers as Buttercup craned her neck as if she was checking out my daughter. With the zeal she normally shows, Lauren snatched up the rainbow reins and placed her hands on the green section. Her side walkers were prepared, arms up, with Lauren's legs pinned beneath their forearms to prevent her from sliding off.

"Have fun," I croaked, heart pounding. As she rode around the ring, Buttercup behaved herself. Lauren looked so tiny on her back. Once, twice they circled. Lauren sat up straight and tall. My heart pumped with every hoof fall, though I knew Lauren's side walkers would prevent her from slipping off. Still, she is my baby. My only child.

At the far end of the ring, they stopped. Usually this meant that Lauren was leaning too far to one side in the saddle. To my eye, she was still sitting straight. I wondered why they stopped and watched as Marcella spoke to Lauren a bit. As they started moving again, to my disbelief, the side-walkers LET GO.

Marcella! You're joking, right? I wanted to shout. Why didn't someone warn me that they were going to do this? Don't they know heart attacks can happen anywhere, to anyone at anytime? Lauren sat straight and tall, as proud as a peacock of her accomplishment and newfound freedom. Buttercup calmly chewed her cud, or whatever horses do, and around the ring they walked, Marcella talking to Lauren the whole time. I smiled to greet Lauren's wide look-at-me-Mom grin. All the while my heart was beating hard, not from fear now, but from excitement and joy and, yes, pride.

When the lesson finally ended and I stood at Lauren's side waiting to catch her as she dismounted, I knew Lauren had made great strides forward that day. The days of side walkers would be over soon. It was a sign of healing. Her surgery had now been proven a success.

Lauren slid off into my arms and begged to pet Buttercup. I reached out as well, rubbing the horse's proud arched neck. I wondered if Buttercup understood the gift she had given my daughter. I owed much to the horse and to those who sponsor her so that she is fed and cared for throughout the winter.

Buttercup bobbed her head and looked back at Lauren and me. Maybe she did understand. Thank you, Buttercup, for carrying my princess gently.

Sandra Moore

To Chutney, with Love

A light hand is one which never feels the contact of the bit with the bars.

François Robichon de la Guérinière

There is an ancient proverb that advises us to "hold a true friend with both your hands." Centuries after that line was written, its advice still rings true. In our busy, chaotic world, a trusted friend is like a fine gem. I'm fortunate to have one such gem in my life—a beautiful mare by the name of Chutney.

In the beginning, Chutney and I were clearly a mismatched pair. I was a shy, insecure teenager; she was a fiery, opinionated mare. Diagnosed with scoliosis, I was forced to wear a back brace for three years. It was a clumsy apparatus that caused me to become the laughingstock of my junior high school class. It was not uncommon to hear kids ridiculing me as I walked by. Some would even go so far as to knock on the brace. Needless to say, whatever self-esteem I did have, plummeted as a result.

Riding was meant to be my escape from such problems. I began the sport at age thirteen, a relatively "advanced" starting age. In the beginning, I rode at a small, backyard-type barn and competed in the friendly atmosphere of 4-H sorts of shows. As I advanced, my pony and I moved to a large hunter and equitation barn, where my lack of skills became apparent. I was a low intermediate at best, while the majority of my new stablemates were elegant equitation riders who had been involved in the sport since toddlerhood. Many competed regularly at high-caliber competition, far beyond my abilities.

The granddaughter of a racing legend, Chutney had been purchased as a weanling at the prestigious Keeneland sale and she had been brought along steadily by a professional. A "hot" horse, she was accustomed to a precise, accurate ride that would best showcase her talents and athleticism. She was far too advanced for me at the time. Nonetheless, I fell in love with her on the spot.

She was stunning, a flashy blood bay with the most expressive, feminine face I'd ever seen and powerful yet floaty gaits. She jumped with her knees up to her nose and with a round bascule that threw you right up out of the saddle. I liked the fact that she was a challenge. A true diva, she'd pin her ears at any horse that passed by.

Showing Chutney was a valuable, though sometimes frustrating, learning experience. She wasn't about to put up with novice mistakes. If I asked her for a certain distance to a fence, she took it, right or wrong. Automatic lead changes? Out of the question. If I asked too roughly, she'd hop; if I didn't ask firmly enough, she'd fail to swap behind. This mare was a perfectionist, which was the one trait we shared. Perfectionism aside, we somehow complemented each other. Where I was weak, Chutney was strong; where I was shy, she was bold.

When I rode her the way she demanded to be ridden—relaxed, with a soft leg, hand and seat—she could, and did, win with the best of them. If I made mistakes, however, she'd express her displeasure, which was usually enough to keep us out of the ribbons. Our show results were based upon how I rode on that particular day, so it was not uncommon for us to be champions one weekend and come home empty-handed the next. These were great lessons beyond the show ring. Life, as we all know, is what you make of it. It's also a series of ups and downs.

While I was riding with an extremely difficult trainer who told me that Chutney and I would never be a suitable pair, a well-known professional rider came to visit the barn. When the pro rode Chutney, he agreed that she was a very complicated ride for an amateur. However, as soon as my trainer left the ring, the rider took me aside and whispered, "I really like this horse, you know. These other kids will learn to look pretty. You, however, will learn to ride." With his words of encouragement, I became even more determined to ride this horse well.

Chutney has been with me through all of the milestones in my life—first prom, SATs, college acceptances, first car, and when my first book was accepted for publication. When my father died of a heart attack when I was eighteen years old, I once again found comfort by Chutney's side. And when the pressures of showing became too much, we'd often sneak across the street into an open field, where we galloped to our hearts' content.

We know each other as well as any lifelong friends do. I know that she loves peppermints but won't give sugar cubes a second thought. I know that she'd give anything to stand outside during a rainstorm, and that when she curls her upper lip, it's a sign that she's not feeling well. And she knows that I sometimes take life, especially riding, a bit too seriously. Whenever I'm feeling low or insecure, I bury my face in her wonderful neck and feel as if nothing in the world could ever hurt me.

Even after being my friend and riding partner for fifteen years, my beloved mare continues to teach me. I recently took up dressage after years in hunters and equitation. As we competed in our first Training Level test, I began to put the familiar pressure on myself. I tensed up and Chutney, in typical fashion, reacted to it by throwing out a huge buck right in front of the judge's box. Years ago, I probably would have cried. Now, sitting on the back of my twenty-two-year-old friend, I could only laugh. It was as if Chutney, in all her wisdom, was saying to me, "It's only a show. Lighten up! It's our friendship that matters." Once again, she was right.

Together we have shared victories and disappointments; celebrated love and lamented loss; and have been there for each other through thick and thin. And somewhere along the way, a shy, insecure teenager became a confident writer, and a novice rider became a capable and effective horsewoman. I'd be lying if I didn't credit much of that success to Chutney.

Regardless of whatever success I've had, I sometimes get that familiar twinge of insecurity. On these occasions, I head straight to Chutney's stall and wrap my arms around her neck—and once again, I feel completely safe and secure, for Chutney is the type of friend that's worth holding onto—with both hands.

Kimberly Gatto

New Life for Rosie

"Mommy, Mommy, can we please keep her?" pleaded my daughter Jackie as the beautiful white pony nudged her pockets looking for treats. Rosie was every little girl's dream pony. She had a beautiful face with big, inquisitive brown eyes and long white eyelashes.

"I'm really in a pinch here," said the young owner. "I'm leaving for college in four days and she can't stay here. There's no shelter and no one can drive out here to feed her. I just need to find her a good home. She's a wonderful horse, I promise!"

"But we haven't even ridden her," I argued.

"Just take her home and try her. You won't be sorry."

"Oh, please, Mommy! I love her! I can't believe it, we're both ten years old!"

I sighed. I was outnumbered.

We moved Rosie to an old dairy farm, where the retired farmer rented out pastures to a few horses. We couldn't catch her during her first couple of days in the pasture. She was having fun, galloping past us with her tail flying. In no time, Jackie—and sometimes her younger sister Chelsea—was riding Rosie around the pasture and on the adjacent trails through the falling leaves for endless hours of fun. Jackie and Rosie were quite a pair. They dressed up for a neighborhood holiday parade and we brought our precious little pony a treat of warm mash on Christmas morning.

Finally, the days were getting warmer and longer and Jackie was making plans for summer fun with Rosie. She had become a member of our family and Jackie's dream of having her own pony had finally come true. Rosie seemed happy, too. It had been a wet and warm spring, making the endless acres of new grass especially luscious. When Rosie wasn't off on adventures with Jackie and Chelsea, she was eating. She had a grass belly, but she wasn't the fattest horse in the pasture, so I wasn't especially concerned.

One day I got the call that every horse owner dreads. "You better come have a look at Rosie," said Roy, one of the other horse owners. "She doesn't want to walk, and she leans back when she's standing. She doesn't seem to want to put any weight on her front feet, but I don't see any signs of any injury."

I thanked Ray and rushed out to the farm. After seeing Rosie, I called our veterinarian. He told me to take her out of the pasture and put her into a smaller space until he could get there. When he arrived, it didn't take him long to diagnose her with laminitis, a condition that affects the internal structures of the hoof. Indeed, Rosie's hooves were very hot and she was leaning back in an effort to take as much weight as possible off of her painful front hooves.

"How did this happen?" I asked Dr. Pickering.

"Marla, simply put, the horse overloads on rich food, which can't be digested normally. A fermentation process in the intestines produces a toxin that enters the bloodstream. The entire body is affected, but certain sensitive structures in the hoof are most prone to damage. When it is extensive, the coffin bone within the hoof can lose its attachment to the hoof wall, and that's very serious."

Dr. Pickering hesitated, then continued. "Sometimes, it even causes the hoof to fall off. Hopefully, we caught this case early enough. Be sure to continue her on these medications and keep her on the diet I've outlined. You'll have to keep her in this small paddock for the next few weeks. Call me if there are any changes at all. Keep me posted, Marla."

Rosie did not like being separated from her little herd and she especially didn't enjoy her new diet. She repeatedly tried to tell us it was all a big mistake.

"Gee, Mom," said Jackie, "I wish there was some way to explain to her that this is for her own good."

"I know, it's pretty frustrating, but she's getting so much better, and we can put some special shoes on her and maybe start riding her again if she continues to improve."

During the sixth week, Rosie got her shoes with a special cushioning on the sole. It looked like she'd be good to go for the summer. But unfortunately, that was not the case.

"Look Mom, Rosie's lying down," my youngest daughter Chelsea exclaimed. It was a hot midday in May and it seemed a bit odd that she would be lying flat out in the middle of her paddock. She didn't look up as we approached.

"Something's wrong—dreadfully wrong. I'm calling the vet," I said.

"It's very hot, try putting some wet towels on her until I get there," advised Dr. Pickering.

We were all glad we could do something helpful while we waited. The veterinarian arrived in no time. "She's crashed," he said. "I had hoped this wouldn't happen. It's impossible to predict which direction laminitis will take. This isn't good, Marla. She might survive today, but her feet may never recover. You might have to consider some other options. Even if we pull her through, she may be unable to walk for the rest of her life."

Dr. Pickering worked tirelessly on Rosie throughout the hot afternoon. We kept busy fetching equipment, holding tubes and refreshing the wet towels. Jackie spent most of her time comforting Rosie through her tears. "Please girl, don't give up. You'll be okay, Rosie. I'll take care of you." Once in a while, Rosie would let out a big sigh. We knew she was in a lot of pain.

Hours later, as the sun was getting lower in the sky, Dr.

Pickering said, "We need to move Rosie. Can she stay in that enclosure next to the barn?"

"Sure," I said, "but how are we going to get her in there?"

"We're going to have to help her the best we can," he replied.

We pleaded with her to get up. She didn't want to step on those tender hooves, but the four of us couldn't carry her. As a last resort, Dr. Pickering picked up her leg and started moving her hooves one step at a time. We did our best to lead her and encourage her and discourage her from lying down. Finally, we made it to the stall that would be her home for the next few months.

"Now you'll have to watch her carefully. She'll need a shot twice a day at first along with these other oral medications. Can you give shots?"

No, I thought. "I'll learn," I said.

"There's one other thing," our veterinarian said, out of earshot of my daughters. "There may come a time when it's too much to ask from Rosie. It may be too much suffering with very little chance of recovery. She may get an infection in her feet. Horses aren't meant to lie down this much. They can develop sores."

"How will I know?" I asked.

"Rosie will let you know," he said. "She'll groan from the pain and she won't be able to get up. She'll let you know when she can't take any more."

Armed with Rosie's multiple treatments and medications, I almost felt hopeless as I watched our veterinarian drive away.

"She'll be okay, Mommy. Don't worry," reassured Jackie when she saw my face. "We'll take care of her. I love her, Mommy. Rosie has to get better."

"We'll do whatever we can. I promise. Now let's get home to get some rest. She's resting peacefully now."

Jackie and Chelsea spent that evening decorating get-well posters for Rosie. The next morning we went to see her and

I gave her the daily medications while the girls hung their signs and posters.

"I know she can't read, Mom," said Jackie, "but I want her to know we're thinking about her when we're not here. It'll make her feel better."

For those first couple of weeks, she didn't show much interest in anything, but she didn't seem to be getting any worse. The veterinarian's words echoed in my mind when I asked, "What if she's in too much pain?" He said I would know.

In the evening, like wolves at the door, a pack of coyotes watched us from across the meadow. Would they come close to the barn? Rosie was unable to defend herself in this weakened state. Was she safe?

Each day, as we arrived at the barn, I started making excuses to keep the girls in the car for a few minutes while I checked on Rosie's condition. I wanted to protect them from the worst. Rosie would glance my way from her stall floor, but when she would see my daughter Jackie come around the corner of the barn, she would struggle to her feet and give a soft nicker. The sparkle would return to Rosie's eyes and I knew this little pony had a chance. But that entire summer we had no idea what each morning would bring.

We had to rebandage her feet every few days with layers of pads and multiple layers of wrap. We worked quickly because it was so painful for her to bear the extra weight on the resting foot while we lifted the one being bandaged. We became quite proficient with the routine. We were Rosie's pit crew.

"Jackie, will you please crush Rosie's pills and mix them with molasses for her before we go?" I asked one morning.

"I already gave them to her," said Jackie. "She eats them out of my hand if I feed them to her one at a time."

The pills were enormous and obviously tasted terrible to Rosie. Most horse owners had to find increasingly clever ways to disguise the taste, and here was Rosie eating them whole when they were offered by Jackie. Because they were offered by Jackie. No one, including Dr. Pickering, could believe how much trust this little pony held in my little girl.

It took more than a year, marred by setbacks, but eventually Rosie's entire front hooves regrew. It took a dedicated veterinarian and a talented farrier and a whole lot of love to get Rosie back on her feet again. And it took a little girl who never stopped believing in her and never stopped encouraging her. It took Jackie.

Jackie showed Rosie at 4-H that spring. Eventually, when Chelsea grew to Jackie's size, Rosie carried her, too, on a couple of Pony Club ratings, which included jumping. Now, Rosie works at our horse camps for five weeks during the summer, taking young horse lovers on some of their first equestrian adventures. Her feet still require special shoes and more frequent shoeing and we pay extra attention to her diet.

Both Rosie and Jackie have reached the age of seventeen together. I have no doubt that the reason Rosie is with us today is because of the total love and devotion supplied by a girl named Jackie who simply wouldn't give up on the incredible heart and spirit she knew existed in her little pony. It was a spirit that Jackie could somehow see in Rosie's eyes.

My youngest daughter Chelsea—who is now riding Rosie and is responsible for her care as her older sister Jackie gets ready for college—put it best when she said, "What I learned from this experience is quite simple—that animals know when you love them."

Rosie is alive today because my daughter believed in her and because she believed in my daughter. As any mother, I always want to see things in my daughters that fill me with pride and wonder. I still remember the get-well posters my girls made for Rosie and realize that they had hope when mine was failing. They showed compassion and helped ease Rosie's suffering. And they learned how trust can be a powerful medicine as Rosie's soft lips took the bitter pills from my daughter's hands and ate them.

What my daughters did for Rosie was to give her back her life. What Rosie did for my daughters was teach them powerful lessons of trust and compassion that will shine on everyone around them for the rest of their lives. I never anticipated when I brought this little white pony into our lives what an incredible gift my family was receiving.

Marla Oldenburg with Bill Goss

Lessons from Lou

A single tear rolled down Lou's face as I talked to her about that boy. Maybe I shouldn't have been surprised by her show of emotion, but Lou was my Quarter Horse mare, and that boy was King, her handsome five-week-old colt.

My husband had bought Lou, a retired racehorse, to occupy my time and mind while I waited out medical disability with a minor heart condition. Lou was four and a half months pregnant, and we both felt stymied by inactivity. Still, we needed to take it easy for a while, and although I couldn't ride, I showered her with love.

Lou had an impressive pedigree, and even with a sway-back pulled low by her ever-growing belly, she was regal. I knew her foal would be spectacular.

We drifted through the days, settling into a comfortable routine while my children were in school. I brushed Lou and scratched her growing belly while I talked and sang to her and cooed to her baby. It seemed to soothe Lou when I sang. I rubbed her head, lightly touching my nose to hers and breathing deeply, willing my spirit and soul into her.

A few weeks before Lou's delivery date, I visited with her former owner. He warned that she might be moody and shield her baby from me. I didn't believe him. He knew Lou as a racehorse. I knew her as a cherished friend. Over the next few days, I watched and waited, wanting to be at her side when she gave birth. Our veterinarian, who had been coming monthly, then weekly, now came almost daily.

Lou waited until we were gone one evening to have her baby. When we drove in, the car's headlights caught the blaze on her face. She seemed to be calling to me, "Come see what I did!"

Then I saw him. A tiny light sorrel colt with a star and a strip on his face and four tiny white stockings on his legs. He was lying on the other side of Lou, peeking out from under her belly. It was love at first sight. I felt as if he were my baby. I walked to the gate, just talking to Lou for a few minutes. Then I inched in and over to her side. She watched me, but she didn't make any menacing moves. Still respecting Lou's maternal privileges, I kept my distance from her baby, talking as I would to any newborn. He recognized my voice and fought his way up onto those little wobbly legs, walking around to nuzzle me as Lou watched.

We bonded closely, Lou, King and I. We were three imperfect creatures sharing one perfect love—an innocent, childlike love that was complete and unconditional. As the days wore on, it became obvious that something was wrong. King's umbilical cord wasn't sealing off as it should and he didn't have the energy to nurse. Although he shadowed his mother, every movement took great effort.

I talked with our veterinarian, who was making frequent visits to check on King. He tried to be encouraging, but the truth was, the chances for recovery weren't good. King had navel ill, a serious blood infection that can occur in newborn animals when bacteria enter the body through the umbilical cord. It typically results in rapid debilitation and usually death.

When King was five weeks old, it was obvious his pain was getting worse. His suffering was comparable to that of a person stricken with severe rheumatoid arthritis. Although the veterinarian gave him cortisone injections to lessen the pain, they never helped for long. The kind practitioner offered me time to think, but there really wasn't anything to think about. I shared King's pain and loved him too much to allow him to suffer. I had kept him alive, hoping, but any longer would be cruel.

On a beautiful, sunny spring morning, with the Houston air still crisp and the world full of new beginnings, I decided on an ending.

First, I talked with Lou. We were both mothers, and my heart ached for her suffering. They say nothing hurts as much as losing a child, and I felt we were both losing one. Although I didn't know how much she could comprehend, I knew Lou was distressed. Her anxious glances in King's direction told me she understood too much to ignore.

I walked over to her hay-strewn stall while the veterinarian talked softly to King. Lou's intelligent eyes examined my tear-stained face as I explained that King was very sick and the doctor was going to take good care of him. I told her we would miss him, she and I. Together, we watched the veterinarian administer the injection that would bring King peace.

I rubbed Lou's velvety muzzle, and she softly snorted. Then I saw the tear roll down her face. We put our heads together and stayed that way for a long while.

When King was finally out of pain, his spirit set free, my husband and I took his body to the back of our pasture to his freshly dug grave, which was under a tree showing the new growth of the season. Lou stood beside me, as still as stone. She watched silent and sad as we gently lowered her baby into the ground.

I stood by the small mound, quietly sobbing. Then the ground around me began to shake with the rhythmic pounding of hooves. Lou circled the pasture, beating the turf hard and solid. She threw her head back, whinnying in the air. Wondering whether she had gone mad, my husband questioned what she was doing.

Through streaming tears, I answered. "She's grieving."

However, I wonder if maybe a little sorrel colt, with a star and a strip and four white stockings, his mane blowing in the evening breeze, ran beside his mama. And if, just maybe, Lou felt King's free gentle spirit racing beside her in the wind.

Edwina Lewis

Bit by the Bug Thanks to Finger Paint

It was a mildly toasty fall afternoon when my mom and I pulled up to my little sister's day-care center to pick her up, just as we did every day. The sized-down schoolhouse sat at the front of a huge farm edged with a crisp white fence. As the tires crunched the gravel driveway, I leaned my head against the car window, closed my eyes and invited the warm rays of sun to dance on my face. The next few moments were so predictable that I knew there would be no reason to open my eyes. The car would stop with a little squeak. My sister would skip from the front door of the day-care building to the car, waving some sort of macaroni artwork and humming an annoying cartoon theme that would repeat like a broken record in my head until I went to sleep. The car door would open, allowing the chatter of chirping birds to flood the hushed interior. I'd soon hear a shuffle as my sister scampered up to her seat. The door would slam and we'd drive away, but only after my mom honked the horn.

This day would be different.

"Oh my goodness," I heard my mom whisper. I opened my eyes and followed her gaze to the front door of the day-care building. A little girl in a yellow dress with disheveled blonde hair and streaks of paint blazing across her face like an extremely colorful army commando scampered up to the car holding her teacher's hand. As the pair came closer, I recognized the mess in a dress as my little sister in disguise.

"Mom, come see. It was finger-painting day!" my sister shrieked with excitement.

"You have quite the finger-painting artist here," affirmed her teacher. "The masterpieces are still a little wet, so we're not letting them go home today, but they are on display."

Powerless against the coercive tactics of the finger-painting artiste extraordinaire, my mom parked the car and followed my bouncing sibling into the gallery. Given this opportunity to scan the grounds of the farm as I leaned against the car, I realized what a great exploration site this would be. The thick, gnarled trees were practically calling my name, inviting me to climb up their branches. I figured my mom would be a while, judging by my sister's exuberance, so I ventured out beyond the day care's boundaries.

Fluttering around the farm like a butterfly riding invisible currents of wind, I ended up in front of a solid wooden gate. On the other side, a vast expanse of sweet-smelling grass and dozens of horses invited me closer. Back at home, I would sometimes pet the neighbor's horses when they hung their heads over the fence to peek in on our backyard family picnics and talent shows. That was the extent of my interaction with these hooved beauties.

I stifled my initial impulse to slip under the fence and boldly cavort with these unfamiliar animals. Instead, I carefully climbed up the fence and sat along the top of the gate. Although I tried to move stealthily, the horses noticed my characteristic lack of grace and subtlety. Some of them popped their heads up from grazing and shot suspicious stares my way. They were eager to continue stuffing their already swollen bellies, so I was able to return to my curious observations undisturbed.

It didn't take long for a chestnut mare with a gray streak in her tail to waddle over (she was quite fat) and welcome me. Not sure how to respond to her surprisingly friendly nuzzles, I jumped to my feet in case I had to run. Then I reached over the fence and allowed my fingers to brush her nose. She tickled my hand with her whiskers. A sudden wave of courage swept through me as I pulled myself back up onto the fence. The mare took a few steps forward, guiding my hands to her long, muscular neck. She welcomed my pats and scratches and, pretty soon, we were engaged in a silent conversation.

After a few minutes of chatting with her, my inhibitions disappeared and I began to wonder what it would be like to gently grab my new friend's mane, slip onto her back and cruise around the pasture.

Looking back on this experience, I don't recall one ounce of doubt or hesitancy. I like to think that the bond formed quickly and with it came unfamiliar confidence and new-found ability.

Before I knew it, my actions zoomed past my thoughts and I slid my right leg over the mare's back, gently rustling her dusty, red coat. The added weight didn't phase the mighty steed. She just stood there, waiting for me to do something.

I think I sat there for about two minutes before my mom came storming out of the day-care building, hands flailing the air. With a hushed but firm voice she tried not to startle my mount while emphatically demanding that I get back on the ground. I wanted to do what she asked, but I wasn't sure how to get down. Before I knew it, a man named Jack, who owned the farm, strolled up to the pasture gate, calming my mother along the way.

"Princess will take care of her," he assured us both. "She's been around the block a time or two."

His weathered hands helped me down, and before I could extend my arm to give Princess's neck a grateful pat, my mom had me by the collar.

The moments that followed went just as you'd suspect. Through the well-deserved verbal lashing (which continued through the drive home and into the night), I peeked over my mom's shoulder and saw Princess standing in the place where I'd left her. She didn't even blink at all of the commotion.

As my mom dragged me back to the car, my teary-eyed sister following behind, I wish I could say I carefully listened to every word like a dutiful daughter, but I'd be lying.

On this day, the car door slammed and we drove away without my mom honking the horn. Although she had no idea how the past fifteen minutes eventually would shape our lives (and our pocketbooks), she noticed something different about me as I stared out the window, desperately trying to catch one last glimpse of my new friend. If she would have stopped screaming, I probably could have told her about the bug that bit me.

All horse lovers know the bug. It doesn't buzz or chirp or hop around. It doesn't stare back at you with big bulging eyes. It lands on your heart, does its job and disappears without a trace. You're not left with a painful sting, itch or welt, just an inexplicable passion that shapes your thoughts, your habits and your dreams. The horse bug was now a part of my fabric.

As my sister sobbed in the backseat, I silently thanked her for the finger-painting masterpieces that weren't dry enough to take home that day. And so, the journey began.

Tiernan McKay

His Special Gifts

During the summer of 1998, my eleven-year-old daughter Liz moved up from a pony to her first horse, and she named him Koda. As is the case with many little girls and their first horses, Liz and Koda immediately bonded and became inseparable.

That fall, after a ride with a friend, Liz did not get the gate latched all the way and the following morning she found that Koda had gotten into the grain. He didn't show any signs of developing founder—an internal deformity of the hoof that is the end result of a complex series of events triggered by overeating. But he had eaten a great deal, so we thought it best to call the veterinarian and take him in to be checked over. Koda was sent home with instructions to keep him moving. If he didn't founder by the weekend, he would be all right.

The weekend came and we thought we were home free. Think again. Sunday morning, Koda was stiff and sore and could not get around. He had foundered. The veterinarian was called, and this time we had medicine to administer, and orders to walk him every two hours and give him shots every four hours.

Liz was devastated. Her horse was dangerously ill and it was because of something careless she had done. She slept with Koda while we took turns on the couch, getting up every two hours. When it rained, she walked him inside the barn. She did everything in her little-girl powers to encourage him to eat. But he steadily got worse.

Neither Liz nor this little horse would give up. He responded only to her. Only she could get him to lift his head or stand. He would nicker for her when she was not there. I would look out the window to see him lying in the yard with his head in her lap and her tears falling on his face. I prayed to God to please not separate these two.

After two weeks and no sign of improvement, our veterinarian suggested that we put Koda down. My daughter was hysterical and I asked him if there was anything else we could do. He told us about a Mennonite horseshoer by the name of Mr. Martin, who lived three hours away and who was known to have had some success saving foundered horses.

After talking it over with Liz's grandpa, we called Mr. Martin and described the devotion of this little girl to her horse, and how hard both were trying. We explained that he was our last hope for pulling Koda through. Without hesitating, Mr. Martin simply said, "Bring him down and let me take a look at him."

The next day, my daughter met her hero. When we arrived at Mr. Martin's, Koda wasn't able to stand in the trailer. The kind horseshoer looked Koda over carefully and in words that were music to our ears, said that he thought he could save this horse. He explained to Liz that she had to be willing to work hard because things were going to get worse before they got better. Liz told him that she would do whatever it would take and, given the sacrifices she already had made, I had no doubt that she would.

With Liz's commitment made, Mr. Martin and his sons welded metal plates onto the bottom of the horseshoes. They applied a homemade concoction to Koda's hooves, then packed them with cotton and nailed on the shoes. Koda was hauled to Mr. Martin's every two weeks for his hooves to be trimmed and the procedure to be repeated. This biweekly regimen went on for three months, then it became every four weeks, then every six weeks for an entire year.

Liz followed every instruction that Mr. Martin gave her, and Koda did everything that Liz wanted him to. With time and lots of love, Koda healed completely and you would never know that he had foundered. Mr. Martin now admits that he wasn't sure Koda was going to make it. What he did know without a doubt, was that Koda would give it his best to stay with his girl.

I think God has a special place in his heart for a mother's prayers and little girls and their horses. He's given men like Mr. Martin extraordinary knowledge and empathy to do good work, and he's blessed us with the power of love. Because of his special gifts, Liz and Koda are inseparable to this day.

Debbie Hollandsworth

Horse at Harvard

Legally Blonde's Elle Woods had her Chihuahua called Bruiser. I have a young Hanoverian gelding named Donovan. So when Harvard Law School accepted me into its fall 2002 entering class, I never questioned whether Donovan would go with me.

As a college student at the small-town, agricultural University of California at Davis, I always had a horse with me, always rode every day, always competed during the school year. Except, that is, for my first quarter, which, not coincidentally, was the least-happy term of an otherwise enjoyable undergraduate career. So I was no stranger to juggling competitions with term papers, veterinary emergencies with final exams and training with daily reading. *I had always done this*, I thought, *what could be so different?*

Turns out, a lot of people thought it would be different. When I told friends and acquaintances, even other students I rode with at Davis, that I planned to take my horse with me to law school, their reaction was invariably, "You're crazy!" "It won't last!" "You can't possibly ride every day while in law school, and especially not at Harvard!" The other law students at Harvard, many of them from big cities, were equally disbelieving. "A horse," they would say in surprise, "How cool! Do you have time to see him most weekends?"

"No," I'd say, "I'm at the barn six days a week!" Then I'd try very hard not to leave a trail of mud from my paddock boots in the dorm hallways and I always removed the horsehair from the washing machines after laundering saddle pads and polo wraps.

But as the semester progressed, I began wondering if everyone was right. Life was so busy! The owner of the barn said she was taking bets on when I was going to collapse. Was I really crazy to try to do this? Then I began to realize that it didn't matter. My friends at the law school would get burned out from the daily pressure of endless reading and paper writing. And I would too. I'd despair that there was no way I could ever do all this work and come out alive. Then I'd go to the barn. Donovan would be there, waiting for me with a look that seemed to say, "What took you so long? I've missed you! Do you have any sugar cubes for me?" I'd groom him, and as I curried his shiny black coat, law school would seem farther and farther away. Then I'd lead him to the mounting block and law school would vanish from my thoughts altogether.

For an hour each day, Donovan and I are the only ones in the world. We ride a supple shoulder-in, a floating medium trot, find that perfect distance to a square oxer or hack through the woods. *Promissory estoppel, res ipsa loquitur, in rem jurisdiction*—who's worried about any of that? All I know is that I am calm, focused and at peace. I am whole.

And each day, upon return to my dorm in Cambridge, the work I had left to do always seems far less daunting, much more doable, even more engaging. I come home every day with renewed serenity and zest for my studies that many law students around me sadly never find.

All during that first semester, widely thought to be the most difficult of three years of law school, I continued to see Donovan nearly every day of the week. His training contin-ued to progress. Twice we met our Los Angeles-based trainer six hours away in New Jersey for a weekend of con-centrated instruction. I even drove Donovan by myself, twelve hours each way, to Virginia to compete in a year-end championship. And we finished reserve champion, a mere fraction of a percentage away from the champion. Much to everyone's surprise, I did all this while keeping up with my daily reading, finishing all my assignments on time, going to class religiously and giving respectable answers when called on by professors using the dreaded Socratic method.

Now that I'm finished with the first semester, I realize that I didn't make it through my first term at Harvard Law *in spite of* having a horse. I made it through *because of* having a horse. Unlike my peers, I have a daily opportunity to escape the stress of school and city life. I have something that relaxes and rejuvenates me and makes me excited to get out of bed in the morning. For this, I realize I am very fortunate. Thank you, Donovan. Thank you for helping me thrive at Harvard Law School.

Jennifer Chong

Tall in Faith

At four pounds, five ounces, umbilical cord wrapped around her neck and delivered five and a half weeks early, Ashley seemed to have more than three strikes against her. Diagnosed with Turner's syndrome and Ollier's disease at age three, this happy-go-lucky child showed little evidence of having endured the trying time of diagnosis and then daily growth-hormone injections and medication to keep her thyroid under control. Her prognosis was good, and although Turner's syndrome could be cruel, Ashley was spared, with only short stature and thyroid disease.

Life seemed to be relatively normal for Ashley until fifth grade, the age where all youngsters seem to hit a growth spurt. Ashley was left behind. She not only felt small in stature, but with all of the kids teasing her, she began to feel small in worth. Ashley was starting to withdraw. As her mother, I was worried. Would she snap out of this funk or would it follow her forever? I had to find a way for her to find herself and be happy with herself.

We had always had horses. Before Ashley and her younger sister Casey were born, my husband and I raised Quarter Horses. After our divorce, I managed to hang on to four precious equine family members. Even though they were the kindest of animals, they were just too big for the girls. I found a riding instructor and the girls began taking riding lessons. This seemed to be a positive experience for Ashley. It didn't matter to these animals that she was smaller than other children. In fact, the horses kind of liked it that way.

Ashley had discovered her passion, but something was still missing. While around the horses, she was bright and happy, but back at school she would retreat into her quiet little world. Ashley didn't have any friends and her grades were barely passing. Then I had a crazy idea. Maybe a pony of her own would give Ashley that friend she so desperately needed.

The search began. On my income as a single parent with a child with more than her share of medical bills, I knew we could not afford a show-ring hunter pony. So we decided to look for a companion that would be honest and form a bond with this child who so needed a friend. Days turned into weeks, weeks into months and we just couldn't seem to find that one special horse. I prayed every day, "Lord, I know you know best. If you see that it is the best thing for Ashley, please help us find her a pony to love, one who will love her in return. And God, she sure would like a white one if you could arrange it." I figured if I was going to ask, I might as well go all the way.

We had almost given up hope. I was now ready to buy the first gentle pony that came along because Ashley was losing faith. She wasn't even excited anymore. We were scheduled to go see a pony one afternoon after work when a friend of mine peeked into my office to tell me about a pony that a friend of his was selling. This friend, Mrs. Jones, had brood mares coming in for foaling and she didn't have room for the pony anymore. The pony had been a brood mare, but she didn't particularly like having babies, so she would have to go. I called Mrs. Jones that very minute and set up a time to see her that afternoon. Mrs. Jones asked me several questions over the phone, wanting to make sure that the pony and her rider would be a good match. After I told her about Ashley, she said, "Lucy is definitely the one." She also was within our budget. Then I inquired about the pony's coat color holding my breath. Mrs. Jones replied, "She is considered a gray, but she is actually all white." I tried not to get my hopes up too high because I didn't want Ashley to suffer yet another disappointment.

When we arrived at Mrs. Jones' farm that afternoon, there stood Lucy in all her middle-of-March glory. She was overweight and hadn't yet started to shed her long winter coat. She also looked as if she'd played in a mud puddle. Even so, I saw potential in the Welsh pony. My daughter did not.

"Let's just look," I pleaded. "We're already here." Trying to be a sport and humor her mother who was trying so hard, Ashley reluctantly got out of the car.

The experienced horsewoman that she was, Mrs. Jones recognized that Ashley could not see Lucy past the mud. "Why don't you go catch her and groom her then you can saddle her up and try her out," Mrs. Jones said, trying to encourage the less-than-enthusiastic little girl. That was enough to do it. If this horsewoman trusted her to be able to handle this task, Ashley would show her that she could do it.

Lucy was a trouper and on her best behavior. Did this pony know something that we had not yet realized? Ashley rode the pony mare in a small arena, where she proved to be a solid, if uninspiring, mover. Ashley was still not excited. "Why don't you take her home and try her for a week?" Mrs. Jones asked. "I think Ashley will like her after she rides her a few times." We scheduled a time to pick up Lucy the following evening.

The next evening when I came home for work, I asked Ashley if she was excited. "I guess," came the reply. Had Ashley given up? "Ashley, will you please trust me on this? I just have a feeling that our prayers have been answered." Again, Ashley seemed to humor me, but she also appeared unable to find the courage to get her hopes up. You see, Ashley really had been wishing for an expensive little show pony that would win blue ribbons—a horse we just couldn't afford.

We brought Lucy home for the trial period and after

Ashley rode her, hope turned into love. We made the purchase and our journey began. Spring finally arrived and we discovered there really was a white pony under all of that dirt and hair. Lucy was put on a diet to get her womanly figure back and she and Ashley began their partnership.

We took Lucy and Ashley to their first show—a backyard affair that we thought would be a good testing ground for them both. Ashley had been taking lessons for about a year, and we had found out that Lucy, in her prime, had shown on the "A" circuit. Lucy now had become the instructor because Ashley's skills had to be polished to ride such an experienced pony.

I held my breath during the first class. I was hoping that this pony would take care of my precious cargo. I must say, during the lineup when I was finally able to breathe, I was quite floored when they announced the first-place winner. This was Ashley's first first-place ribbon. The look on her face was worth all the fortunes in the world. After congratulations were extended, I excused myself for a few minutes to go around to the back of the trailer and let my tears of joy finally fall. I also whispered a thankful prayer.

Lucy has been in our lives for more than two years now. The bond and love between Lucy and Ashley is incredible. They have won many ribbons together and won the champion title in their division at the 4-H state fair this year. Ashley has found a sport where being tall doesn't matter and it has filtered over to other areas in her life. Her grades have gone up to honor roll. She is the vice president of her 4-H club. She was voted Student Council class president, has made the high school cheerleading squad, and we just found out yesterday that she has been nominated for the homecoming court.

Once upon a time, it was hard to get this child to go to school, and now she is talking about which college she will attend. One thing hasn't changed, though—Lucy is still her best friend.

Mitzi Santana

"I suppose it wouldn't be a bad job if
they didn't run those steel rods through you."

Carousel Horse. *Reprinted by permission of Steve Sommer and Francis Brummer.* ©2002
Steve Sommer and Francis Brummer.

6

AND . . .
THEY'RE OFF!

In the darkest days of depression and war,
a horse named Seabiscuit elevated
our country's spirit and embodied
the qualities we cherish in our horses;
heart, drive, loyalty, love and playfulness.

We respectfully dedicate this chapter
to the memory of

SEABISCUIT
May 23, 1934–May 17, 1947

A true champion that still inspires us today.

© CORBIS BETTMANN—SEABISCUIT LEADS WAR ADMIRAL BY TWO

An Unlikely Trio of Hope

Horse sense is the thing a horse has which keeps it from betting on people.

W.C. Fields

"Floss, tell me the Biscuit story again, please," I pleaded. To the day she died, none of her grandchildren called my wispy Irish grandmother "nana" or "grandma." She was Floss, short for Florence, to all of us—same as she was to everyone else.

Floss settled back in her chair and her eyes saw something far beyond our tiny living room in Philadelphia. I sat at her feet, ready to travel back in time with her, to relive the magic of her memories.

In the early 1900s, making a place in a new world meant marriage and a family for every beautiful Irish-Catholic girl. Floss was no exception. As the Great Depression gripped our country, Floss struggled, as many did, with raising a large family. Her struggle bore an atypical twist—her husband had left her for another woman.

In those days, few options existed for an abandoned woman raising six children on her own. Fortunately, some of her neighbors suggested an unusual opportunity and before long Floss became a part-time bookie. Her work put food on the table and kept her brood in good graces with people she knew would protect her and her family.

Every time she shared a story from her past, I felt the bittersweet emotion that filled her soul. I knew the empathy she felt for the underdog, empathy engendered from her own experiences. Empathy acquired from doing what had to be done to get by.

I reached up for her hand and squeezed it as much in anticipation of the good story as to let her know I was there. She smiled, squeezing back, then began.

"Lass, the Biscuit was the ugliest horse you'd ever laid a pair of eyes upon. His first race was down in Florida at Hialeah but he didn't break his maiden for another sixteen starts, and almost fifty before he won a race of any consequence."

"First time I heard the name Seabiscuit, some fool wanted a deuce to win in an allowance race at Rockingham. I could tell this fella didn't have that kind of money to be wagering, but I gladly took the bet, thinking of my vig. As I was paying off the win the next day, I remember thinking to myself, *I want to get a look at this Seabiscuit.*" Her eyes twinkled at the memory.

"'Twasn't a problem getting into the barns and paddocks in those days. When Seabiscuit was on the card, I made the races and started paying attention to the Biscuit and his handlers. Pretty soon, I had lots of company."

"The trainer was a ghost of a man—looked like smoke, like death warmed over. That horse was a handful most of the time, and a lazy son of a gun the rest." Shaking her head softly, Floss gave a short chuckle. "The trainer, Smith, he had a gift. You could see that horse and the ghost talking to each other without words. Like both of them knew they were out of second chances and this was the end of the line."

"They had this handsome jockey, a redhead named Cougar, who used to pick up boxing matches when he couldn't find a mount. He was tough as nails and had desperation in his eyes. I knew that look—saw it a lot in those days."

Floss paused, and I knew without her having to say so that the desperation she had seen in the eyes of many during those days had just as often been in her own. She continued, "Turns out Cougar was an Irish who had ended up in Canada. His real name was Johnny Pollard and I don't know whether I was more taken by the horse or the jockey. Both of them had the mischief in their eyes," she chuckled softly again.

"When Pollard was up, the Biscuit settled. Pollard knew the Biscuit's quirks and let him have his rein. He ran like a duck and liked to mess with the other horses—horses do that you know, play with each other. The Biscuit, he'd lay back and let them come right up, side-to-side, get them feeling like the match was theirs, then he'd look them in the eye and take off like a bullet." Floss laughed out loud at that.

"It was something to see, those three. 'Course most folks just saw Cougar and the Biscuit. Only us that liked the ponies paid any attention to Smith."

"Folks who didn't know anything about horses were betting money on the side they didn't have. Naturally, most of the time I was happy taking book on the Biscuit. That horse was a blessing on four feet. Don't know what we would have done if he hadn't come along. Folks loved betting when they were pulling for the underdog. Being the underdog was something they understood."

I nodded.

"Seabiscuit wasn't a sure thing, ran hot and cold for a long time until he came into his own. I think he got bored and liked to stir up the pot now and then. Then that darn Smith would scratch him from big races when folks had traveled hundreds of miles just to see him run."

"Those three—they were fixed on winning and they paid some high prices for that desire, but lassie, they put on a show. They saved a lot of souls in those years. I know some folks believe those souls were damned from doing the jig with the devil and betting good money they didn't have, but that horse gave people something to look forward to, something they could dream about. Never saw so many people without hope get so excited about a horse."

Floss's eyes cleared and she focused on the sights and sounds outside the little living room in Philly.

"Yeah, I fell in love with that horse. Never been another like him before or since, and you know, girl, I've been watching the ponies all my life."

"I know, Floss," I whispered.

"Not another like him," she said again. "Nary a one kept me dreaming or filled me with hope like that, that's for sure."

Theresa Peluso

[AUTHOR'S NOTE: *In November 1938, 40 million people listened to the radio broadcast of Seabiscuit's victory in a much-anticipated matched race with War Admiral. The Biscuit set a track record at Pimlico for the mile and three-sixteenths, winning by four lengths in just a minute fifty-six. Two years later he captured the elusive win at the Santa Anita Handicap and retired to Charles Howard's Ridgewood Ranch where he passed away peacefully in 1947 at the age of fourteen.*]

Ride the Yule Tide

When your ship comes in, it just might be a horse.

Jan Jasion Cross

It was some kind of cosmic thing that took me there. I certainly did not go for the money or the atmosphere. Pocono Downs in late November was, in fact, quite depressing—the temperatures averaged about twenty-five degrees by post time for the first race each evening. Plus, there was a nice, comfortable job waiting for me in Florida for the winter months. A leading New York trainer had offered me a position as an assistant trainer and exercise girl. It was a job I had prayed for. I finally had fallen on my head enough times to realize that my waning career as a jockey was becoming more dangerous than lucrative.

I would have gone straight to Florida and strolled the sunny blessed beaches for a few weeks while I waited for the New York outfit if I hadn't gotten sidetracked by two of my best friends. Russ and Jackie were a hardworking young couple, and I had won a few races on their cheaper horses at a Philadelphia track. They were heading to Florida, too. But first they were going to ship part of their stable to Pocono

Downs, in Wilkes-Barre, Pennsylvania, to win some races and lose some of their cheap claimers—horses who compete in races in which all entries are up for sale at a specified price. Somehow, they convinced me that I should accompany them. We were staying for only a few weeks, they told me, and we would win lots of races. I packed halfheartedly.

We shipped in one afternoon the week before Thanksgiving. The roads were becoming slick from the falling sleet. Our little caravan slid through the stable gate and down a hill that bottomed out at our assigned barn. My little car had no snow tires. If it had, I probably would have made a quick U-turn and hightailed it south, but there was no way my car was going to make it back up that hill. We unloaded the horses from the van and headed for the little apartment that we would share for three weeks, sipping hot chocolate laced with whiskey and dreaming of the big bets we would cash.

I had made a pact with myself not to ride for any trainer but Russ at Pocono Downs. There was that job waiting for me in Florida and I did not want to risk getting on horses I did not know for trainers I did not know. But pacts are made to be broken.

Stabled next to Russ and Jackie's string at barn "T" was an odd sort of outfit. The Boyd racing stable had traveled to Pocono Downs from a little track out West. A few days after our own arrival, their battered old Ford pickup had chugged in, toting a rusty two-horse trailer. The entire stable consisted of two aged geldings. The two old warhorses received plenty of attention, because the trainer, Sally, was accompanied by her husband, elderly father and young son. The little boy, Scott, was a towheaded, courteous and attentive eleven-year-old. I asked how it was that he got to skip school and live at the racetrack with his folks. Scott told me that just as soon as the family could get some money together, they would be going home for Christmas. Then he would return to school. Home, Scott told me, was in Arkansas.

Sensing that the Boyd stable could not afford an exercise

rider, I volunteered to gallop their two horses for them. Sally readily accepted my offer. One horse, Bart, galloped an easy mile every morning, but the other horse, a black gelding named Coaly, was a wee bit off in the left ankle and usually was ponied alongside Russ's stable pony for his daily exercise.

Within hours of arriving at the track, little Scott asked Russ and Jackie if he could work for them for wages. I am sure that Russ had no clue as to what duties Scott would perform, but he did not hesitate to put the little boy on his payroll. From then on, Scott hustled about the barn all morning, cheerfully holding horses for baths, bedding stalls, raking the shed row and helping me clean tack. Russ paid his little right-hand man his wages daily. Scott would thank him politely and hurry off to join his folks down the shed row. The entire clan would then stroll over to the track kitchen for breakfast. I don't think they ever left the racetrack grounds.

Three weeks went by, and my calendar was lined with Xs that ended with the date of my departure for Florida. By December 15, Russ had run and lost the last horse he wanted to part with. He was making shipping arrangements, and I was planning to get my gear out of the jocks' room and settle up with my valet Paul. Our neighbors down the shed row had not yet raced Coaly or Bart.

On December 16, I went to the jocks' room after morning workouts to retrieve my belongings. But when I requested my tack, Paul gave me a look of consternation. "You can't leave," he said. "You have a mount tonight in the ninth race." He pulled a folded list of the day's entries from his back pocket and passed it to me. He was right. I was named on Coal Bay in the ninth. I asked Paul if he had seen the form on Coaly. "Uh-huh. If this horse wins tonight, there are snowmen in hell," he replied. "Gonna take off?"

I nearly let the word "yes" slip through my badly chapped lips when I caught sight of something out of the corner of my eye. It was little Scott. The racetrack cherub had come dashing out of the racing secretary's office with the entries list in his hand. He was jumping up and down like a young antelope as he raced back to the barn area. "No," I said. "I guess I'm riding tonight."

That evening before dinner, I borrowed Russ's *Daily Racing Form* to study Coal Bay's past performances. He had not seen a winner's circle since he was seven, and he would be nine years old in a few weeks. The chart writer had summed up Coaly's last three efforts as "dull," "outdistanced" and "tired early." These performances had been in cheap claiming races. Tonight, Coaly was entered in an allowance race, a higher level of competition.

At 6:30 I went to the jocks' room to await my last ride at Pocono Downs. God, was it cold out! As I donned my riding garb, I thought to myself that riding a 60 to 1 shot on a night of freezing temperatures was not a terrific way to end one's race-riding career. Such was fate. When the call went round the jocks' room for the ninth race weigh-in, my valet informed me that it was ten degrees outside. I put on an extra-heavy turtleneck shirt after weigh-in and stuck my gloves and boots into the sauna for a last minute toasting before venturing out.

In the paddock, my teeth chattered as Sally told me that Coaly was a cold-weather horse. The old gelding did look good. His coat was thick and shiny. His large hazel eyes were bright with anticipation. I glanced over at our competition. One horse stood out: the betting favorite, Fast Exit, had just shipped in from New Jersey, but I knew him well. I had ridden Fast Exit when he won his first race a couple of years before at a Jersey Shore track. With that race, I lost my "bug," the weight allowance given to apprentice riders until they chalk up a certain number of victories, and the trainer I was riding for promptly fired me. Another memorable day in my career. The same trainer still saddled Fast Exit, and I waved stiffly at him as he met my stare. Suddenly, Coaly and I had a mission. We had to beat Fast Exit for old times' sake.

When the gates opened, Coaly shot out like a bolt of black

lightning. We easily took the lead, with Fast Exit alongside. My old Coaly was running like a fine-tuned sports car. In fact, Fast Exit seemed to be having trouble keeping up. I signaled to Coaly, and we easily left the favorite in the dust. From the quarter pole to the wire, we raced along, just Coal Bay and me. At the eighth pole, I started grinning and posing. To the wire we coasted, four lengths ahead of the favorite.

Coaly pulled up kindly and galloped back to the winner's circle like a gentleman. He was my hero, and I patted his glistening neck tenderly as we posed for the picture. Sally, her husband, father and little Scott were surprisingly calm during the brief victory ceremony. "We knew he could do it!" Scott declared. I thanked them all for a most memorable ride.

The next morning, I went to the stables at eight. I was packed and ready to head to Florida. But before I hit the highway, I needed to see my new friends one last time. I headed over to the two stalls where Coal Bay and his stablemate had been bedded. The stalls were empty. I was quite upset to find the Boyd stable gone without notice. Russ walked down the shed row and stood by my side as I stared misty-eyed at Coal Bay's empty stall. "They were already gone when I got here this morning. They must have loaded up in the middle of the night," he said. "I think something was left for you on their tack-room door."

I walked slowly to the end of the shed and pulled the piece of white construction paper from the door. It was a crayon drawing depicting a huge black horse in a winner's circle; his jockey had been given a large red nose like that of Rudolph the Red-Nosed Reindeer. A family of four was grouped at the horse's head.

I smiled as I read the neatly hand-printed caption at the bottom of the picture: "COAL BAY—WINNER—WE ARE GOING HOME FOR CHRISTMAS," and, in smaller letters, "Thanks, Jan. We love you, [signed] Scott." Only then did I realize why I had come to Pocono Downs.

Jan Jaison Cross

Racehorse Poor

"Why is he eating his mama's manure?" I asked my daddy as we stood looking through the fence at our new weanling. "That means he's a good one," he replied in his all-knowing tone. That's all I needed to hear because my daddy knew everything there was to know about a horse. While we stood in the barn that morning, Daddy wrote the check for what would be our first racehorse. "I'll have a winning racehorse if I have to sell everything we have," I remember him saying. That didn't seem like such a sacrifice in my seven-year-old mind. After all, horses were the only thing that Daddy and I considered sacred.

We sat around the dinner table that evening trying to create a name that would sound good being bellowed from a track announcer. It was a family ritual. With each new horse we purchased, Mama would create a masterpiece for the palate and as we ate, everyone jotted down on bits of paper what the newest little one should be named. Our new weanling's grandfather was Misty Flite, so we tried every combination using Flite and finally came up with something we all agreed would sound exciting as it echoed around the track. And so it was. The little sorrel colt with no particularly outstanding features was named Starflite.

As the brisk spring turned to summer, Starflite grew while

he stood lazing in the warm sun. We moved him to my grandfather's dairy farm, where we had created a makeshift horse facility. Starflite lived next to the Holsteins and shared a fence row with my prized pony Patty. The only growth he seemed to experience that summer was in the region of his head and belly. "He sure isn't much to look at," Daddy would say as he meandered out to get him for another lesson in ground work. It was during those lessons that Daddy was exposed to the restive side of Starflite. Watching from a perch on the fender of our horse trailer, I offered moral support as Daddy cussed and spit and tried in vain to get the youngster to enter the trailer. But nothing moved that horse any closer to getting in. Daddy tried coaxing and then he tried to direct Starflite in with a whip. Exasperated, Daddy finally lost all sense of rational thinking and kicked the horse in his big hind end. As Daddy wailed, my grandfather appeared from nowhere, quickly assessed the situation and immediately fell to the ground rolling in laughter. "It's broken!" Daddy yelled. "Help me get this boot off while I can," he squalled.

Summer faded to fall and all too quickly fall was transformed into a cold Ohio winter. The horses were put up out of the ice and snow in a spacious garage that had been converted into a horse barn. With high-protein grain and all the alfalfa he could eat, our baby was becoming a beautiful young stallion. His ground lessons continued and Daddy's toe mended nicely. Only a slight bend to the left and a black toenail were left as a reminder. When Starflite was moved to a training track, he walked quietly into the trailer like a perfect gentleman.

As the earth started to melt from the long cold winter and teacup-size tulips took their place in my mother's garden, the time had come for the fine young stallion to have a rider on his back. The trainer Daddy hired was a stout older gentleman, "One of the finest horsemen in this county," according to Daddy. Bill really seemed to get inside the mind of a horse. He had some of the finest horses I had ever seen, and we were sure he could "get the run" out of Starflite.

The first task was to get a saddle on the horse's back. And a task this was. "Whoa!" Bill would holler. "Easy, now." Starflite moved in ways I didn't know were possible for a horse. He made an art of dodging the saddle that Bill was trying to toss on his back. Up, back, kick, strike. *Whoa, that hoof was too close to Daddy's head!* I had never seen anything like the circus that I was watching here. The men and the horse were covered in sweat, slobber and even a stray sling of Bill's chewin' tobacco. The battle went on for hours, until finally the great horse gave way. Bill eased the saddle onto Starflite's back, and the horse gave the last snort he had in him. "If he has half that much heart on the track, we've got ourselves a winner," Bill said.

Lessons became much easier for Starflite in the months that followed. Once he was saddled, he was asked to do what he loved best: run. Several mornings a week he was exercised by our new jockey, Jerry. Each time he would come off the track, Jerry would compliment the workout. "*She* did a great job today!" he would shout from Starflite's back as he lazily strode past us. I hated the very sight! I wanted to be a jockey, sitting proudly on Starflite as he burst from the gates. I wanted to feel the wind in my face so fierce that it would bring tears to my eyes. Most of all, I wanted to be on Starflite's back the first time he stepped into the winner's circle. There was one slight problem. I was only nine years old. Daddy allowed me to hand walk our horse after his workouts and remove his protective leg wraps. Then I would feed and water him. I felt important in the grand scheme of things, so I settled for what I could get.

For a young stallion, Starflite was gentle and never gave anyone who was kind to him any trouble. Jerry, in particular, was very fond of him. "She's going to be a great one!" he'd say. And Starflite proved that in his schooling races. Jerry pushed him to be a winner as they prepared for their first real race together. "She's ready," he said one morning as they came in from a fast workout. "Why does Jerry always call him 'she'?" I asked Daddy. "Maybe he calls them all she, like people do when they refer to a boat," was Daddy's answer. I didn't like it, though, and insisted that Daddy talk to Jerry about it. My perpetual complaining finally got to Daddy and he casually asked Jerry one day why he called Starflite "she." "My apologies Slim," he said to Daddy. "You mean to tell me that horse is a stallion? All this time I thought he was a mare because he is so quiet!" "Just thought you should know," Daddy said, even though he didn't care if Jerry called him Mutt as long as Starflite crossed the finish line first.

The big day finally arrived: our first official race for our first real racehorse. My mother was all aflutter, cooking fried chicken right outside his stall on a Coleman stove. Mama always has believed everything should start with a good meal and, wow, can she lay one out! Starflite stood patiently in the crossties as I brushed him. He was so large now that my head came only to the middle of his chest. Although everyone around him was bouncing around, Starflite was the picture of calm and serenity.

As we devoured my mother's feast, Bill prepared my parents for what was to come. "Don't be disappointed if we don't run in the money today," he said. "He's young, this is his first time out and the crowd here today may startle him."

Before long, the call came for the eighth race and the post parade emerged from the tunnel as the bugle began its familiar tune. My heart was beating so fast I could barely breathe. The announcer made his way through the list of names—which included those of the horses as well as their trainers and owners. When he got to "Starflite, owned by, trained by, and ridden by," I decided we had chosen a great name for a racehorse, after all. Once through the field, the horses cantered off toward the gates, every horse that is, but Starflite, who casually walked and then sped up a bit into a Western pleasure-type jog.

He had drawn the Number 3 position, so he and two others entered the gates quietly and waited for the other horses to load. The horse in the Number 9 spot was giving the gate men all kinds of trouble. He reared and kicked, and it took several men to shove him in. "This isn't good," Mama said. "Starflite will get upset. He hasn't seen anything like this." Simultaneously, we looked down the gate to the Number 3 position. We could just see the top of our horse's ears because he had his head so low, and I couldn't believe my eyes. "His legs are crossed Mama!" I yelled.

Starflite was standing quietly and appeared to be thinking, *Calm down so we can get this over with and get back to the barn.* The announcer called, "And they're off!" and the young horses leaped from the gates, trying to find their personal path to victory. Every horse in the race, that is, except Starflite. Apparently, all the commotion had caused him to dose off.

Suddenly, he leaped from the gate with such a stride he was right on the tail of the other horses. What happened in those next eighteen seconds was a blur. The blood was rushing through my head at such a powerful rate I couldn't hear or see what was happening down on the track. Then, as if being awaken from a nightmare, I heard my mother scream, "He won!" I was standing frozen in time, as if all the blood had been drained from my body. I couldn't move.

My mother, on the other hand, was winning her own race. She had taken the stairs out of the grandstand three at a time, knocking over women and small children. When she got to the turnstile, she discovered that it had collected several people exiting the stands, so she jumped it—cleared it just like a fine Thoroughbred. I didn't know Mama had it in her. She was running as if there were the possibility that the winner's circle would disappear if she didn't get there in an instant.

When she finished her endurance course, she was standing alone in the winner's circle. Starflite was still on the backstretch and Daddy was with Bill, standing out on the track waiting for the winner to arrive.

There is no feeling that equals the one that overcomes

you on your way to the winner's circle. It is the culminating moment of years of planning and hardwork that begin with the decision of which mare to breed to what stallion. Through the foal's arrival and his passage from fractious weanling to clumsy yearling, you plan, you dream, you hope. All of the joy and heartache that accompany raising a racehorse can never be expressed in words, but it all comes together in that tiny piece of dirt.

There is nothing like it. Starflite's first win picture—along with all his other win pictures and accomplishments—still hang in our study today. Those mementos are surrounded by similar pictures of his brothers and his offspring. Each has an individual story—some of humor and some of sadness—but none will ever take the place of Starflite. He holds a special place in the heart of everyone he encountered. He possessed a certain kindness with which only a few of God's creatures are blessed. We were "racehorse poor" in Daddy's words, but rich beyond compare with what matters most: love.

Carol Wade Kelly

Happy Horses

Surely, I don't believe superstition brings you good luck! But I'm told it works even if you don't believe in it.

Niels Bohr

I took a friend of mine, George, to the races one sun-splashed Saturday afternoon. Our weekend sojourn to Santa Anita Park was George's first trip to a racetrack. It was also the first time he had ever laid eyes on a Thoroughbred. The day proved to be educational for both of us—teacher and student—as the racehorses once again proved what great equalizers they truly are.

Spending an afternoon at the racetrack is nothing new to me. As editor of a monthly horse-racing magazine, it is among my chief responsibilities to chronicle the races. There are few things I enjoy more in this world than watching Thoroughbreds compete. During a good day at the races, we all try to catch a flash of brilliance here or there, a hint of promise that tomorrow big dreams will come true, that the horses we're watching today will be champions at year's end. "Hope springs eternal," they like to say in this business. It's true.

My passion for Thoroughbreds dates back to childhood. In fact, I can't recall a day I didn't trot off to school without a *Daily Racing Form* in my backpack, tucked in along with all the other semester's required reading. As the years progressed and my knowledge and understanding of the industry expanded, I delved into studying pedigrees and their influence on a Thoroughbred's performance at the racetrack. Today, more than two decades later, and after more than ten years in the business, I am still learning this fascinating game and all of its nuances.

Anytime an opportunity presents itself to introduce someone new to the sport of Thoroughbred racing, I leap at the chance. George, in his seventies, had always admired the majesty of horses, but only from afar, from books and what he'd seen in movies. His hands had never touched the strong neck and thick shoulder of a Thoroughbred. His eyes had never met the eyes of a racehorse or witnessed a furious stretch drive between two rivals, each bent on beating the other. I wanted our afternoon at the races to be something personal for George. I wanted him to make a connection. I wanted him to see how magnificent these racehorses are up close and personal. I wanted him to appreciate the teamwork, the strategy, the preparation and dedication that go into a winning or, for that matter, a losing effort at the races.

As the runners prepared for the second race, a six-furlong turf sprint, I walked with George down to the saddling enclosure for a better vantage point from which to view the jockeys saddling up before heading out onto the track. The horses bounced around there, some of them on their toes, ready to strut their stuff on the track. Trainers offered last-minute instructions to the riders as eager owners and friends gathered around for a listen. Crowds of fans leaned against the white fence framing the saddling ring, hoping to catch a glimpse of something that might possibly point them in the direction of a winner: a thumbs-up from a trainer, an owner's especially large entourage, the look in a horse's eyes, anything at all that may signal that a winning effort is on tap.

I spent much of the time in the walking ring with George sharing the backgrounds of the horses competing in the race, talking about their bloodlines, their siblings, trainers, jockeys, past performances and running styles. I even went so far as to point out what I know about a horse's body language and how various actions translate into terms easily applicable to any athlete readying himself for competition. George absorbed it all like a child at his first baseball game. He was making a connection.

Despite my occasionally lengthy dialog, George had his sights set on a long shot. I alerted him to the host of risks and questions associated with wagering his money on a horse with 20 to 1 odds. My warnings, however, fell on deaf ears. George stood firm. I, on the other hand, backed the classiest runner (at least on paper) in the field. We returned to our table in the clubhouse and continued our discussion of the race as we waited for the runners to make their way to the starting gate.

As the horses began to load, George said that he felt a little nervous. I told him not to worry, six more races remained on the day's program, and he would surely cash a winner before we were through.

I kept close watch of the race's early stages through my binoculars, describing to George that his runner was racing along in midpack. As the field entered the far turn and headed for home, George switched his focus from my race call and fixed his gaze to a nearby television set which offered him a much clearer view of what was transpiring on the track below.

As the runners charged through the stretch, my 2 to 1 favorite slid through an opening on the rail. He appeared full of run and was, without question, on his way to a resounding victory. I was confident that he was the right horse, so confident that I took the liberty of betting a small saver ticket on the favorite for George, just so he'd have a winning ticket to cash first time out when my selection streaked across the finish first.

But before I uttered a word, George's 20 to 1 shot kicked into high gear in the middle of the racetrack. With an apprentice jockey up, the long shot collared us inside the sixteenth pole and posted the upset. George couldn't believe it. I was stunned. With George shaking his head in disbelief at his good fortune, we watched the horse jog back for his winner's circle snapshot. The young jockey's smile was as large as the one on the face beside me. I was smiling too, hoping George had bet a saver ticket on his horse for me.

There is no greater feeling for a new fan at the racetrack than cashing a ticket for the very first time. With George clutching tightly to his winning ticket, I escorted my friend down the stairs to the mutual windows. After some convincing, George parted with the ticket. In exchange, $43.80 came back across the counter. He pocketed the return on his investment and we headed back up to our third-floor table.

As I began poring over the *Form* to study the runners in the next race, I asked George what led him to his winning selection. Without missing a beat, he replied simply, "He looked happy. He just looked happy."

So much for pedigrees, power ratings, past performances, track variants, trainer–jockey combos, post positions and the like. Years of working around horses and the racetrack, and all it took to cash a winning ticket that day were a gut instinct and happy eyes.

We departed the track a couple of hours later. George had given $20 back in losing wagers, but left in the plus column for the day, a victory for sure. As for me, my years of handicapping experience delivered as many winners as George had on the day—one. My winning horse paid $7.20 to win.

As we exited the track, I stopped to purchase the next day's *Form*. George asked why. After a dismal showing at the windows the logic made perfect sense, and I replied, "Looking for happy horses George, looking for happy horses."

As the adage says, "Hope springs eternal."

Michael Compton

Down the Stretch He Comes,
Hanging on for Dear Life

There is something about the outside of a horse
that is good for the inside of a man.

Sir Winston Churchill

Like many of life's bad decisions, it seemed a good idea at the time.

We have all made them: choices that in retrospect seem, well, kind of crazy. Youth is often involved.

Some might think of people they dated or, worse, married. Every August, when the ponies are running up in Saratoga Springs, I think of a date I once had with a horse with no name.

It was fan appreciation day, an annual event when the New York Racing Association throws open the gates to the historic Saratoga Race Course and welcomes horse-racing fans to an afternoon of food and fun, and maybe a death or two. But I'm getting ahead of myself.

I had been asked, and for some reason had agreed, to be a jockey for a day, joining seven other members of the area press. The media race was to be a highlight of the afternoon. It's clear to me now it was just someone's not-too-subtle revenge on the local newshounds.

When I arrived in the paddock area, eight of the sorriest-looking horses I've ever seen were tied to the whitewashed fence—a reassuring sight to a guy who had ridden but twice. I remember being instantly drawn to a gray horse with a swayback and hooves too large to lift. She seemed older than the rest, content perhaps just to saunter around the racecourse at her own leisurely pace. My kind of gal.

I never got her name. She only gave me that you-are-such-a-fool stare—the one animals like to share with people on such occasions.

I willingly signed a waiver that said if I were killed, crippled or crushed, it was all my own fault. I couldn't sue for damages. And then I was handed one of those head-hugging helmets favored by jockeys. I put it on, snapping the strap under my chin.

As my friends lined the rail, waving and laughing as friends do when they know someone is about to make a fool of himself, I slowly rode onto the deep dirt of the track, my knees tucked tight to my chin. It's a position I could not get into today. I barely got into it then.

My horse entered the starting gate without protest, unlike some of her feistier competitors who balked and backed away. I sat smug and silent, happy with my choice.

And then, without notice, a bell rang, the gates flew open and my old gray mare suddenly morphed into the racehorse she once had been. I don't know if it was the bell, the gate snapping open or if someone had blown a dart into her rump, but she took off down the track, lickety-split. A bullet.

There wasn't enough time to see my life pass before me, let alone to scream. I clung to her mane, and the farther we flew down the track, the more I could feel my body leaning to the right. One more furlong and I would be hugging her belly. My only consolation was that I would be rounding the first bend by then, riding away from the twenty thousand people who had come to witness this media massacre.

Just about the time I was sure I was going down, the old gray mare pulled up short, veered off to the rail and abruptly came to a halt. She was done. Finished. So was my racing career.

I didn't win that August afternoon twenty years ago, but I had no regrets.

Instead, as my friend Nancy likes to say, I had "a moment." Even better.

Craig Wilson

Track Meet. *Reprinted by permission Steve Sommer and Francis Brummer* ©*2002 Steve Sommer and Francis Brummer.*

Allez Mandarin

My English mother was a wartime bride. My father, an American, worked for Mobil Oil. I lived in several countries until I was four, then we returned to England. On one visit to my grandparents in Kent, when I was nine years old, I first became aware of my uncle Fred, and my passion for horses was born.

My grandfather was a private trainer for a Kent fruit farmer. Uncle John was Granddad's assistant and he kept scrapbooks of his brother's riding career. After lunch I sat with John as he added clippings from Fred's exploits of the previous day into his fourth overstuffed book. I began to thumb through the other books and was in awe that a relative of mine could get so much press and ride so many winners.

On the drive home, I quizzed my mother about her brother's career. Mother told me about going to the movies with my father in Morocco in 1957. To her surprise, The Pathe News showed Fred winning the Grand National on a horse called Sundew. This was the first she had heard of Fred's win. I was in awe that my uncle was on the news in Morocco, and I wondered what it would be like to be a jockey.

Many times as I pedaled down the road to school, I would race people walking on the sidewalk or driving in a car or truck behind me to the nearest landmark. I imagined I was Fred, driving to the finish on one of his great wins. I usually held on to win.

One day, I looked behind me and saw a bus pulling on to the road I was on. I began peddling like mad, imagining I was Fred riding a horse named Mandarin in the French Grand National. I was lost in the moment, hearing the whirring of the chain, the rattle of the fenders, the singing of the tires on the hot road, the pounding of my pulse in my head and my labored breathing. The winning post was still far off. I was beginning to tire. The roar of the bus got louder and louder. The smell of the diesel fumes got stronger. The harder I peddled, the louder the noise got. But I was Fred riding Mandarin, the bus was the French horse Lumino. The heat of the day starting to take its toll, my legs started to shake. I wasn't going to get beaten. I kept peddling, refusing to give in. As I reached the winning post, the bus roared past me. Too tired to peddle any more, I imagined how Fred must have felt after his epic ride aboard Mandarin in 1962.

Uncle John had devoted several pages to Fred and Mandarin. On the first page was a photo of Fred and Mandarin coming off the course at Auteuil. Mandarin had his head down. Fred looked exhausted. "What happened here?" I asked my uncle. "Have a closer look at the picture," John answered.

I noticed Mandarin's bit hanging by his side. "That was Fred and Mandarin in the Grand Steeplechase de Paris," he explained.

"Surely, he couldn't have raced with a broken bit?" Slowly, we began to thumb the next pages of the scrapbook. My uncle John told me the story. "Your uncle Fred and Mandarin had a lot of success before going to France to try to win France's biggest race. They had won the Cheltenham Gold Cup in England and several other top races together.

"The day before the race, Fred came down with a terrible stomach virus. He felt absolutely wretched on his arrival in France the day of the race. He was in no condition to ride in a race, but he wouldn't give in. By the time of the race, Fred was still feeling pretty sick. Once he got on Mandarin, he was grateful to find that his old partner was feeling well. At least one of them was fit to race. Fred was very much aware that the reputation of English racing hinged on their performance.

"Once the race was off, Mandarin settled in among the leaders. At the third jump, disaster struck."

"What happened?" I cried.

"His bit snapped," John continued. "It happened just as they approached the six-foot privet hedge, one of Auteuil's most difficult jumps. Mandarin and Fred landed safely, but what lay ahead was truly daunting: three and a half miles around a twisting, turning track and twenty-four jumps with no way to steer except for Fred using his legs and slapping the reins."

"Didn't Mandarin try to run off or run out? Surely, he could have run out if he wanted to?" I asked.

"No. He was normally a free-running horse, but he never varied his speed. There were four fences before the next bend. Mandarin was always a bold jumper and he jumped these well. One jockey turned his horse into Mandarin. That, along with Fred's strong legs, got Mandarin around the first turn. Mandarin was now settling down into a rhythm. It was as if he was determined to do his best despite the setback.

"The other jockeys weren't helping now, but they didn't hinder Mandarin either," Uncle John continued. The next part of the course had no railing and it split in three different directions. Mandarin was going left when he needed to go right. Fred put all his weight on one side and was just able to get him to keep the correct course.

"Then Mandarin made a jumping mistake, almost falling at the water jump. He pitched Fred up his neck. It actually was a good thing though. It gave them a lead around one of the turns.

"With about a half-mile to go, Mandarin was going well within himself. Fred began to think that he might have a chance to win. Then fate dealt another cruel blow. Mandarin bowed a tendon. Fred felt his mount falter for a few strides and lose about four or five lengths on the leaders. But Mandarin was not about to give up. Fred had no way to stop him.

"Coming to the last fence, Mandarin was in front. Fred, weakened by a stomach virus, and Mandarin, hurt but refusing to give in, were about to win. Then from out of the pack came the French horse Lumino with a strong run. Fred was urging Mandarin on. The broken bit was dangling uselessly by Mandarin's shoulder, his brow band stuck between his ears. Push kick, push kick, Fred encouraged his brave partner on. They had come too far to let Lumino catch them now.

"The closer Lumino got, the louder the crowd got. *'Allez Mandarin. Allez Fred,'* the crowd roared, 'go on Mandarin, go on Fred.'

"Mandarin was going slower and slower. Horse and rider were fatigued beyond the limits of their endurance. Push kick, push kick, the ill Fred reaching down into reserves of strength only a few champions possess; Mandarin doing likewise. Neither horse nor rider was willing to admit defeat. Lumino was catching up with every stride. Fred could now hear the thud of his rival's hooves on the turf, the rhythmic squeaking of the saddles, the heavy breathing of Lumino at his knee, and the pounding of his pulse in his helmet as the winning post inched ever closer. Just past the winning post, Mandarin came to a walk. The old campaigner knew where the winning post was.

"Walking off the track, Fred was exhausted and dejected. Mandarin had his head down. Neither jockey knew who had won. A loud murmur spread among the crowd. Had Mandarin held on? Only the photo finish would tell. The loudspeaker clicked on and the crowd went silent. Then the roar of the crowd told the story: Mandarin and Fred had held on to win."

The final picture in the scrapbook told it all. The jubilant team: Fred, giving weak smile, and Mandarin, picking up his tired head as if to say, "We did it Fred, we did it." My passion for racing was sparked that day by the great feat of Mandarin and my uncle Fred in France. Separately, Mandarin and Fred were champions. Together, they proved to be immortal.

Thomas Peevey

The Fastest Mule in the West

She has thirteen-inch-long ears and a distinctive birth-mark on her rump that inspired her name. Although she measures just 14 hands tall and weighs only 800 pounds, she has carried imposts of 134 pounds and won fifty of fifty-seven races. Her exploits have made her the darling of northern California racing fans and have even earned her space in *The New York Times* and *Sports Illustrated*.

She is a ten-year-old female mule, or mollie, named Black Ruby. Some people have even called her the Secretariat of mule racing. It's a title that emits a chuckle from her proud owners, Mary and Sonny McPherson.

"Black Ruby's won a lot more races than Secretariat ever did," they tell everyone.

Foaled in Utah, Black Ruby is half donkey, half Quarter Horse–Thoroughbred mix. When she was barely three, she fell out of a moving trailer and severely injured her hind legs. Her right hind ankle still bears scars from the ordeal, but it hasn't bothered Ruby one bit. Like the Energizer Bunny, she just keeps on winning and winning and winning.

Although the record books credit her with fifty-seven races, Black Ruby actually has made closer to eighty starts. When she was a young mule burning up the bush tracks in Nevada, she was often called on to race more than once on a given afternoon, but the rules state that only one race a day can be counted. In the unpredictable sport of horse racing, she is considered such a sure thing that most tracks accept only straight win bets on her and some tracks even refuse to take bets on her at all.

For the McPhersons, the Black Ruby saga began in 1996. They live in Healdsburg, in the California wine country, and share a twelve-acre ranch with about twenty racing mules and an occasional Thoroughbred. Twenty-one years ago, Sonny lost the lower part of his right leg when his truck collided with a tree, but that has not stopped him from becoming an activist for the mule-racing movement in northern California.

He and Mary first became aware of Black Ruby's prowess when they sent their best mule, Fancy, to race against her in Winnemucca, Nevada. Fancy was a champion in her own right, but Black Ruby simply smoked her.

"Sonny looked at me and said, 'I want that mule,'" Mary remembers.

They bought that mule and her legend has continued to grow. So did Black Ruby's legion of fans. Blessed with an incredible winning spirit, she is almost impossible to catch once she makes that charge for the wire. This fierce competitiveness has made her a five-time world champion and pushed her earnings to $185,850, a record for a racing mule.

A few years ago, the McPhersons discovered for themselves just how difficult Black Ruby is to catch when she got loose at their ranch and headed for the hills. Sonny jumped on his John Deere tractor and gave chase.

"Every time I'd get close, she'd take off again," he said. "All you could see were her ears. I was afraid she'd hurt herself before I could catch her. She had a race in four days. She won it anyway and set a track record."

Another who knows all about chasing Black Ruby is her archrival Taz. In forty-three races together, the eight-year-old jack has finished second to Ruby approximately thirty times.

He is also the only mule to beat her more than once.

Their rivalry succeeded in making mule racing quite pop-ular during the summer of 2002. Thoroughbred tracks even started clamoring for personal appearances by Black Ruby and Taz. The first to step forward with a proposition for a promotional event was Del Mar Racetrack in north San Diego County, which offered to stage a betless $10,000 winner-take-all matched race between the two mules on September 8, 2002.

For the first time, mule racing left its humble but spirited roots in Nevada and the northern California fairs to enjoy the rarefied atmosphere of Thoroughbred racing. Del Mar has been the scene of quite a few memorable match ups, Seabiscuit's 1938 victory over Ligaroti being the most famous. No one expected how seriously this seaside track would be infected with mule mania. The match took on greater importance when Taz defeated Ruby in a race at Sacramento two weeks prior to September 8. The two mules moved into Del Mar and became instant celebrities. Even the most die-hard Thoroughbred trainers wanted to have pictures taken with them.

Ruby's fans were hungry for revenge, and revenge is what they got. She jumped out of the gate running and never gave Taz a chance to catch her, winning by a comfortable two lengths. Black Ruby and Taz met again six days later for another $10,000 winner-take-all matched race at the Los Angeles County Fair in Pomona. Running without blinkers for the first time and carrying five pounds more than Taz, Black Ruby appeared beaten in the final fifty yards. But her great fighting spirit kicked in at that point and she came back and caught Taz right at the wire to win by a nose.

"Black Ruby knows exactly where the finish line is, and she just refuses to lose," Mary said after that particularly exciting victory. "She always seems to find that extra gear, call it 'mulepower' if you will."

Black Ruby made it three in a row against Taz before she called it quits for the season. And what a finale it was.

Carrying seven to fourteen pounds more than her competitors, including Taz, she won the 440-yard American Mule Racing Association Gold Cup at Fresno in world-record time.

After that race, Black Ruby removed her running shoes and settled down for the winter at Mary and Sonny's ranch. Just as she has done for six previous winters, she bossed the other mules that share the pasture with her and enticed them to join her in games of chase. She was always the one flying in front.

"Even when she's playing, she's competitive and the others just let her have her own way with things," Mary adds. "She has made it a hard-and-fast rule that she eats first at feeding time. She's the queen bee, and she knows it."

Debra Ginsburg

Mules-R-Us

Mules-R-Us. *Reprinted by permission of Boots Reynolds.* ©2003 *Boots Reynolds.*

Da Hoss

The Breeders' Cup was always a legendary event in my mind. Ranking alongside the World Series and the Super Bowl, it truly is the culmination of a racing season, with the greatest champions in the world on hand to challenge one another in a test of speed and stamina over several distances and a variety of surfaces. I remember watching it on television while growing up. As the only horse lover in a family of nine, it wasn't easy gaining access to our only family television set for four straight hours on a Saturday afternoon. When I was successful in this endeavor, however, everyone else refused to join me and I was forced to take up the role of announcer of each race, convinced that everyone wanted to watch it with me, but they were heavily engaged in other duties at the time. Therefore, it was my obligation to verbally broadcast each race as it unfolded to the entire household with great enthusiasm.

I was a racing fanatic. I grew up with The Black Stallion and his unforgettable conquest of Sun Raider and Cyclone. As a boy, I would drag the piano bench into my bedroom, fasten a Western riding saddle to it and envision myself in the greatest races of the day aboard any number of the greatest racehorses of the day.

Now here I was at the Breeders' Cup, not merely in

attendance, but actively engaged in a necessary role along-side all of the Breeders' Cup employees. How I had landed that internship, I still do not know. Nevertheless, I was there. My duties were to attend to the needs of the horse-men, the trainers, the grooms—anyone who had anything to do with the actual horses.

As fortune would have it, my position afforded me the opportunity to gain unprecedented access to the greatest horses of our time. It was 1998 at Churchill Downs, and the likes of Silver Charm, Skip Away and Gentleman had gathered in Louisville, Kentucky, to test their mettle on racing's greatest stage.

It just so happened that in a rather quiet barn, one gone fairly unnoticed and fairly undisrupted by the ever-present media, was a horse on the verge of legendary status. I could vividly remember calling a race a few years prior in my living room that featured his name, a name that will go down in my personal racing history because it belonged to one of the greatest milers of all time. It was Da Hoss.

To call him a warrior is an understatement. Plagued by injuries throughout his career, with aching knees and swollen ankles, Da Hoss had charged his way into the history books with a dominating victory in the Breeders' Cup Mile at Woodbine in Canada in the fall of 1996.

But this was 1998, and Da Hoss was getting along in age. At seven or eight years old, he was considered by many to be past his prime. It had been two years since I'd even heard his name, and yet he was here. "What a joke," I heard people say. "This reminds me of Rick's Natural Star," another added, referring to a horse who did not belong and who fared rather poorly in a prior Breeders' Cup, causing quite a ruckus among the media.

I couldn't believe what I was hearing. Da Hoss was a champion—a proven champion—yet it became apparent that his fan club had dwindled significantly since his last championship appearance. And who could blame them? We're talking the Breeders' Cup here—a racing

extravaganza that had catapulted the careers of Cigar,
Sunday Silence, Ferdinand and more. It was a day that had
offered the public some of the most awesome showdowns
in racing history. This was the big time. It was for real, and
I began to fear for my friend in Barn 39.

But fear or not, I watched each day as Da Hoss made his
way to the track. He churned up the turf course like a real
competitor. Nothing that I could see would stop me from
believing that this would, indeed, become the comeback of
the decade. I became so confident that I even began to make
my predictions known among the Breeders' Cup crew.
"He's back," I touted. "It's Da Hoss in da mile," was my
battle cry of the week.

The day we had all been waiting for arrived, sunny, crisp
and ripe for the challenges that lay ahead. Churchill Downs
was everything I had imagined. The trademark twin spires
gleamed and the fans streamed in. This was the day champions would be made. As the races progressed, I worked
steadily between the winner's circle and the paddock, assisting in a variety of ways, including having the winner's
blanket and flowers on hand after each race. But my
thoughts were on Da Hoss. The papers had reported and I
had personally witnessed his trainer, Michael Dickinson,
walking and studying the turf course for the perfect route
Da Hoss's jockey would endeavor to travel. Mr. Dickinson,
the "Mad Genius" they called him, had even asked his girl
friend to walk the turf course in stiletto heels so that he
could measure how hard or soft the going might be.

I don't recall the exact order of the races that day. Things
happened so fast and without pause that the only thing
clear to me to this day is that the mile race was upon us, and
the horses were making their way through the track tunnel,
out onto the course. As the horses passed my position I
whispered, "One more time, big guy. Just one more time."

The horses loaded into the gate, which was an incredibly
intense, beautiful and emotional experience. Then the gate
flew open and the athletes emerged, a colorful blur. They

were gone and churning around the clubhouse turn before I could even locate Da Hoss's position in the race. I turned to find the television monitors, strained to hear the announcer over the crowd, searched intently for anything to indicate his progress.

Down the backstretch they charged, all well in hand and approaching the halfway point. As they sped into the far turn, they came together, fourteen horses in all, each with superior breeding, superior care and training, and each within range of grasping the greatest prize of all. Not a horse among them was decidedly out of the race at this point. Yet they were so tightly bunched that no clear leader could be determined as they sprinted into the stretch.

I raced to the rail and saw my hero. He was there among them and as I had predicted, he had charged to the front in an awesome display of talent and fury. On he drove. And then he was second. A talented chestnut by the name of Hawksley Hill had taken over and was now in charge of the race. Maybe seventy-five yards remained, and my hero's fate seemed to be decided. But this was no ordinary horse, and this was no ordinary race. Like Ali on the ropes or John Elway backed up on his own three-yard line, Da Hoss rallied. He rallied like a demon.

If you look at the Breeders' Cup's archived pictures today, you will see photographs from the stretch run of this race. You will see two horses leading the field, nearly dead even and only strides from the finish line. One horse on the outside clearly is running his heart out, but the one on the inside is different. The fire of his effort is palpable. With his head and neck stretched to their limits, Da Hoss is visibly gritting his teeth against his competitor on the track as well as against years of toil and punishment. The look of determination in his eyes is unmistakable and inspiring, so much so, that it will make you weep. For courage, for love, for fun . . . it is impossible to imagine just what force made him move on. But he did. He won. He earned his victory by the narrowest of margins, and it took several minutes for the track officials to evaluate the finish before a decision was announced.

Upon hearing the results, I wept. I wept for joy, for the pain my hero must have been feeling, for the winning ticket in my pocket. Then I ran down the paddock tunnel to my friends and embraced the first one I saw. "Da Hoss in da mile!" I screamed. It had truly been something to behold.

My hero doesn't race anymore and as a gelding, he cannot be bred so there is no possibility that he ever will have off-spring in racing's limelight. However, he is still around. You can see him for yourself should you ever journey to the Bluegrass State. They've got him on display in the Parade of Breeds at the Kentucky Horse Park. Just down the path is the Hall of Champions. Da Hoss, two-time Breeders' Cup Mile Champion. What a horse.

Ky Mortensen

Girly's Gift

Tom and Bonnie Gerdes were as excited as two kids on Christmas morning. The cinder-block paddock they stood in at Hawthorne Race Course in suburban Chicago didn't reflect their festive mood. It was December 15, 2001, but there was nary a wreath, ribbon or bow anywhere. There weren't even any chestnuts among the seven fillies waiting to be saddled for the sixth race. But there was one, nick-named Girly, who was responsible for the gleam in the Gerdes's eyes. She was the first Thoroughbred born and raised by the couple's modest racing operation.

The bay filly's registered name was White O Morn, coined after John Wayne's cottage in the movie *The Quiet Man*. The two-year-old was preparing for an improbable start in the Illinois Breeders Debutante Stakes.

The race, restricted to fillies conceived or born in Illinois, carried a $91,350 purse, by far the richest race for the Gerdes. Bonnie knew that the contest would be a tough one for her untested filly. But Girly was in great racing condition both physically and mentally. Maybe her effort would be good enough for her to finish among the top five and get a check for her owners. Even a fifth-place finish (which represented three percent of the purse) would be more than enough to recoup the $250 gamble the couple had taken in nominating the filly to the race in July. Because so many things can go wrong with a Thoroughbred, Bonnie considered it a moral victory just to have made it to the race.

The Debutante would be the third start in only twenty days for the daughter of the sire Seattle Morn. White O Morn's first two races came against state-bred maidens (horses who have yet to win their first race) at six furlongs (three-quarters of a mile). In her debut, the bay finished eighth in a ten-horse field at odds of 18 to 1. She won her second race by a half-length at odds of 10 to 1 in a pedestrian time (1:16.43). Today, she would race after only a week's rest and run in her first event of more than a mile. It appeared that the odds might be stacked against her.

The wagerers demonstrated little faith in White O Morn at the betting windows. The odds board listed her as a 30 to 1 shot. The field was topped by several tough-looking competitors. The odds-on favorite, Summer Mis, was a daughter of Preakness Stakes-winning Summer Squall. Earlier in the year, Summer Mis had zipped past Illinois-bred maidens by fourteen lengths at Arlington Park, Chicago's premier racecourse. Another Debutante starter, Penny Pit, entered the race undefeated in two open-company starts.

With many of the competitors coming from high-profile stables, White O Morn's more humble origins also did little to stimulate interest among the betting public. The Gerdes, after all, were relative unknowns in the Illinois racing community. Trainer Mike Mokry had been on and off the backstretch many times during his career. Uriel Lopez was a regular in the Chicago jockey colony, but he struggled for race victories.

But that didn't bother Bonnie and Tom, who began to fall in love with each other and with horse racing in 1980.

Following their marriage in 1982, they claimed a sprinter named UC Awarewolf. He won his first race in their racing colors. They were hooked.

Despite their early success, the couple figured that their lark into racing would be costly. So they entered with a realistic understanding of the risks involved and, with their trademark good humor, they named their racing operation Three Good Legs Stable.

Though races are handicapped on paper, they aren't run that way. The Gerdes felt White O Morn would be competitive despite her odds. As the horses were saddled, Bonnie was gripped by the exciting and nerve-racking emotions that most owners experience. Not once did she think about the farm, where the financial situation was so bad, that she had made the last property-tax payment with a credit-card check. Nor did she think of that day, five years before when she'd nearly lost her life.

It was 1996. The Gerdes owned six horses. Each day after work, Bonnie, a postmaster for the U.S. Postal Service, and Tom, a buyer and seller of warehouse equipment, happily tended to the horses' needs at the public stable where they were boarded.

One night at the stable, Bonnie noticed that UC, now a pleasure horse, was reluctant to put weight on his rear right foot. Lost in her concern, Bonnie broke a cardinal rule. She approached the Thoroughbred from behind without letting him know she was there.

UC Awarewolf startled and kicked with both rear feet. His right rear hoof hit the left side of Bonnie's face. After getting the horse back in his stall and telling someone to call 911, Tom sat with Bonnie. As she struggled for breath, Tom repeatedly cleared blood from her nose. The injuries were quite serious. Bonnie's left eye had been displaced from its socket, and her face swelled to four times its normal size. Before the ambulance left the stable, paramedics shocked Bonnie's heart several times to get it into a regular rhythm.

In a coma, Bonnie was given a fifty-fifty chance of making it through the night. Even if she did, the prognosis was not encouraging. The injuries to her brain could cause altered vision and hearing, and trigger changes in her long-term memory, personality and behavior. The chance of permanent brain damage was likely. For the first three nights, Tom never left Bonnie's side in the hospital.

Bonnie awoke after nine days in what Tom described as a childlike state. She improved dramatically during her three-week hospital stay, which included surgery and two weeks of physical therapy. She then went to a rehabilitation center for ten more days to improve her motor skills.

The results of her recovery were miraculous. She suffered no brain damage. After three plastic surgeries, the only visible reminder of the accident was a small depression beneath her left eye. However, Bonnie would learn to live with the loss of most of the vision in her left eye.

Through it all, the couple never lost their resolve or their love of horses. With Tom's help, Bonnie got back up on a horse only two months after the accident. In 1998, they bought a cow farm outside Chicago and began the long process of converting it into a horse farm. They had realized their long-held dream of living a life with horses. They were off.

Yes, they were off, Bonnie now thought as the fillies broke from the gate for the Debutante. Bonnie had taken great care to position herself in her new lucky spot inside the Hawthorne grandstand. That's where she had stood when White O Morn won her first race.

Summer Mis took the lead with Penny Pit close behind. White O Morn was settled in fourth along the rail, seven lengths back. The field never changed positions through the first half-mile of the 11/16-mile race.

On the final turn, White O Morn began to move, but she was still four lengths behind Summer Mis with only about a quarter of a mile to race. Bonnie was in a tizzy, even more so because her breath against the cold glass in the grandstand had fogged her eyeglasses. She used track announcer Peter Galassi's race call to paint a mental picture.

In the stretch drive, jockey Lopez angled White O Morn to the outside, but Summer Mis still looked strong. The Gerdes and their twenty-five-person entourage were lost in the thrill of the moment. Girly moved into second, but still had to make up two lengths on the leader. Suddenly, Summer Mis began to weaken. Under Lopez's continued urging, White O Morn surged ahead for the victory.

The winner's circle scene was pure joy. Improbable victory is the sweetest of all.

The impact of Girly's achievement caused the gleam in the Gerdes's eyes to glow long after that memorable day. The $54,810 winner's purse solved the couple's money problems at the farm. And there was a little extra financial windfall. The tickets held in most of the party's trembling hands were worth $63.40 for each $2 win ticket.

White O Morn was voted the Illinois two-year-old filly reserve champion of 2001 and brought her owners more recognition with an award from the Illinois Thoroughbred Breeders and Owners Foundation.

Ever since the accident one simple poem has never been far from Bonnie's mind. It reads: "Yesterday is history. Tomorrow is a mystery. Today is a gift. That's why it's called the present." Every day the Gerdes squeeze every drop of living out of their beloved life with their horses. And every day they can't help but think about their icing on the cake: Girly's gift.

Dave Surico

The Destiny of Edgar Brown

A chorus of "Amazing Grace" lifted skyward as the mourners gathered around the grave to pay their last respects. Edgar had lived a long life, eighty-eight years before the Lord called him home. Many stories of his life were told in the days and hours preceding Edgar's funeral in March 2002 and it was impossible to hear a story about him that did not involve his horses.

Edgar's life, most of which had been spent in the mountains of Montana, revolved around horses. After he and Jo married, they began raising cattle on the Helena valley's lush meadow grasses and, with the purchase of Shammy and Shalali (Sha-lay-lee), Edgar began developing a reputation as a horseman.

Shammy and Shalali, both American Quarter Horses, were nearly identical twins. They were big, stout sorrels with white strips from forehead to nostril. Under Edgar's tutelage, they developed into confident ranch horses capable of quietly sorting cattle and dragging calves to the branding fire.

Over the years, Edgar's horse herd grew, as did his reputation as a horseman. His early equine protégés were mounts for Edgar and Jo's four children, who participated in youth and amateur rodeo events and qualified for the

National High School Finals Rodeo on horses their dad had bred, raised or trained.

Soon after, Edgar turned his full attention to training horses and moved his family to the old homestead just south of Helena, where he built an indoor training facility and purchased a young stallion that he felt had promise as a sire. Destiny Leo Jag was only a yearling and an injury had rendered him unable to be ridden. However, his pedigree, his temperament and his conformation were exceptional, and Edgar knew this horse would produce champions. Edgar contracted a sign to be painted, and then he hung it beside the highway a short distance from his training facility. The sign read, "Producing horses with a Destiny to show, to run, to win."

And win they did. Edgar's horses had a definite influence on the Quarter Horse industry throughout the western United States. Edgar spent the late 1950s and 1960s training show horses while breeding and raising colts sired by Destiny Leo Jag. On a bet, he once hushed a crowd by entering the showring on a horse wearing no bridle and then, following a flawless reining performance, exited to a thundering ovation!

It was near this time that another sorrel, strip-faced horse entered Edgar's and Jo's lives. They knew this foal was special the moment they laid eyes on her. Destiny Leo Jag and the mare Herfano had produced an exceptional filly. When she was a mere yearling, Edgar hauled this gem they named Destiny Jagetta to numerous Quarter Horse shows, where she was undefeated and occasionally was selected the show's Grand Champion. As Jagetta matured and developed, Edgar added more events to her repertoire: Western pleasure, reining and dally team roping. She excelled in all, rarely placing out of the money.

By now, everyone in Montana's Quarter Horse circles knew of Destiny Jagetta, yet few realized how close she was to becoming a legend. Jagetta had earned enough points in halter and performance classes to meet the criteria established for the American Quarter Horse Association's most coveted prize, Supreme Champion. Yet there was one remaining criterion to fulfill: racing.

Not one to sidestep a challenge, Edgar forged ahead with his prized mare. Her siblings were performing well on the racetrack for some of the northwest's most noted trainers, and Edgar knew Jagetta also was special. Unfortunately, he didn't know beans about training racehorses. As fate would have it, his son-in-law did.

Like the rest of Edgar's and Jo's children, their youngest daughter married a man who shared her interest and devotion to horses. A reputable racehorse trainer in his own right, their son-in-law was certainly capable of training Destiny Jagetta. However, Edgar chose to work with his son-in-law and others, all the while keeping close tabs on his beloved mare and doing the majority of the training himself.

The sun shone brightly on that warm July day when Edgar's and Jo's horse career reached that juncture between showing horses and racing them. Just the day before, Edgar had shown Destiny Jagetta in halter at these very same fairgrounds. She had won yet another Aged-Mare class and was named the show's Grand Champion Mare. Now, in nervous anticipation, the family waited as she paraded to the starting gate for her first race, an old maid of five years among the breed's two-year-old maidens.

In a rush, it was over. The gates had sprung wide, and the horses had hurtled toward the finish line as the crowd roared. Jo was so nervous she couldn't watch, yet when the starting gates flew open and the announcer called, "They're off!" Jo sprang to her feet screaming, "Come on baby! Come on baby!" encouraging her sorrel, strip-faced mare to give her all.

The dust settled and photos were developed, and in an amazing display of versatility, this Grand Champion show mare had won her first race! Destiny Jagetta, Edgar and Jo were on their way to a Supreme Championship, and just as they were well known and respected on the horse-show circuit, Edgar and Jo were on their way to becoming a noteworthy team in horse-racing circles as well.

It took nary a year, but soon only one more AAA rating stood between Jagetta and her Supreme Champion award, so Edgar entered her in a race in Helena.

She didn't win that race, although she certainly tried. She always tried. But this time it didn't matter that she didn't win. Jagetta ran fast enough to earn the speed rating she needed for her second AAA. Edgar and Jo had bred, raised and trained a Supreme Champion!

It was these stories the mourners told: the stories of sorrel strip-faced Quarter Horses that, in turn, told the story of this horseman they had come to honor.

When the priest began the graveside service, the stories ceased and a hush fell over the small cemetery overlooking Edgar's hometown. In grief and sorrow, the mourners prayed, when, in awe and disbelief, someone looked up and saw a figure on the hill just above this little country cemetery. With a polite interruption of the service, the mourners were invited to look toward the skyline, where on the edge of the old homestead in a pasture long-ago ridden by a grand horseman, stood a single sorrel, strip-faced horse watching the proceedings.

The family had chosen to cover the casket at the end of the service, so when the final blessing had been offered, the mourners' voices sang one final verse of "Amazing Grace" as the casket was slowly lowered into the grave. Shovels then appeared from horsemen's pickup trucks as Edgar's family, friends and neighbors joined in to bring closure to a life well-lived. And when shovelful after shovelful of granite had covered the casket, the sorrel horse on the hill quietly turned and disappeared over the horizon.

Jeff C. Nauman

A Tap on the Shoulder

In mid-1992 my uncle went into the hospital for the last time. His health was failing rapidly, and there was little left that medicine could do. JD, as we called him, was my father's older brother, now in his eighties. With still-black hair and a quiet manner, he loved "the horses" and followed the game daily.

When I'd go to visit him in the hospital, we'd just sit and pass the time. JD never talked much to begin with and he was no more talkative now. So any chance I had to create a diversion, I did. One day, I noticed in the next day's entries a horse named Pass the Vazul. Now, that's not a great name for a Thoroughbred, but it was worth a hunch bet for an eighty-five-year-old Italian.

"Hey, JD, I'll bet this one for us."

"Yeah, okay," was his unenthusiastic reply.

I bet $10 and sure enough, this hunch was a good hunch. The horse paid $11.80 to win, and our ticket was worth $59. Although that's not a lot of money, it was worth a story and a good laugh on my next visit.

Now, I didn't get back to the off-track betting shop to cash the ticket. There was no rush to cash the ticket, so it stayed in my wallet. Actually, I forgot about the ticket entirely until a few weeks later when JD passed away. It was only then that I remembered the bet and pulled out the ticket. I decided then that I wasn't ever going to cash it. A few days later it was placed in my favorite uncle's jacket pocket at his wake. It seemed only right that a horseplayer should leave with a winning ticket in his pocket, even if it was worth only $59.

The unreasonable fondness for the ponies that my uncle and I shared was not lost on those who know us. Shortly after the funeral, my aunt approached me and gave me an off-track betting ticket she had found in a drawer at home. JD had made the bet before he went into the hospital for the last time. She asked me to check and see if it was a winner. It read: $6 to Win, Letter B, 4th Race, Belmont, June 28, 1992. I checked it. It was a loser. But I didn't trash the ticket. It was the last bet JD ever made, so I put it in my wallet and forgot about it.

That ticket stayed in my wallet among other scraps of paper until sometime the next summer. Then one day, while I was at the teller's window at the bank, it fell out as I was fumbling with my driver's license.

I hadn't thought about the ticket, or JD for that matter, in months. I looked at the ticket and was struck by the irony. Today's date was June 28, 1993. The same day as the ticket one year later.

There was no doubt in my mind what I'd do next. I went straight to the off-track betting shop.

I bet $6 to Win, #2 (a new designation that replaced Letter B) in the 4th Race at Belmont. And then I made the same bet for my dad.

I cashed these tickets when the horse won. It paid $19.80 or a total of $59.40 for each winning ticket.

I went to my dad's house and put the money on the table.

"What's this for?" asked my dad.

For the first time, I told him the whole deal. The first bet, the ticket in JD's pocket at the wake, the ticket in my wallet, the date, the $59 and everything else. All he said to me was, "JD tapped you on the shoulder."

I can't argue with that.

Basil V. DeVito Jr.

Unbelievable Kentucky Derby Tale

*Sadie's right, that track is crooked! Lora May, it
isn't the track, it's the horses. They fix things up
amongst themselves.*

Joseph L. Mankiewicz, *A Letter to Three Wives*

The first Saturday in May is almost here, which means a
bunch of three-year-old horses with Onewordnamesaslong-
astheirtails will be running for the roses.

Ah, the Kentucky Derby. The most exciting two minutes
in sports and the only day of the year anyone drinks mint
juleps.

Everyone has a favorite Kentucky Derby story, and this is
mine. Actually, it is my great-uncle's.

It happened back in 1955, when Unc drove back east to the
bluegrass of Kentucky in a brand-new red convertible. He'd
made a $500 down payment and was dead set on paying off
the balance with a winning ticket on Swaps with the great
Bill Shoemaker aboard in the Derby.

As the car dealer had advised in order to break in the new
engine, Unc drove fifty-five miles per hour on the freeway the
whole way. It took him five long, hot days with no air condi-
tioning except the gritty wind in his face to reach Louisville.

Along the way, somewhere in New Mexico between Albuquerque and hell, Unc got a flat tire. Fortunately, it was five o'clock so it had cooled off to around a hundred degrees. Cost him five bucks to get it fixed.

It was about then that Unc noticed something, something you probably noticed a while ago. Fives. Everywhere Unc looked, the number five kept popping up.

It was a sure omen, Unc reasoned. After all, he had been born on May 5 in "none of your dang business what year!" as he always said. May, of course, is the fifth month.

Speaking of fifths, Unc was known to imbibe now and again later in the day, so maybe it wasn't an omen he had seen after all.

Anyway. On the morning of the Kentucky Derby on the first Saturday in May in 1955, Unc awoke with a jolt. He looked at the alarm clock. You guessed it. Five-till-six: 5:55.

"Did I mention I was staying at a Motel 5?" Unc would say, obviously embellishing his tale.

He raced down to the corner liquor store, still in his pajamas, and got the *Daily Racing Form*. He looked down to the fifth race. A horse named Five On Me was entered. In the Number 5 post position. At 5 to 1 odds.

That was the instant Unc realized what he must do. Forget Swaps in the Derby. Fate demanded he bet his bankroll on Five On Me in the fifth race. Back in his motel room, Unc pulled his suitcase out from under his bed and dug out his stash of cash from one of his dirty socks. He counted it. One hundred, two hundred . . . five hundred dollars.

He added the money from his wallet. Twenty, forty, fifty . . . fifty-five.

As if that wasn't eerie enough, he had two quarters and a nickel in his pants pocket.

Unc took a taxi to Churchill Downs. Yellow Cab number 5, by the way. The fare was five bucks. He tipped the cabbie the fifty-five cents change from his pocket. Superstitiously, Unc went to the fifth window and bet his last nickel, all $550, on Five On Me.

And they were off. Five On Me got a slow break from the gate and was dead last in the twelve-horse field as they headed around the first turn.

Then Five On Me started to make up ground. He was eleventh. Then tenth. The reddish chestnut moved up to eighth heading down the backstretch.

Unc cheered him on until his lungs hurt.

Turning toward home, Five On Me was seventh and still gaining. At the one-eighth pole, he closed in on the leaders.

Roaring down the homestretch, it was a five-horse race, and Five On Me was one of them.

Unc roared. He yelled. He shook his fist and cursed, "Come on, you sonufagun! You can do it!"

A photo finish.

Unc held his breath and waited for the results.

The omen came true. Five On Me was—what else—fifth!

Woody Woodburn

The Funny Cide of Life

A New York-bred gelding and six lifelong friends renewed the spirits of America during a history-making campaign for the Triple Crown in 2003. This average and unassuming group and their horse became a testament to the old adage that "good things happen to good people."

Funny Cide and the Sackets Six, as the buddies were dubbed, brought America to its feet, cheering on the underdog and drawing more people into horse racing than have watched in years.

Funny Cide thrust his owners, which includes the Sackets Six and four other partners, into the coveted winners' circle in no uncertain terms after stalking the pacesetter and winning the Kentucky Derby by one and three-quarter lengths. His run in the Preakness left everyone but the horse breathless, winning by an astounding nine and three-quarter lengths, a showing that came close to breaking the long-standing record of ten lengths set in the first Preakness run in 1873 by Survivor.

As I reminisced with one of the Six about our high-school years, the enthusiasm about recent wins and a date with destiny on June 7, a mere fourteen days away, was kept to a dull roar.

These friends from Sackets Harbor, a small village in upstate New York, had children in college, businesses to run, retirements to fund and mortgages to pay. They were an unlikely group to be investing in racehorses, but doing so gave the close-knit group another way to enjoy the camaraderie the friends had always shared.

Brothers Mark and Pete were good students and active in the local sports programs. JP (Jon) was the life of everyone's party, while Harold came from a large family and never caused any trouble, preferring to stay out of the limelight. We expected Larry to do well someday; he was a popular kid and knew how to throw a party. Jackie loved sports and excelled at anything he tried, always ready with a smile on his face—win or lose.

Their personalities haven't changed, and if the town wasn't decked out in Funny Cide memorabilia and reporters weren't hovering around, you wouldn't know this group of middle-aged men was at the heart of Thoroughbred racing history. Moreover, at times it seems neither do they.

They were your average kids, growing up on Lake Ontario, close to the Canadian border. Summers were spent cruising around the Village, hanging out on the corner, playing baseball or football, or swimming at the "Jump-Off" and daring each other to dive off the bridge. Fall brought pep rallies with the student body, athletes and cheerleaders marching from the school, through town to the cliffs along the lake, where the bonfire was set and school spirit was ignited along with the blaze. The Six were usually at the head of the pack. Maroon and gray were the school colors, colors worn by Funny Cide today.

Upon graduation the boys scattered to make their mark on the world. Some went to college, some went into business; all married and started families. Everyone stayed in contact.

Before I talked to any of these men about their experiences with Funny Cide I knew what they would say. I knew they would be humble and in awe of their success. I knew they would say it was the horse that was the hero and not them. I wasn't disappointed.

When I talked to Mark it felt like we had just had coffee at the local diner. Characteristically warm and friendly and happy to share his feelings, I could "hear" the big grin on his face and the pride in his voice.

He began the conversation about Funny Cide by telling me, "There were 34,000 or so racehorses born three years ago and I am still in awe that we were lucky enough to find Funny Cide. It just blows my mind. How did *we* ever end up with the *one* horse that could do it? We've always bought New York-bred horses, that's all part of it—a horse born right here at home."

Mark continued. "The first race Funny Cide ever ran, the jockey told us that he had 'potential' and that he might be a winner. The second race he ran, the same jockey told us that 'the lightbulb went on. *This* horse could win the Kentucky Derby.' I said, 'Yeah, sure, okay,' but didn't quite believe him. When we bought Funny Cide we thought he had potential for smaller races and we would be happy if he consistently placed."

In relating their purchase of Funny Cide, Mark said, "When we bought Funny Cide, things were tight and we didn't have much money to invest in anything. Something told us to take a chance—to go for it. All we expected was to *maybe* get our investment back, definitely have some fun following him to races and hopefully make a little profit. We never in our wildest dreams thought that Funny Cide would take us to the Kentucky Derby."

In a moment he will never forget, Mark recalls, "I was walking from the barn to the track with Funny Cide the day of the Derby and looked up at the stands full of thousands of people. All I could think was, *I still don't believe this is happening. How did we get this lucky? What did we ever do to deserve this?*"

Thoughtfully Mark said, "We own part of America's horse. He's the horse for the people, for the little guy."

As we finished talking, Mark summed it up by saying, "It's all about Funny Cide, not us. We haven't done anything special; we just invested in a dream. He's helped us promote our town and showed the world that there *is* life above Albany, that the North Country exists.

"We've been able to show the world what a wonderful town we live in and what great people are here. We didn't take a chance on Funny Cide when we bought him; he took a chance on us. This little horse has helped us show the world that sometimes the dreams of the little guy *do* come true; that what goes around, comes around. If you try to be a good person and give back to your community somehow, someday it will come back to you. Funny Cide rewarded us all in far greater ways than we ever deserved."

As I said, this is an unassuming group of men. They all share a sense of humility, loyalty to their community and love for their family. A family that has grown by thousands since that unforgettable Saturday in May.

They take no credit for their fame; they give all the glory to this little New York-bred horse that has more heart than the whole town of Sackets Harbor put together.

When Funny Cide can't race anymore, they will still be there for him. No matter what happens on June 7 at Belmont Park, Funny Cide's home track where he is undefeated, they will be grateful every day of their lives for the chance to be included in his success and to have owned a piece of America's horse.

Chris Russell-Grabb

[EDITORS' NOTE: *On May 28, Funny Cide turned in a sharp workout, his first since the Kentucky Derby and the Preakness. Trainer Barclay Tagg proclaimed him to be "sound, healthy and happy." As we went to press with this book, anticipation of a twelfth Triple Crown champion was reaching a fever pitch. The last horse to win all three races was Affirmed in 1978. Success at Belmont on June 7 will bring a $5 million bonus to the owners of Funny Cide. Regardless of the outcome, there is no doubt June 8 will find the Sackets Six enjoying a cup of coffee or a cold beer on the porch talking about the ride of their lives, having lived the American dream.*]

7

HORSE...
CETERA

I *have pulled your plows to feed your families.*
I have carried your flag in parades to
celebrate your independence.
I have run with all my heart for that buckle
hanging on your belt.
I have shown you the world from my back,
And now we'll show the world together,
You are America, and I am your horse—
America's Horse.

Reprinted with permission of
American Quarter Horse Association©

They Neigh, I Pay

Although I'm a veterinarian, I don't proclaim to be an expert on horses.

I'm just the guy who brings home the bacon to a household consisting of my knowledgeable, horse-obsessed wife Teresa and daughter Mikkel. However, I do know something that they don't seem to understand or care about. After years of following their footprints and accompanying hoofprints, I've come to the startling conclusion about the essence of having horses in your life: They neigh, I pay!

I used to hear the adage that the best way to make a lot of money with horses is to start out with a lot more money. Trust me, that statement's more fact than fiction.

The purchase of your first horse is a harbinger of what's to come. You buy horses from people who make used car salesmen seem like choirboys and pay only about twice as much as you should. Every horse offered for sale is one of a kind, a special bargain just for you, a horse that never has been and never will be lame, is as gentle as a baby, loads easily into a trailer, is the one that the owners will sacrifice only to a good home. Yours, sucker.

You buy the horse. So far, so bad. Although your bank account has been lanced and has started bleeding, you don't feel the pain at first.

Next stop, the local tack store, where you test-ride a handmade one-of-a-kind saddle with a special seat. They always throw in the part about the seat being special, both for comfort and style, making it even more difficult to pass up a saddle that they say will almost certainly appreciate in value. Throw in blankets, halters, reins, brushes, combs, clippers, helmets, gloves, clothing and jewelry, and you've got yourself a small fortune invested already. Ka-Ching!

Then comes hay, sweet feed, high-priced nutritional supplements, feeders, buckets and, yes, even toys for horses. Ka-Ching!

But wait, your anemic bank account has just been minimally hemorrhaging until now. When the need arises to transport the horses from point A to point B in style, you just hit an economic artery. After becoming the proud owners of a new Ford F-250 V-10, crew-cab pickup, pulling a four-horse, slant-load Featherlite horse trailer with custom graphics, it's time to call the bank for a major transfusion. Ka-Ching! Ka-Ching!

Your yearly salary will show signs of needing a transfusion when your wife and daughter decide to show horses. It starts out low-key with local 4-H shows and competitions but rapidly escalates into big regional shows and eventually, huge national shows. At every step, I hear the words of my late father Bob, "The price of playing poker just went up," as we climb the ladder of financial brinkmanship to the top of the horse world.

Now your family surfs the Web and subscribes to a dozen horse magazines, looking for "the" winning horse to add to the collection. In a game that makes human personal ads seem both understated and true by comparison, the ads about horses claim that each is a national champion of some sort, a sure winner, sacrificed only for, you guessed it, a good home. Yours.

Everybody wants to see a video of the horse that they may want to buy, and soon your mailbox is stuffed with videos coming from the four corners of the United States and Canada. Your VCR is white-hot from watching them over and over, and your eyes squint from viewing grainy videos, shot in low light. Everybody says, "The pictures lie, he really is a lot better than what you see on the video." Yeah, right. False deadlines come and go, and you continue your frantic search.

Then—eureka!—you find him. The horse that has all the coveted abilities to win: head held low enough to scrape the ground with his forehead, trotting so slowly you'd swear you're watching a slow-motion replay, able to be steered by just the trainer in the stands moving her legs.

As you arrange for your panel of horse experts to view the video, someone always finds something about the horse that nobody else noticed and that kicks the prospect out of the running. At that point, like lemmings, everybody agrees, "Yeah. It's there. I didn't see that until you pointed it out. You don't want him."

Me? I see nothing, but I nod my head in agreement so that everybody thinks I'm one of them and certainly not a veterinarian who can't see something so apparently obvious about the health or stealth of a horse.

Now it's Christmastime, and even though you still don't have a horse for next year's shows, that doesn't stop you from going ahead and buying your daughter a custom show saddle with more silver than a Navajo gift shop, a hand-tooled belt buckle with her name in big letters, show clothes, new boots and much, much more. All dressed up for Christmas photos, she looks silly, kind of like Hollywood meets north Idaho. Ka-Ching!

Finally, after months of searching for the equine version of Mr. Right, you're so thoroughly exhausted and dizzy that you just buy the next horse that comes along. That way, you can tell everybody, and especially yourself, that after much consideration, you have indeed, found the perfect horse. But this horse needs a special trainer to reach his potential and, of course, it's best for the horse to live at the trainer's whose housing is better than yours. Ka-Ching! Ka-Ching! Ka-Ching!

Your IRA now eats hay and you need to call the Loan Arranger!

Well now, as much as I hate to admit it, as far as investments go, the ROI (return on investment) is actually great when you buy a horse. You have a wife and teenage daughter who obsess together, train together and travel to shows together. They draw close as they share the thrill of victory and the agony of defeat.

You sit in the stands, jostling elbow to elbow with the other dads, eagerly taking the twentieth video of the season as your daughter and her horse enter the arena. You marvel at the symphony of a 125-pound girl riding a 1,300-pound one-horsepower sports car. Your heart races and your palms sweat as the judges line up the entries to announce the awards.

When your daughter takes a blue ribbon, your wife and daughter hug at the arena gate and you get choked up with pride and joy. It's one of the greatest feelings in the world. But it's short lived.

For tomorrow, you're up at the stalls, manure fork in hand, tossing into the cart what remains of your retirement. Ahhh, I love the smell of horse manure in the morning!

Marty Becker, DVM

Of Great Horses and Men

Spending that many hours in the saddle gave a man plenty of time to think. That's why so many cowboys fancied themselves philosophers.

                                                    C.M. Russell

That's the ugliest horse I've ever seen. Now wait a minute, let me think on that. Yep, that's the ugliest horse I've ever seen.

I was only eight years old the first time I laid eyes on that horse. Up until that time in my life, I had not even considered the fact that there might be an ugly horse anywhere. Even the mules on the ranch where my dad worked weren't that ugly and they're ugly by design. It turns out that this horse's looks were also by design. It seems this horse's owner, plus the horse's purpose, had a lot to do with how he looked.

Picture this: a beautiful black stallion prancing on a hilltop, his mane flowing and tail shimmering in the sun as he rears up to fight the wind in a mock battle. Then he charges off down the slope to his perfect little band of mares and foals, protecting them from harm. How many times have you seen that on TV or in the movies? Isn't this how we visualize the perfect stallion?

Now picture this: a roman-nosed black stallion with a

white patch between his eyes that looks more like a scar than a patch. His mane has been roached low on each side, then grown out to about five or six inches, giving his neck the appearance of being deep and wide. His forelock is long and matted with burrs. His tail has been roached like that of a mule then grown out to where it looks like a fan. His fetlocks, too, have been clipped and grown back long enough to touch the ground. It's obvious that he has been kept in a small lot that has a mud hole in it because he has dried mud and dirt caked all over him.

You'd have thought that his owner had never seen a brush or a currycomb and you would never have guessed that he was an AAA running Quarter Horse. In reality, he was very pampered back at the ranch. He had his own barn, paddock and a personal groom. But it was to his owner's advantage that the horse looked scruffy sometimes. He was run only in matched races because there were no recognized tracks in Oklahoma at the time. The dirt and mud made it easier to match and raise the stakes on what appeared to be an ugly ranch horse.

I had just arrived in Pawhuska, Oklahoma, the day before to spend the summer of 1943 with my favorite aunt and uncle, who managed a stud farm just out of town. My uncle had been quite a racehorse man in his younger years, winning some pretty big races, but health problems had kept him close to home the last few years. His name was Albert Reynolds and he was known as a starter at all the local race, meets and matched races. He was a man you could depend on to give you a fair shake at the gate. If your horse lost the race, it wasn't because he didn't get a fair start. However, there's one little thing about Uncle Albert that I feel compelled to reveal and it's something that too many other people found out the hard way. You should never match him in a horse race. In all the years I knew him, he never lost.

On this day, he was about to start this high-stakes match race of 350 yards. It was between a good-lookin' sorrel blaze-faced horse owned by an Osage Indian family and Ol' Ugly.

I'm sure this horse had a more respectable name, but in the years I knew him I can never remember anyone calling him anything you could print except "that old ugly stud." He belonged to a local rancher by the name of Ben Johnson.

It seems that Ben also had quite a reputation around this neck of the woods for matching horse races. But Ben's reputation went far beyond ranching and racing horses. He was also a world champion steer roper and later Pawhuska, Oklahoma, would dedicate an annual memorial steer-roping event to their favorite son. This soft-spoken cowboy produced a son, Ben Johnson Jr., who also won a world champion title in team roping before going to Hollywood, becoming an actor and winning an academy award for his role in *The Last Picture Show*.

Now, Ol' Ugly was coming down the track toward the starting gates in a slow lope, ponied by a nice-looking bay horse ridden by a man named Dee Garrett. Dee also owned a ranch west of Pawhuska and dabbled in runnin' horses himself. He later owned a running Quarter Horse mare named Miss Pawhuska and a stallion named Vandy. The colts from these two horses produced a lot of changes in the record-book standings for sires.

Well, it was post time. Both horses were at the gate; nothing left to do but run 'em. "Who you ridin'?" Ben asked the Indian.

"My youngest," he said, pointing to a little kid about six years old. "And you?" the man asked Ben.

"I'll ride this boy," Ben said as he put his hand on my shoulder. " This your boy, Albert?"

"He's my nephew," my uncle replied.

"Good enough for me," exclaimed Ben. "Let's saddle 'em and run 'em!"

Before I even had time to react or understand what had just been said, Ben picked me up by the seat of the pants and the back of the collar and set me up on the big stallion. I had never ridden a stallion before and now I was piloting one in a match race! His neck alone was thicker than the horses and mules I had been riding at home. To say I was scared was an understatement.

Don't I get a say in this? What am I supposed to do? Am I going to die if I don't do it right? Why me? The only reason I wasn't throwing up was because there was something lodged in my throat. I think it was my heart, trying to pound its way out through my ears.

"Lift your legs," Uncle Albert said, as he was tossing an elastic overcinch across them to Ben on the other side. "This will keep you from falling off," he explained as they cinched it tight under the big horse. At this point, the horse and I were one. I could feel every ripple of every muscle in his back. I just couldn't feel my legs.

"Listen to me," Uncle Albert commanded. "If you get in trouble, like he falls down or somethin', you just straighten out your legs and the cinch will pop right off." Uncle Albert seemed to think that being up here on this horse wasn't trouble enough.

Ben led the big horse into the gate and then crawled up by his head to steady him while the other horse was being loaded.

"Here," he said, as he crossed the reins. "Hold these like this in one hand."

He then took off his belt, put it around the horse's neck, through the throatlatch of the bridle, and buckled it. I remember the sun glistening off the big gold and silver buckle.

"Get a death grip on this belt with your other hand and don't let go. Now listen to me. Here's what I want you to do," he instructed as I looked up at him. "When the gate opens you just try to shove the bit out of his mouth and scream!"

"Not a problem about the screamin' part," I tried to say, but nothing came out. As I looked back down the long straightaway toward the grandstand and all the people, to my surprise the starting gate and the horse's head were both gone! Just as the sound of the steel gates banging open came to me, I felt my arms being jerked out of their sockets and my head was suddenly snapped back. The big horse had dropped out of the starting gate a-runnin'! The death grip I had on the reins and belt, along with the overcinch, made sure that I went with him.

Never before had I felt such a force of power. The surprise of the start must have cleared my throat as I found myself screaming, first from shock, then sheer fright, then excitement. My eyes were filled with tears from the force of the wind and from the dirty mane, where my face was now buried. I took a short breath and screamed again as we blew by the eighth pole.

I was suddenly becoming aware of my situation. I was still alive, I was in a horse race and I was winning! I looked back and could see the blaze face of a sorrel horse in the distance. As I turned back to the task at hand, we were going by the grandstand and the finish line.

The big horse's ears were up and flicking back and forth. I had just ridden and won my first race! Now what? I pulled back on the reins, but he took the bit in his mouth like a vice, laid his ears back down and picked up speed. By the time I realized I was in a dilemma, another problem appeared. We were running out of track. The straightaway ended and we were at the turn. The big horse changed leads and ducked into the turn with such force that it was all the overcinch and my new grip on the reins could do to stay on top.

When we hit the backstretch, his ears came up again, but he didn't turn loose of the bit. Just as I realized that my peril wasn't improving and I still might die, I caught a glimpse of Dee Garret on the pony horse next to the outside rail. He swooped in and picked up the outside rein and pulled the big horse up. I was really lucky that Mr. Garrett had been there in the backstretch to save me. Years later, it occurred to me that he probably was more concerned about Ol' Ugly's safety than about saving me from certain death.

As we slowed down and were turning around to head back to the grandstand, he proclaimed, "Well, kid, you won that one pretty handy." Then he took the cigar out of his mouth and added, "You can stop screaming now."

Boots Reynolds

Of Great Horses and Men

Are You a Real Horse Mom?

Blind with love, my daughter has cried nightly for horses, those long-necked marchers and churners that she has mastered, any and all, reining them in like a circus hand.

Anne Sexton, "Pain for a Daughter"

You know you're a Horse Mom when:

1. You spend three days and nights in a cramped trailer in a dusty (or muddy) lot behind the horse barns for your vacation.

2. Your colleagues at work ask how your weekend was, you exclaim, "Great!" and then wonder how to explain exactly what was so great about sitting around a cold and drafty or hot and muggy (choose one) barn, getting dust in your eyes and hay in your teeth while your child alternated between giddy euphoria and sullen despair (depending on the judge, the horse's behavior and other factors imperceptible to a mere parent).

3. You realize you have graduated from nights spent walking a fussy or colicky infant around the bedroom

to nights spent walking a fussy or colicking horse around the barn.

4. You find horse-treat nuggets at the bottom of your daughter's clothes hamper and are inordinately pleased that at least you didn't find horse-treat mush at the bottom of the washer when you took her wet clothes out (this time).

5. You are glad to see your child eating vegetables as she takes turns biting from the same carrot with her horse.

6. One of your greatest life achievements is learning to back a trailer around a corner into a parking space without denting either of the much fancier trailers on either side.

7. Raking a brush through your hair and slapping on a hat qualifies as putting on your makeup.

8. Your daughter asks to borrow your hairbrush and you retrieve it later from her tack box, full of long, coarse hair (not yours or your daughter's).

9. The friendly farm veterinarian asks you to "Come here and hold this," and without gloves—you obediently grab the horse's tongue to hold it aside while his teeth get worked on.

10. You can hem a pair of show pants with safety pins and duct tape in thirty seconds flat.

11. The equine feed bill is a bigger portion of your family budget than the human feed bill.

12. Ditto the medical bills.

13. And shoes.

14. You wish your child would spend more time hanging around the mall. It would be cheaper than what's required for all the time she spends hanging around that horse.

15. You cry when your child comes in dead last in her show class. You also cry when she comes in first.

Barbara Greenstreet

Horse Lovers Are
Really Sick People

Did you ever stop to wonder what exactly it is about horses that makes so many people fall obsessively in love with them?

One contributing factor is the number of horse-related stories so many of us read as kids. *Black Beauty, The Black Stallion, My Friend Flicka,* CW Anderson's *Billy and Blaze* stories, *Misty of Chincoteague, King of the Wind* . . . the list goes on and on. And, of course, every horse-mad girl (and boy) that I've ever known has a collection of Breyer horse models. But what exactly is the unknown thing that pushes a normal kid to ask, over and over again, "Mommy, Daddy, when can I have a pony?"

I have long believed that it is very easy to fall in love with horses. Why shouldn't it be? They are beautiful, powerful animals; the stuff of fantasy and legend. They are an integral part of our country's history and the rest of the world's as well. The very fact that a mere person can bond to and form a partnership with such a large and intelligent creature has inspired art, literature and myth throughout the ages. But how . . . why . . . what makes it happen?

I have a theory about that. I believe that the love of all things equine, the true love, is a virus. Most people are carriers of the infection. Many will suffer the symptoms at some point in their lives, usually late childhood to mid-teens. Then there are those who are terminal, destined to exist in the grip of the horse-love virus for their entire life span.

What other rational explanation could there be to explain the intense emotional, physical and financial sacrifices we make for our horses? Why on earth would a normal, sane person dedicate all of his or her time to grooming a very big animal that is going to roll in the mud as soon as he gets back outside? It certainly can't be considered typical behavior to spend the better part of the day picking bits of poop out of a stall with a pitchfork, or spending all of one's free hours in a barn. And why would anyone even want to be at the barn when the weather is soggy, freezing or hot enough to melt your eyeballs? The concept of horse ownership seems to defy all logic.

It starts innocently enough. The average young girl rides a carousel horse for the first time. Not long after, she graduates to pony rides. One Christmas morning, she receives a toy horse or her first copy of *Black Beauty*. Her parents notice their little darling clipping pictures of horses out of magazines and making a scrapbook. Her weekly allowance is deposited into an elaborately decorated, equine-themed coffee can for the future horse-purchasing fund. The Barbie dolls are shoved into the closet and replaced with Barbie's horse, Breyer models, Grand Champions, or whatever other brand the local toy shop carries. Christmas rolls around again, and the obliga-tory letter to Santa simply begs, "Please bring me a pony."

Her parents chuckle to themselves, "Oh, she'll grow out of it," and in some instances, they could be right. There are those who escape the clutches of the virus. Puberty hits and the rush of hormones occasionally is strong enough to extin-guish the infection. But not always.

If the virus persists, the requests for driving lessons are now accompanied by those for riding lessons. The coffee-can fund is in the bank and the horse-crazy teenager is looking for a part-time job to raise additional cash. Instead of rock stars and athletes, posters of galloping horses cover the bedroom walls. Books on stable management and horse care join the well-read storybooks on the shelf. Horses are scribbled on the covers of notebooks. Book reports and class projects consistently revolve around an equine subject. Shopping expeditions always include a quick side trip to the local saddlery. No, she may not own a horse, but she already has riding boots, a hoof pick, brushes and a halter, all displayed in a place of honor in her bedroom.

If the parents are willing to treat the symptoms, the victim may get riding lessons. If she is truly fortunate (and her folks have the cash), she might actually get a horse. Then there are those poor, sad souls, the riders without horses. Perhaps college got in the way, or marriage and motherhood. The virus is still there; nighttime finds the subject tossing and turning, dreaming of a morning gallop across verdant fields. Oftentimes, these folks may have to wait until the mortgage is paid and the kids have moved away before being able to satisfy the needs of the disease.

I am not trying to scare you by telling you all of this. I only seek to warn you, to let you know what to expect in yourself or younger members of your family. You see, I speak from experience. I am a terminal horse-love virus patient. It hit me early, when I was about three and had received my first Breyer model horse. It stayed with me through my childhood, up to college and into adulthood. My parents were very understanding, and provided therapy during my teen years in the form of riding lessons and a big, black gelding named Shadow.

I'm in my late thirties now. My family still loves and supports me. They never fuss when I miss weekend gatherings because I need equine treatment. They don't comment when I can't spend money on them, because I've already spent it all on my horse. If the basement in my house is full of tack, horse blankets and other equipment, they just smile and walk around it. And at Christmas, there are as many gifts for my horse under the tree as there are for me. They know the virus can't be fought, only accommodated.

One of my best friends recently had a baby. I went to visit them both and brought a stuffed pony for the new little girl. In a crib full of toys, it was the only thing she would hold on to. The contagion has been passed again.

Cristina Scalise

Me and Minnie Pearl

The American male, at the peak of his physical powers and appetites, driving 160 big white horses across the scenery of an increasingly hopeless society, with weekend money in his pocket and with little prior exposure to trouble and tragedy, personifies "an accident going to happen."

John Sloan Dickey

I stood on my knees in the back seat of the 1942, black, four-door Ford and put my elbows on the headrest of the front seats where my mother and daddy were sitting. I was going to ride in my first horse show.

Bubbling with an unfounded childlike confidence fueled by my excitement, I had no doubt that I would win my class. I had only one question. "Daddy, what am I supposed to do when the man tells me to canter?"

My daddy, a six-foot tall, 230-pound bear of a man with a Tampa Nugget cigar stuck in one corner of his mouth, replied, "When the man says canter, you trot your horse."

My mother, a short, stocky but pretty woman with black hair, turned toward the back seat, faced me and added, "Don't worry about it, Tommy. You're only four years old. No one expects you to canter the horse." Although her words were supportive, I sensed my mother's nervousness. I knew she didn't want me riding in the show, but as usual, my father had the deciding vote on what happened around our house.

I had grown up around horses. My daddy, whose main business was a grocery store, ran a riding stable on the side. I had been sitting on a horse from the time I could sit up. Our trainer would put me on a horse, hook a lead line to the animal, and I would follow him wherever he went. Recently, I had graduated to riding on my own without the lead line.

My horse was Minnie Pearl, a big, ugly, full-grown, dark bay mare with a head that looked like a mule's. My father trusted Minnie Pearl, and I had learned to ride on her rather than on a pony, which would have been more my size. Minnie was gentle and considerate as she proved the day I fell off and got my foot tangled in the stirrup. I was so short I couldn't even touch the ground with my hands as I hung from the side of the horse. Minnie just stopped and started grazing, waiting until the trainer came to liberate me. At four, I had no fear. I remounted and was off again.

When we got to the show at the Burlington City Park, I walked around the grounds, feeling grown up in my white, short-sleeved shirt, tan riding britches—the kind that flared out on the sides—and my brown riding boots that came up to my knees. I strutted around, aware of the "isn't he cute" glances I was getting from the adults in the crowd.

I walked to the ring, where classes already were underway. Bleachers were set up on one straightaway of the ring and they were about half full of people. Most people seemed to prefer to watch from along the rail, propping their arms and elbows on the top rail. I noticed the grandstands on one side of the ring, nearly full with people. I was too short to see over the top rail, but I got a good view of the action by peering between the top and lower rails. Several times, I got pelted with dirt clods flying from the horses' hooves as they moved around the ring. Worried that I would get my riding outfit dirty, I moved away from the ring. I found a big rock several yards away and climbed up on it. From this perch, I watched the bustle of horses and people.

When it was time for my class, I found my daddy and our trainer, who were at our trailer with Minnie Pearl. Back at our barn, I had a mounting box for getting on Minnie, but we hadn't brought it along to the show. So my daddy lifted me on to Minnie's back while the trainer held her reins. The trainer led Minnie, with me on her back, to the ring to wait for our class.

I don't remember what kind of class it was—probably a pleasure class. It was not a class for kids. Everyone else in the class was an adult. I sat on Minnie at the gate to the ring, surrounded by adult riders, waiting for the preceding class to end.

As the gate opened and I started in the gate, a man I didn't know thrust a stick at me and said, "Here, boy. Use this on that old horse."

I took the stick and entered the ring.

Remembering my daddy's instructions, I turned Minnie to the right and urged her into a trot, keeping to the rail, trying to stay out of the traffic. After a minute, the announcer said, "Walk your horses. Please walk your horses."

I reined in Minnie to a walk. After a few seconds of walking, the announcer said, "Canter. Canter your horses."

The class was crowded with at least fifteen horses. Horses started passing me one after the other. I had never cantered a horse before, but something possessed me to whack Minnie across the rump with that stick. She took off, much too fast for good form. We were passing every other horse in the class as she carried me pell-mell around the ring.

Suddenly, I was Roy Rogers, Minnie was Trigger and we were heading off a cattle stampede. I was having the time of my short, but reckless, life. The wind cooled my face and flapped my shirttail as Minnie and I circled the track.

The crowd went crazy, laughing and cheering. Above it

all, I could my mother yelling, "Herman, Herman. Get him, Herman. He's cantering. He can't canter."

The announcer said, "Walk your horses. Please walk your horses." I pulled Minnie to a walk. The crowd and my mother stopped yelling, but there was soft laughter and a buzz in the crowd.

The next direction from the announcer was, "Reverse. Reverse and trot your horses." I turned Minnie's nose to the outside rail of the ring until she was headed in the opposite direction, kicked her in her flanks and started posting to her trot.

After we had trotted for a couple of laps, the announcer again slowed us to a walk and followed with the canter command. Once again, I whacked Minnie on the flank and sped around the ring. The crowd came alive again, yelling and screaming, but they couldn't outyell my mother, who again yelled for my father to do something.

After the last canter, the announcer had us line up on the infield grass, following the directions of the ringmaster. We sat still on our horses while the judge walked from one end of the line to the other, looking over horses and riders. He wrote his selections on a piece of paper and gave them to the announcer, who called out the winners.

With each named called, my excitement waned. I wasn't among the winners and I was embarrassed as I walked Minnie Pearl out the exit gate with the other losers. As I neared the gate, I saw my father waiting for me there, a big grin on his face, the ever-present cigar in the corner of his mouth. I felt better. My daddy was proud of me and all around me adults were congratulating me, telling me how well I had done.

That confused me. I couldn't understand why I didn't get a ribbon if I had done so well. One thing I wasn't confused about, I'd just had the most fun I'd ever had on the back of a horse and I wanted to do it again, and next time I'd win a ribbon.

I spent the rest of the day exploring the creek and the big

rocks of the city park. Minnie Pearl grazed contently waiting to be trailered home. Finally, as we climbed into the car for the trip back home, my father said, "I have a surprise for you. After your class, the judges got together and decided you deserved a special prize for your showing today. They've asked me to give you this."

He pulled out a purple ribbon and handed it to me. I didn't know what place purple represented, but I didn't care. I proudly pinned the ribbon to the pocket of my white shirt and fell asleep before we got home, dreaming of my next adventure on horseback.

Tom Truitt

"Hey, mister, when you finish her horse,
would you build me one, too?"

Build Me One, Too! *Reprinted by permission of Boots Reynolds. ©2000 Boots Reynolds.*

Attitude

My friend Janet Dean ran her horse Shanghai through the gate. She was riding well, leaning for leverage as they circled the first orange barrel. She could feel her chaps flapping against her leg and knew the barrel was teetering but would stay up. She rode Shanghai all out for the second barrel. This was a good ride. She knew it.

The angle was perfect on the third barrel and Janet's heart raced as she yelled, "Go, go!" and dirt flew from the horse's hooves.

They raced back through the outdoor arena gate where her dad stood with a stopwatch.

"Yeah," Janet screamed. "Yeah!"

She let Shanghai take a wide circle back toward her father. "Well?"

Mr. Dean had on jeans, a checkered shirt and a Jayhawk's cap. He shook his head. "Not as good as last year," he said.

"But it felt so right."

"Maybe you're a better rider this year. Maybe you're helping the horse rather than the horse helping you. It might be time to start a new horse. Old Shanghai has to retire sometime. If not this year, the next, or the year after."

Dust blew across their arena. Janet patted Shanghai on the

shoulder. "Darn good horse, though," she said, shaking her head.

The hottest horse she could find and afford was an unbroken two-year-old, a little mare named Bistro. Her friend Angie had bred her just south of the Kansas border, in Oklahoma.

"She's a brat," Angie said.

Janet and her father stood leaning on a gate across the eight-stall barn. Angie was inside with a plastic bag tied to a whip.

"What do you mean, 'brat'?"

"You'll see." Angie let the little red mare out of her stall. Bistro's trot was light and she appeared to float across the barn. Angie waved the plastic bag.

Bistro had a white stocking on her right hind leg. Pop! She nailed Angie's bag with one kick.

"Dang!" Janet's father said. "I don't know about this."

"Let's see her outside," Janet said.

They took the mare out into the pasture. Bistro was quick, running toward the fence at full speed and spinning around after a sliding stop. She'd dig her hooves into the ground and throw dirt. She kicked up spray as if the dirt were water and she loved coming as close to the fence as she could without crashing into it at full speed.

Janet's eyes got big. "She's athletic."

"Yeah, but 'brat' could mean killer," her father said.

"Let me see her in the stall," Janet said.

Angie led the horse back to her stall and Janet spent several minutes nose to nose with Bistro. It looked like a case of pure love.

"Oh boy. Here we go," her father said.

The first problem came when Angie delivered the mare to Mr. Dean's ranch. Bistro wouldn't unload. She locked all four legs and it took thirty minutes and five men before they got her out.

"I've never seen a horse that wouldn't *unload*," her father said. "Won't go in a trailer . . . sure. That I've seen, but not this!"

Bistro was a sweetheart in the stall with Janet, but outside . . . well, outside, she was a brat.

Janet's father hired a cowboy to break her so that she could be ridden. He quit after the mare rose up on her hind legs and walked him into the corner. Bistro didn't just rear up, she walked on two legs like a man.

The cowboy scooted out of the stall on his belly and said, "I quit."

Janet wasn't allowed to watch the next cowboy. Her father hired tough Bill Hooley and told him to use the whip if he had to.

All Bill remembered was a white hoof in his flak jacket and looking up from the ground to see Bistro bucking through the barn. Bistro crashed through the metal fence across the door and would have ended up in Colorado if she hadn't been bucking with her head down. She ran into a stock trailer and knocked herself out just for a moment.

They were able to lead the stunned horse back to her stall without anymore trouble. Everybody looked at the broken metal fence and scratched their heads.

Bill Hooley handed the whip back to Janet's father and kept on walking. "Getting tough ain't gonna work," he said as he climbed into a black Ford 150. "That horse doesn't *want* to be broke."

The next morning they found Bistro running free in the barn. Mr. Dean looked at the stall. "Too smart," he said. "Now she's letting herself out. That's what's wrong. She's too smart for her own good."

Bistro nuzzled Janet. Her head was over Janet's shoulder. Janet looked at her dad.

"Don't even think about it," her father said. "Someone else has to break her."

"Well who? I'm fifteen."

"I dunno, but not you."

They found a young ex-marine, raised on a ranch in Utah. Rode broncs for a while until it hurt too much. His name was David and he was tall and taut like a rodeo man.

"I'll try it," he said. "But nobody goes near her for one month. Not even Janet. No visits to the stall, no hugging, no nothing. Bistro has to be totally dependant on me. I feed her. I water her."

Janet said, "I love that horse, David. We've got a bond."

"My way or not at all," he responded.

Janet looked at her father and he nodded.

So, Janet began spying on them from the side door. She didn't let Bistro see her.

David spent the first day just standing in Bistro's stall with his back turned to the horse. By day two, Bistro would throw her head over his shoulder, begging for attention, but David ignored her.

David did the feeding. David did the watering. David cleaned the stall.

On day three, David led Bistro out into the barn. He put a rope on her and worked her in a circle for a while. Then Janet was surprised to see him give Bistro a Mountain Dew. The horse grabbed the plastic bottle in her teeth, threw her head back and downed it in quick gulps.

By day six, Bistro was saddled. "You can watch," David told Janet. "Besides, I might need you to call the hospital."

Janet's grin was weak.

David put one foot in the stirrup. Bistro bounced a little. "Whoa. Whoa!"

David put a little weight in the stirrup and finally raised himself off the ground. The horse edged sideways. "Stop it." David got down.

He tried again. Bistro stood still.

David took off the saddle and gave the horse a Mountain Dew.

"What are you stopping for?" Janet asked.

"You think I didn't want to throw my leg over? Oh yeah, I did." He patted Bistro's neck. "But this horse needs patience."

The next day, he was riding Bistro at a walk. The day after, they loped.

At the end of the month, David handed Janet the reins. "You're going to have to ride sometime," he said. "This horse will always be a one-person horse and she needs to know she's yours."

Janet smiled. She hopped on Bistro and they walked around and around the barn.

"Good thing she's got a couple of years," her father said.

David just nodded and opened a Mountain Dew for himself. "They'll be something special by then. They're both smart. Which one you gonna send to college?"

Mr. Dean just blinked.

Gary Cadwallader

"Broke? Yeh, he's broke the corral,
the stall and the wagon!"

A Frosty Georgia Morning

On a frosty Georgia morning, in our old Ford truck, Dad and I drove down the dirt road to the barn on the way to check on our horses. We made an odd, silent pair. I was an awkward twelve-year-old on the brink of womanhood, suspended in the ugly-duckling stage. Dad seemed to have pulled back lately, and I was unsure of his love now that I was no longer little or cute. One thing was certain, though, we both shared a passion for our horses.

A cold snap had swept into the valley overnight. Peanut, my favorite of our seven horses, had given birth to her first colt the day before, and although we had seen the foal right after she delivered, I was eager to get back to the farm and run my hands through the colt's thick chocolate coat, softer than any stuffed animal.

We were excited about this colt, the son of Sunny, our proud Arabian stallion with a wild streak, and Peanut, who was plump and white with brown markings and a scooped nose. Although my uncle argued that Peanut was really a very large pony, she was my favorite mare. Dark brown with black mane and tail, our new colt promised to offer the best of both his parents: gentleness and strength. Daddy let me name him and I called him Pride.

Dad drove our pickup to the pasture gate and we climbed

out in the crisp air. As I pulled on my gloves, I saw Daddy glance in the direction of the iced-over pond. Peanut stood alone at the pond's edge. Her ears perked up when she saw us and she ambled over. Dad spoke to her.

"Hey, girl. Where's your baby?" Peanut answered by simply moving closer to Dad, searching for a treat. She was a big baby herself.

"Get her some oats. I'll find the colt," he said. I ducked into the tack room where the feed was stored, scooped up some of the sweet-smelling feed and came back out to the barn's main aisle to see Peanut staring into one of our open stalls. I found Dad in the stall, down on his hands and knees, patting Pride, who was lying on his side.

"Come on, boy, stand up," he urged, but Pride didn't respond. Dad put his hands near the colt's muzzle, over the nostrils. He turned to me with a grim expression. "I think he's frozen." I couldn't believe it.

"Are you sure?" I asked. "Maybe he's asleep." I moved around by Pride's head, gently stroked his neck and ran my fingers through his cool, soft coat. "Wake up, Pride." I wanted to see a quiver, but there was nothing.

"Peanut must have left him alone and when the temperature dropped last night, he fell asleep and froze," he said. I looked over at Peanut stuffing herself with oats, oblivious to the plight of her new colt. At that moment, I hated my favorite mare.

"Why did she leave him?" I asked, choking back tears as I continued to stroke Pride's fine coat. Daddy stroked alongside me.

"It's not her fault. She's a new mama, she didn't know any better," he said. I tried not to cry, but a tear escaped, slipped down my cheek and landed on the motionless colt. Dad must have seen. Suddenly, he put his strong arms under the colt's limp body and scooped him up into his arms.

"Open the tailgate," he ordered. I ran ahead of him to the truck and pulled down the tailgate. Dad lumbered along awkwardly under the weight of the limp colt. I scrambled up in the truck bed just before he gently laid the foal next to me.

"Hold onto him," he said. I wrapped my arms tightly around Pride's downy neck and we pulled off, headed toward our old farmhouse, now vacant for the winter. There, I held open the back-porch door while my father carried the colt in his arms, up the stairs. What was he doing?

"Open the door," he said. I reached up for the hidden key and unlocked the door. He struggled through the doorway, angling the colt several ways before finally passing into the kitchen. "Open the oven," he instructed. I hesitated. He was scaring me, but I obeyed. Gently, he lifted the colt onto the open oven door, turned the oven on low and began rubbing his hands back and forth across the colt's body. With heat and love, my dad was trying to coax the colt back to life. I joined him.

"Come on, boy, come on," I said, rubbing the colt's neck and sweet face. Dad and I worked together for some time but we didn't say much. I felt miserable that I hadn't been there when Peanut had abandoned him, but as I worked along with Dad to try to save Pride, waves of sadness were replaced with a sense of purpose.

The room grew uncomfortably warm and we stopped working for a moment to slip out of our jackets, then we continued our efforts for another twenty minutes. The colt still didn't move. Dad gave a final pat to Pride's neck and spoke.

"Do you think he's going to come around?" he asked. I ran my hand along Pride's neck one last time and felt the fluffy, cold coat pass under my fingertips. I answered Dad with a somber shake of my head. Despite our efforts, we had lost the fight.

We stopped at my uncle's house down the lane to see if he could help Dad bury Pride in the back pasture. Dad explained what had happened and our efforts to revive the colt in the warm kitchen.

"Now why'd you do a stupid thing like that?" my uncle asked. He had been around farm animals his entire life.

"You know you can't bring somethin' frozen back to life. Didn't you learn that in college?" Dad gave me a sidelong glance.

"We needed to try," he said. My uncle shook his head in dismay.

"Craziest thing I ever heard," he said. But I knew my dad wasn't crazy. He had attempted the impossible for me. I knew then how much Dad loved me.

A few weeks later, our prissy Welsh pony Flicka was due to foal. Against Mama's strong objections, Dad loaded her into the trailer and brought her to our city home. Together, we broke up a bale of hay and spread it all around the concrete floor of our garage, which was attached to our house. He unloaded Flicka, took her inside the garage and shut the door against the cold. A few days later, Flicka gave birth to a healthy colt, whom I named Banner. For the next few weeks, until the cold passed, our entire house had an overpowering smell, but Dad and I were happy. Mama? She counted the days until spring!

Janie Dempsey Watts

The Waltz

You can tell a gelding, ask a mare, but you must discuss it with a stallion.

Author Unknown

As I once told my daughter Suzy and grandaughter Kaitlyn, the waltz is a beautiful dance, but you should choose your partner carefully. I know that seems to be a curious remark, but perhaps you will allow me to explain.

Every day, before and after school, I had a part-time job working on a farm that had fifteen Thoroughbred horses. In addition to mucking out their stalls, I had to enter each one and pour six to eight quarts of oats into the feeding pan, which hung on the back wall. Hay came from the loft above and water from a hose that we pushed through the bars, thereby saving time.

These expensive, high-spirited animals weighed approximately a thousand pounds, so we all wore steel-toed boots for protection. On this particular day, I had stayed after school to play basketball, and I still wore my sneakers because I intended to return to the game after finishing my chores. The horses, whinnying loudly, didn't appreciate my tardiness.

One of the horses had the show name of Bismarck, however, we quickly gave him the nickname Woodhead because he possessed a serious personality disorder. Whatever he thought was in his best interest usually collided head-on with the comfort and safety of the person unfortunate enough to be in proximity to where he intended to go.

Each stall was made of wood on the bottom and steel bars on the top. A large Dutch door provided entry. By opening only the bottom part and ducking down, I could quickly deliver the oats to the bucket located in the rear corner. Getting the oats there reminded me of driving toward the basket when I played basketball. The hungry horses challenged me by trying to get at the oats in the same way that a good guard tried to stop me from advancing on his basket. Bismarck, I mean Woodhead, rarely failed to get his oats before anyone ever got near his bucket. Eating was his goal and he never minded being called for fouling.

Less hearty employees feared Woodhead's combative charge, so they would open the bottom part of the door and pour the oats on the floor. Straw came up to the horse's knees, so this cowardly behavior encouraged him to eat his bedding, thereby increasing his chances of getting sick. In Woodhead's case, the caretakers just didn't care. He'd put fear into anyone daring to enter his stall.

Hazardous duty, like good basketball, requires intuitive action. I'd pretend to swing a punch at his head and he would back off, but only for a second. His retreat made it possible for me to swiftly cross the stall floor and slam dunk the oats into his bucket. He always managed to eat half of them before I got out the door. This time, as he stretched his neck for the oats, I swiped at him with my left fist, instead of my right, and connected. Ouch! He truly deserved his stable name. Babying my hand slowed my slam dunk, giving Woodhead time to attack again. He stepped on my foot.

Horses do not like to step on foreign objects—Woodhead included. He immediately lifted up his hoof. Of course, he continued consuming his oats without regard for my

suffering—none of this would interrupt his meal. My shouting into his ear set the stage for the dance of death. Having
a sneaker on instead of my steel-toed boots resulted in
increasing the decibels of my painful cry. Woodhead had
just experienced one of the few times I had hit him.
Screaming next to his ear persuaded him not only to lift his
foot off my foot, but to shy to the right.

At this point, I became conscious of another problem
beyond my immediate pain. My sneaker lace had somehow
gotten caught between his shoe and his hoof. When
Woodhead shied right, my foot followed. He literally tried
to sweep me off my feet. How could I refuse him? In desperation, I grabbed for his neck and clung for dear life.

The waltz began.

Keeping step with my partner made me cry out each time
that his left front foot hit the floor. Each cry into my partner's ear encouraged him to dip and twirl faster. Holding on
to his neck became less a matter of good form and more a
matter of survival. If I'd fallen, I was sure that he would have
kicked me to death.

The word waltz comes from German and means to roll,
turn about or tumble. These steps didn't appeal to me.
Bowing to my deteriorating interest, Woodhead accelerated
from the waltz to the jitterbug. I had no choice but to go
along. While I provided the music by screaming into his ear
in steadily increasing octaves, he turned and leapt. The pain
in my foot became unacceptable. My dance ticket had worn
out. No one was going to try to cut in on this made-for-each-
other couple.

Somehow, I had to reach down and dislodge the lace. I
tried this once. Fortunately, as I let my right arm slip off his
neck, Woodhead danced us into a corner. Instead of falling, I
hit the wall and ended right back cheek to cheek. If the wall
hadn't stopped me, I would have gone down, and our dance
would have quickly ended. He needed lessons, and I told
myself I would give him a free one with a shovel, as soon as
we broke up.

After a while my screams turned to moaning in his ear, "OH! OH! OH!" each time his hoof crushed my foot. Perhaps he thought I had gotten romantic because of my grasping and gasping. No one ever tried to embrace him before, so this physical closeness had to confuse him. A look into his big brown eye gave no indication he felt loved. In fact, he had a look of intense fear and hatred for his partner.

Round and round we went. Stomp your partner's foot. At this point, my foot felt like a soft banana. The pain had gone beyond feeling. It no longer hurt quite so much. I couldn't get the lace loose and didn't dare let go of his neck. Woodhead did not like his dance partner, and I'd had my fill of him, too. As we passed his oat bucket for the umpteenth time, he stopped to sup. The lace simply released. Thanking him for the dance, and not bothering to curtsy, I dove for the door and ended up in the aisle rolling around in pain.

At the emergency room, the doctor laughingly said, "Well, what have we here?" I wanted to kick him, but that would have added to my foot's discomfort. The nurse removed the sneaker in order to X-ray my foot. It immediately blew up like a football. I had left a basketball game to go dancing with a horse and ended up with a football shaped foot. Would you believe the X-rays showed not one single bone broken? Guess old Woodhead turned out to be light on his feet after all.

The very next morning, I entered the stall next to Woodhead's and stuck a long flexible funnel through the bars and into his bucket. Then I pored in eight quarts of oats.

I would later become a great engineer.

William Geen

Guard Duty

I was eleven when we arrived in the refugee camp in Austria, after having fled our war-torn country, Hungary, in 1947. The camp, located on the outskirts of a small town, was dismal, but at least all of our immediate needs were taken care of and we were grateful to the Lord for that.

The people who ran the camp set up a school for the children and organized a scout group. Soon I was a Girl Scout and even went to a scout camp that summer, held in the beautiful Tyrol region of Austria.

The scout camp, located in the wooded mountains of Alm, was quite a nice setup. On one side of a clear, rushing creek were the tents for the girls and our troop leader, Mrs. Kovacs. On the other side, the boys and Mr. Kovacs, the other troop leader, were camping out. But we went for our meals on the boy's side and the nightly campfire was held there as well.

These campfires were always the highlight at the end of the day. We girls, with Mrs. Kovacs, would cross the little bridge that went over the creek and join the boys around the fire, singing songs, telling stories and playing games. All of us had a wonderful time beneath those beautiful, tall, whispering pine trees that covered the entire area.

To teach us courage and responsibility, I guess, our two troop leaders soon devised a plan. Every night, while the rest of the troop trekked across the bridge to the boys' side for the campfire, one girl would stay behind as the sole guard. This girl was given a whistle in the event she became scared or needed help of any kind, but other than that, she would be alone in the big dark woods for a couple of hours. If she blew the whistle, she would be heard and help would arrive within a few minutes, the leaders told us.

Most of the girls, at eleven and twelve years old, were not happy with this arrangement, but complained only to each other about it. Nevertheless, the ones who got early turns seemed to do their job well, never once blowing the whistle while sitting in the dark for two hours. But the stories they told each other later, of strange noises coming from the pitch-black woods, frightened the dickens out of the girls who hadn't yet had a turn.

"I heard terrible grunting and I was sure a bear was coming to eat me," a girl named Anna told us as we lay in the tent that night.

"So why didn't you blow the whistle?" I asked, chills running up and down my spine.

"Because I didn't want everyone to call me a chicken," Anna replied. "And I'm glad I didn't. The bear went away after a while. I'm lucky he wasn't hungry."

"I heard strange noises when I was on guard," another girl piped up. "It sounded like a woman crying. I even called out to her, but there was no answer. I decided it must have been a ghost and that she finally went to haunt someone else. But Mrs. Kovacs said it was probably only an owl. I still think it was a ghost, though."

"I wonder if there are any wolves in these woods? My turn is coming up soon," still another girl asked.

"Mine, too," I said, "and I can tell you one thing: If I get scared, I will blow the whistle. I'd rather be called a chicken than be eaten by a bear!"

So the following night, my turn to be the guard arrived. Mrs. Kovacs placed the whistle, hung on a long string, around my neck and handed me a flashlight.

"Remember, we'll be just across the creek. If you get scared, blow this whistle," she said, smiling at me. The other girls glanced back at me as they walked away, glad it wasn't their turn. Then they were all gone.

I sat down on a campstool in front of my tent, my heart already pounding too fast, butterflies doing a jig in my stomach. I could see the campfire across the creek and hear the distant singing voices. Everything would be all right, I told myself, glancing uneasily around the now pitch-dark camp and woods. The other girls had survived their two hours as guards, and so would I.

I looked up above the towering pines, and saw the stars and a crescent moon in the sky. I inhaled the wonderful smell of the pines. I began to relax and feel quite good. This wasn't so bad. In fact, it was nice to be alone in the quiet woods, I decided, and I began humming a little tune to entertain myself.

Suddenly, I heard a noise. A very loud thump! Thump! Then it stopped. "Who's there?" I called out. No reply. Then I heard a rustle, followed by more thumps. The noise was getting louder and louder. Again I called out. For a moment there was stillness followed by more thumps. Was my imagination playing tricks on me? I stood up, peered into the woods toward the noise and called out once more. This time the rustling became more frantic and the thumps became louder. There was something or someone out there. It was real, not my imagination and it was heading my way!

What if my friends were playing a trick? Would I be the only one to call for help and forever be known as "the chicken"? Resisting the urge to blow my whistle, I tried to think quickly. It couldn't be a wolf, I thought right away. A wolf would sneak up without all that noise. It had to be a bear and it was getting too close for comfort. I hugged the wall of the cabin and stared deeply into the woods, the thump, thump, thump growing louder and coming closer. I could feel the vibration each thump commanded. Whatever was coming was large, larger than a little girl could handle.

It certainly wasn't a ghost, and must be bigger than a bear.

As I raised the whistle to my lips, the huge thumper of the night came crashing into view and stopped right in front of me. I shined my flashlight on him.

"Snort! Snort!" went the thumper, bobbing his head up and down.

"You're a horse!" I shrieked, spitting the whistle out of my mouth. "A big, giant horse! Hello there, boy. Where did you come from?" I held out my hand as I talked to him. The horse's muzzle touched my fingers gently. He snorted again. I boldly reached up and patted his head.

"There, there, boy. You must be lost or something. I'm sure they'll find your owner in the morning. Meanwhile, you can keep me company, because I don't like to be alone in the dark and maybe you don't either," I said as I continued patting him. "Maybe my guardian angel sent you my way, just so I wouldn't be scared."

The horse snorted again. I wondered if I had something in the tent I could give him as a treat.

"You wait here. I'll be right back," I told him, creeping into the tent and feeling around for the box of keks that I'd saved. "Here. I think you'll like these, boy." Keks were a kind of cookie-cracker combination that was very popular in Austria at the time, and we had each received a packet in case we got hungry between meals.

The horse did, indeed, like the keks, and wanted more and more. Soon my package was empty. I walked around the camp boldly now, my visitor behind me the entire time. Noises I heard no longer frightened me. I had a guardian with me. I was actually sorry to hear voices crossing the creek as the others were returning.

"Look, Mrs. Kovacs, I had company tonight," I called out to them. "So I wasn't alone at all."

"A horse! Look girls, Renie has a horse with her," one of the girls shrieked excitedly as a whole bunch of them gathered around my companion and me.

"Where did he come from?" "I wonder whose horse he is?"

"Weren't you frightened when he came?" And many other questions followed. Mrs. Kovacs then blew the whistle, and her husband, from the boy's side, came running across the creek.

"He probably belongs to the farm nearby. We'll check with the farmer in the morning," Mr. Kovacs said, going back to get a rope. "We'll tie him to a tree for tonight."

The following morning, some boys went to the farm, and it turned out that the horse had gotten out of the fenced pasture and galloped through the woods. Until he found me, that is!

"I had a horse just like this one in Hungary," I told the farmer when he came to get my companion. "I used to ride him all the time. Then we had to sell him because of the war."

"Well," he said, "you can come and ride Rudy while you're here. He is pretty gentle and he seems to have taken a real liking to you."

And that's what I did. I went to ride Rudy several times before we went back to the refugee camp and all of the other girls considered me the bravest of the guards for not blowing my whistle when I heard a thump in the pitch-dark night.

Renie Szilak Burghardt

Battle of the Titans

I have worked for years to establish a good reputation as a horse trainer. My horses are easy to catch, they stand tied, take their shots without theatrics and hold up their feet when asked. Even Gem.

Gem is 12 hands of unrepentant, buckskin-colored obnoxiousness. I tell her she's undisciplined, spoiled and the reason that ponies have such a bad reputation. She says she missed her calling in life. Despite four legs and a tail, she's an actress at heart. She thinks that Hollywood needs her. Sometimes I almost believe her.

She mastered the art of impersonation by watching TV through the living-room window. I changed all the door knobs so she can't join us inside anymore. In her Shirley Temple disguise, she's everybody's darling, so cute and sweet. When she's practicing her Dennis the Menace routine, even the chickens hide. But her most stunning achievement is her Alexis Colby impersonation. She can even copy those hard-eyed, conniving expressions, and she watched *Dynasty* just twice!

Recently, I needed two colts shod and Gem's feet trimmed, so I called my farrier. When he found my schedule wasn't going to match his, he said not to worry. Just put the horses in the corral. He had done them all before without a problem. He could turn them out when he was finished. I agreed and blithely went on my way. He was a big, good-natured fellow who had owned and trained horses all his life. Everything would be fine.

The farrier arrived. Gem was standing at the gate to meet him in her Shirley Temple disguise. He caught her and took her over to his pickup parked inside the gate to the pasture. He pulled out his wooden toolbox with the dowel handle. She rubbed his back while he trimmed her feet. She was cooperative if overly affectionate.

He rubbed her ears and turned her loose. She followed him back over to the corral while he caught one of the colts. He had to shoo her out of the way so he could lead the colt out. Back at the pickup, he picked up the young horse's left front foot. Gem stuck her nose over his shoulder to see what he was doing. He shoved her away, so she went around to the other side and stuck her head under the horse's belly to see what the shoer was doing. That made the colt nervous, so the farrier chased her away. Put out, she morphed into Dennis the Menace mode as she wandered back over to the pickup and began nosing through the tools. She dumped a box of horseshoe nails in the dirt.

"Go away," the farrier yelled, slapping her on the rump.

Satisfied now that she had his undivided attention again, Gem came to help, nosing through the dirt where our shoer was trying to pick up the nails. He swatted her hard and chased her off. Alexis Colby emerged.

Ears back, she stared at him. He ignored her and returned to the colt. He lifted a foot and tucked it between his knees. Seconds later, the colt jumped forward. The farrier held on and growled at the youngster. A few seconds later, the colt lunged harder.

The farrier stood, only to see Gem peering innocently at him from behind the colt. When the man turned his head toward the colt, Gem flattened her ears and threatened to bite the youngster who promptly jumped forward again.

This time the farrier chased her across the irrigation ditch.

"And stay there!" he growled, shaking his file at her.

They swapped glares as he returned to the colt. He was shaping a shoe on the anvil when something grabbed him by the belt and jerked him backward. He staggered, arms windmilling for balance. Gem bounced by, tail in the air and head waving. Score two for the pony.

He grabbed a halter. She couldn't be a pest if she was tied up. She teased him. He could scratch her rump or back but not her neck. Finally, he smacked her with the lead rope. She bolted back across the irrigation ditch.

But Alexis was just warming up. She sneaked up and grabbed the colt's halter rope and tried to lead him away. She stole the hammer off the anvil and dropped it in the dirt. She found the farrier's good hat in the back of the pickup, pulled it out and stomped on it. She dumped his water jug. Each time he tried to retaliate, she pranced back across the irrigation ditch out of reach.

It was into this battle of the titans that I arrived. Unobserved, I opened the gate and walked into the pasture in time to see Gem grab the dowel handle of the toolbox in her teeth and carry it across the irrigation ditch. Left with only a hammer and a mouthful of nails, the farrier erupted from under the colt, face mottled with rage. Whuffling through his moustache and the nails in his teeth, he brandished the hammer at his tormentor. Eyes glittering, Gem slung the box back and forth. Nippers, files, hoof knives, nails and other shoeing tools flew everywhere. When the box was empty she flung it away too, and stood glaring at him, head high, daring him to top that.

He roared.

"Gem!" I yelled, appalled.

She whipped her head around, eyes wide. A look that said "uh-oh" appeared on her face and she bolted into the pasture.

The farrier jerked his hammer down at the sound of my voice. He turned back to the colt and nailed on the shoe.

I picked up the tools Gem had scattered, dusted off the

farrier's hat, refilled his water jug and apologized repeatedly for my little darling's behavior. Monosyllables were the only reply. Gem watched from the far end of the pasture.

I held the other colt and paid the farrier when he finished. He loaded his tools and climbed into his pickup and started it.

"Thank you," I said hesitantly.

"Mmm," he replied.

He turned around and I opened the gate. Racing hooves sounded behind me as the farrier started through the opening. Gem thundered into the yard, head out, ears flat, eyes focused on the retreating pickup. I slammed the gate in her face and she bounced away, tail flagging. Alexis wins again.

So much for my reputation. Anybody know a good farrier?

Lynn Allen

Great-Grandma Hazel and the Sidesaddle

I remember finding great-grandma's sidesaddle in the barn in the late spring of 1971. It was covered with barn dust, the soft dark green fuzz that feels kind of silky between your fingers. You don't dare to blow it, though, because it always seems to end up in your nose.

I managed to find some saddle soap and a sponge and when the saddle was clean, I caught one of the ranch horses in the pasture to see if the saddle really would fit a horse. I caught the only one that was gullible and brought Acey Duce to the barn. I saddled him the best way that I could figure out because there were more straps to that saddle than I knew what to do with. It had two horns on it, and I knew that I had to put my right leg over and around the top one, then my left leg had to go under the bottom one that curved down.

I was quite curious about the sidesaddle. I knew that it was the only way for a lady to ride in times long past. There was only one stirrup to this saddle and it was covered with a very small piece of leather, I guessed to keep one's foot from sliding through. A little purse was sewn to the right side of the saddle, and there were latigo strings on the skirts at the cantle. I was very fascinated by the saddler's design, but wasn't sure how to ride in it or even if I had put the darn thing properly on the horse.

Grandma was in her kitchen with my mom, my great-aunt and a lady from town who worked for Grandma. They were very busy cooking lunch for the hay crew that was due in any minute to be fed. I tied Acey Duce to the orchard fence and then asked Grandma if she would show me how to ride in the sidesaddle. Her answer to me was "No." She didn't have time at the moment. I must have seemed pretty sad at her response because she looked at me and said, "Wait until the hay crew is fed and the kitchen is cleaned and I will show you."

Grandma was sly. She was hoping that I would get bored and tired of waiting for her, put the horse and the saddle away and that would be the end of it. Unfortunately for her, I was very determined to learn how to ride in this saddle. I was still sitting at the back-porch door waiting for her two hours later when she finally poked her head out and said, "I see that old horse is still standing there!" I jumped up and nodded.

Grandma was four feet, ten inches tall and maybe ninety-eight pounds when soaking wet. She was also a woman of very few words. She walked out to the apple orchard where Ace was standing patiently, waiting to see who was coming and what we were doing. Grandma looked over the saddle and the straps and checked the cinch. "My dear," was all she said while undoing one strap and rearranging a few buckles. She led Ace to a convenient spot and mounted him.

Now poor old Ace had no idea what was going to happen. When Grandma got herself settled comfortably in that saddle, she picked up the reins and took off flying across the pasture in front of the house. She jumped the big irrigation ditch and kept on running across the pasture. She then pulled a sliding stop, did the prettiest rollback to the right and ran that fat Quarter Horse right back the way he had come. She jumped the ditch again, slid to a stop in front of me, then very ladylike and daintily swung her legs to the side and slid down from the sidesaddle. She walked up to me, handed me the reins and said, "That, my dear, is how you ride sidesaddle."

My jaw was hanging down and I was shocked at seeing my eighty-year-old great-grandma ride like that. I asked her if she would teach me the art of riding aside that summer. Once again, she told me "No." For the second time that day, the look on my face must have softened her. She asked me, "Why in the world would you want to ride with both legs on one side when my generation fought to put our legs on each side?" I couldn't answer her. I only asked again if she would teach me to ride in that saddle.

Bless her heart, she did and we had a wonderful summer in 1971. I learned to ride and I liked it so much that I entered the local horse show in the fall. Unfortunately, Grandma had a stroke in late-summer and she passed away before she ever got to see me compete. Since that summer, I always ride in her honor and I know in my heart that she is watching from above and smiling every time I ride like a queen.

Dottie McDonald Linville

Trail Etiquette

There is a certain universally understood etiquette among trail riders. For instance, you don't run your horse up on another horse's rear end or gallop off without checking with the rest of the group first. And it is customary to shout out a warning to the riders behind you when you pass a potential hazard. By yelling "bottle!" or "wire!" or even "turtle!" you alert them to the obstacle in their path so that they can avoid it. The system usually works well, but not always.

I had been at the new barn only a summer, but had spent most of those weeks exploring the extensive trail system with new friends. Riding for hours on end in open spaces was a welcome change after years of being confined to a ring. I'd spent all that time showing and training, but now I felt that I finally was riding. My Appaloosa mare Geri had also settled into the new routine and was getting very trail-savvy.

One morning in early fall, a group of five of us headed out for a trail ride over terrain I was still unfamiliar with, but that the rest of the group knew well. At one point, the trail flattened and widened out, the perfect place for a gallop. The group started out at a good clip, with Geri and I bringing up the rear.

Then, ahead of me, I heard a cry of "hole!" I mentally thanked the rider for the warning and cast my eyes downward to watch out for the hole. Stepping into a hole while galloping could be disastrous for both horse and rider. A few seconds later, I heard another warning shout of "hole!" from a different rider, and I looked down with even more earnestness. Then, I heard a third shout of "hole!" this time from the rider just in front of me. Yet, as frantically as I scanned the ground, I still saw no signs of a hole.

I began to wonder, were they shouting "hole" or could it be something else? I looked up just in time to see a four-foot-tall metal *pole* rushing toward me. The pole marked a county-owned gas line and it had a huge sign on it, making it clearly visible to anyone who wasn't looking down for a hole. Had I not overreacted, I would have left Geri alone to take us safely past the pole. After all, she wisely had kept her eyes on where she was going and was on course to pass just to the left of the pole. But I panicked and tried to get a horse who was going at a full-out gallop to change direction in the space of four strides. All I succeeded in doing was to pull her off balance and even closer to the looming metal protrusion. As a last-ditch effort, I pulled my right foot out of the stirrup and bent my knee to draw my leg up, a move that can keep your knee from hitting the arena gate at the walk, but isn't nearly as easy at a gallop. As we flew past the pole, the center of my shin slammed into the metal bar.

My howl of pain brought the ride to a quick halt. I grabbed my throbbing, bleeding shin and muttered expletives punctuated with the word "pole," as the rest of the group looked on in confusion. "Didn't you hear me yell 'pole'?" someone asked. "Yes, but I thought you said 'hole.' I was looking for a hole, not a pole." I give the group credit for stifling their laughter until it was obvious I hadn't broken a bone.

Three years later, with the scar on my right shin fading, I tend to forget about my painful collision that fall morning. That is, until I'm out riding in a group with someone who does remember. On those days I hear the cries of "bottle!" and "wire!" and "large metal rod sticking straight up out of the ground, Christine!"

Christine Barakat

The Gift of a Dream

There was probably no greater horse lover on the planet. I subscribed to three horse magazines and my bedroom was wallpapered with photos, calendars, cutout pictures and paint-by-number artwork. A young teen, I lived, breathed and dreamed horses. I saved for weeks to buy a huge wall-sized poster of wild horses running through a river, their manes flowing and hooves flying—it was beautiful. I had found it on the back of my dad's *Enquirer* and had carried the ad around with me for ages until I had enough money to send away for it.

My obsession with horses was so great that I kept sugar cubes in my jacket pocket on the miraculous chance that I would somehow run into a horse I could befriend. More than anything, I wanted to ride. As consumed as I was with all things equine, I had never actually ridden a horse.

My parents had friends who owned horses, and although I was never allowed to ride them, we visited often and I always brought my sugar cubes and felt immense pride at my knowledge of the proper way to feed them: hand up, palm flat, trying not to squeal when the velvety, slobbery lips whisked them off my hand. It was the highlight of my week to visit them. I longed to throw my leg over the black one's back, sliding John Wayne style into place, winding my hands through the horse's mane and riding off into the sunset. Not that I even knew how to do it, but that didn't stop me from daydreaming.

My best friend Stacey was also a horse lover. Since the sixth grade, we had spent hours and days cutting out horse pictures for our walls, fantasizing of being grown, married and owning neighboring horse ranches, where we'd do nothing but ride to our hearts' content. No one but Stacey understood how much I longed to ride a real horse, (and a black one at that.) Stacey had been riding several times and I was green with envy as she described her days of riding with her family. I would have given anything to go with her even just one time. But we were poor and couldn't afford the rental fees, so I had to wait and dream.

The summer we were thirteen, Stacey and I made plans to go to Lake Comanche in northern California, an hour from where we lived. We were thrilled to be spending our first day on an outing without parents. We packed our bathing suits, lunches and hiking shoes and chattered every night about what we would do with the whole day to ourselves. The day finally came and Stacey's mother drove us to Lake Comanche. Stacey and her mother were both strangely quiet on the drive up and I caught them several times exchanging mysterious smiles and even giggling, as though there were some secret joke between them.

We finally arrived at the lake and Stacey's mother gave me a big hug. Then she said, "Have fun!" with twinkling eyes, and drove off, leaving us on the hot, dusty road that I knew didn't go to the swimming area.

"Where are we?" I looked at Stacey.

She just smiled and said, "C'mon." She walked down the dusty path and disappeared over a hill, leaving me wondering where on earth we were.

I ran to catch up to her and saw her standing next to a horse corral, her arms through the fence, happily petting a brown mare.

"Wow!" I scrambled down the hill and hopped onto the

fence rail, surveying the crowd of horses milling about in the shade of a great tree. It was an incredible scene for me. I had never seen so many horses in the flesh and I felt as if I were dreaming.

Stacey looked at me and just grinned. "Pick one," she told me.

"What?"

"Pick one. We're going to ride. I saved up so we could rent two horses all day!" She fairly exploded as she finally let her secret out.

I just stared. I couldn't believe that she was doing this for me. What kind of thirteen-year-old does this for a friend? It was an incredible gift. I couldn't believe that I was going to ride a horse. A real horse. Me. On a horse. All day. Wow.

I finally absorbed it all and threw my arms around her. We laughed and giggled and danced around. It was a golden moment that still brings tears to my eyes, twenty-five years later.

I looked carefully at the horses and spotted him. He was the horse of my dreams: black with gentle eyes and a flowing mane. I couldn't have wished for a more perfect horse. He was beautiful.

We told the man who ran the stable which horses we wanted, and even though my head was in the clouds, I listened to the rules and watched him saddle my dream horse. When he asked me if I knew how to ride, I nodded and hoped that what I'd read in magazines and books could be applied in real life. I was shaking.

The man gave me a leg up and told us where the horses could rest in the shade and drink at the river. I felt like I was in a movie. John Wayne, move over. The saddle creaked and I loved the sound. I loved it all: the horse smell, the dust we kicked up, the feel of the reins in my hands, even how sore my legs were getting. I was in heaven.

The day was a dreamy, sunny, perfect day. My horse was patient as I learned how to handle him and we got along from the start. I learned to canter and Stacey and I even raced through the hills, laughing blissfully and living out our dream. The day drew to an end and the sun splashed a brilliant wash over a golden day that I've never forgotten. In the years that have passed since that magical summer day, I've ridden many more times. But never has any gift meant more to me than that of a thirteen-year-old girl to her best friend. It was the gift of heart, of soul—the gift of a dream.

Susan Farr Fahncke

Confessions of a Horse-Show Father

It can be set down in four words the best of everything. The best hay, oats and water.

Sunny Jim Fitzsimmons

"For sale: Registered QH gelding. Shown by thirteen-year-old girl. To good home only."

I'd just walked in the door when Andrea, my eleven-year-old daughter, waved a newspaper in my face, the ad circled in bright red. With dramatic sighs, she announced that she absolutely could not face life anymore without a horse of her own. I thought we had solved the life-with-horse-crazy-daughter problem when I agreed to riding lessons at the local stable. But we both knew I would give in to Andrea eventually. I always did. I never could resist those golden ringlets circling her head like angel fluff, or her husky little voice telling me I was absolutely the best Daddy in the whole world.

And so I agreed, somewhat naively, that if we could find "something nice" in the neighborhood of $300, I'd pop for a horse.

The following Saturday, we drove out to see the QH gelding listed in the ad. Susan, Andrea's riding instructor, came along to make sure he would be a suitable mount for her student.

"Smooth-gaited and very responsive," she said after trying him out. "Yes, he is a suitable mount for a starter horse."

For Andrea, it was love at first sight.

"Oh, Daddy," she cried. "I just love Pancho. He is absolutely the one I want."

I reached for my checkbook, congratulating myself that we'd found a suitable mount, and I still had enough of my weekend left for a round of golf. I looked expectantly at the horse's owner. After all, how much could a starter horse cost?

"Thirty-five hundred dollars," he said, not even cracking a smile.

I gulped. Whatever happened to the "something nice for three hundred dollars" I thought we were pursuing?

"What's your best offer?" I asked. "This is more than I planned to spend on a starter horse."

"This is a registered Quarter Horse," he replied, his voice dripping with indignation.

Aha, so that's what QH meant.

"I'll think about it," I said.

The ride home was agonizing. In the back seat, Andrea shed elephant-sized tears as she waved a mournful good-bye to her suddenly beloved Pancho. But I remained steadfast. We'd find a horse all right. But not for that kind of money.

Golf dates evaporated as we ran down every promising horse-for-sale ad. We drove fifty miles to follow up on the ad stating, "super disposition." We found a gentle-natured plow horse with a head a yard long and feet like dinner plates. The "green-broke but gentle" horse, we vetoed immediately when he knocked down his handler while trying to get out the barn door.

We ended up back at the home of Pancho, and I wrote out a check for 3,500 bucks. There went my new golf clubs. But my angel showered me with kisses. "You're the absolutely *best daddy* in the whole world."

Heck. Who needed new clubs? I could play another year with the old ones.

Like every father suddenly thrust into horse ownership, I learned that buying the horse was only the beginning. I hadn't even recovered from the $3,500 hit, when Andrea informed me that Pancho needed saddle, bridle, halters, brushes. At the saddle shop I discovered the prices of "proper" horse equipment to be on par with a trip to Disney World. Seven hundred, fifty dollars for a skimpy little saddle that looked like an oversized pancake.

"But it's a Stubben," Andrea sighed wistfully. "They're totally the best."

Well, if a horse of her own could keep my daughter's attention on four-legged creatures, rather than two-legged ones with raging hormones and body piercing, I was all for it. We emerged from the saddle shop loaded down with, among other things, the Stubben saddle and a checkbook now even lighter.

I admit, when watching Andrea ride her new horse for her lessons, I puffed up like a peacock, even though I didn't have a clue what she was doing. One day, the instructor mentioned a fun show at the stable, and would I like to enter Andrea and Pancho? One look at my daughter's face and, of course, I wanted to.

"I need a proper outfit now that I'm going to show," she announced. Back to the saddle shop. You guessed it. You don't find a proper outfit without another hefty swipe at the checkbook.

At the fun show, I stood at the rail watching horses rumble by, sending clouds of dust into my face, which was becoming the same color as the ring. Andrea emerged from her class, all smiles, clutching a dinky scrap of yellow ribbon. It seemed she had placed third in horsemanship (third out of four, but who's counting?). The radiant look on her face almost made me forget that I had turned down a complimentary round of golf at The Wilds to be there for her triumph.

More shows followed and, believe it or not, I was getting into this horse-showing stuff. In one class, Pancho suddenly broke into a gallop, lapping the field.

"That's my daughter on the brunette horse," I bragged to the woman next to me. "She's beating everybody."

"Way to go Andrea,'" I yelled as she flew by.

"She's supposed to be trotting," the woman sniffed and moved away.

My darling came out of that class ribbonless. One look at her tear-stained face and I knew I was in trouble big time. How could I have embarrassed her by yelling at her in front of the whole world? She could die, absolutely die. But there were other shows where she came home with ribbons and radiant smiles. Hugs for Pancho. Hugs for Daddy, too.

One day, Andrea told me about a Quarter Horse show in Hutchinson. One small problem. We needed a trailer. Back to the want ads. I found a used two-horse trailer and plunked down another 2,500 bucks.

"How do you plan to haul it?" the trailer seller asked.

It just happened he had a truck for sale. There went my plans for the new runabout for the lake cottage I had hoped to buy. But I had a show horse now and a daughter who thought I was wonderful.

The season progressed. I dropped more money and we accumulated more equipment and more ribbons. Andrea now competed in Western classes, as well as English, requiring a whole new complement of saddles, bridles and show outfits. And I was hooked, a helpless victim of the lure of the show ring: beautiful daughters, beautiful horses; every weekend a total commitment in time, money and energy. There were no more weekends at the lake or golf tournaments with the pros, and I didn't even care. When my daughter came out of the ring with a blue ribbon, I could hardly wait to sign up for another show. The scraps of colored ribbons hanging from the mantel came to about $500 per inch, I figured, but what the heck. We were going after that high-point trophy!

My addiction pumped along at an alarming speed as I made plans for the next year's season . . . a new trailer perhaps, with attached living quarters for the out-of-state shows . . . a better truck to pull the new trailer . . . possibly a new horse. As the riding instructor had said, Pancho was a suitable starter horse, but if we were serious about showing, we needed a better one (another unwritten rule in the horse business: the present horse is never good enough).

After two years of this crazy lifestyle, I came home one evening to see one of those two-legged boy creatures I had worried about, sprawled in my recliner watching the latest episode of *Star Trek*.

"I'm not going to the stables tonight," Andrea announced with one of her dazzling smiles. "Kevin and I have something else planned."

"What about Pancho? What about your lesson?"

"Janie's taking my lesson tonight. She's riding Pancho this weekend because Kevin asked me to the school dance."

It was then I noticed the dazzling smile was aimed at Kevin, not me. In spite of my efforts and the enormous holes in my bank account, my Andrea had sailed into the uncharted waters of puberty, deciding boys were more fun than horses and they smelled better. I wouldn't be watching my beautiful daughter in the ring anymore. No more bragging rights about owning an almost-champion show horse.

Gradually, I have conquered my addiction. I'm selling the equipment and recouping some of my losses. Part of me even looks forward to getting my own life back: the golf games and the cool runabout for the hoped-for lake cottage.

But what about Pancho? I'm still attached to that little brunette horse who totally took over my life for two years. With a lump in my throat, I placed the ad in the newspaper:

"For Sale: Registered QH gelding. Shown by thirteen-year-old girl. To good home only."

J.L. Lindstrom

Who Is Jack Canfield?

Jack Canfield is one of America's leading experts in the development of human potential and personal effectiveness. He is both a dynamic, entertaining speaker and a highly sought-after trainer. Jack has a wonderful ability to inform and inspire audiences toward increased levels of self-esteem and peak performance.

Jack currently has three wonderful horses living in his stable and rides with his wife Inga, his son Christopher, and his step-daughter Riley.

He is the author and narrator of several bestselling audio- and videocassette programs, including *Self-Esteem and Peak Performance, How to Build High Self-Esteem, Self-Esteem in the Classroom* and *Chicken Soup for the Soul—Live*. He is regularly seen on television shows such as *Good Morning America, 20/20* and *NBC Nightly News*. Jack has co-authored numerous books, including the *Chicken Soup for the Soul* series, *Dare to Win* and *The Aladdin Factor* (all with Mark Victor Hansen), *100 Ways to Build Self-Concept in the Classroom* (with Harold C. Wells), *Heart at Work* (with Jacqueline Miller) and *The Power of Focus* (with Les Hewitt and Mark Victor Hansen).

Jack is a regularly featured speaker for professional associations, school districts, government agencies, churches, hospitals, sales organizations and corporations. His clients have included the American Dental Association, the American Management Association, AT&T, Campbell's Soup, Clairol, Domino's Pizza, GE, ITT, Hartford Insurance, Johnson & Johnson, the Million Dollar Roundtable, NCR, New England Telephone, Re/Max, Scott Paper, TRW and Virgin Records. Jack is also on the faculty of Income Builders International, a school for entrepreneurs.

Jack conducts an annual eight-day Training of Trainers program in the areas of self-esteem and peak performance. It attracts educators, counselors, parenting trainers, corporate trainers, professional speakers, ministers and others interested in developing their speaking and seminar-leading skills.

For further information about Jack's books, tapes and training programs, or to schedule him for a presentation, please contact:

Self-Esteem Seminars
P.O. Box 30880
Santa Barbara, CA 93130
phone: 805-563-2935 • fax: 805-563-2945
Web site: *www.chickensoupforthesoul.com*

Who Is Mark Victor Hansen?

In the area of human potential, no one is better known and more respected than Mark Victor Hansen. For more than thirty years, Mark has focused solely on helping people from all walks of life reshape their personal vision of what's possible. His powerful messages of possibility, opportunity and action have helped create startling and powerful change in thousands of organizations and millions of individuals worldwide.

He is a sought-after keynote speaker, bestselling author and marketing maven. Mark's credentials include a lifetime of entrepreneurial success, in addition to an extensive academic background. He is a prolific writer with many bestselling books such as *The One Minute Millionaire, The Power of Focus, The Aladdin Factor* and *Dare to Win,* in addition to the *Chicken Soup for the Soul* series. Mark has also made a profound influence through his extensive library of audio programs, video programs and enriching articles in the areas of big thinking, sales achievement, wealth building, publishing success, and personal and professional development.

Mark is also the founder of MEGA Book Marketing University and Building Your MEGA Speaking Empire. Both are annual conferences where Mark coaches and teaches new and aspiring authors, speakers and experts on building lucrative publishing and speaking careers.

His energy and exuberance travel still further through mediums such as television (*Oprah,* CNN and *The Today Show*), print (*Time, U.S. News & World Report, USA Today, New York Times* and *Entrepreneur*) and countless radio and newspaper interviews as he assures our planet's people that *"you can easily create the life you deserve."*

As a passionate philanthropist and humanitarian, he's been the recipient of numerous awards that honor his entrepreneurial spirit, philanthropic heart and business acumen, including the prestigious Horatio Alger Award for his extraordinary life achievements, which stand as a powerful example that the free enterprise system still offers opportunity to all.

Mark Victor Hansen is an enthusiastic crusader of what's possible and is *driven* to make the world a better place.

Mark Victor Hansen & Associates, Inc.
P.O. Box 7665 • Newport Beach, CA 92658
phone: 949-764-2640 • fax: 949-722-6912
FREE resources online at: *www.markvictorhansen.com*

Who Are the Coauthors?

DR. MARTY BECKER is passionate about his work fostering the affection and connection between animals and people we call, "The Bond." Marty coauthored; *Chicken Soup for the Cat & Dog Lover's Soul, Chicken Soup for the Pet Lover's Soul* and *The Healing Power Of Pets,* which was awarded a prestigious silver award in the National Health Information Awards for 2002.

Dr. Becker is featured on ABC-TV's, *Good Morning America,* writes a weekly column for over 350 Knight Ridder newspapers and hosts two new nationally syndicated radio programs, *Pets Unleased* a two-hour live talk radio program and a two-minute pet vignette, *The Pet Update.*

A contributing editor for *Dog Fancy* and *Cat Fancy,* the world's most popular pet magazines and a frequent contributor to *Reader's Digest,* Marty is the Chief Veterinary Correspondent for *Amazon.com* and has been featured on ABC, NBC, CBS, CNN, PBS, and in *USA Today, USA Weekend, The New York Times, The New York Daily News* and *Washington Post.*

Marty and his family enjoy life in Northern Idaho and share Almost Heaven Ranch with two dogs, six barn cats and five Quarter Horses; Chex, Gabriel, Glo Lopin, Pegasus and Sugar Babe.

Contact Marty Becker at:
P.O. Box 2775 • Twin Falls, ID 83303
Phone: 208-734-8174 • Fax: 208-733-5405
Web site: *www.drmartybecker.com*

GARY SEIDLER founded U.S. Journal and Health Communications with his coauthor and former partner, Peter Vegso, over twenty-five years ago. Retiring in 1999 and relocating to Los Angeles, Gary is a Thoroughbred owner and breeder who enjoys the energy and enthusiasm of racing. Gary devotes his time to expanding his nonprofit foundation, which sponsors a summer camp for at-risk kids and to producing documentaries which promote health, wellness and recovery.

Contact Gary Seidler at:
1450 Bella Drive • Beverly Hills, CA 90210
Phone: 310-246-1639• Fax: 310-246-1797
e-mail: *gary@horseloverssoul.com*

PETER VEGSO continues to grow the businesses he and Gary founded over 25 years ago. Health Communications' first *New York Times* bestseller appeared on the list in 1985. Recognized by *Publishers Weekly* as the #1 Self-Help Publisher, HCI is guided by their mission statement "Making a difference in the lives of our readers and the people they come in contact with."

Diversification within Peter's businesses includes; a professional publishing and conference division, U.S. Journal Training, which serves the mental health community, and Reading, Etc., a custom design and architectural elements company which includes two retail stores.

Peter enjoys his 140-acre Thoroughbred breeding and training facility in Ocala, Florida, where the hardest working manager in the world, Chuck Patton, handles daily operations. It is their intention to not only win the Kentucky Derby but also the Triple Crown before their spirits leave this planet.

Contact Peter Vegso at:
3201 SW 15th Street • Deerfield Beach, FL 33442
Phone: 954-360-0909• Fax: 954-360-0034
e-mail: *peter@horseloverssoul.com*

THERESA PELUSO met Peter Vegso and Gary Seidler in 1981 and got acquainted with horses through the partner's interest in Thoroughbreds soon after. Prior to that, her only connection to horses was her Irish grandmother, who loved the ponies and jumped at the chance to move to Florida in the early 1960s to be near Hialeah Park.

While working on this book, Theresa was introduced to these intuitive animals through the eyes of the writers. Through their stories she came to understand what a powerful bond we all share with horses, and developed a spiritual connection to the community of warm, generous people who graciously shared their world—and the incomparable world of horses—with her.

Contact Theresa Peluso at:
3201 SW 15th Street • Deerfield Beach, FL 33442
Phone: 954-360-0909 • Fax: 954-418-0844
e-mail: *theresa@horseloverssoul.com*

Contributors

Lynn Allen says it's her mother's fault that she's horse crazy. As a toddler, she threw Lynn on a horse instead of carrying her around the barnyard while she did chores. Since then horses, cows and agriculture have been Lynn's passions. A free-lance writing career helps support those expensive habits.

Judy Pioli Askins grew up behind Belmont Racetrack where she developed her lifelong love for horses. She has enjoyed twenty-seven years in television: writing, producing, directing, acting, teaching and coaching. Her devotion to Parelli Natural Horsemanship, and her special brand of humor keep her workshops and coaching sessions in great demand.

Christine Barakat is a lifelong rider who gave up hunter equitation for combined training. She later gave that up for trail riding with friends. She has worked in both the United States and Europe as a riding instructor, stall mucker and groom. She is currently an editor with *Equus* magazine.

Teresa Becker resides in Bonners Ferry, Idaho with her veterinarian husband Marty and two beautiful children, Mikkel, age seventeen and Lex, age thirteen. A physical education teacher with a master's degree in athletic administration, Teresa now dedicates her time exclusively to enjoying life with her family which includes cats, dogs, fish and horses.

Denise Bell-Evans and her husband Dave raise horses for English disciplines on their Amarugia Horse Farm. The horses include stallions, brood mares, youngstock and riding horses. Denise, whose active lifestyle was curtailed when diagnosed with MS, concentrates on enjoying farm life and family, which includes her five children and her grandson.

Francis Brummer was born on a farm west of Dunlap, Iowa. After nine years sailing in the Navy, he became a professional cartoonist in 1954. Having sold over 35,000 cartoons worldwide in his career, Francis is semi-retired and draws about six hours per week. We appreciate his collaboration with Steve Sommer on the cartoons in this book.

Sissy Burggraf was born in a small town in southern Ohio. After working for eight years as a vetinary assistant she opened Lost Acres Horse Rescue and Rehabilitation. LAHRR was established in 1994 as an alternative to euthanasia, slaughter or abandonment for abused, neglected or injured horses. Visit LAHRR at *www.geocities.com/sblahrr*.

Renie Szilak Burghardt was born in Hungary, and came to the U.S. at the age of fourteen. A free-lance writer, her works has appeared in *Chicken Soup for the Christian Family Soul* and many other anthologies. She lives in the country and loves nature, animals, gardening, reading and spending time with family and friends.

Sharon Byford-Ruth is the author of, *The Arabian: A Guide for Owners*. With her business partner, Betsy Teeter, Sharon operates Legendary Arabians, home of the champion Arabian stallion, Aul Magic+/, at Caliente, California. Sharon is the proprietor of Book Stall, an Internet store for books about Arabian horses, new and out-of-print *www.horsebooks.com*

Gary Cadwallader lives in Kansas City, Missouri. He raises American Saddlebreds. His stories have appeared in *Canter* magazine, *Literary Potpourri* and *The Phone Book*.

Patricia Carter is a forty-nine-year-old horse lover from Toronto, and mother of a now eleven-year-old horse-crazy daughter. Sharing their love of horses has been an incredible experience for her family, one which has given them countless hours of laughter and pleasure.

Jennifer Chong and Donovan, a young Hanoverian, have been partners since he turned three. Donovan is making a name for himself in dressage, but he also enjoys jumping and hacking out. Jennifer is a student at Harvard Law School and her first book, *To the Nines: A Practical Guide to Turnout and Competition Preparation,* will be available in 2003.

Diana Christensen is the owner of Shalimar Farm in Louisiana where she enjoys the company of four Andalusians, one Welsh pony and one Peruvian Passo. Her moniker, "Diana Dancing Horses," gives you an indication of what she enjoys most about her equine dressage partners—they're great dancers!

Diane M. Ciarloni has served as editor for *Speedhorse/The Racing Report* for the past eighteen years. She has written *Legends I*, which focuses on legendary horses of the past, and contributed to *Legends II* and *III*. She's a consistent contributor to *Guideposts* and its series of animal anthologies. Her work has been cited in *Best American Sportswriting*.

Michael Compton is the editor of *The Florida Horse* magazine, published by the *Florida Thoroughbred Breeders' and Owners' Association* in Ocala, Florida. Michael serves on the Board of Directors of the Public Education Foundation of Marion County and is married with two children. Some of his earliest memories were of attending the races and watching Affirmed in 1978–79 with his late father and grandfather.

Mary Gail Cooper is a school librarian who lives in North Carolina with her husband of twenty-seven years. Two of their children have started college; one daughter lives at home. They still have three horses and an assortment of cats and dogs.

Jan Jaison Cross has enjoyed her career as a jockey, riding in several hundred races at tracks in New Jersey, Pennsylvania and Florida, as well as her time as a trainer and bloodstock agent. In 1999 she began teaching high school in the horse country of Marion County, Florida. Today Jan rides the trails on her 17 hand ex-race horse Cookies.

Barbara A. Davey and her husband live in Verona, New Jersey. She works in public relations and fund-raising and is the author of *Does God Have E-mail?* a collection of inspirational short stories. Barbara's story "A Legacy in a Soup Pot," appears in *Chicken Soup for the Woman's Soul*. Her e-mail address is *wisewords2@aol.com*.

Kris DeMond lives in Pennsylvania with five Percherons, two Appaloosas, an American bulldog, an ornery kitten and a thirty-nine-year-old pony who is still used in the lesson ring when *she* "feels like it." Kris runs a small riding/driving lesson business and offers the carriage for weddings and other fun affairs.

Basil V. DeVito Jr. has more than twenty years experience in the sports business. He has held positions in the NBA, The National Thoroughbred Racing Association, the WWE and the XFL. He also authored the *New York Times* bestseller, *WrestleMania: The Official Insider's Story*.

Christina Donahue and her husband Don own Stonecrest Farm, located just outside of Charlotte, North Carolina. They raise rare Egyptian Arabian horses, which are renowned for their beauty, intelligence and loving dispositions. Chris is in the process of writing a series of children's books about the adventures of an Arabian filly.

Susan Farr Fahncke is the author of *Angel's Legacy* and has stories in many *Chicken Soup* and other inspirational books. She is the founder of 2TheHeart.com and teaches online writing workshops. Susan can be reached through her Web site or at *editor@2theheart.com*.

Lisa B. Friel is a free-lance writer and photographer based in Alexandria, Virginia. Her work appears in popular publications including *USA Equestrian, Virginia Horse Journal* and *Horse & Hound*. Lisa is an amateur rider and competes in the Ladies Sidesaddle Division.

Kimberly Gatto is a professional writer and lifelong horse owner. She is the author of *Michelle Kwan: Champion on Ice* and *An Apple A Day*, with two additional sports titles currently in publication. Kim enjoys dressage and eventing with her two horses Chutney and Grace.

Bill Geen, a retired executive, lives with his wife Barbara in upstate New York. Bill's love of horses started sixty years ago. He shares his experiences with horses and lessons he's learned along the way in letters to his grandchildren which will be featured in a new book entitled *Letters from Grandpa*.

Debra Ginsburg, a staff writer for *California Thoroughbred* since 1985, is a member of the National Turf Writers Association. Her work has appeared in *The Chronicle of the Horse, Backstretch* magazine and *Winning Connection*. She is working on a mystery novel involving horse racing and a book about California's equine millionaires. Contact Debra at *debieg@ctba.com* or (800) 573-2822.

Bill Goss appears monthly on Animal Planet and his stories have been published in *Reader's Digest, Maxim, Daily Word, Chicago Tribune*. He wrote *The Luckiest Unlucky Man Alive* and *There's a Flying Squirrel in My Coffee: Overcoming Cancer with the Help of My Pet*. Contact him at P.O. Box 7060, Orange Park, FL 32073 or *www.BillGoss.com*.

Barbara Greenstreet is a writer, educator and "horse mom" living in western Washington state with a menagerie of children and pets ranging from honeybees to horses. She has been published in *Northwest Baby & Child, WritersLounge.com, WeeOnesMagazine.com, In the Family, Big Apple*

Parent, Wildland Firefighter, Massage, and *Horse & Rider.*

Starr Lee Cotton Heady, granddaughter of homesteaders, now lives in Florida. She is a Certified Horsemanship Association (CHA) instructor in English and Western riding and a licensed mental health counselor. In addition to sharing her private life with horses, StarrLee uses horses in private practice and provides equine assisted psychotherapy for a nonprofit organization (*www.traversekids.org*).

Laurie Henry, a former "Dove Girl" for Dove Soap, shares life in Aqua Dulce with her husband of twenty-six years. They have four children and two grandchildren. As the kids have grown and moved on with other interests, horses remained in Laurie's life and especially in her heart. Her best friend for the past eight years has been Sonny Boy.

Kimberly Graetz Herbert is the editor of *The Horse: Your Guide to Equine Health Care,* a monthly not-for-profit magazine focusing on the health, care and management of horses. A contributing editor to *The Blood-Horse,* the Thoroughbred industry's oldest weekly news magazine, she is the mother of two and lives on a small farm in Central Kentucky.

Debbie Hollandsworth's close-knit family consists of her husband, two teenagers and three brothers. They live adjacent to her parents' 240-acre family farm, where they raise miniature horses and background cattle, and stable the horses and teams the family enjoys riding. Debbie owns a restaurant at the local sale barn.

Paula Hunsicker is a horse breeder and a free-lance writer. Her work has appeared in the National Reined Cow Horse Association's publication, *The Stock Horse News,* and *Performance Horse* magazine.

Jennie Ivey lives in Cookeville, Tennessee, and owns and rides both Quarter Horses and Tennessee Walking Horses. She is a columnist for the Cookeville *Herald-Citizen* newspaper and the coauthor of *Tennessee Tales the Textbooks Don't Tell,* a collection of stories from Tennessee history. She can be contacted at *jivey@multipro.com.*

Dr. Michael Johnson is an author, national columnist and cowboy. His latest release, *Cowboys and Angels,* was named Best Non-Fiction Book of 2002 by the Oklahoma Writers' Federation. Michael lives on a horse farm in Idabel, Oklahoma.

Carol Wade Kelly, her husband Jeff and son Taylor manage a small ranch that consists primarily of retired racehorses. Starflite retired from the track as a four-year-old and after a very successful breeding career, died peacefully in his stall of heart failure in 2000 at the age of twenty-nine.

Roger Dean Kiser lives in Brunswick, Georgia, with his wife Judy, also a writer. Roger is the author of *Orphan, a True Story of Abandonment, Abuse and Redemption.* He has authored and/or coauthored twelve books in four countries. Visit Roger and enjoy his work at: *www.rogerdeankiser.com/index.htm.*

Jeanette Larson was born with the "horse-lovers virus." After spending years starting colts, training dressage horses, galloping race horses and then retraining dressage and race horses for new careers, Jeannette retrained herself and is now a magazine editor. She enjoys her four remaining horses while trail riding on the weekends.

Edwina Lewis is a nonfiction writer and a writing instructor at the University of Houston-Clear Lake. Her inspiration is her family—husband, children, grandchildren, dogs, rabbits and chickens—and her large extended family. She is currently working on *For My Father's Love,* a book about father/daughter relationships.

J.L. Lindstrom realized a lifelong dream when the family moved to a ten-acre "ranchette" where they have raised and shown horses for over twenty years. Now a golden-ager, the ground is too hard and the bones too brittle for riding, so the love for horses is expressed through writing and painting.

Dottie McDonald Linville lives with her husband and two sons in Indiana where she raises Blue Black Arabian horses. You can meet Dottie and her Arabians at *www. juniperdesertarabians.com.* Dottie is a certified instructor and judge with the World Sidesaddle Federation, Inc. and president of the Hoosier Ladies Aside. For more information on riding sidesaddle visit *www.hoosierladiesaside.com.*

Vikki Marshall owns Destiny Farms Sporthorses, breeder of Thoroughbred performance horses. She successfully competes in hunter and dressage, breeds and trains her own horses and retrains horses who have been neglected. Currently writing a novel about experiences in the equestrian sports industry, Vikki has received honorable mention in the 2002 *Olympiad of the Arts* short-story competition.

Tom Maupin, Stacy's dad, is forty-three years old and was introduced to the wonderful world of horses by his wife Crystal. Horses have introduced them to a wonderful network of friends, and have given them the opportunity to continually improve their marriage, lives and health. They trail ride as often as they can.

Tiernan McKay is a free-lance writer based in Scottsdale, Arizona. Her magazine articles focus mainly on health, travel, Christianity, sports, and of course, horses. She continues to ride and show hunter/jumpers.

Jennilyn McKinnon grew up loving horses in the small town of Mendon, Utah, and the love affair hasn't ended. A wife, busy mother of five children, registered nurse and author, Jennilyn has had several stories and poems published. She is currently working on her first book.

Nancy Minor lives with her husband David in the Texas Hill Country.

John L. Moore is an award-winning journalist and novelist who ranches north of Miles City, Montana, with his wife Debra. They are ordained ministers and the parents of two grown children, Jess and Andrea.

Sandra Moore is a mother, pastor's wife and writer—in that order. She is a contributor to *Living Miracles: Stories of Hope from Parents of Premature Babies* from St. Martins Press. If you have a premature child, she'd love to hear from you. E-mail her at *smoore@innernet.net.*

Ky Mortensen was raised on a small alfalfa farm and now lives in Lexington, Kentucky with his wife and son. After serving a two-year Mormon mission in Spain, he returned to the U.S. to complete studies in equine science at Colorado State University. Currently he is Director of Industry Relations for the American Association of Equine Practitioners.

Jeff C. Nauman, Edgar Brown's grandson, is a rangeland management specialist and logistical officer for wildland fire suppression efforts in Idaho. He and his family raise Quarter Horses and compete locally in reined cow-horse, team penning and 4-H events, while promoting AJKyle's Meat Co. (*ajkylenauman@orofino-id.com*), their grass-based, meat-protein business.

Marla Oldenburg lives in Seattle with her daughters Jackie and Chelsea. Their horses Rosie, Mona and Mesa live on a friend's farm, where they all ride and operate a horse camp in the summer. Marla spent many years competing on the West Coast hunter/jumper "A" circuit. Her favorite horsey times are now spent bringing kids and horses together.

Pat Parelli's career is highlighted with diversity, from rodeoing to teaching Olympic competitors. Pat is applauded worldwide for his system of natural horsemanship that uses psychology, love, language and leadership. When not traveling the globe teaching people to teach horses, Pat is at home in Colorado or Florida with his wife Linda.

Mark Parisi's *Off the Mark* comic panel has been syndicated since 1987 and is distributed by United Media. His *Rim Shot* comic panel appears weekly in *Billboard* magazine. Mark's humor also graces greeting cards, T-shirts, calendars, magazines, newsletters and books. Lynn is his wife/business partner and their daughter Jenny contributes with inspiration (as do three cats).

Thirza Peevey began writing two years ago after decades in the horse industry and four years as a teacher. She has been published in several *Guideposts* series, including *Listening to the Animals* and the upcoming *Be Not Afraid.* She is currently working on two novels and was a 2003 winner of the Guideposts Biennial Writer's Contest.

Thomas Peevey has worked in the Thoroughbred industry since leaving high school in England in 1971. While in England, he worked for his uncles, Fred and John Winter, to learn the Thoroughbred business. He moved to Kentucky in 1981 to continue his career. Tom has been published in the *Guidepost* series, *Listening to the Animals.*

Tom Persechino is Senior Director of Marketing for the American Quarter Horse Association, where his mission is to connect people to horses. Growing up in Oklahoma, Tom was an active 4-H show participant who later went on to work at Oklahoma City's Remington Park Racetrack before joining AQHA in 1993.

Rhonda Reese, a former schoolteacher, is a columnist and staff writer for her community newspaper in Jacksonville, Florida. Married to her minister husband for almost three decades, Rhonda can usually be found at home spoiling her nine rescued—once skinny—strays, now basking in luxury as happy fat cats.

Boots Reynolds has designed greeting cards for Leanin' Tree Publishing for over twenty years, and his cartoons are a monthly feature in *Western Horseman* magazine. Boots is a founding member of the Cowboy Cartoonists International, and is currently working on a series of humorous paintings depicting historical events and rodeos in the West, as well as a recipe book on beans at his studio near Hope, Idaho. Visit his Web site: *www.sagebrushes.com.*

Jane Douglass Rhodes grew up riding American Saddlebreds in Louisville, Kentucky. She now lives in rural San Diego on Janra Ranch with her true love, three dogs and—alas!—no horses. There, she writes personal narratives and cocreates Gourditos and other whimsical artwork. E-mail her at *janedogranch@mindspring.com.*

Jan Roat is a ranch wife, mother, grandmother, free-lance writer and photographer. She has written and published with *Pine Ridge Rambling* for five years, before that with *West Bench Meandering* for twenty years. Jan is also field editor for *Country* magazine and associate editor for *Taste of Home* magazine.

Monty Roberts travels the world demonstrating his nonviolent approach to starting horses. Monty is the author of three bestselling books: *The Man Who Listens to Horses, Shy Boy* and *Horse Sense for People*. His latest release, *From My Hands to Yours* is a training manual using Monty's methods. Visit his Web site: *www.montyroberts.com.*

Robin Roberts, who has been a horse-show mom for many years, is now entering the show ring herself in the APHA Novice Amateur Division. She spends much of her time riding and writing, and finds them both challenging and rewarding. Robin is currently writing stories for children.

Melody Rogers-Kelly began dancing professionally at age fifteen. She performed on Broadway in *A Chorus Line*, on CBS television's *Two On The Town*, traveled to over sixty countries, and has appeared in movies. Melody is a certified riding instructor for the North American Riding For the Handicapped Association (NARHA), and enjoys a successful real-estate career in Beverly Hills.

Chris Russell-Grabb is a registered maternity nurse, and has been involved with horses for over forty years. She currently owns and operates, VS Belgians in Sodus, New York, with her husband Dennis. They raise and show registered Belgian draft horses, mini donkeys and Spotted Drafts.

Mitzi Santana and her two daughters live in Virginia. Mitzi was raised around horses, riding before she could walk. Mitzi has enjoyed many disciplines in riding, but admits her favorite is a trail ride with her family. She is an active 4-H volunteer for the Horse N Around Fluvanna 4-H. Contact her at *msantana@cstone.net.*

Cristina Scalise has volunteered with the Equine Rescue League of Leesburg, Virginia, for the past twelve years. Although she dearly loves all of the fifty or so hoofed residents of the League, Albert has a very special place in her affections. Ms. Scalise invites interested readers to visit the League in cyberspace at: *www.equinerescueleague.org.*

Jerri Simmons-Fletcher is an aspiring author and songwriter. She has two American Quarter Horses, Lily and Tucker, whom she loves very much. She is currently attending college and is directing a youth praise team.

Steve Sommer has been a cartoon gag writer for about twenty years. He currently writes and publishes an agricultural advertising cartoon calendar called *Country Chuckles*, and lives in

Merna, Nebraska. We appreciate Steve's collaboration with Francis Brummer on the cartoons in this book.

Carole Y. Stanforth is a freelance writer whose romance with horses began twenty-five years ago when her husband loaned money to a struggling local businessman. He defaulted and repaid the loan with four Quarter Horses, which ultimately became a herd of thirty, including miniature horses. Her husband says it was the most expensive business deal he ever made.

Joyce Stark was born and lives in Scotland. She has traveled widely throughout Europe and the U.S. and says her main hobby is "people." She has had her works published in the *Chicago Tribune, Saturday Evening Post, Rosebud, Highlander* and many publications in the U.K. Contact her via e-mail: *joric.stark@virgin.net.*

Stephanie Stephens is a print and broadcast journalist based in Laguna Niguel, California, is an expert in the equine and pet genres. She syndicates a radio show, *Animal Magnetism,* and hopes for an end to pet overpopulation. With a master's in journalism from New York University, Stephens's work has appeared in more than thirty magazines. You can visit Dan Shaw from "The Guiding Sight" at *www.danandcuddles.com.*

Gayle Stewart has seen her work published in *Equus, Horse Illustrated, Horse of Course, Oklahoma Today, Dallas Morning News, Kansas City Star, The Daily Oklahoman* and *The Denver Post.* In 2001, one of Gayle's pieces was honored with the USA Equestrian Media Award for best magazine article in an equestrian publication.

Dave Surico is a sports writer who lives in the northwest suburbs of Chicago with his wife Lynn and their two children.

Marguerite Suttmeier was a flight attendant for United Airlines for thirty-two years until she retired to a ranch in North Idaho with her husband of thirty-one years. Tom and Marguerite have four horses, one dog (a heeler named Josie Wales) and four cats. She enjoys cross-country skiing, walking, drawing, reading and quilting.

Sandra Tatara has two grown sons, and expects her first grandchild in August 2003. She paints in several mediums, raises registered Quarter Horses, which have competed in pole bending and barrel racing events, and enjoys trail riding. Sandra has had several short stories published and has a novel awaiting publication.

Tom Truitt was born in Burlington, North Carolina in June 1940. Tom has been a teacher, assistant principal, principal, assistant superintendent and superintendent of schools. Currently he is serving as executive director of the Pee Dee Education Center (a consortium of eighteen school districts) in Florence, South Carolina. Tom is married with one son and two granddaughters.

Tracy Van Buskirk has been riding horses since she was small. She loves both horses and creative writing but has never done either professionally. Tracy describes the opportunity to bring both interests together for this book as "a wonderful experience." She can be reached at *kriksubnav@hotmail.com.*

Theresa (T.C.) Wadsworth-Peterson raises APHA and AQHA horses. Her father put her on her first horse and now, some forty years later, T.C. trains horses and raises her own foals, as well as mini-Schnauzers. She enjoys rodeos and cow horse competitions, and especially being in the middle of her remuda.

Janie Dempsey Watts has strong roots in northwest Georgia, where she and her family enjoyed their ponies and horses. She has been published in newspapers and magazines, and recently completed *Moon Over Taylor's Ridge,* a novel with elements of romance, mystery and Cherokee history. She holds two journalism degrees.

Janice Willard, DVM, MS, is married with two children and lives on a small farm in Idaho shared by horses, goats, sheep and llamas. The household also includes several dogs, cats and a very officious parrot. Janice and her husband are veterinarians and Janice studies animal behavior, is passionate about music and loves to sing. Contact *Janice at janwill@turbonet.com.*

Robin Traywick Williams is chairman of the Virginia Racing Commission and the author of *Chivalry, Thy Name Is Bubba,* a collection of humorous, general-interest newspaper columns. She lives on a farmette in Crozier, Virginia, with her husband Cricket, their daughter Katie, and a full complement of cats, dogs, horses, fish and groundhogs.

Craig Wilson's column, *The Final Word*, appears Wednesdays in *USA Today*. Random House published a compilation of his columns, *It's the Little Things: An Appreciation of Life's Simple Pleasures*, last year and he is at work on his second book. He lives in Washington, D.C., with his partner Jack, and their dog Murphy. Contact Craig at *cwilson@usatoday.com*.

Woody Woodburn is an national award-winning sports columnist for *The Daily Breeze*, in Torrance, California. Featured in *The Best American Sports Writing 2001* and *Chicken Soup For The Baseball Fan's Soul*, he is married with two teenagers and is currently working on breaking three hours in the marathon (even if he has to do so on horseback). E-mail him at *Woodycolum@aol.com*.

Laurie Wright is happily married to a Special Forces soldier and the mother of two beautiful girls. Owner of a small breeding and training operation in Colorado, Laurie's passion is Arabians because of their incredible generosity of spirit, extremely engaging personality, and how easy they are to train.

Gerald W. Young (1908–2001) wrote stories throughout his life. In public relations for over forty years, he lived out his retirement on the Ohio farm where he and his wife, Carrie, raised ponies. Gerald was a former director of the Welsh Pony Society of America. We thank Carrie for sharing his work with readers.

Permissions

We would like to acknowledge the many publishers and individuals who granted us permission to reprint the cited material. (Note: The stories that were written by Jack Canfield, Mark Victor Hansen, Marty Becker, Gary Seidler, Peter Vegso or Theresa Peluso are not included in this listing.)

The Racking Horse. Reprinted by permission of Rhonda Reese. ©1999 Rhonda Reese.

A Rocky Rescue. Reprinted by permission of Diane M. Ciarloni. ©2002 Diane M. Ciarloni.

Cowboy Heart. Reprinted by permission of Roger Dean Kiser. ©2002 Roger Dean Kiser.

Shadow. Reprinted by permission of T.C. Wadsworth. ©1999 T.C. Wadsworth.

Old Twist. Reprinted by permission of Tom Maupin. ©2002 Tom Maupin.

A Silent Bond. Reprinted by permission of Tiernan McKay. ©2003 Tiernan McKay.

Daddy Always Said "Yes" to Horses. Reprinted by permission of Teresa Becker. ©2002 Teresa Becker.

Syd and Roanie. Reprinted by permission of Judy Pioli Askins. ©2002 Judy Pioli Askins.

A Horse with Heart. Reprinted by permission of Jerri Simmons-Fletcher. ©2002 Jerri Simmons-Fletcher.

Sleeping Baby. Reprinted by permission of Jennilyn McKinnon. ©2002 Jennilyn McKinnon.

A Gift of Gold. Reprinted by permission of Robin Roberts. ©2002 Robin Roberts.

Chance of a Lifetime. Reprinted by permission of Denise Bell-Evans. ©2002 Denise Bell-Evans.

Throwing My Loop. Reprinted by permission of Michael Johnson. ©2000 Michael Johnson.

The Language of Horses. Reprinted by permission of Monty Roberts. ©1997 Monty Roberts.

Riding the Edge. Reprinted by permission of Jane Douglass Rhodes. ©2002 Jane Douglass Rhodes.

Big Brother Is Watching. Reprinted by permission of Don Keyes. ©2002 Don Keyes.

God Bless Little Horse Lovin' Souls. Reprinted by permission of Patricia Carter. ©2002 Patricia Carter.

Encounter with a Dangerous Spy. Reprinted by permission of Woody Woodburn. ©2000 Woody Woodburn.

Standing Ground. Reprinted by permission of Starr Lee Cotton Heady. ©2002 Starr Lee Cotton Heady.

That Ol' Black Magic. Reprinted by permission of Diane M. Ciarloni. ©2001 Diane M. Ciarloni.

One Good Horse. Reprinted by permission of John L. Moore. ©1992 John L. Moore.

Take a Deep Seat. Reprinted by permission of Gary Cadwallader. ©2002 Gary Cadwallader.

Sgt. Reckless, a Mighty Marine. Reprinted by permission of Boots Reynolds. ©2003 Boots Reynolds.

The Guiding Sight. Reprinted by permission of Stephanie Stephens. ©2002 Stephanie Stephens.

The Stallion and the Redwing. Reprinted by permission of the estate of Gerald W. Young. ©1992 Gerald W. Young.

A Change of Command. Reprinted by permission of Sandra Tatara. ©2002 Sandra Tatara.

From One Mom to Another. Reprinted by permission of Chris Russell-Grabb. ©2003 Chris Russell-Grabb.

A Leap of Faith. Reprinted by permission of Gayle Stewart. ©2002 Gayle Stewart.

Riding in the Alaskan Bush. Reprinted by permission of Laurie Wright. ©2003 Laurie Wright.

Instincts of a War Mare. Reprinted by permission of Christina Donahue. ©2001 Christina Donahue.

The Man Whisperer. Reprinted by permission of Joyce Stark. ©2003 Joyce Stark.

The Pilon. Reprinted by permission of Nancy Minor. ©2002 Nancy Minor.

Shawnee. Reprinted by permission of Jan Roat. ©2002 Jan Roat.

The Wedding. Reprinted by permission of Kris DeMond. ©2002 Kris DeMond.

Chicken Soup
for the Soul®

Improving Your Life Every Day

Real people sharing real stories — for nineteen years. Now, Chicken Soup for the Soul has gone beyond the bookstore to become a world leader in life improvement. Through books, movies, DVDs, online resources and other partnerships, we bring hope, courage, inspiration and love to hundreds of millions of people around the world. Chicken Soup for the Soul's writers and readers belong to a one-of-a-kind global community, sharing advice, support, guidance, comfort, and knowledge.

Chicken Soup for the Soul stories have been translated into more than 40 languages and can be found in more than one hundred countries. Every day, millions of people experience a Chicken Soup for the Soul story in a book, magazine, newspaper or online. As we share our life experiences through these stories, we offer hope, comfort and inspiration to one another. The stories travel from person to person, and from country to country, helping to improve lives everywhere.

Share with Us

We all have had Chicken Soup for the Soul moments in our lives. If you would like to share your story or poem with millions of people around the world, go to chicken-soup.com and click on "Submit Your Story." You may be able to help another reader, and become a published author at the same time. Some of our past contributors have launched writing and speaking careers from the publication of their stories in our books!

Our submission volume has been increasing steadily — the quality and quantity of your submissions has been fabulous. We only accept story submissions via our website. They are no longer accepted via mail or fax.

To contact us regarding other matters, please send us an e-mail through webmaster@chickensoupforthesoul.com, or fax or write us at:

Chicken Soup for the Soul
P.O. Box 700
Cos Cob, CT 06807-0700
Fax: 203-861-7194

One more note from your friends at Chicken Soup for the Soul: Occasionally, we receive an unsolicited book manuscript from one of our readers, and we would like to respectfully inform you that we do not accept unsolicited manuscripts and we must discard the ones that appear.

Chicken Soup for the Soul
Loving Our Cats

Our 101 BEST STORIES

Heartwarming and Humorous Stories about Our Feline Family Members

Jack Canfield
& Mark Victor Hansen
edited by Amy Newmark

We are all crazy about our mysterious cats. Sometimes they are our best friends; sometimes they are aloof. They are fun to watch and often surprise us. These true stories, the best from Chicken Soup for the Soul's library, will make readers appreciate their own cats and see them with a new eye. Readers will revel in the heartwarming, amusing, inspirational, and occasionally tearful stories about our best friends and faithful companions—our cats.

978-1-935096-08-5

We are all crazy about our dogs and can't read enough about them, whether they're misbehaving and giving us big, innocent looks, or loyally standing by us in times of need. This new book from Chicken Soup for the Soul contains the 101 best dog stories from the company's extensive library. Readers will revel in the heartwarming, amusing, inspirational, and occasionally tearful stories about our best friends and faithful companions—our dogs.

978-1-935096-05-4

Chicken Soup for the Soul

What I Learned from the Cat

101 Stories about Life, Love, and Lessons

Jack Canfield,
Mark Victor Hansen & Amy Newmark
With a foreword by Wendy Diamond,
pet lifestyle expert as seen on *Today* and *Greatest American Dog*

Cats are wonderful companions and playmates that brighten and enrich the lives of their "staff," but they're also amazing teachers, often leading by example! Cat lovers, both lifelong and reluctant, share their feline-inspired lessons about determination and perseverance, self-confidence and self-acceptance, and unconditional love and loyalty. Any cat lover will nod, laugh, and tear up as they read this new collection of 101 amazing stories.

978-1-935096-37-5

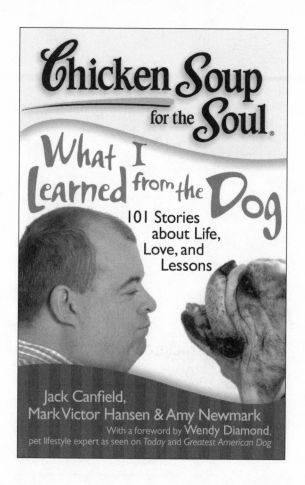

Chicken Soup for the Soul.

What I Learned from the Dog

101 Stories about Life, Love, and Lessons

Jack Canfield,
Mark Victor Hansen & Amy Newmark
With a foreword by Wendy Diamond,
pet lifestyle expert as seen on *Today* and *Greatest American Dog*

An old dog might not be able to learn new tricks, but he might teach his owner a thing or two. Dog lovers will recognize themselves, or their dogs, in these 101 new tales from the owners of these lovable canines. Stories of learning how to be kinder, overcome adversity, say goodbye, love unconditionally, stay strong, and tales of loyalty, listening, and family will delight and inspire readers, and also cause some tears and some laughter.

978-1-935096-38-2

Chicken Soup

www.chickensoup.com

for the Soul

Philippines: repression and resistance

PHILIPPINES

REPRESSION & RESISTANCE

PERMANENT PEOPLES' TRIBUNAL SESSION ON THE PHILIPPINES

KSP

First published 1981 by KSP Komite ng Sambayanang, Pilipino

Copyright © KSP 1980

0 906968 03 8

Typeset by Grassroots Typeset, London NW6. (01-328 0318)
Printed in Great Britain by Whitstable Litho Ltd, Kent.

Distributors:
United Kingdom: (For booksellers and libraries) *Marram Books*
101 Kilburn Square, London NW6 6PS, UK.
KASAMA, BM Box 758, 21a Old Gloucester Street,
London WC1N 3XX, UK.
Europe: *KSP*, Admiral van Genstraat 26 bis 3572 XL Utrecht, Holland.
Asia: *RCPC* PO Box 2784 Kowloon Central Post Office, Hong Kong.
North America:*Tribunal Report*, c/o PO Box 24737, Oakland CA 94623, USA.

vi

Contents

The Case of the Bangsa Moro People / 225

The Verdict / 263

Appendices

Map of peoples' resistance in the Philippines

The Permanent Peoples' Tribunal session on the Philippines

National Democratic Front spokesperson

Moro National Liberation Front spokespersons

Glossary

Bahala Na	A Filipino phrase expressing a 'let fate takes its course' attitude.
Bangsa Moro	The official name of the Muslim people in the Philippines.
Barangay	Village.
Barangay Brigade	Units of men, women and youth organised under the Barangay Brigades Programme.
Barangay Tanod	Selected youth in the Barangay Brigade who are trained for military and surveillance activities against 'subversives'.
Barangay Training Programme	This is a Marcos Government Training Programme for men, women and youth and includes ideological and military training, culminating in initiation rites which requires them to be on military reserve.
Barrio	Village.
'Blue Book'	This is a reference book of actual or potential dissenters which is kept at Manila International Airport. Security agents check the names of travellers against this list.
Bolo	A broad-bladed implement with many uses especially on the farm, for cutting sugar cane etc.
Bukluran ng Manggagawang Pilipino	A alliance of militant unions founded in Manila on 1 May, 1975.
Bulletin Today	A government daily newspaper, published in Manila.
Camote	Sweet potato.
Carabao	Water buffalo.
Cavan of Palay	Cavan is a term applied to the measurement of rice. Palay is the Filipino word for pre-milled rice, to distinguish it from bigas, which applies to milled rice. One cavan has a volume capacity of 75 litres.

Colorums	The Colorums waged revolts in Mindanao 1923 - 1924. On a lesser scale, they also rebelled in Negros, Rizal, Batangas Laguna Pampanga and Tarlac.
Decree	During Martial Law Marcos ruled by issuing laws and regulations — some were called Presidential Decrees.
Encargado	This term dates from the period of Spanish colonialism and is the word applied to a Hacienda overseer.
'First Quarter Storm'	This refers to the waves of mass demonstrations in Manila of the 1960s and early 1970s.
Gabi leaves	Water cress leaves.
Hacienda	This word dates from Spanish colonialism and refers to the tracts of land owned by a landlord who extracts large surplus through exploitation of tenants.
Hectare	This is equivalent to 2.471 acres.
Hukbalahap	The Anti-Japanese People's Army (Filipino name).
Ilaga	A terrorist gang trained and armed by the Philippine Military to terrorise the people of Mindanao.
Illustrado	This word dates from the Spanish period and refers to the Filipino Nationalist intellectuals who emerged before the outbreak of the Philippine Revolution 1896.
Kababayan	Organisation of Filipino Migrant Workers in Rome.
Kabataang Makabayan (KM)	The Nationalist Youth Movement
Kaingin / Kaingineros	This is a Filipino word meaning to burn. It refers to the practice of snidden agriculture, that is, burning scrubs and trees in overgrown mountain areas, as a preparation for cultivation. Kaingineros are those farmers who practise this form of cultivation.
Kalon system	A complex peace pact among Tinggian communities, which is a basis for self organisation of law and order among this tribal peoples of the mountain areas.
Kapatid	Organisation of Relatives and Friends of Political Prisoners.
Kasama	An organisation of militant workers in Manila.

Katipunan ng mga Gurong Makabayan	Union of Nationalists Teachers.
Kilusan ng Bagong Lipunan (KBL)	New Society Movement — President Marcos' New Society Political Party.
Kilusan Mayo Uno	May 1 movement of militant workers unions.
Kilusan para sa Katarungan at Kapayapaan	Ecumenical Movement for Justice and Peace.
Letters of Instruction	Forms of Presidential edicts during Martial Law.
Luyo-luyo	A mutual exchange of labour practiced among the peasants, providing needed labour during planting and harvesting and also as a source of funds during emergency.
Makabayang Samahang Pangkalusugan	Underground organisation of Health Workers.
Malacanang	This is the Palace Residence of President Marcos and previously the residence of former Presidents as well as of American and Spanish Governor Generals.
Manghihilot	A local barrio person who treats sick people with massage.
Masagana 99 Programme	This is a government programme to increase rice production through the use of special seedlings, needing fertilizers and pesticides, which the peasants can finance only through bank loans.
Masaka	A government sponsored organisation of peasants promoting the Marcos land reform programme.
PKP	Partido Komunista ng Pilipinas — Old Communist Party founded 1930.
Presidential Decree/Proclamation	Form of Presidential Edict during Martial Law.
Rebolusyonaryong Kilusan ng Magsasaka	Revolutionary Mass Movement of Peasants.
Rebolusyonaryong Kilusan ng mga Manggagawa	Revolutionary Mass Movement of Workers.
Sacada	Workers on sugar plantations.
Samahang Nayon	A government sponsored organisation of peasants promoting the Marcos Land Reform Programme.
Tungro	A Filipino word referring to a disease affecting rice plants.

Abbreviations

ADB	Asian Development Bank.
AFL-CIO	American Federation of Labour -Congress of International Organisations.
AI	Amnesty International.
ASSO	Arrest, Search and Seizure Order.
AWOL	Absent Without Leave.
BAECON	Bureau of Agricultural Economics.
BEPZ	Bataan Export Processing Zone.
BFD	Bureau of Forestry Development.
BGF	Barrio Guarantee Fund.
BLISS	Bagong Lipunan Sites and Services.
BMA	Bangsa Moro Army.
BT	*Bulletin Today.*
CARBDP	Cotabato-Agusan River Basin Development Project.
CAT	Citizen Army Training.
CHDF	Civilian Home Defence Force.
CIA	Central Intelligence Agency (US).
CLUP	Civil Liberties Union of the Philippines.
CMT	Citizen Military Training.
CNL	Christians for National Liberation.
COCOFED	Coconut Federation.
CPC	Cellulose Processing Corporation.
CPP	Communist Party of the Philippines. (Re-established 1968).
CRC	Cellophil Resources Corporation.
CUFA	Committee on Un-Filipino Activities.
DEPZ	Davao Export Processing Zone.
DPI	Department of Public Information.
EFF	Extended Fund Facility.
FAPE	Fund for Assistance to Private Education.
FFF	Federation of Free Farmers.
GO	General Order.
HMB	Hukbong Magpapalaya ng Bayan.
HUKS	Hukbo ng Bayan Laban sa Gapon. (Hukbalahap)
IMF	International Monetary Fund.
INP	Integrated National Police.
JUSMAG	Joint US Military Advisory Group.
KBL	Kilusan ng Bagong Lipunan.
KM	Kabataang Makabayan.

KMU	Kilusan Mayo Uno.
KSDR	Kalinga Special Development Region.
LI	Letter of Instruction.
METROCOM	Metropolitan Command.
MISG	Military Intelligence and Security Group.
ML	Martial Law
MLG	Marxist-Leninist Group.
MNLF	Moro National Liberation Front.
MOLE	Ministry of Labour and Employment.
NASSA	National Secretariate for Social Action.
NDC	National Development Corporation.
NDF	National Democratic Front.
NEDA	National Economic Development Authority.
NMPC	National Media Production Center.
NPA	New People's Army.
NPDSP	Nagkakaisang Partido Demokratiko Lolyalista ng Pilipinas.
PHIVIDEC	Philipine Veterans Industrial Development Corporation.
PANAMIN	Presidential Assistant on National Minorities.
PC	Philippine Constabulary.
PCSPE	Presidential Commission to Survey Philippine Education.
PD	Presidential Decree.
PKP	Partido Komunista Pilipinas — Old Communist Party — founded 1930.
RP	Republic of the Philippines.
SEATO	South East Asia Treaty Organisation.
TFD	Task Force Detainees.
TUCP	Trade Union Congress of the Philippines.
UP	University of the Philippines.
UNICOM	United Coconut Mills.
US	United States.
USAID	United States Agency for International Development.
US - RP	United States - Republic of the Philippines.
WB	World Bank.

Foreword

The Nuremberg Tribunal, established after the Second World War, created a precedent for the application of the principle that leaders of governments and their subordinate officials are responsible for their acts and can be brought to account before an international legal instance. It affirmed that crimes under international law are committed, not only through violations of the laws of war, but also through acts which are an attack on humanity itself. After the Nuremberg Judgement in 1946, the General Assembly of the United Nations affirmed those principles of international law which had been identified by the Charter of the Tribunal and in its judgements. The General Assembly then directed the International Law Commission to formulate those principles so that they might be codified for future generations. In 1949 the International Law Commission formulated what are now known as 'The Nuremberg Principles'. These are:

1. Any person who commits an act which constitutes a crime under international law is responsible therefor and liable to punishment.
2. The fact that internal law does not impose a penalty for an act which constitutes a crime under international law does not relieve the person who committed the act from responsibility under international law.
3. The fact that a person who committed an act which constitutes a crime under international law acted as Head of State or responsible government official does not relieve him from responsibility under international law.
4. The fact that a person acted pursuant to order of his government or of a superior does not relieve him from responsibility under international law, provided a moral choice was in fact possible to him.
5. Any person charged with a crime under international law has the right to a fair trial on the facts and the law.

And then the International Law Commission went on to set out the crimes which are punishable under international law, including crimes against peace, war crimes and crimes against humanity.

By 1954 the International Law Commission had furthered the work of promoting an international criminal jurisdiction when it finalised the Draft Code of Offences against the Peace and Security of Mankind, but unfortunately that Code is still being considered by the General Assembly, and so far no machinery has been devised whereby the Code and the Nuremberg Principles might be implemented.

It is therefore not surprising that, given the delays on the part of governments, many people became impatient of the institutional void which exists between codified and established principles of international law and the application of those principles to reality. In fact, for many, legal rules had ceased to bear any relation to the reality of the events taking place in the world. Wars continued to be waged, weapons of mass destruction were stockpiled, minorities were oppressed and large numbers of people victimised, tortured or massacred. It was the concern of such people which led in 1967 to the establishment of the 'Bertrand Russell War Crimes Proceedings'. The Russell Tribunal, as it came to be called, assembled a distinguished 'jury of conscience' to hear of the crimes being committed in Vietnam. It voiced the protest of the world's public at the crimes against humanity and violations of the laws of war which were blatantly taking place in South East Asia. Since then, several 'public opinion' tribunals have considered violations of human rights in other parts of the world.

The problem of course is that the principles and standards of post-Nuremberg international law are still not adequate to embrace the full range of aggressive anti-humanitarian activities which, in the modern world, are carried on, not by individuals, but by multinational corporations and international financial institutions steered by boards of directors. A new corpus of legal principles was needed, and in 1976 Lelio Basso and a group of his associates sought to fill this need when they formulated the Universal Declaration of the Rights of Peoples (the Algiers Declaration). Then, in 1979, the Basso Foundation organized the establishment of a permanent International Peoples' Tribunal which would function as a permanent institution to express the voice of concerned public opinion, and would apply not only well established rules and principles of international law, but also those emerging new principles reflected in the Algiers Declaration.

The case brought before the International Peoples' Tribunal on behalf of the Filipino and the Bangsa Moro Peoples, the proceedings of which are contained in this book, was one of the first cases before that institution, and it is unusual for the range of issues it raised. I believe that it will be of considerable interest to lawyers in that it refers to the international humanitarian code of law and principles which governments and individuals are now bound to observe; it also points out those newer areas of law with which lawyers must concern themselves in this world of institutionalised violence and inhumanity.

The book is of vital interest as well to students of the Philippine situation and those who are interested in the Third World generally; the information is concrete, up-to-date and wide-ranging, from the role of the International Monetary Fund and the World Bank to the day to day living experience of workers, peasants, students or cultural minorities. The situation in the Philippines is not unique of course, and many Third World peoples will recognise their own dilemma in the Philippine experience.

Finally the book is a demonstration of one of the most remarkable features of modern life, the power of mass communication. No longer can governments or institutions conceal their activities from public scrutiny; their actions will be seen, heard about and read about — and the public will react to what it sees, hears and reads. One day there will be an International Court of Human Rights which will impose sanctions and punish wrongdoers. In the meantime the wrongdoers may go unpunished, but they will not be forgotten.

Those who have participated in this work have rendered a valuable service to the cause of human rights and lawyers working in this field.

Sean MacBride
April 1981.

Introduction

From 30 October to 3 November, 1980, the Permanent Peoples' Tribunal (PPT) met at the University of Antwerp, Belgium, to examine the appeals presented by the National Democratic Front of the Philippines (NDF) and the Moro National Liberation Front (MNLF) on behalf of the Filipino people and the Bangsa Moro people respectively.

The PPT is an international group of jurists, intellectuals, political, labor and church leaders who took part in the three sessions of the Bertrand Russell Tribunal II on Latin America in the early seventies. They decided to continue the work of enforcing not just the individual but the collective rights of peoples in international law, and drafted the *Declaration of Rights of Peoples*, also known as the *Declaration of Algiers*, after the city where it was proclaimed in 1976. The main figure behind this endeavor was Lelio Basso, an Italian senator, who thought of establishing a permanent international body to which organized peoples could appeal for the defense of their rights and for recognition of the justness of their struggle.

The PPT was formally inaugurated in Bologna, Italy on 29 June, 1979. It has a distinguished list of members who act as jury. For the session on the Philippines, the member-jurors were George Wald (President), Bishop Mendez Arceo, Richard Baumlin, Harvey Cox, Richard Falk, Andrea Giardina, Francois Houtart, Ajit Roy, Makoto Oda and Ernst Utrecht. (see Appendix No. I).

Before its session on the Philippines, the PPT had already examined the situation in Western Sahara, Argentina and Eritrea. In February 1981, it held a session on El Salvador which was widely covered by the international press because of the critical situation in this Central American country.

The appeals of the NDF and the MNLF were submitted to the PPT on the day of its inauguration. The PPT accepted them as valid and appointed two joint committees to prepare for the session: the Filipino People's Committee (better known under its

Filipino acronym KSP, (*Komite ng Sambayanang Pilipino*) and the Moro People's Committee. They were each composed of three PPT-appointed members and three members appointed by the liberation movements. A Belgian Steering Committee was later set up in Antwerp to provide the necessary infrastructure.

Preparatory work for the tribunal consisted in gathering the materials to be presented to the jury, both written documentation and visual evidence (photographs, slides, films). More than 3,000 pages of personal testimonies, basic reports, political positions and other documents were put together — the most comprehensive presentation so far of the case of the resistance in the Philippines at the international level.

The task of relating these materials to the various international laws and thus make, not just a moral but a legal case, was assumed by Muireann O'Briain from Ireland who acted as lawyer for both the NDF and the MNLF.

At the same time, since the PPT is a people's tribunal, the preparatory work had another aspect — the campaign for solidarity among other peoples of the world for the NDF and the MNLF. Inside the Philippines, the appeals were discussed by groups of workers, peasants, students and other organizations who sent more than 9,000 petitions to the PPT. Other liberation movements and solidarity networks, political and labor organizations, progressive church people and other progressive groups and individuals were informed and showed their solidarity by giving material support for the session. More than 6,000 letters and petitions came from Europe, the USA, Canada, Hong Kong, Japan, Australia and New Zealand, calling for the condemnation of the US-Marcos dictatorship and international recognition of the NDF and MNLF.

The government of the Philippines and of the United States of America were duly informed of the charges presented against them through their embassies in Italy (where the PPT is incorporated) and in Belgium (where the session was to take place). Both were invited to send a representative to the Tribunal to state their case. The US embassy in Rome acknowledged receipt of the letter, but the Philippine embassy chose to remain silent. At the opening of the session, PPT General Secretary, Gianni Tognoni informed the jury of the steps taken. However, in February 1981 the Office of the President of the Philippines has reacted to the judgement of the PPT by issuing a 10-page answer. (See Appendix No. VIII).

The Tribunal hearings were structured in such a way as to alternate comprehensive reports, personal testimonies and visual evidence. The basic reports on the economic repression of both Filipino and Moro peoples were delivered by Dr Joel Rocamora of the Southeast Asia Research Center, Berkeley, California, while that on the political repression of the Filipino people was given by Dr Walden Bello of the University of California.

Witnesses who had come from the Philippines to testify were: Victoria de los Reyes, a peasant member of the New People's Army, Perla Silangan, a student, Antonio de la Cruz. a union leader, Salud Torres, a defector from the Ministry of Public Information, and Wada Taw-il, a representative of the Cordillera people in Northern Luzon.

The presentation of the case for the Filipino people was climaxed by the address of the NDF spokesperson, Luis Jalandoni who presented the NDF as the framework of unity and coordination of a fast-growing mass movement aimed at the armed overthrow of the US-Marcos dictatorship and the establishment of a united front government.

The case for the MNLF was presented by Abdurasad Asani, head of the information office of the MNLF, Hatimil Hassan, and Parouk Hussin. Asani traced the historical basis for the Moro people's claim to sovereignty and explained how the MNLF, the vanguard organization of the Moro people, has now a de facto government which has assumed civil functions in its controlled zones all over the Bangsa Moro homeland. Hassan expanded the presentation on the MNLF, providing an overview of its history and politics. Hussin, a doctor, testified about the genocidal proportion of the military campaigns waged against the Moro people.

On the basis of such wealth of information and documentary evidence, the jury produced a verdict that is considered a historic breakthrough by both liberation movements. Following the provisions of the Declaration of Algiers and other international documents, agreements and treaties, the PPT severely condemned the regime of President Marcos in the Philippines and the US government for their role in the economic, political, military and cultural repression of the people. It also affirmed the authority of the NDF and the MNLF to 'enforce the rights of their people, by armed struggle if necessary', thus recognizing a 'belligerency status' which would enable the two liberation fronts to legally receive assistance from established governments and other international bodies.

For the MNLF, the formal recognition by the PPT contributes to the recognition already accorded it by the governments of the Islamic Conference. For the NDF its recognition as legitimate representative of the Filipino people is a significant first step in establishing the legal basis for a future revolutionary government.

But this legal and judicial aspect is only half of the PPT session on the Philippines. The other half is the popular manifestation of support and solidarity. Around 500 attended the session, most of them members and sympathizers of support groups from Belgium itself, Holland, Germany, Italy, Sweden, England, Ireland, France, USA, Canada, Hong Kong and Japan. The cultural evening drew even more participants as performances by Indonesian, Malaysian, Chilean and Belgian groups enriched the variety of support group presentations. Finally, a solidarity manifestation was held in which various political parties, liberation movements, trade unions, women's organizations, church groups and other progressive bodies sent messages, some of which were read by their representatives.

This collection of papers from the PPT session on the Philippines is being published in line with the continuing campaign for international political and material support for the struggle of the Filipino and Moro peoples led by the NDF and the MNLF. The political isolation of the US-Marcos regime and the legitimization of the NDF and the MNLF by the PPT is a step toward recognition and endorsement by other international bodies, including the United Nations. The various support groups can use these materials to further build an international solidarity movement for the people who struggle in the Philippines.

It is this continuing struggle, with its steady accumulation of victories, that provides a firm basis for seeking international political and material support. It is also this struggle which is the important expression of solidarity of the people in the Philippines with the struggles of all peoples throughout the world.

Komite ng Sambayanang Pilipino (KSP)
Admiral Van Gentstraat 26bis
3572 XL Utrecht,
The Netherlands
April 1981

The appeal of the Filipino people to the PPT

The Filipino people have long suffered under semi-colonial and semi-feudal exploitation and oppression and have many times risen up in resistance against this oppressive system.

On 21 September, 1972, Ferdinand Marcos, the incumbent President, imposed martial law in the face of a national democratic mass movement which was challenging the US military bases and other special privileges, fascism and the growing militarisation of society, feudal structures of land ownership, government corruption and other forms of oppression.

At that time, US imperialism was on the verge of defeat in Indochina and sought to strengthen its remaining line of defence in Asia (Thailand, Malaysia, Indonesia, Philippines, Taiwan, South Korea).

Under martial law conditions, the Marcos regime, supported by US imperialism, has intensified the political, economic and cultural oppression of the Filipino people and has committed grievous war crimes against significant sections of the population, including genocide against the Moro people and against the Igorot people.

For this reason, having read the Universal Declaration on the Rights and Liberation of Peoples approved in Algiers on 4 July 1976, we, the undersigned Filipino citizens, request that the International Tribunal of Peoples be convoked to deal specifically with the situation of the Filipino people and to hold a trial against:

a.   US imperialism, and
b.   Ferdinand Marcos and his military regime on the following grounds:

1. US Control of the Philippines

Continued US control of the Philippine economy, politics, culture and military has been assured by a series of unequal treaties signed between the United States Government and subservient Philippine administrations in complete disregard of the interest of the Filipino people. To this day, the United States continues propping up the Marcos regime through huge amounts of economic and military aid. Until now it maintains more than twenty military bases and stations, approximately 16,000 troops, some of which have been directly involved in operations against the Filipino people.

Among the unequal treaties are:

- the US-RP* Treaty of General Relations (4 July 1946)
- the US-RP Military Bases Agreement (1947)
- the US-RP Military Assistance Pact (1947)
- the US-RP Mutual Defence Pact (1951)
- the Agricultural Commodities Agreements.

* US (United States); RP (Republic of the Philippines)

2. Political Repression

Since martial law was declared, more than 60,000 Filipino citizens have been arrested and imprisoned without trial and charges; many languish in jail for years. Most have been subjected to brutal physical and mental torture. A considerable number have been murdered and some have never been heard of after arrest. Military *safehouses* have been extensively used for the torture of prisoners. Recently, instead of taking prisoners, the military has resorted to the so-called *salvaging* policy, i.e. the outright killing of arrested persons or the massacre of citizens in their homes.

In imposing martial law, not only did Marcos confirm the 1971 suspension of the writ of *habeas corpus*, but he opened the way for indiscriminate arrest and prolonged detention. Public demonstrations are prohibited under heavy penalty.

Upon the imposition of martial law, all print and broadcasting communication media were closed down by the military and subsequently put under strict control and ownership of the Marcos regime. Whereas, previously, the press in the Philippines was internationally recognised for its outspokeness, now there is only a controlled and muzzled media.

The Marcos regime has severely curtailed the rights of the workers, especially the right to strike and picket through General Order No. 5 of 22 September, 1972, Presidential Decree No. 823 of 3 November, 1975 and the new Labor Code that became effective on 1 November 1974. The procedure prescribed for settling labour disputes is heavily weighted against the workers.

Marcos has used a series of fake referendums to legitimize his dictatorial and martial law regime. On 7 April, 1978, he organized fraudulent elections to establish a sham parliament and present a facade of democracy.

While Marcos remains an instrument of US imperialism, he has made pretenses to be a leader and spokesman of the Third World and is trying to manoeuver himself into the non-aligned movement. In 1976, he hosted the Group of 77 Conference and read out the Manila Declaration in UNCTAD IV in Nairobi. He tried unsuccessfully to join the non-aligned Conference in Colombo but hosted UNCTAD V in Manila in May 1979.

3. Economic Repression

There has been a general impoverishment of the Filipino workers and peasants who comprise about 90 per cent of the population. There is a deliberate policy to keep the workers' wages down in the face of soaring inflation.

On the other hand, the transnational corporations (North American, Japanese and Europeans) have been accorded special privileges which increase their profits while allowing the intensified exploitation of the Filipino people and crushing local industries.

Free trade zones have been created to let the US and other corporations have permanent economic enclaves which legalize their own even greater exploitation of Philippine labour and allows unlimited repatriation of profits as well as other privileges.

In the face of determined people's opposition at home, the transnationals are exporting pollution to the Philippines without adequate safeguards for the life and health of the affected population. A clear example of this is the *Kawasaki* sintering plant in Mindanao.

Mass eviction of peasants have been perpetrated by transnational corporations, especially the fruit companies, in acquiring and extending their plantations.

The nuclearisation of the Philippines is being initiated with a US$1 billion Westinghouse reactor in Morong. This plant will be located on a major earthquake zone, close to four active volcanoes, just six miles away from the entrance of the US 7th Fleet, Subic Naval Base. Besides the direct harm presently inflicted on the 11,000 poor farmers and fishermen of Morong, millions are now threatened by an explosion or a massive nuclear radiation accident. No storage site for radioactive wastes is available in the country.

The land reform program of Marcos, which is put forward as the cornerstone of the regime's so-called *New Society*, has in reality further impoverished the peasants. Not a single poor peasant has benefited from this program.

World Bank funded 'development' projects are causing massive dislocations of national minorities and entire mountain peoples as in the case of the Chico River Basin Development Projects whereby 100,000 Kalingas and Bontocs of the Igorot peoples are threatened with the loss of their ancestral lands and rice terraces. The forced evacuation of these peoples at gunpoint has already begun.

In the cities, hundreds of thousands of slum dwellers are subjected to the demolition of their homes and forced eviction without any adequate provision for re-settlement. Millions of others are threatened by the same. The regime's justification for these mass evictions is the implementation of World Bank and Asian Development Bank financed projects which will benefit transnational corporations and local commercial interests.

Working women are exploited even more through lower wages, sexual exploitation, discrimination and reduced benefits that go below international standards.

Taking advantage of the dire economic situation of the people, the Marcos regime promotes prostitution as a lucrative enterprise and a tourist attraction. Around the US military bases, cities have sprung up whose principle source of income is prostitution and night clubs.

Because of the depressed economic situation, tens of thousands of Filipinos are lured to work abroad hoping for better wages and living conditions. The vast majority, however, suffer exploitation abroad with the collaboration of the Marcos regime. Some forms of this exploitation are discrimination in wages and living conditions, job insecurity and bribe extortions by Marcos bureaucrats.

The Marcos government has a policy of exporting workers. The target is 36,000 every year. The 1.2 million Filipinos overseas, including seamen and construction workers who are forced to sign a contract to send back 70 per cent of their salary through Philippine banks, will earn $1 billion in foreign exchange in 1980. This will make it the No. 1 dollar earner for the Philippines.

4. Cultural Repression

Scores of nationalist journalists, poets, writers, painters, members of the entertainment world, religious and intellectuals have been arrested and detained. Some have been tortured and a few have been killed. Among the foreigners, some have been deported.

The alienating 'New Society culture', a pseudo-nationalist culture which extols Marcos as the 'father of the nation' and systematically but subtly infuses submissiveness, is imposed through youth seminars (*Kabataang Barangay*), the educational curriculum, popularised songs and slogans and a controlled mass media.

Upon imposing its colonial rule on the Filipino people in 1898, US imperialism also imposed its culture. English became the medium of instruction. The educational curriculum glorified the American way of life while obliterating the rich tradition of the Filipino people. This has created a colonial mentality and an alienated culture among the people. This alien culture is still imposed through movies, television shows, comics, advertising, songs and US products.

In an effort to boost his regime's image at the international level, Marcos has repeatedly offered to host costly sports events, international beauty contests, cultural events and international conferences. He has mis-spent hundreds of millions of dollars not only for hosting such spectacles but also for building huge ostentatious edifices for this purpose, such as the Philippine International Convention Center, the Cultural Center and Folk Arts Center.

The Marcos regime's educational policy is geared to serve the expansionist needs of the transnational corporations. Soon after the imposition of martial law, Marcos approved the recommendations of the Ford Foundation and sponsored a study made by the Presidential Commission for the Survey of Philippine Education (PCSPE). These recommendations, which aim to produce vocationally skilled manpower for the transnationals, are now being implemented.

The health system does not serve the needs of the majority of the people. It is western-oriented, institution-centred and technologically sophisticated. It caters to the elite. While the great majority of the people still suffer from chronic malnutrition, a high rate of infant mortality and diseases such as tuberculosis and schistosomiasis, millions of dollars are spent on the

Heart Center in Manila and only a small per cent of the national budget is allocated to the rural health program. US imperialism actively promotes and funds population control programs in order to make the people believe that large families are the cause of their poverty. Coercive measures are also taken to enforce sterilisation and population control.

The Marcos regime shows complete disregard and contempt for the culture and sacred traditions of the national minorities. As these cultural minorities oppose this repression, the Marcos regime attempts to divide them through bribery, scholarships, and other means. The chief instrument of this is PANAMIN (Presidential Assistance for National Minorities).

War Crimes

As the people rise up in armed resistance against their repression the Marcos regime pursues a policy of aggression and genocide.

In South Philippines, as the Moro people resolutely wage their just struggle, the Marcos regime has launched a policy of genocide and is conducting a war of extermination including the use of napalm and chemical warfare.

In the mountains, a policy of genocide is increasingly being used against the Igorot people who resist the Marcos regime's repressive policies, massive dislocations caused by the government's so-called 'development projects' and attempts to annihilate their culture.

In the countryside, millions of Filipinos have been displaced and have to live the life of refugees. In strategic hamlets and in refugee camps, the needs and welfare of the people are callously disregarded.

US troops from the US military bases in the Philippines are increasingly participating in direct military operations against the Filipino people. Their interference has escalated from the presence of military advisers to that of green berets; from the US-RP civic action teams to joint US-RP military operations.

The US government has increased its military aid to the repressive apparatus of the Marcos regime. From 1969 to 1976, it poured in US$247.1 million worth of military aid. Since martial law was declared, the amount of aid given has more than doubled. For fiscal year 1979 the Carter Administration has requested a total of $37.3 million in military aid for the Philippines.

Many high officers of the Philippines Army and Police, including top intelligence agents and notorious torturers, have received special training in military training camps in the United States. Some are also trained in the Federal Republic of Germany.

People's Resistance

Despite the continuous and brutal oppression of the US-Marcos regime, as outlined in this appeal, the Filipino people have built up a well organized and widespread resistance. The on-going and intensifying struggles of the workers, peasants, fishermen, slumdwellers, national minorities, students, the church sector and other progressive groups are concrete proof of this.

Approximately a quarter of a million workers are launching concerted militant actions and undertaking systematic political education. One million peasants are organized and give systematic support to the New People's Army (NPA). A further nine million look to the leadership of the NPA for organization. The NPA was established on 29 March, 1969, and has grown from sixty guerillas with 35 rifles to several thousand armed troops operating in 41 provinces and supported by a people's militia several tens of thousands strong.

The National Democratic Front (NDF) unites this widespread resistance of the Filipino people. The basis of unity for these national democratic organizations and mass movements is the *Ten Point Program* of the NDF, issued on 24 April, 1973 and re-affirmed and elaborated on 12 November, 1977.

We, the undersigned Filipinos, considering the above mentioned charges request the Permanent Peoples' Tribunal to:
1. Judge, condemn and denounce US imperialism in the Philippines and the present Marcos dictatorship.
2. Recognise the just struggle of the Filipino people.
3. Recognise the NDF and the NPA as legitimately representing the genuine interests of the Filipino people.

The National Democratic Front of the Philippines

The appeal of the Bangsa Moro people to the PPT

The Bangsa Moro people (in the southern Philippines) have, in the last 32 years, suffered untold misery under Philippine colonial domination and oppression. It was on the declaration of Philippine Independence in 1946, upon the evil collusion between American imperialism and its Filipino puppet leaders, that the Bangsa Moro national homeland of Mindanao, Basilan, Sulu and Palawan was criminally annexed to the territorial jurisdiction of the Philippine State.

After Philippine Independence, and the criminal annexation of the Bangsa Moro homeland, the Bangsa Moro people have several times risen upon in armed struggle against Philippine colonial rule. But instead of recognising their rights to self-determination and to a free and peaceful existence, the Philippine colonial regime, aided and supported by American imperialism has, in fact, intensified its colonial oppression and economic and cultural repression including, in the last ten years, a systematic campaign of genocide of the most vicious and most brutal kind.

Now, therefore,

Having read the historic document, *Universal Declaration of the Rights of Peoples*, announced in Algiers on 4 July 1976 which consecrates, among others, a people's right to political self-determination, right to existence and economic rights;

Aware that these basic rights of the Bangsa Moro people are being grossly and systematically violated by the Philippine colonial regime and its US imperialist collaborators;

And, knowing that, in an effort to advance the rights of all oppressed and colonized peoples, the International League for the Rights and Liberation of Peoples is convening an International Tribunal in Bologna for the trial of colonial and oppressive regimes;

I, the undersigned, by authority of the Chairman of the Central Committee of the Moro National Liberation Front and on behalf of the Bangsa Moro people in the southern Philippines, as well as in my capacity as official representative of the

Front, being Director of the Front's relations office in Tripoli, Jamahiriya, hereby present this appeal and strongly request that the Philippine colonial regime and its master, US imperialism, be put on public trial before the Tribunal in order to expose their crimes against our people and humanity, on the following grounds:

Philippine Colonial Domination and the Bangsa Moro People's Right to Self-Determination

It is a matter of historical fact that the Bangsa Moro people have been an independent people. They had an independent government under the Sultanate of Sulu in the Sulu archipelago and the Sultanate of Maguindanao in the island of Mindanao.

When Spanish colonialism came to the Philippines, it tried to conquer the Bangsa Moro people by force with the aim of establishing colonial hegemony in the area. But the Bangsa Moro people courageously defended the integrity of their homeland. The famous Spanish-Moro wars lasted well over 333 years, from 1565 to 1898, hence, Spanish colonialism never gained any permanent foothold or influence until its withdrawal from the Philippines when America took over colonial possession of the Philippine islands.

American colonialism in the Philippines, like its Spanish predecessor also tried to conquer the Bangsa Moro people by force. But again, the Bangsa Moro people waged a heroic armed struggle to defend their freedom and independence. The war against American colonialism lasted from 1900 to 1914. Realizing the futility of its military efforts to subdue the Bangsa Moro people, American colonialism proclaimed a policy of attraction. Despite this new policy, however, America did not completely win over the Bangsa Moro people, especially the masses who carried out, and suffered most, the brunt of the war.

At any rate, recognizing the distinct and separate character of the Bangsa Moro people from the Filipino people, American colonialism pursued its colonial administration in those areas of the Bangsa Moro homeland which came under its nominal control through the so-called Moro province.

In 1946, America granted the Philippines independence. But through the evil collusion of American colonialists and their Filipino puppet leaders, the Bangsa Moro national homeland of Mindanao, Basilan, Sulu and Palawan was arbitrarily and criminally annexed to the newly-born Philippine State. This annexation was done over the vehement objection of the Bangsa Moro people and in complete disregard of their inalienable right to national self-determination and to set up their own free and independent Bangsa Moro State. This was how the Bangsa Moro people fell under Philippine colonial rule. Today they have taken the historic decision to break off the shackle of this colonial imposition.

2. Economic Exploitation, Repression and Discrimination

In a sweeping move to extend its colonial authority to the Bangsa Moro homeland, one of the first acts of the Philippine State was to divest the Bangsa Moro people of their ancestral land by declaring all lands as part of the public domain. Ownership of all natural resources, mineral, forest, agricultural, and marine wealth, was thereby taken over by the Philippine colonial State, and their exploitation and utilization were thrown wide open to big Filipino capitalists and their foreign masters, mostly giant American corporations and multinationals.

After the annexation, a policy of settler colonialism was vigoriously pursued whereby hordes of settlers from the northern and central part of the Philippines were brought down to all parts of the Bangsa Moro homeland especially Mindanao. This was followed by a systematic landgrabbing scheme whereby poor and unsophisticated Bangsa Moro peasants and farm owners were dispossessed of their ancestral land and forced into less fertile and less habitable mountainous regions.

The settlers, with the aid and support of the government, or in connivance with unscrupulous government bureaucrats, were given ownership titles to lands which were hitherto the ancestral possession of the Bangsa Moro peasants, thus depriving the latter of their basic source of livelihood. Those who have managed to secure land titles under the alien torrens system have been terrorized into vacating their farmlands. Such lands as those vacated by their owners are immediately seized by the settler-newcomers or by their fanatical terrorist gang, if not by regular officers and men of the Armed Forces of the Philippines.

Multinationals, mostly Americans, and big Filipino capitalists are given special privileges and incentives to establish and expand their business corporations in the Bangsa Moro homeland. This is especially true in the case of several fruit companies which acquired and expanded their plantation areas through forcible eviction of peasants who, for generations, have occupied those lands.

In industries which have been established in the Bangsa Moro homeland, no indigenous Bangsa Moro capital is given equity participation in investment. The workers are also imported from the northern and central parts of the Philippines. The native and indigenous people are not given any chance to be employed, or if there are few who are at all fortunate enough to be given jobs in such industries, they are no more than temporary manual workers completely denied any chance to bargain for their workers' rights such as job security, better wages and better working conditions.

There is gross discrimination in all facets of social life. In health service, education, appointments to government positions and private and semi-government corporations, the Bangsa Moro people, particularly Muslims, are discriminated against because the regime's education system, being under tutelge and control of the American system, foster the colonial attitude of 'a good Moro is a dead Moro', an American aphorism which means that the Moros are bad, savage and treacherous, overlooking the fact that the history of the Bangsa Moro people is more brilliant and colorful than other national groups in Asia.

3. The Marcos Regime's Campaign of Genocide

Not content with its colonial imposition upon the Bangsa Moro homeland, the Philippine colonial regime, abetted by massive US support of its military arsenals, has launched a campaign of genocide against the Bangsa Moro people. This genocidal campaign began under the dictator, Ferdinand Marcos, in March 1968 when 68 young Muslim trainees were mercilessly massacred on Correigidor island by their training instructors who were all officers of the Armed Forces of the Philippines. Until today, many of the almost 300 young trainees are still missing.

Afterwards, in 1969, the Marcos regime, through its fascist Armed Forces, unleashed their Ilaga paramilitary terrorist front to massacre and indiscrimately kill innocent Bangsa Moro civilians. Witness, for example, the massacre of 70 Muslim men, women, and children right inside a mosque in barrio Manili, Carmen, Cotabato on 19 June, 1971; the massacre of 17 innocent Muslim civilians in Bual, Tulunan, Cotabato on 17 September, 1971; the massacre of 37 innocent Muslim men and women in Tacub, Kauswagan, Lanao del Norte on 22 November, 1971 and many other massacres and mass killings between March 1968 and September 1972. In the meantime, while all these grisly killings were going on with impunity, the fanatic Ilaga terrorist front, organized, trained and led by officers and men of the Armed Forces of the Philippines were plundering, looting and burning Bangsa Moro villages and towns especially in the regions of Cotabato, Lanao and Zamboanga.

In September 1972, President Marcos imposed martial law in the Philippines. He assumed dictatorial power and militarized society; he abolished the Philippine congress and made the Supreme Court a rubber stamp of his presidential whims and caprices. The press and communication media were put under strict government control. Two months later, in November 1972, the regime declared war against the Bangsa Moro people and utilizing composite military forces from the Army, Constabulary, Navy and Air Force, launched search-and-destroy oprations starting on Jolo island followed by other search-and-destroy operations in Cotabato and other parts of the Bangsa Moro homeland, killing in the process several hundreds of innocent civilians and burning their houses.

Under Martial Law, the crimes of the Marcos regime increased ten-fold in magnitude and severity. With increased regular troops deployed all over the Bangsa Moro homeland, assisted by their terrorist paramilitary forces, the military went on a rampage, killing around 500 civilians in the period from February to June 1973 in Lebak, Cotabato; followed by the bombing and razing to the ground of the entire village of Tuburan on Basilan island in July, 1973; and the burning of Jolo City on 8 February, 1974 by naval cannons, artillery fire and napalm. Massacres followed after massacres, victimizing men, women and children.

To emphasize the magnitude of the genocidal crimes of the regime committed against the Bangsa Moro people, here is what one report has to say:

> About 2,000 women, civilians and children buried by Army at Malisbong, province of Sultan Kudarat. About 7,000 civilians have evacuated to upper Kolong-Kolong and Kran, Sultan Kudarat province. Every now and then moneyed Muslims are being picked up as suspects for giving aid to the rebels. They are being released for certain monetary consideration.

This top secret report entitled, *For the President's Eye Through (Information) Secretary Tatad*, was prepared and submitted to President Marcos by a certain Atty. Leloy Caniedo, a member of the Philippine military investigation team that inquired into the widely known army crimes and abuses against Bangsa Moro civilians in South Cotabato in December 1974. Indeed, the widely publicized Mai Lai massacre of Vietnamese by American troops in Vietnam would be dwarfed by the savagery of the Marcos military in the southern Philippines. (More details of massacres and list of towns and cities burned or destroyed will be supplied at the proper time.)

In the cities and urban centers, the regime's army conduct systematic arrest, torture and liquidation or salvaging of small traders and merchants suspected of anti-government activities. In Jolo, for example, anyone whose residence certificate shows that he comes from Patikul, would be arrested, tortured and liquidated without any question asked. Fishermen out at sea with their vinta outriggers are strafed with machineguns or bombarded with naval cannons.

The armed forces of the Philippines and their paramilitary terrorist front violate with impunity the honor and dignity of our women; in some cases, the women are forced to submit to the carnal lust of the brutes in the presence of their husbands. And in many cases, they are raped first and murdered afterwards. Infants are stamped to death under the soldiers' boots or just bayoneted to death.

Consistent with the regimes policy of genocide, the Marcos military defoliated farmlands and agricultural crops. Work animals are forcibly taken from their owner or merely shot dead to reduce the people's capacity to work for their livelihood. Poisonous chemicals are dropped from the air, poisoning water supply in the countryside and causing widespread disease and epidemic.

Hand in hand with the physical extermination of the Bangsa Moro people, the Marcos regime through its barbaric armed forces, is out to liquidate the Bangsa Moro people's culture. Such sacrilegious acts as burning of mosques and Islamic schools are as common to the Marcos terrorist army as shooting innocent civilians. The pages of the Holy Quran are used as sanitary papers. Several of the massacres of innocent civilians have in fact been committed by the Philippine military while the victims were in the midst of prayer in the mosques.

As a result of ten years of continuous and unabated acts of violence and savagery in pursuance of Marcos' and his regime's genocidal policy, around 90,000 innocent Bangsa Moro civilians have to date already died in the hands of the barbaric Armed Forces, no less than 250,000 houses and thousands of mosques and madrasas (Islamic schools) have been burned and reduced to ashes. The Marcos genocidal war has further made millions of peaceful Bangsa Moro masses refugees in their own homeland. These refugees are today exposed to disease, starvation and famine, moving from place to place and in constant danger of being massacred or killed. Furthermore, an estimated 130,000 refugees have already fled to the East Malaysian State of Sabah whose life situation is today similar if not worse than the Vietnamese 'boat people'.

4. The Role of US Imperialism

The United States maintains large military bases in the Philippines, ensuring effective US control of Philippine political, military and economic life. Hence, because of such control, the Philippine regime gives US monopoly capital, multi-nationals and consortia virtual no-limit privileges and incentives in the plunder of all natural resources, including oil and minerals, in the Bangsa Moro homeland. To service the need of US fruit companies for land, for example, poor Bangsa Moro peasants are forcibly evicted from their ancestral farmlands.

To make sure that the Philippines would remain a US client state, the United States imperialist strategy is to keep the Philippines poor so that it becomes even more subservient as it relies on heavy doses of US economic and military assistance. Without such assistance the Martial Law political infra-structure would soon collapse in the face of the gathering force of democratic Filipinos opposed to the dictatorship and of the Bangsa Moro people's liberation struggle in the southern Philippines.

In recent years, alarmed by the fast growing strength of the Bangsa Moro people's struggle which threatens US economic interests, not only has the US government increased military aid to the martial law dictatorship of Marcos, but the US has resorted to direct intervention in the Marcos genocidal war against the Bangsa Moro people by allowing American jets from the huge Clark Air Base to participate in bombing missions over Mindanao in the south of the Philippines.

What is more ominous, however, is the fact that as a result of a revised US-Philippine military bases agreement concluded early this year, aside from assuring huge amounts of military aid to the reactionary Marcos regime for the next five years, the

United States may now participate in security activities such as counter-insurgency operations, providing for legal justification for direct US troops involvement of a Vietnam-type war in the north and central parts of the Philippines and more so in the Bangsa Moro homeland.

I strongly request that this appeal be heard by the Tribunal; that the Marcos regime and US imperialism be tried and condemned before the bar of world public opinion for their crimes against our people and humanity; and that the Tribunal recognize the inalienable right of our people to national self-determinaion as well as their legitimate aspiration for nationhood like other free nations of the world. I would like to add that the Bangsa Moro people today is a cohesive national group, with its own history and culture, customs, traditions and habits distinct and separate from the Filipino people, with the contiguous territory historically recognized as their own.

Most Respectfully Submitted:
for Nur Misuari
Chairman
Central Committee
Moro National Liberation Front

Abdurasad Asani
Director
MNLF Information Office, Tripoli
10 June 1979

THE LEGAL BRIEF

**The Filipino People and The Bangsa Moro People
at the suit of the National Democratic Front (NDF) of the
Philippines and of the Moro National Liberation Front
(MNLF)of the Southern Philippines**

versus

**Ferdinand Marcos, the Government of the Republic of the
Philippines and the Filipino Individuals and Families more
Particularly listed in the First Schedule Hereto**

and

The Government of the United States of America

and

The International Monetary Fund and the World Bank

and

Banking and Finance Capital
Bank of America
First National City Bank
Chase Manhatten Bank
Daiichi Kangyo
Philamlife Insurance Co.

Oil and Energy
Caltex Petroleum Corporation
Royal Dutch Shell Oil Co.
Mobil Oil Corporation
Westinghouse Electric Corporation
General Telephone and Electric Co.

Extraction and Semi-processing of strategic raw materials
Mitsubishi Metal Mining Co.
(Atlas Consolidated Mining and Development Corporation)

A. Soriano Y Compania (Benguet Consolidated Inc.)
Marcopper Mining Co. Corporation
Marinduque Mining and Industrial Corporation
Philippines Sinster Corporation (Kawasaki Steel Corporation)
Mitsubishi Group

Agricultural Exports
Castle & Cook (Dole, Philippines)
California Packing Co. (Del Monte)

Strategic Industries
B.F. Goodrich Co.
Goodyear Tire & Rubber Co.
Firestone Tire & Rubber Co.

Food and Detergents
Unilever
Proctor & Gamble
Pepsico International

Drugs
Abbot
Pfizer

Machinery
International Harvester Co.

Cars
Ford Motor Co.
General Motors Corporation
Toyota

Trading
Cargill Industries (Granexport Corporation)

The Charges

Ferdinand Marcos, the Government of the Republic of the Philippines, and the Filipino Individuals and Families more particularly listed in the First Schedule hereto are charged with:
i.   Violation of the Rights of Peoples.
ii.   Violation of Human Rights.
iii. Crimes under International Law including genocide.

The Government of the United States of America is charged with:
i.   Violation of the Rights of Peoples.
ii.   Conspiracy and complicity in crimes under International Law.
iii. Incitement to and conspiracy in genocide of Filipino minorities.

The International Monetary Fund and the World Bank are charged with:
i.   Violation of the Rights of Peoples.
ii.   Violation of the Provision of their Charters.
iii. Aiding violations of Human Rights.
iv.   Inciting the commission of genocide and crimes under International Law.

Bank of America, First National City Bank, Chase Manhatten Bank, Daiichi Kangyo, Fil-Am Life Assurance Company, Caltex Petroleum Corporation, Royal Dutch Shell Oil Co., Mobil Oil Corporation, Westinghouse Electric Corporation, General Telephone and Electric Co., Mitsubishi Metal Mining Co., A. Soriano Y Compania, Marcopper Mining Corporation, Marinduque Mining and Industrial Corporation, Philippines Sinster Corporation, Mitsubishi Group, Castle & Cook, California Packing Co., B.F. Goodrich Co., Goodyear Tire & Rubber Co., Firestone Tire & Rubber Co., Unilever, Proctor & Gamble, Pepsico International, Abbot, Pfizer, International Harvester Co., Ford Motors Co., General Motors Corporation, Toyota, and Cargill Industries together with the corporations and companies more particularly listed in the Second Schedule hereto are charged with:

i.   Violation of the Rights of Peoples.
ii.   Violation of Human Rights.
iii. Inciting the commission of genocide and crimes under International Law.

Introduction

When the Permanent People's Tribunal was established in June 1979 at Bologna, Italy, under the auspices of the Basso International Foundation for the Rights and Liberation of Peoples, a request was made on behalf of the Filipino and the Moro peoples by the National Democratic Front of the Philippines and the Moro National Liberation Front of the Southern Philippines that the Tribunal should hear their complaints of massive violations of human rights and the rights of peoples in the Philippines by President Ferdinand Marcos, his government and the elite who support him, by the Government of the United States of America, by the international financial institutions and by certain international businesses and corporations. This request was acceded to by the Executive Committee of the Tribunal. The NDF and the MNLF present herewith a Brief in two parts of the charges and complaints they prefer against the accused parties, and of the evidence they propose to present in support of those charges and complaints. The MNLF Brief also contains an application for a determination by the People's Tribunal of the right of the Bangsa Moro people to self-determination.

This case is brought by opposition fronts because the

Government of the Philippines is not the legitimate representative of the Filipino people or the Moro people since its members were not democratically elected by a free election process. It is a government of the elite and for the elite (less than 4 per cent of the population) and maintains power only through a martial law dictatorship. In the course of this case it will be shown that elections and referenda in the Philippines do not give a voice to the people. As a result, the grievances of the people can neither be expressed to its government or by its government.

Of the Plaintiffs, on the other hand, the NDF unites the widespread resistance that exists among the Filipino people to economic, political and cultural repression in the Philippines. It represents the main organised resistance with members coming from all sectors of Philippine society: workers, peasants, and farmworkers, fishermen, slumdwellers, national minorities, students, teachers, health workers, and other professionals, businessmen, church personnel and others. Its Ten-Point Programme, proclaimed on 24 April, 1973, and reaffirmed on 12 November, 1977, represents the genuine aspirations of the majority of the Filipino people and provides a framework for the cooperation and coordination of all who struggle for national liberation and democracy against what is termed the 'US-backed Marcos dictatorship'. At present the NDF and the resistance forces it unites count over one million formally organised members and have the active and reliable support of over four million, three-fourths of which are in the countryside. Their influence extends to a much bigger number.

The New People's Army (NPA) is the main armed group of the resistance forces under the NDF. Aside from fighting, it helps organise and educate the people in the countryside and implements land reform step by step. It was established on 29 March, 1969 and presently has several thousand armed troops supported by five times as many people's militia. It operates in 26 guerilla fronts spread over 40 of the 70 provinces in the Philippines.

The second Plaintiff, the MNLF, has united resistance to the campaign of colonialism and genocide being waged by President Marcos and his government against the Bangsa Moro people of the Southern Philippines since 1972. Its program aims at complete political independence for the entire Bangsa Moro homelands of Mindanao, Basilan, Sulu and Palawan. The Bangsa Moro Army was formed by the MNLF in 1972 and has waged an outright armed struggle against the armed forces of the Philippines since then. The Bangsa Moro Army and the MNLF has the support of the Moro people of the Southern Philippines who represent over 60 per cent of the population there.

There are other smaller opposition groups in the Philippines, represented by the traditional elite opposition and some social-democratic groups. The elite opposition tends to limit its goals to a change of government and its members are generally part of the privileged minority themselves. The social-democratic groups, together with other more spontaneous and transitory formations, tend to develop working relations with the NDF as their experience and study make them realise the need for the comprehensive program and strategy that the Plaintiffs offer.

The Tribunal is requested to recognise the NDF, together with the NPA, as the legitimate representatives of the Filipino people and to acknowledge their right to present this case on behalf of the Filipino people.

The Tribunal is requested to recognise the MNLF, together with the Bangsa Moro Army, as the legitimate representatives of the Moro people, and to acknowledge their right to present the application for a determination of their right to self-determination and the charges of genocide and war crimes on behalf of the Moro people.

Documentation

As explanatory material, the Tribunal will be presented with the following documents:

1. Philippines 1980. An NDF Publication.
2. Neo-Colonialism: Root of our Discontent. (1979) Published by the Civil Liberties Union of the Philippines (C.L.U.P.)

The Historical and Political Contexts in which the Charges referred to the Peoples Tribunal have arisen.

The Philippines is an archipelago consisting of over 7,000 islands with a total land area of 115,000 square miles. It has extremely fertile agricultural lands and vast forest, mineral, marine and power resources.

The Filipino and the Moro people now number about 48 million. About 75 per cent of them live in largely underdeveloped rural areas, earning a poor livelihood as tenants, farmworkers and fishermen.

About 85 per cent of the people are of Malay stock. The Malays came in three waves; the first around 250 B.C.; the second between the first and the thirteenth century who became the main ancestors of the Tagalogs, Ilocanos, Pampangenos, Visayans and Bicolanos; and the third in the 14th and 15th centuries came with the Arab traders and religious teachers who laid the foundations of Islam in Mindanao and Sulu. The Filipinos speak some 100 dialects, but Tagalog has become the principal base of the national language now called Filipino.

The early social units were 'barangay' consisting of 30 to 100 families. Property was mainly communal. In Mindanao and Sulu, sultans reigned over several barangays in a more advanced economic and social state of organisation. By the 16th century when the Spanish came, the people had developed an extensive agricultural economy, as well as mining, lumbering, shipbuilding, and weaving. They had a literature and music and had developed the visual arts.

Due mainly to the lack of political unity in the Philippines, the Spanish were able to impose a colonial rule over most of the country by 1580, except for the Muslims in Mindanao and Sulu, and the Igorots in Northern Luzon, who continued to resist. A colonial and feudal system was imposed by the Spanish whereby large areas were taken over as *encomiendas* under the Spanish crown, the colonialists and the religious orders. The petty nobility of the barangays then became the lesser landlords. In the 18th century the cultivation of export crops was imposed and the remainder of the land acquired into private ownership.

Over 200 revolts and uprisings took place during the Spanish colonial period, in opposition to the tributes and forced labour imposed on the native population. A national, anticolonial, revolution began in 1896 and quickly spread through the whole country. By June 1898 the Filipino forces were in control of virtually all of the Philippines. In April 1898 the United States of America declared war on Spain. The Americans attacked the Spanish in the Philippines with the support of the Filipino forces to whom they had given assurances that, on the defeat of the Spanish, Filipino independence would be respected. However, the Spanish negotiated separately and secretly with the Americans, and by the Treaty of Paris in December 1898, Spain ceded the Philippines to the United States for 20 million dollars. Soon after, the Philippine-American war began and continued until 1901. After that the Americans ruled by force of arms and the people's resistance was confined to guerilla activity.

The people's resistance was, however, of such proportions, that between 1900 and 1901, the number of American troops had to be increased from 70,000 to 126,000 distributed in 639 military posts. Torture, burning of villages, looting and massacres took place on a vast scale to try to quell the resistance. Various laws were passed penalising with death or long prison sentences those who resisted US rule. Philippine jails were so badly overcrowded that many prisoners died in prison; the death rate in one prison in 1905 was 438 per 1,000 inmates.

The reason that the Americans wanted control in the Philippines was to gain entry for its commerce in China and the rest of Asia, for which the Philippines provided a forward base. The Philippines itself also provided a market for American goods and a source of cheap raw materials. In 1909 the Payne-Aldrich Act provided that American goods could enter the Philippines duty-free and in unlimited quantities. All quota limitations for imports to America from the Philippines were abolished in 1913. By 1933 the Philippines purchased 64 per cent of its total imports from the United States, and 83 per cent of its exports went to the United States.

A Philippine Assembly was established in 1907, but only participation of the native elite was possible, and the real power lay with the American Governor-General. The masses were kept from participating in elections by the restricted suffrage which ensured that only representatives of the native elite could be elected. Political parties were allowed only with the approval of the American Governor-General. The cultural Americanisation of the Filipino people was achieved through the adoption of English as the medium of instruction and the public school system.

But despite the systematic consolidation of American rule, unrest still persisted. In 1923 the *Colorums* (peasants and urban poor) staged scattered uprisings in Surigao, Agusan, Samar, Leyte and Nueva Ecija. In 1927, 26,000 sugar workers rose up in several provinces of Visaya against their landlords. In 1935, 60,000 organised peasants called *Sakdalistas* rose in rebellion in many areas. Workers rebelled as well, including 100,000 in 1903 who staged a mass demonstration against American imperialism. From 1925 until the end of the thirties, numerous strikes took place in factories, ports, mines etc.

In 1934 a Constitutional Convention was established by the Tydings-McDuffie Act, which was to frame a Constitution. However, the Act specifically directed the inclusion in the Constitution of all reservations of powers and privileges of the United States, and the Constitution even had to be approved by the American President before submission to the Filipino people.

During the World War which began in 1939, Japan launched attacks on US bases in the Philippines, and Manila was occupied by the Japanese in 1942. Other parts of the Philippines were also occupied. The Nacionalists Party, which was the largest party of the Commonwealth government, split, with one faction supporting the United States, and the other, the Japanese. In October 1943 the Japanese set up a so-called 'independent republic' in the Philippines, with its supporters at the head of the government. Resistance to the new colonialists continued, mainly organised by the Communist Party of the Philippines, which created the *Hukbalahap* (the anti-Japanese People's Army) and was particularly successful in Central and Southern Luzon. When the Japanese were finally defeated, the United States then re-took control of the Philippines.

Formal independence was finally granted to the Philippines in 1946, but the economic domination of the country by the United States still continued with the cooperation of the opportunistic elite in the Philippines. The instrument of US control over the nominally independent former colony was the Philippine Trade Act of 1946, commonly known as the Bell Trade Act. This Act was drafted and debated in the US Congress and designed to conform to the needs of American interests. Passage of the Act in the Philippines was made possible not only by the genuine support of the pre-war exporting interests, which would benefit from the reconstruction of the old economy, but also by an element of bribery, since release of funds from the US Rehabilitation Act was made conditional upon Philippine acceptance of the Bell Trade Act. The Act demanded parity rights for Americans to exploit natural resources and operate public utilities, the continuation of free trade until 1954 and the placing of the Philippine currency under American dictation.

American domination of the economy continued even after the expiration of the Bell Trade Act. When it expired in 1954, the Laurel-Langley agreement extended parity rights in all kinds of business for a further twenty years. That agreement ended in 1974, and was replaced by a new trade agreement in October

1979 (the Collantes-Murphy Agreement). The text of the agreement was not released, but it was announced that no duties would be imposed on certain Philippine products entering the United States, and that there would be reductions on duties on other goods. The point about the agreement is that the export incentives will benefit only the elite of the Philippines who control the export industries, and that it continues and confirms the export-oriented strategy of the Philippine economy. It is on the basis of this export-oriented strategy that International Monetary Fund and World Bank loans are granted, and it has its roots in a concept designed to limit the industrialisation of the Philippines to labor-intensive industries catering for a foreign market, and to link the natural resources of the country to the requirements of the developed countries. Its success is dependent on a cheap labor policy and a floating rate.

United States domination of the Philippines has also been achieved through military agreements. In 1947 the Military Bases Treaty gave the US extra-territorial control over 200,000 hectares of Philippine territory, free of rental payments. On this land, 23 military bases have been established throughout the country. This Treaty was amended in 1979 on the basis that the President of the United States would obtain additional funding for 'security assistance' for President Marcos. The additional funding promised totalled $500 million for a five-year fiscal period. (Congressional Record 5th February 1980). The United States-Republic of the Philippines Military Assistance Pact of 1947 provided for American involvement with the armed forces of the Philippines through a joint US Military Advisory Group. In 1951 the US-RP Mutual Defence Pact gave formal rights to the US military to military intervention on Philippine territory when required, on the grounds of so-called 'mutual defence', and guaranteed the right of US troop movements of any part of the country without Philippine consent.

The present US annual military aid to the Philippines includes 25 million dollars in grant military assistance, 50 million dollars in foreign military sales credits, 20 million dollars in security supporting assistance (police, communications, equipment), and 700,000 dollars in military training. There is also a programme of concealed military assistance which is termed 'aid for self-reliance'. The President of the United States has also promised to give 'prompt and sympathetic consideration to requests for specific items of military equipment... and to requests for the sale of other military equipment which (the Philippine) government may wish to purchase through US government or commercial channels' (Letter of 4th January 1979 President Carter to President Marcos).

The Philippine government's own military allocation is P5.5 billion out of a total national budget of P34.3 billion.

Resistance to the American and Filipino elite manipulation of the economic and political life of the country has continued throughout the years since independence, but since 1970 has reached massive proportions. In early 1970, at the start of Marcos' second term as President, tens of thousands of students, workers and other citizens staged a series of militant demonstrations against the Marcos regime and the domination of the economic and political life of the country by the United States. Even after President Marcos had suspended the writ of Habeas Corpus in 1971, huge demonstrations were held in Manila and other cities. In the countryside the New People's Army gained more support from the peasants, and in the cities militant strikes were launched by workers.

As the storm of resistance grew, President Marcos declared martial law on 21 September 1972. Thousands were arrested and imprisoned, democratic rights were suppressed, the media was silenced and Congress was abolished.

The martial law regime still continues.

Documentation

As additional explanatory material, the Tribunal will be presented with the following documents:

1. *Country Paper: Philippines.* Prepared by the National Secretariat of Social Action, Justice and Peace (NASSA) for the General Assembly of the Asian Partnership for Human Development. September 1979 and update April 1980.
2. *Makibaka: Join Us in Struggle.* A documentation of resistance to martial law in the Philippines. Second edition 1979. Published by Filipinen Groep, Holland.
3. *Les Philippines: Le Reveil d'un Archipel* by Charles Foubert. IDOC (Italy) 1980.

Economic Repression of the Filipino People

The economic situation in the Philippines is one of complete repression of the majority of the people. The instigators of this repression are the American Government through a series of unequal treaties through which the American control of the Philippine economy is assured, secondly President Marcos and his government, who continue to enforce the said treaties, and who accord special privileges to the United States government and to multinational corporations in the interests of their own enrichment and that of their friends, the Filipino elite, particularly the large landowners and businessmen who exploit their workers and deny them the means of earning an adequate livelihood, the international monetary institutions, who set the overall structure for the continuation of underdevelopment and find projects which exaggerate the distortions of the Philippine developmental process, and finally the multinational corporations which exploit and perpetuate the situation offered to them for their own profit, and without regard to the welfare of Filipino workers.

The present economic situation shows a gross lopsidedness in the distribution of income, severe underdevelopment in rural areas, and the majority of the population without adequate food, shelter, health, education, transport or communication facilities. The balance of payments deficit of $8.3 billion is unprecedented, as is the balance of trade deficit of $400 million, and inflation is estimated at an unprecedented 27 per cent per annum.

The Plaintiffs will show that it is the policies and actions of the accused parties concerning the Philippine economy which have caused these discrepancies. In particular it will be shown that the said policies and actions have resulted in:

Widespread poverty to the extent that 90 per cent of the population have an income which is inadequate for their basic needs. 84 per cent to 91 per cent of Filipino workers are paid wages which are below subsistence level, according to the Ministry of Labour (Philippine Labour Review 1977). Real wages of workers have declined steadily since 1972. Actual take-home pay for an industrial worker in 1980 is P29 per day. Yet the National Economic Development Authority estimated in August 1980 that a worker would require P72.19 per day to support a family of six, based on requiring P47.55 per day for food, and P24.64 per day for other basic necessities.

Homelessness, mass evictions from homes and inadequate basic housing. Development projects involving the building of dams, air bases, naval bases etc. benefit large corporations, large landowners or the United States, and lead to the eviction, by force or otherwise, of people from their homes. For example, the building of four dams on the Chico River would dislocate 100,000 Bontoc and Kalinga people, while the building of the Tandag-Togo dams at Surigao del Sur will dislocate almost 3,000 Monobo families. In the urban areas, millions of squatters live in shacks in shanty towns, without space, water or sewage. They are often evicted, their shanties demolished and they are forcibly resettled. The National Housing Authority estimated in 1977 that 86,000 new housing units had to be built each year for ten years, and that 82,000 other households needed to be resettled. Yet the houses built in 1978 represented only 24 per cent of the target for that year.

Hazards to life and health through industrial and nuclear pollution. Industrial waste is allowed to pollute the atmosphere which affects the health of workers, and the seas which then pollute the water and destroy fish-life and consequently deprive fishermen of their livelihood. The nuclear plant at Morong, Bataan, does not comply with US Nuclear Regulatory Commission standards, and in any event is geodetically unsafe. The American bases house nuclear missiles and the areas of the bases are consequently prime targets in the event of nuclear war.

A high rate of infant and adult mortality by reason of poverty and inadequate health care. 74 out of every 1,000 Filipino infants die before their first birthday. A Philippine Governmental enquiry published in December 1978 showed that in 75 provinces and 61 cities of the Philippines, 78.58 per cent of the children suffered from malnutrition (National Nutrition Council and National Nutrition Service of the Ministry of Health). Disease and malnutrition cause death also to large numbers of the adult population.

Child labor. 18 out of every 1,000 Filipino workers are under 15 years of age. In 1976, 3.1 million children of school-going age were either working or looking for work. It is estimated that the present figure is 3.6 million. Such children work to supplement the family income and because money for school expenses is not available. 90 per cent of working children are working 40 hours per week and upwards, and are badly paid, earning between P2.67 and P4.83 per day. In agriculture, children from the ages of 6 and 7 are working in the sugarcane fields.

Sexual exploitation of women. Financial hardship forces many women into prostitution, particularly around the American military, naval and air bases and in the tourist industry.

Exploitation of industrial and agricultural workers, tenants and farmers. Working conditions of industrial workers revolve around the management's compulsion for profit, resulting in long working hours, high quotas and strict regulations. Overtime is often compulsory, the working conditions unhealthy and hazardous, the social security benefits inadequate or non-existent, and no job security. The right to strike was prohibited by General Order No. 5 of 22 September, 1972, and Presidential Decree No. 823 of 1975. Agriculture workers suffer from lack of job security and a lack of control over their working conditions, since they are entirely dependent on the large hacienderos. Their incomes are even lower than those of industrial workers with a minimum wage of only P7 per day for sugar workers in 1978 and P4.75 per day for other agricultural workers. Tenants and small farmers suffer from high production costs because of the cost of fertiliser and insecticides, and they are also hit by government taxes and compulsory contributions to government land reform schemes. The Government's Land Reform Program supposed to emancipate the agricultural tenants has benefited only 1 per cent of them, and the price of the land available for them to purchase is not controlled. Moreover the program excludes vast areas of agricultural land. Even the World Bank assisted programs such as at Samar, Cagayan, Mindoro, Bicol River Basin and Palawan are political in motivation, and do not succeed in eliminating the true source of the rural crisis, namely the semi-feudal organisation of rural society. An evaluation of the USAID (Agency for International Development) aid for the years 1977 and 1978 showed that from a total of $107 million spent on development projects, only $66.7 million benefited the needy. The Export-Import Bank loans require no monitoring at all in relation to the effects of its loans on the poor. The US Commodity Credit Corporation Export Credit Sales Program has financed sales of food to the Philippines out of which the Philippine authorities have made huge profits at the expense of the poor. The World Bank increased its loans eleven-fold after martial law. Its projects for 1976-1978 totalled $1,023 million, yet only $597.0 million actually benefited the needy. Of the other projects, many were priced out of the reach of the needy or the result was the displacement and dispersal of rural communities. The Asia Development Bank projects totalled $405.5 million for 1976-1978, almost half of which did not benefit the needy at all.

The IMF aid, of which the Philippines was the largest recipient in the Third World, is given without concern for social equity. Instead the Fund has exerted considerable pressure to have rice and milk prices raised, wages held down and agricultural, health and education programs cut.

Exploitation of women workers. They suffer extremely low wages, long working hours, lack of medical and maternity benefits, overcrowding and bad working conditions generally.

Exploitation of migrant workers. There are millions of Filipinos who have had to leave their country to seek work and to be able to send money home to their families. They suffer exploitation from government agencies, labour contractors and travel agents in seeking to leave the country, and then from employers in developed countries where they work for low wages in menial jobs.

The evidence in this section will show that all the accused parties, by their actions, and/or their policies have violated fundamental rights of the Filipino people expressed in the Universal Declaration of the Rights of Peoples. These fundamental rights are the right to its natural wealth and resources, the right to a fair evaluation of its labour and to equal and just terms in international trade, the right to pursue its own path to economic development without any foreign interference and the right to the conservation and protection of its environment.

The Plaintiffs seek a finding that the disregard by the Defendants of the provisions of the Declaration constitutes breaches of obligations towards the international community as a whole, and the Filipino people in particular. The Plaintiffs seek a Declaration that unequal treaties, agreements and contracts concluded by the Defendants in disregard of their rights are of no effect and that they are entitled to compensation for the loses caused to them by the violations of their said rights. And they seek a Declaration that there is a duty incumbent upon all the members of the international community to re-establish the fundamental rights of the Filipino people in view of the seriousness with which they have been disregarded.

The evidence will also show that President Marcos and his government have violated the rights recognised in the International Covenant on Economic, Social and Cultural Rights, which said Covenant was ratified on behalf of the Government of the Philippines on 7 June 1974. The rights violated include the right to the enjoyment of just and favourable conditions of work, including fair wages, equal pay, safe and healthy working conditions, equal opportunity and reasonable limitation or working hours, the right to form trade unions, the right to strike, the right to social security, the rights of children to protection from economic and social exploitation, the right to an adequate standard of living, the right to freedom from hunger and the right to enjoyment of physical and mental health.

President Marcos and his government have also violated provisions of certain International Labour Organisation (ILO) Conventions, including, but not limited to, the Convention on Freedom of Association and Protection of the Right to Organise (1948), the Convention on Medical Examination for Fitness for Employment in Industry of Children and Young Persons (1946), the Convention on Night Work of Young Persons Employed in Industry (1948), the Convention on the Minimum Age for Admission of Children to Industrial Employment, the Convention on Night Work of Women employed in Industry (1948), the Convention on Equal Remuneration of Men and Women Workers for Work of Equal Value, and the Convention on Workmen's Compensation for Accidents.

These accused have further permitted and encouraged the Filipino elite who support them to disregard the provisions of the said Covenant and Conventions in relation to their own workers. The Filipino elite, and more particularly the persons named in the First Schedule hereto, have duties to the community to which they belong, duties inherent in international humanitarian law and specifically acknowledged in the Preamble to the International Covenant on Economic, Social and Cultural Rights. They have violated the rights guaranteed to their workers in the Covenant and the ILO Conventions, and have therefore failed in their responsibilities under those agreements.

The Plaintiffs further allege that the accused international corporations and businesses have a responsibility to maintain the standards set in Conventions of the ILO and the International Covenant on Economic, Social and Cultural Rights, and that they have failed in that responsibility and are accessories to the violations of the Conventions and the Covenant.

In relation to the international financial institutions, the Plaintiffs allege that they are in breach of the provisions of their own Charters and that they are contributing to violations of human rights.

The Plaintiffs ask the Tribunal to condemn these violations and to bring them to the attention of the United Nations Organisation and the International Labour Organisation through the International League for the Rights and Liberation of Peoples.

The Evidence will consist of:
1. An outline of the structure of the Philippine economy and of the role therein of the international financial institutions, the multinational corporations, the Government of the United States and the Government of the Philippines, which will be presented by Dr. Joel Rocamora, of the South East Asia Resource Center.
2. The verbal testimony of a Filipino worker who has direct knowledge of the life of workers in the Philippines and of workers abroad and of the workings of the *Philippine Labour Code*.
3. The verbal testimony of a Filipino peasant who had direct knowledge of the life of the peasants and tenant workers in the Philippines and the workings of the *Land Reform Program*.
4. The verbal testimony of a Filipino woman, describing the particular exploitation of women in the Philippines.
5. The verbal testimony of a Filipino migrant worker, describing the specific conditions of exploitation of Filipino migrant workers.
6. Excerpts from the film entitled *For People or For Power* made by Radharc, (Ireland) 1978.
7. Excerpts from slide shows dealing with Kawasaki workers and the Banana Industry.

As additional evidence, the Tribunal will be presented with the following documents:
1. Robin Broad, *International Actors and Philippine Authoritarianism*,Princeton, June 1979.
2. Edberto M. Villegas, "The Philippines and the IMF/World Bank Conglomerate", *Third World Studies: The Philippines and the Third World Paper Series* No. 17, May 1979.
3. *Filipina Workers: A Case of Exported Women Workers.* Published by Migration Secretariat, WCC January 1980.
4. *Philippines: Workers in the Export Industry.* Pacific Research, USA March-June 1978.

5. "Kawasaki Steel Corporations's Sinster Plant in Mindanao". Published in 'Free Trade Zones and Industrialisation in Asia', *AMPO* Review 1974.
6. *Some are Smarter than Others.* A study prepared by Filipino businessmen and professional managers, 1979.
7. "The Philippines: A Captive Economy". Published in *People Toiling Under Pharaoh*, Report of the Action-Research Process on Economic Justice in Asia: Urban Rural Mission Christian Conference of Asia 1976.
8. *International Policy Report: Aid to the Philippines — Who Benefits?* Published by the Centre for International Policy, Washington D.C., October 1979.

Political repression of the Filipino people

On the 21 September 1972, President Marcos declared a state of martial law in the Philippines. Martial law has meant the suspension of democratic forms of government, and instead a dictatorship of the President who rules by Decree, using the military to enforce the decrees. The rule is an oppressive one in which detention without trial, killings and intimidation have been sanctioned and tolerated in order to quell any attempt at opposition. The political situation in the Philippines is therefore one of complete oppression of the majority of the people.

The declaration of martial law was made without reference to Congress (in contravention of Art. VI section 6 of the 1935 Constitution of the Philippines). The Supreme Court power to review the constitutionality of laws, orders or regulations (Art. VIII, section 2, 1935 Constitution) was squashed by General Order No. 4 of 22 September 1972. Presidential actions and the actions of all military personnel thereby become exempt from judicial review. The excuse for the declaration of a state of martial law was an alleged 'Communist threat', but the 1971 Senate Ad Hoc Committee Report had found 'no clear and present danger of a Communist inspired insurrection or rebellion'.

Arbitrary arrests of hundreds of individuals took place, including the arrest of three senators, three congressmen, two governors and three newspaper publishers. Many of those arrested are still in detention. There was an executive prohibition on all forms of public protest imposed, the writ of Habeas Corpus suspended, newspapers, television and radio stations closed, and government employees were arbitrarily dismissed.

A new Constitution was ratified in January 1973 without a

plebiscite by rigged citizens' assemblies, and martial law was extended indefinitely. Military tribunals now adjudicate over crimes which, on any pretext, are claimed to relate to the issues of national security or subversion. The civil courts are in any event now subservient to the President since he extracted and holds undated letters of resignation from the judges and has abolished security of tenure for judges.

There are now thousands of political prisoners in detention, and the use of torture against them has been found to be widespread. 'Salvaging' or assassination of persons is commonplace. Prisoners are detained without charges or trial, there is no enforceable right to due process of law, no habeas corpus and no investigation of complaints of ill-treatment and abuses.

There is no freedom of expression or association, the media remains controlled, and there are no free elections. Military atrocities and abuses committed against civilian populations are numerous. In the island of Samar, for example, after several years of military build-up and many reports of military abuses, there has been an increase in reported atrocities since the end of June 1979. Reports have been detailed of killings, strafing of villages, torture, rapes, arbitrary arrests and detentions, lootings and evacuation of thousands of people from their homes. Complaints against the military number 54,000 per year, but there is no effort to discipline or punish those responsible for the abuses. The economic interests underpinning military escalations is often seen in the concentration of military forces and operations in areas rich in natural resources.

While the political control of the country is in the hands of the President, the fact that he remains so firmly in control is due in large measure to the military and financial assistance which he receives from the government of the United States. Martial law had become necessary in the eyes of President Marcos because of the increasing public outrage in the Philippines at the economic policies which he was pursuing with the encouragement of the United States, and at the privileges and powers of the elite. In order for these policies and privileges to continue, stricter control over the people and the media was required.

After the declaration of martial law, military assistance from the US to the Philippines increased to $40 million per year. From 1974, the Philippines began to receive arms and equipment under a special credit sales program from the US to the Philippines increased more than three-fold after 1972. The Philippine police and army personnel receive training from US personnel in all areas of police and military activity including intelligence, and US personnel and equipment are even used in military operations in the Philippines.

The vast military assistance which the US gives to the Philippines is therefore one of the major factors in the continuation of the Marcos dictatorship, and the Plaintiffs contend that the responsibility for events can be placed both on the dictator himself and on the US government. The international financial institutions and the international corporations and businesses are not without responsibility either. For them, the excesses of martial law have meant stability, and because of the political restrictions and in particular the restrictions on workers, they have simply taken advantage of the political situation to exploit Filipino workers for the sake of profit.

The evidence in this section will show, and the Plaintiffs claim, that by the actions of President Marcos and his government, which have taken place with the knowledge and support of the government of the United States, the Filipino people have been deprived of their right to determine their political status freely and without foreign interference. They have further been deprived of their right to a democratic government representing all the citizens and capable of ensuring effective respect for the human rights and fundamental freedoms of all, contrary to the provisions of the Universal Declaration of the Rights of People.

The Plaintiff seeks a finding by the Tribunal that the deprivation of these rights constitutes a breach of the obligations of both the Philippine and the American governments towards the international community as a whole, and the Filipino people in particular.

Furthermore the Plaintiffs ask the Tribunal to find that certain inhuman actions of the martial law regime, including torture of prisoners, salvaging and massacres carried out against a civilian population, constitute crimes under international law, for which the individuals and officials responsible, including the President and the Minister for Justice, should be amenable to criminal sanctions.

The Plaintiffs ask the Tribunal to find that the support of the government of the United States to the Marcos regime in military aid and advice amounts to conspiracy and complicity in crimes under international law, and is therefore itself a crime under international law.

The Plaintiffs ask the Tribunal to find that the international financial institutions are helping to prolong and sustain the excesses of the martial law regime by the financial support for the Marcos government, and that they are consequently inciting the commission of crimes under international law, which is itself a crime under international law. The Tribunal will be referred to the Draft Code of Offences against the Peace and Security of Mankind adopted by the International Law Commission (Ref:A/CN.4/SER.A/1951/Add.1) and in particular to Article 2 thereof, and to the Draft Articles on State Responsibility adopted by the International Law Commission and in particular Articles 19 and 27 thereof.

The Plaintiffs seek a Declaration that persons injured as a result of crimes committed against them, and the families of persons killed as a result of crimes committed, are entitled to compensation by the party or parties responsible.

The Plaintiffs also seek a Declaration that there is a duty incumbent upon all the members of the international community to re-establish the fundamental civil and political rights of the Filipino people in view of the seriousness with which they have been disregarded.

The evidence will also show that President Marcos and his government have violated fundamental rights of the Filipino people specifically recognised in the International Covenant on Civil and Political Rights. This Covenant has not been ratified by the government of the Philippines, and indeed since 1972 it would be impossible for it to do so. Nevertheless it will be submitted that the most important rights enumerated in the Covenant are in any event established principles of international law, and that by denying these rights to the Filipino people and by the suppression of all forms of democracy, President Marcos and his government are in breach of their obligations under international law and under the Charter of the United Nations. In particular, the rights of life and to freedom from torture or from cruel, inhuman or degrading treatment or punishment are rights which are recognised as fundamental under international law, and which there is a clear duty on all States to respect, even in times of emergency. The other rights violated include the right to liberty and security of person, the right to be informed of any charges, to be brought promptly before a person or body with judicial power, and to trial within a reasonable time, the right to the remedy of Habeas Corpus, the right to a fair trial (the minimum guarantees for which are set out in the Covenant, Art. 14(3)), the right to privacy, the right to freedom of expression, including the right to information, the right to peaceful assembly, the right to freedom of association, and the right to take part in the conduct of public affairs, including the right to vote at genuine elections.

The Plaintiffs submit that while the Covenant and international law does permit derogation from the obligations of States to respect these rights in time of public emergency which threatens the life of the nation, no such emergency did exist in 1972 when martial law was proclaimed, and does not exist now. Consequently the Government was not entitled then and is not entitled now to any derogation. And they ask the Tribunal to declare accordingly.

The evidence will consist of:

1. The verbal testimony of Walden Bello who will testify on political repression in the Philippines, including the detention, torture and murder of political prisoners, the suppression and control of the media, the rigging of elections and referenda, the political control of the courts and military abuses.

2. The verbal testimony of a witness who has been in detention and tortured.

3. The verbal testimony of a witness who has seen and experienced martial law in operation in the Philippines for a number of years and can explain its effects from the point of view of the ordinary person.

4. The films *Collision Course* made by the BBC Panorama program, 1976, and excerpts from *Catacomb Church* made by Radharc/RTE in 1978.

5. The Reports of the FFP (Friends of the Filipino People) and AMLC (Anti-Martial Law Coalition) Investigating Team to Luzon, Visayas and Mindanao in 1978 entitled *Conditions of the Filipino People under Martial Law*.

6. The Report of the International Commission on the Militarisation of Samar, Eastern Visayas, entitled *Militarisation of Samar* and published by the Resource Centre for Philippine Concerns, Hong Kong, October 1979.

As additional evidence, the following documents will be available to the members of the Tribunal:

a) *Political Detainees Update* published by the Task Force Detainees (Association of Major Religious Superiors).

b) *Human Rights and Martial Law in the Philippines*, Report
    of the FFP and AMLC Investigating Mission 1977.
c) *Report of a Mission to the Republic of the Philippines*
    published by Amnesty International (Second Edition in-
    cluding the Reply of the Philippine Government).
d) Report of the International Commission of Jurists on *Mar-
    tial Law in the Philippines*.

Cultural Repression of the Filipino people

The ancient cultures of the Filipino people have been submerged
over many years beginning with the Spanish colonial rule. The
Spaniards used religion to control and colonise the Filipinos,
and since 1898, the Americans used education to do the same
thing. However, while the Spanish left little influence behind
them apart from the Catholic religion, American culture has
dominated the pattern of learning in the Philippines to the present day. Since American rule, English became the medium of
instruction, history learning was American history, and the
educational curricula glorified the American way of life. Even
since independence, the alien American culture continues to
dominate through the vast consumer imports from the United
States.

In recent years, a pseudo-nationalist culture has been imposed on the people by President Marcos. This 'New Society'
culture is geared towards achieving a submissive people who
look to Marcos as their great leader and benefactor. It is imposed
through the controlled mass media, through the educational curricula, through bribery and corruption in the civil service and
through repression of artists and intellectuals.

A training drive for barangay (local council) brigades in
operation since 1979 is designed to inculcate New Society
philosophy and values as well as Marcos' political ideas among
barangay brigade leaders. The barangay brigade training program is in fact a nationwide scheme to develop a personality cult
of Marcos and high officials in the regime. The program ends
with the induction of participants as barangay kawals (community soldiers) sworn to defend the New Society with their lives
and pledged to total commitment to its leaders.

Cultural repression is manifested also in the inequalities of
cultural and educational opportunities. Poverty denies to many
educational opportunities, as families are forced to remove their
children from school in order to work on the land or to help sup-

port the family in other ways.

In addition to the general cultural repression, there is actual annihilation of distinct cultural groups taking place or being attempted. The most obvious examples are the Bangsa Moro people in the southern Philippines and the Igorot people in the area of the Chico Dam project. All of these peoples are suffering cultural genocide for the sake of the profit of the ruling elite and international business corporations. In the case of the Bangsa Moro people, they are being massacred outright, and their homes destroyed. In the case of the Igorot people, they are being displaced from ancestral self-sufficient homelands in the mountains, and will disintegrate as cultural entities as well as die of starvation in the lowlands. The alleged aim of the Chico and similar projects is to improve the energy resources for the people as a whole, but in fact it is the elite who will benefit, and millions will suffer the loss of homes and livelihood in the process. Many projects, such as road-building, are ostensibly for the development of the rural areas. But in fact they are designed for military purposes, namely the seeking out and crushing of NPA support, and are carried out under the supervision of military advisors.

Many so-called development projects are funded with the financial assistance of the United States and other developed countries. However, the majority of the aid is not even intended to help the poor. An agency-by-agency review by the Centre for International Policy in Washington (see documentary evidence No. 6 in Chapter 4 above) has suggested that between 1976 and 1978 only 22 per cent of US aid went into projects directly benefiting the poor. The rest went for tobacco loans, insurance for a Bank of America branch office, military aid, rural electrification priced out of the reach of the poor, and balance of payments loans conditioned on the adoption of government policies that reduce real wages for the poor. In that same period, military aid increased by 138 per cent.

The evidence in this section will show that President Marcos and his government by their actions and policies have denied to the Filipino people as a whole the right to the respect of its national and cultural identity, the right to preserve and develop its own culture, and the right not to have an alien culture imposed on it, contrary to the provisions of the Universal Declaration of the Rights of Peoples.

Furthermore the evidence will show that all the accused parties have denied to certain Filipino minorities the very right to existence, and that such minorities have been subjected to massacre, torture, persecution, deportation or living conditions which have compromised the identity and integrity of the people to which they belong, contrary to the provisions of Sect. 1, art. 4 and Sect. 6, art. 19 of the said Declaration.

The Plaintiffs seek a finding that such disregard by the Defendants of the provisions of the Declaration constitutes breaches of obligations towards the international community as a whole and the Filipino people and certain Filipino minorities in particular.

The Plaintiffs seek a declaration that the prejudice resulting to Filipino minorities from disregard for the Universal Declaration of the Rights of Peoples must be totally compensated for by the accused parties, that the said minorities have the right to retain possession of their territories or to return thereto, and that profits accruing to the accused parties or any of them in violation of the provisions of the said Declaration shall be amenable to restitution.

And the Plaintiffs seek a declaration that there is a duty incumbent upon all members of the international community to re-establish the fundamental rights of the said Filipino minorities in view of the seriousness with which they have been disregarded.

The evidence will also show that the accused parties have committed, conspired to commit or incited the commission of acts of genocide within the meaning of Art. II (a), (b) and (c) of the Convention on the Prevention and Punishment of the Crime of Genocide 1948.

The Government of the Philippines ratified the said Convention on 7 July 1950 and it will be alleged that it is clearly in breach of its obligations under the said Convention. The Government of the United States has not ratified the said Convention, but it will be argued that genocide, as defined in the said Convention, is in any event a crime under international law, and recognised as such by General Assembly Resolution 96(I) of 11 December 1946, for which the State is responsible. The Tribunal will again be referred to the Draft Code of Offences against the Peace and Security of Mankind and the Draft Articles on State Responsibility adopted by the International Law Commission and to the Nuremberg Principles formulated by the International Law Commission and approved by the General Assembly of the United Nations.

It will be argued that the international financial institutions as agents of States are obliged to act in conformity with international law. In helping to create or encourage conditions in which genocide is committed, they become guilty of complicity in and incitement to the commission of crimes under international law.

It will further be argued that the international corporations and businesses which have participated in, encouraged and profited by, cultural genocide in the Philippines share responsibility for it within the framework of Nuremberg Principles of International Law and the decisions of the Nuremberg Tribunals.

The Plaintiffs seek findings of crimes of genocide committed by all the accused parties, their officials, servants or agents.

The evidence will also show that President Marcos and his government have violated certain rights of the Filipino people recognised in the International Covenant on Economic, Social and Cultural Rights, ratified on behalf of the government of the Philippines on 7 June 1974. The rights violated include the right of a people to its own means of subsistence and to the free pursuit of cultural development, the right to an education directed to the full development of the human personality, and the right to take part in cultural life.

The Plaintiffs ask the Tribunal to condemn these violations and to bring them to the attention of the United Nations Organisation through the International League for the Rights and Liberation of Peoples.

The evidence will consist of:
1. The verbal testimony of a member of a Kalinga tribe who will describe the effect of 'development' on his people.
2. The verbal testimony of a witness who has direct knowledge of and experience of the educational system in the Philippines and of the cultural repression which it manifests.
3. The verbal testimony of a witness on Filipino writers.
4. Document: *Mis-Education of the Filipino* by Renato Constantino.
5. Document: Training Manual Barangay Brigade Members.
6. Document: *Tribal People and the Marcos Regime*, South-East Asia Chronicle Issue 67, October 1979.
7. Slide show.
8. *The Uprooting of a People in Kalinga, Apayao*, Asia Forum on Human Rights, Hong Kong, 1980.
9. Chronology of Events and Military Activities and

Harassments in Chico Dam area from January to April 1980.

10. *Militarisation Comes to Chico*, Cordillera Committee on Justice and Peace, 1980.

11. *Squatters in their own land* by Ben & Nilo Langa-an. 1980.

The Filipino people's Resistance and the National Democratic Front (NDF)

Wherever there is repression there will be resistance. This historical truth is evident in the history of the Filipino people; more than 200 revolts against Spanish colonial rule, culminating in a national revolution, the Philippine-American war and subsequent guerilla war against American colonial rule, the resistance against Japanese occupation, and the various armed and non-armed struggles against Philippine governments that were seen to serve foreign interests and not the welfare of the majority of the Filipino people.

As martial law has intensified the economic, political and cultural repression of the Filipino people, so also it has provoked more widespread and more intense resistance. There's hardly any province in the Philippines that has not witnessed some protest and resistance activity, although the extent and level vary considerably. Some groups oppose martial law and the monopoly of power, others link this to sectoral demands, like the right to strike and genuine land reform; still others link these to the general subservience of the government to foreign, especially American, interests. The levels and forms of struggle are also varied; open statements, legal suits, indoor and outdoor assemblies, open and secret organising, legal and illegal strikes, delegations and marches, urban armed actions and rural guerilla war.

The NDF represents two significant developments in this continuing resistance of the Filipino people. First of all, like the Declaration of Algiers, it does not limit itself to individual and political rights, but advocates the economic, political, social and cultural rights of a people. Its comprehensive program summarises and carries forward the historic and current grievances of the Filipino people. Secondly, the NDF recognises the historical right and responsibility of the people to use all possible forms of struggle to achieve their goals. Hence it wages both legal and illegal, unarmed and armed struggle in the spirit of Sect. VII, art. 28 of the same Declaration. The NDF recognises the initiatives of various groups and sectors, seeking resolutely to unite them into one coordinated and effective force.

Programs of the National Democratic Front (NDF) and of the New People's Army (NPA)

The NDF and the NPA have certain programs which are their guides for the course of the revolutionary struggle, its political direction, the land problem, and health. They ask the Tribunal to consider these programmes.

The Ten-Point Program of the NDF

Proclaimed first in April 1973, the program calls for the overthrow of the 'US-Marcos Dictatorship' and the establishment of a coalition government, the nullification of unequal treaties, the nationalisation of property, and the re-establishment of democratic rights for the people. It calls for support for the armed struggle being waged by the New People's Army (NPA) and the Bangsa Moro Army, and for support for the struggle of national minorities for self-determination. It promotes a program for land reform and also promotes the protection of national jobs, national capital and national culture.

Basic rules of the New People's Army

Working mainly in the countryside, the aim of the NPA is to transform backward villages into advanced political, military, economic and cultural bastions of the people's revolution. It believes in an alliance of the working class and the peasantry as being the true foundation of a broad democratic unity. Its main strategic principle is the waging of a protracted people's war from rural bases. These bases serve as the rears for the emergence and expansion of guerilla zones, and also for the advance of all other forces of the people's democratic revolution. The NPA envisages three strategic phases in the people's war, throughout which it retains the political initiative because it integrates revolutionary theory with revolutionary practice, and because it is closely linked with the masses. It regards the overthrow of US imperialism, of the comprador bourgeoisie, of the landlord classes and of the bureaucrat capitalists in the Philippines as its revolutionary duty.

The Revolutionary Guide to Land Reform

This programme serves as the basic guide for the NPA and the Barrio Organising Committees in carrying out the agrarian revolution. The Land Reform Program has as its minimum goal the drastic reduction of land rent and the elimination of usury, and as its maximum goal the free distribution of land to the tillers who have no land, or who do not have enough land. It also aims at the betterment of wages and living conditions of farm workers on landed estates. To implement the program, land reform committees are to be established at every level to supervise land reform work.

The National Democratic Health Program
The National Democratic Health Association, an association of numerous health workers, has a Seven-Point Health Program for the health sector. The program calls for the nationalisation of the health industry, and reliance on local capital, materials and entrepreneurship, and for the development of low-cost in-digenous alternatives to costly imported drugs. It opposes the use of health as a tool of the regime, seeks to expose the duplicity of government-sponsored health programs, and to direct the resources of the health agencies to the needs of the broad masses. It seeks to develop health programs to strengthen the revolutionary mass movement in the urban centers and in the countryside. It encourages health workers to render direct support for the armed struggle through participation in the People's Army as health workers. It upholds the rights of the health workers to organise and fight for better conditions of pay and employment, and promotes the reorientation of the health education system towards nationalist and democratic values. It promotes solidarity with all progressive health workers abroad and seeks their support for the revolutionary struggle.

The Tribunal will be presented with copies of all the above programs and representatives from the NDF and the NPA will be available to explain same and to answer questions from the Tribunal.

Having considered the evidence presented before it, and the above programs of the Plaintiffs, the Tribunal is asked to find that the fundamental rights of the Filipino people have been seriously disregarded, and that the Plaintiffs have the right to enforce them even, in the last resort, by the use of force.

Application for a Determination by the People's Tribunal of the right of the Bangsa Moro People to Self-Determination.

The Moro People, at the suit of the Moro National Liberation Front (MNLF) apply to the People's Tribunal for
a)   A Declaration that the Bangsa Moro people have a separate

national and cultural identity from the remainder of the Filipino people.

b) A Declaration that the national homelands of the Bangsa Moro People are the islands known as Mindanao, Basilan, Palawan, and the Sulu Archipelago.

c) A Declaration that the Bangsa Moro homelands were wrongfully annexed into Philippine territory between 1935 and 1946 and that the Bangsa Moro People have been and continue to be deprived of their homelands.

d) A Declaration that the said deprivation is illegal.

e) A Declaration that the Bangsa Moro People are entitled to establish their own independent state within the area of their own homelands.

f) A Declaration that the MNLF is the legitimate representative of the Bangsa Moro People, recognised as such by the Islamic Conference.

g) A Declaration that the combatants of the MNLF are entitled to the protection of the humanitarian laws of war.

h) A Declaration that the maintenance by the Philippine Government by force of colonial domination over the Bangsa Moro homelands is a crime under international law.

The application is based on the following factors:

1. The Bangsa Moro People have a cultural, ethnic and religious identity which is distinct from the remainder of the people of the Philippines.

2. They were a distinct political entity until 1898 when Spain sold the Philippines to the United States of America, and included the Bangsa Moro homelands, over which the Spaniards had never succeeded in maintaining colonial authority. American sovereignty over the homelands was accepted by the Moros in general until 1935 when a Constitutional Commission was established and a Commonwealth Government formed, and preparations made for the granting of independence to the Philippines. At that stage, the Moros protested at being included with the remainder of the Philippines in the independence plans, and expressed a wish to remain for the time being under American rule. The provisions envisaged for them in a Philippine Constitution were highly discriminatory, and they objected strongly to being incorporated into one State with the Christian Filipinos. However, they were arbitrarily made subordinate to the

Commonwealth Government and later the Republic of the Philippines.

Armed rebellion was constant since 1946, in Luuk, Sulu, in 1948, an armed rebellion led by Masa Kamlon began which was to last for seven years. Another rebellion was led by Datu Tawan-Tawan in Lanao around the same time against the colonial settlers in the Kapatagan area. In 1960 Hajal Ouh led a movement for the independence of Sulu, Basilan and Zamboanga from Philippine domination. Then in 1968 the Muslim (later changed to Mindanao) Independence Movement was launched. Finally it was the MNLF which emerged as the last link in a chain of resistance against Philippine colonialism.

In 1974 the MNLF declared in a Manifesto the emergence of the Bangsa Moro Republik, and the severing of all political, economic and other ties with the Government of the Philippines. Subsequently the MNLF were asked by the Islamic Conference to negotiate with the Philippine Government within the framework of preserving the territorial integrity of the Philippines. This they did, and restricted their demands to political autonomy. Negotiations reached the stage in December 1976 that an Agreement (known as the Tripoli Agreement) was signed by the MNLF and the Philippine Government which allowed for a ceasefire and for the establishment of an autonomous government for the Muslims in the southern Philippines. However, ten months later the agreement was violated by the Philippine Government and the war began again. Talks were scheduled to start again in April 1980, when it was announced in Manila that the Tripoli Agreement was no longer valid. The MNLF was thereby freed from its commitment to political autonomy, and has reverted to its original demand for complete independence for the Bangsa Moro people.

3. Today the Bangsa Moro homelands can still be distinguished geographically from the remainder of the Philippines as areas where the majority of the population are Moro and would choose independence from the Philippine State.

4. The Bangsa Moro homelands are potentially a viable economic unit, since they are rich in natural resoures and the land is fertile.

5. The National Democratic Front of the Philippines recognises the right of the Bangsa Moro people to determine their own political and economic status.

6. The Islamic Conference has granted Observer Status to the MNLF since May 1977, thereby recognising the MNLF as the only legitimate spokesman and representative of the Bangsa Moro people.

7. The legitimacy of the claim of the Bangso Moro people is assured by the Universal Declaration of the Rights of Peoples (Algiers Declaration), by the Charter of the United Nations, and by the Declaration on the Granting of Independence to Colonial Countries and Peoples (G.A. Res. 1514 (XV) 1960).

   The Moro People have never freely determined their political status, so that they have in fact remained under colonial domination even as part of the Republic of the Philippines.

   Until the people have freely determined their status, they retain the right to do so.

   The Philippines is not justified in retaining colonial domination by force or otherwise over the Bangsa Moro homelands on the basis of territorial integrity, since at the time of annexation, the Moro people had expressed opposition to becoming part of the Philippine state, and were given no opportunity to determine the destiny of their own territory.

   In any event, the Philippine Government has violated the duties imposed on it by the Charter of the United Nations, and has consequently forfeited any authority it might have had over the Bangsa Moro homelands. Article 73 of the Charter of the UN applies not only to trust or mandate territories but also to territories under a colonial regime, and obliges all administering authorities to respect the cultures of residents in the Non-Self-Governing Territory, to promote their overall advancement and to ensure them just treatment. The Philippine Government has violated the purposes and principles of the Charter in its dealings with the Moro people and thereby forfeited its own authority over them.

The following will be used in support of the Application:

1. Document: *Moros — Not Filipinos*. A summary of the political history of the Bangsa Moro people by Abdurasad Asani.

2. Maps of Muslim areas from 1521 - 1939 and at the present time.

3. Copy Treaty between the Sultan of Sulu and the United States of America, 1842.
4. Copy Agreement between General John C. Bates, US Army, and the Sultan of Sulu, together with certain Sulu Chiefs, signed at Jolo, August 20, 1899.
5. Lanao Protest, 1935.
6. Speech of Congressman Bacon of New York in the United States House of Representatives sponsoring House Bill No. 12772 which sought to remove the Moro Country from the Philippine Islands (US Congressional Records, House, 6 May, 1926, pp. 8830 - 8835).
7. *MNLF Turns Full Circle.* A summary of the recent political developments concerning the Bangsa Moro homelands, by Abdurasad Asani.

The above documentary evidence will be presented by Abdurasad Asani, a student of political science and representative of the MNLF in Tripoli.

Charges of Economic Exploitation and Repression in the Bangsa Moro homelands

Economic exploitation of the Moro territories by the Defendants can be distinguished from such exploitation in the rest of the Philippines. It began in a serious way with the Resettlement Program under which land was arbitrarily granted in the Southern Philippines to settlers from other areas. In 1913, agricultural colonies were created by Act No. 2254 of the Philippine Commission in Cotabato Valley, with families from Cebu in the Visayas. A year later, in 1914, Act No. 2280 of the Commission created the Momungan Agricultural Colony in Lanao for American soldiers who wanted to settle in the area. As a result of these colonisation schemes and those which followed, streams of settlers came to different parts of the Bangsa Moro homelands. American and Filipino capitalists also moved in B.F. Goodrich Co. began operating a rubber plantation in Basilan in 1919, Goodyear Tire and Rubber Co. started business in Zamboanga in 1929, and now has two large plantations in Mindanao. Del Monte opened its pineapple plantation in 1926.

The settlement program discriminated against the native population in that the Christian settlers were entitled to own more than double the amount of land that natives could own. Christian settlers also got priority for land grants and were given ancestral land actually occupied by natives. When the National

Land Settlement Administration was created in 1939, whole areas were selected as sites for settlement projects. Native Muslim inhabitants were then uprooted and forcibly moved out.

Such programs have continued over the years so that now the settlers number about two million, compared to an indigenous population of 6.2 million (1970 figures). The multinational companies and the settlers now own vast tracts of land in the southern Philippines, with the added advantage of holding legal title documents to those lands. Displaced indigenous populations, not having title documents, have therefore no remedy against their dispossession. The resettlement programs have therefore caused even greater economic exploitation and disruption in the Bangsa Moro homelands than in the remainder of the Philippines.

Another distinction between the economic repression in the Philippines generally and that in the southern Philippines is the fact that Muslims suffer from racial discrimination. They are second-class citizens in their own homelands, being discriminated against in employment, education and the provision of services generally. The Plaintiffs will show that Muslims encounter more difficulty in obtaining jobs in the public sector and in industry than other Filipinos, that the educational system completely ignores the existence of their culture, history and heritage, and that less public services are available for their communities than for other Filipinos.

The evidence in this section will show, and the Plaintiffs will contend, that all the Defendants have conspired to deprive them by force of their natural wealth and resources, and of the right to choose their own economic system and pursue their own path to economic development freely and without foreign interference, contrary to the provisions of the Universal Declaration of the Rights of Peoples.

The Plaintiffs further contend that they have been deprived of their right to respect for their identity, traditions, language and cultural heritage, and of the right to participate on an equal footing with other Filipinos in public life, again contrary to the provisions of the said Declaration.

The Plaintiffs seek a finding that the disregard by the Defendants of the provisions of the Declaration constitutes breaches of obligations towards the international community as a whole, and the Moro people in particular.

The evidence will also show that not only has the Philippine

Government violated the provisions of the International Covenant on Economic, Social and Cultural Rights, as alleged in the
First Part of this Brief, but that it has also violated the International Convention on the Elimination of All Forms of Racial
Discrimination, a Convention which has been ratified on behalf
of the Government of the Philippines.

The Plaintiffs ask the Tribunal to condemn these violations
and to bring them to the attention of the Committee on the
Elimination of Racial Discrimination of the United Nations
through the International League for the Rights and Liberation
of Peoples.

The Plaintiffs seek a finding that the resettlement programs
are illegal, being a misuse by the Philippine Government of its
administrative authority over the Bangsa Moro homelands, and
contrary to the purposes and principles of the United Nations
Charter, and that the lands appropriated are liable to re-
confiscation by the Bangsa Moro people.

The evidence will consist of:

1. The evidence of a Filipino economist and based on the
   documents *Economic Exploitation, Repression and
   Discrimination* and *The Role of US Imperialism Economic
   Aid for Control — Control for MNCs Profit* Part I by Ab-
   durasad Asani.
2. A Moro witness will describe discrimination against
   Muslims.
3. *Our Land for Others / Our Lake for Others*, by Lindy
   Washburn. Research Bulletin of Dansalan Research Center,
   Marawi City, Philippines.

Charges of Genocide and of War Crimes against the Bangsa Moro People

The problem of the political repression of the Bangsa Moro
people in the southern Philippines has to be looked at separately
from the repression in the Philippines in general. The Bangsa
Moro people seek liberation from the Philippines, and to set up
a separate state. And the reaction of the Philippine government
to their cause is particularly harsh. It is contended by the Plaintiffs that a policy of genocide is directing the armed forces of the
Philippines, against not only the Bangsa Moro army, but against
the Moro population as a whole. They also contend that
unlawful weapons and unlawful methods of warfare are being
used. Napalm bombings, the use of chemical weapons, the raz-

ing of whole villages, shootings and massacres of civilians are commonplace, and already 90,000 Moros have been killed, 250,000 homes destroyed, and thousands of mosques destroyed since 1970.

But it is not only in response to the liberation ideals of the Bangsa Moro people that genocide is taking place. The Philippines has vast natural resources in the southern areas and it is these riches which are at the heart of the problem. As has been stated before, the Philippine government has tried to colonise the area since the 1950s when President Magsaysay launched a policy of opening up Mindanao to Christian settlers, which meant the displacement of Muslim peasants from their ancestral homelands. This policy paved the way for the acquisition of vast tracts of fertile land in Mindanao by US and Japanese multinationals as well as by big Filipino comprador-landlords and politicians. Opposition by the Moros eventually culminated in resort to force of arms. A massacre took place in 1968 of Muslims by a Christian terrorist movement supported by the Philippine Government, and it was after this that the Moro independence movement, with the aim of liberation from the colonial-type regime, became a national movement. The genocidal policy of the Philippine Government became entrenched and escalated after the imposition of Martial Law in 1972.

The bombings, massacres and other outrages have been well documented by the MNLF, and the evidence in this section will clearly establish the existence of a campaign of genocide in the Bangsa Moro homelands. The main perpetrators of genocide are of course President Marcos and his government. However, they are actively supported by the Government of the United States of America, which, through its military assistance agreements, allows American planes, bombs, equipment and personnel to assist them.

The Plaintiffs will argue that both governments, their officials, servants and agents, are committing or conspiring to commit genocide within the meaning of the Convention on the Prevention and Punishment of the Crime of Genocide.

They will also argue that both governments, their officials, servants and agents are committing crimes against peace, war crimes and crimes against humanity, contrary to the principles of International Law, recognised in the Charter of the Nuremberg Tribunal and the Judgement of the Tribunal as formulated by the International Law Commission and approved by the General

Assembly of the United Nations.

The Plaintiffs will also argue that those members of the Filipino elite who support the genocidal campaign of the Government and benefit from the war effort in terms of contracts and land grants are guilty of incitement and conspiracy to commit genocide.

The Plaintiffs will argue that the international financial institutions, as agents of States, are obliged to act in conformity with International Law, and that in helping to create or encouraging conditions in which genocide is committed, they become guilty of complicity in and incitement to the commission of genocide and crimes under international law.

Finally it will be argued that the international corporations and businesses which have profited by genocide and other crimes committed against the Moro population share responsibility for it within the framework of the Nuremberg Principles of International Law and the decisions of the Nuremberg Tribunal. The Plaintiffs seek findings of crimes of genocide and of crimes against peace, war crimes and crimes against humanity committed by all the accused parties their servants or agents.

The evidence will consist of:

1. Document: *The Campaign of Genocide*, by Abdurasad Asani.
2. Document: *The Undeclared War in Southern Philippines*, by Robin Osborne.
3. MNLF Document: *Some Sampling of Bombing Operations and Ground Assault Carried Out by the Marcos Regime's Army*.
4. Statistical Analysis: Massacres; Destructions of villages, towns, mosques etc.
5. Special: *Asian Wall Street Journal* "Philippine Moslems take Refuge on Sabah, but Status is Murky".
6. Film by Thierry Roland made in 1977.
7. Film: *The Undeclared War in Southern Philippines*, by Denis Riechle, 1975.
8. Photographs of war damage, war victims and the Bangsa Moro Army.
9. *The Role of US Imperialism* (Part 2: US Military Assistance) by Abdurasad Asani.
10. Verbal testimony by a member of the MNLF.

The Moro People's Resistance and the MNLF

The MNLF is the only organisation which represents the mutual solidarity of the Bangsa Moro People. It will present to the Tribunal its Manifesto of 28 April 1974 and the Press Statement of its Chairman made on 17 April 1980.

The Manifesto declares the establishment of a Bangsa Moro Republik, and the securing of a free and independent state by armed struggle. It identifies the Bangsa Moro people as being committed to the establishment of a democratic system of government in which all citizens, including Filipino, will be entitled to equal rights. The Bangsa Moro people are, however, committed to the preservation of their Islamic culture without prejudice to the development of other religions of indigenous cultures. They are also committed to respect for the Charter of the United Nations and the Universal Declaration of Human Rights, and to world peace through mutual cooperation among nations.

The MNLF asks the Tribunal to endorse its aims.

Representatives from the MNLF will be available to answer questions from the Tribunal.

First Schedule

Emilio Abello
Jose Abello
Fortuna Marcos Barba
Roberto Benedicto
Rodolfo Cuenca
Eduardo Cojuangco
Ramon Cojuangco
Herminio Disini
Inday Escolin
Juan Ponce Enrile
General Romeo Espino
Manuel Elizalde
Fred Elizalde
Antonio D. Floirendo
Elizabeth Keon Marcos
Josefa Marcos
Lloyd Velez Marcos
Mariano Marcos II
Pacifico Marcos
Judge Pio Marcos

Sixto Jn. Orosa
Ramon Orosa
Antonio Ozaeta
Alfredo 'Bejo' Romualdez
Benjamin 'Kokoy' Romualdez
Ricardo Silverio
Simeon Marcos Valdez
Geronimo Velasco
Luis R. Villafuerte
Cesar Zalamea

And the following families:

J. Campos
Duavit
Enriquez
Ilusorio
Nieto
Oledan
Roman
V. Recto
Rustico-Tantoco
De Venecia

THE CASE OF THE FILIPINO PEOPLE

Testimonies on Economic Repression

US imperialism and the economic crisis of the Marcos dictatorship.

by Joel Rocamora

More Filipinos are poor today than at any other time in the history of our nation. More poor Filipinos are malnourished. More malnourished Filipinos are dying.

This year, the Marcos government will export 300,000 metric tons of rice, the staple food of Filipinos. This amount of rice could feed nine million people, one out of five Filipinos for one whole year.

In May of this year, Arturo Tanco, Minister of Agriculture in the Marcos regime, said that he found it ironic that there should be many malnourished Filipinos when the Philippines produces so much food.

If so many Filipinos are malnourished, why is the Marcos dictatorship exporting so much rice? Why do its ministers find only irony in what, by any measure, is a monstrous crime?

The last eight years, the martial law years, have been years of growth for the Philippine economy. According to the government, the total value of goods and services — the Gross National Product (GNP) — grew from P55.5 billion in 1972 to an estimated P220 billion this year. In 1972, only 6.7 percent of exports were manufactured goods. Last year, Mr. Marcos recently claimed, 34 per cent of exports were manufactured goods. Philippine industrialization is well underway, Mr. Marcos proclaimed.

The last eight years have indeed seen an acceleration of

Prof. Joel Rocamora, Writer and Staff of the *South East Asia Chronicle* economic growth in the Philippines. But behind every glowing government statistic lies the agony of a people whose livelihood has deteriorated at a rate faster than the economy has grown. What kind of economy is this that produces more victims the more goods it produces?

Marcos and his economic managers — his American trained technocrats — often deny that living conditions have deteriorated for the Filipino people. On those occasions when they are forced to acknowledge problems, they say that Filipinos of today have to make sacrifices in order to set the basis for more sustained economic growth in the future.

Even by this standard, the Marcos dictatorship still has to be judged an utter failure. Far from making headway in solving the basic problems of the Philippine economy, the economic policies of the Marcos dictatorship have only made them worse. Inflation, unemployment, chronic balance of payments deficits, an expanding foreign debt — these and other structural problems bear down more heavily on the economy today than at any time in the past.

Are all of these economic problems the result of economic policies of the Marcos dictatorship? The answer is unequivocally, yes! But at the same time the responsibility has to be shared by the United States for the economic policies of the Marcos dictatorship are as much a creation of the United States as they are the creation of Marcos and his technocrats.

In a more important sense, the responsibility of the United States is even greater. It was the United States which created the current, distorted structures of the Philippine economy. It was during the period of American colonial rule that the dependent, raw material-exporting character of the Philippine economy was set. It was the United States that established the legal and economic framework that froze Philippine society into the semi-feudal, semi-colonial, and bureaucrat capitalist mould.

Marcos' role has been that of establishing the framework of repression required by the intensification of exploitation in the past few years. He has also supervised the translation of the economic strategy of US imperialism into specific policies. When the resistance in the Philippines speaks of the US-Marcos dictatorship, therefore it is not a matter of rhetorical overstatement but a simple summation of the basic reality of Philippine society.

Poverty amidst plenty

What then is the current state of people's livelihood in the Philippines?

Almost two-third (63 per cent) of the Philippines' 47 million people live off the land. Six of the country's top ten exports are agricultural products. The share of agriculture, fisheries and forestry in the GNP rose from P11.7 billion pesos in 1970 to P47.1 billion pesos in 1978. For the first time in decades the Philippines is self-sufficient in rice, national production having risen from 4.3 million metric tons in 1965 to 7.25 million metric tons in 1979.

According to a study by University of the Philippines economists in 1971, 69.3 per cent of all rural families had incomes below that required to buy enough food. Four years later 71.3 per cent of all rural families lived below this 'food threshold'.[1] Of all the families in the country with less than enough income to buy food and other necessities, over 80 per cent were in the rural areas in 1971. There is no reason to believe that the proportion has changed since that time.

An even more startling set of statistics is provided by the government's Bureau of Agricultural Economics (BAECON). According to a 1980 BAECON study, the real net income of rice farmers, the most numerous in the country, dropped by a phenomenal 53.4 per cent between 1976 and 1979. The main reason for this decline, according to BAECON, is that while production expenses went up by 21 per cent during this period, the government-controlled price of rice went up by only 2 per cent.

Conditions among farm workers are no better. Although the sugar industry has recovered from a five-year slump with greatly increased world market prices for sugar, very little of this has been passed on to the notoriously oppressed sugar workers, the *sacadas*. A survey of coconut farmers and farm workers in December 1976 showed that 90 per cent of them lived below the poverty line of $1,000 yearly income set by the Ministry of Social Services and Development. Given this, one can only imagine the impact of the collapse of the world market prices of coconut products early this year.

Other social indicators show that rural inhabitants consistently suffer lower standards than urban inhabitants. Despite the high national literacy rate, 15 per cent of the rural population have not had any formal education, while 70 per cent have completed only the elementary grades. In the field of medical services, the ratio of health manpower (doctors, nurses, mid-wives and sanitary inspectors) to the rural population is 1:1,603 people while the urban ratio is 1:559[2] Meanwhile, every year thousands of medical personnel, unable to find jobs in their own country, flock to the US where they fill that country's most undesirable positions.

The decline in rural incomes has been matched by a decline in the real wages (money wages adjusted for inflation) of urban workers. In the period from 1972 to 1978, real wages declined by as much as 39 per cent. This decline is particularly noteworthy in that it is higher than at any other period in recent Philippine history. Thus where the decline in real wages in the period between 1955 and 1965 was only 13 per cent, and between 1965 and 1972, only 3 per cent, in the first two years of martial law alone, real wages declined by 30 per cent.[3].

The steady decline of urban workers' is certain to accelerate further in the wake of the 25 per cent inflation in 1979 and the estimated 20-25 per cent inflation this year. To illustrate the gross inadequacy of workers' wages, where a day's wages bought 19 chickens for the American worker in 1977, and 9 chickens for a worker in France, a day of Filipino worker's wages could buy only three-quarters of a chicken.

Another way of illustrating the inadequacy of workers wages is to measure it against his family's needs. According to the government's Wage Commission, the daily earning requirement for an average worker's family is P63.22 (US$9). Even after the recent increase in minimum wages and allowances, the effective minimum wage is less than half of what is required. As a result, according to a University of the Philippines School of Economics study, some 60 per cent of Philippine urban families fall below the poverty threshold.[4]

Workers and peasants are not the only victims of martial law economic development. While top civilian and military bureaucrats and managers of local and foreign corporations are enjoying vastly increased wages and perquisites, school teachers, nurses, students, and other members of the so-called middle-classes are reeling from the impact of inflation on their fixed incomes. Even college professors from top universities such as Ateneo and the University of the Philippines have to take on two or three jobs in order to maintain their standard of living.

As difficult as the situation is for the urban wage earner, his or her condition is still better than that of many others. Among

those listed by the government as 'gainfully' employed are:
1. in Manila alone, some 30,000 scavengers, people who rummage through garbage cans for bits of paper, bottles and tin cans;
2. uncounted thousands who sell cigarettes and chewing gum by the stick, or boiled peanuts, bananas, sweets and assorted other materials in tiny, movable street corner stalls;
3. bar hostesses, massage parlor attendants, stripteasers and prostitutes who number over 100,000 in Manila and some 30,000 in the U.S. military base towns Angeles and Subic Bay.

If scavengers and prostitutes are among the most oppressed of urban residents, in the countryside the conditions of the Moro people and tribal Filipinos are particularly bad. Already victimized by landgrabbers, by logging concessionaires and multinational agribusiness, the Moro people in the past twelve years or so have also suffered from the burning of their homes and farms, the desecration of their mosques, and in many instances, the outright massacre of men, women and children by government troopers or government-sanctioned goon squads such as the infamous *Ilagas*.

Tribal Filipinos face an organized attack on their culture and livelihood in the name of progress and benevolence. Over two million tribal Filipinos have already been pushed out of their lands and into government reservations. Many others, among them the Kalingas of Northern Luzon and the T'boli's of Mindanao are threatened with the flooding of their homes and farms by government hydro-electric projects.

The rapid deterioration of working and living conditions under martial law has created yet another category of the oppressed — the migrant worker. According to the government, as many as 1.5 million Filipinos have left the Philippines as immigrants and contract workers. Abroad they work as professionals, sailors, household help, construction workers and a variety of other jobs. On the whole, they earn more abroad than in the Philippines. But they also suffer exploitation and oppression.

Even before migrants leave the Philippines, they are prey to hundreds of illegal recruiters who cheat them in the process of securing travel papers. They often have to work at jobs below that which they trained for. Doctors work as medical orderlies, nurses as nurses' aides, lawyers as clerks. Contract workers are paid less than they are promised or forced to work long hours without overtime pay. They are subjected to racial discrimination, and often live in squalid living conditions without being able to complain for fear of being sent home.

Wherever you look in Philippine society, whatever sector of the population you examine, you will find that living conditions are deteriorating rapidly. The poor are not only getting poorer, there are increasing numbers of people becoming poor both in absolute and proportional terms. It is also very clear that the long-term trend towards the deterioration of people's welfare intensified tremendously during the last eight years of martial law.

The Economic Crisis of the Sixties

When Marcos declared martial law in 1972, he also proclaimed a 'New Society'. Peasants will be 'liberated from centuries of feudal bondage,' Marcos said. A new era of rapid industrialization and overall development will replace decades of stagnation. The last eight years have shown that, for the vast majority of the people, there has certainly been no 'New Society'.

But there is at least one way in which Marcos is right. The martial law years do represent a distinct stage in the economic history of the Philippines. It is a stage marked by the application of a new set of economic policies in an attempt to surmount the economic crisis of the sixties. In order to understand Marcos' resolution of the crisis, we have to examine its component parts carefully.

It was, firstly, a crisis in Philippine agriculture, a crisis brought about by the exhaustion of easily available land by the mid-sixties. Up until this period, increases in both export and food crop production derived mainly from increasing the amount of land under cultivation. Thus, in the period between 1950 and 1955, the average annual increase in area harvested was 4.9 per cent. Ten years later, in the 1960 to 1965 period, growth had declined to only one per cent per year.

The declining growth rate in agriculture also meant a decline in its capacity to absorb new workers. The agricultural employment growth rate went down from 3.7 per cent annual growth between 1955 and 1960, to 1.7 per cent between 1960 and 1965, then to an extremely low 0.2 per cent between 1965 and 1970. Agriculture's share of total employment declined from 61.2 per cent in 1960 to 50.4 per cent in 1971.

The crisis in agriculture was felt most strongly in the rice sector not only because rice is the staple food of Filipinos but also because the large majority of Filipino farmers are rice farmers. Under pressure from the expanding export crop sector, rice hectarage declined from 3.2 million hectares in 1960 to 3.1 million hectares in 1970. The annual growth in rice production also declined from 3.7 per cent average annual growth in the decade of the fifties to 2.3 per cent in the sixties. Although large increases in output were registered in the late 'sixties with the introduction of high yielding rice varieties — the so-called miracle rice — output gains from this source were quickly exhausted. The rice surpluses of 1968 and 1969 were followed by deficits that required over 400,000 tons of rice imports in 1971 and again in 1972.

The stagnation in agriculture pushed larger and larger numbers of rural inhabitants into the urban areas. But because industrial sectors were growing at a pace not much faster than in agriculture, there were few urban jobs available. Where manufacturing, for example, had been the fastest growing sector of the economy in the fifties, in the 'sixties the growth in manufacturing output averaged only five percent per year. Manufacturing's share in employment actually declined from 12.1 percent in 1960 to 11.3 percent in 1974.

Another measure of the crisis of the economy during the sixties was the stagnation in Philippine exports. Between 1964 and 1969, export receipts grew by only 2.7 per cent annually and actually registered declines in 1967 and 1969. As a result, Philippine balance of trade deficits rose from an average of $34 million a year between 1964 and 1966 to $270 million per year between 1967 and 1969. This difficult financial situation was made worse by the net outflow of $2.7 billion dollars in profit remittances, withdrawal of investments, and amortization of private sector loans[5] in the period between 1964 and 1972.

In order to pay for these ballooning balance of payments deficits, the government resorted to heavy short-term borrowing. Election year 1969 was particularly bad, for President Marcos used all available resources to buy his way into a second term as President. The following year, the Philippines was literally bankrupt. More than half of the country's estimated $1.5 billion in export receipts was needed to service the country's foreign debt.

In exchange for rescheduling the country's due loans and a small additional $37 million 'stabilization' loan, the Marcos government had to agree to devalue the peso by as much as 60 per cent. While this arrangement enabled the Marcos regime to overcome its financial crisis, its impact on the population was disastrous. The lower foreign exchange prices of Philippine exports generated an increase in the volume of exports, but at the same time imported agricultural input prices rose even faster due to the combination of the devaluation and other inflationary pressures. Thus, rural real incomes actually went down on average. In urban areas, the real wages of skilled and unskilled workers plummeted by 30 index points in 1973 and 1974 alone.

The economic crisis of the late sixties also precipitated a crisis in the political sphere. While we cannot go into the details of the political crisis in this paper, we should take up those aspects of this crisis that had a direct bearing on economic trends during this period. In general terms, the political crisis of the late sixties was characterized by the deterioration of the liberal democratic political system which mediated competition between different factions of the ruling class on the one hand, and the increasing assertiveness of peasants, workers and segments of the petit-bourgeoisie such as the students, on the other.

During this period, workers actively pushed for higher wages and better working conditions through strikes and other actions. In 1969, for example, more workers went out on strike than in any other year between 1965 and 1975. Real wages actually increased between 1967 and 1969, the only time in the period between 1955 and 1979 that an increase of this magnitude was registered.

In the countryside, increasing numbers of peasants began to resist landgrabbing and tenant eviction and to call for lower land rents. A variety of methods, including large numbers of cases filed before the Court of Agrarian Relations, plus demonstrations and other mass actions were used. These actions were led initially by reformist organizations such as the Federation of Free Farmers, and later, by more radical organizations led by the newly re-established Communist Party of the Philippines and its military arm, the New People's Army.

The economic demands of workers and peasants also took shape as political demands. Working together with students and other segments of the petit-bourgeoisie, plus a number of national bourgeois elements faced with increased competition from foreign investors, workers and peasants served as the social base of a fast-growing radical nationalist movement. This movement exposed the dominance of foreigners, especially Americans in the economy and called for greater national economic self-reliance. Together, the various elements in this movement pressed their demands in strikes, street demonstrations, a wide-ranging propaganda movement and even in elite-dominated political institutions. It was during this time that economic nationalism found expression in decisions of the Congress, the Supreme Court and the Constitutional Convention.

The Economic Strategy of the New Society

The economic and political crisis of the sixties was 'resolved' through the declaration of martial law in 1972. In particular, a regime based on fascist repression was installed in order to stop the growing nationalist movement and to destroy people's organizations capable of mobilizing resistance against the dictatorship's plan for intensifying economic exploitation.

In quick order, strikes and demonstrations were banned and progressive youth, worker and peasant organizations declared illegal. The Congress, where national bourgeois elements were gaining strength, was disbanded. The Supreme Court was emasculated and its nationalist decisions superceded by a whole series of presidential decrees encouraging foreign investment. As then Board of Investment Chairman Vicente Paterno put it: 'The logic of foreign investments to participate in the generation of exports of labor-intensive manufactures seems clear and incontrovertible, but the country needed martial law to implement it.'

Having eliminated the political obstacles to its implementation, the Marcos dictatorship quickly implemented a new economic strategy. Working under the guidance of the World Bank and the International Monetary Fund, New Society technocrats imposed a radical reorientation of the Philippine economy along the following lines:

1. unrestricted flow of foreign investments and profits;
2. dismantling of the protective tariff structure;
3. industrialization for export markets, not for internal Philippine market;
4. rationalization of the export sector through the centralization of the marketing of several export commodities in government hands; and most importantly,
5. provision of cheap, unorganized labor.

The legal and logistical superstructure for increased foreign investment — the Investment Incentives Law and the Bataan Export Processing Zone — was established before the declaration of martial law. The shaping of the labor force took place after. By holding money wages down through a policy of labor repression, and at the same time, forcing real wages down through inflation, the Marcos dictatorship succeeded in making Philippine labor the cheapest in all of Asia.

The impact on wages was immediate and dramatic. In that broad industry category called 'Manufacturing' for example, the rate of exploitation (surplus paid to the capitalist/wages paid to the worker) rose by 180 per cent between 1971 and 1975. This increase is particularly significant in that it occurred in a relatively short span of five years. In the preceding fifteen year period (1956-71), the rate of exploitation rose by only 78 per cent. From 1973 to 1974 alone, the first two years of martial law, the rate increased by as much as 110 per cent.

For the worker, this means that, out of every peso of total net output he produced (total output less raw materials and depreciations), his share decreased from P0.36 in 1956 to P0.09 in 1975. From another vantage point this means that whereas in 1956, the worker worked two hours and 53 minutes to produce the value of his wages, by 1971 he was spending only one hour and 57 minutes. Four years later, he was working a total of only 44 minutes for himself, leaving the value of the other 7 hours and 16 minutes of his labor to be appropriated by the capitalist.

Given these favorable conditions, it is not surprising that foreign investment began to come in soon after 1972. According to the Central Bank, direct foreign investment between 1970 and 1972 totalled only $16.3 million while profit remittances and other payments totalled $87.8 million. In the three year period subsequent to the declaration of martial law (1973-75), direct investment, predominantly American, totalled $362.1 million.

Investments by Filipino businesses also accelerated during this period. While total investments declined from P468.6 million in 1968 to only P284.4 million in 1970, it jumped tenfold to P2.5 billion in 1974. In his budget speech in June 1980, Marcos claimed that from 1972 to 1979, investment rose at an average annual rate of 27.5 per cent. A good part of these new investments went into manufacturing for export, in the process pushing manufactured exports from 6.7 per cent of total exports in 1972 to as much as 34 per cent in 1979.

Two other government programs, the promotion of tourism and the export of contract workers abroad have been successful in generating foreign exchange. The government has aggressively promoted tourism by subsidizing the construction of tourist hotels and other facilities, by sponsoring attention-getting events such as international beauty contests, championship boxing, chess tournaments and conventions of all manner of groups from the Pacific Body Builders to, of all things, an international human rights conference. The most important element in the growth of tourism, however, has been the government's thinly-veiled encouragement of sex tours especialy for Japanese male tourists.

The same brazen disregard for the impact of government programs on the people involved has also been evident in the promotion of labor exports. In the case of merchant seamen, for example, the government itself negotiates contracts which call for wages some 70 to 80 per cent below international rates. When Filipino seamen go on strike in protest, the government sends its diplomatic officials to threaten retribution and striking seamen have been blacklisted and in some cases arrested upon their return to the Philippines.

In the countryside, the government initially focused on increasing rice production. By vastly increasing investments in irrigation, pushing the use of high-yielding rice varieties, fertilizer and pesticides, and most importantly, initiating a large, non-collateral credit program for rice farmers, the government succeeded in raising rice production from 5.1 million metric tons in 1972 to 7.25 million metric tons in 1979. This program was of particular importance to the regime because of the need to supply cheap food to the urban working class. If urban workers' real wages were to be lowered as the government planned, they should at least be fed.

In an attempt to compensate for the wildly fluctuating international prices of the country's main export crops, sugar and coconuts, the government has also promoted the production of new crops such as feed grains and palm oil. In the last few months alone, the regime signed contracts with large multinational agribusiness such as Sime Darby, to open up as much as 100,000 hectacres of land for the production of palm oil.

Export-Oriented Growth or Accelerated Underdevelopment?

It cannot be denied that martial law economic policy has generated growth in the Philippine economy. But if its impact on people's livelihood has been disastrous, what has been its effect on the economy as a whole, on chronic problems such as balance of trade deficits, unemployment and inflation?

Let us consider the Philippines' balance of trade situation under martial law. This is a crucial measure of success or failure because the basic premise of export-led growth is that it is necessary to expand exports as fast as possible in order to have the foreign exchange needed to buy capital goods for industrialization. The balance of trade deficit for 1980 is expected to be more than $2 billion, more than the total balance of trade deficit between 1960 and 1974.

Part of the reason for this is the fast growing Philippine oil bill, but of greater importance is the high import requirement of the country's new export-oriented manufacturing industries such as electronics and garments. In 1970 the Philippine import bill for raw materials and intermediate goods (excluding oil) was $432.1 million. By 1979, this bill had grown to $2.5 billion or 40.5 per cent of all of the country's imports. If one adds to this the 30.8 per cent of Philippine imports devoted to capital goods, most of which goes to these export-oriented manufacturing industries, the total bill goes up to over 70 per cent of all Philippine imports.[6]

Another way of looking at the value of these new export-oriented manufacturing industries is to look at one of the two largest, the garment industry. According to a recent study of the industry,[7] 'About 56 per cent of the export values are actually imported raw materials and only 44 per cent (the value added thanks to the Philippine garment worker) originated from the Philippines. Since 30 per cent of this value-added is profits which may be repatriated, the 'net benefit' to the country in terms of income paid to Filipinos out of every dollar of garment exports is only 31 cents.'

Another reason for the country's ballooning balance of trade deficit is the deterioration of its terms of trade, a process that has been particularly pronounced under martial law. Using 1972 as a base year (100), Philippine terms of trade declined to 71 index points in 1978. This means that in order to buy the same quantity of imports in 1978, it had to export 42.8 per cent more than in 1972.

In turn, the Philippines' balance of trade deficits have necessitated the rapid expansion of the country's foreign debt. In 1972, the foreign debt was $2.2 billion. By mid-1980, it had grown to a gargantuan $11.04 billion, more than five times larger in a span of only eight years. To get a sense of the proportion of this debt burden, it should be pointed out that it is now over a third of the country's total production (GNP), whereas it was only 23 per cent of GNP in 1972. To service these debts, the Philippines will pay close to $1.5 billion this year. If incoming loans are excluded, the country will pay way more than 20 per cent of its foreign exchange receipts, the widely acknowledged danger point.

What is the connection between these trends and inflation, one of the main causes of the decline in urban real wages and farmers' incomes? The fast rate of increase of prices of Philippine imports is one of the main sources of inflation, for higher import prices, say of oil, are quickly passed on to consumers. In pushing to increase exports the government has also fueled inflation by cutting down the supply of available goods within the country. Of equal importance, the push to export has also resulted in the imposition of world market prices on locally produced products sold within the country.

The country's large foreign debt has also fueled inflation since a good part of this debt is used to finance infrastructure projects which do not, in the short run, increase the stock of goods available within the country. Because more than half of the foreign debt is incurred by the government, debt service payments have become a larger and larger component of the budget. Debt service payments of the government increased from P1.1 billion in 1979 to P2.54 billion this year, an increase of 131 percent, the largest increase in any single item of the budget.

The rapid increase in the government budget, from P6.8 billion to P35.4 billion between 1975 and 1980 alone, has also generated tremendous inflationary pressure because more and more of the budget is spent on non-productive activities such as the military. Moreover, a larger and larger proportion of the budget is financed simply through the creation of new money. In addition, inflation is generated because an increasing portion of government revenue comes from indirect taxes (21.1 per cent in 1973 to 27.9 per cent in 1978) which are quickly passed on to consumers in the form of higher prices.

What has been the impact of New Society economic policies on unemployment, another major problem of the Philippine economy? According to the government, unemployment in the last few years has averaged below 5 per cent of the workforce. Careful examination of government statistics show, however, that in fact unemployment may be as high as 40 per cent. The government's statistical system excludes five million housewives who are jobless, 3.4 million out-of-school youth without jobs, and some 442,000 people who gave 'assorted reasons' for not wanting to work, plus another 146,000 unemployed who although wanting to work were not looking for work during the survey period. If these nine million are considered part of the labor force, the number of unemployed in the country rises to 9.6 million or 40 per cent of the population above age 15 who are able to work.

The impact of New Society policies in the countryside has been equally devastating. Although manufactured exports have increased significantly, the Philippines remains a mineral and agricultural product exporting economy. The push to increase exports has therefore fallen heavily on the peasantry. Between 1970 and 1976, for example, the amount of land devoted to sugar and coconuts increased by 663,000 hectacres.

Other government programs have served to increase pressure on the already beleaguered peasantry and exacerbated the process of land alienation and concentration of land ownership in fewer and fewer hands. Government programs for increasing rice production, for example, require large expenditures for seeds, fertilizer and pesticides. Thus while production has indeed increased, 'marginal' farmers with tiny farms and little capital have been forced to sell out to larger farmers with increasing frequency. The government's corporate farming program has also had the same effect.

The victimization of Moros in the south and tribal Filipinos in other parts of the country are also the result of government programs. Because Mindanao is one of the few remaining areas for agricultural expansion, the increases in agriculture export crop hectarage have had their strongest impact on Moros in Mindanao. The accelerated program of hydroelectric projects for irrigation and rural electrification often affects tribal peoples whose lands are flooded when dams are built.

Even government agrarian reform programs have ended up working against the interests of the peasantry. When land reform was proclaimed soon after the declaration of martial law in 1972, it was supposed to include more than one million rice and corn farmers. Eight years and reams of government propaganda later, a grand total of 1,600 farmers-tenants have received title to their land. Some 70,000 other farmers have become 'amortizing owners' but according to confidential World Bank memos, the default rate on land reform amortizations ranges to as high as 80 per cent in a number of areas. With this level of default on amortization payments it is unlikely that many of the farmers in the program will end up actually owning their lands after the 15-year amortization period.

Finally, the Marcos dictatorship has added a new wrinkle to the perennial problem of corruption. Where past presidents were satisfied with salting away a few million dollars in Swiss banks, Marcos, his relatives and his cronies have used martial law powers to wrest control of whole sectors of the economy. Two of Marcos' closest associates, Roberto Benedicto and Juan Ponce Enrile, for example, control the sugar and coconut industries, the two biggest export moneymakers for the country.

Let me illustrate this point by telling the story of how Marcos' Defence Minister Enrile acquired control over the coconut industry. Soon after martial law was declared, the regime imposed a large levy on copra. This tax was supposed to be for the purpose of subsidising mass consumption items such as cooking oil which use copra as a raw material. In practice, only 14 per cent of this levy was ever used for the subsidy. The rest of the funds were allowed to accumulate in a private bank, United Coconut Planters Bank, specifically created as a depository for these funds. After seven years, industry sources estimated the fund at approximately US$800 million.

The administrator of the Philippine Coconut Authority, the government's watchdog agency for the industry is Defense Minister Enrile. The chairman of the Board of United Coconut Planters Bank is the same Minister Enrile. With substantial funds already at his disposal, Enrile then moved to weaken the position of the coconut mills, the key instruments of economic control over the industry. Enrile did this by arranging for a set of export taxes and other government regulations which made it more profitable to export copra instead of coconut oil, a move which incidentally contravenes the government's policy of promoting processed raw material exports.

By promoting the export of copra, Enrile deprived the coconut mills of their raw material, in the process, pushing several of them to near bankruptcy. Enrile then founded UNICOM (United Coconut Mills), a private corporation, and started using levy funds to buy out financially hard-up mills. Enrile also arranged for a presidential decree which required other mills to 'affiliate' with UNICOM thereby creating, at one stroke, a cartel, controlling the whole industry.

The impact of such uses of martial law powers for private gain is again illustrated by Enrile's control over the coconut industry. When Enrile took over the industry, world market prices for coconut products were at an all time high. In an attempt to defend its profits when the price of coconut exports plummeted this year, UNICOM lowered the price at which it bought copra faster than the fall of the export price. This created a drop in the incomes of coconut farmers that has been more severe than might be expected from, the drop in export prices. Since some 15 million people are dependent on the industry, the impact of Enrile's form of corruption has been indeed, significant.

US Imperialism and Philippine Underdevelopment

The increasing impoverishment of the Filipino people in the last eight years of martial law rule is the direct result of the economic policies of the Marcos dictatorship. But where do these policies come from? They are, in the first instance, the result of direct and indirect pressure from the United States and US-controlled multilateral lending institutions such as the World Bank (WB) and the International Monetary Fund (IMF). Secondly, they represent an attempt by the US-Marcos dictatorship to preserve and extend the semi-feudal and semi-colonial society created by US imperialism. In order to understand the political economy of the US-Marcos dictatorship, therefore, we have to go back in time and examine how contemporary Philippine society was shaped by US imperialism.

The role of the United States in the economic life of the Philippines goes back to a period earlier than the arrival of Admiral Dewey in 1898 and the subsequent American conquest of the country. In the early decades of the 19th century, the growth of export agriculture and the gradual integration of the Philippines into the worldwide imperialist system was spearheaded by English and American commercial houses. These enterprises provided credit, technology, and foreign markets for Philippine abaca, sugar and other agricultural products. Because of their role, some historians described the Philippines at that time as an Anglo-American colony, although it remained in Spanish hands.

Given prior American interest in Philippine export agriculture, it should not be hard to understand why the Philippines quickly developed a classical colonial economy — an exporter of raw materials and importer of manufactured goods — once it formally became an American colony at the end of the 19th century. The colonial trade pattern was formalized by the Payne-Aldrich Tariff Act of 1909 which stimulated 'free trade' throughout the period preceding World War II. The production of raw material exports increased tremendously, expanding to include new products such as copra and coconut oil, pineapples, rubber and mineral products such as gold and copper. Most of this trade was with the United States. By 1941, just before the outbreak of World War II, 80 per cent of Philippine foreign trade was with the United States.

When the US granted independence to the Philippines in 1946, it made sure that the Philippines remained a US dependency in political and economic terms. The provision of war damage assistance to the war-torn country was made conditional upon the granting of parity rights to US citizens. Parity gave rights to American citizens and corporations equal to those possessed by Filipinos with respect to the ownership, use, exploitation and development of natural resources and the operation of public utilities. Philippine dependence on raw material exports was assured through the continuation of free trade and later through a system of gradually increasing tariffs set by the repatriation of the peso profits of American businesses in the country, the Philippine monetary system was tied to the dollar, whose value in pesos could not be changed without the approval of the US.

The agreement concluded at that time between the two governments also prohibited the Philippines from imposing export taxes until 1956. This prevented the use of a weapon 'that could have been effective both for protection against uneconomic terms of trade losses, and also for the transfer of some income from traditional exports to other sectors.'[8] Finally, under the agreement, "The US President was given discretionary power to withdraw any or all of the substantial economic concessions granted to the Philippines upon indication of nationalistic pressures being applied to US interests."[9]

The impact of this agreement can be seen in the $273.17 million average annual trade deficit of the Philippines from 1946 to 1949. The severe balance-of-payments problem in 1949 led to the sending of the Bell Economic Survey Mission in the following year. It was during this period, at the instigation of the US government, that the strategy of 'import substitution industrialization' was inaugurated. The components of this strategy included:

1. foreign exchange controls to limit the outflow of foreign currency;
2. import controls;
3. encouragement of local manufacturing of consumption products.

On the face of it, the strategy seems to go against the standard 'free trade' orientation of US imperialism. In order to understand this seeming contradiction, it must be remembered that the Philippine ruling class was severely fragmented at this time in the aftermath of the 1949 election, and, of greater importance, it faced what at the time appeared to be a strong threat from the Huk movement. Under the circumstances, the US could not allow the economy to go bankrupt.

To assure the continued viability of the economy and the extensive American stake in it, the US concluded an agreement with the Philippine government[10] which required close American supervision over economic policymaking. Commenting on this arrangement, nationalist leader Claro M. Recto said: '... after the Bell Mission ... and in implementation of the recommendations embodied in the report, our government signed an agreement in 1951 under which they accepted a motley crowd of American advisors. They are present in every branch of the national administration. They prepare our budget, they make our economic planning. They even prepare the President's message to Congress dealing with economic policies.'[11]

A review of the period shows that American businesses did not exactly suffer. Taking advantage of their privileged position, Americans invested heavily in import-substitution manufacturing as a way of going over the high tariff walls. Despite exchange controls, American businesses repatriated an average of $85.7 million a year from 1949 to 1960, a figure so high that it averaged 33.15 per cent of the country's international reserves during the same period.

The consumer goods component of Philippine imports declined from 28 per cent in 1950 to 17 per cent in 1957, and growth of manufacturing averaged a respectable 11 per cent annually during the whole decade. But most of the new manufacturing enterprises were in fact no more than assembly or packaging plants and did not set the basis for self-sustaining industrialization. Because a large proportion of new products were really luxury goods, at least in the Philippine context, their potential market was limited.

Import-substitution manufacturing also required high levels of equipment and raw material imports such that, even with exchange controls, balance of trade and balance of payments deficits began to go up in the latter half of the decade. After a particularly large balance of payments deficit in 1957, the US began to push for decontrol. After initial resistance by the Garcia administration, exchange and import controls were gradually lifted, culminating in the devaluation of the peso in 1962.

Why did the US push for devaluation at this period? Filipino scholar Edberto M. Villegas explained it this way. 'US policymakers viewed control as not being at all detrimental to American investments in the Philippines, but, on the contrary, as shielding them from competition. But the price for the protection afforded US businessmen in the Philippines was, in the eyes of the IMF, an overvalued Philippine peso in terms of the dollar. The gain of American investors in the Philippines was a loss to American importers since the latter had to pay higher prices for Philippine products because of an overvalued Philippine currency ... Full decontrol was allowed by the US-IMF group in 1962, since by that time US investments were already sufficiently entrenched in the Philippine economy ...'[12]

The politics of the 1962 devaluation marks the first time that the US used the IMF as an instrument to impose its will on the Philippines. This point is forcefully brought out by Miguel Cuaderno, Central Bank governor during that period, in his memoirs. Cuaderno reports that the IMF would have supported a plan he proposed that would have stopped short of devaluation had it not been for the intervention of the State Department.

The 1962 devaluation had a wide-ranging and devastating effect on the Philippine economy. The devaluation of the peso from P2 to $1, to P3.90 to $1 doubled the peso cost of imported raw materials and the peso coverage of the foreign debt. As a result, manufacturing growth decelerated from the 11 per cent average annual growth in the fifties to 4 per cent annually between 1960 and 1965.

Devaluation, conversely, served to return raw material exports to their premier place in the economy. Under the impetus of a 75 per cent increase in the peso earnings of every dollar of export proceeds, export volume expanded by 32 per cent between 1962 and 1963. Where the area planted to export crops had fluctuated around 1.5 million hectares between 1951 and 1960, by 1966 it had expanded to 2.3 million hectares.

The rapid expansion of export crop production during this period was partly at the expense of rice production. Because the rate of growth in rice production declined from 4.4 per cent annually in the 1949 to 1955 period, to only 2.1 per cent annually between 1958 and 1965, rice prices went up and helped to drive up the rate of inflation. Combined with the inflationary impact of the higher peso cost of imports, higher rice prices drove the inflation rate from an annual average rate of 1.3 per cent between 1949 and 1962 to 6.1 per cent between 1962 and 1967.

The rapid increase in exports initially boosted the country's balance of payments position such that the total deficit between 1960 and 1964 was a modest $115 million. By the end of the decade, however, deficits climbed back up to levels even higher than in the late fifties. Between 1965 and 1969, the total deficit was $874 million.

The Philippines' mounting balance of payments deficits set the basis for the virtual institutionalization of the role of the IMF as the watchdog of US imperialism. In exchange for a $300 million US stabilization loan and a smaller $36.7 million loan from the IMF in 1962, the Philippine government agreed to 'abide by a standby agreement which laid down the country's year-long program for handling her balance of payments deficit under IMF supervision ... From 1962 on, the Philippine government, because of constant borrowings from the IMF-WB conglomerate and restructuring of her debts, has been submitting yearly stabilization programs to the Funds under various stand-by agreements.'[13]

The more the Philippines borrowed, the stricter IMF control became. In 1970, when the Marcos government realized that it could not pay its debt service payments for the year, its creditors agreed to a restructuring of their loans only on the condition that the government accept the IMF recommendations for correcting the country's weak financial position. Filipino economist Alejandro Lichauco summed up the situation at this time by saying that: 'by the time a member (of the IMF) makes it their drawing (as the Philippines did in 1970), it has virtually relinquished its economic sovereignty to the Fund. The Fund for all practical purposes, dictates the member's economic policies. It dictates not only what the borrowing country's foreign exchange policy should be, but, far more important, what the character of the entire development strategy should be.'[14]

The 1970 devaluation was only the precursor of an even more stringent set of economic policies inaugurated by the declaration of martial law in 1972. One does not have to look for CIA spies drafting Marcos' martial law declaration to establish US complicity. Martial law repression is a necessary component of the economic strategy of the US-Marcos dictatorship. As such it is of no great relevance that it was Marcos rather than the US President, Richard Nixon, who signed the martial law declaration.

Apart from the explicit IMF role in the formulation of Philippine monetary and fiscal policy, World Bank documents also provide direct evidence of its role in the formulation of overall economic policy. A March 1976 World Bank memorandum,[15] for example, says:

The Bank's basic economic report proposes a broad framework for future development which the Government has accepted as a basis for its future development plans ... The Bank can play a major role ... because the government is receptive to bank staff advice.

The other role played by the US has been that of guarantor of the financial viability of the Marcos dictatorship. Thus direct US aid to the regime, both military and economic, doubled immediately after the declaration of martial law. Of greater importance, the IMF and the World Bank came through with a $45.5 million and $22 million loan in 1972. The IMF-WB stamp of approval, moreover became the basis for vastly expanded borrowing from international commercial banking sources.

As if the 1970 level of IMF control over the economy was not enough, the Marcos dictatorship in 1976 became the first Asian country to avail of the IMF's Extended Fund Facility (EFF) loans. According to IMF rules, a country can qualify for EFF loans only if it is suffering 'serious payments imbalance relating to structural maladjustment in production, trade and prices and is prepared to implement a comprehensive set of corrective policies covering a period of two to three years.' These conditions are so stringent that only 8 other countries have availed of EFF loans and as of 1979, the Philippines was the only country in the IMF which had completed the whole program.

This year, 1980, the World Bank-IMF combine added yet another instrument to its arsenal for controlling the Marcos regime policy. Until this year, World Bank influence had been largely worked out through the Bank's projected loans and through its role in the formulation of development plans. This role is not insubstantial for World Bank project loans have accounted for an average of 40 per cent of all development loans provided to the Philippines. Through its role as organizer and permanent chair of the Consultative Group of Philippine creditors formed in 1970, moreover, it can mould the overall structure and direction of development lending to the country.

With the inauguration of a new lending program called 'Structural Adjustment Lending' this year, the WB has appropriated powers strikingly similar to those of the IMF. As with the IMF's Extended Fund Facility program, the Philippines is the first borrower, the 'guinea pig', as Finance Minister Cesar

Virata unabashedly says. The *Asian Wall Street Journal* (Oct. 8, 1980) aptly describes the program this way:

'... the loan is by no means without strings. The World Bank doles it out in successive tranches, or installments, each to be earned by compliance with the bank's recommendations for changes in tariff, taxation, and investment policies. With the sugar coating of quickly disbursable funds goes the bitter pill of tough, administrative reforms'.

Each intervention by the IMF-WB combination is supposed to be for the purpose of providing remedies for the Philippines' chronic balance of payments and other structural problems. In practice, IMF-WB intervention has exacerbated these problems because the full thrust of IMF-WB policies has been to strengthen US control over the Philippine economy, the main source of these problems to start with. American economist Cheryl Payer sums up the IMF-WB impact by saying:[16]

'With every cycle of "crisis" and "rescue" by the IMF and WB ... the Philippines becomes more indebted to foreign creditors, less able to manage its own resources, more inflationary, and more prone to renewed "crisis". It is a vicious cycle indeed.'

Strike the Roots

This review of the Philippine economic situation and its history has shown:

1. the accelerated deterioration of people's livelihood under martial law;
2. that this deterioration is the direct result of the economic policies of the US-Marcos dictatorship;
3. that these policies represent an attempt to surmount the structural crisis of the economy in the decade of the sixties, and finally,
4. that the recurrent crisis of the economy is built into the semi-colonial and semi-feudal economic system created by US imperialism.

This analysis suggests that the economic problems of the Filipino people cannot be solved without the destruction of the Marcos dictatorship. The continued existence of the dictatorship depends upon its ability to sustain profits for those social forces which support it. Since these profits, in turn, cannot be generated without the increasing impoverishment of the Filipino people, they are left with no other choice but to destroy the source of their suffering.

As the economic crisis of the Marcos dictatorship deepens, the possibility that Marcos will be replaced by another puppet of US imperialism also looms closer. Such a change may result in a temporary decrease in repression. But unless the whole economic structure is radically altered, continuing economic deprivation will generate more resistance which, in turn, will bring about a return of repression. In the final analysis, the only lasting solution to the economic problems of the Filipino people is to strike at their root — to sever the links which bind the Philippines to US imperialism.

Notes

1. Mahar Mangahas, *A Critique of the 1975 FIES.*
2. Blondie Po, 'Rural Development and Rural Organizations', Report to *FAO*, April 1978, p.22.
3. F. Briones, R. Oliveros, L. Panganiban, *Labor-Capital Relations and the Incidence of Work Stoppages*, U.P. School of Economics, 1978; *Ibon*, 40 (15 April, 1980).
4. op. cit., Mangahas
5. Direct foreign investments during this period totalled only $117.36 million while loans of the private sector totalled $463.6 million for a total inflow of $580.9 million. Set against this were $264.9 in profit remittances, $106.59 million in withdrawal of investments, and a gargantuan $2.9 billion in debt service payments (private sector only) for a total of $3.2 billion in outflow. *Invisible Receipts and Disbursements (1964-73)*, Foreign Exchange Dept., Central Bank.
6. NEDA 1976 Statistical Yearbook; IMF, *Philippine Recent Economic Developments*, July 29, 1980.
7. *Ibon*, 29 (October 31, 1979).
8. John Power and Gerardo Sicat, *The Philippines: Industrialization and Trade Policies* (NY: Oxford University Press)
9. Hawes, op. cit., page 8.
10. The Quirino-Foster Agreement on Economic and Technical Cooperation.
11. Quoted in Robin Broad, *International Actors and Philippine Authoritarianism*, pages 17-18.
12. Edberto Villegas, 'The Philippines and the IMF-WB Conglomerate', *Third World Studies*, 1979, Series No. 17, page 8.
13. Villegas, op. cit., page 9.
14. Alejandro Lichauco, 'The IMF-WB and the International Economic Order', *Impact*, XI (December 1976), page 412, Quoted in Hawes, page 20.
15 Michael Gould, *Philippine Country Program Paper*, March 26, 1976.
16. Cheryl Payer, *The Debt Trap*, (Penguin Books, 1976).

Testimony of a worker

The martial law government not only provides management with laws that allow the suppression of workers, it also engages in direct suppression of workers...

I am Antonio de la Cruz. I used to be a union leader at an appliance manufacturing firm in Manila and a union organizer in other factories. I have been placed under 'preventive suspension' because I led a strike and because of my other union activities. What has happened to me is happening to other Filipino workers under the US-Marcos dictatorship. It is therefore on behalf of Filipino workers that I testify before this tribunal.

'Preventive suspension' is only one of the many methods provided by the martial law labor code for management to stifle the workers' exercise of their rights. According to this provision, a company can suspend a worker *indefinitely*, on the ground that he *might* cause trouble. The company doesn't need to prove the worker's guilt.

I was charged with sabotaging company operations, work stoppage, and violation of Presidential Decree 823 which prohibits strikes. My case was dragged through various agencies till it reached the Supreme Court. It has been there for the last 7 months, with no prospects of an early or a favourable decision.

But let me first tell you my experience as a worker before I was suspended. In 1977 my take-home pay was P14.00 a day (including allowances), while my family of four needed P31.65 or was all we could afford for our food, which consisted of two eggs at P1.00, 1 kilo of rice P2.10, ⅓ kilo of dried fish at P2.00. I spent P3.60 daily for my transportation fare to and from the factory. For the cooking gas (kerosene) we paid P0.80. For our drinking water we bought a can of water everyday costing P0.70 a can. A small room in a slum area without toilet facilities cost us P3.00 a day. All this amounted to P13.90 which was all my take-home pay. These expenses did not include our other basic necessities like milk, fruit for the kids, sugar, coffee, toothpaste, lard, laundry and bath soap and others. To buy these, we often skipped meals or reduced further our expenses for viand. There were even times when we had only rice and coffee for a meal.

Our living conditions got worse everytime I absented myself from work, or when someone got sick, which usually happened every month. I was forced to borrow money from usurers, who charged interest rates as high as 20 per cent a month. To pay for my debts I had to work overtime 4 times a week. This has adversely affected my health. My wife tried to look for a job to boost our income. But she was turned down by all because she is married and without a high school education. Under this condition I could not give my family even a rare treat. I could not buy toys for my kids.

At present the Manila workers' take-home pay is supposed to be P29.00 or US$3.93 a day. This is barely enough for an adequate diet. But this amount is received by only one out of every four workers, since the government has many laws exempting companies, especially foreign-owned ones, from paying the set wages. Most companies, in fact, do not pay the minimum wage. The Employers Confederation of the Philippines reports that only 30 percent of employers pay the minimum wage, and the Ministry of Labor admits that it is only 10 percent.

There are many factories that do not pay the workers the minimum wage and neither do they implement wage increases decreed by the government. The factories which pay the old minimum wage, though they did increase the workers' wage, this increase did not correspond with the decreed rate. Furthermore, workers who were paid above the former minimum wage did not get any increase at all, on the grounds that the decree did not specify across-the-board-increases. This practice then disregards years of service. In our factory, workers employed for 5 or 10 years receive almost the same wages as workers employed for only a year.

Another measure to cheat the workers of their just wages is the merit rating scheme where workers are evaluated for job effectivity. Workers who are favoured by management get high merit points, while those active in union work or are assertive of their rights get low ratings, hence, no merits and no wage increase. When the company has to pay the merit increases, they give it just before the government decrees the wage increase and it is able to pass off the merit increase as the new minimum rate.

The same measure applies to benefits won by unions through collective bargaining agreement. The benefits are given only after a long delay and just before the government announces changes or reforms for labor. Thus it is not surprising to find workers in San Miguel Corporation, a multinational company owned mostly by Americans, receiving P30 to P35 a day even if they had been with the company for 30 years; or to find workers in Yupangco Cotton Mills receiving P9.85 a day, in spite of the fact that the company had a net income of P32 million in 1976-77. Workers in mining firms like Benguet Consolidated and Lepanto Consolidated are paid P225 to P322 a month instead of the minimum P325.50 a month set by law in 1978.

In labor-intensive garment industries, companies like Aris Glove manage to pay wages lower than the minimum by employing pieceworkers who are paid according to the number of articles they produce instead of the hours they work. A study by the University of the Philippines Law Centre in 1973 found 39.8 percent of all garment industries used this system of piecework. Unemployment and underemployment have further reduced our wages. Although the government claimed that there were only 818,000 (4.35 percent) unemployed in 1978, the actual figure of the unemployed should be 9.80 million (38.4 percent) if we include the many categories not accounted for in the government statistics. There are over 1.9 million people who are underemployed, and this would bring the figure of those who are not in gainful employment to at least 11.7 million, which represents 46 per cent of the workforce.

From January to June 1980, around 300,000 workers were dismissed from work, purportedly due to increases in the price of oil and other materials, economizing and all other invented reasons. Many workers were put on a rotation basis (thereby diminishing working hours), particularly those in garment and textile factories such as Master Shirt, Ding Velayo and Top Form. Rotation basis was also employed in Northern Motors and in the Manila ports.

Also adversely affected are the 50,000 jeepney drivers in Metro Manila area. The state has already implemented its Integrated Transport System project. In September 1980, double-deck buses of the state-owned Metro Manila Transit have taken the main routes previously used by the jeepneys which are now relegated to secondary routes. As a result, the jeepneys will not have passengers to pick up because the people will look for rides along the main routes. The drivers, consequently, will be included in the fast growing majority of unemployed and underemployed. Militant workers, particularly the leaders, are always threatened with preventive suspension.

I was only one of the 6,000 labor leaders and union members who were given preventive suspension in 1977. Others were the 300 workers at the Engineering Equipment Incorporated, 200 workers at Greenfield and Santiago, 127 workers at Solid Mills, 121 workers at Gelmart and 7 at Impact, plus many others.

Our cases take from 6 months to 3 years before resolution. The Ministry of Labor's own records show that of every 1,000 cases of preventive suspension, only 13 have been decided in favour of the workers. Even those who win their cases are faced with the problem of the implementation. Besides, they are reinstated without backwages. Together with low wages and job insecurity, workers suffer from poor and inhuman working conditions. In the factory where I worked, if we absented ourselves because of sickness we were scolded. We were then threatened with dismissal. In order to use our legal rights to vacation and sick leave, we still have to struggle and bargain with the company. Many of us were not paid our rightful sick leave benefit and we were even charged with being *awol* because we couldn't present a doctor's certificate. But we couldn't present such a certificate for the simple reason that we couldn't afford to have ourselves examined by a doctor. Besides, those who did have such a certificate were still not accepted by the company doctor who wanted us to go exclusively to his clinic. But that would have meant additional expenses in exchange for superficial treatment, often just Aspirin, no matter how serious our illness was.

Oftentimes the doctor wouldn't authorize our going home even if we suffered from fever or over-fatigue in the middle of our shift. We had to finish the shift. On one occasion a co-worker had to have a tooth extracted. He couldn't go home because he would be charged as *awol*. But he couldn't ask his supervisor because the supervisor would have asked for the doctor's certificate. So he had to continue working.

The company often set very high quotas. To insure reaching this we were forbidden to talk with our co-workers. Even our going to the toilet was timed: 3 minutes for urinating and 5 minutes for defecating. Just one violation of rule was enough to get us suspended, with the threat of dismissal or forced resignation. That's why we couldn't even take our break at the canteen. To walk over to the canteen would take 7 minutes and we had only a 15 minute-break. So we were forced to stay with the bad smell of chemicals and the heat of the plant rather than risk overextending our break-time.

If we couldn't reach the quota, we were forced to go on overtime. If we didn't, we could be classified inefficient and that would prevent those of us who were probationary from being classified as permanent and the casuals from being classified probationary, not to mention the loss of any pay increase. The law provides for a definite period after which a worker must become regular, but this is not often followed. In the case of the La Tondena workers, 1,100 casuals had been such for 6 or more years by the time they went on strike in October 1975.

If there is overproduction or if sales are slow, whether we like it or not, we are forced by the company to go on vacation for one or two weeks without pay. The company invents excuses like major maintenance of machinery or installation of new facilities. Together with these moves, they lay off many casuals.

In labor-intensive companies, the conditions are worse. Most garment workers complain of heat exhaustion. Fainting and dizziness are common among workers in Triumph International, a foreign-owned firm making brassieres. At Gelmart, a dress and glove firm owned by an American, a worker said: "The factory is very hot. Because of the sudden change in temperature when we go out, our bodies are prone to sickness." It was also in this factory that fire broke out and killed 11 workers, with 53 others injured.

At Dynetics, an electronics firm, two women workers were suspended for going home too early after overtime on Sunday which was supposed to be their rest day. They both had the supervisor's permission. One had influenza and the other had to meet her parents who were arriving from the province. Yet the labor code provides that workers should not be asked to work overtime on their rest day.

Workers in the electronics industry tend to suffer from eye defects after three years of employment. Others complain of acid burns, skin rashes from epoxy resins and other allergy reactions due to solvents like trichloroethylene. Even if they are given gloves and masks, they do not use them because these would slow them down and they would fail to reach their quota. Besides this, they are not required by the company to use them and in fact are not taught about the need for protective devices. Of course the company benefits from not having to spend on such protective equipment and training.

Depressed Working Conditions

Ramada Hotel, one of the most expensive hotels in Manila, is owned by an American. The cooks, waiters, roomboys, bellboys, porters and other workers are treated worse than the pets of the tourist-guests. They are forced to work almost 12 hours a day for a P10 daily wage, cheated of the service charges due to them, denied their emergency allowances and night differential and given spoiled soup and fish for their meals!

Under martial law there is a general ban on strikes. While this is especially oppressive, it is not the only measure used to suppress our right to organize and fight for our rights. Under martial law, the simple act of workers deciding to form a union has become a life and death question. A union's decision to strike becomes a life and death issue.

When 800 workers at Manila Paper Mills went on strike in 1977, all of them were dismissed from their jobs. When workers at Greenfield and Santiago, a garment firm with 1,800 workers, formed a union in mid-1977 their officers were dismissed and the members were suspended from work. At Triumph International, 56 union leaders and stewards were terminated from work when the union went on strike to protest about the taking away of P10 from their P60 monthly allowance.

At Solid Mills, a garment factory, management withheld 65 centavos from the daily allowance of P2. To protest about this, the workers went on slow-down strikes for two months before going on a three-day strike. Production went down by half. Management grilled workers individually to find out who the leaders were and hired informers to keep suspects under surveillance. The company also raised production quotas and made a 4-hour overtime compulsory. Workers were transferred from one section to another to prevent them from launching any concerted activity.

In the company where I worked I learned from the oldtimers that the workers had made three attempts to form the union. In the first attempt the company harassed and intimidated the leaders who were forced to resign from the company. During the second time, the workers' unity was already strong due to the influences of the workers' and students' movement in Manila in the early 1970s. They went on strike in order to be recognized by the company. All the strikers, 400 of them, were fired from their jobs for participating in an illegal strike.

After 5 years, the Supreme Court upheld the workers strike. But it was provided in the order, that the workers should be reinstated without back wages. So the workers appealed to Malacanang. Up to the present, the case is still pending decision.

In their third attempt, the workers successfully established the union and I became the vice-president in 1974. In 1976-1977 organisations of workers became active again under the umbrella of the Bukluran ng Manggagawang Pilipino (Bukluran). Previously, the umbrella organisation that performed this role was KASAMA, a militant workers' organisation. This workers' organisation was unable to remain legal after martial law was declared.

Bukluran

Bukluran ng Manggagawang Philipino is an alliance of militant unions in Metro Manila. It was organized on 1 May, 1975 and was highly active in the La Tondeña strike on 24-25 October. In this strike, 1,100 casuals demanded that the workers be granted permanent status. Management conceded after a long and militant struggle.

Aside from being involved in strikes, Bukluran works closely with other sectors, like students, urban poor and the religious in launching mass actions. Mass actions took place on the following dates: 1 May, 1976, 10 October, 1976, 1 May, 1977 and 23 September, 1977. Due to its growing support among many groups, the government branded it as subversive on May 1977.

In the midst of mass actions and widespread struggles for rights and justice we launched a strike in our factory. Our strike was illegal because the Department of Labor denied our notice of strike. This was inspite of the fact that we met the requirements for holding a strike, as provided in PD 823, which limits strikes to non-vital industries and prohibits strikes within a mandatory 30-day cooling period. Our company does not fall in the vital industry category. There was a deadlock in the Collective Bargaining Agreement negotiations. We had also abided by the 30-day cooling off period. But under the law, the President or any of his representatives, such as the Secretary of

Labor, could call off any strike which they claim threatens the national security and economy. So our notice of strike was denied by the Department of Labor.

As a matter of fact, over 90 per cent of the more than 400 or so strikes launched by workers throughout the country in the period 1975-1978 were "illegal", in that they were in defiance of PD823. Because of this almost all of these strikes resulted in mass arrests as well as indefinite detention and torture of some of the leaders.

It is a known fact that the martial law government not only provides management with laws that allow the suppression of workers, it also engages in direct suppression of workers, especially with the use of military units.

During the strike at La Tondeña, 515 workers were detained supposedly for violating curfew laws. A planned demonstration against the ban on strikes had to be dropped because of mass arrests of workers in 1976. I will not enumerate the many union leaders and members who have been arrested, tortured and detained. The latest case is that of the Kilusang Mayo Uno leaders who were arrested during a raid on their offices. For Attorney Arellano, KMU general secretary, this is the third arrest.

Because of the problems of low wages, poor working conditions, job insecurity and outright suppression of our rights to organize, the need for strong and militant organizations of workers is doubly called for.

But this is where we face one more problem, namely, the false labor leaders who deceive and cheat us and whom the martial law government and US imperialism control and support. These labor leaders try to teach us that management and workers are harmonious partners in developing industry and that unions should be kept far from politics. They conveniently neglect to mention the harassment we receive from management, over and above our being exploited. They ignore the heavy hand of martial law politics that represses us.

Worse than these false doctrines, these labor leaders engage in outright selling off of workers during collective bargaining agreement negotiations. They are not satisfied with the union dues they have already stolen from us. They also lead us into draining and senseless struggles due to union-raiding and the petty rivalries between them.

For example the 11,000 workers at Gelmart Industries are made to hold certification elections every 3 years because of fighting among various fellow federations. In 1974, the workers managed to form their own independent union and won the elections, but management refused to recognise it and placed the elected union leader under preventive suspension.

The 8,000 workers at San Miguel Corporation also suffer from divisions caused by the rivalry of yellow union leaders. Often such struggles last 4 to 6 months at the expense of the workers' welfare.

These labor aristocrats are supported by the government in line with its "labor structure" program. The Marcos regime wants to form one federation per industry. On paper such a plan seems to be reasonable. To implement this, the government sponsored the formation of the Trade Union Congress of the Philippines (TUCP), under the leadership of the two chief labor aristocrats: Roberto Oca and Democrito Mendoza. The Ministry of Labor was ordered to help the TUCP to cleanse the workers' movement of "radical" unions.

In 1977, 5,640 of the 7,000 registered unions and federations were refused recognition. Because of this, many independent unions were harassed, if not broken up, because they could not provide Collective Bargaining Agreement, financial report, and other technical requirements of the Ministry of Labor. Other unions were forced to join one of the officially recognized federations. This is what our union had to do.

The American-Asian Free Labor Institute has its part in fostering the kind of unionism and union leadership as represented by the TUCP. Its purpose is to conduct intelligence work at the unions and to develop leaders whose main task is not to be genuinely representative of workers' interest, but to prevent the radicalization of the workers.

I have stated before you the case of exploited workers. I have been denied justice by the Philippine Supreme Court. I appeal to you now to stand in judgement, not for myself alone, but for the Filipino workers whom I represent, and we ask you to denounce and condemn the US-Marcos dictatorship. We ask you to recognize our struggle and unite with us in our fight for a just and full life, not only for Filipino workers, but for all the Filipino people.

Testimony of a peasant

Sometimes they had to work the whole day and night because the landlord would set a deadline.

I am Victoria delos Reyes, 23 years old and a peasant. I will speak before you about my own and generations of peasant exploitation.

My mother is of peasant-fisherman origin in one of the coastal areas in Southern Luzon. As I was told, my mother was orphaned at the age of fourteen and was adopted by a sympathetic peasant relative. She earned a living by sewing on buttons for tailors and working as a hired hand during rice planting and harvesting seasons. She was able to finish secondary education.

My father is a peasant whose parents were the early settlers in one of the mountainous areas in Southern Luzon. My grandparents were able to transform areas in the mountain into rich source of rice, corn, tubers, bananas, camotes and coffee, with only one carabao, a plow, a hoe, a bolo and tremendous amount of sweat and determination. My grandmother also wove baskets, made hats and mats which she bartered for fish in the town center.

During Magsaysay's term as president (1954-1957), the land cultivated by my father's family became a homestead. Many settlers from all parts of the country, particularly Southern Luzon, were given the 'promised land' of 25 hectares per family but these lands were mostly located in dense forest areas or on rocky terrain. Years and years of painstaking toil made it possible for the settlers to produce rice and vegetables for their daily subsistence. The rice paddies were irrigated by rivers flowing through the settlement areas.

When my grandfather died, my father inherited 'ten fingers'. I will also inherit from my father 'ten fingers' — which means that our one legacy as peasants is our capacity to till the soil.

By 1966, land disputes began. The homestead which was about 130 hectares of rice and coconut was being claimed by a powerful landlord. He had 'legal papers' of ownership, and when the barrio was named after him, it became very difficult to assert our rights over the land. My parents, possessing no legal papers of ownership, were forced to become his tenants and we became part of a hacienda.

Life in the hacienda was demanding. My mother had to wake up at 3 a.m., boil camote for breakfast and prepare lunch for my father. She would wrap rice mixed with coconut milk, gabi leaves and dried fish, in banana leaves, give it to my father who worked in the plantation. Then she left for the kaingin herself. I did my share by attending to the feeding of the chickens and pigs, and cultivating the vegetable patch in our backyard.

On the coconut plantation, my father had to work hard and for long hours. The harvest season for coconuts comes every 45 days and the preparation for copra-making is tedious. For two weeks, my father had to pick thousands of coconuts, husk them, cut them in halves, dry them under the sun and bake them in the kiln. Because my father could not do all this work alone, he had to hire some of our relatives and I would also help, often sacrificing school work. Sometimes they had to work for the whole day and night because the landlord would set a deadline. They also had to guard the copra from being stolen or burned in the kiln.

My father not only had to provide for the labor but also shoulder most of the expenses for copra-making. He had to pay hired hands for weeding, cleaning and cutting the old trees. He had to feed our relatives during copra-making besides giving them a small amount of money. The cost of producing copra amounts to P324.00 per hectare (approx. 3,000 coconuts). The breakdown of expenses are:

P160 for paying about 20 hired hands, P8 each during the whole harvest season.

P60 for picking the coconuts from the trees.

P60 during husking.

P24 for breaking the nuts and baking in the kiln.

P20 for transporting the copra to the buying station.

The total sale of the copra is P1440, out of which my father would get one-third (P480.00), while the landlord gets two-thirds.

This is aggravated when there are typhoons and pestilence, because we are still forced to meet the two-thirds share of the landlord, not to mention the share of the encargado who is the hacienda manager.

As a result, my father has to borrow constantly from local money lenders at the rate of one cavan of palay for every P50 so to meet the expenses of copra production, to pay for my education and to survive during seasons of low productivity. Money for medical needs or emergencies is another problem.

In spite of the abundance of crops and fruits in the hacienda all the peasant families have to subsist on boiled camotes. Often, one can hear the children asking their mothers, "Mama, why are we always eating breakfasts?" — not knowing the terms for lunch or dinner because camote is the only food and it is associated with breakfast. Coconut-based products like margarine, bath or laundry soap and candies are all a rarity.

The coconut tenants became more and more dissatisfied with the conditions in the hacienda. As owner-cultivators once, they had known better days, and so there was great dissatisfaction with life in the hacienda. The landlord then introduced the Coconut Federation, more popularly known as COCOFED, an organization initiated by landlords claiming to be of service to the coconut farmers. The COCOFED promised the tenants the following:

1. the farmers would be assured of selling copra at a profit by setting up buying centers all over the country. This was necessary due to the fluctuating price of copra and the proliferation of copra dealers who buy copra at very low prices;
2. an insurance scheme providing P10,000 for the farmer in case of accidents or physical incapacity and the farmer would have to pay only 55 centavos every harvest time;
3. productivity would be increased by the creation of tractor cooperatives;
4. scholarships for children of coconut farmers would be made available.

Up to now, I have yet to see my father collect his insurance money after he met an accident and was rendered unfit for work. I had to quit school because we did not have a stable income and I could not get any scholarship from the COCOFED. We never got an opportunity to use a tractor either. We did see a lot of COCOFED T-shirts worn by some landlords and dealers at copra-buying stations but it made us very angry because they were buying copra at 75 centavos a kilo. Where did all the alleged benefits go?

The rice and corn tenants are doubly burdened in the hacienda. I wish to focus on the fate of tenant farmers under Presidential Decree 27, which is supposed to free the Filipino tenants from the bondage of the soil.

Tata Goring, an uncle of mine, had tilled the land for 38 years in the same hacienda where we are. He was informed that he could own the land if he met the following conditions:

1. that he becomes a member of the *Samahang Nayon*, a cooperative-type association of farmers organized under the government's land reform program.
2. that he joins the *Masagana 99* Program, which promotes the use of fertilizers, pesticides and special high-yielding variaties of rice, known as miracle rice, to increase production.
3. that his share from the harvest is about 75 per cent and this share will serve as a steady source of amortization payment.

It all seemed simple for Tata Goring, he imagined himself becoming an owner of the land and getting legal papers after 15 years. Together with other tenants, Tata Goring joined the Operation Land Transfer, a step towards becoming a landowner, where tenants are given land transfer certificates.

After several years, Tata Goring discovered that his land transfer certificate did not free him from incurring debts. The constant threat of his land being mortgaged due to inability to pay the amortizing fees; the costly measures of the Masagana 99 Program, which dictates that the farmers must get their fertilizers, seedlings and pesticides from a specified source at fixed prices; and increasing irrigation fees. All these became problems because of the rising cost of rice production and the low price of rice and corn.

Together with other members of the Operation Land Transfer, Tata Goring made an acccounting of the cost of rice production based on a farm of 3.5 hectares. The expenses can be broken down as follows:

Even under normal conditions, Tata Goring was spending

P17,998.00 but is only able to earn P17,710, thus incurring a deficit of P228.00 a year.

The farmers also discovered later that the seedlings being loaned to them, like the so-called miracle rice, were chemically dependent. The fertilizers given to them would sometimes be spoiled and the pesticides did not really protect the rice plants from a disease called 'tungro'.

The Samahang Nayon did not become an effective vehicle in staving off the economic difficulties of the farmers and so Tata Goring and other tenants organized a *luyo-luyo* or a mutual-exchange-of-labor-type brigade. The luyo-luyo provided the farmers with the needed labor during planting and harvest seasons and also a source of funds during emergencies.

While all the difficulties with the Land Reform Program were becoming pronounced, the relations with the landlord and the encargado were also becoming very tense. The landlord resented the fact that the tenants had joined the Operation Land Transfer. He took advantage of the situation by issuing orders through the encargado that no fruit or crop or any part of the coconut tree can be gathered free by tenants. All pig-raising projects by the luyo-luyo were prohibited and all those hired by the plantation would have to work very hard. The landlord set up a watchtower with a giant spotlight and a private army to guard the hacienda. All the measures were geared at making life very harsh for the farmers in the hacienda. The encargado saw to it that the farmers worked very hard without rest. Once, he even pointed his gun at Tata Goring for taking a siesta. He berated the farmers resting with Tata Goring, "You are all lazy people! You deserve less!". Tata Goring stood up and said, "We are kind to our animals. We put our carabaos under the shade and splash them with water at noon. If you want us to work harder, you must allow us to rest. But remember, we are not animals."

At the age of seventeen, I could see the greying hair of my parents. The long lines of wrinkles on their faces marked the long hard years of toil. I was wondering about their 'ten fingers', what they had brought them and what I was supposed to do with mine.

Life outside the hacienda was just as harsh. Our neighbor's son, Caloy, 25 years old, sold his carabao and plough, and together with other farmers sought jobs outside the farm. I heard that they were being recruited by an agency as construction workers for Saudi Arabia. His sister, Lina, who was about my age and who is my childhood friend was recruited by another agency for employment in Manila. Their younger brother, Armando, 19 years old, enlisted as a trainee in the Philippine Army. I found out later that Caloy never got to Saudi Arabia. Lina become a bar girl entertaining men in Manila and Armando was sent to Mindanao to fight. Tata Goring had to move out of his land because it was mortgaged and he ended up fishing in one of the coastal areas to survive.

There are many more cases of economic dislocations with hacienda farmers and peasants in neighbouring barrios. The worsening economic conditions attracted pro-government and anti-government groups to come to our place. We heard about an organization of farmers called MASAKA and its members would explain that the interest of the farmers could only be protected by a real peasant organization. Its objectives were directed towards land reform but when some of the tenants joined the MASAKA, they found out that it was promoting the Marcos land reform program. The farmers were disappointed because they knew that there was still no genuine land reform.

Talks about the New People's Army also reached our barrio. During one graduation celebration in the school hall, the hacienda encargado was riddled with bullets while dancing, and died on the spot, bathed in his own blood. The military said that the NPA killed him while others said that it could have been the landlord because the encargado's wife was his mistress.

Whoever did it, the people were happy about the death of the encargado because they were freed from his abuses. I was beginning to be curious about the NPA. Once, I overheard Tata Goring whispering to my father about a group of guerillas who might spend a night in our home. I decided to ask my mother about the NPA and she described them as good people who help oppressed people, especially the peasants. She also told me about my grandfather being sympathetic to the Huk guerillas, and that her family used to hide the guerillas during the Japanese Occupation. My grandfather died protecting these guerillas and so my mother knew the consequences of helping guerillas.

It was one moonlit night that we were awakened by Tata Goring. My father looked at my mother and beckoned her to light the kerosene lamp while he quietly looked through the small window opening. He opened the door and Tata Goring came in with four companions carrying long rifles. My father tried to calm our dog which had started to bark and my mother asked me to brew coffee and boil camotes. The four companions were introduced as friends, and they were members of the NPA. One of them was a woman and she approached me introducing herself as Ka. Mila. That night, my parents and Tata Goring discussed with them the problems and concrete conditions of the peasants in our place. I was impressed by these visitors. I got to sleep beside Ka. Mila and when I became more at ease, I started to ask her about the NPA. "Are you not afraid to carry a gun and walk in the dark?" I eagerly whispered. "Is it hard to be a woman guerilla?"

Mila responded warmly to all my questions. She shared with me her experiences as a peasant woman and how she became politically conscious. I will always remember how her voice became very firm when she said, "When we die, it is better to die fighting for freedom."

The armed propaganda units of the NPA frequently visited us. The discussions with them made me conscious of the need to be of more help to them. I was no longer contented with just cooking for the NPA and so I asked Ka. Mila about how to become more useful. She embraced me and said, "You can join us and become part of the armed propaganda unit."

It was on a warm evening when I kissed my parents good-bye. With their blessings and hugs of endearment, they entrusted me to the waiting comrades. My father blessed me and the comrades. "I cannot join you anymore in the mountains because my legs are already weak," he said, "I have only one child to do the task for me, but my heart goes with you in our struggle for justice and democracy."

Testimony of a migrant worker

This year, 1980, the Philippine Government aims to earn $1 billion from migrant Filipinos.

I am Celia Soliman, a Filipina working with *Kababayan*, an organization of Filipino migrant workers in Rome, Italy. I shall speak about the situation of migrant workers abroad, especially in Europe. My presentation will include testimony from migrant workers who are not able to testify here themselves. These migrant workers are unable to be here because of two reasons: one is their fear of speaking out in public due to their legal status; the other is their work situation, the near impossibility of getting time off from work.

I will begin with a case involving Filipina migrant workers in Belgium late last year and early this year.

In November and December 1979 the Belgian police for foreigners, arrested and subsequently repatriated some twenty Filipina women, who had been illegally employed in Belgium as domestic workers. These women, however, had been unaware of their illegal status since the travel agency which processed their travelling documents in Manila had neglected to tell them — despite the fact that they paid for it — that the Belgian government no longer grants new work permits to foreigners. The women were kept under administrative detention, meaning in jail, pending their repatriation. Aware of the fact that they had been victimized by illegal recruiters and travel agencies in their home country, and had also, in some cases, been exploited by their employers in Belgium, the Ministry of Justice decided not to file any charges against them.

A four-month period of silence ensued without further police action being taken. This interval was used to give the case some prominence in the local press, but even more so abroad, in order to alert possible candidates for emigration from the Philippines or other countries about the suspension imposed by Belgian authorities on the issue of labour permits to foreign workers. At the same time reports from Manila confirmed that the travel agency propagating this human traffic had already replaced its contact person in Belgium who had been arrested along with the others. It was clear that there was no intention whatsoever from their side to give up this profitable trade. The women who had been repatriated in December had either been provided with a free ticket for a second chance abroad or were bribed into silence by the travel agency. Only two resisted these offers and decided to sue the travel agency before a Philippine court.

A second wave of arrests, involving illegally employed Filipina workers in Belgium, occurred during the last week of April 1980. This time, the women were either registered in the municipality where they stayed or had applied for a work permit under the au-pair status. Other Filipinas who were employed by foreign embassy or NATO personnel, and as such cannot be touched by Belgian law, were questioned as to the whereabouts of their friends.

One woman was picked up on Tuesday, 24 April, to be followed by seven more arrests. All had been invited for an interview regarding their applications for work permits. However, instead of the promised interview, they were questioned and placed under administrative detention. (Commission for Justice and Peace, Tweekerkenstraat 17, 1040 Brussels, Belgium).

This is not an isolated case. Similar incidents have occured and are occuring in many countries of Europe. These women and the thousands of other Filipinos like them are part of the Philippine government's export of labor trade. In 1978, 45,000 Filipinos left the Philippines to work in 103 countries in line with the government's program to sell its labor force. They are among the thousands who are making migrant work one of the top dollar earners for the Philippine government. This year, 1980, the Philippine government aims to earn $1 billion from migrant

Filipinos. The *Far Eastern Economic Review* of 26 September 1980 writes:

> In only five years the Philippines has graduated into the first division of labor-exporting nations, with a present ranking, according to the Ministry of Labor and Employment (MOLE), of No. 7 worldwide. The marketing of talent, muscle and training brought foreign exchange remittances of an estimated $1 billion in 1979. That compared impressively with merchandise export receipts of $1.74 billion. The number of men and women placed abroad in 1979 represents a four-fold increase over the previous five years.
>
> The Philippine government began their big push to sell labor abroad in 1974, when the total outflow of 'land-based' workers, as opposed to seamen, totalled 11,614. In the first six months of this year (1980), the flow was 44,621, in addition to 34,056 seamen (21,540 in 1974). The total recorded outflow between 1974 and 1980 was 492,255 (268,774 'land-based'; 223,541 seamen).

The exact number of Filipino migrant workers in any country is never known. Many of them enter the country as tourists and stay on to work. In Britain there is an estimated 20,000 Filipino migrant workers working as domestics, hotel workers and hospital workers. In Germany there is an estimated 6,000 working as nurses or mid-wives; in Spain, 6,000; in Italy, over 15,000, working mostly as domestic workers.

Most of the Filipino migrant workers who come to Europe are women, a large percentage of whom are professionals: nurses, teachers, midwives, social workers. They are forced to accept low income jobs and work long, hard hours. They are silent victims of exploitation.

Their exploitation begins in the Philippines. Because of the government's encouragement to find work abroad, hundred of legal and illegal recruiting agencies fleece money from the Filipino migrant workers to process their papers. The same *Far Eastern Economic Review* article states:

> ... the industry is being plagued by an undiminishing number of so-called 'illegal recruiters' — fly-by-night operators who sell promises of overseas jobs that do not exist ... MOLE experts say operators first advertise in newspapers or simply spread the word in a town or neighbourhood. Respondents are initially charged about

P300 (US$40), supposedly for passport and other expenses. The victim is later told that a job is available, perhaps as a housekeeper for the fabulous monthly pay of US$300 plus room and board. A similar position brings less than P100 in most Philippine households, so when the recruiter adds that it will cost anywhere from P3,000 to P15,000 in advance, to secure the contract, many do their best to comply. Families sell their working animals and even their land, borrow from loan sharks and take on extra jobs, all expecting that within a year everyone will be amply repaid ... there are already serious questions about the ability or willingness of the Marcos regime to take rigorous steps against the illegal recruiters. Corruption is also considered a problem. In cases where victims have been jailed overseas after flying to non-existent jobs, operators had been able to obtain not only passports which passed Philippine immigration scrutiny, but also official exit permits. More significantly, while illegal recruitment grows, MOLE studies show that nearly all operators charged so far have got off almost scot-free. Some blatantly resume business while out on bail.

What does this mean to the Filipinos who are victims of these agencies? Here are some of their statements:

1. I was happy and excited. What I did not understand was that after I was already in the plane, I was asked for my return ticket. The agency's representative came just before the plane left. I was excited. So, I just signed everything. He got my return ticket, even my travellers cheques of $250. All I had was $5 when I arrived in Rome. I immediately got a job but my first employer was a bad man. I was stranded for six months before I could find another job.

2. I was met in Rome by the agency's representative. He said that the Italian government prohibits the giving of work to foreigners, especially Filipinos. I did not know if this was true or not. Suddenly I felt very weak. I went out of Rome and found a job cleaning a theatre, a school, a gymnasium and a swimming pool. And I received only 3,500 lire (about $4.00) a day. Oh it was very hard. My body and mind could not bear it! I said to myself, I will just go home to Manila. Anyway, I still had my return ticket. When I tried to confirm my flight, the airline said my ticket was a stolen ticket. They took it away from me. I was able to get back to Manila

only with the help of my relatives who spent P9,000. What I am wondering now is, how can I pay back my debt. Moreover, I had sold a lot of my possessions ...

3. From Manila, we flew to Paris. There we were instructed to take a train to Brussels. We were told we would find jobs in Brussels ... After one year we were arrested. Some of us were imprisoned. Others were expelled, and put on a plane back to the Philippines. I feel deeply the loss of P15,000 which I spent in order to leave the Philippines. What is our crime? Is it right to penalize and accuse us? Is it a crime to work in another country? We cannot find work in our own country.

The dream of finding better conditions abroad than in the Philippines becomes a nightmare. Often the promised job does not exist. Sometimes it means being forced into prostitution. For others it has meant forced marriages to allow them to work in another country. For all, it holds untold pain, suffering and loneliness.

In Italy, most Filipina migrants end up as domestic workers. Once in Italy, they are again at the mercy of unscrupulous agencies and employers because of their precarious situation as clandestine workers. Not knowing the language of the country, they are usually kept in ignorance of the labor laws which are meant to protect them, and of their rights as workers, concerning job security, insurance, minimum pay, holidays and time off. It is not unusual to find the Filipina domestics working ten or twelve hours a day, completely uninsured, at less than minimum pay with their airfare illegally deducted from their already meagre pay by their employer.

This is how some Filipinas describe their work:

1. Sometimes I cannot bear to think about our conditions here. It is like being in prison. It is so lonely just being by myself. Just think how long the hours of work are. Besides having to do heavy work, there is no overtime pay. I am given the responsibility over their children. Sometimes I am ordered to clean the car or to garden or to decorate the house. So, I do not even get a full day off which I am supposed to be entitled to have. And it is so cold here in this small room!

2. The food given is lacking. Sometimes, you are even insulted. If you are not strong your head will break and you might even think of committing suicide.

This is all part of the nightmare: the hard work and the inner pain; the incomparable sadness; the separation from home and loved ones; the adjustment to a new culture and a new language; legal papers to worry about; anxiety about the police; the low and inadequate salary; the debts incurred to come and which have to be repaid ...

Domestic work means cleaning a whole house, cooking, washing a heap of dishes and glasses, hands soaked in cold and hot water, washing and ironing, getting shouted at when a mistake is made, burns in the hands, a painful reminder of where the Filipino migrant worker is and what she is. And still through it all, she is supposed to remain 'joyful and smiling' because that is what her employer expects of her.

The Filipino migrant workers have asked themselves: how long will it last? The anxiety of not having legal papers that can help make life a bit more secure; the injustice of not receiving even the minimum wage for domestic workers; of having no one to defend their rights.

From among their ranks has come the answer itself. 'Even if we are afraid, we must organize ourselves. It is only when we are organized that we can help ourselves.' 'There are so many of us — why don't we get organized?'

In Italy, several labor organizations have expressed their interest in the case of the Filipino migrant workers. They have offered their services and the services of a team of lawyers to help the migrants. They are trying to work to have laws passed to give the migrants the same rights as Italian workers.

From among the migrants, the seeds of their organization is already beginning. They realize that only in organizing themselves will they be able to fight to defend their rights, to work for better working conditions and to be able to face the world with dignity and self-respect.

The roots of the problem remain, however. These are:

1. Marcos' political and economic policies which force thousands of Filipinos to go abroad to find jobs due to unemployment at home.
2. The policy of using migrant labor to get foreign exchange.
3. The collusion between the Philippine government and legal and illegal travel and employment agencies.
4. The inadequate information and protection given by the Philippine government to Filipino workers abroad.

Testimony of women

Because of their double oppression (economic and male domination), women have found their way into the resistance and the National Democratic Movement.

I am Perla Silangan, aged 22, a college student in the Philippines. I am testifying on behalf of the Filipino women.

Filipino women compose more than one half of the Philippines' population of 48 million. They are of all classes. The vast majority of Filipino women, therefore, belong to the oppressed and exploited masses. Already oppressed and exploited with our male counterparts, we Filipino women, are additionally oppressed simply because we are women.

I have experienced this additional oppression in my family. My family belongs to the middle class or petty bourgeoisie. My father being a government employee and my mother a teacher. My mother would teach me that the place of woman is in the home and her crown of glory is the success of her children and that the man is the breadwinner of the family. My brothers were free to go wherever they wanted. They didn't have any restrictions nor did they have to do housework, while we, women in the family, had to do everything. This discrimination was heightened when I became involved in the struggle for liberation. I had to be away from home most of the time then; my work of organizing and mobilizing students plus my studies made it impossible for me to perform household chores. I was castigated not just for my involvement but also for neglect of duties as a woman member of the family, and for my insistence on being treated equally with my brothers.

They insisted that women should not take part in such

political activities because this is men's work. Furthermore, this involvement interfered with my household duties. This conflict intensified with my parents, my sister and my brothers.

Even when we would go on visits to friends of the family, I also noted the women were treated by the men as inferiors. While the men relax and talk about national politics and the international situation, we women, have to go to the kitchen and prepare the food or look after the children. Women are not allowed to participate in the discussions. They are relegated to the background and are expected to know nothing of the society or the world. Their world is confined to the home.

If as a member of the middle class I already had to experience such oppression and discrimination, how much more is the oppression felt by my sisters who work in factories and farms or are employed in private and government offices or in the entertainment business?

Exploitation and Oppression in the Tourism and Entertainment Industry

Thousands of my sisters have fallen into additional degradation by having to work as a-go-go dancers, hostesses, sauna bath attendants, call-girls and prostitutes because of desperate poverty and unemployment. The government encourages this use of women in the tourist industry, which *Asia Women's Liberation*, a Japanese magazine, bluntly calls 'prostitution tourism'. There are about 120 flesh shops in Manila's tourist belt; 21 are accredited by the Ministry of Tourism and licensed by City Hall. Each shop has 80 to 200 hospitality girls employed by accredited tour agencies. (*Bulletin Today*, 21 August 1980). Typically, a large Japanese operator will advertise a 'package tour' to the Philippines in cooperation with a Manila agent. The deal includes everything from shopping to hotel, and women who are either chosen from pictures in Japan or selected in person in one of the large clubs.

These men pay an average of US$60 for one night with a woman. But a woman receives very little of this money. The following is a rough breakdown: clubowner — US$15; local guide — US$10; Japanese guide — US$10. Total US$60. The woman receives between US$4.25 and US$5.75 from the owner's share. (Source: A. Lin Newman, "Hospitality Girls in the Philippines", in *Southeast Asia Chronicle* Jan - Feb. 1979). Hospitality girls are more concentrated in areas where many foreigners are, notably US military bases in Angeles and Olongapo. Many of our sisters who have to prostitute themselves are barely out of their teens with the youngest at 14 or 15. The government classifies the hospitality girls as professionals under section 679 of its Labor Code but does not give them the rights accorded to professional workers.

Let me tell you about Beth, a sauna bath attendant who lives in the outskirts of Tondo. She comes from a middle peasant family. Though poor, they were able to send her to high school. She decided afterwards to go to Manila to work because there were no job opportunities in the province. She left home at the age of 18.

In Manila, she soon discovered that her educational attainment was not enough to get her a good job. Offices in Manila only look for college students or graduates. In the end she got a job as a waitress in a Chinese restaurant. A year later, she met and lived with a married man whom she thought loved her more than his own wife. She found out too late that he only wanted her body. He left her when she got pregnant. Her parents, disapproving of her actions, disowned her.

After giving birth, Beth continued working as a waitress but her pay of P8.00 was insufficient to feed 2 mouths. The baby needed milk and nourishment. With the increases in the prices of rice, food and other basic necessities they could no longer live on her wages.

Finally, she swallowed her pride and took a job in a massage parlour. The salary was about the same as in the restaurant, but she could double the amount with tips from the tourists, especially the Japanese who frequented the place. She could earn more, but she had to be prepared to go to rooms. Beth despised the job, but was forced by poverty and the needs of her child.

Like Beth, there are many more of my sisters in the provinces who are driven by rural poverty to the cities. But jobs in the cities are scarce and the wages low. Out of necessity many women are forced to work in the hospitality industry.

Exploitation and Oppression of Women Peasants

By the middle part of 1980, my work brought me to the rural areas. It was then that I saw the conditions of peasants and national minorities under this 'New Society'.

Women peasants share the burden of feudal exploitation

suffered by the whole class. The peasantry suffers from the exploitative landlord-tenant relationship, usury, price manipulation, and are forced to give free menial services to the landlords. However, the woman peasants suffer further exploitation. In doing the jobs on the farm, like transplanting, weeding, harvesting and drying, the women are paid much less than the men. Such underpricing of the labor of the peasant women can be shown in the following examples. In Hacienda Recato in Bicol, women farm workers are given only P5 to P7 a day while the men receive P10 - P12. In Hacienda Miranda in Central Luzon, the women workers are given P12 - P15a day while the men receive P20 - P24.

Aside from this, the typical role of a woman in the rural community is that of a mother and a housekeeper. Housekeeping, for which she is not paid, is more than a full time job, every day of the year. Even if the woman works with her husband on the farm she still has to shoulder the full responsibility of the household work. Men in general do not help with domestic chores.

Rural women compared to their urban counterparts suffer more deplorable conditions. Their educational attainment is much lower than that of the urban women, only 25 per cent have completed elementary education even though it is free. This lack of education is caused by extreme poverty and the traditional preference of male over female in career opportunities. Due to poor nutrition and the lack of medical facilities in the rural areas, childbirth can be hazardous to both mother and child. The incidence of miscarriage and infant mortality is alarmingly high at 47 per cent.

Moreover, the heightened militarization of the countryside under the Marcos regime brings additional problems to the peasants, especially the women. I would like now to talk about the case of Ka Lina, a peasant woman.

I met Ka Lina in Bicol, June 1980. She is 27 years old, married, with 5 children. She is a victim of military atrocities in Bicol: her husband is dead, two of her children were wounded, and her left arm was amputated as a result of the atrocity perpetrated by the Philippine constabulary. This is how it happened:

They were peacefully sleeping one night when all of a sudden they were awakened by the sound of gunfire. Her left arm went numb. She discovered that a bullet had hit her. Then she heard someone shouting from the outside that those wounded would be treated and those dead would be left inside the house. When she went outside, she saw that there were Philippine Constabulary (PC) men outside. They took her husband to the Municipal Hall because he was dead. Her children were left beside her. One child was hit in the head and in the back. The other was hit in the stomach and on the knee.

Twenty-four PC men attacked their house — all armed with high powered armalite rifles. They suspected that there were NPAs inside their house. The PC themselves found out that there was none. It was only her husband, herself and her five children who were in the house.

When the PC found out that there were no NPAs inside the house, they took her and the wounded children to the hospital. Her husband was left in the Municipal Hall, and her three children who were not wounded were left with their neighbors. In the hospital her left arm was amputated and the wounds of her two children were treated. The PC only paid the expenses for their hospitalization and medicines for a few days so she had to go to her parents who are also poor, to seek assistance and she got help from them. The PC maintained that this assistance actually came from the NPA.

Her eldest son who was hit in the knee is now lame, the other became mentally ill, and the younger ones are still suffering from shock. They cower in fear whenever they see persons carrying guns.

Military atrocities like this happen all over the country and affect men and women alike. But when soldiers commit abuses women usually suffer the additional assault of being sexually abused.

Cristina — A Woman Worker

I would like to tell you about Christina, a woman worker whom I met and interacted with during a study on the condition of women in the Philippines. This study on women took eight months.

When I first met her, Cristina was only nineteen and was working as a sewing machine operator in Capital Garments Industry, Metro Manila. This company employs 90 per cent women workers. Cristina has been working since the age of fifteen to help out her family.

Cristina has to produce a quota of $500 worth of goods per day to earn a minimum standard rate of P13.50 (less than

US$2.00). However, she can only sew $450 worth, which is the most her fellow workers can produce as well. She has to work overtime in order to reach this quota, but she does not receive any money for working overtime. The workers who fail to reach the quota receive a warning, or lose their jobs. Even after working in the firm for five years a person can still be given notice for failing to achieve the quota. Cristina, in order to reach the quota, refrains from going to the toilet when she needs to. Even if she is hungry she works through the lunch break of thirty minutes. Because the canteen is very small, she simply sits on the floor of the factory to eat her food. And still she has no guarantee of permanency. The management can fire a person anytime, without prior notice.

Another problem, she says, is the management's practice of depressing wages below the minimum. They impose a training period of 6 months for each new worker. During this period the trainees receive P6.00 per day (less than US$1.00) with no emergency living allowance and before the 6th month is reached many are laid off. This is done to avoid regularization of casuals. The workers are laid off for a few weeks or sometimes months and then rehired with a new contract. Because of this, the workers cannot earn enough to meet the subsistence requirements of the average Filipino family. Even with two family members working full time in this company, it is still not possible to earn enough for their needs. For this reason, in many families, like Cristina's, the mother and two or more daughters are working in factories to help make ends meet. These women start work at an early age to contribute to the support of their families. Most of them have only completed elementary school education before starting to work.

The National Minority Women

Our national minority sisters, like the peasant women, have to be mothers and housekeepers, as well as having to work on the farm.

While they are encouraged to attend meetings, women do not in general have much influence in decision making. They may express their opinion occasionally, but their words do not carry much weight.

The national minorities suffer from harrassment by the military. Apart from this military terrorism, the women are also victims of the sexual violence committed by the soldiers of the government.

A Catholic publication, ICHTYS, in its 10 January, 1978 issue, documented a case of six women being raped at the PC Ababba headquarters during an evacuation and relocation of the people in Northern Luzon.

Apart from these acts of atrocities, soldiers prey on the native women, luring them into committing sexual acts by promises of marriage. Most of those deceived are later abandoned by the soldiers when they become pregnant.

Even pregnant women are not free from abuses by the military. In an incident in Pikit, Northern Cotabato, on 22 September, 1979, after the barrio was raided and ramsacked, and some of the men tortured, resulting in the death of one, the soldiers then assaulted a pregnant woman which resulted in her giving birth to a still born baby. Her husband, Belnate Ayob, recounted his wife's ordeal:

> My pregnant wife and my sister were told to go down to the kitchen, and there my wife was told to undress. Then the soldiers poked the butts of their rifle at her belly. The next morning, as we feared, she started having pains and gave birth prematurely to a dead baby. (See *Tribal Forum*, January - February, 1980, page 17.)

Women in the National Democratic Movement.

Because of their double oppression, women have found their way into the resistance and the National Democratic Movement. Women in the revolutionary struggle fight side by side with the men against the people's enemies in the armed struggle in the countryside and in the underground movement in towns and cities. However, we women, aside from facing up to the basic problems of Philippine society, have our own struggle to wage. Because even among those of us who are already in the revolutionary struggle, many, especially male comrades, have feudal and bourgeois attitudes towards women. One of the ways this manifests itself is in the structure and bias in job assignments. For instance when I first joined the movement my job was to type and file papers. When, after six months, I wanted to learn and develop organizing skills, it took a lot of persuasion before I was assigned to the rural areas. Later, when I was ready to take the responsibility of organising peasants in the 'white areas' — i.e. areas outside the guerrilla zones — I had to convince the male comrades once again of my ability to do so.

This feudal and bourgeois attitude can be and should be

corrected. In numerous incidents women have shown in discussion and practice that they are as capable as the men.

The national democratic struggle cannot be a total people's effort without the participation of women who compose half of the population. But we women also believe that aside from participating with the men and children in the struggle, we should persevere in the distinct struggle which will liberate women from the added exploitation and domination of the 'male authority in this semi-colonial and semi-feudal society'.

We salute our sister comrades who have served and died for the people! They are models of truly liberated womanhood for all Filipino women.

Testimonies on political repression

The forms, functions and causes of political repression in the Philippines

by Walden Bello

The Authoritarian Viewpoint

Every regime constructs a rationale for its existence, a philosophical justification that both reveals and obscures the essence of that government. The Marcos state is no exception. Yet, it has been exceptional in one sense: it has been more explicit than others in its rejection of the ideals of democratic rule and popular representation that peoples have universally struggled for since the eighteenth century. In the classic words of the dictator himself during the fourth month of martial law, "The times are too grave and the stake too high for us to permit the customary concessions to traditional democratic processes."[1]

In its effort to make the dictatorship respectable, the regime has elaborated the ideology of 'constitutional authoritarianism'. The first premise of this ideology is that the Filipino people are incapable of democratic government. The Ministry of Public Information does not mince words: "We Filipinos are a people whose flamboyant self-indulgence is legendary. Most of us live by the day, and *bahala na* (nor let fate take its course) for tomorrow. Among such an aimless people Marcos is remarkable."[2]

Given our alleged congenital incapacity for self-rule, the dictatorship contends that the first and main aim of the government is to establish order and authority. As the 'remarkable' leader himself declared during a visit to the United States in April 1980, "All that people ask for is some kind of authority that

Prof. Walden Bello — Writer, Berkeley, USA.

can enforce the simple law of civil society.''[3] Moreover, Marcos fancies his system to have universal application — to be a 'third way for the third world'. For, from what he regards as the teeming, 'undisciplined' masses of the underdeveloped world, "Only an authoritarian system will be able to carry forth the mass consent and to exercise the authority necessary to implement new values, measures and sacrifices.''[4]

Order, not representation; authority, not democracy — the formulation may be new and attractive, but the essence of the prescription is not. Here, in new language, is the old principle of reaction that was disguised as 'benevolent despotism' in eighteenth century Europe, 'enlightened stewardship' in American imperial ideology, and Mission Civilatrice in French colonial doctrine. Even in its new formulation, the theory is hardly Third World in origin, as Marcos claims. It is lifted, almost word for word, from the work of Samuel Huntington, the Harvard political scientist who justified the carpetbombing of Vietnam's rural areas on the grounds that it was creating an urban, modern society; and legitimized by invoking the authority of that spokesman of cynical and weary American liberalism, Robert Heilbroner.[5] The only novel feature is that its practitioner, despite his contempt for the Filipino people, presents himself as one of us.

Uprooting Democratic Habits

Old habits die hard. The pre-martial law system of elitist, formal democracy was certainly far from ideal, but the Filipino people's aspirations for genuinely democratic government have been much too ingrained to be uprooted overnight. The dictatorship has thus been forced into perverse attempts to cloak its authoritarian essence with democratic forms.

The Question of Constitutionality

The social contract between governors and the governed is enshrined in the written constitution. So sacred is the notion of formal constitutional contract that no dictatorship can afford not to fabricate one. Again, the Marcos dictatorship is distinguished by the fact that it claims to rule under *two* constitutions — the 1935 charter of the pre-martial law Republic and the 1973 Marcos constitution. The dictator claims to derive his power to declare and maintain martial law from the 1935 charter and his absolute authority from the 1973 constitution.

Mr Marcos claims to be both president by virtue of the 1935 constitution — which he, at the same time, declares to have been superseded — and prime minister under the 1973 constitution.[6] This, of course, defies all canons of constitutional law and, indeed, all the arts of legal casuistry.

Yet the even greater outrage is that the 1973 Marcos constitution is clearly illegal. It was rammed through by pro-Marcos members of the Constitutional Convention on 30 November, 1972, under full martial law conditions, with the intimidating presence of the military in the hall, and with the political opposition in jail or in hiding. The document was then 'ratified' in January 1973 by what the *New York Times* described as 'obviously figleaf' citizens assemblies hastily convened for the occasion, in order to circumvent the legally necessary national referendum.[7] The social contract between Marcos' regime and the Filipino people is non-existent. The whole elaborate edifice of the martial law state rests not on law, but on a foundation of arbitrary power.

The Separation of Powers
To the authoritarian mind, democracy is time-consuming. The give-and-take of democratic decision-making is seen as a 'democratic stalemate'. Thus, the principle of the separation-of-powers or checks-and-balances, so central to the democratic tradition and the fragile product of centuries of struggle against tyranny, is dismissed by ideological spokesmen of the regime as a Western, Lockean institution irrelevant to the Philippine experience: But, like the written constitution, it is another one of those addictions from which the regime cannot easily wean the Filipino people: thus, the Marcos constitution provides, grudgingly, for the existence of a National Assembly and a Judiciary. But the relationships among the Executive, the Legislature, and the Judiciary are, both in theory and practice, quite different in the Marcos state from those in a democracy.

The concept of the Legislature checking the Executive has been banished and replaced by a relationship of pure subservience. The role of the Interim National Assembly is to provide a modicum of legitimacy for the initiatives of the dictatorship and refine them for public consumption. Perhaps, most revealing in this regard is the opinion of Cesar Virata, one of the regime's top technocrats, regarding the greatest virtue of the National Assembly: "We can now get major legislation passed in a month-and-a-half, whereas previously it would have taken no less than six months.''[9] This 'efficiency' rests on the fact that the Assembly is almost completely dominated by members of the dictatorship's New Society Party (KBL), who were installed in office during the fraudulent parliamentary elections of April, 1978. Indeed, so subservient are these legislative 'fiscalizers' that they now wish to erase even the facade of legislative independence by proposing to formally legislate the granting to Mr Marcos of the power to 'prolong the detention period for persons charged with crimes against national security and to exercise such other powers as he may deem necessary and proper to execute'.[10]

The judiciary has suffered a fate even worse than the legislature: it has become an arm of the repressive apparatus of the state. Military tribunals responsible only to their commander-in-chief, Ferdinand Marcos, have systematically usurped jurisdiction over political cases from a timid, cowering civilian judiciary.

"Martial law is to law what martial music is to music," former US Attorney General Ramsey Clark once observed.[11] The state of justice in the Philippines today, which might be said to be court martial writ large, provides a perfect illustration of Clark's dictum. All steps of the criminal justice system, particularly in the area of 'political crimes', are effectively dominated by the military: suspects are apprehended by military security agencies, imprisoned and tortured at military camps like Fort Bonifacio and camp Aguinaldo, prosecuted by military lawyers, and judged by military commissions. In spite of repeated promises by the dictator to turn over political cases to civilian judges, military tribunals continue to reign supreme over these courts.

The quality of martial justice is perhaps most clearly revealed in the well-publicised showcase trial of the torturers of Ms Trinidad Herrera, the famous leader of Manila's urban poor. Despite overwhelming evidence that would have secured their conviction in a civilian court, the two military men were shielded by a barb wire of military procedure that was systematically biased against their accuser, resulting in their acquital by a tribunal of colleagues who concluded that Ms. Herrera had inflicted the torture marks on herself![12]

The meek submission of the civilian judiciary to the executive is one of the lowest points in the history of the legal profession in the Philippines. No voice of protest was uttered when Mr Marcos demanded and got the undated letters of resignation from appeals and lower-court judges. Nor was there the slightest resistance to Section 9 of the Transitory Provisions of the Marcos Constitution which made the continued tenure of the justices of the Supreme Court dependent on the whims of the dictator.[13] Indeed, not only was there scarcely a protest, but some justices of the Supreme Court, like their colleagues in Chile, have gone out of their way to justify and attempt to popularize martial law. At the August 1977 Conference on the International Legal Protection of Human Rights in Manila, Associate Justices Fred Ruiz Castro and Enrique Fernando asserted that human rights and martial law were not only not contradictory, but that they were complementary. Then, without blushing, they went on to articulate the regime's grand Catch-22: that the martial law system was constitutional because the Supreme Court had examined all challenges to it and declared them insufficient or irrelevant.[14]

Perhaps the most appropriate verdict on the state of the separation of powers is still that made by the Amnesty International in 1976:

"... Stripped of its jurisdiction and independence, the judiciary of the Philippines has become totally ineffective in preventing the violations of human rights.

... The rule of law under martial law is authoritarian presidential-military rule, unchecked by constitutional guarantee or limitation."[15]

Representation

The casting of the ballot with free choice is the primordial act of representative democracy. Unable to dispense with the ballot before a people who have been socialized to regard it as the fountainhead of democratic legitimacy, Ferdinand Marcos, like his colleague Augusto Pinochet in Chile, has resorted to rigged referenda and elections. The precedent for the cynical manipulation of the electoral process was set during the 'ratification' of the Marcos constitution by 'Citizens' Assemblies' in early January 1973. Primitivo Mijares, former chief propaganda spokesman for the regime and self-described as the 'Joseph Goebbels of Marcos', had this to say of the results at hearings at the US Congress:

... There really was no referendum at all, the votes reported to the President by a Committee ... (were) manufactured by this group and I was part of this group. We were able to arrive at the figures reported to the President by simply going over the election figures of the previous elections and then deciding how many votes we will report against. We even were very careful and saw to it that we reported abstention votes.[16]

Mijares' revelation was learned the hard way by Fox Butterfield, correspondent of the *New York Times*, who was apprehended by guards and pushed down the stairs after accidentally walking into a vote-tampering session by Marcos' Commission on Elections while covering the 17 April, 1978 elections to the Interim National Assembly.[17]

Backstage fraud, however, gave way to open terrorism during the local elections of January 1980, which saw the Marcos party, the New Society Movement (KBL) win over 94 per cent of all governships and 91 per cent of all mayorships.[18] Troops were openly used to deliver votes, and in what was probably the most blatant case of fraud, 500 school teachers were herded into a room and forced to file election returns favouring the local Marcos candidate.[19] The elections were so fraudulent that Mr Marcos thought it the better part of political wisdom to admit his party had cheated, while relegating responsibility to his subordinates. "No press release can hide the truth," admitted Teodoro Valencia, the regime's current most favored propagandist, who, perhaps inadvertently, revealed that Mr Marcos' subordinates "thought that victory at any price was what the president would find pleasing."[20]

The Fundamental Political Freedoms

Freedom of Speech and Freedom of the Press

"What happens," asks O.D. Corpuz, the New Society counterpart of Hitler's Alfred Rosenberg, "if the right of free expression is exercised against the government?" His answer: "The right of free expression is not justified if it tends to create a danger to the state. No government in the world tolerates, much less protects, sedition and rebellion in the guise of free expression."[21]

Equated by the New Society's Hobbesian minds to sedition in a Third World context, the freedoms of speech and the press were the first victims of martial law. The first item of Presidential Proclamation 1081 directed the Secretary of National Defense to:

take over and control or cause the taking over and control of all such newspapers, magazines, radio and television facilities and all other media communications, wherever they are, for the duration of the present national emergency or until otherwise ordered by me or my duly designated representative.

In the next few weeks, 404 media were seized by the military, including 26 major circulation magazines, 600 television channels, 312 national and provisional radio stations.[22]

Letter of Instruction No. 1 was followed by General Order No. 2-A, which ordered the arrest of the nation's leading journalists; and by the notorious General Order No. 19, which decreed it a crime to spread political rumors — the so-called edict on 'rumor-mongering'.

The iron fist of martial law did not exempt media belonging to the Catholic Church, five of which have been ordered closed since 1976. Nor has it failed to touch foreign correspondents, many of whom have been harassed, arrested or eased out of their jobs like Bernard Wideman of the *Far Eastern Economic Review*, or expelled, like Arnold Zeitlin of the Associated Press.[23]

The contempt with which the New Society regards freedom of speech is perhaps best symbolised in the way it treated Saturnino Ocampo, former vice-president of the National Press Club and business editor of the *Manila Times*: he was forced fed human waste by his military torturers — an act reminiscent of the punishment visited by the Chilean folksinger and guitarist, Victor Jara, whose fingers were broken one by one while being taunted to sing. It is indeed worthwhile to recount more fully for this audience the barbarities visited on this fervent defender of free expression and nationalism, who is one of the regime's longest held political prisoners.

Blindfolded and manacled, he was seated in a rattan chair and given electric shocks by taping on his wrist one end of live wire and pressing an electrically charged spoon on his penis and testicles. His torturers also poured Cola drinks on his lower torso and on the points of electric contacts to maximise the shock effects. At the same time, his interrogator slapped him hard on both ears, pulled back his head by his hair, struck his oesophagus with finger flicks, twisted his nose and hit his head with fists. Still refusing to answer questions he was stripped naked and cola drinks and cold water were poured all over his body ... The electrically charged spoon was repeatedly pressed on several parts of

his body, like the   hands, thighs, testicles, penis, groin, ab-
domen, chest, nipples, shoulders, neck, chin, face and nose ... He
was also beaten with a stick on his thighs and legs and the soles
of his feet. He was spat upon. His mouth was forced open and
he was fed with human excreta. To open his mouth, his throat
was sqeezed or tightly gripped until he vomited. Lighted cigarettes were placed on his nipples, on the corner of his mouth and
his toes. His torturers kept saying that they could leave him inutile or mentally deranged.[24]

Freedom of Movement

'Population control' in more senses than one, might be said to
be the regime's basic policy towards the Filipino people. Control
is exercised through curtailment of the freedom of movement of
Filipinos. The declaration of martial law in September 1972 was
accompanied by the imposition of a midnight curfew which was
in effect nationally until late 1977 and continues in force in
many areas deemed 'sensitive' until today.

Letter of Instruction No. 4, issued the very day martial law
was declared, banned Filipinos from travelling abroad. Travel
rights, according to the International Commission of Jurists,
continue to be restricted 'to exact from those in opposition to
the government from criticizing or carrying out anti-government
criticism abroad'.[25] The Manila International Airport has
become, in effect, an international checkpoint, where the names
of travellers entering or exiting the country are scrutinized by
security agents against a 'bluebook' containing the names of real
or potential dissenters.

The freedom to move on the part of poor people has recently
been sharply curtailed by the introduction of the regime's
'Return to the Province Program'. Under this scheme, rural
families will be prevented from migrating to Manila. Current
residents of the city will be issued identification cards to separate
them from those the government regards as 'intruders'. According to the governor of Metro-Manila, the government "will see
to it that the family really boards the boat or the bus going
home".[26] Is this not the embryo of a pass system like South
Africa's, except that in place of race as the criterion of
discrimination, we have class?

Academic Freedom

The institutionalization of academic freedom prior to martial
law made Philippine centers of learning among the most vibrant

in the world. Martial rule has sought to turn them into intellectual graveyards. Government security forces have systematically and periodically converted the campus into a hunting ground for suspected activists. The threat of detention and harassment has effectively stifled the free exchange of ideas, forcing the enterprising student or professor to resort to Aesopian formulations of political and social criticisms. The more outspoken and forthright risk certain arrest, like the many student leaders who have been apprehended since April for attacking the regime's master plan for fascist socialization — the National Education Act of 1980.[27]

The National Education Act will complete the intellectual castration of the Philippine university system by formally taking away from the university community and handing to government technocrats the fundamental right to determine what to teach, who may be qualified to teach, who may be admitted to study, and how instruction will be carried out.[28]. Indeed, more than academic freedom is involved in this matter, but the very ability of the university to train free thinking individuals. This World Bank-supported effort seeks no less than a radical reorientation of Philippine education from the cultivation of critical intellectuals and scholars to the mass production of apolitical technicians.[29]

Fundamental Human Rights

In the world of Thomas Hobbes, the father of modern authoritarian ideology, the people surrender their political and civil rights to the absolute monarch in exchange for the latter's protection of their lives, limb and property. Thus, the 'war of all' is replaced by the placid social order of despotism in which life becomes nasty, less brutish, and less short.

The world dominated by Mr. Marcos is constructed on the principles of Hobbes; and like all Hobbesian worlds, reality is very different from ideology. The regime staked its legitimacy on its promise to provide basic security for life and limb. But it is now, in fact, the major threat to the Filipino's life and limb.

The Writ of Habeas Corpus

The abolition of the writ of habeas corpus, the fundamental legal protection of the citizen from arbitrary arrest, has permitted the regime to apprehend and detain over 60,000 people over the last eight years.[30] In 1979 alone, at least 700 long-term political prisoners were identified by the Task Force for Detainees, the internationally respected human rights surveillance organization. To these were added 1,302 new political arrests.[31] Contrary to the dictator's periodic promises to empty his jails of political prisoners, there is a revolving-door quality to the penal system. In 1979, for instance, the places of 510 political releases were more than filled up with 1,302 new arrests.[32] Indeed, a Kafkaesque bureaucratic logic appears to govern a militarized penal system whose security staff has developed a vested interest in jailing people. "Detention centers no longer exist to keep prisoners," asserts Sister Mariani Dimaranan, head of the Task Force for Detainees. "Rather, prisoners are maintained to keep detention centers functioning. Officers and guards would ask me: "But, Sister, what would happen to us if the president declared amnesty for all detainees?"[33]

A great number of political detainees have no formal charges lodged against them. Indeed, the serving of the so-called Arrest, Search, and Seizure Orders (ASSOs) — a device decreed by the regime to give its arbitrariness a touch of legitimacy — continues to be more the exception than the rule. ASSOs for most people are made up after arrest, if at all.[34] Especially in the rural areas, many detainees are kept for long periods with no formal charges lodged against them. Many Muslims arrested and detained, according to Sister Mariani, do not even possess records of detention. This leaves their fate completely in the hands of local camp commanders and guards — a system of 'arbitrariness within arbitrariness'.[35] Solitary confinement with no end in sight is the fate of well-known and popular dissenters, among them are the most exemplary fighters for social justice of the younger generation of Filipinos, like Jose Maria Sison, Juliet Sison, Bernabe Buscayno, and Victor Corpus.

Torture

For critics and dissenters in the Philippines today, to be merely arrested and imprisoned is lucky. In fact once the writ of Habeas Corpus is abolished, the only effective legal barrier to further acts of arbitrariness against helpless political captives is removed. Torture has become a sinister institution in the Philippines. As Amnesty International asserted in 1976, "The Republic of the Philippines ... has been transformed from a country with a remarkable constitutional tradition to a system where star chamber methods have been used on a wide scale to literally torture evidence into existence."[36]

Techniques of torture have ranged from modern, 'scientific' methods like the application of severe shock by means of electric transceivers to medieval ones like spreading hot pepper over lacerated bodies.[37] For women, capitivity holds special terrors, for in addition to physical pain, the detainee often faces sexual abuse; if not gang-rape by her captors. The fear, pain and shame of a woman under torture comes out vividly in the following account.

> About 10 to 20 men swelled the ranks of those already in the room. They threatened to kill me, get my relatives and torture them in front of me. They slapped my face and hit me in the thighs. They threatened me with a sharp edged bolo knife against my throat. They gave me the MERALCO treatment. MERALCO is the supplier of electricity in the city. An agent forcibly removed my blouse and bra and unzipped my fly. Another brought in a hand-cranked electric generator used as a military telephone. Still another forced me to drink glassfuls of water and poured ice-cold water over my body. It was to intensify the shock ... The exposed wires were attached to my bare little toes ... The current shot painfully through my body. I screamed and pleaded ... While pouring water, several agents mashed my breasts, while one contented himself by inserting his finger into my vagina after failing to make me masturbate.[38]

The perverse fascination with the abuse of sexual organs by the regime's experts in the application of pain often times extends to their male captives as well. Sixto Carlos, formerly a professor at the University of the Philippines, recounted his treatment after arrest in April 1979:

> One of the most painful things I experienced all day was continuous pounding of my testicles. One of the agents sat on a sofa by my knees. By means of what seemed to be a small wooden hammer, my testicles would be hammered by quick sharp blows ... This hurt very much. While I would be writhing from the pain, they would strike me on the chest, cursing me ... "If this lasts any longer, your balls will break," I heard someone say.[39]

The security apparatuses of authoritarian regimes have often attracted sexual sadists and other psychotic types. The Marcos regime is no exception.

Salvaging and Disappearances

The recent assassination by government security forces of Macli-
ing Dulag, the internationally renowned leader of the Kalinga
people's epic struggle against the Chico River Dam, has drawn
world attention to the phenomenon of 'salvaging' in the Philippines. Salvaging, the ominous military codeword for summary
execution, is a technique familiar to those who have followed
events in Argentina and Chile. It is the regime's 'quick and easy'
solution to the problem of international attention focused on its
concentration camps. Dead men, reasons Marcos, tell no tales to
the press or to Amnesty International. The standard military explanation is that the victims of salvaging are 'NPA terrorists'
killed in 'an encounter' or 'shot while trying to escape'.
However, investigation by such agencies as TFD and the
respected National Secretariat for Social Action (NASSA) has
revealed that the victims are usually ordinary civilians in areas
experiencing extensive militarization, like the island of Samar.[40]
Indeed, salvaging is but the most extreme punishment visited on
peasant communities that are also subjected to arbitrary exac-
tions of food, properties, and women by occupation troops[41]
that now rival in unpopularity the Japanese Imperial Army during the Second World War.

The magnitude of the problem of summary execution is indicated by the fact that in 1979, there were 115 documented cases
of likely salvaging by the military.[42] Also probably salvaged were
another 35 people most of whom 'disappeared' while under
military custody.[43] Since 1975, in fact, at least 78 people have
vanished into thin air after arrest, despite consistent inquiries.[44]
The problem, in all probability, surpasses documented cases.
For as Sister Mariani of TFD has noted, "There is a saying
among Muslims that Muslim captives rarely reach a detention
center alive."[45]

One of the most notorious cases of disappearance, that of
Jessica Sales, a faculty members of the University of the Philippines, remains a mystery, bearing witness to the tenacity of
bureaucratic secrecy. Arrested on 31 July, 1977, Jessica has been
seen at least four times in the company of intelligence
operatives. The military has been unofficially circulating rumors
that she was killed in an encounter with the NPA in April 1977,
but more than three years later, her family continues to be
denied official notification of her fate.[46]

The victims of salvaging are often tortured heavily before
execution: and, indeed, the tribulations of some victims do not

end with their death. Zoilo Francisco, a young resident of
Northern Samar, was shot to death immediately after arrest and
reappeared the next day as a bloody head mounted on a stake.[47]
Zoilo's fate was shared by at least 50 others in Samar in early
1979 whose heads were displayed by soldiers belonging to the
notorious 60th Constabulary Battalion, together with 35 ears.[48]
This gothic practice apparently serves three purposes: it satisfies
the troops' craving for 'personal trophies': it saves the time and
effort that would otherwise be involved in dragging bodies to
headquarters; and, most important, it strikes fear of the military
in the population.

In the last eight years, life has indeed become more nasty,
more brutal and shorter for larger numbers of the Filipino
people exposed to the predatory behavior of the Marcos state
machine. When a government systematically threatens and takes
the lives of citizens, when it becomes the principal threat to their
physical well-being, then the government is no longer entitled to,
nor should it expect the loyalty of the people. All the great
historical documents of political democracy, including the
American Declaration of Independence, affirm that in situations
like that of the Philippines today, citizens not only have the right
to armed self-defence but to rebel. Other governments have been
popularly overthrown for less.

Social Rights: The Rights to Shelter and Choice of Residence

In return for abolishing their basic political rights, the Marcos
regime promised not only to safeguard the basic security of the
Filipino people but to deliver economic prosperity.

The rationale of this policy was articulated thus by the head
of the Foreign Ministry, General Carlos P. Romulo: "In poor
developing countries the first priority of the common man is
where his next meal will come from. He does not worry about
the niceties of whether he can listen to a speech or read a certain
editorial. His first priority is his stomach, and his family's
stomach ... "[49]

Yesterday, we all heard eloquent and well-documented
presentations by different witnesses that revealed that instead of
delivering prosperity, Mr Marcos has foisted both economic
repression and economic depression on the Filipino people.
Yesterday's witnesses have already touched on the dismal state
of the rights to gainful employment, strike, and to freely organize
unions. I would just like to dwell briefly on two very important
personal and social rights — the right to live where one chooses
and the right to a roof above one's head. Both of these basic

freedoms have been grossly abused by a government whose military operations and rural and urban development schemes have displaced millions of Filipinos.

Military Displacement

The 'free-fire' zone is one of the most brutal and indiscriminate tactics devised in modern warfare. Intended to isolate the popularly supported guerillas from the peasantry, the 'free-fire zone' involves the forced relocation of people from their farms and homes and the conversion of the affected area into hunting ground where anything that moves is fair game for the military. First perfected by American troops in the Philippines in 1899 and later used extensively in Vietnam, the free-fire zone has been one of the favorite tactics an increasingly desperate Marcos has resorted to in the futile effort to stamp out the growing resistance.

Right after the declaration of martial law, 50,000 peasants were forcibly relocated from 100 to 200 villages in Isabela Province in a manoeuvre to deprive the New People's Army of mass base.[50] Base-denial operations, to use the military lexicon for refugee-creation, have also been carried out in parts of the Bicol regions, Quezon Province, Montanosa, the island of Samar, and throughout Western Mindanao and Sulu.

One of the most massive recent operations took place in Samar in 1979, as some 10,000 troops drove some 50,000 people in 65 interior towns to refugee centers which were so crowded that, according to a NASSA report, 'sleeping has to be done in shifts'.[51]

Mindanao is, of course, the land of refugees ... an uprooted mass of humanity created by an army intent on depopulating the Muslim countryside and shifting the population to more controllable refugee centers in certain areas like Cotabato City and Zamboanga del Sur. Military overkill, or the employment of tremendous firepower had resulted, as of 1976, in the destruction of 535 mosques, 200,000 houses, and 35 towns and cities.[52] In 1974, the government admitted having created more than one million refugees in its genocidal war in Mindanao — surely a conservative figure.[53] The refugee problem in the south has, indeed, become an international problem, necessitating close examination by all those agencies now concerned with other South-east Asian refugees. It has been estimated that at least 300,000 people have been forced to take refuge in the neighboring Malaysian state of Sabah.[54]

Urban Displacement

The rights to freely choose one's residence and have a shelter over one's head have also been repeatedly violated in the case of the urban poor. In 1974, the regime expelled almost 100,000 people from their residential sites near their areas of work in the center of Metro-Manila.[55] To remove what she termed 'eyesores', Imelda Marcos had 60,000 people forcibly relocated in preparation for the October 1976 World Bank-IMF Conference.[56] The World Bank has, in fact, given assistance to the regime in these people-expulsion efforts: both are now cooperating in an effort to relocate 2,000 recalcitrant families in the Tondo area of Manila in order to expand port facilities to serve multinational corporate interests.[57]

The anger of those displaced by the regime was perhaps best summed up by one refugee who told the *New York Times*: "We are Filipinos. Why are we Filipinos out here while all the foreigners are in Manila in those big buildings?"[58] In her usual unique fashion, Madame Marcos, in another context, provided the answer: "Why do I build a heart center or a convention city instead of urban mass housing? I believe that we just mustn't do that. I don't believe in building houses for everyone because I don't want our people to be mendicant."[59]

Relocation and Genocide

The grandiose scale of the development projects of the dictatorship has been paralleled by the deep misery they have inflicted on people. The building of the nuclear power plant in Morong, Bataan, for instance, involved the forced eviction of numerous households, expropriation of their fields, destruction of fish-spawning grounds, and disruption of a town of 11,000 people.[60] But perhaps the most severely affected by the regime's violation of the right of residence are the national minorities or oppressed peoples. Much has already been said of the conflict in the Chico River area, where the Kalinga and Bontoc peoples are desperately fending off the regime's attempt to flood out 3,419 acres of one of the world's most energy-efficient agricultural systems and uproot 100,000 people.[61] The Kalingas and Bontocs, however, are not the only minority peoples being driven out of their ancestral homes. The whole conflict in the south stems from Manila government-backed efforts by direct expropriation or the fraudulent use of western land titles. The Tinggians in the province of Abra are being robbed of their lands by the giant

Cellophil Corporation controlled by Marcos' cronies.[62] And in the Lake Sebu area in Mindanao, the T'boli people are facing the same dilemma as the Kalingas in the north: to die opposing a government dam project or allow itself to be evicted and live the rest of one's life as part of a deracinated mass.[63]

The relation of the authorities in Manila to the minority peoples has always been one of internal colonialism. But never has this condition been more stark than in the current period, when the Marcos regime is, objectively, creating the conditions of genocide by depriving these peoples of their fundamental right to live and die in their ancestral lands.

The Marcos Regime: An Arbitrary Government?

The present government of the Philippines has often been described as an arbitrary regime. If by arbitrary we mean that no legal or moral barriers constrain the regime from violating the rights of its citizens, then the description is accurate. But if we mean that the repression of the people takes place at the whim and fancy of our current rulers, we are mistaken. There was a time when, for many people, the favorite explanation of Marcos' defeated and outwitted rivals in the elite sufficed: that the roots of repression lie in the dictator's incurable lust for power. More and more people, however, have become too uneasily aware that there is something all too systematic about the administration of coercion to allow it to be attributed to the personal whims of an arbitrary, autocratic personality. And many have become too conscious of the striking similarities among the structures of domination forged by Marcos, the Chilean dictator Pinochet, and the late but unmourned trio of the Shah of Iran, Park of South Korea, and Somoza of Nicaragua to permit the Philippine dictator to be dismissed as an historical aberration.

No, Marcos is no accident, and much as his propagandists would like to convince us that he is an exceptional figure that seeks to uproot Philippine history from its normal channels, his dictatorship is a creature of history — a desperate expression of the clash of historical currents, a twisted but inevitable manifestation of the accelerating conflict between broader social forces. There is, in other words, an historical inevitability to the emergence of this regime. To grasp this, we must first of all give up the idea that the making of our internal history has been in our control. We cannot penetrate the essence of the Marcos dictatorship unless we first understand that since the turn of the century, the Philippines has been integrated into an imperialist network, the dynamics of which has determined and continues to determine our destiny as a nation.

The Historical Roots of the Dictatorship

Colonialism and the Creation of the National Elite

The Philippines came under US control at the turn of the century when US troops were ordered to crush a national movement that had just thrown off the yoke of Spanish colonialism, by a president who claimed that his mandate came from the Divine himself, or herself. There was, however, nothing heavenly about the conquest: it took 150,000 colonial troops, employing such methods as water torture, rope torture, strategic relocation and outright massacre more than three years to break the back of the national resistance. In the end, as many as 600,000 *gugus*, as the Americans termed the Filipinos, died — a figure of genocidal proportions, considering that it amounted to a little over a tenth of the total population in that period.[64]

The Philippines was appropriated for its raw materials, especially sugar, and to serve as a stepping-stone to China — the great prize of American capitalists who had feverish dreams of fabulous fortunes made by being able to sell one shirt to each of the 600 million Chinese. But added to these basic economic aims was the strategic one that was best articulated by the man in charge of the colonial war effort, General Arthur MacArthur, father of the more famous Douglas, who would later serve as the first and only Field Marshal of the Philippine Army. The Philippines, he told Congress in 1901, constituted:

> the finest group of islands in the world. Its strategic position is unexcelled by that of any other position on the globe. The China Sea, which separates it by something like 750 miles from the continent, is nothing more or less than a safety moat. It lies on the flank of what might be called a position of several thousand miles of coastline: it is in the center of that position. It is therefore relatively better placed than Japan, which is on a flank, and therefore remote from the other extremity: likewise, India, on another flank. It affords a means of protecting American interests which with the very least output of physical power, has the effect of a commanding position in itself to retard hostile action.[65]

This rationale or variants of it have been repeated to the US

Congress countless times since then by Pentagon officials as a justification for continued American military presence in and military aid to the Philippines.

Pacification was a bloody affair which lasted well into 1916. To accomplish it, the colonial authorities founded the Philippine Scouts, an adjunct of the US Army, and the Philippine Constabulary, a national police force that has constituted the repressive backbone of colonial and neo-colonial rule ever since. Together with American troops, these mercenaries put down a series of nationalist and peasant revolts, like that of Macario Sakay in Southern Luzon from 1902 to 1906, and later, that of the Colorums in 1923-24.

Mindanao and Sulu proved to be the most stubborn areas to drag into American colonial control; and to bring this about necessitated the invention of the 45 caliber revolver and the wholesale massacre of Muslim communities at the Battle of Bud Dajo in 1906 and the Battle of Bud Bagsak in 1913 — slaughters carried out by American troops assisted by the Philippine Constabulary.[66] Romanticized in such pre-war colonial films like *Uncertain Glory*, starring Gary Cooper, this fact must be underlined today: that the presence of the Philippine Constabulary in the South began as part of an imperial effort to subjugate what the Americans called Moroland.

Pacification was rapidly followed by the conversion of the Philippine economy into an appendage of the US economy. The Payne-Aldrich Act of 1909, which decreed the free flow of US manufactured goods into the Philippines, and Philippine raw materials into the United States, saddled the country with an agriculture-based economy and systematically stamped out any attempt at industrialization. The captive character of the colonial economy is shown in the fact that whereas Philippine trade was more equally distributed with other parts of the world in 1896, by 1935, seventy-two per cent of it was with the United States.[67]

American colonialism, however, suffered from one major problem: by the time the United States matured as a colonial power, colonialism as a system of metropolitan control had become both disreputable and obsolete. Independence movements were steadily on the rise throughout the non-white world; and in the Philippines, even America's firmest allies among the *ilustrados* or mestizo elite had to mouth slogans of independence in order to maintain some semblance of legitimacy in the public eye.

The US therefore began to experiment with methods with which to maintain the political and economic benefits of empire while shedding its outward forms — in other words, to prepare the ground for neo-colonialism. The solution eventually arrived at under the clever leadership of administrators like William Howard Taft and Francis Burton Harrison, came to be popularized as 'tutelage for democracy'. This involved the establishment of an educational bureaucracy designed to inculcate colonial and capitalist values in the mass consciousness; an army closely patterned on that of the United States and responsive to US influence; and a formal democratic system centered on an executive, legislature, and judiciary copied directly from their American counterparts. This model of formal, constitutional democracy, however, masked the real basis of power, which was a partnership between the United States and the Filipino landed oligarchy. The terms of this contract between the white colonizer and the mestizo elite had been worked out very early on, as far back as 1900, when the illustrados deserted the First Philippine Republic en masse: in return for loyalty to the United States, the system of semi-feudal control they exercised over the Filipino peasantry would be preserved by the colonial adminstrators. Indeed, it was the Americans who actively forged the various local elites into a national ruling class.

After a brief interruption by an inter-imperialist war, which saw Franklin D. Roosevelt sacrifice 70,000 Filipino troops in Bataan in 1942 for no other strategic purpose than to save American military prestige, the Second Philippine Republic was inaugurated, appropriately enough, on 4 July, 1946.[68]

The Second Republic and Neo-Colonialism

The Second Philippine Republic was launched with a hated ilustrado collaborator of the Japanese as chief of state. The Manuel Roxas administration pretty much set the pattern of political life for the next 26 years: power in this formal democratic regime was exercised by the landed oligarchy through patronage, massive corruption, and the legalized repression of groups defined outside the political pale, like the Communists. The chief mechanism of elite control was the two-party system. Born in the colonial period, it combined the worst features of feudal paternalism with the worst features of American patronage politics. As the late Senator Claro M. Recto noted:

It is to be deplored that our major political parties were born and nurtured before we had attained the status of a free democracy. The result was that they have come to be caricatures of their foreign model with its known characteristics — patronage, division of spoils, political bossism, partisan treatment of vital national issue ... Through their complacency, the new colonizer was able to fashion, in exchange for sufferance of oratorical plans for independence, and for patronage, rank and sinecure, a regime of his own choosing, for his own aims, and in his own self-interest.[69]

For the class in command, politics was the art of protecting narrow class interests, and public office was a system of institutionalized looting. This philosophy was perhaps best captured in the classic statement made to President Elpidio Quirino by Senate President Jose Avelino:

If you cannot permit abuses, you must at least tolerate them. What are we in power for? We are not hypocrites. Why should we pretend we are saints when in reality we are not?[70]

Not only did the Republic carry the burden of a corrupt and chronically short-sighted landed class. It was also trapped by a network of unequal laws and treaties that constituted a double guarantee for the protection of US interests against the influence of mavericks like Recto. Let us briefly mention the most important of these:[71]

- The Parity Amendment to the Constitution, rammed through in 1946, gave Americans equal rights as Filipinos to exploit the natural resources of the country;

- the Laurel-Langley Agreement of 1954 extended Parity rights to agriculture and industry;

- the US-Philippine Military Bases Agreement of 1947 legalized the presence of over 20 military bases and installations and stipulated that 'the armed forces of the US may serve on Philippine military establishments wherever such conditions appear mutually beneficial ...

- the US-Philippine Military Assistance Pact of 1947 provided military aid, training and advice to the Philippine Armed Forces through the Joint US Military Advisory Group (JUSMAG);

- the US-RP Mutual Defence Pact of 1951 bound the Philippines to go to war on the side of the US against a third country;

- the Southeast Asia Treaty Organization Treaty, the brain-child of the McCarthyist John Foster Dulles, committed the Philippines to the 'defence' of other Southeast Asian elites threatened by popular revolutions;

- the Economic Assistance Act of 1954 provided for the concerted penetration of the Philippine economy by US assistance agencies like USAID.

Loaded down with unequal treaties and controlled by a class that was totally insensitive to national development, it is not surprising that the people did not rally to the defense of the Republic against the armed insurrection of the Huk or HMB revolutionary movement in 1948. It was the CIA and JUSMAG that stepped into the breach. The political strategy of the counterrevolution was directed by Col. Edward Lansdale, one of the most effective CIA operatives in Southeast Asia, who established the Office of Psychological Warfare, cultivated the image of Ramon Magsaysay as a 'man of the masses', and created the land resettlement program EDCOR.[72] Former CIA director Allen Dulles himself admitted that 'the various covert steps ... in suppressing the Huk rebellion in the Philippines' represented one of the first major attempts at secret warfare by the agency's covert operations department established in June 1948.[73]

Lansdale was complemented on the military side by JUSMAG, under General Leland Hobbs, which reorganized the Defense Department and provided military assistance,[74] down to the squad level, to Philippine military units going after the Huks. "Certainly," asserts one US army expert in counter-insurgency, "the Joint US Military Advisory Group in the military field and the International Cooperation Administration in the economic sphere did splendid jobs and contributed immensely to the defeat of Communism in the Philippines."[75]

One of JUSMAG's 'splendid jobs' was to author the Anti-Subversion Act,[76] a key instrument in the witch-hunts coordinated by the Congressional Committee on Un-American Activities, so memorably immortalized by Woody Allen in the movie *The Front*. Under the Act, scores of Filipinos were stripped of either their jobs or their reputations, and some were sentenced to long terms in prison, including Amado Hernandez, a labor leader and one of the finest poets ever produced by our people.

An era of stifling McCarthyism blanketed the country between the early fifties and the mid-sixties — a direct spinoff of the McCarthyist period in the United States. Leftist sentiment was suppressed, leftist books were banned, travel to liberated countries was prohibited, and the slightest expression of independent thinking earned one the label of 'Red' or 'Pinko' Militant anti-nationalism and pro-Westernism were assiduously cultivated by such groups as the American Jesuits through organizations like the Student Catholic Action (SCA). In addition to their activities in education and the student movement, the Jesuits and like-minded clerical groups created anti-Communist labor unions, like the Federation of Free Farmers and the Federation of Free Workers, and had a hand in the formation of unabashedly pro-Western political groups like the Progressive Party and the Grand Alliance, headed up by Raul Manglapus and Manuel Manahan, two of Lansdale's influential protegees.[77]

The US did not, however, leave everything to the Jesuits: the McCarthyist period was one of intensive penetration of the Philippine economic, political and cultural life by the US Agency for International Development (USAID) and the CIA. USAID projects sought to turn peasants' attention away from land-tenure problems to 'rural beautification'.[78] Together with the Office of Naval Research of the US Department of Defense, AID promoted, through the Ateneo de Manila University's Institute of Philippine Culture, a number of studies of the political and social attitudes of Filipinos for purposes of prediction and control.

The CIA, through the Congress for Cultural Freedom, set up *Solidarity Magazine* and *Solidarity Bookstore* to encourage 'positive nationalism' and the Asia Foundation to coopt rising bright young artists and intellectuals with grants. Working hand-in-hand with the AFL-CIO, the agency also sought to penetrate Philippine Labor and transform it into an anti-communist force under yellow trade union leadership, established in 1968.

In more sinister fashion, CIA station chief Gen. Ralph Lovett and US Ambassador Raymond Spruance calmly contemplated poisoning Claro Recto. Lovett later revealed that "they finally decided not to do this ... but the basis of their decision was pragmatic considerations rather than moral scruples."[80] The most effective CIA project, however, was the 'rationalization' and unification of the Philippine police forces, which it coordinated with USAID. Directed by Frank Walton, who had earlier headed up similar police reorganization efforts in South Vietnam and Iran, the effort resulted in the creation of the Integrated National Police (INP) and Metrocom, a 6000-man inter-urban paramilitary force that was born just in time to rescue Marcos from the explosion of mass nationalism that engulfed the country in the late sixties.[81]

The Crisis of Neo-Colonial Control

The structural contradictions of the Republic could be suppressed neither with McCarthyism, token reformism, nor repression. By the late sixties, the crisis that had been briefly surmounted with the defeat of the HMB in 1954 reemerged in full force. This time it was terminal in character.

There were several dimensions to this crisis. There was, first of all, the intense inter-elite competition for political power, which had clearly run out of control. The 'equilibrium' of the Philippine Republic had rested partly on the unspoken rule among different factions of the elite that each would get its chance to control the government machinery. This unwritten rule of corrupt patronage politics was broken in November 1969, when a combination of massive fraud and electoral terrorism handed Ferdinand Marcos another term as president. No president had been reelected since 1946. Political competition soon came to take on predominantly extra-constitutional forms, like vendettas carried out by heavily armed private armies of the political bosses, some of which numbered over 1,000 retainers. 'Warlord politics' reminiscent of China in the 1920s began to rule the country, its violence perhaps best illustrated in the assassination of Floro Crisologo, a Marcos ally who controlled the key province of Ilocos Sur. Crisologo was 'blown away', as they say, in a fashion reminiscent of a scene from *The Godfather*: he was shot in the head, reportedly while receiving communion at the Vigan Cathedral.

A second dimension to the crisis was the bitter conflict between the interests of the nascent entrepreneurial class that had emerged in the fifties in Philippine industry as a result of the accidental protection afforded by foreign exchange controls, and the thrust of US investors to more completely open up the Philippines to the free flow of US capital and manufactured exports. Controlling huge amounts of surplus capital, but confronted with high labor costs and a declining rate of profit in a slow-growth domestic economy, US corporations were stepping up their drive to more fully exploit Third World markets, resources, and above all, labor. This anti-protectionist, pro-devaluation, and pro-foreign capital lobby found its expression in the Marcos elite and ranged itself against a nationalist industrial class and intelligentsia supported by a ballooning nationalist mass movement. The Constitutional Convention, assembled in 1970 to rewrite the basic law of the land, was swiftly thrown into deadlock between these two groups.[82]

As the upper classes were divided in internecine strife over political office and over the response to US capital, thousands of youths, workers, and peasants burst beyond the straitjacket of post-war electoral politics and rocked the country with massive demonstrations, marches, and strikes for anti-elite and anti-American ends. Originally intended as a means of coopting, fragmenting, and defusing mass demands through patronage politics, the formal democratic system began to turn into what the elite regarded as an uncontrollable and dangerous mechanism once important sectors of the middle class and the lower classes refused to operate within the coordinates of patronage.

The massacre of students demonstrating in front of Malacanang Palace in January 1970 ignited the 'First Quarter Storm', an explosion of mass nationalism that observers compared in significance to the May 1919 national-cultural revolution in China. This movement was able, between 1970 and 1972, to acquire such influence as to intimidate a normally conservative Supreme Court into issuing a number of decrees revoking preferential rights for American investors.[83] This reawakening of the masses from the cynicism and resignation of the McCarthy era under the bold leadership of the National Democratic movement was the most alarming aspect of the crisis of the neocolonial republic — the factor that finally wedded American capital to the dramatic move of the Marcos faction of the elite to monopolize power in September 1972. The sigh of relief collectively expelled by American business interests came in the form of a telegram to the new dictator:

> The American Chamber of Commerce wishes you every success in your endeavor to restore peace and order, business confidence, economic growth and the well-being of the Filipino people and nation. We assure you of our confidence and cooperation in achieving these objectives. We are communicating the feelings of our associates and affiliates in the United States.[84]

It is not surprising that the essence and outcome of the crisis of government in the Philippines exhibited remarkable parallels to that in Brazil in 1964, Chile in 1973 and Uruguay in 1974. For the turbulence in the Philippines is part of a larger, international headache for the United States: the growing obsolescence of a system of mass control that it has propelled throughout the Third World as an answer to the challenge of national liberation movements in the post-war period.[85] In these societies, three of which — the Philippines, Chile and Uruguay — had achieved the reputation of being the most durable constitutional democracies in the Third World — the people were beginning to use for their own class-ends a constitutional machinery originally designed to ensure elite control. Like the proverbial Dr Frankenstein, the United States and the ruling groups in these three societies had no choice but to blow up their own creation.

Nor should it be a cause for surprise that the solution to the crisis of formal democracy was everywhere the same. Brazil blazed the way to a new formula in 1964: an authoritarian government keeping down the masses through systematic, scientific repression and resting on an alliance among the military, multinational corporations, technocrats and local bureaucrat capitalists.[86]

Essential Features of the Marcos State

An Exceptional State of Imperial and Class Rule

The martial-law regime represents a fundamental shift in the imperial and elite domination of the Filipino people. Marcos had described his regime as a 'crisis government'. In this he is right: martial law is the crisis government of the ruling class, an exceptional state of class rule where the cooptative and persuasive devices that accompany normal imperial and class control have been jettisoned in favor of a regime of sheer repression. Martial law strips away the obfuscating layers of formal democracy and reveals the coercive relation that is at the core of the dependent imperialist state.

Reliance on repression has necessitated an expansion of the military from 60,000 men prior to martial law to 250,000 today. The expansion in numbers has been accompanied by a proliferation of roles for the military. Provincial and local military commands have effectively supplanted governors and mayors as the real basis of decision and power in local areas. The politicization of the military has been legitimized with the ideology of the army as a neutral technocratic agency. As Defense Minister Juan

Ponce Enrile puts it, "If the situation arises ... that our civilian sector is unable or unwilling to carry on the job of pushing through the reform program of the President, the military will have no alternative but to take over the job, even if it would involve taking over purely civilian functions."[87] Or in the high and mighty language of the Armed Forces Civic Action Manual:

> Many military leaders in the underdeveloped countries were trained in the West ... These indigenous military structures represent, historically speaking, the peculiar product of the most highly industrialized civilizations yet developed ... As a consequence, these establishments are imbued with a spirit that is tied to rapid technological progress. In a sense, they often represent islands of modernity in the troubled seas of pre-industrial societies striving for modernity.[88]

The reality of military behaviour, however, is quite distant from the ideology of technocratic militarism. 'Civic action' has been translated into the enrichment of the upper echelons of an officer corps that expects to be rewarded for its loyalty. Officers have been awarded key positions in the economic fiefdoms of bureaucrat capitalists like Enrile or Eduardo Cojuangco, raised to highly paid administrative positions in state economic agencies like the National Oil Company or the National Electrification Administration, or rewarded outright with their own fiefdoms, like the large agro-industrial corporation PHIVIDEC, which has been described as 'the largest of all proposed and ongoing industrial estates'.[89] Other military personnel, according to a knowledgeable observer, "have been allowed to take over the rackets of members of Congress and protection rackets run by local policemen at soaring rates of interest".[90] Still others have resorted outright to pirate capitalism by grabbing land from minority groups like the Mangyans of Mindoro.[91]

Martial law has indeed, only greatly expanded the field of operations of an institution that is thoroughly stamped with a parasitical and mercenary character. In the 1950s, JUSMAG adviser Gen. Joseph Harper likened the Philippine Army's relationship to the people to that of "US Army units stationed at the cavalry and frontier posts throughout Indian country during the opening of our Western frontier".[92] The comparison is as apt today as it was then.

Centralization and Concentration of Power

The current regime represents the forcible unification of the Philippine elite under the hegemony of the Marcos faction. The quasi-feudal autonomy of the regional and local political dynasties has been broken; and resources of political and economic power that were more dispersed in pre-martial law Philippines have now been concentrated by Marcos and his henchmen. At the same time, the strategic placement of loyalists within the different arms of the national state apparatus has converted it into a powerful, well-coordinated machine to attain factional and, ultimately, class objectives.

The history of early modern Europe is filled with the ultimately futile struggle of feudal lords defending local privileges against centralizing monarchs. The final product was the Absolutist State, which represented the centralized redeployment of the power of the feudal class against the spreading challenge of lower-class peasant revolts.[93] Bearing in mind the limits of historical analogy, something akin to this has happened in the Philippines: the Marcos state represents the centralized redeployment of the power of the Philippine ruling class in order to better contain the revolutionary thrust of the lower classes. Some elements of the old elite, like the Roxases, Aquinos, and Laurels, may not like this. Indeed, some of them, like the Lopezes, have had to be sacrificed. But the concentration of power in the Marcos faction is essential to the survival of the neo-colonial ruling class as a whole.

This centralization of power, it must be noted, has proceeded with the active encouragement of US-dominated agencies like the CIA and the World Bank. The CIA's role in centralizing the police has been mentioned. For the World Bank, centralization of power has been perceived as a prerequisite for a more efficient and more all-sided penetration of the Philippines by foreign capital: it reduces the 'irrationalities' or 'uncertainties' faced by foreign investors and aid agencies in dealing with a myriad of competing and oftentimes conflicting factions and interest groups. As the Bank approvingly noted in a 1976 confidential memorandum, "Changes in the Government's development policy were supported by a significant improvement in economic and financial management. In addition, the proclamation of martial law in 1972 and the abolition of Congress provided the Government with almost absolute power in the field of economic development."[94]

A very clear illustration of Bank-supported administrative and political centralization was the creation of the Metro-Manila Government out of several cities and municipalities in 1975. It was the Bank that was the greatest lobbyist for such a development, and when the new governmental unit was created in 1975, with Imelda as its head, World Bank Vice-President, George Votaw asserted, "The Bank strongly supports the establishment of a Metro-Manila Government and stands ready to assist the government ... "[95]

The Ascendancy of Bureaucrat Capitalism

Not only has martial law accomplished a forcible unification of the Philippine ruling class: it has also displaced the center of gravity of class power from the traditional landed oligarchs to Marcos' coterie of new and old rich elements. Composed of Marcos' relatives and cronies ensconced in the private sector, conservative technocrats in key economic and financial agencies of the state, and selected members of the military class who have sworn filialty to Marcos, this clique has effected a radical redistribution of wealth within the Philippine elite.

Bureaucrat capitalism refers to the use of strategic positions in the state for the accumulation of private wealth.[96] The modus operandi of the Marcos group ranges from the piratical expropriation of rivals, like the Eugenio Lopez clan that has been divested of a business empire ranging from communications to energy, to more subtle tactics like the creation of a government-backed private monopolies like UNICOM, controlled by Defense Minister Enrile, which took over the coconut industry last year, or semi-governmental marketing boards like the Philippine Sugar Commission, headed by well-known Marcos frontman Roberto Benedicto. Benjamin Cojuangco, Pacifico Marcos, Herminio Disini — these are the beneficiaries of the immense opportunities brought about by the centralization of corruption that martial law has accomplished.

The US-Marcos Dictatorship

The principal aspect of the Marcos regime is, of course, that it is the open, terroristic rule of US imperialist capital. The different dimensions of US economic penetration under the Marcos regime have been thoroughly documented by other witnesses. Let me just dwell briefly on the political aspects of the relationship between Marcos and the US.

First of all, the Marcos government, lacking any viable mass base, is completely dependent on US political and military support for its survival. Despite the low-profile diplomatic support for Marcos in the early years of martial law, the regime has the basic approval of the US government. As a US Senate

Foreign Relations Committee report on the attitudes of key US officials toward martial law asserted in 1973:

> We found few if any Americans who took the position that the demise of individual rights and democratic institutions would adversely affect US institutions. In the first place, these democratic institutions were considered severely deficient. In the second place, whatever US interests were — or are — they apparently are not thought to be related to the preservation of democratic processes ... US officials appear prepared to accept that the strengthening of presidential authority ... will enable President Marcos to introduce needed stability: that these objectives are in our interest: and that ... military bases and a familiar government in the Philippines are more important than the preservation of democratic institutions, which were imperfect at best.[98]

A more dramatic indicator of US support for martial law was the 106 per cent increase in military assistance to Marcos in the first three years of martial law, compared to the figure for the three years preceding it — $166.3 million in contrast to $80.8 million.[99]

US aid to Marcos has consisted principally of weapons for counterinsurgency. As Admiral Thomas Moorer, then chairman of the Joint Chiefs of Staff, asserted with candor in 1974: "The security assistance material program ... are designed to provide mobility, firepower, and communications ... the three basic elements required to combat insurgency forces."[100] Weapons which have been or are being delivered to Marcos include the F-5E Tiger jet fighter, which was specifically designed for counterinsurgency: the M-113 armed personnel carrier: and the Bell UH-1 helicopter, the mainstay of the helicopter-based anti-guerrilla war waged by the United States in Vietnam.[101] Recently, the US has also sent Marcos OV-10 aircraft,[102] which gained notoriety from their use against Fretilin Independence guerrillas by Indonesian troops that invaded East Timor in 1977.

US aid to Marcos has included the training of hundreds of armed forces officers in counter-insurgency in US military schools like Fort Benning and the US Army Intelligence School or in the Philippines itself at the hands of US 'mobile training teams'.[103] This has been complemented by the training that USAID and the CIA have jointly imparted to scores of military and police agents in surveillance, torture, and terrorist tactics in such shadowy places as the International Police Academy in

Washington, D.C., the FBI National Academy, and the Border Patrol Offices in Texas, the site of explosives and terrorist training that was graphically exposed in Costa Gravas' *State of Siege*. Between 1972 and 1975 alone, 99 Filipino police agents were graduated from these programs.[104] Although the Public Safety Program was reported to have been phased out in the mid-seventies, by then it had most certainly contributed its critical share in institutionalizing "the most advanced techniques of information and confession extraction from political suspects, like the common use of electric shock, subtle psychological torture, and selective beatings — methods remarkably similar to those employed in Brazil, Korea, Vietnam, Iran and Uruguay."[105] In addition to providing security training for his police, the CIA has also provided Marcos assistance in improving his image through the agency's public relations firm Doremus.

Economic aid provided by the US through agencies like AID has always been tied to counterinsurgency aims. Some aid projects, however, are more directly counterinsurgent in character than others. As part of the US Bases Agreement, for instance, the US is providing the regime $200 million for development schemes designed to pacify the areas around Clark Air Base and Subic Naval Base, where NPA guerrillas enjoy significant popular support.[106] Similarly, the USAID-backed Bicol River Basin Development Program and the Provincial Rural Development Program, staffed with former members of the notorious CORDS pacification effort in Vietnam, were launched in direct response to the growth of the revolutionary movement in rural areas.[107]

Indeed, even such seemingly neutral programs as rural electrification, supported by USAID to the tune of $250 million, are stamped with a counterinsurgent purpose. Now being touted as the regime's most successful rural development program, rural electrification, according to AID consultant Judith Tendler, "received a major political and financial commitment from the government because it was seen as crucial to one of its basic objectives — to win support away from the Communists in the countryside".[108] This relationship between electricity and counterinsurgency was appropriately described by one AID officer as "planting the flag in bandit country".[109]

Formal Democracy or Dictatorship: The Human Rights Debate

In 1978 and 1979, slight cuts in US aid to the Philippines were made by the Congress on 'human rights grounds'. Rather than view these as acts of altruism or a pained conscience, let us strip away the layers of noble Kennedyite rhetoric and see them for what they really were moves resulting from contradiction within the US elite and between the elite and the American people. The popular legitimation of official support for repressive regimes that characterized the Nixon era was especially difficult during the mid-seventies, when a wave of popular disgust and disillusionment over US foreign policy swept the population after the US defeat in Vietnam. This contradiction exacerbated a debate between those sectors of the American elite like Ted Kennedy and Rep. Donald Fraser who remained committed to the old system of domination through formal democratic means and those, like Henry Kissinger, Jimmy Carter and the upper echelons of the State Department, who saw more realistically the changed realities in the Third World that had provoked the authoritarian response. The debate within the elite was conducted in the language of human rights, but its essence could be reduced to the question: Should US dominance in the Third World be mediated through formal, bourgeois democracies or authoritarian regimes?

It was at this point that the issue of US military bases became extremely useful. For the dominant sector of the US elite, it provided a way of circumventing the dissatisfaction of the American people and stifling dissent among the minority sector of the elite. By invoking 'national security' and cultivating an image of Marcos as a Third World nationalist figure, the Carter administration has been able to violate both the letter and the spirit of Section 502B of the Foreign Assistance Act — a piece of legislation enacted as a concession to US public opinion that prohibits the provision of aid to any government "which engages in a consistent pattern of gross violations of internationally recognized human rights".

The Bases Agreement of January 1979 promised Marcos $300 million in military aid and $200 million in militarily-relevant economic aid in the period 1980-84. The current annual aid of $70 to $75 million more than doubles the aid figure of $31.7 million in 1979. The agreement, indeed, does not only guarantee an increase in aid to the dictatorship at a time of increasing turmoil. It also explicitly provides for the participation of US troops in security activities off the bases[110] — an area which can be arbitrarily defined to include from 100 or 200 miles from bases boundaries. That this provision was included is no mystery: the bases are surrounded by areas in which the New

People's Army is particularly strong. Indeed, 80 per cent of the province of Pampanga, in which Clark is located, is now estimated to be under the political influence of the NPA. The security cordon of American troops, warns George Kahin, the noted Cornell University specialist on Southeast Asia, may become the 'tripwire' for larger US troop involvement.[111]

The question of human rights is now hardly ever invoked when US policymakers discuss the Philippines. Even the handful of liberal opponents of the elite consensus on the Philippines now argue in terms of *realpolitik*. As one liberal congressman put it during the deliberations on foreign aid in February 1980, the US "must not lose the bases in the long run through the application of a policy designed to save them in the short run". In his view, the US ought to encourage moderate forces in order to prevent the emergence of a 'radical liberation front' that could become 'an umbrella for the disaffected' like the Sandinistas in Nicaragua.[112]

But what the US elite has learned from the events in Nicaragua and Iran in 1979 is that there is no viable alternative to authoritarian regimes as a means of neo-colonial control during this period. From both countries, the American elite has drawn the lesson that pressuring allies to make even cosmetic concessions may only open the floodgates of radical opposition that would inevitably destabilize these dependent regimes. Very revealing in this regard was the response of William Sullivan, the State Department-CIA hatchet man who served as the last US ambassador to the luckless Shah, when asked what lessons the US had to learn from the events in Iran: "When a dictator liberalizes, he falls."[113]

Sullivan's dictum is especially relevant to his former assignment, the Philippines, where the clock cannot be turned back to the late sixties. For Marcos has, over the last eight years, so successfully smashed the mass base of his hapless rivals within the elite at the same time that he has so successfully stirred up mass opposition, that any measure of liberalization would work, not to the strategic benefit of moderates friendly to the United States but to that of the mass-based nationalist and revolutionary opposition.

The US Bases and the US-Marcos Threat to the Third World

The preservation of a strong authoritarian regime keeping the Filipino masses in line has become even more crucial to the US as it feverishly mounts its global counter-offensive against liberation movements. In response to the breaches in the imperialist fortress created over the last six years by liberation struggles in Indochina, Southern Africa, Nicaragua, and Iran, the US enunciated the 'Carter Doctrine' in February 1980. Vowing to counter with force any attempts by 'outside powers' to threaten US interests in the Persian Gulf, President Carter reinstated direct intervention as a formal principle of US foreign policy, after a decade during which that principle had fallen into popular disrepute.

The bases in the Philippines, being the most forward large-scale US military installations in Asia, have been described by Asst. Sec. of State Richard Holbrooke as "central to our strategic position in the Indian Ocean".[114] They now constitute the 'principal logistical base' of the American military build-up in the area — a role highlighted by two well-publicized excursions to the Indian Ocean at the height of the erosion of US influence in Iran by two Subic-based carriers, the Kitty Hawk and Constellation.[115] Subic also served as the jump-off point and training center for a 1,800-man marine brigade that accompanied warships in the Indian Ocean — a function that prefigures the use of the bases as the Western Pacific springboards of the 100,000-man Rapid Deployment Forces currently being stitched together by the Pentagon.[116]

Indeed, in the current strategy of American-led counter-revolution, the bases are meant not only to be the logistical center for Indian Ocean deployment but also to serve as a back-up for US troops in Korea and to support possible US intervention in the event of conflict in Southern Africa and the Near East. As Gen. Freddie Poston, commander in chief of Clark, boasted in 1978: "I can have Phantoms into fields in East Africa twelve hours after they leave here."[117] These multifarious interventionist schemes can proceed efficiently only if these bases are surrounded by a *cordon sanitaire* provided by a mercenary regime. *That regime is in place.*

The late Senator Claro Recto once wrote somewhere that, "The US bases constitute a dagger poised at the throat of Philippine sovereignty". We might add that both the bases and their security force, the Marcos dictatorship, are also poised against the independence and freedom of the Third World. This dictatorship is not a 'new force' in the Non-Aligned Movement, contrary to what its propagandists would have us believe. It is a Trojan Horse in the midst of those movements and governments that are genuinely struggling against imperialist counterrevolution, repression, and exploitation.

Alternatives to Marcos

The character of the Marcos dictatorship as a state completely dependent on US imperialism clarifies the answer to the burning issue: Which of the political alternatives now being presented to the Filipino people best serves to achieve their goals of justice, freedom and independence? While we cannot address this matter thoroughly in this presentation, such a major issue necessitates a few comments.

Is the elite opposition the alternative for the Filipino people? Will the people turn back to those old faces etched in their memory for their keen participation in the pre-martial law system of institutionalized plunder?

Surely, a political force, the main leaders of which have admitted close association with the CIA in the 1950s, is suspect, to say the least. An alternative that seeks to be installed in power by the United States by fanning American fears of the growth of the national democratic movement under martial law is, indeed, no alternative at all for our people. For just as certainly as day turns into night, these promoters of the illusion of a return to the good old days of elitist democracy will find that, if awarded the reins of power, they themselves will have to resort to terrorist dictatorship to contain the effervescent, escalating mass movement against inequality and foreign domination. Shortsighted and class-bound as always, these gentlemen do not understand that it was not Marcos that produced the dictatorship, but that the all-sided crisis of neo-colonial control demanded and produced the Marcos dictatorship.

Can the Filipino people rely on the so-called Social Democrats? The rhetoric of social justice that these Christian gentlemen offer seems attractive. But can we seriously accept a program that attacks Marcos and the Philippine elite as the principal enemy of the Filipino people but compromises and hems and haws on the question of US imperialism? This reflects a fundamental failure to understand that the Philippine elite and its system of control have been molded by the US and periodically remolded to fit the conjunctural needs of imperialism.

But perhaps the essence of Social Democracy is revealed in its position toward the nationalist left. How sincere is a force that views Marcos and the National Democratic Movement as equal threats to the Filipino people?[118] Indeed, that makes the left the target of more attacks than Marcos? Yet the Social

Democrats' present position of rhetorical ambiguity on the question of imperialism and their militant anti-communism are consistent with the historical record. The ideological precursor of Philippine Social Democracy first appeared in the 1930s as a cleric-led movement that interpreted Catholic social thinking in a conservative fashion and admired Francisco Franco of Spain. It emerged as a significant force at the time of the Huk uprising of the 1950s, when it teamed up with the CIA to oppose its program of 'Social Justice' to an armed struggle for land and liberation. Not surprisingly, some of the famous Col. Lansdale's key lieutenants, like Raul Manglapus, were also the stars of the Jesuit-influenced movement. It is not coincidental that Jesuit social thinking, under a new brand name, Social Democracy, has reappeared today. For this is a period of rapid growth of the left, of the National Democratic Movement.

Finally, does the old Communist Party, the PKP, offer the Filipino people a viable alternative? Surely, this is absurd. A group that would attack US imperialism but paint Marcos as a nationalist who can be persuaded and cajoled into taking progressive steps misses the fundamental lesson that the Filipino masses have absorbed in the last eight years that the Marcos dictatorship is the main agency, the armed terrorist force of US imperialism. The following statement blazoned in the party program drawn up in 1977 requires no comment from us:

> The Marcos administration wants to assert Philippine sovereignty, yet it is not strong enough to demand total and immediate withdrawal ...[119] One of the strongest and most decisive of Filipino presidents, President Marcos has succeeded, through martial law powers, he has effectively and adroitly been wielding, in steering the country away from total dependence on imperialism, however limited this effort may be. This foreign policy, strengthening the role of national government in economic planning, the search for new indigenous political structures, diversification of trade, and the enhancement of Filipino culture.[120]

When the PKP formally laid down its arms in 1974 and pledged cooperation with the dictatorship under the illusion that it was forming a united front with Marcos against US imperialism, it was, in fact, thrown into a united front with US imperialism against the Filipino people. This move was but the latest step in a long history of tragic errors and miscalculations that have consistently derailed the people's movement and thoroughly discredited the PKP as a progressive force. Of these people, one can repeat the old adage: "With friends like these, who needs enemies?"

There is only one force that has displayed consistency, firmness, and dedication in the struggle against imperialism and dictatorship in the last 15 years. This consistency, based on the accurate analysis that the dictatorship and imperialism are one, has now borne fruit in a broad mass movement and people's army that, interestingly enough, is regarded unanimously by Marcos, the elite opposition, the White House, and the Social Democrats as the principal strategic threat to the US position in the Philippines. That force, that movement is unmistakable; its ascendancy, inevitable. Certainly, it has appeared as such to the best and more sincere individuals in both the PKP and the Social Democratic groupings, who courageously broke with their respective groups rather than accept foreign domination.

Honorable jurors:

Allow me to conclude by repeating about Marcos what one Chilean political prisoner once said of Marcos' colleague and brother-in-arms, Augusto Pinochet: "If he did not exist, imperialism would have had to invent him." But if there is, to the Marcos dictatorship an historical inevitability, is not its fall as well a historical necessity? We ask you to render a verdict of guilty on all the charges that the Filipino people have brought against the dictatorship. I thank you.

Notes

1. *New York Times*, 21 January, 1973
2. Juan Gatbonton, *President Marcos: A Political Profile*, Manila, Ministry of Public Information, Republic of the Philippines, April 1980
3. Ferdinand Marcos, *The Third World Alternatives*. Speech prepared for the American Newspapers Publishers Association Convention, April 1980, p. 23.
4. *Ibid.*, p. 25
5. See Robert Heilbroner, *The Human Condition* (New York: Harper, 1974).
6. Constitution of the Republic of the Philippines, Manila, Bureau of Printing, 1972, p. 47.
7. *New York Times*, 18 January, 1973. See also reports on the Constitutional Convention in *New York Times*, 30 October, 1972; and *Ang Bayan*, Special Release, 5 December, 1972.
8. See, among others, O.D. Corpuz, *Liberty and Government in*

the New Society, Manila, undated.
9. Comments at the Asia Society, Washington, D.C. 1 October, 1980.
10. *Agence France Presse*, 10 September, 1980.
11. US Dept. of State, *Country Report on Human Rights Practices for 1979* (Washington, D.C.: US Govt. Printing Office, 1980), p.509.
12. See John Caughlan, "Torturers on Trial", in *Human Rights and Martial Law in the Philippines* (Oakland, Ca.: National Resource Center for Political Prisoners in the Philippines, 1977), pp. 3-8.
13. William Butler et al., *The Decline of Democracy in the Philippines* (Geneva: International Commission of Jurists, 1977), p. 45.
14. See accounts by Peter Weiss, "World Peace Through Martial Law?" in *Human Rights and Martial Law in the Philippines*, pp.9-13.
15. Amnesty International, *Report of an Amnesty International Mission to the Republic of the Philippines* (London: Amnesty International, 1976), p. 56.
16. Primitivo Mijares, Testimony in Subcommittee on International Organization, US House of Representatives Committee on International Relations, *Human Rights in South Korea and the Philippines: Implications for US Policy*, 94th Congress, First Session, 17 June, 1975, p. 306.
17. *New York Times*, 8 April, 1978.
18. *Agence France Presse*, 14 Feb. 1980.
19. *Agence France Presse*, 12 Feb. 1980.
20. *Philippine Times*, 31 March, 1980, pp. 11-12
21. Corpuz, *ibid.*, p. 12.
22. *Agence France Presse*, 10 July, 1973.
23. *Reuters*, 6 Nov. 1976
24. Association of Major Religious Superiors in the Philippines, Women (AMRSPW), *Political Detainees in the Philippines, Book Two* (Manila: AMRSPW, 1977), p. 46.
25. Butler et al., *ibid.*, p. 30.
26. *Asia Record*, August 1980, pp. 8-9
27. Paul Icamina, "Student Demonstrations: Legitimate Grievances or Subversion?", *Asia Record*, Sept. 1980, p. 7.
28. *Ibid.*
29. Before his arrest, UP Collegian editor Bobby Coloma had written that the Act "must be seen as a result — and intended instrument — of a subtle but nevertheless vicious scheme to regiment Philippine education in accordance with the demands of foreign vested interests." *Ibid.*
30. The 60,000 figure is that cited by the International Commission of Jurists as of August 1977. Thousands more have been arrested since then, with 1302 in 1979 alone. See Butler et. al., *ibid.*, p. 32.

31. Task Force Detainee (TFD), *Quarterly Report: Political Detainees* (Manila: TFD, October-December 1979), p. 119
32. *Ibid.*, pp. 119-120
33. *FFP* (Friends of the Filipino People) *Bulletin* (Washington, D.C.), April-May, 1979, p. 8.
34. "Martial Law and Human Rights", *FFP Occasional Papers*, Vol. 1, No. 1 (Feb. 1980), p. 7.
35. *Ibid.*
36. Amnesty International, *ibid.*, p. 57.
37. TFD, *Political Detainees Update*, Vol. 3, No. 10, p. 4. This describes one notorious instance of the use of "hot pepper" method.
38. Quoted in Don Luce, "Life and Death in Prison", in *Human Rights and Martial Law in the Philippines*, pp. 17-18.
39. Quoted in "Sixto Carlos Severly Tortured", *Solidaridad II* (Hong Kong), No. 17, Jan.-Feb. 1980, p. 2.
40. *NASSA News* (Manila), Vol. 11, No. 8, August 1979, p. 5.
41. *Ibid.*
42. TFD, *Quarterly Report*, Oct.-Dec. 1979, p. 121.
43. *Ibid.*, pp. 111-115.
44. Ibid.
45. *FFP Bulletin*, ibid.
46. "Martial Law and Human Rights", pp. 3-4.
47. Earl Martin, "6oth PC — Butcher Battalion Terrorizes Northern Samar", *Philippine Liberation Courier*, Vol. 3, Nos. 9-10 (September-October, 1979), p. 8.
48 *Ibid.*
49. *New York Times*, 11 September, 1978, p. 5.
50. *New York Times*, 22 October, 1972.
51. *NASSA News*, ibid.
52. Abdurasad Asani, "Muslim Assesses Martial Regime", *Signs of the Times*, 2 October, 1976, p. 37.
53. *Social Welfare in Development: Annual Report FY 1973-74* (Manila: Department of Social Welfare, 1974), p. 38.
54. Estimate provided by Abdurasad Asani, MNLF spokesperson. This contrasts with the undoubtedly deflated figure of 150,000 refugees provided by Rear Admiral Romulo Espaldon, Southern Philippines military commander. *Agence France Presse*, 8 October, 1980.
55. Dept. of Social Welfare figure, cited in *The Refugee Crisis in the Philippines* (Chicago: Anti-Martial Law Coalition, 1977), p. 23.
56. *Ibid.*, p. 20.
57. See *Congress Task Force Washington News Service*, "West German Mission Lambasts Controversial World Bank-Funded Projects", 6 Sept., 1980.
58. Quoted in *The Refugee Crisis*, p. 20.
59. Quoted in *ibid.*, p. 19.
60. Walden Bello, Peter Hayes and Lyuba Zarsky, *500-Mile Island: the Philippine Nuclear Reactor Deal*, Vol. X, No. 1 (1979), p. 27.

61. Dean Alegada, "The Price of Progress in the Philippines — the Igorots", in *Conditions of the Filipino People Under Martial Law* (San Francisco: FFP and AMLC, 1979), p. 13; see also Charles Drucker, "The Price of Progress in the Philippines", *Sierra*, Nov.-Dec. 1978, pp. 22-26.

62. *Philippine Liberation Courier*, Vol. 3, Nos. 9-10, Sept.-Oct. 1979, pp. 6-7.

63. "Two Voices, One Theme: Dams", *MSPC Communications*, Jan. 1978, p. 25.

64. This section is based on a number of historical sources: Amado Guerrero, *Philippine Society and Revolution* (Oakland: International Association of Filipino Patriots, 1979), pp. 16-28; Renato Constantino, *The Philippines: A Past Revisited* (Quezon City: Taal Publishing, 1975), pp. 198-341; Steve Shalom, *US-Philippine Relations: A Study of Neo-Colonialism*, Ph.D. dissertation, Boston University, pp. 38-94; and Jonathan Fast and Luzviminda Francisco, "Philippine Historiography and the D-Mystification of Imperialism: A Review Essay", *Journal of Contemporary Asia*, Vol. 4, No. 3, 1974, pp. 344-58.

65. Quoted in William Manchester, *American Caesar: Douglas MacArthur 1880-1964* (New York: Dell, 1978), pp. 48-49.

66. Guerrero, *ibid.*, p. 19.

67. Constantino, *ibid.*, p. 301.

68. See the account in Manchester, *ibid.*, pp. 279-283.

69. Quoted in Renato Constantino, *The Filipinos in the Philippines and Other Essays* (Quezon City: Malaya Books, Inc., 1971), pp. 49-50.

70. Quoted in Stephen Shalom, "Counter-Insurgency in the Philippines", *Journal of Contemporary Asia*, Vol. 7, No. 2, 1977.

71. Guerrero, *ibid.*, pp. 68-72.

72. Lansdale's exploits are documented in his book, *In the Midst of Wars* (New York: Harper and Row, 1972); see also Shalom, *ibid.*, *The Pentagon Papers* (New York: Bantam, 1971, pp. 135-36); and Walden Bello and Severina Rivera, eds., *The Logistics of Repression* (Washington, D.C.: FFP, 1977), pp. 34-35.

73. Memorandum for Lawrence Houston, CIA General Counsel, from Allen Dulles, April 21, 1964, Dulles Collection, Mudd Library, Princeton University. See also Letter of Allen Dulles to Harry Truman, 7 Jan. 1974, from the same collection.

74. Shalom, *ibid.*

75 Major Boyd Bashore, US Army, "Dual Strategy for Limited War", in Franklin Mark Osaka, ed., *Modern Guerrilla Warfare* (New York: Free Press, 1962), p. 200.

76. Robin Broad, *International Actors and Philippine Authoritarianism*, Princeton University, New Jersey, June 1979, unpublished, p. 25.

77. Lansdale, *ibid.*

78. Walden Bello, "Cultural Imperialism in the Philippines", *Philippine Times*, July 1975.

79. On CIA and AAFLI, see Lenny Siegel, "Asian Labor: The American Connection", *Pacific Research and World Empire Telegram*, Vol. 6, No. 5, July-August 1975; also Don Thomson and Rodney Larson, *Where Were You, Brother?: An Account of Trade Union Imperialism* (London: War on Want, 1978), pp. 65-68.

80. Thomas Buell, Interview with Ralph Lovett, Manuscript Collection 37, Naval Historical Collection, US Naval War College. Cited in *Philippine Liberation Courier*, June 1980, p. 7.

81. See Bello and Rivera, *ibid.*, pp. 28-30; also Broad, *ibid.*, and Michael Klare, "The Police Apparatus of USAID", *Philippine Information Bulletin*, Vol. 1, No. 1 (1973).

82. The nationalist position was exemplified in the document entitled "Directive Principles of State Policy" which called for "an integrated, nationalistic and socially oriented economic plan that shall effectively promote rapid industrialization ...". Cited in Broad, *ibid.*, p. 36. The pro-foreign capital lobby's big gun was technocrat Gerardo Sicat, who drew up the faction's position in the influential *Economic Policy and Philippine Development* (Manila: National Development Authority, 1972).

83. The "Quasha Decision" ruled that lands acquired by Americans since 1946 had been acquired illegally and subject to forced sale or confiscation before or after 1974, when parity rights would come to an end. Another court decision barred foreigners from holding executive jobs in American oil, labor, and mining companies after 1974. See National Committee for the Restoration of Civil Liberties in the Philippines, *Report to the Senate Foreign Relations Committee on Martial Law in the Philippines and US Relations with the Marcos Administration*, Washington, D.C., June 1973, mimeo.

84. Quoted in Samuel Bayani, "What's Happening in the Philippines?" *Far Eastern Reporter* (Nov. 1976), p. 26.

85. See Organizing Committee for a Human Rights Grassroots Movement, *Human Rights in US Foreign Policy: An Historical Perspective*, New York, October 1977, mimeo.

86. On the Brazilian model, see Peter Evans, *Dependent Development: The Alliance of Multinationals, State, and Local Capital in Brazil* (Princeton: Princeton University Press, 1979).

87. Cited in Broad, *ibid.*, pp. 29-30.

88. Home Defense, *Military Civic Action* (Manila: Armed Forces of the Philippines, undated), p. 166.

89. Kudo Junko, "Mindanao in May 1976", *AMPO* August 1976, p. 25.

90. Primitivo Mijares, Testimony in Subcommittee on International Organization, *ibid.*, p. 472.

91. *Ibid.*

92. Bashore, *ibid.*, p. 201.

93. See Perry Anderson, *Lineages of the Absolutist State* (London: New Left Books, 1975).

94. World Bank, *The Philippines: Priorities and Prospects for Development, Basic Economic Report* (classified version), Washington, D.C., 19 March, 1976, p. 1.
95. Memorandum of World Bank vice president George Votaw to Robert McNamara, Washington, D.C., 18 Nov., 1975. The opportunist character of this alliance is indicated elsewhere in the memo, where Votaw writes, "Mrs. Marcos has identified herself with a few showcase projects, which we consider ineffective and which are a bit of a joke even among knowledgeable Filipinos."
96. A good description of the dynamics of bureaucrat capitalism is found in Joel Rocamora, "Bureaucrat Capitalism — A Classic Case", *Philippine Liberation Courier*, Vol. 3, No. 11 (Nov. 1979), pp. 5-7
97. *Some are Smarter than Others*, Manila 1979, mimeo.
98. US Senate Committee on Foreign Relations Staff, *Korea and the Philippines* (Washington, D.C.: US Government Printing Office, 1973).
99. Bello and Rivera, *ibid.*, p. 8.
100. Cite in *ibid.*, p.14.
101. *ibid.*, pp. 20-23.
102. Asst. Sec. of State Richard Holbrook, Testimony before US House of Representatives Committee on Foreign Affairs, 21 Feb., 1980.
103. Bello and Rivera, *ibid.*, p. 15.
104. Philippine graduates in police training, as of 1977; list obtained through Freedom of Information Act by John Kelley, editor of *Counter-Spy Magazine.*
105. Bello and Rivera, *ibid.*, p. 30.
106. USAID, Presentation to Congress, FY 1980, Washington, D.C., 1980.
107. Bello and Rivera, *ibid*, pp. 54-57
108. Judith Tendler, *Rural Infrastructure Projects: Roads and Electrification*, Paper prepared for Bureau of Program and Policy Coordination, USAID, October 1978, p. 70.
109. Interview with AID Philippines Capital Assistance Project Officer, 20 December, 1978, Washington, D.C.
110. Article III, Paragraph Six of the Executive Agreement.
111. Testimony before Subcommittee on Foreign Operations, US House of Representatives Committee on Appropriations, 6 April, 1979, p. 7, mimeo.
112. "Sending a Signal to the Philippines", *Congressional Record*, 5 February, 1980.
113. Personal communication from Don Luce, who visited the US Embassy in Iran together with Ramsey Clark in January 1979.
114. Asst. Sec. of State Richard Holbrooke, Testimony before House of Representatives Subcommittee on Asia-Pacific Affairs, 21 February, 1979.

115. Larry Niksch, "Philippine Bases: How Important to US Interests in Asia", *Congressional Research Service Issue Brief*, 2 January, 1980, p. 7.
116. Michael Klare, Institute for Policy Studies, January 1980.
117. Quoted in "Withdraw US Bases from the Philippines!" (*FFP* broadsheet), 1978, p. 3.
118. See the analysis of the Social Democratic program in *Liberation* (Manila), Vol. VIII, No. 2, February 1980, p. 14.
119. Partido Komunista ng Pilipinas, *For An Independent and National Democratic Philippines* (Philippines: PKP, July 1977), p. 71.
120. *Ibid.*, p. 85.

Testimony on militarization and military atrocities

The parents also suffer great fear... because of the high incidence of torture, rape and even murder of those held in custody.

I am Victoria de los Reyes. I stand witness to the military atrocities being inflicted on the people by the Philippine government since martial law was declared. September 21, 1972 marks the day of military rule throughout the country. Proclamation 1081 changed the daily life of many people.

Our barrio used to be a very peaceful place. We would walk the streets freely and visit friends. When martial law came, our evenings were disturbed by the entry of the military and our activities were curtailed. Checkpoints were set up along certain points of the municipal road. Everyone was required to have a new residence certificate and one should have a curfew travel pass to travel during the night. Lights were supposed to be out by seven in the evening.

After some time, there came an order for all firearms to be surrendered to the military. A truckload of homemade rifles, Japanese and American rifles, some single-shot guns and mostly pistols were confiscated from the people in our barrio and neighbouring barrios. Even my father's airgun was confiscated and nobody was allowed to carry sharp or bladed objects, not even a toothed kitchen knife.

Soon afterwards, we started hearing gunfire from the near-by detachment of the Philippine Constabulary (PC). "Those are from the military training activities," the authorities would explain to the people. Later some of our friends found out that the military were training their guns on them.

It was my grandmother who would say, "It's terrible! It's more terrible than the Japanese soldiers during the war!"

At first, I could not understand why the military were training many men inside the camp but it did not take long before I started to see a pattern and understand terrorism by directly experiencing it.

The military organized civilians into the Civilian Home Defense Force Units or CHDF, to insure peace and order in the countryside and to watch out for subversives. Most people recruited into the CHDF in our place were town thugs and notorious elements. The CHDF would hang around public places like bus terminals, stores and the market place to wait for farmers bringing in their produce to the town or merchants selling products. They would harass the farmers or merchants and extort money from them. If anyone resisted, he was muzzled, beaten or branded a subversive. Identification cards were confiscated and people were intimidated whenever the CHDF elements were drinking or restless.

Often innocent civilians were abused for no reason by the Philippine Constabulary soldiers or their CHDF companions. I will present certain examples of barrio folks being mauled or physically abused by the military.

Narding was a young man from a neighboring barrio. One day his mother asked him to buy rice in town. Early in the morning, Narding set out to walk the 15 kilometer distance to town. He reached the town safely, bought the rice and started to look for a place to get breakfast. He was stopped by a CHDF with an armalite. "Is that for the NPA?" accosted the armed civilian. "No," Narding answered calmly. The CHDF got angry and dragged Narding towards a group of drinking CHDF and Narding was hit, kicked and battered with an armalite. A man pointed his gun at his mouth and tried to force him to declare his family as NPA supporters. When Narding resisted and they could not make him talk, another man threatened to kill him if he did not give his money and rice. Narding had no choice but to give his rice and breakfast money (P2.50). It was only then that he was allowed to go and he got home after noon, exhausted, sore, hungry and very angry.

During a barrio dance, a civilian was kicked and whipped with a gun by a PC sergeant until he vomited blood. The man tried to protect a woman whom the sergeant tried to kiss and molest in front of the barrio folks. The CHDF elements accompanying the sergeant searched him and when they found his small knife, he was charged with "possession of deadly weapons" and was detained.

Not only were barrio folks intimidated by the military and its CHDF. They were often robbed of their farm animals and produce. Mang Pedro, a farmer in our barrio, found his pregnant cow missing. When he looked for it, he saw its head and skin near the military detachment. He looked for more traces and found pieces of its meat hanging from the roof of the military outpost.

Cattle-rustling became more rampant inspite of the presence of the guardians of peace and order, the PC and the CHDF. The continuous cattle-rustling of a gang linked with a government official and the constant drinking activities near the detachment, made these elements more notorious.

Women in the barrio were no longer safe to walk on the streets, for the military personnel could get very rowdy and pick women they saw and fancied.

Aside from putting up with the CHDF and the PC soldiers, barrio folks have to get involved in the Barangay Brigades Program. The Barangay Brigades Program divides the training of barrio and town residents into the Ladies Brigade, the youth brigades and the Barangay Tanod. Of the three groups, the Barangay Tanods are particularly selected and trained for military campaigns against subversives. Most of those recruited into the Barangay Tanods are very young men and they become very aggressive. These Barangay Tanods have been called *Barangay Tagay* (tagay being a Filipino term for a measure of drink) or *Barangay Salakay* (salakay meaning to attack). They conduct surveys of residents, sometimes during the night, and often kitchens are raided of their food and pans whenever the Barangay Tanods conduct their search. It is also not uncommon to hear of rape because most of the women and children stay in the house during the harvest while the men guard the fields.

The Ladies Brigade is another feature of the Barangay Brigades Program. Mothers, local women officials and adult women are required to attend an intensive, live-in, three-day seminar. They wake up at 5 a.m., are made to go through some military drills like climbing very steep places or crawl under narrow tunnels. The food is limited to the barest essentials. In the evening, the women are asked to make pledges of allegiance to the New Society and to Marcos and Imelda in particular. The last session is made dramatic with everyone holding a candle and all have to take the oath of loyalty to the New Society.

The Youth Brigades Program, which started as the *September 21 Movement* of Marcos, is to create a youth base and source of New Society cadres. The training of youth is similar to the initiation of fraternities wherein one can only belong to a group when he has proven himself a man, a macho and is totally convinced of the goals of the New Society.

Whoever does not participate in these brigades is put under surveillance and harassed by the Barangay Tanods, or the CHDF or the PC. It becomes worse when these groups bicker among themselves, for they take it out on the poor civilians if they cannot get even with each other.

When I became a member of the New People's Army, I encountered a number of cases of military atrocities. I will present a few to illustrate the repressive measures in the countryside. For the first one I quote an interview with a local cadre in Northern Central Luzon:

"I am also a victim of military atrocities in our barrio. Two of my children died because of them. My husband was arrested and mauled by the army. On my part I was threatened and maltreated in words. I was forced to produce as evidence, a gun like that. I said I don't have anything to give.

Then this happened, after the funeral of my sons. There were thirty-eight of us, including our children, grandchildren, relatives, and a group of old men and women who could hardly walk due to old age, when an army truck intentionally banged the jeep that we were riding. The Army truck bumped the jeep several times until it was totally crushed. Almost all of us were severely injured, bathed in our own blood and in a state of shock. One of my cousins died on the spot. After placing us in this helpless condition, the army went further into formation and deployed themselves as if those bodies lying in from of them were their enemies. Without the help of the masses, the people in the barrio where the incident took place, we could not have been brought to the hospital. One of my children suffered a fractured bone in his foot. My teenage daughter suffered a laceration on the breast. On my part, I suffered a bone fracture in the hip and it's almost one month now that I could hardly move. My husband was also badly hurt and also suffered a fracture in the ribs. My other children were injured and also suffered fractures. None of us could work on the farm for more than one month. That is why it is the masses, the people in the barrio, who attend and work on our farm.

Until now, we still feel the pain. I could no longer attend to the farm unlike before when I assisted in the farm activities. My husband also could no longer go to the farm because of pains in his ribs.

Even though we were intentionally bumped, that devil army did not even bother to help us.

What we had used for our emergency treatment were the donations given by the masses on the death of my son. We were taken to the hospital only because of these donations although these were not enough to defray all the expenses. We were discharged from the hospital not fully recovered. We also did not have cash to buy our medicines, so we had to employ the service of the *manghihilot*. It was only from this method that we recuperated and were able to walk again."

This is the story of Ka Binsing, the daughter of a peasant in the Bicol Region.

"My name is Ka Binsing. I am 16 years old and I finished grade VI only. My parents are poor peasants. I would like to relate the atrocities committed by the military against me and my family.

It was almost 4.00 o'clock in the morning when some 17 armed military men came and fired at our house, not even bothering to see if there were civilians inside. They fired at us continually. I was hit in the left leg, then in the right leg, then another time in the right leg and then another time in the left. My mother was shouting out of fear because I was already crying from pain and they thought I would die.

It was already 7.00 o'clock in the morning when they stopped firing. They searched the house and stole some of our things. They were looking for evidence. After some searching for half an hour, they took us to the hospital.

At the hospital, the army men instructed us to tell those who would inquire what happened to me — that I fell down from a Pili tree. And that if an army man come to visit us in the hospital, we should tell that he is a relative. At the hospital, the army told the doctor to treat us. I stayed four months in the hospital.

When we were discharged from the hospital, the army told us not to sue because they would produce evidence against us, that we were members of the NPA.

---

manghihilot — local barrio person (man or woman) who treats sick people with massage and local herbs.

The Philippine Army did not pay for damages and from then on did not bother to come back.''

I will relate now, further examples of military atrocities.

Zoilo Francisco, 42 years old, and a father of four, is the husband of Maria Morillo. He was a farmer in Barangay Giadgavan, Pambujan, Northern Samar. He and his family had just been moved out from an evacuation site in Pambujan to Barangay Dona Anacita of the same town. He was killed by Philippine Constabulary operatives of the 60th Philippine Constabulary Battalion last 7 August, 1979 at around 2.00 o'clock in the afternoon. His head was severed from his body and his stomach was slashed until his intestines came out.

A couple of minutes before he was murdered, Philippine Constabulary troopers led by Crespotin Lukban, went to the shack of Zoilo and found him taking a bath. He was ordered by the military to dress up immediately because he was allegedly being summoned to an interrogation in the *poblacion*. Zoila passively heeded the order and went with the military. When they had passed the bridge, his wife heard four consecutive gunshots. She immediately searched for the residence certificate of her husband in the used pair of trousers of Zoilo and found out that he had left it. Knowing the importance of this document, she quickly asked her children to bring this to their father. After a few minutes the children came home crying and reported to their mother that their father was killed by the military — his head severed from his body. Next day, they found his body near a coconut tree a few meters away from the provincial road on the other side of the Pambujan Bridge. Zoilo's head was displayed at the municipal hall.

The cases of this type of atrocity are not new in the province of Samar. Two sackloads of severed heads that were brought to Lao-ang, a town near Pambujan, have been reported by the local townspeople. According to them, when the military are tired of carrying bodies they have murdered, they just cut off the heads of the victims and bring them to the municipal building. In the detention center of Palapag, 32 human ears were displayed for the view of passers-by. Many more unreported incidents of massacre, rape, torture, forced evacuation, theft and other military abuses are common stories narrated by the residents of the above mentioned towns of Samar.

One of the owners of a coconut plantation narrated that his harvest of 5,000 coconuts had been reduced to 2,000 nuts because of the practice of target shooting by the military soldiers. They have made life very difficult for the townspeople wherever they went. In Gamay, as in other areas, the people who had evacuated earlier due to militarization, were ordered back to their barrios. The military, at the same time, called on the NPA to surrender. They threatened to intensify the militarization on the civilians if this call was not heeded.

Aside from the cases of military abuse, it is not uncommon for quarrels among the soldiers to end up in gunfights, causing great fears among the civilian population. These incidents, however, are seldom factually reported.

One such incident occurred in June 1979, at Can-avid, Eastern Samar, when a clash between rival military groups resulted in some casualties. This was reported in *Bulletin Today*, 23 June, 1979, as follows:

"... Lt. Col. Sabas Imbong, PC Commander of Eastern Samar, reported that an army soldier was killed and seven others were wounded when a team led by 2nd Lt. Eriberto Padernalla of Phil. Army's 19th Infantry Battalion was ambushed last Wednesday. The incident took place in the vicinity of Can-avid. The team was on its way to Taft after escort duty in Dolores when ambushed, Imbong said ..."

While this report may appear credible to the readers of the *Bulletin Today*, the residents in the Can-avid area know well that this is a cover-up to conceal the indiscipline of the military.

I wish to talk about a dear friend who was detained and tortured by the military. His name was Darwin. We used to spend long hours together, learning from each other and from the people.

He and I shared a lot because he was poor and kind. When he began to encounter a lot of economic difficulties, he quit school and searched for ways and for people who could teach him more about changing the life of the poor. He joined the resistance movement and became an artist for an underground paper. He was caught by the Military Intelligence Service Group (MISG), brought to a safe house and was tortured continuously for three days. The military stripped him, poured water into his mouth and tried to string him up but this made it impossible for them to extract information. Then they started putting bullets between his fingers and squeezed them everytime he refused to answer questions. Still, Darwin refused to say anything and this made the interrogator very angry. He was beaten next and whipped with a gun. Darwin was beginning to feel very faint and the MISG asked for the dynamo to be brought into the room.

Darwin had resolved that he would never reveal any information no matter how painful the torture would be and so when the military tied exposed wires to his fingers and toes, forced him to drink water and started to send electric shocks into his body, Darwin was able to withstand the torture without giving any information. The military decided to play Russian roulette on him. A sergeant put one bullet in his gun and cocked his gun and pointed at Darwin's left temple. The sergeant did not get to shoot Darwin because an order came from his superior to release Darwin and to use him as a tracer.

Darwin was able to elude the military and went back to his underground work. He was killed later in an ambush and the enemy cut off both his hands and feet, pulled his tongue out and paraded his dead body in the town with a soldier shouting to the people, "Look at your hero! This is your NPA! This is your hero!"

Activists are not the only ones who suffer under the heavy hand of the military. Innocent parents and relatives are often harassed and sometimes even held as hostages, if the military cannot find people they want to arrest. The parents also suffer great fear and anxiety when their son or daughter is arrested, because of the high incidence of torture, rape and even murder of those held in custody.

The US-Marcos dictatorship has ten fingers, five weaving a soft glove, and the other five clenched in an iron fist in the form of the military. Often, the peasants get the iron fist treatment.

Testimony of a former government employee

As a whole the mass media in the Philippines is heavily censored and virtually under the control of the regime.

I am Salud Torres. I will speak of my experiences as a government employee from 1972 to 1978 in the Department of Public Information, now called the Ministry of Public Information.

The Department of Public Information (DPI) is as old as the Marcos martial law regime. It has been created to be the state's direct arm in the control and supervision of mass media, and to be the state's propaganda machine.

But tremendous as these powers are, I came to realize that the military, represented by the Department of National Defense (DND), is more powerful than the DPI. I was able to work in the DPI not because I had the capability for the job, not because I had a friend heading a certain DPI unit, but above anything else, because the military granted me the right to work. Then and now, every applicant to a government position must first secure a military clearance. If military files show that the applicant has any subversive involvement, whether true or fabricated, the applicant is denied the job, and could be arrested and detained.

There is no longer any distinction between what we call temporary and permanent government employees. In the pre-martial law days, government employees were assured of the right and privilege to job security, after rendering long years of service to the government and passing the civil service exams. At present all government employees are subjected to regular military clearance. Any suspicion or charge of subversion will mean job termination. In most cases, this 'subversive record' tactic has been used to expel government employees to make way for Marcos loyalists, relatives and friends.

I can very well remember my first personal experience of what we called 'military phobia'. It was on 21 September, 1973, the first martial law anniversary, that Marcos declared a holiday for government offices. However, government employees were required to go to the Luneta Park in Manila where Marcos would deliver his speech. Attendance would be checked. I joined the 'loyalty' march, stood among government employees, listened to Marcos' long speech, not because I believed in him, not because of the one-day salary deduction for those who would be absent, but because I did not want to invite any 'special' attention from the National Intelligence and Security Agency (NISA) unit in our office.

As I have already mentioned, the DPI performs two functions. As an instrument to control mass media, the DPI has the following tasks: granting of permits for the operations of mass media establishments (publications, radio and television stations, printing presses, advertising agencies); monitoring publications, radio and television programs, films, theatre, and even advertisements, for any subversive content or insinuation. For the latter, we follow the guidelines set by the DND and the DPI. As a propaganda machine, the DPI, on the other hand, has the following tasks: to project Marcos' rule not as a martial law regime but a 'New Society' (a term coined by Marcos when he declared martial law); to portray the Marcos couple as true leaders of the Filipino people; to develop national and world public opinion favorable to the state; to trumpet about government projects so that the people will think that these projects are really for their welfare and development.

The control of the granting of operation permits is a manoeuvre to make mass media pliant and subservient to the state. If a publication, for instance, gets critical of the state, the DPI simply revokes the operation permit. Thus, mass media establishments are in the hands of the Marcoses and their relatives and business associates. For instance, the first newspaper to be published after the declaration of martial law, the *Philippine Daily Express* was owned by a Romualdez, a relative of Imelda Romualdez Marcos. To date, of the three major publication networks in the country, two are owned by the Romualdezes, the third by a certain Hanz Menzi, a Marcos business associate. One of the major television and radio networks is owned by Roberto Benedicto, another close Marcos business associate.

In actuality, there are two ministries monitoring mass media: the DPI and the DND. Violations of the state's guidelines on mass media will mean suspension or job termination, blacklisting from the state controlled mass media, or a military 'invitation'. One recent case I can give you is connected with Dulag Macliing's death. Macliing was a Kalinga national minority leader, very vocal and very active in his people's resistance against the state's Chico river dam project that will inundate their ancestral lands, the very source of their livelihood. One night, a group of military men came to Macliing's house, and riddled him with bullets. For publishing the fact, two writers, Maria Ceres O. Doyo and Rene Villanueva, and an editor, Leticia Jimenez Magsanoc, were individually 'invited' by a military panel which subjected them to interrogation, insults and warnings.

Through the DPI, Marcos used the mass media to deceive the people as to the military nature of his rule. He has coined the term the 'New Society', and has instructed the mass media to popularize it. Noting that the phrase 'under the New Society' was used, whether intentionally or unintentionally, there came an instruction to the mass media that from then on, the phrase 'in the New Society' was to be used. This is to make the public feel and believe that they are part and parcel of the martial law regime, because the phrase 'under the New Society' obviously carries a repressive connotation.

The mass media projects that there is peace, order and stability in the country. And so, during the early years of martial law, news on encounters between the military and the NPA or the MNLF, were totally banned. The people got to know about these encounters eventually. Sensing that this prohibition only widened the credibility gap between the state-controlled mass media and the people, the state has allowed the publication of encounter news provided they follow this formula: the NPA and the MNLF are always on the losing side (they surrender, they suffer more casualties, they are outnumbered, those who are able to escape are wounded, etc.); the women fighters are referred to as amazons, the men fighters as terrorists. More often than not, the news of these encounters ends with the sentence that firearms and subversive materials were confiscated from, or left behind by, the amazons and the terrorists.

The state uses the mass media to project Marcos and Imelda as true leaders of the country. In newspapers, for instance, particularly during the early part of martial law, it had been the policy always to have the photos and headlines on the Marcos couple. It was not unusual then, that the entire front page was devoted to the activities of the Marcos couple, the inside pages containing editorials, columns and write-ups on the government's 'development' projects. There was a very strict policy then regarding the use of photos. For Marcos, he should be shown either smiling, or serious but dignified, as the father of the land, as the leader of the 'New Society'. Imelda, on the other hand, should be shown always looking refreshed, beautiful, smiling and there are many photos of her embracing old people, carrying in her arms a malnourished child, surrounded by and shaking hands with poor people. The objective is to project her as the protector of the poor and the needy. Imelda has her 'compassionate society' which the mass media also plays up. Her photos should not only be compassionate looking but beautiful. During those early years of martial law, all photos of Imelda for national newspapers and magazines must come only from Malacanang, these photos were screened and okayed. It was also an instruction then that photographers should not take full-body photos of her. Why? Because in journalism, there is the term 'top-heavy', referring to a page lay-out wherein the top-half looks heavy because the concentration there of bold headlines and news makes the lower half look thin and light. Imelda is 'top-heavy' with her skinny legs, and so, the instruction against full-body photos. I also remember that one time, she telephoned our office and called the attention of my boss to her photo published in a national newspaper, in which she looked haggard. She instructed our boss to 'remind' the editors to be very careful and selective in using her photos. To please Imelda, publications often used what is considered Imelda's favorite photo, taken years back when she was slimmer and prettier. We call that photo the 'Mona Lisa' photo, because of the similar pose and the attempt to portray an enigmatic smile.

Through the DPI I have discovered how the mass media is manipulated to create public opinion favorable to the regime. Long before a certain decree is to be announced, we already churn out articles and paragraphs to be sent to columnists for insertion in their sections and editorials. Everyday, the people, through newspapers, radio and television, are bombarded with propaganda so that those who are not yet politically conscious get into the trap of acceptance and believing. I can cite many instances of this:

1. Everytime the regime wants to hike oil prices, long before it makes the formal announcement, the mass media harps on blaming OPEC for raising oil prices. What is not being published is the fact that the state hikes oil prices so that it can get more oil taxes, so that the oil multinationals can extract more profit from our people.

2. During the passage of the Investment Incentives Act, the mass media stressed the fact that we lack capital and technology to industrialize; and that only the foreign investors can supply these needs. They concealed the fact that these multinationals only seek to plunder the wealth of the nation and to exploit our labor.

3. Whenever the call for the lifting of martial law is strong, the newspapers and television are saturated with news of the upsurge of crimes and violence, the increased activities of MNLF in Mindanao, and the NPA in Luzon and Visayas, and so on and so forth.

Issues of foreign publications containing articles critical of the US-Marcos dictatorship are banned in our country. Some of these are the *Far Eastern Economic Review*, Newsweek, *Time*, *Life*, etc. Despite the banning, just the same, for those who are lucky enough to get hold of smuggled copies of said issues, and for those who came to know by word of mouth, the mass media puts out its defence of the state. One specialist in this field is the most powerful and most favored columnist in the country today, Teodoro Valencia.

The mass media sings halleluja to all the government 'development' projects. Our office was the one handling press releases for Imelda's projects such as the Cultural Center of the Philippines, Folk Arts Theater, Nutrition Center of the Philippines, Population Center, Philippine Heart Center for Asia. The latest addition to these projects, is a Children's Hospital, again another grandios building. All of these are in Metro Manila. Other Imelda projects are the **Bagong Lipunan Sites and Services (BLISS)**, and her own version of the Green Revolution, which takes the form of backyard-planting.

We wrote on the CCP (Cultural Center of the Philippines) and the FAT (Folk Arts Theater) to enhance Imelda's image as the 'patroness of art', a title which she likes and thinks she deserves.

The Nutrition Center of the Philippines, Population Center, BLISS, Green Revolution, Philippine Heart Center for

Asia, the Children's Hospital — these are used to show and prove to the people that she has much concern, devotion, sympathy and love for the poor and the needy. These are the showcases of her so-called compassionate society for the Filipino people and for the world community.

But the real facts concerning these projects and buildings, hidden from the people, are:

1. The CCP caters exclusively to the taste of the rich, both foreign and local. Apart from the prohibitive cost of the tickets, the Center itself is situated far from the public transport routes, making it inaccessible to the ordinary people. On top of this, a poor man, dressed in his best attire, would still look shabby in the company of the affluent people, clad in fabulous clothes and glittering jewelries, and feel out of place in the atmosphere of the plush carpets and magnificent chandeliers.

2. While the high brow elitist art and culture is the main diet in the CCP, the Folk Arts Theatre (FAT) is being projected as the platform for the expression of the popular culture of the people. In fact, the word *folk* in the Folk Arts Theater is purely ornamental. The building itself was constructed to hold the *Miss Universe Contest* in 1974. The government hosted the *Miss Universe Contest* to allay the fears of the foreign investors as regards peace, order and stability in the country. Since its inception the Folk Arts Theater has mainly been used for pop and rock groups, both foreign and local.

3. The much publicized Philippine Heart Center and the Children's Hospital, built with public funds, have some of the most advanced medical equipments in the world, but they are virtually inaccessible to the ordinary people because of their location and the high cost of medical fees. Imelda Marcos is in fact planning to build another prestigious clinic — the Lung Center of Asia — in Metro Manila. Thus the Marcos government is in fact using the country's money to provide first class service to the rich minority who can pay their way into these hospitals. In the opinion of many Filipino doctors what is needed are numerous small clinics and health centers throughout the country, within the means and reach of the general populace, rather then a few exclusive and impressive buildings in the city.

4. The American funded Nutrition Center of the Philippines and the Population Center Foundation of the Philippines were purportedly built to help Filipinos ungrade the quality of their food, and secondly to control the birth-rate. As a matter of fact these Centers are used as tools to deceive the people as to the true causes of their poverty and exploited conditions. The propaganda of these Centers lays the blame of malnutrition and overpopulation on the poor people themselves, for their lack of knowledge of proper diet and family planning. In this way they hide the fact that the actual cause of these problems is poverty which is a result of economic exploitation.

5. As for Imelda's housing project, BLISS, contrary to the propaganda, no ordinary person can afford to buy even on installment basis, any of the housing units. To qualify for an housing loan a couple would need a monthly income of P3,000 to P5,000, a salary which few professionals receive. Nurses, for instance, receive only P500 a month, while doctors average P1,000 a month.

As a whole the mass media in the Philippines is heavily censored and virtually under the total control of the regime. An example of this control is the suppression of the coverage relating to the Marcos couple's 25th wedding anniversary celebration, held in 1979. Originally it was planned that a basilica, which would have cost anything from P50 million to P185 million, be constructed. The Marcos couple were to ride to the basilica on a silver chariot, drawn by white horses imported just for the occasion. These details were leaked to the public, and due to vehement reactions, particularly from the church sector who refused to be involved in the basilica issue, these plans were scrapped. The wedding anniversary was then held in Malacanang Palace which had to be specially renovated and refurnished for the occasion. Among other things, expensive chandeliers were imported. The local mass media was not allowed to cover the wedding anniversary and so the majority of the Filipino people did not know that a royal happening had taken place in their midst.

I came to know about the wedding anniversary through underground publications and through a smuggled copy of *Life* magazine (this particular issue was banned). The *Life* magazine showed the Marcos couple walking down the aisle, strewn with red roses, while in another photo Imelda praying with her diamond-beaded rosary. The rites were followed by a grand ballroom dance and other celebrations, till the early hours of the morning. The Marcos couple gave silver bell souvenirs to their guests, among whom were the jetsetter friends of Imelda, Christina Ford, Sean Connery and lesser known European royal blood personalities. The jetsetters came to the country per invitation of Imelda. To cover up the real purpose of their visit, it was played up in the mass media that the jetsetters came to attend the opening of a holiday resort, and that their presence was advantageous to the country because they would invest in that resort and in other business ventures. It was first-class entertainment and hospitality for the jetsetters, and the high point was a cruise in the presidential yacht with the Marcos couple leading the eating, wining, dancing and singing.

Later, when the news of the grand wedding anniversary festivities, which were estimated to have cost around P100 million, became known to the people, the Marcos loyalists defended them by saying that couples can only celebrate their 25th wedding anniversary once in a lifetime, and that the Marcos couple had spent their own personal money, so why all the fuss.

Through time my position as a government propagandist, while at the same time supporting the resistance movement against the US-Marcos dictatorship, became too difficult for me to live with. These questions kept bugging me: Am I really committed to the movement? Where is my self respect as a writer? Do I really believe in my political convictions? Can I just close my eyes and continue in this dual existence? In the final analysis whose interests do I really serve?

These questions have made me realize that in doing state propaganda work, I am a tool of repression, and at the same time, I am an object of repression. As a propaganda writer, I deceive the people because I tell them lies, all lies. I am their enemy too. But like the majority of the Filipino people, I also suffer exploitation and repression. I am not free to write. I do not have job security. There is always that fear of the military — of being suspended from work, terminated from my job, blacklisted, arrested, detained or even liquidated.

Finally, I decided to leave my job as a state propaganda writer, and work full-time for the movement.

Testimonies on cultural repression

Testimony of a student

For every 100 students who enter elementary level only 42 reach grade 6, and only four reach high school.

I am Perla Silangan, age 22, a political science student of the University of the Philippines. I have been a member of the *Kabataang Makabayan* since 1978. I am here to testify about the Philippine educational system.

The Philippine educational system is composed of 3 levels: elementary which is over 90 per cent public (there are 51,786 public elementary schools compared to only 1,880 private elementary schools); high school with an almost equal division (2,825 secondary public schools and 2,019 for secondary private schools); and the collegiate level which is 80 per cent private (247 for public and 677 for private). (*Ibon*, 15 June, 1980).

Various surveys have shown the deteriorating quality of education at all levels. In the elementary school level alone, the Educational Program Implementating Task Force found out that on the average, elementary school graduates have learnt only two-thirds of what they should have learned, and the subject which the elementary school graduates seem to have learned the least, are those traditionally considered basic to elementary education, like reading, mathematics and language. Facilities are inadequate and the teachers, overworked with tasks other than elementary education, are stifled by the Administration. ('Profile of a Sixth Grader: Notes on the Study Outcome of Elementary Education', *FAPE*, June 1976).

The school officials in the elementary level pointed to the continuous progression system as the primary cause for the present deterioration of the elementary education. (*Bulletin Today*, 8 May, 1978). The continuous progression system allows every pupil to be automatically promoted to the next grade at the end of every school year. In 1979, the Minister of Education and Culture, Juan Manuel, reported that at least 45 per cent of grade six pupils in the country's public elementary schools are illiterate, unable to read or count. This was attributed by Manuel to incompetent teachers and officials, shortage of necessary instructional materials, inadequate facilities and poor socio-economic conditions of the people.

'One of the reasons for the deteriorating quality of education can be attributed to incompetent teachers.' But why are the teachers incompetent? It is because teachers in public schools are poorly paid and are overloaded with subjects. Aside from this, they are forced into many non-teaching activities by the Ministry of Education and Culture. How can a teacher cope with this.

My mother is a public school teacher. She teaches eight hours every day. This activity takes up almost all her time and yet the government still imposes several activities to which she must attend or be reprimanded by the principal. The government has made it the duty of the teachers to assist in mock referenda and elections. It also passes memoranda to public school teachers and students to stage a welcome every time President Marcos or a visitor arrives. During public symposiums of the president, all teachers and students are made to attend, to fill the empty seats in the auditorium, to show to the local and foreign press that he has a large audience and sympathizers. Aside from these, there are still government programs which the teachers are again obliged to attend — like tree planting programs on Saturdays, and the *Alay Lakad*, a compulsory energy-saving walk. Most of the time my mother comes home tired and exhausted, and yet has to work on her lesson plan for the following day. She and her fellow teachers work for more than eight hours a day almost seven days a week without additional compensation and for a very meagre salary.

The monthly minimum wage rate of public elementary school teachers was P517 until it was adjusted to P574 in August, 1978. In October 1979, when inflation was estimated to be 22 per cent, their salaries were increased to P603 with an additional P50 per year for clothing allowance. In Maryknoll Mission (MM) private schools, elementary and high school teachers received P380-P650 a month while a non-MA college teacher received P750-P850 a month. College professors get only P500-P900, excluding deductions for medicare, retirement, social security and loans (*Ibon*, 15 June, 1979).

This explains why many teachers are forced to engage in more menial sidelines: selling sweepstakes, cosmetics and underwear. (*Bulletin Today*, 30 November, 1978).

The question of teachers' salaries has generally received less publicity than other complaints against the educational system. Nevertheless, it affects educators' morale and subsequently the quality of education we students receive.

Meanwhile as the government grossly neglects elementary and high school education, high school graduates go to college with very little knowledge and are not prepared to do the rigorous studies a college student has to face. Coupled with this problem, they are also faced with the greed of the school management which is more interested in profit than in providing a good education for the students. Students in the universities and colleges face grave problems in the kind of education they are getting.

Commercialization of Education

On 21 May, 1980, we students lobbied at the Ministry of Education and Culture to protest against the proposed 15 per cent tuition fee increase. We pointed out that education has been turned into big business. One of the reasons cited for the proposed increase is the large losses attributed to greater maintenance and operational costs, and heavy taxes imposed by the government on private schools. The proprietary schools like the University of the East and the Far Eastern University are treated by the government as corporations. The Bureau of Internal Revenue taxes them as such. The Bureau of Customs collects tariff duties. A special 15 per cent import tax is levied on their imports of educational materials and equipment. But while these schools complain of great losses, their profits have soared to millions of pesos. *Business Day*, a weekly magazine, reported that as early as 1975, universities and colleges in Metro Manila were having an annual net income of more than P4m. FEATI University, University of the East and the Far Eastern University are among the top 1,000 corporations.

Furthermore, as tuition fees go up every year, there has been no improvement in the quality of education we received. Facilities are also inadequate. In FEATI University alone, there are more than 50 students crammed into a small and dingy room, with dirty dilapidated walls, and the windows are facing the noise and traffic of one of the busiest shopping centres in Metro Manila, Santa Cruz, while at their back is the foul smell of the Pasig River. The rooms are very hot during summer because of poor ventilation, and dripping wet during the rainy season because of the cracks in the walls and ceiling. The administration constructed new buildings, but they built without consideration for the students' comfort and welfare. They also lack chairs and laboratory equipment. On top of this, we students cannot buy the necessary books and school supplies because of the ever increasing prices. We content ourselves with borrowing books from the library. But the library has only one textbook for 200 students.

FEATI University is one of the big universities which jacks up tuition and other school fees almost every year, without making corresponding improvements in school facilities and services. In this manner, the capitalist educators reap as much profit as possible at the lowest cost.

The rising cost of education prohibits an increasing number of our youth from acquiring formal higher education. For every 100 students who enter elementary level only 42 reach Grade 6 and only four reach high school.

On the other hand, there are schools and institutions under the direct supervision of the government like the University of the Philippines, Central Luzon State University and others. These schools and institutions specialize in engineering and technological courses to produce technicians, bureaucrats and technocrats for the managerial manpower requirements of the multinational corporations. The government boasts of a P4,000 expenditure for each student every year. However, of this amount only P317 is spent on the student and the remainder is used by the school administration. Before martial law, the share of the Department of Education in the national budget was 30 per cent. Today it is down to 12 per cent. (*Daily Express*, 20 June, 1979). For 1980, education was only allotted P3.5 billion out of the total budget of P41 billion, only a poor second compared to the military budget of P5.5 billion.

Meanwhile, the total expenditure of a nursing student for four years in a provincial private college is already P31,500 (*Liberation*, Manila 1979). How much more will it cost in Metro Manila?

Suppression of Democratic Rights

Since the imposition of martial law, Marcos has tried to silence the students into passivity. He banned the student councils, made student organizations illegal and stopped all campus publications. It was only after years of protests and struggle that they were allowed to operate. In my school, UP, it was only on 7 February, 1978, that the student council was restored. Our newspaper, *Philippine Collegian*, though allowed to be published, is subject to the censorship of the government through the Philippine Council of Print Media and the school administration. The situation in our school is similar to the other universities and colleges. Coupled with these, any students or persons who do not agree with the government are branded 'subversives', therefore an atmosphere of fear hangs over our classrooms, as our teachers and some of the students veer away from political issues and criticism of social ills, lest they be considered 'subversives' and be arrested. The issuing of Arrest Search and Seizure Orders (ASSOs) for students by the Ministry of National Defence, is a common occurence. Students sometimes just disappear, to be found later in one of the prison cells of the Marcos regime.

The latest batch of students to be arrested in our school (UP) was on 26 September, 1980. These included Martin Babiano, Victoria Bariga, Felizardo Colombo, Romulo Cruz, Ramon Duran, Dante Esquivel, Enrico Fos, German Ilagan, Florentino Inogo, Jade Joy Lim, Roland Pascual, Romina de los Reyes, Emilio Rivera III, Luz del Rosario, and Leoncio Yap. As of 2 October, they were detained in Camp Bicutan (*Philippine Collegian*, 2 October, 1980). They are only a few of the many students arrested since the imposition of martial law because of their principles and political beliefs.

This heightened militarization can also be seen upon entry to our universities. In my school, University of the Philippines, hordes of military agents, informers and police, prowl the campus to spy and harass student militants. Quasi-fascist groups sponsored by the government like YADO, the Vanguard, Kabataang Barangay Chapters, CAT and CMT have also been set up to buttress the network of suppression.

In my experience as a college student, I noticed that there are many college courses that prepare students to enter elite companies and MNCs, and subjects that are irrelevant and useless to our society. Our educators, meanwhile, even propose the dropping of history because they think that it is dead and useless (*Bulletin Today*, 21 June, 1978). At first I could not understand their values. When I reached my third year in college and read volumes of books, I got angry with all my teachers from elementary to high school, who taught me the wrong things about society and the benevolence of America. I was lucky that I corrected my knowledge on important issues such as these, that greatly affected my thinking process. But how about the thousands of my classmates who were not given the same opportunity to read the right books. They will be totally brainwashed. Later, I also realized that it was not the fault of my teachers. They were also victims of the same kind of education. Then I started analyzing the whole situation.

Before I entered college, I was made to take an exam, the National College Entrance Examination that determines whether we should enter a university or take up a vocational course. This written examination was instituted by the government following a recommendation of the Presidential Commission to survey Philippine Education. This Presidential Commission is composed of scholars of the Ford Foundation. They emphasise the technical and vocational training of students. Another recommendation was Parliamentary Bill 524, titled an 'Act providing for the establishment of an Integrated System of Education'. The proposed bill, if approved, will provide for the entire educational system to be under the jurisdiction of the Ministry of Education and Culture. It will not only virtually suppress the democratic rights of students in schools and universities in all levels, but as former UP President Salvador P. Lopez puts it, "The bill will make universities adjuncts of state apparatus".

Slowly, we the general populace, through the educational system, become part of a system which does not serve the interests of the people or the nation.

Testimony on writers under martial law

To attract the best writers these government offices offer high salaries to those who will work as... propaganda writers.

I will speak on the repressed condition imposed by the U.S.-Marcos dictatorship on Filipino writers.

Before martial law, Filipino writers were already economically oppressed. Then and now, even the most widely circulated magazine pays a measely sum for a poem, essay or short story. Thus, writers cannot be creative writers — they must have another source of income, whether it be teachers, researchers, underwriters, copywriters, thesis and term paper writers.

Nevertheless, the writers of pre-martial law days had something to be happy about. There were many publications to choose from — national/commercial as well as campus. Though the income from these sources may not have been much, at least, writers were able to write and relay their ideas to the reading public.

Under the martial law regime, the writers suffer not only economic repression but also political repression. All publications were closed down when Marcos declared martial law on 23 September, 1972. Schools and colleges were shut down to put a check on the militancy of the academic sector. These moves naturally dislocated the writers, many of whom were teachers. It is no exaggeration to say that during this time, many of them and their families and dependents practically starved.

While closing down all avenues of dissent, the Marcos dictatorship was at the same time strengthening its propaganda machinery to cover up the regime's military character, to project

Marcos and Imelda as the true leaders and protectors of the
land, to make the people believe that the state was doing everything for their welfare and development.

Towards these goals, the state created the Department of
Public Information (the DPI, now elevated to ministry level)
whose function is not only to supervise and control the mass
media but also to provide propaganda materials for local and
foreign use. The National Media Production Center (NMPC)
was also created, to produce propaganda films, advertisements
and publications. Since then, the NMPC takes care of multi-
media coverages (press, radio, television and film) of all
"historic" activities of the Marcos couple in the Philippines and
abroad.

Also, information and publication units of government offices, in particular, those at the ministry level and those dealing
with Imelda's projects, were enlarged and given huge funds for
their smooth operations. And to attract the best writers, these
government offices offer high salaries to those who will work as
government information writers, in other words, propaganda
writers.

It is in this context of the lack of job opportunities in the
private sector, and in the face of the attractive high salary offered by the government information agencies, that many
writers find themselves in the employ of the US-Marcos dictatorship.

Once inside the government's propaganda machinery, it is
now very easy for the writers to be coopted by the regime. Aside
from high salaries, propaganda writers usually are not required
to observe regular office hours because "they are writers". High
salaries and flexible working hours — these are some of the ways
employed by the state to pamper its propaganda writers, to the
envy of rank and file government employees.

Money comes easy for the more talented writers in the
government propaganda machinery. Here, writers can avail
themselves of "sidelines" or extra jobs, for instance, speech-
writing for Marcos and Imelda or any cabinet member. A writer
is paid over P1000 for a speech. Many writers, when being offered the job of speech-writer for the Marcos couple and the
cabinet members, find it difficult to resist the temptation.

A writer can prepare a speech in a matter of a day or so.
The income from one speech alone is enough to cover a writer's
economic needs for a month or two. So a writer in the government employ need not seek another source of income from

teaching, researching, copywriting or thesis and term paper writing.

The government holds regular seminars to assess the effectiveness of its propaganda work and the quality of its publications. I remember in one seminar the subtle attacks on the government policy in some of the articles were pointed out. Our department boss gave us those "inspiring" words: "Always bear in mind, you don't bite the hand that feeds you."

Aside from the DPI and the NMPC, the state also employs outside services to improve its propaganda. I remember a case where a literary writer was asked to do a special write-up on the Masagana 99, a part of the government's so-called land reform program.

This propaganda project was aimed to make the farmers believe that they really needed Masagana 99 and that they would really benefit from it. The material was to be written in a popular style, easily readable by the farmers. It was suggested that the writer should stay for sometime with a peasant family in a barrio, so that his writing would capture the local flavour, thereby rendering it more acceptable to the farmers.

No expenses would be spared for this project: the writer was told that he could name his price, and all facilities, such as transport, researchers etc. would be readily available to him. He was told that he need not hurry with his decision. The state in the meantime would be looking for a barrio where a peasant family had really benefited from the Masagana 99 project.

This propaganda project was later shelved because they could not find a barrio where a peasant family had really benefited from the Masagana 99, not even in the Nueva Ecija, the province that was being developed as the showcase of the state's land reform programme!

State-sponsored contests also proliferate these days — with big cash prizes for films, music, literature, radioplay and teleplay. For the films, there is the Imelda-sponsored Metro Manila Film Festival; for literature, the contests of Imelda's Cultural Center of the Philippines (CCP); for music, the CCP sponsored Popular Music Foundation of the Philippines; for radioplay and teleplay, the MPI's contest. The themes and subject areas that artists can explore and develop are clearly defined by contest rules. For guidance, there is the Presidential Decree No. 1081 or the Anti-Subversion Law.

The government has used these contests and big cash prizes to manipulate the talents of writers for its own ends. A case in point is the grand prize winning epic in the CCP sponsored contest. This epic eulogized the Pantabangan Dam and hailed it as a great success of the 'New Society' development program. However, this was a complete distortion of the fact. The truth is that the dam destroyed the livelihood of the Pantabangan people of Nueva Ecija.

This is what happened in Pantabangan:

When the Pantabangan people first heard of the plan to flood out their town and to relocate them, they resisted. Their main reason was economic — the Pantabangan people were mostly farmers and the land was their source of livelihood. The other reasons could be classified as cultural: they were born on that land; they grew up there; their parents and their ancestors had lived and died on that land. The Pantabangan people were afraid to lose their town and with it their memories and the history of their people.

But the state allayed all the fears of the Pantabangan people, by promising compensation for their lands, crops, trees, properties and everything they would lose because of the dam project. The people were promised subsidies and loans, new lands, jobs, houses and other facilities. Because of these promises, the people agreed to be relocated.

For this decision, the Pantabangan people have paid a high price. Particularly during those early years of resettlement, it was ironic that the Pantabangan people were living beside a dam, yet, they did not have water. They had to cross hills and go down the river for their water. As a result of using river water, some people got sick. A number of them drowned when they took their bath or washed their clothes in the river. The people were now idle and yet at the same time were starving because the new lands were not yet suitable for farming. There were also many anomalies in the compensation payments and in the allotment of new lands. In most cases, the funds and the lands were monopolized by the people in power. Some got paid for their lands and properties, but what they received was less than their properties' real value; others got paid later, but by that time, the value of the pesos was less than it used to be; others did not get paid at all because the legality of their property ownership was questioned.

Deprived of their main source of income, land and trees, the people soon used up whatever money they had. Most of them decided to leave the resettlement area, and they went to Manila to look for jobs. There, the Pantabangan people have joined the ranks of the unemployed and the underemployed.

This tragic fate of the Pantabangan people was not recorded at all in the award winning epic of the CCP literary contest.

It would come as no surprise if despite the military atrocities in the Kalinga-Mountain Provice, where the Chico Dam is being built in the face of fierce opposition from the people there, a song, film, short story, novel, epic, play, radioplay or teleplay on the 'noble', 'glorious' Chico River Dam will win an award in one of the state-sponsored contests.

This propaganda, whether blatant, or disguised as art and culture, is at least addressed to adults who may be able to discriminate between fact and fiction. What is much more pernicious is the assault on the minds of young children which is now being carried out. Imelda has employed the services of a group of writers to produce children's books. According to Imelda, it is not enough that the country tackles the problem of malnutrition — if there is the problem of the stomach, there is also the problem of the mind, or mental malnutrition. To complement her so-called nutrition program, she has thought of the "mental-feeding program". For this, Imelda has allotted P40 million for the production of children's books which are distributed in the cities and the barrios. These children's books seek to inculcate in the impressionable young minds the values of the Marcos' "New Society"; the adulation of the "First Family"; the glorification of the regime's "development" projects.

In suppressing the freedom and creativity of the Filipino writers the Marcos regime hopes to deny the people the knowledge of the realities of the present Philippine society.

The National Democratic Front combats this repression and struggles for the rights of the Filipino writers to identify the problems in society and to articulate the genuine aspirations of the people.

Testimony on cultural minorities

Today under martial law, we believe that our culture, beliefs, traditions, indeed our very survival and existence as a people are threatened.

I am Wada Taw-il, an Igorot from the Cordillera of Northern Luzon in the Philippines. I have come as a representative of my people and as a witness against the systematic atrocities of exploitation and oppression inflicted upon us as a people.

Including our Muslim brothers and sisters, we number around six and a half million people, or 16 to 18 percent of the total Philippine population. We are composed of more than 60 distinct groups. We are the Igorots of the Mountain Provinces of Kalinga-Apayao, Bontoc, Benguet and Ifugao; the Tinggians of Abra; the Manobos, Subanon, Bilaan, Bagobo, Ata, T'boli, Tagakaolo, Higaonon, Tiruray, Mandaya, Mansaka of the South; the Mangyans of Mindoro; the Gaddangs, Ikalahans and Dumagats of Nueva Vizcaya; the Ibanag of Cagayan Valley; the Negritoes of Zambales, and others.

Our lands are in the remote interiors throughout the length of the Philipine archipelago. We are dependent on our lands in many ways. As farmers, the land is the basis of our survival. We are skilled in our farming practices and have few other options for successful livelihood. We cannot compete in the cities or labor markets as equals.

The land means much to us! Our history is bound to our lands. Fields handed down through generations are both economic assets and a statement of tribal history — a link with past ancestors. The forests and fields have spiritual significance for us, as the homes of powerful natural forces that are to be respected and cherished. They are also the resting place and homes of our ancestors.

The development and improvement of our lands are the fruits of the collective efforts of deceased ancestors. We, the living, have the grave responsibility to care for the land and the dead. Allowing the submersion or destruction of our land means a breaking of this awesome responsibility, an act of desecration against grave-sites and homes of the spirits. But what is more frightening is that it means our death as a people.

We have developed our own extensive and complex system of political organization, including the peace pact — which we have used as an effective deterrent against intruders. From the coming of the Spaniards to the eventual take-over of the Americans, we resisted all forms of foreign invasion.

As a people, we are treated as ignorant, uncivilized and not Filipino. We are discriminated against in terms of education, health, housing, electricity supply and other services. Typical of the pervading attitude against us is the statement of the present Minister of Foreign Affairs, Carlos P. Romulo, when in the 1960s he said: "The Igorots are not Filipinos!"

Today, under martial law, we believe that our culture, beliefs, traditions, indeed our very survival and existence as a people are threatened. We believe that the government is pursuing policies that can only be described as genocidal.

To support these claims, I have here written and documented facts gathered from personal experiences of other individuals and groups of national minorities.

**The Government Program and its effects
on the Cultural Minorities**

One of the most far reaching and damaging parts of present government policy which affects minorities is its energy program. The government has existing plans to build more than 40 major dams. Almost all of these dams are to be built on lands at present occupied by national minorities. The dams will submerge our best farmland, the settlements, graveyards and sacred sites of many peoples. It is estimated that more than one and a half million minority Filipinos and another half million poor farmers will be impoverished and dislocated by these dams.

These dams would not only displace communities of people, but would destroy the whole tribal economy of some peoples. The government has now passed special regulations empowering the National Power Corporation to restrict or even prevent farming within the watershed of dams, and to forcibly expel anyone breaking these rules. These rules would deny the people the means of basic subsistence that has been theirs for centuries. In my home — the Cordillera — the government has immediate plans for eight dams and further proposals for at least seven more. Already the Ifugao people who number more than 100,000 and live in the watershed of the Magat Dam are being prevented from clearing new mountain farms. They are forced instead to plant trees on their old clearings. This will bring hunger to the Ifugao. But at the very time that the ordinary people are being prevented from continuing their farming practices, new logging concessions are given within the watershed. Local officials, including the governor and assemblyman of Ifugao, now have commercial logging concessions within the area. So, control over the cutting of trees is only imposed on the poor farmers but not on the rich concessionaire.

The energy program for the next ten years was planned to cost more than $14.5 billion but recently Marcos made an announcement that this program must be implemented in only five years. So our situation has become even more critical.

The proposed energy supply increase is not to meet local needs but is planned as an incentive to foreign investment. The whole program is heavily financed and backed by the World Bank, Asian Development Bank and USAID. Most of the Bank money is being spent on construction and equipment paid straight out to foreign heavy engineering contractors. In the Cordillera, on the Ambuklao dam, it was Guy Atkinson and Co of the USA; on the Magat Dam it is Voest Alpine and Brown Boveri from Europe; on the Chico, it is Lahmeyer of Germany.

The government makes propaganda that these dams are a sign of progress and prosperity for the nation and will improve the quality of life, especially for the rural poor. But we in the Cordillera ask, "Whom does it really help?" We know it does not help us and we are the most neglected sector of the rural poor. We gain no share in the benefits of these dams, while our livelihood and culture are to be destroyed. We are to be sacrificed. Even Marcos says this.

In 1956 the Ambuklao Ibaloy were moved off their land. There was no adequate compensation, no place for relocation. After 25 years when the dam is already choking to death with silt the people still have no land. When they were on their land, they were promised relocation but when the dam was built and they were no longer a threat, there was no relocation.

The government says that dams will bring electricity and irrigation to the lowland peasants but these people still live in poverty. They cannot afford the high costs of electrical appliances or even irrigation pumps and rentals. The benefit is only to rich landlords in the Cagayan Valley, men like Defense Minister Enrile, Local Government and Community Development Minister Rono, President Marcos and a handful of others, all of whom have large tracts of land in the Cagayan Valley that will be irrigated by the Chico and Magat dams.

The dam program that has been worked out for the Philippines by the World Bank has come to be priority only under martial law conditions. When the Chico was first considered for damming in the 1960s the project was indefinitely shelved because of the social costs involved. But by 1973 under martial law when the people had no voice, it was no longer thought necessary to even ask for the people's opinion or even inform them. In Kalinga and Bontoc, we first learned of the project when survey teams invaded the valley. The people angered by such deceit, ejected the teams.

In July 1974 the survey teams came back with a military escort and abused the people, especially in Cagaluan, Kalinga, where three boys were lined up and soldiers used submachine guns to shoot coconuts off their heads.

We tried petitions and legal appeals to the government and the World Bank, thinking that no one would knowingly destroy the culture and livelihood of the 80,000 people of the Chico. But Marcos avoided meeting our delegations. He made excuses and one delegation that went to Manila to plead for their land was turned away because the President was too busy they said "with the preparations of the *Miss Universe* contest"!

Only when it was clear that the people would fight for their land and would have support in Manila and elsewhere did Marcos take notice. The people adopted the tradition of our peace pact which is strong among us to call for unity in the defense of our lands.

It was at this point that the attempts to trick and deceive and divide us really began. Marcos' Minister Melchor announced the suspension of all work in the Chico Valley and the indefinite postponement of Chico II dam in the heart of the mountains. But it is clear now that this was a conscious trick. There has been no attempt to bring the issue of Chico II up for further discussion but plans for its construction have gone ahead. Construction is now scheduled to begin within 3 years.

At the time of Minister Melchor's announcement the government had fears that the Chico would become another minority problem which could spark off an all out war like that of the Muslims in the south. Marcos has an agency, the PANAMIN (Presidential Assistance on National Minorities), to deal with its minority problem but like the government it does not represent the people but the big business that seeks to exploit their lands. Who the PANAMIN serves is very clear by looking at the people who control it. These people are some of the biggest capitalists in the Philippines like Elizalde, Ayala, Soriano & Cabarrus, and working for them are, both serving and retired military officers including those who have been trained in Vietnam in counter-insurgency programs.

PANAMIN was established without even one representative of a national minority as a member. It does not represent or serve the interests of the minority people. Under martial law it has become the government's instrument of repression against minorities. The documents we present show that the PANAMIN, like the state it serves, has had to resort increasingly to armed oppression; and that now, the major item of the PANAMIN Budget is for its own security not for minority development.

Within months of the announcement of suspension of all work at Chico, PANAMIN and its head Manda Elizalde himself showed up in Kalinga, to work on the people. He arrived in November like an early Father Christmas, giving out gifts of basketballs, whisky and blankets; and for the community leaders there was money and the offer of jobs. Elizalde even offered money to satisfy himself with our women. Elizalde expressed concern over our case and promised to help take it to the President. He gathered community leaders together and took them to Manila. But there they were kept under guard and were pressured and tricked into signing their support for the project.

As a result, Marcos announced the creation of Kalinga Special Development Region (KSDR) to give special attention to this poor region. But the whole of the Cordillera is neglected and in need of development; our roads are bad, hospitals few and schools inadequate. Why then did the KSDR only cover the area affected by the dam? KSDR was an attempt to dupe the people into surrendering their land. Within KSDR scholarships were offered to people as long as, and only if, they supported the government.

Worst of all the PANAMIN turned the people against each other. The Basao were armed by PANAMIN in their tribal war with the Butbut people who are well known for their opposition to the dams. The Basao were given more than 40 high-powered rifles. Because of the many guns several Butbut and Basao were killed. As a result the border area between Kalinga and Bontoc was virtually closed by the feuding and the unity of the peoples was badly affected.

But opposition continued even though the PANAMIN, backed by the military, became increasingly abusive and violent. When the troops tried to establish a camp to guard the dam site, 250 Kalingas dismantled the camp and marched 25 kilometers in defiance of martial law curfew regulations to return the camp equipment to the Provincial military HQ. The people also effectively boycotted the 1977 referendum. The elders said that we could not take part because any sign of co-operation with the government would be twisted to make it seem that we supported the dam. Because of these two actions, more than 100 people were arrested and detained without trial. Most of them were held during and over the planting season so that they had nothing to eat. The church had to organise emergency relief for families that had not been able to farm because of the arrests.

We approached World Bank representatives in Manila who repeated the promise of Robert McNamara that the World Bank would not fund the Chico project in the face of opposition from the people; but they lied and they have continued to fund the project despite our opposition. They have also funded other projects like that on the Magat river and elsewhere.

The people's fight for their rights against the Marcos government has taught them many bitter lessons. The resistance of the Kalinga gives hope to other people in the Philippines, thus the government has to send its troops into the province to silence us.

There have been many and horrible abuses against my people. Many of these abuses are documented and show that contrary to the government's assertion that military abuse is rare and incidental, in fact it is common and systematic. None of the soldiers identified to have committed the severest abuses of murder, torture, arson and rape have ever been made to pay.

To cite just a few of the abuses committed:

● 25 October, 1977 in Tanglag Lubuangan, the 55th Infantry

Battalion PC led by two identified NCOs burned down two houses and stole or destroyed heirlooms valued in excess of P30,000.

- In January 1978 a farmer, Ruben Ta-ilan, was picked up by identified 55th PC officers. The next day his dead and mutilated body was found by the roadside.
- In April 1978, two elders of Ngibat Tinglayan were shot and killed. And in an operation launched by the 60th battalion, the whole village was subjected to mortar attack causing extensive property damage.
- In June 1978, a 16 year old girl, Norma Kikilaw, sick and confined in Lubuagan hospital, was raped by two identified PC.
- In July 1978, a river ferryman was wounded when he was shot in the mouth by a soldier who refused to pay his fare on the ferry.
- In September 1978, the Chico IV dam site area and all the land around the village of Tomiangan was declared a Free Fire Zone. The people of the village could only enter or leave the village with military permit, and a strict 3.00 p.m. - 9.00 a.m. curfew was imposed which effectively stopped the people from working their land. As their fields were within the Free Fire Zone, many were afraid to do any work on their land. For the people there was foc   shortage and hunger and the PC were able to take advantage of the situation. For food and sport they have shot virtually all the villagers' cows and carabaos grazing in this area.
- In October 1978, in Batong Buhay Pasil, indiscriminate mortar shelling of the community led to the killing of a small child.

In April 1980, Macli-ing Dulag, the spokesman of the Kalingas was murdered by the 44th Infantry Battalion. Macli-ing was a powerful opposition spokesman and the best known of our leaders. He was shot down inside his own house in the night by men since identified and admitted by the government to be members of the 44th Infantry Battalion under the leadership of Lieutenant Adalem. On the same night in the same village an attempt was also made on the life of Pedro Dungoc, another of the Kalinga opposition spokesmen.

Macli-ing was well known to the government for his opposition. His village had hosted two major Peace Pact celebrations called to discuss the dam problem and unite the people and strengthen them in their opposition. He had been offered bribes by Elizalde which he refused.

His murder was a further proof to us that we could not expect justice within the present system where even our most respected spokesmen are just gunned down like animals. The people all know that we must be prepared to defend our land if we are to survive. And we are happy to join the NPA and unite with the other poor Filipinos in fighting for a better society.

We ask this Tribunal to recognise that the struggle of the Tribal Filipinos and other oppressed sectors of Philippine society, is a just struggle and that we have the right to resist the genocide and oppression that we face.

Logging operations in cultural minority homelands

I would now like to talk about logging operations in the lands of my people in the Cordillera Mountains of Northern Luzon. This is the Cellophil Resources Corporation (CRC), established in 1973 as part of the Herdis business empire of Herminio Disini, a relative by marriage of Imelda Marcos.

The Herdis Group first came to the Cordillera in 1972 when they did survey work in the province of Abra and were accompanied and guarded on their mission by members of the Presidential Guard. Later we came to see the presence of the Presidential Guard as one of the signs of President Marcos' class involvement and personal interests in CRC.

In 1973 and 1974 CRC and Cellulose Processing Corporation (CPC) were granted concessions of 99,565 hectares and 99,230 hectares respectively. But the CPC has no separate existence from CRC. It has the same owners and uses the same workers and equipment as CRC. The reason for the existence of the CPC was only to evade the regulations of the Bureau of Forest Development (BFD) that restrict logging concessions to 100,000 hectares; The joint CRC-CPC concession is 198,795 hectares and covers the lands of the Tinggians of Abra, the Kalingas and Isnegs of Kalinga-Apayao, the Bontocs of Mountain Province and the Kankanai Mountain Province and Ilocos Sur.

The CRC plans to strip the pine forests of these mountains to feed a pulping mill. Foresters have all along voiced doubts about the capability of the concession to provide enough timber for the massive 66,000 tons per annum capacity pulp mill. The demands of the mill from the 198,000 hectares are so great that severe deforestation is predicted.

Despite the environmental problems this would cause, CRC has gathered many backers. The major foreign stockholders in CRC are Bauminter Corporation of Switzerland with 18 share holdings (P15.2 million), Mitsubishi Rayon, Daicel and Marubeni Corporations, all of Japan, collectively own a further 12 per cent.

In addition the capital outlay for the project was raised from a syndicate of Banks made up of the Union Bank of Switzerland, Banque del Benelux of Belgium and Krediet Bank NV of the Netherlands. This funding helped foreign construction companies to win the contract for building the plant. In this construction, Spie Balignolles of France, Summa Kumagai of Japan and Atlantic Gulf and Pacific of the USA were involved.

We are afraid that our lands will become denuded and barren like those of so many of our brother tribal Filipinos in the other parts of the country. During this decade, 170,000 hectares of the forests of the Philippines have been denuded every year by logging. Yet exports of wood have continued.

But we Igorots cannot afford and will not allow our lands to be denuded. We are dependent upon our forests for so many things and their destruction would mean our death as a people. This can be explained by looking at Abra which is the home of the Tinggian peoples.

The Tinggians were first to be affected by CRC because their lands are nearest the mill. For the Tinggians this struggle is crucial because most of their ancestral land and settlements are within the concession. The Tinggians number approximately 55,000. They are a distinct cultural group, with their own languages, traditions and political institutions based on communal decision-making led by village elders. Between communities there is a complex peace pact or *Kalon* system which is the basis of law and order in the mountain areas. The people live in largely self-sufficient valley bottom settlements between the steep mountains, and their economy is based on terraced wet-rice cultivation, river fishing, kaingin farming, hunting, raising cows and pigs, and making handicrafts from forest materials.

We feared that logging on the scale and style that CRC planned would lead to erosion causing siltation of the people's fields and the rivers, and driving the fish away. We feared also that CRC by cutting the trees would disturb the ecological balance which would affect the supply of water to the people's fields. Furthermore, the company also planned to use the river for floating logs to the mill which would destroy the people's fish traps and irrigation schemes. While below the mill the polluted waste discharged would be a further threat to fish supplies.

Our fears about the destruction of the environment were increased by the knowledge that the company did not need to reforest in the uplands, as CRC, in cooperation with the Philippine Government and World Bank, have plans to establish a tree farm project on Tinggian pasture lands in the future. This project is part of a bigger World Bank funded program by which forests are to be licensed to corporations which will use the land for mixed logging and commercial farming. The government National Economic Development Authority (NEDA) says, and I quote:

> The project involves the transfer of kaingineros to resettlement areas which shall be cultivated by agricultural corporations for forest and agricultural crops. Kaingineros shall be employed on wage basis and shall be allotted 1,000 sq. meter home lots to enable them to do backyard gardening to supplement their wages.

This project would affect 400,000 families within the 1978-1983 period. The Tianggians at first tried to use the law against CRC. They had a good case: first, CRC declared a concession area of 98,000 hectares in excess of the legal limits; second, the Bureau of Forest Development (BFD) granted the concession without the required public notification; third, the company failed to comply with the Forestry Administrative Order No. 11 which demands that concessionaires exclude the lands of resident minorities from their concession; and fourth, CRC plans to operate in four critical and protected watersheds: the Chico, Pasil, Abulog and Abra. But the people's appeals were consistently ignored. The people also made demands to the company for provisions which would protect their lands. The company only made promises but did nothing.

At the First Inter-tribal All-Tinggian Peace Pact the elders put to the BFD that the ancestral lands should be excluded from the concession. Both the BFD and the company denied the people's rights. The BFD representative asserted that under the law based on the old Cordillera Forest Reservation Act and the Martial Law Presidential Decree No. 705, it *is the people who were the squatters and the company who had the rights.*

Through all their protests and actions the people saw very clearly the tie-up between company, the military and the President, so that the company with this backing was free to do almost anything to achieve its ends. The following illustrates this.

When CRC decided to build the mill next to the river, it bought 60 hectares at Gaddani, Tayum, Abra. Some people refused to sell out so the company intimidated them by using their bulldozers to pile up earth all around their land, cutting off water supply and access trails. Then because of local corruption only

P1.30 per square meter compensation was paid instead of the agreed P3.00 per square meter. The local mayor and others got the remainder.

From the beginning the Presidential guard have been deployed in the province as company security and also as undercover agents. The provincial commander, Lasaten, was active in support of the company and would label anyone who criticised the company as subversive. The province was in September 1977, placed under the governorship of Arturo Barbero, the son of the Under-secretary of the Ministry of Defence, Carmelo Barbero. In 1977 PC Major Cuyupan, who is not even a Tinggian or an Abrenian was appointed directly by President Marcos to be the Mayor of Tineg, Abra, where CRC planned to begin operations. Later in March 1979 when CRC changed plans and intended to begin work in Malibcong, Major Cuyupan, still on military service, was again appointed by the President to be the Mayor of Malibcong.

Through their bitter experience the people have come to the conclusion that only by taking up arms would they have any chance of defending their lands. And so we give active support to, and join, the NPA.

Despite the stepping up of the people's resistance, the company continues to operate. Logging roads have been built and the company is now trying to keep up its schedule of cutting 200 trees a day. The extensive logging leaves whole mountain sides bare. The mud from erosion has already ruined fields and fishing during the summer of 1980. This is a hungry time and fishing is very important at this time of the year. This year below the logging areas there are no fish. At the mill the pollution problem is much worse than expected, not only is the water below the mill undrinkable but the fish are dying and people who bathe in the river get skin diseases. In addition, the factory is pouring out smoke and dirt, and the noise is so loud that it is difficult to even hold a conversation in the neighboring village. The government through its provincial military arm, the Philippine Constabulary, carries out a campaign to silence any opposition. Examples are many but the following incidents should suffice to bring home my point.

During my visits to relatives and friends, people complained of harassments and the surveillance of their homes and activities. Suspected oppositionists to CRC and supporters of the NPA are trailed by military men wherever they go. I too experienced and observed this so many times.

In the rainy season of 1979, work in the fields of Bangilo and Mataragan was totally disrupted when the military Mayor, Alfredo Cuyupan, demanded the evacuation of all farms. This was part of a military operation to deny NPA its mass bases. At the same time in Sallapadan, a dozen community leaders were also arrested and detained without trial. Later, whole communities of people were deceptively told to raise their right hands before high ranking military officials sent by Barbero and have their pictures taken. Government controlled media headlined them as NPA surrenderees the next day.

25 January, 1979 saw the infiltration of the Tubo Inter-Tribal Peace Pact. Military men in civilian clothes were all around the place. Again, on 30 March, 1979, the provincial government and provincial military command through Major Alfredo Cuyupan forced all the delegates to the 2nd Bangilo Inter-Tribal Peace Pact to go back and attend a government-military sponsored seminar instead.

Last summer, many church workers and personnel were either arrested, detained or chased out of the province.

Conclusion

The peoples of the Cordillera suffer from national oppression brought about by US imperialism. We also suffer all the basic oppression and exploitation experienced by other sectors of Philippine society, except that the oppression of the minorities is made harsher by systematic discrimination. We suffer because of the insatiable hunger of international capital for more raw materials and natural resources, the remaining supplies of which are now concentrated in our lands. The building of the dams and the logging operations of CRC are but two of the many examples we tribal Filipinos could cite as genocidal acts carried out in the interests of profit and being posed as development.

Don't mistake us. We are not a backward-looking people. Like others, we want development and we want to improve our lives and the lives of the next generations; we want better education, better health and better services. But we want to control this development in our land and over our lives. And we demand a share both in decision-making and in the benefits of development. We do not recognize the right of the Marcos regime, or the World Bank, or anyone else, to steal our lands, forests and other resources. We do not recognize their right to dictate to us or exploit us. We believe in the justness of our struggle. We are ready to fight and defend our land with our lives.

Thus in unity with other oppressed sectors and groups in the Philippines, on behalf of the Cordillera peoples and other Philippine National Minorities, I appeal to this body to recognize the justness of our struggle against the US-Marcos dictatorship and to support our cause to bring about a genuine Philippine national democratic society.

Testimonies on Resistance

The presentation of the
NDF spokesperson

Honorable President of this Session of the Permanent People's Tribunal, honorable members of the jury, comrades and friends, ladies and gentlemen:

September 21 of this year marked the eighth anniversary of martial law in the Philippines. For Ferdinand Marcos it meant eight uninterrupted years of absolute power. But for the Filipino people, it has meant eight long years of intensified economic, political and cultural oppression, unprecedented in post-war Philippine history.

Marcos has called his martial law government by different names: crisis government, constitutional authoritarianism, new society, and even democratic revolution. His propagandists have even coined a new term calling it 'a smiling martial law'.

But no amount of demogoguery can hide the reality: martial law *is* military dictatorship.

US Imperialism the main prop of the martial law regime

Our contention that US imperialism is the main instigator and supporter of the Marcos martial law regime rests, first of all, on the evidence of highly increased US military aid to the Marcos regime. Official US military assistance to the Philippines from 1969 to 1972 was $80.8 million. From 1973 to 1976 it more than doubled to $166.3 million.[1] This trend of increased US military aid was capped by President Carter's assurance in January 1979 of $500 million of military aid over the next five years.

Moreover, US economic aid to the Marcos regime, under the various categories of 'official aid', 'aid from US government corporations', and 'aid from US controlled multilateral agencies', increased almost threefold from $1041.2 million from 1969 to 1972, to $2922 million from 1973 to 1976.[2] It is not at all surprising, then, that the US Chamber of Commerce in the Philippines was the first to congratulate Marcos on martial law and pledge full cooperation with the martial law regime.[3] The fact that US Ambassador Byroade met with Marcos on the eve of martial law[4] only adds to the evidence of US complicity in the imposition and prolongation of martial law. Other sources point to the approval and wholehearted support of US embassy officials and virtually the entire American establishment in the Philippines for the Marcos martial law regime.[5]

The imposition of martial law in the Philippines was clearly in line with the *Nixon doctrine*, aimed at counteracting the growing anti-imperialist movement in our part of the world, a movement which in 1972 was threatening the interests of US monopoly capitalists guaranteed under the 1935 Philippine Constitution, the Parity Amendment of 1946 and the Laurel-Langley Agreement of 1954. The declaration of martial law paved the way for the 1973 Constitution, now appropriately called the Marcos Constitution, and various Presidential Decrees guaranteeing and enlarging US imperialist interests.

Thus, Marcos got his autocratic powers and unrestricted opportunity to amass personal wealth, while the US monopoly capitalists continued the plunder of the country's economic resources.

Intensified economic crisis and exploitation

Today, clear signs of a rapidly deteriorating situation of the Philippine economy are everywhere to be seen. The external debt rose to an all-time high of $11.04 billion by June 1980,[6] almost 50 per cent higher than the 1981 budget of only $7.2 billion.[7] The unemployment rate is computed at 40 per cent of the labor force[8] and inflation is running at well over 20 per cent.[9] Indeed, the economic crisis has reached the proportions of the crisis during the Japanese occupation of World War II.

As a result, the Filipino people, especially the masses of workers and peasants, are suffering intensely. In some areas, they have taken to eating camote and other root crops due to rice shortages and high food prices.

On the other hand, foreign monopoly capitalists, the big comprador bourgeoisie and landlords continue to reap huge profits, limitless benefits and privileges for themselves.[10] Among those who have prospered under martial rule, the most visible are the new-rich elite who are close relatives and associates of Marcos.[11]

At the core of this bleak scenario is Marcos' development plan. Essentially, it has placed the Philippine economy overly dependent on foreign capital. The overriding consideration of Marcos' economic policy is foreign investments. And to attract foreign investments, wages must be kept down,[12] or 'competitive', as his technocrats would put it.

There is a second component to this development program, which is to make available to foreign investors the supply of raw materials and semi-processed commodities.

It is with this twin package of cheap labor and ample but cheap raw materials and semi-processed commodities that Marcos attracts foreign investments.

For American and Japanese multinational corporations, this open-door policy means profit and more profit. Profit from the colonial exchange of commodities, profit from direct investments and profit from the practice of international usury. An underdeveloped Philippine economy means profits for US imperialism and an opportunity to transfer the crisis in its homeland to its semi-colonies like the Philippines.

Political and military repression

We all know that exploitation such as we have experienced in the Philippines could not continue to exist without repression. US imperialism knows very well that political unrest is bad for business.

In the first place, martial law was aimed at suppressing the surging anti-imperialist movement. The dictatorial regime curtailed all democratic rights, freedom of speech, freedom of assembly and movement, freedom of association and freedom of the press. Strikes were banned.

Eight years of martial law saw more than 60,000 citizens arrested and detained without trial or even the benefit of formal charges.[13] Many were subjected to electric shock treatment, water torture, pistol-whipping, rape and other forms of torture. A considerable number have disappeared without a trace.[14]

In southern Philippines alone, around 90,000 people have

died at the hands of the barbaric armed forces of the government. No less than 250,000 homes have been reduced to ashes. Live babies and small children were known to have been crushed beneath the soldiers' boots; women raped in the presence of their husbands; and corpses buried in mass graves.[15]

Elsewhere, hundreds of thousands have been forced to evacuate their homes and farms to give way to the military operations and infrastructure projects of the Marcos regime. Among the most widely known and opposed government projects are the Chico River Dam project that threatens to displace 100,000 Igorot people, and the Westinghouse nuclear plant in Morong, Bataan that threatens the livelihood of 11,000 farmers and fishermen and endangers the lives of millions. Wherever the people put up resistance, the military never hesitate to use force, as the recent killing of Chico Dam oppositionist and Kalinga leader, Macli-ing Dulag aptly proves.[16] Massacres, abuses and atrocities happen very frequently. There has been ample documentation of such military abuses and atrocities.[17]

While the biggest number of victims of military abuses come from the peasants and farmworkers, cultural minorities and fishermen, there are also many cases of arrests and torture of workers, urban poor, and students.[18] Progressive church people who have dared to air their indignation at such atrocities and stood by the people's struggles have been subjected to arrest, imprisonment, inhuman treatment, and even kidnapping and murder in some cases.[19]

Marcos shoots the gun and Washington provides the bullets, as well as the training of many of Marcos' military officers,[20] including the most notorious torturers. The highly increased US military aid to the Marcos regime and the personal assurance of President Carter for more aid and weapons have already been stated above.

'Normalization' and other forms of deception

Martial law is despised by the Filipino people. It is also increasingly being exposed internationally. Therefore it has become necessary for the US-Marcos dictatorship to sugarcoat its fascist character. Bowing to pressure from his imperialist master, Marcos now dangles the promise of 'normalization'. He assures his political rivals of a nominal share of political power on the condition that they capitulate to him first. Fraudulent elections and referenda have been stage-managed time and again, each one calculated to put up a facade of democracy.[21]

Fascism is a double-edged sword. One side of it is military force, the other is deception. Through the mass media, deception propaganda is dished out on a massive scale. Almost everywhere, slogans that are meant to delude the people are broadcast: 'Plan your family, reduce population growth', 'conserve energy', 'Eat the right food'. All these may seem logical and sensible. But in the context of Philippine political life, they constitute an oblique way of making the people blame themselves for their poverty.

In the field of education, textbooks and subjects extolling 'the virtues' of the fascist regime have been introduced. The US-Marcos dictatorship has restructured the country's educational system to serve US interests. Recommendations of the US-financed Presidential Commission to Survey Philippine Education (PCSPE)[22] have been implemented and the Education Act of 1980[23] is being pushed to ensure government control on all levels of education. These so-called 'reforms' have further entrenched US control over the Philippine educational system. Now, its direction is clearly to serve US interests, that is, by creating technocrats, skilled and semi-skilled workers for imperialist-controlled enterprises.

United Front for Resistance

Exploitation and oppression are inevitably met with people's resistance. Counterrevolutionary violence is met with revolutionary violence. The heroic Filipino people will never submit to foreign aggressors and their local underlings.

The current revolutionary struggle traces its proud tradition to the more than 200 revolts during the 300-year Spanish rule, to the 1896 Philippine Revolution which crushed the Spanish colonial forces, to the valiant people's struggle to preserve their newly-won freedom against US imperialism at the turn of the century, to the workers' struggles and peasant uprisings in the 1920s and 1930s, to the anti-Japanese guerilla war during the 1940s, to the people's war waged by the old people's army in the 1950s, and to the resurgent urban and rural revolutionary movements in the 1960s.[24] This revolutionary tradition and the comprehensiveness of the struggle made it easier to forge unity based on revolutionary objectives even before martial rule was instituted in 1972.

Martial law has intensified the people's misery tenfold. But it has also left the US-Marcos dictatorship extremely isolated both in the Philippines and the international community. It was intended to strengthen and protect the ruling system, but instead, it has further jeopardized its very existence. Martial law has fanned the flames of people's resistance.

There exists today a broad united front committed to the armed overthrow of the US-Marcos dictatorship and to the establishment of a united front government truly representative of the people.

The firm foundation of this broad united front and its main strength is the active support and participation of the toiling masses.

In the 26 guerilla fronts established by the New People's Army (NPA) throughout the country, over 5 million peasants, farmworkers, fishermen and members of cultural minorities give active support to the revolutionary armed struggle. They offer food and shelter to the NPA guerillas, warn them regarding enemy movements and help them get in and out of the area safely. At the core of these millions are 800,000 active members of revolutionary organizations led by 40,000 mass leaders of the localities. The 26 guerilla fronts embrace a total population of 10 million in 4,000 barrios in 300 towns and 40 provinces.[25]

In September 1979 there were already 80,000 industrial workers directly led by NDF forces, while 150,000 workers were in organizations receiving guidance from the NDF. The latest upsurge in the workers' movement, seen in the mass rally of some 25,000 workers and their supporters last 1 May,[26] indicates that the number of workers in the urban revolutionary mass movement has increased by several tens of thousands. This latest upsurge is a result of an effective rectification of work in the urban areas.

On the basis of the active support of the toiling masses, especially of the peasants, farmworkers, fishermen and members of cultural minorities and the growth of their revolutionary organizations, the New People's Army has grown and strengthens itself in the course of resolutely waging people's war to overthrow the US-Marcos dictatorship. Starting with only 60 Red fighters and 35 rifles in 1969 in one district in a Central Luzon province, the NPA has grown to several thousand full time guerillas operating in 26 guerilla fronts in 40 provinces. These full time NPA guerillas are actively assisted by armed people's militia 5 times bigger than the number of full time guerillas.

These 26 guerilla fronts constitute the foundations of guerilla warfare in the Philippines. Among these, 13 are relatively large, covering from 12 to 33 towns; 6 are medium-sized, covering from 8 to 11 towns; and 7 are relatively small. Among the latter, 6 cover from 5 to 7 towns, while a newly opened one covers 3 towns. Every guerilla front has its own NPA local command, a guerilla force, people's militia and mass organizations capable of carrying out guerilla warfare and growing in the course of people's war.

These fronts are located in different major islands, strategically situated so as to divide and overstretch enemy forces throughout the archipelago. There are 4 in northern Luzon, 7 in Central Luzon, 2 in southern Luzon, 7 in the Visayas, and 6 in Mindanao. These fronts comprise not only remote mountainous areas, but also the lowland plains and reaching even town centers and cities.

In most guerilla fronts, the NPA has reached company strength. Full-fledged guerilla units carry high powered rifles while most of the people's militia are armed with simpler rifles and homemade guns.

In all fronts, the NPA has proven its capability to wipe out or disarm oversized enemy squads. In certain areas, such as Samar, the NPA has been able to seize town centers for a limited time.

Many fronts have withstood enemy campaigns involving up to 7,000 fascist troops. Not only has the NPA successfully used shifting tactics to avoid being crushed in such a situation, it has actually been able to launch tactical offensives in the midst of such an encirclement campaign of the enemy.

The NPA does not limit itself to guerilla operations. While it has wiped out thousands of government troops, enemy informers, despotic landlords and others who bring harm to the people, the NPA assists the revolutionary masses in the implementation of the Revolutionary Guide to Land Reform of the Communist Party of the Philippines. This guide calls for the free distribution of land to the peasant masses as its maximum goal. Its minimum goal is to reduce land rent to 10 per cent, eliminate usury, and raise farmworkers' wages. This work for agrarian revolution and the concrete fruits which the rural masses enjoy from its implementation are the strongest reasons for the enthusiastic support for the NPA. In addition, the NPA helps the masses in production, helps them organize their cooperatives and associations, provides them with political education, teaches them how to read and write, and attends to their health problems.

The NPA enjoys the warm support of the masses. As one peasant put it, "The rich and the government have their army. We too have our army, the New People's Army." A farmworker in Negros was asked if he and his co-workers would support the NPA, should the NPA come to their area. He answered: "Support the NPA? Of course not! We will *join* it!"[29]

Playing an essential role in the broad front of resistance is the re-established Communist Party of the Philippines. At its first congress in December 1968, it summed up the history of the revolutionary movement in the Philippines, formulated the program for a people's democratic revolution, and set out firmly on the path of armed revolution. Accordingly, on 29 March, 1969 it founded the NPA. It leads the NPA and it has developed its party organizations in 12 regions of the country. It has developed revolutionary mass organizations in the rural and urban areas while also setting up a revolutionary underground as the firm base for legal and semi-legal mass struggles. Its numbers have grown from several scores of Party members at the end of 1968 to several thousand cadres and members at present.

The revolutionary student movement is also an important part of the broad united front. In July and August of this year, some 250,000 students in over 30 colleges and universities in Metro Manila launched boycotts, marches and other protest actions in a concerted movement for democratic reforms in the educational system as well as exposing and opposing US imperialism and the Marcos dictatorship. At the core of this student movement is the underground youth organization, *Kabataang Makabayan* (Nationalist Youth), which was founded on 30 November, 1964.

Many progressive teachers have joined the student protest movement and have formed their own underground organization, the *Katipunan ng mga Gurong Makabayan* (Association of Nationalist Teachers). In like manner, progressive health workers — nurses, doctors and other health personnel — have formed their underground organization, *Makabayang Samahang Pangkalusugan*, and have announced their national democratic health program.

The Christians for National Liberation (CNL), the underground national democratic organization of Church personnel, counts several hundred active members and hundreds of sympathizers among Church people. The CNL, founded on 17 February, 1972 assists organizational work among the toiling masses, while also doing political work within the Church sector.

The National Democratic Front comprises an active membership of over one million with the following underground organizations as members: the CPP, the NPA, the *Rebolusyonaryong Kilusan ng Magsasaka* (Revolutionary Movement of Peasants), the *Rebolusyonaryong Kilusan ng mga Manggagawa* (the revolutionary movement of workers, which grew partly from *Bukluran* which was founded on 1 May, 1975 and was declared illegal by the Marcos regime in 1977), the *Kabataang Makabayan* (Nationalist Youth), the *Katipunan ng mga Gurong Makabayan* (Association of Nationalist Teachers), the Christians for National Liberation (CNL), and the *Makabayang Samahang Pangkalusugan* (Nationalist Association for Health). Other organizations, such as those of women and cultural minorities, are in the process of being formed — to a great extent they are already functional on the local (municipal), provincial or even regional levels. In due time, after this healthy development of coordination in the local or regional levels, they could elect their national bodies and be represented in the NDF formally.

Since announcing its 10-point program in April 1973, the NDF has worked hard to develop the unity and cooperation of all democratic forces throughout the country. The organizational work of the NDF extends to legal organizations, legal institutions and even within the government itself. Underground NDF cells continue to multiply in various sectors. Outside the country, the NDF has established effective links with several progressive movements, organizations and individuals:

Through its official organ, *Liberation*, it issues timely situationers and initiates or coordinates mass campaigns.

Also in the broad front of resistance to the US-Marcos dictatorship are other significant forces. The one waging the strongest struggle among them is the Moro people in southern Philippines resolutely waging an armed struggle for self-determination. The Moro National Liberation Front (MNLF) and the Bangsa Moro Army (BMA) pin down large numbers of government troops in big battles, thus setting significantly favorable conditions for the expansion and consolidation of the NPA's guerilla fronts.

In accordance with its line of exerting utmost efforts at developing unity and cooperation of all revolutionary and democratic forces in the Philippines, the NDF expressly supports the just struggle of the Moro people and the MNLF and BMA.

Many legal and semi-legal organizations have sprung up in opposition to the US-Marcos dictatorship. While they do not belong to the NDF, they too form part of the broad front of resistance and contribute in varying degrees of significance to the overall struggle against the US-Marcos dictatorship. Among the most consistent and active are the Civil Liberties Union of the Philippines (CLUP) led by Senator Jose W. Diokno, the *Katipunan para sa Kalayaan at Kapayapaan* (Ecumenical Movement for Justice and Peace) which documents and protests against abuses of the government troops, the Task Force for Detainees (TFD) of the Association of Major Religious Superiors in the Philippines which renders services to detainees and also documents and protests against torture and other forms of maltreatment of political prisoners. The political prisoners, themselves, have formed their organization and issue statements regularly supporting popular issues and mass struggles while waging their own struggles to defend their rights and improve their conditions in prison. The *Kapatid*, organization of relatives and friends of political prisoners, work for releases and help cope with the needs of the political prisoners.

Within the group of social democrats (often called *socdems*) of the *Nagkakaisang Partido Demokratiko Sosyalista ng Pilipinas* (NPDSP — United Democratic Socialist Party of the Philippines)[30], a group split away from the Intengan-Gonzales leadership in 1978. This group criticized the strong anti-communist and anti-NDF line of the socdems and wanted to engage in genuine organizational work among the masses. This group expressed sympathy for the program and work of the NDF. In like manner, the Marxist-Leninist Group (MLG) broke away from the old party, the *Partido Komunista ng Pilipinas* (PKP) in 1973. The MLG refused the PKP line of collaborating with Marcos and attacking the national democratic movement. They decided to wage militant struggles, in some areas also armed struggle, against the US-Marcos dictatorship. In the course of such struggles, especially after the PKP leadership openly surrendered to the Marcos regime in October 1974 and agreed to collaborate with the dictator, the MLG chapters in the provinces and in Manila have drawn closer to the NDF.[31]

Even among Marcos' political rivals both on the national and regional and local levels, the NDF — on a selective basis — has been able to forge alliances that have benefited the open mass struggles of workers, students and urban poor on certain occasions. Indeed, among the political rivals of Marcos, two main trends have appeared. One is to capitulate to Marcos hoping to get a little share of political power and economic privileges. The other is to increase the struggle against Marcos. It is among the latter that the NDF is able to prudently forge limited alliances.

Besides the organized resistance led by NDF forces and the consistent opposition of legal and semi-legal organizations, there are also spontaneous protests and mass actions, such as strikes and demonstrations. These spontaneous mass actions add to the total effect of isolating the US-Marcos dictatorship. Those who participate in these mass actions tend to draw closer to one or another of the NDF forces. For, while the NDF does not comprise the totality of the resistance, it does present the most comprehensive program and an effective leadership and coordination.

In June of this year, the NDF re-issued its call for national unity and republished the 12 November, 1977 reaffirmation of its 10-point program.

Allow me to read out the main points of this program:

1. Unite all anti-imperialist and democratic forces to overthrow the US-Marcos dictatorship and work for the establishment of a coalition government based on a truly democratic system of representation.
2. Expose and oppose US imperialism as the mastermind behind the setting up of the fascist dictatorship, struggle for the nullification of all unequal treaties and arrangements with this imperialist power and call for the nationalisation of all its properties in the country.
3. Fight for the establishment of all democratic rights of the people, such as freedom of speech, the press, assembly, association, movement, religious belief and the right to due process.
4. Gather all possible political and material support for the armed revolution and the underground against the US-Marcos dictatorship.
5. Support a genuine land reform program that can liberate the

peasant masses from feudal and semi-feudal exploitation and raise agricultural production through cooperation.

6. Improve the people's livelihood, guarantee the right to work and protect national capital against foreign monopoly capital.

7. Promote a national, scientific and mass culture and combat imperialist, feudal and fascist culture.

8. Support the national minorities, especially those in Mindanao and the mountain provinces, in their struggle for self-determination and democracy.

9. Punish, after public trial, the ringleaders of the Marcos fascist gang for their crimes against the people and confiscate all their ill-gotten wealth.

10. Unite with all the peoples fighting imperialism and all reaction, and seek their support for the Philippine revolutionary struggle.

Faced with a stronger and broader united front, the US-Marcos dictatorship can be expected to try and cut up the comprehensiveness of this struggle and dilute the 10-point NDF program.

We can therefore expect that US imperialism will try to sell various types of pseudo-nationalism, especially those types that are devoid of anti-imperialist content. This can be done by US imperialism either in consonance with or separately from the Marcos clique. The notorious CIA has been known to have supported anti-Marcos but not anti-imperialist groups. One such group, the socdems, tried to approximate the 10-point NDF program. It is selling another type of strategy and tactics, one that does not appear to negate armed struggle but equates it with anarchist urban guerilla activities. They have, however, failed to delude the people.

US imperialism can be expected to try to divide and rule the mass movement. It will use every means to discredit the NDF. In fact, it will not be a surprise if CIA Filipino agents will pose as revolutionaries in international forums.

But the NDF program, which exposes an all-rounded anti-fascist, anti-imperialist and anti-feudal struggle, will expose the pseudo-nationalists and pseudo-revolutionaries.

Appeal

In line with our 10-point program, we uphold the principle of self-reliance. The Philippine revolutionary movement relies basically on its own efforts. This principle proceeds from the conviction that the mobilization of the broad masses of the Filipino people is the key to the successful overthrow of the US-Marcos dictatorship.

However, while adhering to the principle of self-reliance, we find it nonetheless an imperative to seek international support and solidarity in the face of the increasing assistance given by US imperialism to the Marcos dictatorial regime. We therefore appeal to the peoples of the world and the progressive countries to extend moral and material support to our revolutionary struggle.

We particularly seek the recognition of many countries, movements, parties and groups in the world. This recognition will render significant political support to our struggle and further inspire the Filipino people in waging its national liberation struggle.

We are determined to resolutely wage our revolutionary struggle so that our people can contribute their share to the world-wide struggle against all forms of imperialism and reaction.

It is inspiring to the Filipino people that the oppressed and exploited peoples of the world are resolutely on the road of revolution. The future of imperialism is bleak. That of mankind is bright.

On behalf of the NDF and the revolutionary Filipino people, allow me to reiterate our greetings and thanks to all of you for this opportunity to speak to you about our struggle.

Notes

1. Walden Bello and Severina Rivera (eds.), *The Logistics of Repression*, published by Friends of the Filipino People, Washington D.C., 1977, p. 8.
2. *Ibid.*, pp. 50-51.
3. Cf. *The Philippines: American Corporations, Martial Law and Underdevelopment*, IDOC, p. 32. The cable read: "The American Chamber of Commerce wishes you every success in your endeavors to restore peace and order, business confidence, economic growth and the well-being of the Filipino people and nation. We assure you of our confidence and cooperation in achieving these objectives. We are communicating these feelings to our associates and affiliates in the United States."
4. US Ambassador Sullivan in *The Philippine-American Relationship*, USIS, 1974, p. 34. Cited in Civil Liberties Union of the Philippines, *Neo-Colonialism: Root of Our Discontent* (A Study Outline), p. 3.

5. W. Scott Thompson, *Unequal Partners: Philippine and Thai Relations with the United States*, 1965-1975, pp. 150-151, and Richard Critchfield, "Dictator or Democrat", *Insight*, July, 1973, p. 46. Cited in Civil Liberties Union of the Philippines (CLUP), *op. cit.* pp. 3-4.

6. Source: Central Bank of the Philippines. Cited in *Balitang Malayang Philipinas*, "8 years of Martial Law: Struggle and Reaction", special issue, 21 September, 1980, p. 6.

7. Source: Central Bank of the Philippines.

8. *Kapatiran Anak Pawis Foundation Research*, August 1979. Cited in *Balitang Malayang Pilipinas* (BMP), "8 Years of Martial Law: Struggle and Reaction", Special Issue, September, 21, 1980.

9. IMF placed the rate of inflation in 1979 at 25 per cent while the Marcos regime claimed it was only 18.8 per cent. With 25 per cent rate of inflation, the IMF put the Philippines with the highest rate in Southeast Asia. For 1980 the estimate is between 20 and 25 per cent. See Joel Rocamora, *US Imperialism and the Economic Crisis of the Marcos Dictatorship*, paper presented at PPT session on the Philippines, 30 October, 1980, p. 5.

10. US investments in the Philippines have earned $3.58 for every $1.00 invested, of which $2.00 have been repatriated. UP Law Center, *The Impact of Transnational Corporations in the Philippines*, June, 1978.

11. *Some are Smarter than Others*, Manila, September 1979, 34 pp. Written by a group of Filipino businessmen. It lists 239 big corporations owned by the Marcos and the Romualdez families, their business partners and dummies.

12. Marcos' address on Silver Anniversary of the Central Bank, 4 Jan, 1974. Cited in CLUP, *op. cit.*, p. 14.

13. Vanya Kewley, *Collision Course*, TV program of BBC, wherein Minister of Defense Juan Ponce Enrile states that since martial law 60,000 had been arrested.

14. Task Force for Detainees (TFD), *Political Prisoners*, Book Three.

15. See also Abdurasad Asani, MNLF, *Appeal of the Bangsa Moro People*, submitted to PPT.

16. Episcopal Commission on Tribal Filipinos (ECTF), *Tribal Forum*, April, May and June, 1980.

17. KKK, Ecumenical Movement on Justice and Peace, Iron Hand, Velvet Glove, published by CCIA of WCC, 69 pp. (1980).

18. For example, last 3 September, 1980, the following worker leaders were arrested: Attorney Ernesto Arellano, General Secretary of *Kilusang Mayo Uno* (May 1st Movement); Mr Vicente Amboy, staff of Association of Nationalist Labor Organizations; and Mr Andres Magtoto, President of Wyeth-Suaco Labor Union. Up to the time of writing this, there is no report that they have been released from detention. From June to August 1980 leaders of the League of Filipino Students have been arrested or hunted by the military. For ongoing reports see

the bi-weekly publication of Task Force for Detainees of the Philippines, *Political Detainees Update*.

19. Carlos Tayag, A Benedictine Deacon who was an active leader among Christians, disappeared on 17 August, 1976 and has never been heard of since. See *Political Prisoners*, Book Three, 1977, published by TFDP.

20. Bello and Rivera, *op. cit.*, pp. 15-16. See also, Chomsky and Hermann, *The Washington Connection*, Southend Press, Boston, 1979, frontispiece.

21. The more recent ones on 7 April, 1978 and January 1980 were met with massive protest actions. On 6 April, 1978 a noise barrage lasting several hours was launched by hundreds of thousands in Manila.

22. PCSPE Recommendations were blocked by strong opposition in Congress prior to martial law as the anti-imperialist movement intensified. After martial law was declared, Marcos decreed the approval of the PCSPE recommendations.

23. This Education Act of 1980 has been the subject, among other issues, of massive student boycotts, protest marches, and other protest actions from July to September this year. See BMP, *op. cit.*, p. 23 for a brief description of the student protest actions.

24. See Constantino, *The Philippines: A Past Revisited* and Amado Guerrero, *Philippine Society and Revolution*.

25. *Ang Bayan*, 29 March, 1980.

26. See *Liberation*, May 1980 for a description of the rally and the issues and significance of the rally, led by the *Kilusang Mayo Uno*. For the growth of the workers' movement in 1975, 1976 and until May 1977, see Filippijnengroep Nederland, *Makibaka!* War on Want; London, 1980. (2nd Edition).

27. TFDP (Bacolod), *Itum, Bitter Times in the Land of Sugar*, 1979.

28. See *Liberation*, Feb. 1980 for a study of the political line of the socdems.

29. See *Far Eastern Economic Review*, 25 October, 1974 for an account of the surrender of PKP leaders. See also, PKP, *For an Independent and Democratic Philippines*, Political Resolution and Program. Adopted at 7th Congress, PKP, Central Luzon, Philippines, July 1977. 122 pp.

Statement of the NPA

Fraternal greetings to all comrades and friends who are gathered in this session of the Permanent Peoples' Tribunal, to place on trial the US-Marcos fascist dictatorship for its numerous and grave crimes against the Filipino people!

Comrades and friends! The struggle of the Filipino people for genuine national independence and democracy has a long and tortuous history. From the 16th to the 19th century, our people waged bitter struggles against the colonial rule of Spain. These struggles deepened and developed into the Philippine Revolution of 1896. The first of its kind in Asia, the Revolution of 1896 which succeeded in overthrowing Spanish colonial rule.

But the victory in the battlefield did not lead to the founding of a sovereign and democratic Philippine Republic. The US imperialists invaded our country and robbed our people of the victory that rightfully belonged to them. To subjugate our people, the US imperialists unleashed a ruthless war of aggression that lasted from 1899 to 1916.

Even after the collapse of the armed resistance in 1914, our people persisted in their struggle against the colonial rulers. Despite the persistent colonial repression, workers, peasants and patriotic intellectuals launched struggles on many fronts. On November 7, 1930, the Communist Party of the Philippines was founded for the purpose of coordinating and giving comprehensive political leadership to the anti-colonial and democratic struggles of the people.

When World War II broke out, the Japanese fascists invaded our country. Like one person, our people rose to resist the Japanese. The Communist Party established the *Hukbo ng Bayan Laban sa Hapon* (Anti-Japanese People's Army) and led the people in guerilla warfare. When the American troops returned, the guerrilla forces had already broken the back of Japanese resistance. Instead of treating the *Hukbalahap* as an ally in the anti-fascist struggle, however, the returning American forces quickly moved to destroy the people's army.

For fear that a full-scale anti-colonial war would break out in the Philippines, formal independence was granted by the US imperialists in 1946. But then, they were confident of the loyalty of the big comprador bourgeoisie and the big landlords whose wealth depended mainly on colonial trade and who, during the previous three decades, were thoroughly trained in subservience to US imperialism. Moreover, the US imperialists demanded and got constitutional guarantees and unequal treaties that safeguarded their interests. Their economic stranglehold on the Philippines remained as strong as ever and they continued to maintain military bases and US troops there.

There was widespread resentment against these neo-colonial arrangements. In 1950, the people's anger exploded into a civil war. The Communist Party reorganised the people's army into the *Hukbong Magpapalaya ng Bayan* (People's Liberation Army) and waged guerilla warfare in the main island of Luzon and later in Panay in central Philippines. The puppet government, with the full support of US military aid and advisers, relentlessly attacked the people's army and the revolutionary mass organisations until they were decisively defeated in 1954.

There were serious strategic and tactical errors on the part of the Communist Party which led to this defeat. Although some small units of the people's army persisted in guerilla warfare in some parts of Luzon, there were also those which degenerated into bandit gangs. During the 1960s and the early 1970s, the center of revolutionary activities shifted to the urban areas.

A new propaganda movement for nationalism and democracy was launched. By the middle and latter part of the sixties, mass demonstrations and rallies denouncing imperialism, feudalism and fascism became more frequent, grew big and strong and spread throughout the archipelago. On December 26, 1969, three months later, the New People's Army was established and guerilla war was resumed. The call for a new democratic revolution reverberated throughout the whole archipelago and won the ardent support of the broad masses.

Martial law was declared in 1972 in an attempt to stop the spread of the people's new revolutionary movement. It was also a desperate move by Marcos and his master, US imperialism, to surmount the economic crisis of the sixties by intensifying the exploitation of the Filipino masses. In order to protect itself from the people's anger, the US-Marcos dictatorship imposed a regime of fascist repression that recalls the terrors of the Philippine-American war at the turn of the century.

But the fascist dictatorship has not succeeded in crushing the revolutionary forces in the cities and the countryside. The people's forces have steadily advanced and gained strength even under these most trying conditions. After a decade of painstaking organisational work among the peasantry, we are now on the threshold of moving into the advanced stage of the strategic defensive in our armed struggle. The day will surely come when the people's strength will prevail and victory will be ours.

We are aware that US imperialism is keenly following events in our country. US imperialism will not take lightly the loss of its Philippine neo-colony. Even now it has already stepped up its military aid to the Marcos dictatorship. US military advisers are active in training, planning and directing "counter-insurgency" campaigns against the New People's Army. We are also vigilant against the threat of direct US aggression in the event that its Philippines puppets have become inutile in containing the revolutionary forces.

It is in this regard that we recognise the important role that international public opinion and support are playing in our revolutionary struggle. To overthrow the Marcos dictatorship, we also have to confront and defeat the manoeuvers and interference of such a powerful enemy as U.S. imperialism.

The New People's Army of the Philippines wishes to express its profound gratitude for the keen interest you have shown in our life and death struggle against the brutal, corrupt and puppet Marcos ruling clique and its U.S. imperialist masters. Your sincere support for this just and noble cause lightens our hearts and further strengthens our determination to carry on the fight no matter what the sacrifices may be.

On our part, we solemnly pledge never to slacken in our efforts until our people are completely liberated from imperialism, feudal and fascist exploitation and oppression. We also pledge to contribute in any way we can to the international struggle to rid mankind of the scourge of imperialism, colonialism, racism and all reaction.

May Our Unity and Friendship Continue to Flourish!

May the Solidarity and Mutual Support among our Peoples and the Peoples of the Whole World Continue to Grow Strong and Bear More Magnificent Fruits!

Message from the workers movement

The US-Marcos dictatorship remains the chief enemy of the Filipino working class and other exploited classes of Philippine society.

It has reduced the entire working class into slaves, who live only when they find work, who find work only when they can be used to further enrich the US-Marcos dictatorship and the entire ruling elite.

The Marcos regime should be condemned for being the most loyal, most vicious labor dealer of US imperialism.

With the imposition of martial rule, it has made the country more favorable to foreign investments. Left and right, it has coughed out investment, agricultural, export and fisheries decrees — all increasing tax exemptions, tariff cuts and other incentives designed to raise foreign profits and the plunder of Filipino wealth and resources.

On the other hand, the US-Marcos dictatorship continues to deny the Filipino workers their basic rights to a just wage, permanent employment, the strike and other democratic liberties.

It has pushed down the minimum wage even below the subsistence level. Along with legislated allowances, the workers' take-home pay supposedly amounts to P26.34 (US$3.50) — barely enough to supply the worker and his family with a nutritious diet. Three out of four workers earn even less than this wage, since the Marcos regime provides foreign and local capitalists with a host of exemptions, notably for export-oriented industries where most foreign investments are.

The US-Marcos dictatorship maintains a vast reserve of unemployed Filipinos to assure that labor will remain cheap. Today they stand at 11.5 million — including peasants driven out of their farms — but the unemployed find no room in factories, since industrialization is being stunted by the continued dominance of US imperialism over the economy.

To prevent chronic unemployment from seething into political discontent, the Marcos regime has resorted to exporting

Filipino workers. As a result, overseas workers have been exposed to inhuman working conditions and other forms of exploitation abroad. Many have been robbed of their hard saved money by illegal recruiting agencies and the government.

On the other hand, the Marcos regime even shamelessly boasts that it has been raking in millions of dollars from the export of Filipino workers and credits itself for 'easing the unemployment problem'.

Export processing zones are being set up all over the country. But these industrial enclaves only spell wages even cheaper than the minimum wage in Metro Manila, inhuman working conditions and other forms of exploitation.

An aggressive training program has been launched purportedly to provide skills to Filipino workers. But in reality, the Marcos regime only wants to assure foreign industries that labor is not only cheap but skilled as well.

As the impoverishment of workers and their families continue to trigger strikes and other acts of protest, the US-Marcos dictatorship fiercely suppresses the democratic rights of workers and other Filipinos.

Strikes have been banned through General Order No. 5 and Presidential Decree 823. The Marcos regime lamely reasons that strikes are banned only in vital industries. But its own list of vital businesses covers almost all factories and industries.

The Marcos regime further betrays its fascist hand with its brutal suppression of workers' strikes. It has now become standard operational procedure for government troops to beat up strikers, arrest and detain them by the score, torture and murder the most militant workers and organizers.

To quash workers' resistance more thoroughly, the US-Marcos dictatorship has armed foreign and big capitalists with 'preventive suspensions' — which are no different from terminations without pay. With this, militant workers, especially union leaders, are fired, even only for trying to organize genuine trade unions and asserting their demands during collective bargaining.

While suppressing local protests, the US-Marcos dictatorship is even more wary of worker organizations which cut across industry lines, and which unite workers with other oppressed sectors of society. These national alliances with clear socialist perspectives demand the nationalization of foreign-controlled industries and genuine land reform.

Such alliances have been branded time and again as 'subversive' and are under tight watch by the regime's intelligence men who pinpoint and arrest 'dangerous leaders and subversive elements'. Only recently, the Marcos regime ordered the arrest of two officers of the *Kilusang Mayo Uno* (KMU), and raided two federation offices. Apparently the regime is troubled with the massive labor day rally the KMU staged last May, student boycotts in the biggest universities, and a partial transport strike by jeepney and bus drivers protesting the recent oil price hike.

The US-Marcos dictatorship will pursue its anti-labor policies and add more to its long list of crimes. US imperialism will not on its own desist from the most systematic and brutal exploitation of Filipino workers it instituted as soon as it set foot on Philippine soil. It will not allow itself to be deprived of the stable source of cheap labor and superprofits it has created for itself.

For these reasons, US imperialism continues to block at every turn the workers' struggle for national and class liberation. It has patterned Philippine laws and policies on labor after its own. The Philippine Magna Carta of Labor is a mere carbon copy of the US original. The concept of collective bargaining was introduced to derail and suppress the anti-imperialist stance firmly adopted by the Filipino workers' movement since the 1900s. The American Federation of Labor stepped in to set up 'labor education' institutions which continue to preach 'rice and fish unionism' and 'harmonious relations', in an attempt to divorce the workers' movement from the national liberation movement.

The Marcos regime for its part, will continue to pander to US imperialism, at the expense of millions of workers and other Filipinos. As the workers' movement surges forward, the regime will increasingly become more repressive, even as it hatches new forms of deception.

The Filipino workers' movement is aware that it must dismantle the massive machinery of exploitation maintained by the US-Marcos dictatorship for almost a century.

Together with other oppressed sectors of Philippine society, the workers' movement struggles to free the country from imperialist domination — through protracted armed struggle and democratic protest actions.

The Filipino working class believe that the solution to its problems lies in the seizure of political power from the ruling class. This will ultimately put the instruments of production in the hands of the workers and the people in order to destroy the roots of capitalist exploitation.

For this reason, the fight for nationalist industrialization and genuine land reform can only be won through a protracted people's war.

The Filipino working class movement believes that only the National Democratic Front can unite the broadest resistance of the Filipino people and throws its full support behind the New People's Army (NPA). It hopes that in due time, the Filipino people will succeed in establishing a democratic government which truly represents the interests of the people — in place of the present reactionary state.

Along with the National Democratic Front (NDF), therefore, we enjoin the Permanent People's Tribunal to:

1. Judge, condemn and denounce US imperialism in the Philippines and the present Marcos dictatorship.
2. Recognise the just struggle of the Filipino people.
3. Recognise the NDF and the NPA as legitimately representing the genuine interests of the Filipino people.

Ang Proletaryo,
official publication of the
Revolutionary Workers' Movement in the Philippines

Message from the Christians for National Liberation

We, the Christians for National Liberation, united with other revolutionary classes, sectors and groups in the Philippines under the National Democratic Front, hail the Permanent People's Tribunal as it conducts a trial against US imperialism and Ferdinand Marcos together with his military regime.

We highly appreciate the concern of so many friends abroad supporting the revolutionary struggle of the Filipino people.

We are deeply grateful to the Tribunal for granting the appeal for a hearing made by the National Democratic Front of the Philippines.

We greet our Moro brothers and sisters in the Moro National Liberation Front who stand with the National Democratic Front at the Tribunal to denounce the US-Marcos dictatorship and assert their right to self-determination.

Too long have the Filipino masses been victimised by US-imperialism and its local lackeys. The Philippines has a long history of people's resistance to exploitation and oppression under a semi-colonial, semi-feudal system.

In the 1970s this resistance reached a high point in a national democratic mass movement to which the Marcos regime, backed by US imperialism, reacted with increasing viciousness. The US-Marcos dictatorship perpetrates the most heinous war crimes against the people.

Progressive Christians have been victimised too. The only reason for this is that they have left the dubious safety of a non-partisan position and have joined the people in their struggle for liberation.

Putting themselves at the service of the workers, peasants, fishermen, slumdwellers, national minorities and students, placing the interests of the masses above their own institutional interest, progressive Christians soon discovered that they are most effective when they are organized as a sector. Learning from the people, they found that their struggle for liberation is most significant when they can further weld their own national democratic mass organization to the revolutionary mass movement.

Over the past eight years, the Christians for National Liberation has kept pace with other mass organizations of the revolutionary classes, sectors and groups. It counts a nationwide membership by the hundreds composed of progressive clergy, professed religious and lay associates from the different Christian churches.

It consistently carries the national democratic line and wields a considerable influence on the various forces of the church sector.

Some of its members have already joined the armed struggle. Others are engaged in direct organizing work with the workers and peasants. Still others are engaged in sectoral organizing or in-service.

Constantly striving to strengthen its unity with all other progressive classes, sectors and groups in the Philippines under the 10-Point Program of the National Democratic Front, Christians for National Liberation conveys its solidarity with all other peoples and groups abroad fighting imperialism, colonialism, racism and all forms of reaction.

We have great faith in the Tribunal's role of exposing before the world the enemies of all peoples fighting for their national liberation.

Christians for National Liberation
Manila, Philippines.
1 October, 1980

Message from the political prisoners

Distinguished and honorable friends:

The United Nations Universal Declaration on Human Rights is today subjected to extreme tests. How far could its moral sanctions stay the hands of repressive regimes that only violate their people's human rights?

The Universal Declaration on the Rights of Peoples approved in Algiers on 4 July 1976 reinforces the human rights declaration. It sharpens the latter to emphasize the justice and legitimacy of people's struggles against repressive regimes, even if it be through the use of arms. The Algiers declaration thus enhances the survival and assertion of human rights.

But declarations are meaningful by themselves only to a certain degree. Their validity and effectiveness can only be gauged by the practical adherence to their guarantees and sanctions. Governments violate the guarantees, peoples struggle to assert them. This has been the general trend in most parts of the world today.

And what of the sanctions? The United Nations has largely been weakened, if not altogether neutralized, in imposing sanctions on erring governments. This is because of the overriding veto, the influences, and the collusions of the big imperialist powers with erring governments. In many cases of a government's violations of human rights of its citizens, an imperialist power lurks behind as instigator and beneficiary.

Only through the people's persevering and united struggles, can human rights be protected from the assaults and abuses of repressive regimes backed up by imperialism.

The Permanent People's Tribunal is a vital instrument for oppressed peoples to seek redress beyond the realm of governments and international governmental organizations. Although the Tribunal may not have the armed might to enforce political or economic sanctions, the moral force at its command — supported by oppressed peoples and by liberated peoples and their governments — can deliver tremendous pressures upon an erring government.

It is in this light that we, political detainees in the Philippines, welcome and urge the Permanent People's Tribunal to sit in investigation and judgement of US imperialism and the Marcos martial law government.

US imperialism has, since the turn of the century, been the leading oppressor of the Filipino people. The Marcos martial law regime is currently its direct arm in oppressing our people.

US imperialism must answer for having implanted and entrenched in the Philippines a semi-colonial and semi-feudal social system that up to this day subjects the masses of our people to economic exploitation, political oppression, and military suppression.

Under this semi-colonial and semi-feudal social system, US imperialism has retained control of the Philippine economy, politics, culture and military, through a network of unequal treaties between the US and the Philippine governments.

Because this imperialist control buttressed by feudal structures in the countryside and the bureaucratic machinery of the state was under siege by the people's national democratic movement, President Ferdinand Marcos imposed martial law on 21 September, 1972.

The situation in the Philippines has since then been characterized by intensified political, economic and cultural oppression and military suppression. In the guise of defending the 'national security', the rights of the people guaranteed by the Universal Declaration on Human Rights have been methodically violated.

Thousands of citizens encompassing a broad spectrum — workers and peasants, urban poor and landless, students and professors, writers and other intellectuals, professionals, and national minorities — have been arrested and detained at one time or another, many indefinitely.

Torture, maltreatment, denial of human and constitutional rights — in some cases outright killing — invariably accompany arrest and detention. And as the people's resistance to martial law intensifies, these inhuman practices are intensified accordingly.

We, political detainees, are living testimonies to these crimes. That is why the Marcos martial law regime is vainly trying to deny our existence. It uses devious terms, such as 'public order violators' or 'POVs' as we are now referred to, if only to evade using the term 'political detainees'.

Distinguished and honorable friends: The Marcos martial law regime, with US imperialism squarely behind it, must answer for all this violence and outrage against the Filipino people.

US imperialists and the Marcos martial law regime should be tried, judged and condemned as one, for all these crimes.

They should be condemned for suppressing the just and legitimate struggle of the Filipino people for national liberation and the dismantling of the oppressive social structures in Philippine society.

Such condemnation shall lend wider support to the Filipino people's national democratic struggles.

Political Detainees
In the Philippines

THE CASE
OF THE BANGSA
MORO PEOPLE

A Case for self-determination

Presentation of the MNLF spokesperson, Abdurasad Asani

Mr. President, members of the Tribunal.

In June last year at Bologna, the Moro National Liberation Front (MNLF), on behalf of the Bangsa Moro people, filed an appeal before this Tribunal alleging, among others, four specific charges against the Marcos regime and US imperialism in the Philippines. The appeal was submitted pursuant to the historic Algiers Declaration and other applicable principles of international law that recognize basic human rights of people including the right to freely charter their own future and destiny.

In the appeal, the MNLF asks the Tribunal for a hearing, during which evidence would be presented to substantiate it, and to issue judgment on the charges raised therein. In addition, the MNLF asks the Tribunal for a declaration of the right of the Bangsa Moro people to self-determination and to declare as follows:

1. That the Philippine presence in the Bangsa Moro homeland of Mindanao, Basilan, Sulu and Palawan is colonial and that the Bangsa Moro people are illegally deprived of their right to self-determination, freedom, and independence;

2. That such colonial presence and domination bring about and are the direct causes of economic exploitation, repression and discrimination of the Bangsa Moro people by the Philippine regime and its local and foreign collaborators;

3. That the Marcos regime in the Philippines is criminally engaged in a diabolical campaign of genocide against the Bangsa Moro people;

4. That US imperialism, through its persistent support and assistance to the Philippines economically and militarily, is guilty of complicity with the Philippine regime in the commission of such crimes;

Mr President, I shall confine my statement to providing the historical basis of the application in the first part of the

Abdurasad Asani — Moro National Liberation Front spokesperson at the PPT session. Director of Information, Tripoli.

MNLF brief. Other MNLF witnesses who are here with me for this trial will deal with the other charges.

To begin with, I would like to draw attention to the document entitled *Moros — Not Filipinos*, which briefly summarizes the political history of the Bangsa Moro people. This document forms part of the dossier for the Bangsa Moro case in this hearing.

In this document, the Tribunal will have ample proof of the fact that our people have led a free and independent, continuous and uninterrupted, existence from the middle of the fifteenth century well up to the beginning of this century. They were a politically organized entity under a sultanate form of government which was patterned after the Arab's Caliphate — inevitably, since the sultanate was founded in 1450 by a learned Arab Muslim said to be from Hadramaut.

The sultanate was not a perfect model of government. It was certainly feudal, and aristocratic. But as an organized institution and an independent political unit, it nevertheless represented the common unity and solidarity of our people's history. It was already an advanced form of state organization, functioning for and commanding the loyalty, obedience and support of the masses of its citizens.

The Emperor of China welcomed the sultan in his court as visiting head of a sovereign state. One Sulu chief, in fact died in China while on a state visit. European powers manifested recognition of the Bangsa Moro people and homeland by signing agreements with our sultan. One such agreement, for instance, was the Wilkes Treaty of 1842 wherein an American scientific expedition led by a certain Charles Wilkes was granted permission to repair to the sultan's port for provisions and protection while in Sulu's territorial water. Another one, the Bates Treaty of 1899, concluded between American General John C. Bates and the Sultan of Sulu following the arrival of US army volunteers in Jolo that year in which the "government of the Sultan" was recognized. This infamous treaty, however, was more designed to prevent the sultan's government from coming to the assistance of the Filipino revolutionaries who were then engaged in a new struggle against the Americans. Copies of both the Wilkes and Bates treaties are found in the dossier. There are many other documents of similar import but they are not now available for the Tribunal's perusal.

All this shows that our people have been a sovereign power for centuries. Indeed, the cohesion achieved by our people serves to explain why Spanish colonialism in the Philippines failed in its repeated attempt to put them under its colonial hegemony.

Following the Treaty of Paris on 10 December, 1898, between Spain and America which saw the formal conclusion of the Spanish American war, the United States succeeded Spain as a colonial power in the Philippines. Initially, the Americans tried to deal with our people as friends. But after subduing the Filipino insurrection in 1902, the Americans, adept at creating provocation in order to find justification for waging war on a people, began encroaching upon the internal affairs of the Moros.

One of their first acts was to create a colonial bureaucracy for the administration of the Bangsa Moro homeland in 1903. This was the so-called Moro Province with political jurisdiction separate and different from the apparatus governing the Filipino people. The United States also unilaterally abrogated the Bates Treaty in March 1904. These twin moves precipitated one of the most bloody episodes in Bangsa Moro history when the heroic Moro fighters found themselves in military confrontation with America until 1914.

During this period events in Europe had their repercussions in our part of the world. World War I broke out and America's attention was diverted to her interests across the Atlantic. The military campaign against the Bangsa Moro people was halted without achieving a clear-cut military victory. But in lieu of force, the Americans shifted to the much-vaunted policy of attraction whereby Moro resistance fighters were persuaded to lay down their arms, to talk peace and cooperation. Casting the colonialist in an image of benevolent and sympathetic friend, it was ironically this policy of attraction that gained for the Americans some degree of acceptance among some Moro leaders. This marked an important colonial breakthrough for the United States in the Bangsa Moro homeland which led to a greater consolidation of their presence.

Meanwhile, a drive toward Filipinization, pressed on the Americans by the Filipino leaders, began in earnest. This drive assumed two facets:

1. increased participation by Filipinos in the colonial bureaucracy, including positions of decision-making in preparation for an early independence for the Philippines,
2. a subtle policy manipulation designed to draw the Bangsa Moro people into unity with the Filipinos under a unitary

Philippine state. This included, first of all, the abolition of the Moro Province in 1914, after which laws enacted for Filipinos were made applicable to the Moros. Secondly, a policy of settler colonialism was vigorously pursued whereby people from northern and central Philippines were brought southward in hordes to be settled in the Bangsa Moro homeland. Started at a time when there was no shortage of cultivable land for the peasantry in Luzon and Visayas, the aim of settler colonialism was to numerically overwhelm the Bangsa Moro population with foreigners, dispossess them of their ancestral land, and present to the world a colonial *fait accompli*.

Naturally, the Bangsa Moro people would not take such a sinister drive as the Filipinization process with indifference and complacency. Their reaction toward the prospect of being forcibly and illegally incorporated into the future Philipine state is reflected in at least two general courses of action which revealed their vehement opposition to such an unjust move. First, the parliamentary one was characterized, in the language of Leonard Wood and William Cameron Forbes who were both familiar with the 'Moro Problem', by 'increasing protest against the prospect of Filipinos ruling over them (Moros)'. The second path was the armed resistance put up by the freedom fighters against the police authority of the Philippine constabulary. According to one report, there were in the latter case, 124 conflicts between Moro armed resistance groups and the Philippine constabulary in the seven years from 1913 to 1920.

The antagonism (difference) between the two peoples led former US Congressman Robert Bacon of New York to describe the efforts at Filipinizing the Moro people as 'an abortive undertaking from its inception'. Bacon then filed a bill in the US Congress in 1926 which sought to separate (restore to their former status in 1914 is more appropriate) the Moro country from the rest of the Philippines islands. One of Bacon's arguments was: while the Filipino people in their lobby for early independence, may claim the right of self-determination for themselves, they have no right and therefore they cannot, pretend to claim that right for or over the Moro people. Only the Moro people themselves are entitled to claim their (own) right to self-determination, freedom and independence. But Bacon's voice was literally lost in the labyrinth of American colonial manipulation and the Filipino lobby.

The speech of Congressman Bacon has also been reproduced as part of the dossier and we submit that the same is of great historical importance to the legitimacy of our people's case at bar before this Tribunal.

Then in the early 1930s, preparation went on for Philippine independence. The US Congress, through the efforts of the annexationists, Manuel Quezon, Sergio Osmena, Manuel Roxas and others, passed the so-called Tydings-McDuffie Law authorizing the convening of a Philippine Constitutional Convention. But no provision whatever was made for the reversion of the Moro country to the Moro people. When the delegates were chosen, Filipinos from the north were made to represent the Moros in the south. The conspiracy to put the Bangsa Moro homeland under Philippine colonial rule and to regard the Moro people as a non-entity was so thorough and blatant that Thomas Cabili, a delegate from Lanao did not sign the final draft of the constitution.

In response to this conspiracy, more than one hundred Moro leaders of Lanao gathered at Dansalan on March 18, 1935. In that assembly, they wrote a strongly worded letter of protest to the US President and Congress, expressing opposition to the annexation of their homeland to the Philippines under the constitution, and warning of the consequences of such a move. The Moro leaders from Lanao told the US government that the Philippine islands, as it is known to Americans, are populated by two different peoples. The Filipinos inhabit the islands of Luzon and Visayas and the Moro people predominate in the islands of Mindanao (Basilan, Sulu and Palawan being generally considered parts of Mindanao). Hence, they said, and I quote: "we do not want to be included in the Philippine independence (for) once an independent Philippines is launched (there will be) troubles between us and the Christian Filipinos because from time immemorial these two people have not lived harmoniously (together)." The *Lanao Protest* is similarly reproduced as part of the dossier.

Finally, under the constitution, a commonwealth government was proclaimed and its flag flew over Moro country. The commonwealth period was to be a transition for ten years under the "benevolent" guidance of America. The year 1946 was set for the final declaration of independence, the severance of direct colonial ties. But before the Moro people could launch any concerted action to express their opposition once more, the second imperialist war broke out in the Pacific, and the euphoria that followed the proclamation of the commonwealth government was swept away by the fury of the war.

Suffering setbacks in the initial stages of the war in the face of the Japanese onslaught, the American forces, unprepared as they were, had to withdraw to Australia and Hawaii. Filipino resistance forces gathered their own strength and fought a delaying tactic while being abandoned by "mentor-protector" America. Meanwhile the Bangsa Moro people fought the Japanese Imperial army as one more colonial invader. But somehow, the scourge had to end and so it was on the ashes of war that Philippine independence was proclaimed in 1946, thereby completing the process of Filipinization colonization of the Bangsa Moro people and homeland.

At that point in history, the Philippines, having been under the colonial domination of Spain from 1565 to 1898 and under America from 1902 to 1946, indeed up to this moment remains a neo-colony, became a colonizer. On the other hand Bangsa Moro people, having resisted virtually tooth and nail the intrusion of western colonialism into their sacred homeland during all those years, fell, by a mere stroke of the pen, under Philippine colonial rule.

No prophetic vision could have been more accurate or analysis of events meore precise in their outcome than what the Moro leaders of Lanao had foretold at Dansalan. For, as the Philippine national anthem was sung in town squares and drums beaten in parades to mark the day of independence, almost simultaneously there were the sounds of gunfire and cries of widowed mothers in some villages in the countryside. Moro resistance fighters immediately took to the hills against what they have always believed to be *govierno a saruwang a tao*, i.e. foreign government.

Mr. President, the Filipino people considered, and rightly so, Spanish and American colonial occupation of the Philippines as illegal and an injustice which had to be redressed. They rose up in revolt against Spain and America invoking the right of a people to freedom and self-determination. By the same token, they cannot now justify Philippine colonial domination over the Bangsa Moro people and homeland. Indeed, they must be the first to recognize this truth. They must cast their support behind our people in our struggle to obtain that right.

We must acknowledge though that it is recognition and adherence to this universal principal that have moved the National Democratic Front, a revolutionary movement led by progressive Filipinos, to formally recognize in its ten-point program the right of our people to self-determination, a gesture that we in the Moro National Liberation Front very much appreciate. This recognition could not have come by magic either. It must have been a result of an in-depth study and discussion on their part, resulting in their correct reading and appreciation of the history of the Bangsa Moro people, and therefore the legitimacy of our people's claim to self-determination, freedom and independence.

Neither are the Bangsa Moro people passive claimants of their right. Aware as they are that Philippine colonialism would not dismantle its colonial edifice of its own accord, they have launched an armed struggle led by a vanguard organization, the Moro National Liberation Front (MNLF) and its military arm, the Bangsa Moro Army (BMA). In a Manifesto dated 28 April, 1974, the Moro National Liberation Front has declared the severance of all ties with Philippine colonialism and the establishment of the Bangsa Moro Republik. Since then the MNLF has been assuming civil functions in its controlled zones all over the Bangsa Moro homeland, acting to all intent and purpose, as a regular organized government. Indeed, I can make the claim here and now that we have all the attributes of a *de facto* government.

Considering the specific condition of our people which is principally composed of rural toiling masses, the Bangsa Moro Revolution and the MNLF adopt the strategy of mass mobilization which gives primacy to the role of the peasants uniting with urban workers, intelligensia, small merchants and artisans as well as civil servants who have been forced to eke out a living under the colonial bureaucracy.

In organizing the masses, the MNLF operates on a committee system with the Central Committee at the top of the structure, followed below by regional or provincial committees, followed further down the structural pyramid by municipal committees and lastly, by the barrio or village committees at the grassroots level. This point, as well as the role of the Bangsa Moro Army, will be explained elsewhere in another MNLF testimony.

With the above manifestation, Mr. President, I wish to conclude my statement by asking the Tribunal to render judgment, as follows:

1. recognizing the rights of our people to self-determination, freedom and independence;

2. declaring that Philippine colonialism in our people's homeland is unjust and illegal under applicable rules of international law relating to colonized peoples and non-self-governing territories;

3. declaring the legitimacy of the present armed struggle of our people led by the Moro National Liberation Front to obtain their rights since it is certain that Philippine colonialism would not withdraw from our people's homeland without force;

4. declaring that the Moro National Liberation Front be entitled to invoke the rules governing the civilized conduct of war, especially those rules governing the protection of civilians and their properties and the humane treatment of prisoners-of-war;

5. demanding that U.S. imperialism withdraw all forms of support from our people's colonial enemy;

6. requesting the United Nations to perform its responsibilities and obligations to our people in hastening our people's march to freedom;

7. and such other judgment that the Tribunal may deem just, proper and appropriate that would vindicate the right of our people to their homeland.

Thank you.

Imperialism, the Marcos regime and the economic plunder of the Moro people

by Joel Rocamora

The Moro people of the southern Philippines are an oppressed, colonized people. They are the victims of a genocidal war waged by the US-backed Marcos regime since before martial law was declared and fascism thereby institutionalized on September 21, 1972. Armed, trained, even advised by US imperialism, the Philippine military has systematically terrorized and uprooted the Muslim population from their homes and their lands. Of a total Muslim population of roughly five and a half million, close to half are now refugees from this genocidal war.

The Moro people have not been passive victims, however. Far from it. Rather, they have waged a heroic resistance to the brutal attacks of the Marcos military, led by the Moro National Liberation Front (MNLF) and its Bangsa Moro Army (BMA). The Moro people are fighting not only for survival but for the recognition of their right to independence from colonization by the US-backed Marcos dictatorship.

The process of wholesale expropriation and marginalization of the Muslim population of the southern Philippines has reached unprecedented intensity since the Marcos regime came to power, and most especially since it declared martial law. By the same token, the resistance of the Moro people to the destruction and occupation of their homeland has achieved new heights during this same period under the MNLF's direction. Yet, the Marcos dictatorship's policy of pacification through extinction of the Moro people is only the most recent and most egregious instance of a long history of colonialism's and imperialism's efforts to open up these rich territories for their uncontested plunder. The MNLF, at the same time, represents the culmination of a long and glorious history of the Moro people's determined opposition to these nefarious designs on their homeland.

To understand the contemporary political economy of Mindanao and the other southern islands, then, it is necessary first to trace the historical development of this region in relation to the world capitalist economy and the various colonial powers —

most especially Spain and the US — who attempted to impose their hegemony over the southern islands in the same way they had done elsewhere in the archipelago.

Spanish Colonial Designs on Mindanao and Sulu

Prior to the arrival of the Spanish conquistadores in the Philippines in the 16th century, the social formations of the various Muslim people were more highly developed than those of the peoples of Luzon and the Visayas. The numerous sultanates which existed throughout the south had already extended their influence with the Visayas, where no comparable state apparatus had existed previously. Even Manila had a Muslim Sultan at the time of the Spanish conquest of the city in 1571, though no stable Muslim community existed there.

Islam was introduced to the peoples of Mindanao and Sulu by Muslim traders who passed through and eventually came to settle in cities like Jolo, which was a key link in the long-distance trade between Arabia and India to the west and China to the north. A substantial Chinese community also settled in Jolo as a result of this trade. The power of the Sultanate of Sulu rested largely on its participation in the lucrative trade in silks, spices and other commodities. The Sultanate of Maguindanao was likewise heavily dependent on trade. There was also a flourishing inland trade on the island of Mindanao, as goods from other lands were shipped up the Cotabato River and the wealth produced in the heartland of this island made its way down the river and out across the seas.

The various Muslim ethnic groups were not solely dependent on trade for their livelihood. The Maranaos were known for the production of upland rice and corn, the inland Maguindanaos for wet-rice cultivation along the Cotabato valley, and the Tausugs and coastal Maguindanaos for fishing as well as shipping. The Samals and Bajao relied wholly on the sea for a living. On the whole, the commercial contact of the Muslim sultanates with the rest of the world was an important source of economic vitality within the various pre-colonial social formations.

Unlike in the north, Spain faced in Mindanao and Sulu relatively advanced state structures and cohesive ethno- cultural groups, with their own leadership in the various sultans and datus and their own warriors and weapon-making capability. Precisely for this reason, Spain never in four hundred long years succeeded in subjugating the Moro people to its colonial rule.

Spain relied on Christian mercenaries from the north to man its invasion forces which carried out repeated raids on the Moro homeland. Failing in its efforts to control the extensive territory of Mindanao, Spain settled instead for severing the ties of long-distance trade between the sultanates and the outside world. Thus, the basis for the relative prosperity of these sultanates were undermined. At the same time, production surpluses were being continually drained off to sustain the armed resistance to the so called 'Moro campaigns'. After four hundred years of warfare and virtual isolation from the rest of the world, the Moro economy and society was by the end of Spanish rule only a pale reflection of the glory it had once been.

Towards the end of the Spanish colonial sojourn in the Philippines, the Spanish authorities had begun to devise a new scheme for the colonization of the south. This strategy entailed the large-scale relocation of by now predominantly Christian peasants from the north to the vast, sparsely-populated frontier of Mindanao in order to colonize it by 'proxy'. Before they could implement this plan, however, the Spanish suffered defeat at the hands of the Philippine revolutionary forces in the north and then surrendered to the Americans; thus, they had to abandon their last military fortress on Mindanao — located at Cotabato — in 1899.

The American Colonial Period in Mindanao and Sulu

What the Spanish colonialists had conceptualized, the American colonialists would soon institutionalize. Before they could, however, they had to suppress the intense struggle waged by the Moros against this new would-be oppressor. For, while the US had agreed with the Sulu Sultanate, this turned out to be a cruel ploy to keep the Moro leadership from responding to the call of the leadership of the new Philippine Republic for unity in the face of a common aggressor. Once resistance in the north had been successfully crushed, the US unilaterally abrogated the treaty on 2 March, 1904, signalling its intent to mete out the same treatment to Moro nationalists it had meted out to Filipino nationalists. Military rule and resistance to that rule in Mindanao continued for the next 10 years until 1913.

Land Rights and Resettlement

At the outset of the US colonial rule, the population of Mindanao and Sulu was still roughly 98 percent Muslim. The other 2 percent consisted largely of non-Muslim minorities. The policy of resettlement and the other land policies initiated during the American colonial period would radically transform the ethnic makeup of the population and cause major disruptions in economic and political power relations in the region.

Government-sponsored colonization of Mindanao got under way in 1912, one year before military rule ended, with an agricultural settlement in the Cotobato Valley. Two more were to follow in 1919, in Lanao and Basilan. Many more followed. US colonialism, the northern Filipino landlord elite and the Christian settlers all benefited in different degrees from this process. On the other hand, the Moro people and other indigenous peoples of Mindanao lost out, with few exceptions.

US imperialism saw the strategic value of gaining control over the vast agricultural, mineral, forest and water resources of Mindanao and Sulu, which lie outside the typhoon belt that spans the northern islands. In order to extend this control, however, it had first to replace customary land rights of Moro society — according to which land is inalienable — with private property rights in land, thereby making it a commodity to be exchanged on the market.

This was accomplished first through the Public Land Act of 1919, which declared the ancestral lands of the Moro and other indigenous peoples public lands. The Manila government thereby reserved to itself the authority to distribute titles to this land, possession of which became proof of ownership. Under this Act, Christians could apply for up to twenty-four hectares of public land, while non-Christians were limited to ten hectares. Either out of ignorance or defiance, most Muslims failed to secure a title to their ancestral lands, and so found Christian settlers had laid claim to them.

While Christian settlers clearly benefited at first from this arrangement, the choicest lands along roadways and waterways were often gobbled up first by northern landlords — usually members or cronies of the Filipino colonial bureaucratic elite — who realized the potential wealth the islands had to offer. These same wealthy landlords from the north also realized the advantage of having such a frontier to relieve the discontent among their own impoverished tenants and the growing landless class in Luzon and the Visayas, which from time to time erupted into open rebellion. Some members of the Muslim elite also obtained title to large tracts of land which they themselves as well as other members of their clans were farming.

The end result of this process has been the creation of a

hierarchy of landholding with wealthy Christian landlords at the top, then a small Muslim landholding elite, followed by a plethora of poor Christian settlers owning a few hectares of land each, with the overwhelming majority of the Moro masses deprived of any land at all, or forced to till marginal lands cleared from the forested mountain slopes. The non-Muslim minorities suffered a fate similar to that of the Moro people, if they had not already been forced long since into the upper mountain reaches.

While the basic legal and institutional framework for the massive displacement of the indigenous population of Mindanao was firmly established by the end of the US colonial period, by far the greatest numbers of settlers have migrated to the south in the period following independence in 1946.

Multinational Corporate Penetration in the
US Colonial Era

Along with the restructuring of land rights and land ownership in Mindanao during the US colonial period, a more far-reaching restructuring of the basic mode of production was progressing. During the Spanish colonial period, the areas of central Luzon and western Visayas had been transformed into plantation economies producing sugar cane for export; abaca, or Manila hemp, was also grown for export in such regions as Bicol, while tobacco became the chief crop of the Ilocano provinces. Mindanao was only integrated into this colonial pattern of development — producing cash crops and supplying the raw materials to industries and consumers in the colonizing country — with the coming of the Americans.

The US had a simple design on the archipelago — to exploit to the fullest its abundant resources to supply US consumers and industry with cheap primary products, while exporting the manufactured goods churned out by booming US factories to the Philippines as yet small markets. The institution of free trade between the US and the Philippines in 1909 tied the fate of the latter inextricably to the whims of the former. US colonial policy towards Mindanao can be understood only in light of this broader design of US imperialism on the Philippines. US soldiers stationed in Mindanao until 1913 were employed not only for pacification of Muslims, but for prospecting and surveying their land. As the US army explained, it was 'a duty to explore the little-known regions of Mindanao and Sulu in order to discover the topography, mineral and agricultural resources and other physical characteristics of the southern islands'.

The wealth they and others after them found is impressive, to say the least. A few statistics make this clear. Today, Mindanao produces 50 per cent of all the corn and coconut in the Philippines, 20 per cent of all rice, 50 per cent of fish, 40 per cent of cattle, almost 100 per cent of all exported bananas and pineapples, 89 per cent of nickel and cobalt, 90 per cent of iron ore, 62 per cent of limestone, almost 100 per cent of aluminium ore, 72 per cent of logs, and 100 per cent of rubber. These figures become even more impressive when one considers that the islands of Mindanao and Sulu cover just over one-third of the total land area in the Philippines and contain less than one-fourth of the total population.

Soon after free trade was instituted and a colonial administrative apparatus had been set up in the south, American, and to a lesser degree, Japanese corporations began moving into the region. In 1919, for example, B.F. Goodrich began growing rubber in Basilan, while in 1926 Del Monte started planting pineapples on a former US military camp in Bukidnon. Three years later, Goodyear began rubber production in Zamboanga. During the same period, Japanese agribusiness corporations were turning Davao into an abaca-growing province. By 1938, Japanese landholdings in Davao amounted to 63,765 hectares.

The 1935 Constitution of the new Philippine Commonwealth prohibited ownership or leasing by private corporations of land in excess of 1,024 hectares. To satisfy the land-hunger of such big multinational agribusinesses as Del Monte, however, the Commonwealth government established a public National Development Corporation (NDC), entitled to lease land in excess of the legal limit from the government. The NDC simply turned around and 'sublet' this land to the big corporations at a nominal rent. Thus was Philpak, the Del Monte subsidiary, able to acquire control over 7,922 hectares of land through a 25-year sublease agreement with the NDC. This roundabout procedure is still used to this day to allow companies like Dole and Del Monte to add to their plantations at little cost. It often happens, however, that the land onto which they choose to expand is already occupied by Filipino farmers. The contract Dole has concluded with the NDC for the use of some 6,818 hectares of pineapple land contains a clause blatantly sanctioning Dole landgrabbing from farmers. 'NDC shall, from time to time, when and as requested by Dole, buy, acquire and obtain title to such additional parcels of land as may be needed by Dole in its operations under the agreement.'

The coconut industry also began to expand into Mindanao in the first few decades of US colonial rule. American soap and margarine manufacturers were increasingly using tropical oils like coconut for raw materials. Mindanao became a key supplier of US demand for coconut, as the Visayas became the main supplier of sugar. Today, 40 per cent of Mindanao's cropland is planted with coconuts. Most coconuts were and still are grown on relatively small farms owned by small and medium landlords. Nevertheless, there are a number of big landlords from the north who own extensive coconut lands in Mindanao. One 196-hectare coconut plantation in Davao del Norte, for example, is owned by a large sugar haciendero from Negros. Eduardo Cojuanco, a close associate of Marcos with extensive sugar lands in central Luzon, is now the biggest coconut landlord in Mindanao. The customary rent paid by tenant coconut farmers to these landlords ranges from 67 to 75 per cent of their harvest. With what remains, the coconut farmer must pay his hired help and buy certain inputs. Little is left over for his own family needs. While it is small consolation perhaps, the Mindanao coconut farmer is not quite as poor as his counterpart in the Visayas or Bicol. Besides the landlords like Cojuanco, the other big profiteers from the coconut industry are the domestic traders, millers and exporters. In the case of copra, 34 per cent of the export value ends up in the hands of domestic traders and exporters. With coconut and copra meal, 58 per cent of the export value accrues to the middlemen and oil millers. Who are these oil millers? There are thirteen coconut oil millers in Mindanao, the two biggest of which belonged until recently to Legaspi Oil Company and Granexport Manufacturing Corporation, the two largest coconut oil producers in the country. The former was owned by a Filipino-Japanese joint venture, the Ayala-Mitsubishi group; the latter by Cargill, a US-based agribusiness multinational. Both were bought in 1979 by the United Coconut Planters' Bank, a creation of the Marcos regime in a move to establish a government monopoly over coconut milling and marketing. The bank includes on its board of directors both Eduardo Cojuangco and Defense Minister Juan Ponce Enrile. Franklin Baker, a subsidiary of the US multinational General Foods, expanded into the Philippines in 1922 and currently has a plant in Davao del Sur producing dessicated coconut for export. Its Philippine operations earn a phenomenal 244.9 per cent return on equity, the second highest of any company in the Philippines.

Summary of the Colonial and Commonwealth Periods
By the time US imperialism granted the Philippines neo-colonial independence in 1946, the parcelling out of Moro and other lands among Christian settlers from the north on the one hand, and multinational corporations on the other, was already well underway. From 1918 to 1948 the population of Mindanao increased from 1.1 million to 2.9 million, or 166 per cent, while the total Philippine population rose by only 86 per cent during the same period. The difference in the rates represents immigration into Mindanao. The basis of the Moro agricultural society — the system of customary land ownership and the ties to ancestral lands — was supplanted by a new system of land ownership based on private property rights and an altogether different mode of production corresponding to it. While this older mode of production still existed in places, it was now subordinated to the requirements of capitalist expansion in the region. The main export industries which began to penetrate Mindanao during this period were pineapple, rubber, and coconuts. Even the Christian settlers who served as a buffer between multinationals and the displaced Moro population would later fall victim to the same forces of capitalist expansion in the region.

The Post-Colonial Period of Expansion into Mindanao-Sulu

The post-colonial period was marked by an intensification of all the economic forces which were set in motion during the US colonial years. On the one hand, the land problem in Luzon and the Visayas continued to worsen, leading to widespread peasant unrest after World War II and to the Huk rebellion in Central Luzon. Mindanao once again served as a pseudo-solution for the northern landed aristocracy who dominated the newly independent government. On the other hand, the post-colonial Philippine administrations perpetuated in all important respects the Philippines subservience to US economic interests. For another decade free trade between the US and the Philippines continued to rule, while the Parity Amendment to the Philippine constitution extended the right of US citizens up till 1974.

Resettlement since Independence
The tide of immigration to Mindanao rose even higher after the Second World War, as land-hungry peasants either moved south on their own or were forcibly moved by the Philippine government as part of its pacification of the Huk rebellion. The influx

continued unabated into the 1970s. From 1948 to 1970 the population of Mindanao increased by roughly 5 million, or 171 per cent, as compared to a 90 per cent increase in the population of the country as a whole. Government resettlement agencies relocated the new settlers in such present-day provinces as Lanao del Sur, North Cotabato, Sultan Kudarat, Maguindanao, Davao and Bukidnon, displacing numerous Muslims in the process. As in the past, these resettlements served as a wedge, ultimately benefitting wealthy Filipinos from the north and agribusiness companies, driven between indigenous Muslim and non-Muslim population and their lands. Thus, a Senate Committee on National Minorities report in 1963 observed: 'Natives in these provinces complained that they were being driven away by in-fluential persons and big companies who have been awarded rights to lands which have long been occupied and improved by the members of the cultural minorities.'

The process of dislocation of Muslims continues up to the very present, but to the pressure of settlers and multinationals on the Muslim population is now added the assault on Muslim communities daily conducted by the Philippine military. As a result of all these factors, the Moro people have literally been pushed to the brink. They have been marginalized and im-poverished by the very same political and economic forces which are unleashing at an unprecedented pace the productive potential of the region. With a single stroke imperialism has completely disrupted the pre-existing social order while replacing it with the order of production for the world market; it has made the Moro and other peoples into squatters on their own land by occupying that land; it has generated increasing misery and poverty for the many while amassing untold profits for the privileged few.

Imperialist Expansion and Consolidation in the Neo-Colonial Era
The post-colonial history of imperialist penetration of the south has been marked on the one hand by diversification into new in-dustries and on the other hand by the continued expansion of its interests in already existing industries. After the war, for exam-ple, the timber industry in the Philippines began to boom. Japan imported large quantities of Philippine logs, lumber, plywood and veneer for use in its post-war reconstruction. In the early 1950s such big US multinationals as Georgia-Pacific and Weyerhauser acquired extensive logging concessions in Min-danao and Basilan. In addition to these concessions, the two

companies established sawmills and veneer plants. Boise-Cascade would soon follow suit, acquiring control over Zamboanga Wood Products to complement its 42,800 hectare timber concession. Currently, over half (or 514 million hectacres) of all forest land in the Philippines covered by timber licenses is located in Mindanao. The timber industry in the Philippines, however, is now finding it difficult to compete with those of Malaysia and Indonesia because of the rapacious logging practices of profit-hungry concessionaires. The forest destruction rate exceeds the reforestation rate by 9:1 ratio. All of the best lands have long been logged over.

Logging operations have a very immediate impact on the livelihood and welfare of the Moro people since historically they have been forced to migrate to the edges or even into the midst of the forests to eke out a meagre existence. The rape of the forests disturbs the delicate ecological balance on which their lives depend. Those trees which signify only pesos to the logging companies represent the difference between water control and flooding, soil conservation and soil erosion to the local people. Ironically and tragically, because the Moro and other indigenous peoples have been forced into the forest to make a living, they may be aggravating this ecological imbalance through the practice of swidden agriculture (or kaingin), which is their only means of survival. Pulp and paper mills, like that of PICOP in Surigao, dump tons of waste chemicals into bays and rivers in Mindanao and elsewhere, with no regard for the thousands of people who depend on fishing in those waters for their living.

Another major area of corporate expansion in Mindanao since the war — in particular since the early 1960s — has been bananas for export. Here again, Japan serves as the principal market. Today, Mindanao accounts for all Philippine exports of bananas, which amounted to $84.1 million in 1978. The choicest lands in Davao del Norte and South Cotabato became banana plantations run by or for Dole, Del Monte, TADECO (partner of United Brands of the US), or Davao Fruits (partner of Sumitomo of Japan). Altogether some 20,794 hectares of Mindanao farmland were planted with bananas for export in 1975. The expansion of banana lands in many cases has meant the encroachment on other croplands. In Davao del Norte, for example, Dizon Farms — a grower for Del Monte — ejected some 200 farmers on the same number of hectares of rice and coconut lands to make way for its banana operations in 1979. Early in 1977, TADECO — owned by Antonio Floirendo, a close crony of Marcos — successfully evicted, with the help of the military, some 700 families from lands adjacent to the company's plantation in Tagum, Davao del Norte. Because of its close government ties, moreover, TADECO also has the rare privilege of employing the inmates of the Davao Penal Colony to work on its plantation at substandard wages. Chiquita bananas from the Philippines are grown with prison labor. In addition the finest road in Davao runs from the heart of the TADECO plantation to the landing dock, where the bananas are put on ships bound for Japan.

Other key industries which have emerged in Mindanao during the post-colonial era include corporate rice and corn farming, sugar, palm oil, and coffee growing, mining, cattle ranching, and tuna fishing. These first developed in response to a martial law General Order issued in 1974 requiring any company with 500 or more employees either to grow or import the grain needs of its employees. Out of seventy such corporate farms serving the needs of some 145 companies, twenty are located in Mindanao growing rice and corn for over half these firms. Among the multinational enterprises involved in corporate farming in Mindanao are Dole, Del Monte, Goodyear, B. F. Goodrich, Ford, Procter and Gamble, Bank of America and Union Carbide. The average size of the corporate farms in Mindanao is 653 hectares, though several exceed 1,000 hectares. They are highly mechanized and exceedingly productive. They use very little labor and enormous quantities of fertilizers and pesticides. These capitalist farms have helped make the Philippines a net exporter of rice in recent years, at the same time that a majority of the children are undernourished. A survey conducted in Mindanao from 1976 to 1978 found that 74 per cent of pre-school children suffered from some degree of malnutrition.

The pattern of development which has characterized these other sectors of Mindanao's economy — sugar, palm oil, cattle ranching, etc. — should by now be familiar: dislocation of Moro and other native peoples; replacement of subsistence production with production for the world market; the generation of a rural wage labor force much larger than can be absorbed by the capital-intensive export crop economy; the forced migration of the growing marginal population to the hinterlands or to the expanding squatter communities of Davao, Zamboanga, Cotabato, Iligan and Cagayan de Oro cities. Even in their new homes the dispossessed have not escaped the undiscriminate hand of imperialist expansion. In the hinterlands they face the threat of further dislocation by timber and mining companies. In the cities they face uprooting to make way for the construction of new factories and the free trade zones to house them; or for new roads and ports to facilitate the export of Mindanao's wealth to the far reaches of the earth. Meanwhile, the people possess neither a home nor the wealth of their land. Davao City is the proposed site of one such export processing zone, where cheap Filipino labor will be brought together with foreign raw materials and machines to produce big profits for foreign electronics, garment or other manufacturers. The mayor of Davao City has warned of the displacement of thousands of residents of Daliao district if construction proceeds as planned. All would probably agree that imperialist penetration of Mindanao has had a devastating effect on the pre-existing mode of production, completely severing the ties of the Moro peasant population to the land. Some might ask however, if the accelerating growth of new export industries is not providing alternative — and perhaps even more lucrative — employment opportunities for the growing landless class. Certainly in advanced industrial societies, the shift of population from subsistence agriculture to industrial or agricultural wage employment, has often been accompanied by increased living standards for the general population. Why not in Mindanao and why, in particular, not for the Moro people?

An answer to this question has two aspects: In the first place, the circumstances surrounding the displacement of the Moro population made it both unnecessary and unfeasible from the point of view of multinational capital to utilize Moro people as the primary labor pool from which to staff imperialist enterprises. On the one hand, the large influx of Christians from the north provided an ample reserve army of labor generally more accessible to these corporations than the Moro population. The latter were generally concentrated in areas of Western and Central Mindanao, where most multinationals dare not venture because of the war. On the other hand, imperialism had already developed a long-standing relationship with the northern population from which the settlers came, and therefore could manage a Christian labor force better. The vast majority of agricultural plantation workers, therefore, are Christians not Muslims. The same holds true for workers employed by industry in the major urban areas.

In such growing industrial centers as Davao City, Iligan City, and Cagayan de Oro, Muslims make up only a minute percentage of the population and an equally minute portion of the labor force. So, to the extent that anyone has benefited from the employment opportunities provided by multinational enterprises, it has not been the Moro people.

The second aspect of the answer to our earlier question has to do with precisely the extent to which these multinational enterprises provide opportunities for economic growth and for higher incomes which would not have existed otherwise. There is a fundamental difference between such foreign corporate investment in Mindanao and agribusiness or industrial expansion within the economies of the advanced industrialized countries. In the latter agribusiness and industrial production are primarily oriented toward the internal market. For corporations to be able to sell their output in that market, incomes must be high enough to buy the commodities produced. The laborers employed by these firms are not only part of the costs of production, but also a large part of the final demand for the goods produced. In the heavily export-oriented corporate economy of Mindanao the situation is entirely different. The people of Mindanao do not serve as the principal market for Dole's bananas or Del Monte's pineapples. From the perspective of these companies, the workers they hire are purely and simply costs of production, to be minimized by whatever means.

Thus, depressed incomes of Mindanao households are perfectly compatible with corporate expansion in Mindanao. Indeed with respect to the actual workforce of these corporations, depressed wages are the direct outcome of multinational profit-making. The profits to be made are indeed enormous. In 1970, Dole's rate of return on equity in the Philippines was 174.3 per cent, for example, while its US rate of return was only 11.2 per cent. The martial law government has played a crucial role as guarantor of the continued availability of a cheap, docile labor force for the exploitation of foreign corporations. The ban on strikes in 'vital' (read export) industries has been the most important weapon in its arsenal, though by no means the only one. Violation of the ban invariably prompts a swift and ruthless response from the regime. Offenders are carted off to prison or harassed and beaten by military or para-military goons. A strike two years ago by workers at the American-owned Findlay Miller lumber company in Zamboanga del Norte was greeted by such a show of strength by the Marcos military.

Martial Law at the Service of Imperialism in Mindanao

The events which led up to the declaration of martial law by the Marcos government in September 1972 were by no means limited to Mindanao. US imperialism's interests in the country as a whole were increasingly threatened in the years prior to martial law by a militant nationalist mass movement as well as by certain members of the legislative and judiciary branches who wanted to limit the prerogatives of foreign capital. The right of US citizens to own land in the country had been successfully challenged in a landmark Supreme Court case. Foreign control of banks was likewise being challenged in the Senate. The infamous Parity Amendment was soon to expire and there was open speculation as to whether or not it would be renewed.

Martial law was designed to succeed where Philippine democracy had proved wanting. It was necessary to ensure not only the preservation of imperialism's premier role in the Philippine economy, but to deepen the economy's integration into the world capitalist system through the imposition of export-led industrialization. Even bourgeois democracy could not be expected to work in imposing on the broad masses of Filipinos the heavy costs of such a strategy, which coincided with the evolving needs of imperialism.

Thus, in the martial law period the Philippine state has served as the guarantor and the advance guard of imperialist interests in the country to a greater extent than in any other period since independence. The nature of the Marcos dictatorship's relationship to imperialism is fourfold: (1) as maintainer of political stability; (2) as ultimate protector of private property rights in land and other means of production; (3) as organizer and discipliner of the labor force; (4) as coordinator and constructor of the necessary infrastructure projects to enhance corporate profitability.

In fulfilling each of these roles the Marcos regime has clearly focused a great deal of its attention and resources on Mindanao. The dictatorship has sought to maintain social stability in the region by wholesale massacre of those Muslims who refuse to be cowed into passivity — who refuse to consent to their own liquidation. In this context social stability is seen to be a highly relative notion, since the Marcos regime itself has been the major source of instability in the region by unleashing its full military might on a largely unsuspecting Muslim population. The complicity of US imperialism in helping the Marcos regime 'pacify' the Moro people is beyond dispute. The upwards of 100 per cent increase in US military aid to Marcos in the four years after martial law as compared with the four years before is ample testimony to this complicity. Up to the present the bulk of Philippine soldiers and military hardware are deployed in the Muslim areas of Mindanao. Much of that hardware comes from the US. US-made fighter planes and even US military pilots are reported to have participated in the bombing of Mindanao in 1974. More recently, the US has once again boosted its annual military assistance to Marcos by over 100 per cent in return for continued use of the US military bases at Subic and Clark, from which those earlier bombing raids were staged. Once again, the Moro people are bearing the brunt of this escalation in US military support for Marcos. According to one estimate, by the end of 1976, 50,000 Muslims had been killed, 200,000 homes burned, two million refugees created, 535 mosques and 200 schools demolished, and 35 cities and towns wholly destroyed. In less than a decade Muslims have been forced to abandon over a million hectares of land because of the war.

As Muslims flee the war, their lands are often claimed by professionals, petty government officials or members of the military, who see the prospect for acquiring wealth in a hurry. Multinational agribusiness and other corporations are more reluctant to rush in to the war-torn areas of western and central Mindanao. These companies have, whether by choice or necessity, limited their landgrabbing activities since martial law mostly to the relatively 'peaceful' regions of northern and eastern Mindanao, where the lands they grab are now farmed mostly by Christians and non-Muslim minorities. The Philippine military and constabulary serve as agents of eviction when that proves necessary, while Bureau of Land officials prepare the necessary paperwork. Bukidnon, Davao del Norte and South Cotabato have been scenes of substantial corporate landgrabbing in recent years. In 1976, for example, members of the Manobo tribe were evicted from their village in Bukidnon to make way for a sugar plantation owned largely by Rodolfo Cuenca. A close friend of Marcos, Cuenca heads the Construction Development Corporation of the Philippines (CDCP), the biggest Philippine construction company with numerous contracts to build government infrastructure projects. Also participating in the sugar venture, known as BUSCO, is Marcos crony and Ambassador to Japan Roberto Benedicto, who heads the Republic Planters Bank and the National Sugar Trading Corporation. The latter controls all sugar marketing in the country.

The Marcos regime's role as organizer and discipliner of the labor force, while not essentially different from that of its predecessors, has taken on heightened importance as a result of the imperialist-imposed export-led industrialization path the regime has pursued and the cheap labor on which the strategy relies. Within this overall strategy, Mindanao has until now been cultivated as a supplier of primary products — agricultural, mineral and forestry — to the world market. What limited export industrialization has occurred in the last few years — mostly of the labor-intensive, light manufacturing variety — has occurred largely outside of Mindanao. The industry which does exist in Mindanao tends to be highly capital-intensive and resource-based — like the cement industry in Davao and Iligan and the Kawasaki Sintering Plant (which uses iron ore) near Cagayan de Oro City. Even plantation agriculture tends to be capital-intensive as compared with subsistence agriculture. Pineapple plantations, for example, employ an average of one worker for every two and a half hectares of land, while the Dole corporate rice farm in Mindanao is reported to employ one farm worker for every 13 hectares. The average land/labor ratio for all Philippine agriculture, by contrast, is 1.4 hectares per laborer. The lack of labor-intensive industries in Mindanao may be partially explained by the relative 'scarcity' of labor or 'abundance' of land in this region until fairly recently as compared with Luzon and the Visayas. In 1975, only 6.5 per cent of the employed labor force in Mindanao worked in manufacturing as compared with a national average of over 10 per cent. As northerners continue to move south in large numbers; this situation is apt to change. As a land shortage and labor surplus takes shape in Mindanao the Marcos regime is beginning to encourage the location of labor-intensive industry in such heavily Christian areas as Davao and Cagayan de Oro. The proposed Davao Export Processing Zone and the PHIVIDEC industrial estate are part of this employment generation effort. Thus, the regime's role of policing the labor force and keeping the lid on labor unrest will undoubtedly become more pronounced in Mindanao in the years to come.

The Marcos regime, finally, has assumed the responsibility — to a far greater extent than any previous administration — of coordinator and erector of the basic infrastructure so essential to the profitable operation of imperialist enterprises in the country. The US-dominated World Bank and the Japanese-dominated

Asian Development Bank have been the two major sources of infrastructure loans to the regime while private banking consortia have likewise been generous. The magnitude of such loans is reflected in the fact that the Philippines has an outstanding external debt of close to P12 billion. Several of the biggest infrastructure projects have been built, are going up, or are being planned for Mindanao. These projects are of four major types:

   a.   irrigation and water control systems;
   b.   power and electrification;
   c.   roadways and bridges;
   d.   portworks and airports.

The centrality of the last three to a development strategy of export-led growth is evident enough. Cheap power generation for industry, reliable and speedy transport of goods — especially perishables, adequate storage, loading and shipping capacity for an increased export volume are essential. The first type of infrastructure project is less obviously but nonetheless importantly related to the strategy. Not only is irrigation essential to realize the full productive potential of the export crop economy, in addition, increasing productivity of rice and corn lands is essential to keep those commodities cheap without the drastic reduction of farm incomes. Cheap rice and corn in turn makes the regime's task of repressing wages all that much simpler. As long as workers' wages buy enough rice or corn to feed their families, they are not so likely to press their multinational employers for wage increases. In addition, with productivity increases in rice and corn the Marcos regime expects to be able to convert more and more cropland to export crops. Already, over half of Mindanao cropland is planted to commercial and export crops, compared to a national average of about 44 per cent. Since Cotabato valley has become an important rice granary for Mindanao, the advantage in terms of this strategy of increasing productivity through irrigation and other means in that area are sizeable.

The most ambitious infrastructure project in all of Mindanao is the Cotabato-Agusan River Basin Development Project (CARBDP), which covers one-third of the total land area of Mindanao. When finished the entire project is expected to cost P15.7 billion. The foreign exchange component of the cost is being financed in large part by loans from the Asian Development Bank (ADB). In addition to the irrigation projects in the Cotabato and Agusan river valleys, many of which are in various states of implementation, there are at least 17 dams scheduled for construction between 1981 and 2000. In most cases these will combine irrigation, hydroelectric power, and flood control. One of the first scheduled for completion — and probably the most controversial — is the Lake Sebu Multi-Purpose Dam in South Cotabato. The T'boli tribe live on the shores of the lake. The damming of the lake will mean the destruction of 3,000 hectares of rich farmland and with it the livelihood of 1,700 T'boli.

Another major hydroelectric dam project along the Agus River in Lanao del Norte is having a devastating impact on the Maranaos, a Muslim people inhabiting the shores of Lake Lanao. The project, financed by the ADB as well as several private banking consortia, is slated to generate close to 900 megawatts of electricity upon completion. Both the agricultural and fishing activities of the Maranaos have been completely disrupted by the destabilization of the water level in the lake. Over 600 Maranao families have been relocated with compensation only for improvements on their lands. One of the key beneficiaries of the Maria Cristina dam — part of the Agus system — has been the Kawasaki Sintering Plant in Misamis Oriental, which consumes an enormous quantity of electricity and in turn spews out large quantities of pollutants. The stories of innundation of villages and farmlands and dislocation of communities without adequate provision for relocation could be repeated with reference to every major dam project in Mindanao.

In fact, every major infrastructure project of whatever type invariably involves dislocation of families, destruction of lands, and disruption of the local ecology. Yet, certain economic improvements clearly derive from such projects. Superficially, the problem is that the losers from such projects — the disenfranchised — are those who can least afford to lose. Moreover, the beneficiaries are usually those who least need the benefits and who could easily afford to compensate the losers — assuming there is any adequate compensation for the destruction of one's way of life. Yet, seldom if ever is fair compensation paid. The government could, at the very least, force big corporations like Del Monte or Kawasaki or big landlords like Floirendo or Cojuanco to pay compensation to those poor farmers and fishermen who lost everything for the sake of cheap electricity and irrigation water which they will never get to use. Yet, for the Marcos dictatorship to do that would be, so to speak, to bite the hand that feeds it. It would be to betray its very nature.

More fundamentally, the problem is that infrastructure projects which could be providing cheap electricity, irrigation water and transportation to the vast majority of people of Mindanao are not and cannot — given the existing system of political and economic power relations prevailing in the region. For the Moro people and other peoples of Mindanao to benefit from dams, irrigation canals and roads, from mines, fields and factories, those basic power relations must be overturned. The stranglehold of imperialism, big landlords and the Marcos dictatorship over the Moro people and the other peoples of Mindanao must be broken. For one decade now the Moro people have been struggling fiercely to free themselves from the deadly grip of this three-headed hydra. More and more, other oppressed and exploited Filipinos are coming to realize the wisdom and justice of their cause.

Sources:

1. AFRIM Resource Centre, *Mindanao Report : A Preliminary Study on the Economic Origins of Social Unrest* (Davao, 1980)
2. Corporate Information Center, National Council of Churches of Christ in USA, *The Philippines: American Corporations, Martial Law and Underdevelopment (IDOC, November, 1973)*
3. *ICL Research Team, A Report on Tribal Minorities in Mindanao* (Manila, 1979)
4. ICL Research Team, *The Human Costs of Bananas* (Manila, 1979)
5. Rad D. Silva, *Two Hills of the Same Land: Truth Behind Mindanao Problem* (Mindanao-Sulu Critical Studies and Research Group, 1979)
6. *Some are Smarter Than Others*, (Manila, 1979)
7. Third World Studies, University of the Philippines, *Mindanao: Development and Marginalization*, AMPO Japan-Asia Quarterly, 4th Quarter, 1979.

The Moro National Liberation Front and the present resistance

by Hatimil Hassan

The present Bangsa Moro Revolution is the culmination of a series of armed struggle waged by the Bangsa Moro people against Philippine colonialism. In the present struggle, the Moro National Liberation Front (MNLF) has taken the vanguard role in providing revolutionary guidance and direction.

Founding of MNLF

The MNLF was founded by young Moro professionals and students who arrived at the conclusion that armed revolution was the only option left for the Bangsa Moro people to take, in order to vindicate their right to their national homeland.

The MNLF adopts the strategy of mobilizing the masses by organizing them to play their revolutionary task, as well as forging and consolidating genuine national unity and solidarity. Masses of our people have become the reservoir of strength for the MNLF and the Bangsa Moro Army (BMA), the military arm of the movement.

International Organization and Policy

The MNLF itself is, in a very concrete sense, a democratic people's organization. It functions on a committee system wherein the masses and the people are organized into village committees at the grassroots levels to which they choose their representatives by popular consent. At the top of the MNLF structure is the Central Committee headed by a Chairman. It has a secretariat that functions both as executive and administrative organ of the MNLF. Within the secretariate are members of revolutionary service organs or agencies that perform various functions by way of implementing the social policy of the organization, such as education, health and medical service, refugee welfare, finance, transportation and communication, supply and the like.

At no time in the history of our people has there been so

much enthusiasm in support of the Revolution and at no time had the people's heroism in the past been as severely tested as it is at the present time.

The MNLF seeks the unity of all oppressed forces in our society — peasants, workers, intelligensia, small merchants and artisans, Muslims, Christians, nature-worshippers, and non-believers in a national liberation struggle to liquidate the presence of Philippine colonial rule in the Bangsa Moro homeland where no exploitation of any kind would be tolerated. It was this oppressive rule that has brought about the existing pattern of social relations in Bangsa Moro society where the elites and landlords are maintained in their privileged social position at the expense of the poor masses, a situation exacerbated by the coming of colonial settlers who after grabbing the lands of the natives, have themselves become oppressive landlords and capitalists.

In a *Manifesto* issued on April 28, 1974, the Moro National Liberation Front announced the severance of all ties with Philippine colonialism. In that manifesto, the MNLF also outlined its strategy for attaining its objectives. More importantly, the MNLF declared its commitment to the principle of constructing, I quote 'a democratic system of government which shall never allow nor tolerate any form of exploitation and oppression of any human being by another or of one nation by another nation as replacement for the sultanate and privileged aristocracy.' (Paragraph IV).

In relation to the Filipinos who have lived peacefully in the Bangsa Moro homeland, the Manifesto states categorically, I quote again, 'those Filipinos who may wish to remain in the Bangsa Moro National homeland after independence shall be welcomed and entitled to equal rights and protections with all other citizens of the Bangsa Moro Republik, provided that they formally renounce their Filipino citizenship and wholeheartedly accept Bangsa Moro citizenship; their property rights shall be fully respected and the free exercise of their political, cultural and religious rights shall be guaranteed.'' (Paragraph V).

Foreign Policy

In foreign policy, the MNLF expressed its recognition and adherence to the Charter of the United Nations and the Universal Declaration of Human Rights. In addition, the MNLF respects and adheres to all laws and conventions binding upon the nations of the world. If I may add, the MNLF is committed to the Third World and non-aligned movement as well as the world wide anti-imperialist struggle.

Today, the Bangsa Moro Revolution has established its apparatus. It had organized as early as 1974 the Supreme Revolutionary Tribunal which has been acting as the judicial arm of the MNLF. The Tribunal is structured down the judicial tier with the organization of the provincial revolutionary courts and municipal courts all over MNLF-controlled zones. The lower courts, systems, operating under the Supreme Revolutionary Tribunal assumes largely civil functions. Cases of misdemeanor, infractions and breach of discipline by the Bangsa Moro Army however, are resolved by Military Tribunals created on *ad hoc* basis by the General Staff of the Bangsa Moro Army. This distinction had to be resorted to, considering that the circumstances in which they operate is one of war and the situation is much too fluid to require more permanent military tribunal for the Bangsa Moro Army.

The Congress

Out of twelve states or regional areas within the Bangsa Moro Republik, the MNLF has organized provincial congresses in nine of them, one after another since 1974. And in April 1974, the Bangsa Moro people's Congress was called for the first time at the National headquarters of the Moro National Liberation Front somewhere in the jungle of Zamboanga. The National Congress was convened by the MNLF to define the specifics of the principles enunciated in the Manifesto of April 28, 1974. The Congress came out with a broader agenda and converted itself into an executive committee to prepare draft documents for its next session in October 1977. But while the Executive Committee was meeting in October, they were bombed and strafed by two F-5 jets, four *Tora-Tora* (T-28) bombers, subjected to air-to-ground rocket attacks by DC-3 type planes and long-range artillery shells. In less than 12 hours one delegate from Davao counted 211 bombs, mortars, rockets and cannons directed to an area less than two kilometers in diameter.

The Bangsa Moro Army

The Bangsa Moro Army is the military arm of the Moro National Liberation Front. Today the BMA numbers about 30,000 regulars organized into 10 provincial armies and so many numbers of zones in each. In addition, a large part of our masses are armed. They serve as kind of barrio defense forces ready to put up immediate defense to protect themselves from unexpected enemy attack.

A very important development in the organization of the Bangsa Moro Army is the creation of the National Mobile forces. This is the crack striking force of the Bangsa Moro Army directly under the General staff. In terms of operational area, the mobile forces are divided into four armies. These are the 1st, 2nd, 3rd and 4th Army. Each army is strategically positioned as to be able to launch tactical dispersal of every force whenever one BMA area suffers severe military pressures. The development of this army is also designed to suit the specific characteristic of our homeland in which they operate, such that whenever analysis of the situation calls for BMA offensive, it could be launched at different points of enemy position simultaneously so as to spread the enemy's forces, thus making them more vulnerable.

The BMA is responsible for liberating vast portions of our homeland. It is now entrenched all over, and indeed since 1974 it has been able to carry out many limited strategic offensives.

The Marcos regime campaign of genocide

by Dr Parouk Hussin

Mr. President, members of the Tribunal.

To date, as a result of a systematic and diabolical campaign of genocide perpetrated by the Marcos regime and his fascist and terrorist armed forces, aided by their imperialist master, the United States of America, more than 100,000 innocent Moro lives mostly children, women and the aged have already perished, about 300,000 dwellings burned down, incalculable worth of properties wantonly destroyed and almost half of the entire population of the Bangsa Moro homeland have been uprooted from their homes, including the over 200,000 refugees now in the neighboring State of Sabah Malaysia. These refugees are duly recognized by the Malaysian Government as well as the United Nations High Commission on Refugees. These violent and savage acts were committed in a span of 10 years or so under the dictatorial Marcos regime. This is not however a recent phenomenon, this is a phenomenon of more than 400 years, from the time of the early colonizers, the Spaniards, then the Americans and now Philippine colonialism.

As we listen, discuss and judge how the Martial Law regime of Marcos commits torture and repression against the Filipino people, there in the Bangsa Moro homeland Marcos' armed forces are continuously perpetrating their crimes in pursuance of the regime's genocidal policy against the Bangsa Moro. The regime does not any more go through such nasty procedure as torturing their victims but they immediately resort to killing, murder and massacres against the innocent Bangsa Moro masses.

Such killings started with the merciless massacres of 68 Moro youths at Corregidor Island in March 1968. That year, the military recruited about 300 Bangsa Moro youths purportedly for commission in the Philippine armed forces special unit. But on the eve of their graduation, the young trainees were murdered in cold-blood by their training instructors, all military officers led by Air Force Major Edwardo Martelino, for allegedly refusing to obey an order. That order, we learned from newspaper accounts and congressional investigations which were conducted in the aftermath of the crime, was to infiltrate Sabah, Malaysia over which the Philippines has filed territorial claims. When they refused to be used as tools by Marcos in his colonial gamble and greed for expansion, they were massacred. Until this very day, many of the 300 trainees are still missing.

When the Bangsa Moro masses demanded justice for the victims at Corregidor Island, the Marcos regime responded by organizing the infamous terrorist gang — the Ilaga. Trained and armed by the Philippine military led by PC officer Col. Carlos Cajelo and Capt. Manuel Tranco, the Ilaga conducted depredation and plunder against Bangsa Moro communities, killing innocent Bangsa Moro people and burning their homes while regular military units stood by and often times assisted them.

The Ilaga armed bands waged widespread extermination campaigns especially in the Cotabato and Lanao provinces. Glaring testimonies to this are the Manili Massacre in Carmen, North Cotabato in June, 1971. About 200 Bangsa Moro people were invited by the colonial soldiers to a peace conference. But while waiting inside the mosque for the conference to start, the colonial soldiers and Ilaga terrorists arrived and instantly massacred them. Only a few of them survived. The Mosque was turned into a graveyard. This was followed by a series of heinous massacres like the ones in Bual, Tulunan, Cotabato in September 1971, where 17 Bangsa Moro civilians were massacred and the 22 November, 1971 massacres of 36 innocent Bangsa Moro people in Tacub, Kauswagan, Lanao del Norte. In all these massacres, the men were beheaded, pregnant women were mutilated and disembowelled and children's ears were cut off. Ear cutting has even become ritualistic on their part. And according to information, they also get blood-money because for every pair of Moro ears, they get P1,000.

In the Tacub Massacre for example, the innocent masses were asked by the Commanding officers of the 4th PC Task Force Pagari to exercise their right of suffrage in a special national election of 22 November, 1972. They were promised security from Ilaga depredation. On the way home after voting the Philippine Army ambushed them, killing 36 on the spot and the rest died on the way while escaping for their lives. Then the Dimataling massacre in Zamboanga del Sur which was ordered by the Provincial Commander and Governor himself. Then the Magdaup, Zamboanga del Sur massacre followed subsequently by the Lebak Massacre in North Cotabato on 27 November, 1971.

Blood-letting is everywhere. And in all these massacres there is an element of treachery as when the 300 trainees of Corregidor were told that they will be trained and commissioned for the armed forces; as when the Manili civilians were gathered for a 'peace conference'; as when the Tacub residents were asked to vote with guarantee of PC security. And among the perpetrators of these treacheries is Marcos himself. This is exemplified by an April 1972 incident which followed upon the massacre in Lebak, a certain Datu Blah Sinsuat sought Marcos' permission to invite the evacuees from Lebak to his municipality at Upi. This man is very loyal to Marcos. In fact, he helped Marcos in his campaign for the surrender of our freedom fighters. However, he was moved by his desire to help the suffering evacuees who were mostly his relatives. Marcos gave him the permission with the assurance that Upi would not be included in the military operation. He was also instructed to raise a white flag at the evacuation center.

Datu Blah lost no time in gathering the evacuees, but no sooner were the helpless, innocent evacuees gathered in the center and the white flag raised, when the Philippine Air Force indiscriminately straffed and bombed the evacuation centers inflicting heavy toll on human lives and properties. When Datu Blah complained to Marcos about the incident, Marcos cabled him back by assuring him that the situation would be looked into and that an investigating team would be sent. What he received as a result were consoling words and alibis by Gen. Fortunato Abat, the Chief of the Central Mindanao Command, that it was a mistaken raid. He was also assured by Marcos and Gen. Abat that similar incidents would not happen again, but they were repeated after one week, and this time, not only Upi were included but the neighboring areas like Babato, Lagitan, Simpac, Mompong, Paligi and Kamalig. And this time not only air bombardments were used but also shelling from naval boats reducing the entire area to ashes.

To the Bangsa Moro people these atrocities of Marcos and his armed forces come not as a surprise. For there can be no greater testimonies to their crimes than the suffering of our people under their blood-soaked hands, children bayoneted to death, infants trampled under the boots of the savage colonial soldiers, women molested and raped (and not content with satisfying their carnal lust, they insert bottles into the Moro women's genitals before they are executed) and aged men are hogtied and often used by these cowardly colonial soldiers to shield them from fire. These are just some of the grim pictures of genocide in the Bangsa Moro homeland. This total extermination only points to the grand design of permanent colonization of our people's national homeland.

Manifestations are very well illustrated in the policy of euphemism and rhetorics in the regime's social approach to the Bangsa Moro situation. The Commission on national integration was created — an act which among other things was designed to effectuate the economic, social, moral and political advancement of the Moros, to render real, complete and permanent the integration of the Bangsa Moro into the Philippine body politic. In this above policy, social advancement means that the Moros should abandon their social practices and traditions which in effect is cultural genocide. This precisely is the message behind the desecration of thousands of mosques.

There are still innumerable lists of massacres and depredations, but I don't like to bore you with statistics. I would just like to refer you to the documents on massacres and destruction reports. Suffice to say that the facts of genocide in the Bangsa Moro homeland is horrible. It defies the imagination.

The Bangsa Moro people have seen and experienced so much pain and suffering but they have endured and are very confident that they shall prevail.

Personal experiences of a doctor in Bangsa Moro homeland

The years 1968-74 before and during martial law, I was connected with a government hospital, then as a public health officer and later as a private practitioner.

The hospital had a 75-bed capacity, located in the capital of a province with a population of nearly a million. The hospital building was dilapidated, equipment was antiquated, drugs and medical supplies were inadequate or, if available, were usually products of fly-by-night drug manufacturers or military, without FDA license, medical and allied staff were very much wanting!

Gastro intestinal, respiratory and other diseases like TB, and malnutrition are rampant, cholera and malaria are endemic. Less than 1 per cent of the people are attended to medically. Hygiene and sanitation are zero. Infant mortality, though no exact statistics are available, are very high. The government, instead of looking into the situation, find satisfaction in having people die without the benefit of medical care. A subtle way of genocide! There is no greater proof of this utter disregard and inhumanity of the government than the statement of Adm. Gil Fernandez, Chief of the Southwestern Command at Zamboanga City who in March, 1973 proudly told the *New York Times* that because he did not have enough troops to spare for the Islands, he had 'ordered a stop to anti-malaria spraying in Tawi-Tawi province so that malaria mosquitoes would now thrive there and help to debilitate the rebels', referring to the Bangsa Moro Army.

I have treated cases of injuries involving innocent civilians who fell victims to the indiscriminate bombings of the Philippine Air Force in which after amputation of multilateral extremities or operations for visceral organ injuries following shrapnel wounds, the colonial soldiers in another act of inhumanity, would take them to military detention as suspected Bangsa Moro Army right from the operating table before they even recovered from anesthesia.

In the days preceding martial law, as public health officer I also did medico-legal work, among other things. I witnessed hundreds of crimes — murders of civilians by military men whose cases were not even brought to court, let alone the savage soldier-perpetrators prosecuted. For example, I have a very clear recollection of an incident in 1970 when two feuding political factions nearly had an armed clash and Philippine Constabulary men came to pacify but, instead, on arrival at the scene, they immediately fired at the protagonists without any provocation at all. Seventeen people died on the spot and several were injured, mostly students and passers-by. As medico-legal officer, I personally did post-mortems on all the dead bodies. They died of bullet wounds inflicted by 50-caliber machine guns, which I wrote in my report. Normally I should be called in to court to testify on this, but until today not a single case was brought before the court. This again demonstrates that in the Bangsa Moro homeland no crimes involving the military, no matter how heineous are ever properly redressed in the Filipino courts of justice — for there are not courts of justice at all, only courts of injustice!

THE VERDICT

General Introduction

The Permanent Peoples' Tribunal operates within the constitutional framework established by the *Universal Declaration of
the Rights of Peoples* (*The Algiers Declaration*) as adopted at
Algiers on 4 July, 1976. After holding hearings in June 1979 at
Bologna, the Tribunal agreed to receive separate, yet joined,
complaints about violations of legal rights, on behalf of the
Filipino and Bangsa Moro Peoples. These complaints were
directed against the Marcos government in the Philippines,
against various specific political, business and military leaders
and their agents, against the United States Government and its
representatives, against specific multinational corporations and
commercial banks, and against certain international financial institutions, specifically the International Monetary Fund, the
World Bank and the Asian Development Bank. A specially
selected jury of ten prominent citizens drawn from the larger international panel of the Tribunal, received oral testimony and
written evidence in support of these complaints, at its Antwerp
session of 30 October - 3 November 1980.

The separation of these two judgements requires comment,
especially as the Tribunal agreed to hear the charges at this single
session. Both the Filipino and Bangsa Moro peoples are joined
in a common struggle against the Marcos government and
against a wider neo-colonial system dominated by the United
States. Their analysis of the issues is identical. The Bangsa Moro
people, living in the southern Philippine islands, have a long
history of separate cultural and political identity, have been victims of a particularly vicious campaign of genocide, and are
devoted to the goals of national self determination for their
5,000,000 or so people. In these respects their circumstances are
different from those of the Filipino people in general and
appear, in balance, to justify two distinct judgements by the
Tribunal.

It should be noted that the Tribunal notified the principal
defendant governments, the Philippines and the United States of
America, of these pending proceedings and afforded them a full
opportunity to participate in their own defence. These invitations were ignored. The Tribunal decided to proceed in their
absence, given its failure to have any means to compel participation and given the seriousness and well-documented character of
the complaints. Furthermore, although its procedures are infor-
mal and non-technical by comparison with the normal court of

law, every effort at fairness was made, including some consideration of possible lines of defence. The whole purpose of the
Permanent Tribunal is to overcome the deficiency in international
society that allows gross crimes of state to persist without notice
or remedy. Our efforts conceive of law as existing on behalf of
people, not to serve the interests of abstractions such as the
sovereign state or the multinational corporation.

In this respect, the Algiers Declaration, drafted and approved
by leading jurists drawn from all regions in the world, challenges
the idea that government and their institutions enjoy a monopoly
over law-making. The Permanent Tribunal is committed to the
notion that individuals, as citizens of the world as well as of their
own country, have the right and obligation to shape emerging
law in accordance with human needs and human values. Such an
obligation is especially strong in the present historical period
where crimes of state are widespread and intense, go unpublished,
and are often committed in concert with international institutions, especially those institutions operating in the economic
sphere. We refuse to sit idly by and watch, without attempting to
remedy, this accumulating record of official abuse and institutionalised repression.

The Algiers Declaration is also a response to substantive
gaps in the law. In particular, many of the peoples of the Third
World are being subjected to a cruel and exploitative transnational system of rule, often known as 'neo-colonialism'. This
system takes different forms in different countries, as the
evidence on the Philippines demonstrates. Yet, there is a common reality of economic plunder by foreign interests, often
spearheaded by multinational corporations and their banking
partners, that is made effective by a militaristic apparatus that
combines internal and international elements of repression.
Conventional international law is virtually oblivious to these
realities so central to the lives of Third World peoples, and so
the Algiers Declaration has been developed and will be applied
to provide a legal instrument of detection and judgement.

At the same time, conventional international law is itself
developing in accordance with the flow of history and under
pressure from progressive elements in international life. To the
extent that international law reflects these progressive tendencies
we draw upon its conclusions to reinforce our findings. We rely,
for instance, on the rules of emerging international law that endorse the legitimacy to claims of national self-determination and
to claims on behalf of the human rights, including economic and

cultural rights, of individuals and groups. We rely, also, on the legal precedents created after World War II when leaders of governments, their officials and even industrialists, were tried for crimes of state and crimes against humanity, which precedents have now been codified into accepted principles of international law. We believe, as the prosecuting governments back in 1945 claimed they believed at the time, that *all* governments, not just governments defeated in war, should be held accountable for obedience to law, if necessary by the peoples of the world, organized as best they can.

Finally, it should be noted that this inquiry into the charges made by the Filipino and Bangsa Moro peoples has been made only after it was evident that there was a complete absence of political will on the part of established forums in the international community to investigate these grievances. We felt obliged under these circumstances to act, given the seriousness of these grievances and their continuing character. Indeed, a failure by the Tribunal to heed the urgent moral and political situation in the Philippines would contribute further to the impression that little or no international resistance exists to those dark and powerful forces at work in the world to devalue human society.

The Fundamental Grievances of the Filipino people

1.   The social and economic situation of the great majority of the people is one of misery and oppression. A 1971 University of Philippines study reports that 69 per cent of the rural people live below the poverty line. In 1975 that proportion rose to 71.3 per cent. Malnutrition plagues 70 per cent of the population and, according to the Food and Nutrition Research Institute, malnutrition causes fully 40 per cent of the mortality. In 1975 unemployment reached 40 per cent which is 9.6 million persons. In Metro-Manila, 1.5 million people live in slums. In the country-side there are 4 million landless squatters.

2.   The situation of the Filipino people is not unique. It is common to most of the Third World countries, dominated as they are by an expanding capitalist economy which, in the present phase of concentration and transnationalization, maximizes and accelerates. As a result, countries like the Philippines are brought into a growing dependency on powerful economic institutions which are then able to dictate policy in the fields of investment, wages, capital repatriation, profit remittances, etc.

This policy promotes, at one and the same time, both economic growth and the impoverishment of the majority of the people. Following this contradictory pattern, the Gross National Product grew from P77,958 million in 1977 to P82,477 million in 1978; the real income of rice-peasants decreased 53.4 per cent between 1976 and 1979; the real income of urban workers fell 39 per cent between 1972 and 1978. While in 1952 the average worker received P0.36 on each peso produced as value, in 1971 the same average worker received only P0.24, and in 1975 only P0.09. Clearly when profit and economic power become the exclusive criteria for production, 'growth' results in a total neglect for human beings and for the natural environment. The internationalization of the market economy thus deprives the people of the right to determine for themselves their economic and cultural fate.

3. It is also true that, in spite of the problems it has in common with other Third World countries, the Philippines is also in some ways unique. It is a former *colony of the USA* and continues to live in an unfinished process of decolonisation; it is tied by a number of treaties and agreements of a political and economic nature to the United States of America. In 1946, parity rights were conceded to US citizens, for persons as well as for corporations. In 1951, the Quirino-Foster Agreement on Economic and Technical Cooperation established the principle of a close American supervision over economic policy making. The Laurel-Langley Agreement of 1954 tied the Filipino monetary system to the dollar, whose value in pesos could not be changed without the approval of the United States of America. This pattern of unequal treaties with the US gave the US virtual control over the Philippine government and opened the door to such treaties with other countries, including especially Japan. It should be added that US investments represent 80 per cent of the total foreign investments in the Philippines and 60 percent of the total American investment in Southeat Asia.

4. The *economic exploitation* of local resources including natural capital, local agricultural and industrial manpower, has been increasing in recent years. This comes from the role played by outside economic powers, particularly transnational corporations and foreign commercial banks. In 1978, there were 324 multinational enterprises, representing 52.6 per cent of the total sales and 66.7 per cent of the total income of the top 1,000 corporations. Among the transnational corporations, agribusiness is an important activity. Four corporations own 27,000 hectares

of banana land. Among them Del Monte which owns 9,000 hectares of pineapple plantations, and Dole. Among the foreign owned mines, Benguet plays an important role. In the industrial field the Mitsui group has important investments and in the banking field the Chase Manhattan Bank should be mentioned.

5.   Through political measures and in particular through the establishment and institutionalisation of Martial Law, now a permanent and indispensable instrument of rule, the Government of Mr Marcos serves as an intermediary for this international economic exploitation, and an agent of local oppression. During the two years preceding Martial Law, foreign investments amounted to $16.3 million and during the two years after it (1972-73) new investments rose to $362.1 million. The increase in the capital of foreign firms which were already present in the Philippines when Martial law was promulgated was 1,000 per cent growing from P83.7 million to more than P1 billion. These increased profits were built on the repressive control of labour and of democratic institutions. General Order No. 5 prohibits the right to strike. Decree No. 21 gives businesses the right to dismiss without notice any worker opposing productive policy. By Decree No. 143 Sunday as an obligatory holiday for workers has been abolished. Decree No. 148 reduced the advantages given to pregnant women. Decree No. 823 reinforced General Order No. 5 by forbidding any foreign organisation to give direct or indirect support to workers organisations, except through the official unions recognized by the Ministry of Labour. Arbitrary arrests of hundreds of individuals took place, including three senators and several priests. Many of those arrested are still in detention. An executive prohibition on all forms of public protest was imposed, the writ of *Habeas Corpus* was suspended, newspapers, television and radio stations were closed, and government employees were arbitrarily dismissed.

6.   Part of the Filipino dominant classes are associated with this exploitation process, building up their wealth and power by participating in political power and through subservient functions in the local operations of international corporations. They have even accumulated massive fortunes through corrupt economic practices. For instance, Defense Mininster Juan Ponce Enrile has been able to acquire control over the entire coconut industry, through his influence in government. At the same time, coconut workers (who, with their dependents, number 15 million people) became the category of workers most affected by

the real wage decreases. The same Mr Enrile also accumulated a great amount of real property.

7. In implementing their policies, the Marcos government has particularly infringed the rights of ethnic minorities, like the Kalingas and the Bontocs for instance, who have been deprived of their land, without proper compensation or relocation, and culturally destroyed. Several leaders of minorities have been tortured and assasinated.

8. The Marcos government has also engaged on a full-scale war against the Bangsa Moro people, using the Philippine army, air force and navy for the bombing of villages. This violent action has been accompanied by mass murders, expulsion of thousands of people from their homeland and has resulted in 200,000 people becoming refugees.

9. The economic policies followed by the Philippine government have been increasingly guided and even framed by International Financial Institutions, such as the World Bank, the International Monetary Fund and the Asian Development Bank. The principal features of such policies particularly since Martial Law in 1972 are: a) unrestricted flow of foreign investment and profit; b) dismantling of the protective tariff structure; c) industrialization of the export sector through centralisation of the marketing of several export commodities and; d) provision of cheap unorganized labor. So, for instance, the extension of sugar and coconut plantations by 663,000 hectacres between 1972 and 1976, resulted in a diminution of rice production (3.2 million tons in 1960 against 3.1 million in 1970) in spite of the population increase, a deficit of 400,000 tons. The average rice consumption is only 76 kgs per year as against 104 kgs in the other ASEAN countries, whereas the necessary minimum is estimated by the WHO at 114 kgs. The foreign aid programs mainly reinforce the same economic policy. The Center for International Policy of Washington D.C. estimates that between 1976 and 1978 only 22 per cent of US aid went into projects directly benefiting the poor. The rest went for tobacco loans, insurance for a Bank of America branch office, military aid, rural electricification priced out of the reach of the poor, and balance of payments loans conditioned on the adoption of government policies that reduce real wages for the poor. In the same period, military aid increased by 138 per cent.

10. The support given by the US government has internal

security dimensions, such as financial contributions for military build up, training for counter-insurgency, legal authority for military units to perform security activities off military bases in Philippine territory. When the military budget of the Philippines passed from P584 million in 1972 to P2.449 billion in 1978 (at the same time as the education budget passed from 1.360 million to 1.499 million), the military assistance of the USA which was P60.2 million between 1970-1972, nearly doubled to 118.8 between 1973-1975. But this military presence of the US has also international dimensions. The US bases serve to control the Pacific and the Indian Oceans and even to intervene in the Middle East. This close relationship between the Marcos regime and the US government belies the former's claim of being a 'non-aligned' state.

11.   Facing such oppression, the Filipino people, having lost most of the democratic means of defence and of expression, has organized itself in underground resistance movements and even in armed struggle, the legitimacy of such resistance arising from the oppression itself.

Fundamental Grievances of the Bangsa Moro people

The situation of the Bangsa Moro people also reflects the experiences of the Filipino people under the Marcos regime of 'permanent' Martial Law described in the preceding section. In this section we call particular attention to the additional experience of repression endured by the Bangsa Moro people.

1.   For centuries the southern islands existed as separate sultanates. Even during the American colonisation of the Philippines, in spite of formal integration, the separate status of the Moros was recognized by special arrangements and policies. It was lost only in the treaty of independence from the US in 1946, which merged the southern islands, in spite of Moro protests, into one entity with the northern Philippines.

2.   The southern islands have had a distinct culture. At the beginning of US colonial rule at the turn of the century, the population of Mindanao and Sulu was 98 per cent Muslim. A program of government-sponsored colonisation with northern Philippine Christian settlers began in 1912. It was greatly accelerated by the Public Land Act of 1919, which declared the ancestral lands of the Moro and other indigenous peoples public lands, title to which would henceforth be issued by the govern-

ment in Manila. The rate of infiltration of Moro areas with settlers from the North has increased markedly since 1946, particularly under the Marcos regime, so that now the Muslims comprise only 60 per cent of the population, Christian Filipinos 25 per cent, while the remaining 15 per cent are distributed among other ethnic groups.

3.   The Southern islands are predominantly rural with few cities. Development in the sense of industrial and large-scale enterprises is new, foreign, and still in its beginnings. The Northern islands are ahead in this regard. For this reason the Moros feel almost as much threatened by Filipino entrepreneurs and exploitation as by the colonial powers. As one MNLF representative said, "We feel that the Filipinos come halfway between the Americans and us." We have the impression that the Moros are struggling to regain their lost farms, to retain their barrio tradition and, if it comes to that, to determine and carry out their own technological development.

4.   The Moros are being subjected to a planned and accelerating program of displacement from their ancestral lands and physical extermination. Of the 5.5 million Moros, roughly half are already refugees, and about 250,000 have emigrated to the Malaysian state of Sabah. It has been suggested that such emigration is being fostered by the present Philippine regime. To put it plainly, the Moros are felt to be 'in the way' in their own homeland, and a policy of displacement and extermination is in progress, reminiscent of that which involved the American Indians when they got in the way of the Western expansion of the white population of the United States.

5.   What is planned for the Southern islands is not primarily industrial development, but exploitation as a source of raw materials and food. In the light industry that has so far been developed by outsiders, the Moros are hardly involved. They are not wanted either as workers or consumers, since major products are intended for export. The Southern islands are fabulously wealthy in resources. At present, Mindanao produces half of all the corn and coconut in the Philippines, 20 per cent of all rice, 50 per cent of fish, 40 per cent of cattle, almost all exported bananas and pineapples, 89 per cent of nickle and cobalt,90 per cent of iron ore, 62 per cent of limestone, almost all aluminium ore (bauxite), 72 per cent of logs and all the rubber. Yet the islands of Mindanao and Sulu cover hardly more than one-third the land area of the Philippines and contain less

than one-fourth of the total population.

6.   That population is now stratified into a small elite of industrialists and landlords, mainly Filipino and foreign, only a remnant deriving from the old Muslim aristocracy, a large number of new Filipino farmers, poor and with small holdings of a few hectares, and the Moros. In his report to the World Bank on 21 September, 1970, Robert McNamara, its President, spoke of what he called 'marginal men'. These, he explained, are not merely unemployed, there is no use for them in the market economy. They are not needed either as producers or consumers. They are not only in the way, their very existence is an embarrassment. The American, Japanese and European entrepreneurs and the Philippine ruling elite apparently have decided to regard the entire Bangsa Moro people as 'marginal' in just this sense, and are proceeding callously and brutally to remove them from their homelands, by displacement and genocide, as impediments to their planned program of so-called 'development' — the exploitation for profit of the rich resources of the southern islands.

7.   The struggle of the Bangsa Moro people, as represented by the MNLF and the Bangsa Moro Army, has achieved significant international recognition. In this context reference should be made to the recognition of the MNLF by the Islamic Conference which led to negotiations, and a consequent agreement (the Tripoli Agreement of 23 December 1976) concluded between the MNLF and the Marcos regime. This agreement represents formal recognition of the MNLF by the Philippine government.

8.   The international recognition of the armed struggle of the Bangsa Moro people places an obligation on the Philippine government to fully respect the provisions of the Geneva Conventions in relations to the combatants of the MNLF. It also places an obligation on international bodies to allow the MNLF to take part in their activities.

Legal Framework

This general situation of severe oppression in the Philippines discloses a vast pattern of illegal and criminal conduct involving numerous specific violations.

The basic Marcos-US role in the Philippines contravenes virtually every provision of the Algiers Declaration, suggesting the severity of the situation facing the Filipino and Bangsa Moro peoples. We call particular attention to the following violations.

The neo-colonial system operating in the Philippines manifestly denies to its peoples the promise of the Algiers Declaration Articles 2 and 3 that "Every people has the right to the respect of its national and cultural identity" and "Every people has the right to retain peaceful possession of its territory... ". Neo-colonialism in the various forms already described violates Article 5's promise of the right to self-determination, as well as the assurance of Article 6 that: "Every people has the right to break free from any colonial or foreign domination, whether direct or indirect... ".

In more concrete terms, in relation to economic matters, Article 8 calls for every people to have "an exclusive right over its natural wealth and resources". Such a fundamental legal assurance is completely inconsistent with the elaborate Marcos-US transnational economic structure that deprives the Filipino and Bangsa Moro people of their rights and illegally confers economic benefits on foreign imperial powers and their accomplices in the corporate and banking world. Furthermore, in concrete terms, Article 10 provides that "every people has the right to a fair evaluation of its labor". Article 11 adds that "every people has the right to choose its own economic and social system and pursue its own path to economic development freely and without any foreign interference". These legal standards are completely undermined by the arrangements governing the economic life of the Filipino and Bangsa Moro peoples, the essence of which, as the evidence shows so convincingly, is to rely upon the fruits of their labor and to deny the country as a whole the benefit of its natural resources and capital producing wealth. In particular, we determine that international financial institutions, including the International Monetary Fund, the World Bank and the Asian Development Fund perform a major role as accomplices in the violation of these main provisions of the Algiers Declaration.

The evidence also demonstrates that multinational corporations violate Article 16 of the Algiers Declaration, to the extent that they locate polluting industries in the Philippines. These offences are particularly serious in those cases where the industry is not permitted to operate for environmental reasons in its country of origin, e.g. the Kawasaki sintering plant in Mindanao.

The evidence also shows that the mistreatment of various tribal peoples in the Philippines was a direct deliberate consequence of this neo-colonial structure. There exist blatant violations of those rights of minority peoples which are specified in Article 19 to 21 of the Algiers Declaration, for which the Marcos regime, its multinational corporate and international financial institutional accomplices are mainly responsible. By dispossessing minority people of their ancestral lands, the Marcos regime has carried out discriminatory policies of a criminal character which have inevitable genocidal effects.

Indeed, the entire repressive apparatus of the Marcos Martial Law system violates the political and civil rights of the Filipino and Bangsa Moro peoples, with the connivance, collaboration and participation of the United States government and its various agencies. Cruel and brutal policies are used to silence opponents and to prevent even the most peaceful forms of opposition to express themselves. Daily existence is turned into a perpetual nightmare by the continuous exercise of arbitrary authority by Marcos' military and paramilitary security forces. These abuses of state power not only violate the Algiers Declaration, but also are condemned by the specific provisions of the Universal Declaration of Human Rights which all governments acknowledge as expressive of binding law.

The net result of the documentation on abuse of peoples' rights is summed up by Article 22 of the Algiers Declaration which concludes that disregard of its provisions "constitutes a breach of obligation towards the international community as a whole".

Relief called for is specified in the Algiers Declaration, Article 23 to 27, and includes the right to receive reimbursement for losses incurred, which covers the excess profits earned by foreign corporations and banks. Article 25 specifically declares further, that unequal treaties, of the sort binding the Philippines to the United States "shall have no effect".

Article 26 calls for the disregard of foreign debt that have "become excessive and unbearable for the people", a description that reflects the situation of the Filipino people and is a direct result of the corrupt and repressive policies of the Marcos dictatorship. Significantly, the commission of these violations is held by Article 27 to "constitute international crimes for which their perpetrators shall carry personal penal liability". The Tribunal regards it important to conclude that the Marcos-US neo-colonial system amounts to a continuing criminal enterprise under emerging international law and that the respective leaders and agents of these governments should properly be held personally responsible.

It is also affirmed by the Algiers Declaration as a matter of legal right, that liberation movements specifically, in this case the National Democratic Front (NDF) and the Moro National Liberation Front (MNLF), enjoy status in international society. They are empowered, by Article 28 to enforce the rights of their peoples, by armed struggle if necessary. The Tribunal would add that given the enormity of the crimes committed by the Marcos regime, that regime has lost its legitimacy and that in its place, these liberation movements are recognised as enjoying the international status of being legitimate representatives of their respective peoples.

This detailed indication of the relevance of the Algiers Declaration to the evidence brought before the Tribunal discloses the general legal framework relied upon to reach our conclusions.

It should be understood, however, that the Marcos regime and the neo-colonial support system would be multiply indictable under traditional international law and punishable for international crimes without reliance on the Algiers Declaration. That is, these defendants would be equally culpable if a proper international court was convened, as indeed it should be, by the United Nations or by the concerted action of foreign governments, as in fact was done at the end of World War II to bring charges against the German and Japanese war leaders, including some of their prominent business leaders.

Particularly relevant in this regard are Article 55 and 56 of the *UN Charter* calling upon the United Nations and its members to assure respect for the principle of self-determination of peoples, and for the promotion of "higher standards of living, full employment, and conditions of economic and social progress and development" and "universal respect for, and observance of, human rights and fundamental freedoms for all without distinction as to race, sex, language, or religion". Also relevant are the *Universal Declaration of Human Rights* and the various human rights covenants and conventions endorsed by the United Nations and its specialised agencies.

Most important as a general legal underpinning for this inquiry are the Nuremberg Principles, first endorsed unanimously by the General Assembly of the United Nations and later formulated in authoritative terms by the UN International Law Commission. These Nuremberg Principles, in their essence, hold individuals and groups criminally responsible for acting against the fundamental rights of peoples, even if their actions are formally undertaken under the authority of the State. One category of substance dealt with in the Nuremberg Principles are 'Crimes against Humanity'; acts and activities involving gross brutality against the civilian population; although restricted by Principle 6(c) to those acts arising in connection with 'Crimes against Peace or War Crimes', the independent criminality of actions against the civilian population in one's own country has by now come to be established in general international law.

Particularly applicable in relation to the complaint of the Bangsa Moro people, but also relevant for the situation of tribal peoples in the northern Philippine islands, is the 'Convention on the Prevention and Punishment of the Crime of Genocide'. Of course, the basic rights of peoples arise from a natural foundation, often expressed as 'the conscience of humanity', that exists quite independently of any formulation of these rights in positive law documents such as treaties and other international agreements.

This recital of the relevant legal framework relied upon by the Tribunal, demonstrates the extent to which the Marcos-US Martial Law and neo-colonial system is a criminal enterprise that needs to be resisted by all elements of the international community concerned with justice, morality, and an effective system of progressive international law. The Tribunal in pronouncing its Judgement is conscious of the urgent need to elaborate more fully the rights of the peoples of the world in relation to grievances of the sort presented in this case.

Judgement on the Appeals of the Filipino people and the Bangsa Moro people

The Tribunal considered the joint complaints separately, yet in view of the interlocked character of the stuggle, framed its judgement on behalf of the Filipino people and the Bangsa Moro people in identical terms.

1.   The Tribunal finds that the Marcos regime by its reliance on 'permanent' martial law and numerous blatant abuses of state power is deprived of legitimate standing as a government in international society and lacks the competence to act on behalf of the Filipino or Bangsa Moro people;

2. The Tribunal finds that treaties and agreements imposed by the United States on the Philippines, admittedly with the complicity of successive Philippine governments, are null and void as 'unequal treaties', and that all obligations incurred under them should cease forthwith. In this connection, the Tribunal declares invalid the latest international trade agreement, signed in October 1979 and known as the Collantes-Murphy Agreement, being a replacement for the expired Laurel-Langely Agreement of 1954. It also finds null and void the Military Bases Treaty of 1974 and its recent extension in 1979 by Executive Agreement;

3. The Tribunal condemns in the most rigorous terms the program of displacement and physical extinction that is now being waged by the Marcos regime against the Bangsa Moro people that has already deprived them of much of their ancestral land and made roughly half of their number refugees and exiles; the cumulative effect of this program has been the commission of the crimes of genocide;

4. The Tribunal considers that the abuses of the Marcos regime have contributed excessively to the degradation of women and to their economic and sexual exploitation;

5. The Tribunal condemns, also, the United States government for its role in sustaining, supporting and encouraging the Marcos regime to act on behalf of its economic and global strategic interests in violation of the rights of the Filipino and Bangsa Moro peoples and calls upon it to cease such activities in support of state crime forthwith, and to renounce all of its 'rights' obtained by way of unequal treaties and to respect from now on the full sovereignty of the country, including the status of the National Democratic Front (NDF) and the Moro National Liberation Front (MNLF) as legitimate representatives of their respective peoples;

6. The Tribunal, in this regard, calls on world public opinion to be especially vigilant of possible attempts by the United States government to replace the Marcos dictatorship with another dependent, neo-colonial regime during this period of increasing popular resistance to a government that has lost its credibility and capability;

7. The Tribunal also notes that the International Monetary Fund, the World Bank and the Asian Development Bank, despite the stated purpose 'to help raise the living standards of the developing countries', are playing a crucial role in sustaining,

supporting and encouraging the Marcos regime, despite its commission of systematic state crimes, and calls upon these international financial institutions to terminate these relationships that abet the violation of the rights of peoples and are responsible for disrupting the life and threatening the very existence of such tribal peoples as the Igorot and Kalinga through their support for high-technology hydro-electric projects;

8.   The Tribunal censures a series of American, Japanese and European multinational corporations for their role in violating the sovereign rights of the Filipino and Bangsa Moro peoples, including their legally protected right to sovereign control over natural resources and calls upon these corporations to cease their activities, compensate the Filipino and Bangsa Moro peoples for the depredation of their resources, and to avoid all further interference in the internal life of the Philippines;

9.   The Tribunal censures also the transnational commercial banks for their role in sustaining the illegal and criminal activities of the Marcos government and of multinational corporations and calls upon these banks to cease their lending activities that reinforce criminal undertakings harmful to the Filipino and Bangsa Moro people;

10.   The Tribunal also denounces the various actions of non-governmental organizations, including the educational, religious and trade union organizations to the extent that they lend support to the Marcos regime by supporting economic projects reinforcing the existing social order, by training a local elite and by misleading workers and peasants, through the formation of fake organizations that pretend to work for the people but are in reality tools of the regime;

11.   The Tribunal finds Ferdinand Marcos guilty of grave and numerous economic and political crimes against his own people and against the Bangsa Moro people and declares him unfit to govern, and subject to severe punishment for his past wrongs, including economic plunder and failure to protect the sovereignty of his country from neo-colonial interventions;

12.   The Tribunal finds the corrupt and plundering Marcos 'entourage' guilty as accomplices and perpetrators of numerous political and economic crimes and declares them subject to punishment by an appropriate criminal tribunal;

13.   The Tribunal acknowledges that the Bangsa Moro people are entitled to the right of self-determination; it welcomes also

the guarantee by the MNLF that should the Bangsa Moro people decide to establish a separate state all minorities are entitled to entirely equal rights irrespective of race, religion or national origin; further, the Tribunal welcomes the common position of the NDF and the MNLF on the crucial issue of self-determination;

14.   The Tribunal concludes that the armed struggle between the Marcos regime and the Filipino and Bangsa Moro peoples qualifies in international law as a condition of belligerency and that, accordingly, the parties should respect fully the provisions of the Geneva Conventions on the laws of war, an observation made necessary by the numerous atrocities committed by the Marcos soldiers over the years;

15.   The Tribunal calls upon world public opinion, progressive governments, organizations and individuals, to lend their support to the struggle of the Filipino and Bangsa Moro peoples to achieve national self-determination, liberation from the Marcos regime and the neo-colonial system of repression.

Appendices

I Member Jurors of the Permanent Peoples' Tribunal, Session on the Philippines

Sergio Mendes Arceo, Archbishop of Guernavaca, Mexico, a leading figure in the progressive wing of the Roman Catholic Church.

Richard Baumlin, legal expert and Swiss Parliamentarian.

Harvey Cox, professor of Theology at Harvard and author of the influential 'Secular City'.

Richard Falk, professor of International Law at Princeton University, and a well-known environmentalist.

Andrea Giardina, professor of International Law at the University of Naples.

Francois Houtart, professor of sociology at the University of Louvain.

Ajit Roy, renowned Indian writer for the 'Economic and Political Weekly'.

Makoto Oda, noted Japanese novelist and vice-president of the Permanent Peoples' Tribunal.

Ernst Utrecht, professor at Sidney University and a fellow of the Transnational Institute in Amsterdam.

George Wald, ex-professor of Biology at Harvard University and Nobel Prize Winner, who served as President of the jury. President of the PPT session on the Philippines.

Muireann O'Briain, a lawyer from Ireland, was the legal representative of the NDF and MNLF.

Gianni Tognoni, the General Secretary of the PPT, was the co-ordinator of the session.

II Full List of Jury Members of the Permanent Peoples' Tribunal

Wolfgang Abendroth — Germany — Philosopher
Rafael Alberti — Spain — Poet and painter
Richard Barnet — USA — Economist and writer
Richard Baumlin — Switzerland — Constitutional lawyer
Madjid Benchikh — Algeria — International lawyer
Amar Bentoumi — Algeria — Lawyer
Canon Burgess Carr — Liberia — Secretary General of the Protestant Churches of Africa.
Guido Calvi — Italy — Lawyer
Ernesto Cardenal — Nicaragua — Monk and poet
Georges Casalis — France — Protestant theologian and writer
Antonio Cassese — Italy — International lawyer
Noam Chomsky — USA — Linguist
Julio Cortazar — Argentina — Writer
Harvey Cox — USA — Protestant theologian and writer

Burhan Dajani — Palestine — Economist
Vladimir Dedijer — Yugoslavia — Historian and writer
José Echeverrìa — Chile — Philosopher of Law
Ole Espersen — Denmark — International lawyer
Adolfo Perez Esquivel — Argentina — Nobel prize winner for Peace
Richard Falk — USA — International lawyer
Ruth First — South Africa — Sociologist and writer
Paulo Freire — Brazil — Pedagogue and writer
Eduardo Galeano — Uruguay — Writer
Gabriel Garcia Marquez — Colombia — Writer
Andrea Giardina — Italy — International lawyer
Giulio Girardi — Italy — Theologian and philosopher
Pablo Gonzales Casanova — Mexico — Former Rector of the
    autonomous University of Mexico
José Herrera Oropeza* — Venezuela — International lawyer
Francois Houtart — Belgium — Sociologist
Kumari Jayawardene — Sri Lanka — Sociologist
Ruiz Jimenez — Spain — Lawyer
Louis Joinet — France — Magistrate
Edmond Jouve — France — Jurist
Alfred Kastler — France — Nobel prize winner in Physics
Jan Kulakowski — Belgium — Trade unionist
Leo Matarasso — France — Lawyer
Sean McBride — Ireland — Nobel prize winner for Peace
Ernesto Melo Antunes — Portugal — Former Minister of Foreign
    Affairs and member of the Revolutionary Council
Sergio Mendez Arceo — Mexico — Archbishop of Guernavaca
Kinju Morikawa — Japan — International lawyer
Gunnar Myrdal — Sweden — Economist
Vicente Navarro — USA — Sociologist and writer
Joe Nordman — France — Jurist
Makoto Oda — Japan — Journalist and writer
Raim Panikkar — *USA* — *Expert in oriental religions*
Andreas Papandreou — Greece — Economist and politician
James Petras — USA — Sociologist
Francois Rigaux — Belgium — International lawyer
Ajit Roy — India — Journalist and writer
Laurent Schwartz — France — Mathematician
Salvatore Senese — Italy — Magistrate
Albert Soboul — France — Historian
M.M. Thomas — India — Protestant theologian (ex-member of the
    Directing Committee of the World Council of Churches)
Enrique Tierno Galvàn — Spain — Mayor of Madrid
Armanda Uribe — Chile — International lawyer
Ernst Utrecht — Indonesia — Sociologist
George Wald — Nobel prize winner in Biology
Adolfo Perez Esquivel — Argentina — Nobel prize winner for Peace

* deceased

III   Universal Declaration of the Rights of Peoples

Preamble

We live at a time of great hopes and deep despair;
a time of conflicts and contradictions;
a time when liberation struggles have succeeded in arousing the peoples
of the world against the domestic and international structures of imperialism and in overturning colonial systems;
a time of struggle and victory in which new ideals of justice among and within nations have been adopted;
a time when the General Assembly of the United Nations has given increasing expression, from the Universal Declaration of Human Rights to the Charter on the Economic Rights and Duties of States, to the quest for a new international, political and economic order.

But this is also a time of frustration and defeat, as new forms of imperialism evolve to oppress and exploit the peoples of the world.

Imperialism, using vicious methods with the complicity of governments that it has itself often installed, continues to dominate a part of the world. Through direct or indirect intervention, through multi-national enterprises, through manipulation of corrupt local politicians, with the assistance of military regimes based on police repression, torture and physical extermination of opponents, through a set of practices that has become known as neo-colonialism, imperialism extends its stranglehold over many peoples.

Aware of expressing the aspirations of our era, we met in Algiers to proclaim that all the peoples of the world have an equal right to liberty, the right to free themselves from any foreign interference and to choose their own government, the right if they are under subjection to fight for their liberation and the right to benefit from other people's assistance in their struggle.

Convinced that the effective respect for human rights necessarily implies respect for the rights of peoples, we have adopted the Universal Declaration of the Rights of People.

May all those who, throughout the world, are fighting the great battle, at times through armed struggle, for the freedom of all peoples, find in this Declaration the assurance of the legitimacy of their struggle.

Section 1: Rights to Existence

Article 1.   Every people has the right to existence.

Article 2.   Every people has the right to the respect of its national and cultural identity.

Article 3   Every people has the right to retain peaceful possession of its territory and to return to it if it is expelled.

Article 4   None shall be subjected, because of his national or cultural identity, to massacre, torture, persecution, deportation, expulsion or living conditions such as may compromise the identity or integrity of the people to which he belongs.

Section II: Right to Political Self-determination

Article 5   Every people has an imprescriptible and unalienable right to self-determination. It shall determine its political status freely and without any foreign interference.

Article 6   Every people has the right to break free from any colonial or foreign domination, whether direct or indirect, and from any racist regime.

Article 7   Every people has the right to have a democratic government representing all the citizens without distinction as to race, sex, belief or colour, and capable of ensuring effective respect for the human rights and fundamental freedoms for all.

Section III: Economic Rights of Peoples

Article 8   Every people has an exclusive right over its natural wealth and resources. It has the right to recover them if they have been despoiled, as well as any unjustly paid indemnities.

Article 9   Scientific and technical progress being part of the common heritage of mankind, every people has the right to participate in it.

Article 10   Every people has the right to a fair evaluation of its labour and to equal and just terms in international trade.

Article 11   Every people has the right to choose its own economic and social system and pursue its own path to economic development freely and without any foreign interference.

Article 12   The economic rights set forth above shall be exercised in a spirit of solidarity amongst the peoples of the world and with due regard for their respective interests.

Section IV: Right to Culture

Article 13   Every people has the right to speak its own language and preserve and develop its own culture, thereby contributing to the enrichment of the culture of mankind.

Article 14   Every people has the right to its artistic, historical and cultural wealth.

Article 15   Every people has the right not to have any alien culture imposed upon it.

Section V: Right to Environment and Common Resources

Article 16   Every people has the right to the conservation, protection and improvement of its environment.

Article 17   Every people has the right to make use of the common heritage of mankind, such as the high seas, the sea-bed and outer space.

Article 18   In the exercise of the preceding rights every people shall take account of the necessity for coordinating the requirements of its economic development with solidarity amongst all the peoples of the world.

Section VI: Rights of Minorities

Article 19   When a people constitutes a minority within a State it has the right to respect for its identity, traditions, language and cultural heritage.

Article 20   The members of a minority shall enjoy without discrimination the same rights as the other citizens of the State and shall participate on an equal footing with them in public life.

Article 21   These rights shall be exercised with due respect for the legitimate interest of the community as a whole and cannot authorise impairing the territorial integrity and political unity of the State, provided the State acts in accordance with all the principles set forth in this Declaration.

Section VII: Guarantees and Sanctions

Article 22   Any disregard for the provisions of this Declaration constitutes a breach of obligations towards the international community as a whole.

Article 23   Any prejudice resulting from disregard for this Declaration must be totally compensated by whoever caused it.

Article 24   Any enrichment to the detriment of the people in violation of the provisions of this Declaration shall give rise to the restitution of profits thus obtained. The same shall be applied to all excessive profits on investment of foreign origin.

Article 25   Any unequal treaties, agreements or contracts concluded in disregard of the fundamental rights of people shall have no effect.

Article 26   External financial charges which become excessive and unbearable for the people shall cease to be due.

Article 27   The gravest violations of the fundamental rights of peoples, especially of their right to existence, constitute international crimes for which their perpetrators shall carry personal penal liability.

Article 28   Any people whose fundamental rights are seriously disregarded has the right to enforce them, especially by political or trade union struggle and even, in the last resort, by the use of force.

Article 29   Liberation movements shall have access to international organizations and their combatants are entitled to the protection of the humanitarian law of war.

Article 30   The re-establishment of the fundamental rights of peoples, when they are seriously disregarded, is a duty incumbent upon all members of the international community.

IV   The Ten Point Program of the National Democratic Front

1.   Unite all anti-imperialist forces to overthrow the US-Marcos dictatorship and work for the establishment of a coalition government based on a truly democratic system of representation.

2.   Expose and oppose US imperialism as the mastermind behind the setting up of the fascist dictatorship, struggle for the nullification of all unequal treaties and arrangements with this imperialist power, and call for the nationalisation of all its properties in the country.

3. Fight for the re-establishment of all democratic rights of the people, such as freedom of speech, the press, assembly, association, movement.

4. Gather all possible political and material support for the armed revolution and the underground against the US-Marcos dictatorship.

5. Support a genuine reform program that can liberate the peasant masses from feudal and semi-feudal exploitation and raise agricultural production through co-operation.

6. Improve the people's livelihood, guarantee the right to work and protect national capital against foreign monopoly capital.

7. Promote a national, scientific and mass culture and combat imperialist, feudal and fascist culture.

8. Support the national minorities, especially those in Mindanao and the Mountain Provinces, in their struggle for self-determination and democracy.

9. Punish, after public trial, the ringleaders of the Marcos fascist gang for their crimes against the people and confiscate all their ill-gotten wealth.

10. Unite with all peoples fighting imperialism and all reaction, and seek their support for the Philippine revolutionary struggle.

V The Manifesto of the Moro National Liberation Front

Manifesto
April 28, 1974

Establishment of the Bangsa Moro Republik

We, the five million oppressed Bangsa Moro people, wishing to free ourselves from the terror, oppression and tyranny of Filipino colonialism which has caused us untold sufferings and miseries by criminally usurping our land, by threatening Islam through wholesale destruction and desecration of its places of worship and its Holy Book, and murdering our innocent brothers, sisters and folks in a genocidal campaign of terrifying magnitude;

Aspiring to have the sole prerogative of defining and chartering our own national destiny in accordance with our own free will in order to ensure our future and that of our children;

Having evolved an appropriate form of ideology with which the unity of our people has been firmly established and their national identity and character strengthened;

Having established the Moro National Liberation Front and its military arm, the Bangsa Moro Army, as our principal instrument for achieving our primary goals and objectives with the unanimous support of the great mass of our people; and finally,

Being now in firm control of a great portion of our national homeland through successive and crushing victories of our Bangsa Moro Army in battle against the Armed Forces of the Philippines and the Marcos military dictatorship, hereby declare:

1. That henceforth the Bangsa Moro people and Revolution having established their Bangsa Moro Republik, are throwing off all their political, economic and other bonds with the oppressive government of the Philippines under the dictatorial regime of President Ferdinand E. Marcos to secure a free and independent state for the Bangsa Moro people;

2. That we believe armed struggle is the only means by which we can achieve the complete freedom and independence of our people, since Marcos and his government will never dismantle the edifice of Philippine colonial rule in our national homeland on their own accord;

3. That the Moro National Liberation Front and its military arm, the Bangsa Moro Army, shall not agree to any form of settlement or accord short of achieving total freedom and independence for our oppressed Bangsa Moro people;

4. That the Revolution of the Bangsa Moro people is revolution with a social conscience. As such it is committed to the principle of establishing a democratic system of government which shall never allow or tolerate any form of exploitation and oppression of any human being by another or of one nation by another;

5. That those Filipinos who may wish to remain in the Bangsa Moro national homeland even after independence, shall be welcomed and entitled to equal rights and protection with all other citizens of the Bangsa Moro Republik, provided that they formally renounce their Filipino citizenship and wholeheartedly accept Bangsa Moro citizenship; their property rights shall be fully respected and the free exercise of their political, cultural and religious rights shall be guaranteed;

6. That the Bangsa Moro people and Revolution are committed to the preservation and growth of Islamic culture among our people, without prejudice to the development and growth of other religious and indigenous cultures in our homeland;

7. That our people and Revolution recognise and adhere to the Charter of the United Nations and the Universal Declaration of Human Rights; and, in addition, they shall respect and adhere to all laws binding upon the nations of the world;

8. That the Bangsa Moro people and Revolution are committed to the preservation and enhancement of world peace through mutual cooperation among nations and common progress of the peoples of the world. Accordingly, they are committed to the principle of mutual respect and friendship among nations irrespective of their ideological and religious creed;

9. That our people and Revolution, upholding the principle of self-determination, support the right of all peoples of all nations in their legitimate and just struggle for national survival, freedom and independence;

10. That the Bangsa Moro people and Revolution shall, in the interest of truth, guarantee the freedom of the press;
11. That, in order to accelerate the economic progress of our war-ravaged Bangsa Moro homeland, our people and Revolution shall encourage foreign investment under terms and conditions beneficial to our people and the investors. Accordingly, those foreign investors in the Bangsa Moro homeland who may decide to continue their economic activities under the revolutionary regime shall be welcomed;
12. That the Bangsa Moro people and Revolution are committed to the principles that they are a part of the Islamic World as well as of the Third World and of the oppressed colonised humanity everywhere in the world.

Therefore, we hereby appeal to the conscience of all men everywhere and the sympathy of all the nations of the world to help accelerate the pace of our people's Revolution by formally and unequivocally recognising and supporting our people's legitimate right to obtain their national freedom and independence. Such recognition and support must be concretised by accepting the Bangsa Moro Republik as one of the members of the family of independent and sovereign nations in the world and giving official recognition to the Moro National Liberation Front.

Done in the Bangsa Moro Homeland, this 28th day of April 1974.

Hadji Nur Misuari,
Chairman,
Central Committee,
Moro National Liberation Front.

VI PPT letter to the US government

To President, Jimmy Carter,
The White House,
Washington, D.C., USA.

Rome, August 25, 1980

Mr President,

I have the honour to inform you that this Tribunal has accepted to examine a complaint on the rights of the Philippine People lodged jointly by the Moro National Liberation Front and the National Democratic Front.

This complaint concerns, *inter alia*, the laws and practices in force in the Philippines.

Following articles 14 and 15 of the Statute of the Tribunal, I hereby inform you the proceedings have been opened and the Tribunal is ready to receive your representatives or any written documents you may wish to file.

Yours truly,

(Francois Rigaux)
President

VII   PPT letter to President Marcos

His Excellency,
The President Ferdinand E. Marcos,
Malacanang Palace,
Manila, Philiippines.

Rome, June 30, 1980

Your Excellency,

I have the honour to inform you that this Tribunal has accepted to examine a complaint on the rights of the Philippine People lodged jointly by the Moro National Liberation Front and the National Democratic Front.

This complaint concerns, *inter alia*, the laws and practices in force in the Philippines.

Following articles 14 and 15 of the Statute of the Tribunal, I hereby inform you the proceedings have been opened and the Tribunal is ready to receive your representatives or any written documents you may wish to file.

Yours truly,

(Francois Rigaux)
President

VIII   The reply from the Philippines President's Office to the verdict of the PPT

This reply was circulated by the Philippines embassy at The Hague to some newspapers in Holland.

Issue: Legitimacy and Competence of the Philippine Government under Martial Law

The legitimacy of a government in international society rests on the acceptance or recognition of said government by the other states. Recognition is evidenced by an act officially acknowledging the existence of such government and indicating a readiness on the part of the recognizing state to enter into formal relations with it. Recognition is essentially a matter of intention. States may or may not recognize the existence of a new government.

To allege that the Marcos Regime is deprived of such standing is a grossly inaccurate accusation. In fact, the Philippines under the leadership of President Marcos has earned the esteem of almost every state in the world. The Philippines is fast emerging as leader of the Third World as evidenced by its being the representative of the said block in different international conferences and negotiations. The Philippines has thus assumed leadership roles in UNCTAD, Economic and Social Council, ESCAP, FAO, World Food Council, WHO, ILO, UNESCO, and other agencies geared towards the upliftment of economically disadvantaged peoples.

The Philippines' status in the international society can be judged by its impressive accomplishments in furthering international relations. As compared to the previous administrations, the New Society government has negotiated/concluded more treaties/agreements, has received more heads of state and other high ranking government officials and has participated/hosted more international conferences. To date the New Society Government negotiated 91 bilateral/multilateral treaties and agreements, received 12 state and 42 official visits of heads of state and high government officials, established diplomatic relations with 29 governments and hosted major international conferences among them, the 3rd Ministerial Meeting of Group 77, UNCTAD, Revision of the UN Charter, IMF-WB Meeting and the Asian Regional Meeting on Economic Cooperation Among Developing Countries.

Issue: Increasing Popular Resistance against Martial Law Regime

That there is increasing popular resistance to the Martial Law regime under the leadership of President Ferdinand E. Marcos is an outrageous fabrication of Filipinos purporting to be representatives of the Filipino people but in effect are people hungry for political power. Further, such accusations are made by Filipinos based abroad who are unaware of the real situation in the Philippines.

For a government to stay in power, a wide political base is needed. Accordingly, if the present government is not enjoying the confidence of the Filipino people, said government would have already been toppled down. Power rests on the people and it is thus the people who dictate the existence of a government.

It is a known fact that the present government has been supported and mandated by the people to act on behalf of the Filipinos in several referenda held in the Philippines. Further, the Supreme Court of the Philippines in the Benigno Aquino, Jr. vs. Commission on Election case ruled that by general referendum of 27-28 July, 1973, the sovereign people expressly authorized President Marcos to continue in office even beyond 1973 under the 1973 Constitution in order to finish the reforms he initiated under Martial Law. The logical consequence is that President Marcos is a de Jure President of the Republic of the Philippines.

Issue: US Intervention in Philippine Affairs and Nullity of Agreement due to Inequality of Concessions.

The accusation that the United States government is sustaining, supporting and encouraging the present government to act on behalf of its economic and global strategic interests in violation of the rights of the Filipino is false and definitely misleading. The fact is that Philippine foreign relations is premised on the policy of self-reliance. Respect for the right of countries to determine their own policies has been emphasized.

Since the advent of Martial Law in 1972, the era of Philippine-United States 'special relations' has come to an end. New relations based on equality, justice, and mutual respect has been stressed. Thus, a re-examination of various economic and security agreements have been undertaken, the outcome of which is the renegotiation and signally of the new RP-US Trade Agreement and the RP-US Bases Agreement.

The most important provision of the new amendment to the RP-US Bases Agreement is the extension of full Philippine sovereignty over the bases, symbolized by the Philippine flag flying signly over these bases, and the designation of a Philippine base commander at each base. These have removed all the ambiguity and doubts that once attended the sovereignty question.

The new RP-US Trade Agreement is also seen as a significant step forward in RP-US relations. It is viewed as an indication of the Philippines' new found relationship with the United States since it was negotiated within the GATT framework between equal partners exchanging trade concessions based on each other's trade interests. The agreement expands opportunities for Philippine trade on a permanent basis not only with the United States but also with other GATT members.

Such treaties and agreements are thus valid as they were negotiated on equality based on each countries' interests.

Issue: Request for Recognition of Belligerency in Southern Philippines

In International Law, a condition of belligerency exists when armed comflict within a state is recognized by the present state and by other states; otherwise, the situation is technically known as insurgency. The question of whether recognition of belligerency shall be extended to an insurgent force is a matter for determination by the recognizing state.

So far, no government or international entity has accorded the Moro National Liberation Front a belligerent status. This stems from the fact that these handful of misguided rebels living abroad in self-exile are not the legitimate spokesmen and representatives of the Muslims in the Philippines. The whole of the Southern Philippine is populated by 12 million people, of which only 2 million are Islamized. The MNLF, therefore, does not represent even one per cent of the Muslim population and not even 0.1 per cent of the total Southern Philippines population. Its claim for representative leadership is therefore ridiculous. Furthermore, a favorable turn in the Mindanao situation is in evidence. The back of the MNLF has been broken. Out of the original seven leaders of the MNLF, five have returned to the fold, and one is dead. In addition, overall peace and order in the South has been confined to containing roving terrorist bands engaged in petty thievery, extortion and harassment of civilians.

Besides such, the promised development of Southern Philippines is being pushed forward through the concerned efforts of local leaders, government workers, and rebel returnees. Muslim leadership today is fully engaged with government not only in the pacification effort, but also in the vital socio-economic development program for Mindanao.

As regards political development, two autonomous regions in the south are now in the process of organizing the Sanguniang Pampook or Regional Assembly. The establishment of autonomous regions in the south is only the start of a long-range plan to enable these areas to enhance their development projects and promote the unity and prosperity of the nation.

Issue: Displacement and Physical Extinction waged by the Government against the Bangsa Moro People

There has never been a Bangsa Moro and the Filipinos of the Southern Philippines are not Moros. Moro is the term of the Spanish colonists for the sea pirates and terrorists who plied the Southern Philippines a few centuries ago. The Bangsa or state recognized in the Southern Philippines during the Spanish colonization and before that, was the Sultanate of Sulu, abolished by the government of the Philippines at the turn of the 20th century. There is only one state now — the Republic of the Philippines.

There has never been a program for displacement by the government, past nor present, of any ethno-cultural group in the Philippines. There was a transmigration of Filipino from the North and the Southern islands to the sparsely populated Mindanao encouraged by the government to speed up economic and political development in the South. Physical extinction is not borne out by facts, because the population in Region IX is 2,446,588; Region XII is 2,211,971; predominantly Muslim. Neither has genocide been committed. Among the Armed Forces of the Philippines serving to contain the rebellion of Maoist-oriented Moro National Liberation Front are thirty-five thousand (35,000) Filipino Muslims from Mindanao. The Commander of the Southwest Command is himself a Muslim Filipino.

Issue: Right of Self-Determination for the Moro National Liberation Front

Respect for the status of the representatives of the people cannot be vested in the National Democratic Front nor the Moro National Liberation Front, because they are only fronts, not truly nor duly elected by popular will as the people's representatives. The assemblymen in the autonomous governments of Region IX and XII for Muslim Filipinos were duly elected in a special and clean election, like those in the National Assembly. They carry the status and respect as the people's representatives. The tribunal does not have the prerogative to declare the representatives of the Filipino people. We elect our representatives.

Furthermore, the Philippine Archipelago is peopled by some 111 ethnic, linguistic and cultural groups speaking 70 major languages and dialects. Despite formal variations in cultural, religious and social practices, all Filipinos throughout the country share a common identity. The Philippines is one coherent nation, organized into one secular and democratic state.

Issue: International Financial Institutions and Transnational Banks: Their Role in the Present Government

It has been alleged that the different financial institutions are playing a crucial role in sustaining the present government. However, such an allegation is incorrect since these financial institutions do not support the present government, rather the Filipino masses who are the end-benefactors of development projects funded by these financial institutions.

The World Bank (WB) and the Asian Development Bank (ADB) finance specific projects being undertaken by the government. These financial institutions invested in agriculture, irrigation, transportation, roads, education, and other economic projects, all of which actually serve to uplift the welfare of the masses. Needless to say, many of these projects are located in Mindanao such as the irrigation projects approved in 1980 by the ADB for Cotabato, Agusan del Sur, Bukidnon, and Davao del Norte, and roads and commercial faucet systems under WB-IBRD packaged for Cotabato, Lanao del Norte, Lanao del Sur, Sultan Kudarat, Maguindanao, Sulu, Tawi-Tawi and many others.

These government programs requiring foreign funding under the present government are definitely in support of uplifting the welfare of the masses specifically the promotion of countryside rural development.

Issue: Multinational Control of Natural Resources

Today, economies are inherently multinational. For no nation on earth can guarantee itself for food, the natural resources, the manufactured goods and the markets that its citizens demand.

The Philippine government has long recognized this fact that although it considered domestic resources as the major source of financing industrial and overall economic development, supplementary foreign capital can help achieve the development goals of the country at an accelerated pace.

The allegation that these multinational corporations are violating the sovereign rights of the Filipino including the right to sovereign control over natural resources, is a misrepresentation of facts by people who are misinformed and unaware of Philippine laws on such matters. To safeguard Philippine interests, the Board of Investments was created to promote and regulate foreign investments. Through the Foreign Business Regulations Act, the Board allows foreign firms to do business in the Philippines provided the operation or activity of such alien firms a) is not inconsistent with the Investment Priorities Plan; b) is not in conflict with the Constitution and by-laws of the Philippines; c) is not adequately exploited or developed by Filipinos; d) will not pose a clear and present danger of promoting monopolies; and e) will contribute to the sound development of the national economy on a self-sustaining basis. Taking all the legal basis/protective institutions to safeguard the rights of the Filipino, there is no way wherein these multinational companies can take advantage and exploit resources which rightfully belong to the Filipino.

Issue: Degradation of Filipino Women

Filipino women under the present government were never degraded nor sexually exploited. In fact, Filipino women were always given the chance to be actively involved in the government's task of nation-building. These women have been active agents of change and development at all levels and sectors of the society. They are in the professions, in government, in business, in education and have raised themselves to the same level as the menfolk in terms of responsibilities and needs of the community.

Based on statistics, 6.94 per cent in the governatorial and vice governatorial posts were occupied by women, and 6.1 per cent and 5.6 per cent in the Mayoral and vice mayoral posts, respectively.

Comparatively, data on the 1971 and 1980 elections show an increase in the number of women elected mayor by 3.1 per cent and vice-mayor by 1.6 per cent.

Likewise, Filipino women are also represented at all levels in the Judiciary and the Foreign Service.

In the Foreign Service, of the 36 councillors, 22 per cent are women and 8 of them are based abroad. 33 per cent of 152 Foreign Service officers are women. It is noted that the 6 women FSO class 1, are all assigned in the foreign service.

Further, 39.57 per cent of employees in the career service and 32.06 per cent in non-career service are female.

The above mentioned statistics show that since the advent of Martial Law, little by little women are easing their way into traditionally male dominated professions which is indicative of the confidence of government in Filipino women as an agent to nation building.

IX Evidence presented to the Tribunal

Basic Reports

1. Prof. Joel Rocamora, South East Asia Research Center, Berkeley, Calif., USA. *US Imperialism and the Economic Crisis of the Marcos Dictatorship.*
2. Prof. Joel Rocamora, *Economic exploitation, repression and discrimination of the Bangsa Moro people.*
3. Prof. Wallen Bello, University of California, Berkeley, USA., *The form, functions and causes of political repression in the Philippines.*

Witnesses

Antonio de la Cruz	Worker
Victoria de los Reyes	Peasant
Perla Silangan	Student
Salud Torres	Writer & ex-government employee
Wada Taw-il	Member of tribal minority
Dr Parouk Hussin	Doctor

Representatives of the plaintiffs

Luis Jalandoni	National Democratic Front
Victoria de los Reyes	New People's Army
Abdurasad Asani	Moro National Liberation Front
Hatimil Hassan	Moro National Liberation Front

Documentary Evidence

1. *Philippines 1980.* An NDF Publication
2. *Neo-Colonialism: Root of our Discontent.* Published by the Civil Liberties of the Philippines (C.L.U.P.), 1979.
3. *Makibaka: Join us in struggle.* A documentation of resistance to martial law in the Philippines. Second edition February 1980.
4. *International Policy Report: Aid to the Philippines — Who Benefits?* Published by the Center for International Policy, Washington D.C. October 1979.
5. *Militarization of Samar* — Report of the International Commission on the militarization of Samar, Eastern Visayas, Philippines. Published by R.C.P.C. Hongkong, October 1979.
6. *Iron Hand, Velvet Glove* — Studies on militarization in five critical areas in the Philippines by the Ecumenical Movement for Justice and Peace.
7. *Tribal people and the Marcos regime*, South-east Asia Chronicle, Issue No. 67.
8. *The Ten-Point Program of the National Democratic Front.*
9. The Health Program of the National Democratic Front.
10. *The Rules of the NPA and the Revolutionary Guide for Land Reform.*
11. *Situationer* — March-April, 1980. Prepared by the National Secretariate of Social Action for Justice and Peace (NASSA).
12. *Country Paper: Philippines.* Prepared by the National Secretariat of Social Action Justice and Peace (NASSA) for the General Assembly of the Asian Partnership for Human Development. September 1979 and update 1980.
13. *Les Philippines: Le Reveil d'un Archipel*, Charles Foubert. IDOC 1980.
14. *The Labor Code of the Philippines and its implementing Rules and Regulations.* 8th edition, 1980.
15. *The Philippines Land Reform Program* Presidential Decree No. 2 of 26 September, 1972.
16. *Conference Internationale du Travail 1979. Rapport III.* Rapport de la Commission d'experts pour l'application des conventions et recommandations I.L.O.
17. *International Actions and Philippine Authoritarianism*, Robin Broad, Princetown, 1979.
18. *The Philippines and the IMF-World Bank Conglomerate*, Edberto M. Villegas. Third World Studies: The Philippines and the Third World Papers Series No. 17, May 1979.
19. *Filipina Workers: A case of exported women workers.* Published by Migration Secretariat, WCC, Jan. 1980.
20. *Philippines: Workers in the export industry.* Pacific Research, USA, March-June, 1978.
21. "Kawasaki Steel Corporation's Sinster Plant in Mindanao" in *Free Trade Zones and Industrialisation in Asia*, by AMPO Review 1974.

22. *Some are smarter than others*. Study prepared by Filipino businessmen and professional managers, 1979.
23. *People Toiling under Pharaoh*. Report of the Action Research Process on Economic Justice in Asia. Published in Urban Rural Mission, Christian Conference of Asia, 1976.
24. *Pumipiglas — Political Detention and Military Atrocities in the Philippines*. Published by the Task Force Detainees: Association of Major Religious Superiors in the Philippines, 1980.
25. *Political Detainees in the Philippines*, Association of Major Religious Superiors in the Philippines: Book 1 (1976); Book 2 (1977); Book 3 (1978).
26. *Conditions of the Filipino People under Martial Law* (1978) and *Human Rights and Martial Law in the Philippines* (1977). Reports of the FFP (Friends of the Filipino People) and AMLC (Anti-Martial Law Coalition) Investigating Mission to the Philippines.
27. *Report of a Mission to the Report of the Philippines in 1975*. Amnesty International (Second Edition including the Reply of the Philippine Government).
28. *The Decline of Democracy in the Philippines*. International Commission of Jurists 1977.
29. *The Mis-education of the Filipino*, Renato Constantino 1966.
30. *Training Manual: Training for Barangay Brigade Members* 1979.
31. *Tribal People and the Marcos regime*. South-east Asia Chronicle. Issue 67, October 1979.
32. *Squatters in their own land*. Ben & Nilo Langa-an. 1980.
33. *Militarisation comes to the Chico Valley*. Cordillera Committee on Justice and Peace, 1980.
34. *The Uprooting of a People in Kalinga-Apayao*. Asia Forum on Human Rights. June 1980.
35. Chronology of events and military activities and harrassments in the Chico Dam Area. Jan-April, 1980.
36. *Moros — Not Filipinos*. A summary of the political history of the Bangsa Moro People by Abdurasad Asani.
37. Treaty between the Sultan of Sulu and the United States of America 1942.
38. Agreement between General John C. Bates, US Army, and the Sultan of Sulu, together with certain Sulu Chiefs, signed at Jolo, 20 August, 1899.
39. Lanao Protest, 1935.
40. Speech of Congressman Bacan of New York in the United States House of Representatives Sponsoring House Bill No. 12772. (US Congressional Records, 6 May, 1926 pp. 8830-8835).
41. *MNLF turns full circle*, Abdurasad Asani.
42. *Focus on a Multinational Evil, The Banana Industry* by Asnada Mennorite Research Group, Colorado.
43. *Our Land for Others*, Lindy Washburn.
44. *Our Lake for Others*, Lindy Washburn.
45. *The Campaign of Genocide*, Abdurasad Asani.

46. *The Undeclared War in the Southern Philippines*, Robin Osborne.
47. *Some Sampling of Bombing Operations and Ground Assault carried out by the Marcos Regime's Army*, MNLF Document.
48. *Statistical Analyses of Massacres, Destruction of villages, towns, mosques etc. 1968 - 1980.*
49. "Philippine Moslems take Refuge in Sabah, but Status is Murky", *Asian Wall Street Journal Special*, 22 May 1979.
50. *Economic Aid for Control — Control of MNC's Profit*, Abdurasad Asani.
51. *MNLF Manifesto*, 25 April 1974.
52. MNLF Press Statement, April 1980.

X   Instruments of International Law Considered

- The Universal Declaration of the Rights of Peoples, Algiers, 1976.
- The Universal Declaration of Human Rights
- The Charter of the United Nations
- The International Covenant on Economic, Social and Cultural Rights
- The International Covenant on Civil and Political Rights
- The International Convention on the Elimination of all Forms of Racial Discrimination, 1965
- The Geneva Conventions I, II, III and IV, and in particular Article 3 thereof
- The Nuremberg Principles of International Law adopted by the General Assembly of the United Nations
- The Conventions of the International Labour Organisation
- The Declaration on the Granting of Independence to Colonial Countries and Peoples